PUBLISHED

Restoring Faith in Reason
A new translation of the Encyclical Letter Faith and Reason
of Pope John Paul II together with a commentary and discussion
Laurence P. Hemming and Susan F. Parsons (editors)

Contemplating Aquinas
On the Varieties of Interpretation
Fergus Kerr OP (editor)

The Politics of Human Frailty
A Theological Defence of Political Liberalism
Christopher J. Insole

FORTHCOMING

Corpus Mysticum
translated by Gemma Simmonds CJ and Richard Price
Henri Cardinal de Lubac SJ

Postmodernity's Transcending

Devaluing God

Laurence Paul Hemming

scm press

The photograph on page xii is reproduced by permission of the
artist from the video *Brontosaurus* © 1995 Sam Taylor-Wood.
Courtesy of Jay Joplin/White Cube (London)

British Library Cataloguing in Publication data

A catalogue record for this book is available
from the British Library

0 334 02992 9

First published in 2005 by SCM Press
9–17 St Albans Place, London N1 0NX

www.scm-canterburypress.co.uk

SCM Press is a division of
SCM-Canterbury Press Ltd

Printed and bound in Great Britain by Biddles Ltd,
www.biddles.co.uk

in memoriam J. Jeremy Walters 1946–2003
Knight Hospitaller of the British Association of the
Sovereign Military Order of Malta
Brother in Christ
requiescat in pace

Räumen ist Freigabe von Orten

Martin Heidegger

Contents

Acknowledgements and Preface

This book has been in preparation for several years. It develops some of the themes of my first book, *Heidegger's Atheism: The Refusal of a Theological Voice*, but is not about Martin Heidegger, although his work and what I learn from him are companions on the way.

As always with a book of this nature, debts of thanks are manifold and deeply owed. I must thank Lieven Boeve of the Dogmatic Theology Department of the Catholic University of Louvain for his kindness in inviting me into a Fellowship, initially for four months, extended to a full sixteen, between April 2002 and December 2003 during which time the heart of the research for this book was carried out. Most remarkable was the conference organized by the Dogmatic Theology Faculty on the penultimate draft of this book, held in Louvain in October 2004. I owe gratitude to the Fund for Scientific Research – Flanders (*Fonds voor Wetenschappelijk Onderzoek – Vlaanderen*) and the Research Council of the Katholieke Universiteit Leuven (*Onderzoeksraad KU Leuven*) for their generous awards which made my time in Louvain and this research possible. Thanks are also due to my colleagues at Louvain who so often encouraged me and allowed me to prove my work with them in seminars and lectures as well as in private discussions; especially to Lieven Boeve, who arranged the conference and Yves De Maeseneer and Tom Jacobs who organized it; to the speakers Kevin Hart and Stuart Elden (whose remarks and suggestions contributed to the final shape of the work), and to Martin Stone, Peter Jonkers and Yves De Maeseneer. My thanks to the faculty members: Mathijs Lamberigts, Georges De Schrijver, Terrence Merrigan and Stijn van den Bossche; and to the student members of the research group Theology in a Postmodern Context: Johannes Ardui, Christophe Brabant, Annekatrien Depoorter, Frederiek Depoortere, Hans Geybels, Tom Jacobs, Joeri Schrijvers and Lea Verstricht.

Those who have been willing to read all or portions of the manuscript and who have offered helpful comments I also owe thanks. To:

Michael Lang *cong. orat.* for his assistance with some of the Greek; Ferdinand Knapp for the idea and subsequent photograph for the cover image of a picture of Olafur Eliasson's presentation in London's Tate Modern Gallery of his monumental *The Weather Project*,[1] as well as for his long-suffering assistance with my (and Heidegger's) German; thanks are due also to Roger Ruston, Christopher Pipe, Mary Matthews and Barbara Laing of SCM Press for the care they have taken in preparation of this book; above all my co-editor, intellectual, and spiritual companion in so much of my working life, Susan Frank Parsons. The book is far improved by their kind suggestions: the persisting faults and errors remain entirely my own. Jeremy Walters, to whom this book is dedicated, delighted in the ideas that lay beneath it and his energy and confidence sped mine as it was written. His sudden death on 2 November 2003, that year unusually the Feast of All Saints, is still mourned.

Small portions of this book have been published in earlier form elsewhere. A rather different version of Chapter 6 was published in April 2004 as '*Analogia non Entis sed Entitatis*: The Ontological Consequences of the Doctrine of Analogy' in *International Journal of Systematic Theology*, Vol. 6 (April 2004). Some parts of a version of Chapters 8 and 9 were given as a conference paper at the KU Leuven fourth international conference of Leuven Encounters in Systematic Theology in November 2003 as 'Are We Still in Time For God? Apocalyptic, Sempiternity, and the Purposes of Experience', published as part of the proceedings of the conference. A part of Chapter 8 was given in a much earlier version as a lecture in the series 'Religious Experience: Issues in Contemporary Dogmatic Theology' in the Faculty of Dogmatic Theology of KU Leuven and published as 'The Experience of God: Aquinas on the Identity and Difference of Divine and Human Knowledge' in the collection *Divinising Experience*.[2]

The translations provided in the volume are in every case my own, although I have made reference to extant English translations. Where English translations of works exist, I have provided a reference to them in the Bibliography. Where I have used critical editions (in the case of Descartes, Hegel, and Nietzsche), I have simply provided the general title of the particular volume and the volume number in the notes to the text. Full information is available in the Bibliography.

---

[1] Displayed in the Turbine Hall of Tate Modern between October 2003 and March 2004.

[2] Hemming, L. P. and Boeve, L., *Divinising Experience*, 2004.

In the case of Heidegger's collected works (*Gesamtausgabe*), I have provided the volume title, year of publication, and volume number, using the now commonly accepted prefix *GA*. All citations of Heidegger are from the *Gesamtausgabe* edition, although the year of first publication of earlier editions or editions first offered by other publishers is given in brackets after the year of the volume cited. Again, full information is available in the Bibliography. For ancient texts (of Plato, Aristotle, Longinus, and Aquinas) I have provided the title, question and article number, section or line number in the manner customary for reference to those texts, with full information on the editions I have used in the Bibliography. Square brackets '[ ]' in the text indicate a word or phrase of my own intruded into a reference or quotation (unless within a parenthesis in a reference in a footnote). Several individuals were invaluable in assisting me to obtain unusual texts and references. My thanks are due to Sam Taylor-Wood, by whose kind permission the image from *Brontosaurus* is included, and to Bruce McCormack of Princeton for a rare German text of Karl Barth's.

The text is intended to be taken inclusively, although I have eschewed throughout the normal paraphernalia of inclusive language. I apologise to readers for whom this is a difficulty; I assure you, there is no intended diminution of women or men in my use.

A symposium was held in honour of *Postmodernity's Transcending: Devaluing God* at the end of 2004. The papers given at the symposium are now available to read in the *Arts Disputandi* e-journal at: http:// adss.library.uu.nl/ courtesy of Utrecht University.

Christmas Eve, 2004

Sam Taylor-Wood
Brontosaurus
1995
Video projection and sound
Duration: 10 minutes
© the artist
Courtesy Jay Jopling/White Cube (London)

I

Introduction

A figure dances, perhaps in a ballet, perhaps to the intoxication of a trance or acid house rhythm. The movements are sometimes slow, and graceful, sometimes more pulsed and anguished. Hands fly above the head or meet gracefully before the belly. The figure is lightly bearded, wirily muscular but thin, almost emaciated. Although naked, the sexual display is inverted in this performance: he could be taken up in any one of a number of sexual identities, and for this reason has barely one at all. Sex so often represents the most immediate and fastest intimacy it is possible for us to establish, and works through such instantly recognizable figures that we are always immediately engaged by images of sex, even when repelled. In overtly sexual imagery the self can always lay claim to what is most intimate about what stands before it without speech, without preliminaries, above all, without the time that is required to dwell with another before he or she becomes intimate to us. Sexual images collapse the work even of sight into its readiest folds. In this sense sex is not sex, but is that drawing out from ourselves whatever we most intimately already know about ourselves, figuring our own desire to ourselves through masking what is already ours by representing back to ourselves all our most immediate lacks. We find ourselves too often in what most appears to be something not of our own at all. Our own embodiment deceives us, as our own bodies are not what actually is most familiar to us but, in every sense, the familiar is that on which our bodies seek to find themselves projected. In sexual imagery what is laid before us is an invitation to discover what it is within us we most want, even when the image itself is nothing that attracts us. In sex, disinterest and repulsion work as much as do attraction and desire, as advertising so cunningly knows with its capacity not just to exploit our most immediate engagements, but also our fears, and the engagements of those with whom we are concerned intimately, so that sex *sells* even at stages or generations removed.

In postmodernity we believe ourselves above all else to have re-

covered a language of embodiment, banishing the dualism said to constitute the Enlightenment – and all that fell before it – and yet, in
that speaking, postmodernity has generated within itself its greatest
tension. To speak of embodiment is not to be embodied, but rather to
direct the appearance of embodiment to some*where*, a place, the place
of language perhaps, or the imaginary, as if simply to *recall* the language of embodiment and to parrot and enact it constantly overcomes
the disjunction between language and the thing of which language
writes and speaks. Language, understood like this, is as a representing,
a mirroring surface on to which embodiment and its immanences are
reflected, a source of exchange and enquiry. Such a use of language, in
other words, is imaginary.

Here, in this dancing figure, however, even the immediacy of sex is
presented as denied, since the dance and its performer refuse an
engagement, or rather unfold an engagement that excludes us from his
gaze – his eyes are almost always closed. Windows stand above and
behind him, but it is night, and they yield only black panes. In the
foreground, a mournful, schmaltzy music plays, with no relation in
rhythm or tone to the dancing. The disjunction between his movements and the music we hear deepens the divide of us from him: occasionally his rhythms fall in with the music, only to fall away again as
swiftly, so that our passing into and out of the jerks that betoken
his world are purely accidental and do not touch us or bind us into
something we can take as common. A small stuffed toy – a dinosaur –
watches the scene, as do a crowd: this is an artwork, a video installation. The installation is called *Brontosaurus*, the artist, Sam Taylor-
Wood.

A remarkable feature of *Brontosaurus* is the involuntary reaction it
provokes in many who find themselves before it. I have witnessed as
often as one in every ten spectators spontaneously give tongue to fury
at sight of it – shouting at the video-screen or barking critically to
companions, to the indifference of the figure, who continues to dance.
Brontosaurus captures well our contemporary situation – it opens up
the relation of human self-understanding within aesthetic representation with huge, yet almost accidental, power. I shall argue in this book
that the human subject – the subject of postmodernity – appears most
accessibly and most constantly under the visual, videographic and
cinekinetic conditions on which *Brontosaurus* relies for its success.
Brontosaurus exemplifies the aesthetic attainment to sublimity in
postmodernity. Here we have a preliminary indication of why the
sublime, as a category in philosophical aesthetics, presents itself as

the persistent thread for this book. For the sublime (in contemporary discourse above all a category of the *visual* aesthetic, and at the same time a category concerned with our aesthetic sense in its greatest degree) is, in all its outermost and loftiest, nevertheless always that which we articulate from our sense of the *within*. It is in this sense, and from a contemporary viewpoint, always something known to me and intimate to me when I am gripped by it. This loftiest and utmost character has, however, often indicated the connection of the sublime with divinity and transcendence. Could it be that the sublime, sufficiently well understood, will allow us to connect the subjectivity of our most inward self-experience with the outermost of what we can know?

For all the attempts to critique and to understand it as decentred, the postmodern subject continues to appear in the light of the place laid out by Descartes, Leibniz, and above all Kant.[1] Take for example, the definition of the subject as 'the loneliness of a being whose being consists in being decentred'.[2] A subject therefore who, lonely, and so *produced* through loneliness (the very essence of the *cogito*), and for whom everything that would satisfy, excite, and give it being is at the same time denied it – or rather (and here is the essence itself) is brought before it in repetitious self-denial – is at the same time confronted with the sheer melancholy that there is denial, and so *things* to deny. Being is, in being, negated. At the very moment where things become things – where enthingment occurs (where else did Kant's *Bedingungen* come from?) – they occur at once as nullified.

The decentredness of the subject is this very indeterminacy: that there is alterity, that which is beyond me *as such*; and that alterity is without meaning. The metaphysics of Marx as much as the modern free market arise on the basis of this indeterminacy, and in making things determinate, which means, in assigning them a value or in setting us the task of the self-assignment of value, the indeterminacy of the subject is evaluated and brought into fundamentally calculable relations. To change the world you must first have decided, in a valuative act, what the world is to be transformed *into* – to succeed economically, you must decide in advance that you can be worth

---

[1] Although I shall discuss Descartes and Kant in detail, I do not intend to discuss Leibniz's nevertheless important contribution. I have alluded to it in Hemming, L. P., 'The Subject of Prayer: Leibniz' Monadology' in Ward, G. (ed.), *The Postmodern Reader in Theology*, 2001, pp. 444–57.

[2] Visker, R., *Truth and Singularity: Taking Foucault into Phenomenology*, 1999, p. 14.

something, that you can assign a value to yourself. Democracy is not the end of hierarchy, it is its beginning; you yourself must decide where in the scale of value you will find yourself to be assigned. Every failure to achieve your proper rank is wellspring to an indignant anger, the fuel of politics and litigation. Hence the loneliness of the subject is neither social nor psychological, and yet it is both at the same time, or rather it constantly tips over into being either – the subject can find no gravity, no centre, and so totters from one sphere of meaning to another, constantly enacting every sphere to which it clutches for the sake of its origin.

If the subject does not spring from out of the world it knows and so is, whence else its source? Except, perhaps (as we shall come to examine), from God, the cause of all things? – or so it seems for Descartes. Except, as we shall repeatedly discover, in postmodernity this source is disbarred, because God is dead, not only in virtue of Nietzsche but because the sheer melancholy of the cancelled enthingment of being in the midst of the world constantly disassembles this god of originating causes who never explains enough, never causes sufficiently, never accounts for all that is, and so – for those who would believe – has constantly to be replaced, and this means re-emplaced, re-enthroned, restored, to the exhaustion of subjectivity itself. The subject, decentred, neither socially, nor psychologically, nor divinely caused, caused *by nothing* in virtue of its very need to be caused, is constantly driven back on itself as a task. Constantly driven back on whatever it can seize upon and so embrace, constantly throwing out its imaginary and seizing upon itself through the images it recovers and through which it recovers. Above all, and for reasons we must examine, it undertakes this as a moral task. I must, because I can!

In postmodernity the subject appears first and most accessibly as pure self-representation, and the aesthetic construction of *Brontosaurus*, where we are challenged to recognize ourselves most forcibly by a figure closed in on itself, sexually ambiguous and infinitely projectible and scalable (larger or smaller) is not accidental. And yet this pure representation of *Brontosaurus* brings before us a body, the body that we are to be. *Brontosaurus* draws attention to the means and mode of its representing by denying representation – by subtracting all the content that should come in the form of the figure's address to us, whilst at the same time emphasizing the potency of the means of the address itself, and exposing all the borders and limits that constitute the self and its dividedness from a world that at the same time is its melancholic other. We are forced to witness our own exclusion from the figure's possession of his self-upliftedness. It is for this reason that *Brontosaurus* excites such anger – and yet, the anger remains moral, and appears as indignation. It is excited by the transgression of the rights of access that we now always assume, not only that we should have to the psyche of another, but that we should have *at our command, effortlessly*. The nakedness of the figure and its overt sexual display, as sex-without-sex, deprives our command and so refuses to allow us to be already in the know, already folded over into collusion with an adult privacy – this figure really is private *without us*. And it does not matter that this man is naked – he is not there to draw us to him, or repel us for that matter. His skin has become his outer clothing, so that what for him constitutes the border between him and world – his real exterior – is, like the lining of a coat, unseen to us, and we see only a folded-out within. This skin to whose outside we are exposed has an inside which contains an inner being who is embodied only insofar as *we* can see. He manifests for us that postmodernity works through surfaces that are to be visible and so *seen* to be. His shuttering eyes pass him rarely through and over to us, for us his limbs are in futile play, not even to a music to which we are attuned in hearing. The black windows through which light may not pass indicate that this monad is a soul without windows to the world, whose privacy we do not disturb. Insofar as we are driven to anger or delight before him, it is we who are exposed, not him. The world has disappeared for him – it is not that he might not open his eyes and re-enter it and so pass back across the threshold of his nakedness to enter the place wherein his indifference has referred to us our *own* gaze. This figure has, in attracting our attention, given up his gaze, and thereby refuses the assembly of the visual field which would constitute us as anything like spectators, a field on which the videographic and cinekinetic normally so urgently depends. He is myself denied. His flapping genitalia are to us a taunt, a thing for him unfelt.

And can we find ourselves at the point of view of the spectating brontosaurus? Are we too, stuffed toys fixing this kinetic figure in a weighting that lends a gravity to a performance that – as Taylor-Wood herself has pointed out – was constructed amidst 'giggling and rolling around laughing'?[3] Or is the toy brontosaurus the trace of the presence of an originating cause? Does the brontosaurus take the place of God, the creator of the heavens and the earth, or is it representative of what God's creating activity has now become and alone how it can be

---

[3] Taylor-Wood, S., 'Interview' in *Sam Taylor-Wood*, 2002.

thought in the videographic and cinekinetic? The question of origination should be understood as the question which asks what lies prior and lays out or makes possible the field of vision for whatever emerges and presents itself to us. As a question it must ask: how? Does it appear in the guise of what this lies-prior has become – a caricature, a phantom of a cause, the whiff alone of history and prehistory's unfolding, that has only mythic and unrepresentable origins, except perhaps as a child's toy that suggest an origin, but only *as a suggestion*, a hint, and nothing more? Has 'god' so shrunk to this?

Is it not that in this installation there are two sets of causes at work: first the question of origins, yes – but of an evolutionary development from what exactly? Origins from out of childhood, perhaps, and so origins articulated in psychoanalysis – figured in a toy, or from a past that some kind of loose Darwinianism might faintly hint at, but never fully thematize? And second, causes thought, not *as* the sexual content of the images, but as what stabilizes that content, what sex itself is now marker for – the most immediate and pressing way in which I find myself prefigured in you, addressed by you and so able to address you? Which is to say, what I can know and take for granted I know about you (that implicates me in you even before we speak, before we address one another – before we should so much as even touch), so that we would not have actually to touch, indeed already to have touched. But is it not that in this touching, I can touch you even though you need never know or even care that you are touched? Is not the postmodern paradox of sex here the same as that of fame, that the famous – for what, means nothing – are famous only because they belong, already, intimately, to all of us who 'know' them without ever having touched them? And is this 'knowing' not the same as the commanding disdain of their being referred to our proprietary imaginations, so that they are at our beck and call, although we never met them? And do they not belong to us so intimately, that they have for public purposes and through the endless dissimulating industries of agents, public relations, glossy parasitic media of gossip and so forth, to construct an intimacy which is never their own – or rather which is always even more their own than their own intimacy really is, because it is more plausible, more obviously, credibly, theirs than the intimacy they actually inhabit for themselves? And should they fall from grace, should the real intimate details of their lives prove publicly unpalatable, is not what is unforgivable, not what they did or do in private, but that they had a privacy at all, a life from which we were excluded, even though we bought our way into it, or were, willy-nilly, pressed into it, so that the fiction of their being at our command while being nothing of the sort is all at once exposed, and we discovered that we had been *lied to*?

Or is it not more complex yet? This intimacy, of course, has in post-modernity a double feature – we already know that what we 'know' of the famous and who they really are is separated, so that the real transgression is the having dared to call attention to the separation (and so not granted us our right of touch-without-touch), so that we can no longer be cunningly in the know about both what we do know and what we are supposed to know that we really don't know – because this is what intimacy now really is, a ventured imaginary for all of us (and not just the famous), a margin of knowing-about-not-knowing, the bits of us that are publicized *as* private – knowing winks that can be endlessly reciprocated, so winding ourselves into each other's pasts (however many we need to explain who we think we are becoming) without our needing ever to dwell there. You can 'know' me, without my ever having dwelt together with you.

The sublime has, across the divide of both the pre- and post-Enlightenment understanding of the structure of the world, been understood to be the experience of the divine. At the same time, the sublime brings to the fore what appears to be the paramount onto-logical moment, the moment of 'seeing yourself sensing'.[4] To 'see' in this way has from the outset meant not actual seeing with the eyes, so much as seeing with the mind. This is the distinction that has been known to us from the Greeks, between νοεῖν, seeing and knowing as thinking, Latin *intelligere, intellectus*, in contrast to the verbs ὁράω, *video*, I see (by looking with the eyes). The fundamental connection between seeing and sensing has as its pure object something that in fact cannot strictly be seen as such, but which discloses itself in the seeing of the mind: this is Aristotle's seeing as contemplating, θεωρεῖν. Contemplation is the consideration both of being insofar as it is being, and being insofar as it is highest being and most divine. Contemplation is, strictly speaking for Aristotle, θεολογία, theology. Contemplation of being, insofar as it is highest being, and insofar as it is most divine.

When we see something that is sublime we must, as it were, look for what it is in what we see that makes it sublime. We must look with

---

[4] This phrase was used by Olafur Eliasson for an installation in the New York Museum of Modern Art between September 2001 and May 2002. The same idea of the sublime is at work in *The Weather Project*, pictured on the cover of this book.

the mind for what in our seeing has compelled us to sublimity. In the history of thinking itself, the sublime has been taken to be the way in which certain (but not all) sensations, experiences, occurrences (if you like), have a divine aspect to them: they disclose divinity as such, by being the highest to which we can attain: highest value. Now, however, when we enquire after highest value, we do so in the wake of Nietzsche's proclamation of the devaluation of the uppermost values, for the sake of a revaluation of all values. The moment where God appears as a value is the moment where God can be taken *as* something. To take something *as* something means that it could be taken as the something that is assigned to it – this value – or another. The value of God becomes exchangeable.

To experience God as highest value is already to know that God can be and has been devalued, and so is to ask who is it that values and devalues God. To ask such a question is already to ask a question about the being of being-human. Because philosophy always asks a question of this kind on the basis of 'what . . .' as in 'what is the structure of this being insofar as it is like *this* and not like *that*', the question which expresses itself as 'τί τὸ ὄν', 'what is this being insofar as it is?' we are tempted to ask the question in terms of the *structure* of the being of being human and the *objects* of human knowledge, of which God may be the first, or least. To ask this question as a description of a thing-in-general is, however, already to take for granted the separation of the 'inner' from the 'outer', the separation of two worlds, which makes possible the video-kinetic appearance of the figure in *Brontosaurus*. Thus we ask 'what is that being over there?' as if it could be anywhere. But the being who asks this question is already in the midst of being, is *being* in itself: it has its own specified 'where'. It is this peculiarity which, because so self-evident, is normally transparent (and in fact invisible) to us, and so enables us to take ourselves as both subject and object at the same time. We are able, once again, to take in view the importance of the sublime because it is concerned at one and the same time with this 'inner' and 'outer' so that it appears to explain the relation of the inner and the outer. How and in what ways is 'perception' (αἴσθησις) 'knowledge' (ἐπιστήμη)? – a question we will discover already to be embedded in the very origins of Western thought.

The sublime indicates a seeking of what is most 'beingful' and divine in what is there to be experienced and known. Because sublimity has been understood in this way, it has been taken as a name for transcendence. And here is the ambiguity which this whole book is intended to expose. What kind of transcendence is delivered in sublime experiences? The temptation for modern philosophers and theologians when they take up the sublime is to say: if upliftment is an explicitly ontological description of existence (of what it feels like to be human, of what experience *is*), and one in which divinity or God or the gods also appears, have we not uncovered an ontological grounding for divinity, God, and the gods? Alternatively, if the sublime is nothing other than our furthest reach and highest value, a divine value which can be exchanged for any other as powerful and sublime, are we not ourselves devalued by the very drive after pleasure and upliftment that is all we can ever know? Is transcendence nothing other than the experience of nothing, of a nihilistic transcendent aim that exists and strikes out only for its own sake? Here is Nietzsche's claim 'what does nihilism indicate? that the highest values have devalued themselves; the aim is lacking: the answer to the "why?" is lacking'.[5] Here we have the two halves between which the modern soul oscillates constantly – God as the eternal, highest value, and our own being thrown back eternally on ourselves, in the ambiguity of the sheer drive into power for its own sake and its concomitant decline. For which of the two does sublimity decide?

And here is the thesis of this book: the sublime is the bringing before myself of whatever occurs in its sharpest form, the form that entrains me *to* whatever is occurring (upliftment is the opposite to, the abolition and disbandment of, boredom; of not particularly noticing what occurs and passes me by). As this, it is both attempting to secure what occurs, and the knowledge of its occurrence. Sublimity is the most originary description of the things that happen, of what-occurs.

Sublimity is therefore a name, not for the experience of an object nor that object's exchangeable and so nihilated value, but for experience as such, experience in itself. Because sublimity is the experience *of* experience, it is not concerned with presence – either as absolute, ultimate presence, the eternal ever-sameness of what is most beingful and divine – God, if you like – nor the eternal recurrence of the same. Both these determinations of eternity, the one of God, the other in consequence of the death of God, are *a*temporal in their structure. As definitions of the eternal and sempiternal, they are definitions of what, strictly speaking, is without time. Quite to the contrary; sublimity is

---

[5] Nietzsche, F., *Nachlaß 1885–1887*, 1988, vol. 12, p. 350f. 'Es fehlt das Ziel; es fehlt die Antwort auf das "Warum?" was bedeutet Nihilismus? – daß die obersten Werthe sich entwerthen.'

the experience not of something eternal, but something temporalizing. Sublimity is a name for the temporalizing of the being of being human. Sublimity is the experience of time. As this, it does not bring us before the transcendent, nor does it lock us into the uttermost experience of immanence. It is a name for transcending, for the unfolding being of being-human. Sublimity is a way of describing ourselves to be in time.

To describe something is at the same time to name something and to know it, to take it into knowing. And here we must take note of something the Greeks knew well and took for granted, and which we have to some extent lost the proper knowledge of. To speak (truly) of something is the same thing as to bring it into the light, to point out what it is, and so disclose it for itself. The verbs φαίνω, to bring to light, to allow to be seen, and φάσκω, to say or deem, have the same root and are really the same word. Here we can hear the entirely proper meaning of the Greek word ἀλήθεια which we translate as truth but which is better understood as drawing out of hiddenness.[6] So we must ask, in connection with the ambiguity of the question I raised earlier, when language speaks, do we speak of what we *already* know, or are we addressed by what is yet to be fully understood by us and yet to come? This is one way of engaging with the difference between what is, insofar as it already is (presence), and what is coming to be (presencing).

This book will therefore attempt to describe the experience of coming to be and presencing. Why if sublimity is transcend*ing* has it been so often understood through transcend*ence*, and so presence? In attempting to explain sublimity as transcending it will therefore be necessary to explain why transcending has constantly been covered over and negated in favour of transcendence. In the course of this we will come to understand something that Martin Heidegger had said in 1924: 'When the philosopher enquires after time, then he is resolved *to understand time from out of time*, respectively from the ἀεί, which thus looks like eternity, but which turns out to be a mere derivation of being-timely.'[7] To come to a proper understanding of presencing will

---

[6] Some will recognize this as 'Heidegger's' understanding of truth. This controversial etymology, connecting truth with λήθη, oblivion, is quite uncontroversially suggested by the 1499 *Etymologicum Magnum* of the Cretan philologist Nicholas Vlastos, with the explanation that the true is that which has 'not fallen under oblivion' (ἀληθὲς τὸ μὴ λήθη ὑποπῖπτον). Vlastos, N., *Etymologicum Magnum*, ed Gaisford, T., 1848 (1499), 62.51.

[7] Heidegger, M., *Der Begriff der Zeit (Vortrag 1924)*, GA64, 2004, p. 107. 'Fragt der Philosoph nach der Zeit, dann ist er entschlossen, *die Zeit aus der Zeit zu verstehen* bzw. aus dem ἀεί, was so aussieht wie Ewigkeit, was sich aber herausstellt als ein bloßes Derivat des Zeitlichseins'. Emphasis in original.

allow us to attain to a more adequate understanding of presence, one that does not fall into the postmodern trap of denouncing all presence as 'metaphysics', and as the metaphysics of presence, something to be derided and reviled as if we were already somewhere far better. The most nihilistic interpretation of Nietzsche's eternal recurrence of the same is as much a metaphysics of presence as the loftiest proclamation of the eternal transcendence of God. Will we, perhaps, in coming into an understanding of sublimity, presencing and presence, better understand divinity and God? If sublimity is not the grounding of God and the gods in the being of being human, from where might we know whom it is God is? This is the same question as: 'What kind of theology is intended or indicated by a discussion of the sublime?' This question we will keep in view as we proceed through the text, but any answer that might be proffered will be left until the very last. Should we attain to it, I hope you will be in a position to welcome the answer when it arrives.

2

Postmodernity's Transcending

Just what is postmodernity? Is postmodernity so difficult to define? If postmodernity points up the succession of epochs, and so names an *event*, then postmodernity becomes installed in the history of thinking. In postmodernity, however, it is always dangerous to locate history in events. Events deceive us by their very factuality, for fact and fabrication are closer often than we dare concede. How much of ourselves is lent to the making of the fact, the thing done, and so made? Are we not right to suspect all things of manufacture, seeking only the purity of whatever is untouched by human hand? The events of yesterday seem too-long past, the happenings of centuries ago still effect our present. Neither, however, is history what we make of the past, even though the past is now made ever more present to us as a region into which we may enter – for the first time, without trepidation, and as ourselves. The past, as that distant, othered place from whence we spring, still lies hidden from us in this and has to be discovered as something yet to be understood, while already it has (as what precedes us) given us to be. The past, insofar as it is just like the present, is not in any genuine sense the past. Or rather, such a past is itself ensnared, and ensnares the present in some middle place, preoccupied with what has been, and unable to look forward, unable, in fact, to draw attention to the past's intimate relationship to forgetting and its own having fallen into oblivion. A genuine understanding of the past lies always before us as a task for the future.

It is a mark of shifts in the epochs of thinking that they arrive, sometimes over centuries, sometimes over decades, but always as if they were already here, so that it becomes near impossible to turn back into their origins and what lies behind them without finding them already everywhere. On this basis already, before ever postmodernity arrived, St Augustine turned out to be Cartesian and Socrates a form of Christ. These more obvious anachronisms conceal a more subtle time-trick, so that we are always taken up short to discover that there were no homosexuals before the *Psychopathia-Sexualis* of

1890,[1] or that interiority meant everything under the heavens rather than inside my head until psychology supplanted cosmology as a way of thinking about human persons. The past is in postmodernity entirely pressed out from the present and its preoccupations. The foremost question that hides itself from us is what these preoccupations are, and herein lies the trick: no matter that the past is far distant from us and a strange land, nevertheless we persist in the view that everyone from the Ancient Egyptians to modern-day Tahiti and beyond could know perfectly well what we ourselves know more perfectly. Did they but move in next-door to us, they should soon enough become as like to us as we are to ourselves.

To move in next door means to become accessible, to become available to us, either by the opening of doors, or cybernetically through the internet, or telephonically, or the whole paraphernalia of the abolition of separation. Distance, temporal or geographical, is constantly worn-out by our immediacy to ourselves. Our very ability to travel great distances in short times merely extends the grasp we have to pull everything closer to us and wear it out more quickly than to confront ourselves with its difference from us. Thus museums of the ancient world have begun to concentrate on showing how *like* our own lives were those of our forebears. The modern-day Museum of London shows Roman Britain as a place of kitchens and bedrooms just like our own – no matter that the social and political conditions, the conditions of thought and religion which these kitchens fed and hearthed are far distant from our own, and made still more distant, even inaccessible, by the effacement of the genuine past for the sake of what in them we most might find familiar.

Perry Anderson argues that 'virtually every aesthetic device or feature attributed to postmodernism – *bricolage* of tradition, play with the popular, reflexivity, hybridity, pastiche, figurality, decentring of the subject – could be found in modernism', indicating the extent to which every trait or tendency in postmodernity can immediately demonstrate its genealogy, its roots, in what immediately preceded it.[2] Anderson brings before us the narrative sequence of the epochs under discussion, finding that postmodernity emerges from modernity. And so a succession is indicated, which, as the hands of a clock move round its face, makes sense to us, and we can see that postmodernity follows

---

[1] von Krafft-Ebing, R., *Neue Forschungen auf dem Gebiet der Psychopathia sexualis. Eine medizinisch-psychologische Studie von Dr. R. v. Krafft-Ebing*, 1890.
[2] Anderson, P., *The Origins of Postmodernity*, 1998, p. 80.

naturally enough from modernity, and even that modernity was preparation for what succeeded it.

Except that the succession does not work in this direction at all, but rather, moves in exactly the opposite direction. What Anderson overlooks is that, in all its variants (now endlessly discussed in the available literature – early or late modernity, the origins of modernity and so forth) modernity is both a production and a fiction of postmodernity's making. Modernity is postmodernity's *product*, generated to explain its difference from what is now named as preceding it. Modernity as such – the way we now conceive it, as if it had ever been there – never existed before postmodernity is named. Prior to this, modernity or Modernism, aesthetic or philosophical, simply named in its broadest sense the contemporary, the up-to-the moment and *avant-garde*, or, more narrowly, certain contemporary aesthetic styles, particularly in architecture, painting or sculpture. Postmodernity is often the conservative bewailment of the decline of 'Enlightenment values' or as one commentator calls it with not untypical disdain, a 'philosophy of despair masquerading as radical chic'.[3] Postmodernity is – in every sense – modernity's decline. Having denounced the poisoning of the academy in postmodernity, our pundit notes in true postmodern style that 'texts do lend themselves to more than one interpretation' and even 'much of what we live with is, in fact, socially constructed', thereby conceding every claim of the very enemy he so forcibly seeks to trounce.[4] The problem these critics of postmodernity confront but cannot explain is the extent to which postmodernity is also a liberation, a deliverer, it would seem, of huge promise. It releases us from the relentless stress of modernity's straining forward for a future that it never quite reaches, never actually manages to assemble. Postmodernity is modernity's relapse into a more comfortable past. What is astonishing in postmodernity – something all its most vociferous critics must address (and for the most part fail to address without themselves lapsing into postmodern ways of thinking) is this: if postmodernity delivers so little (and hence the invitation to deride it) why so many are seemingly contented with the little it delivers.

In this they fail to understand the fundamental political consequences of postmodernity – that the emancipatory movements of modernity have had a conclusion, namely the very destruction of the victim tribe that each and every emancipation claimed first to

---

[3] Berman, M., *The Twilight of American Culture*, 2001, p. 63.
[4] Berman, *The Twilight of American Culture*, 2001, p. 65.

recognize and assemble, and then to liberate. Every identity – social, gendered, sexual, is driven up into a new being and then tossed aside for what comes next. The Left is stranded wailing at the wall, as feminism ebbs in the waves of a successively quiescent tide. Postmodernity places and displaces – literally, in that it frees persons from the determining locus of political hierarchy – it disbands peoples as real entities (whilst constantly erecting fictive nationhoods and castes) and at the same time makes possible their continued life in this displacement. Every drive for a new identity decays into nostalgia for the pinnacle that, once attained, was already passed.

Perhaps the most repeated definition of postmodernity is the 'end of all grand narratives'. This, the very *quoting of the quotation*, although it encapsulates postmodernity's essence, is itself marked by a postmodern degeneration. A reference to Jean-François Lyotard's *La condition postmoderne*, in fact cites by misquoting that text. The very self-evidence that announces postmodernity announces in its very breath its freedom towards its origins. For the 'end of grand narratives' is more accessible, more immediately correspondent to experience, the experience of effacement and erasure that postmodernity *is* in daily life, than its genuine root. It does not fall out accidentally that postmodernity's most easily accessible definition is marked by postmodernity's capacity for caricature and decay.

Lyotard actually calls the postmodern condition 'a crisis of narratives' and 'incredulity towards metanarratives'.[5] Metanarratives are not themselves stories or narratives as such, but rather those things that make my own self-narrating possible: they allow me to tell my story within a wider context, a context I can take for granted. This making-possible, which is a standing-over that allows something else to occur, is, if you like, what a grand narrative or metanarrative is supposed to do. Above all postmodernity is the triumph of the visual, and especially the kinetic visual, whose exemplification is the videographic and cinematic. The standard of self-evident truth – worth a thousand words, a picture never lies – is symptom and emblem of postmodernity's perpetual cycle of decline.

The mechanization and instantaneity of the electro-kinetic and cybernetic radically reconfigure the question of the whole, but do so only because of possibilities which already stood out before us, already available long before the technological means for fulfilling them arose (indeed it could not have arisen without first the means for

---

5 Lyotard, J.-F., *La Condition postmoderne*, 1979, p. 7.

understanding them having been in place). In this there is a question of causes, for the underpinning and underlying is not easy to configure or address, particularly as postmodernity itself is *itself* characterized as what I can narrate from the here and now to give account of what lies before me, so that causes only appear to work narratively and are endlessly reconfigurable to my own unstable identity, an identity I first have constantly to posit before proceeding to its causes.

How is this positing undertaken? In postmodernity the imagination comes to the fore – but leaves open the question of what the imagination is, so that in every instant where I enter into question I take hold of myself by an imaginative means and then proceed to the question at hand. Thus in postmodernity the real and the imaginary collapse constantly into each other, or rather the imaginary is constantly to be realized more than simply personally – thus, cinekinetically, cybernetically, in advertising, televisually, in fact through any medium which is constituted by a field of vision. Jean Baudrillard speaks of these effects in their most extreme form when he says: 'What no-one wants to understand is that the *Holocaust* is *primarily* (and exclusively) an event, or rather an object, that is *televised*.'[6] Baudrillard adds: 'the media are the producers not of socialisation, but of exactly the opposite, of the implosion of the social in the masses.'[7] If the medium is the message – the consequences of which for Baudrillard are far from exhausted – then 'only the medium can make an event',[8] which means that the medium conditions and determines what the event is and how it appears. The analogy with architecture forces itself upon us – the frame, alien from what it supports, and forgotten because hidden from sight, nevertheless determines the shape and appearance, the very possibilities available, of what it supports. What it supports, however, need bear no visible or immediate reference to the frame. This is the very basis of postmodern architecture – not that from a certain point buildings (or, to be more accurate, their façades) became assemblies of eclectic reference to the styles of other periods, but that when technically this architectural bricolage became possible, it became required. Formerly the outward appearance, the 'look' of

---

[6] Baudrillard, J., *Simulacres et Simulation*, 1981. 'Ce que personne ne veut comprendre, c'est que *Holocauste* est *d'abord* (et exclusivement) un événement, ou plutôt un objet *télévisé*.' Emphases in original.

[7] Baudrillard, *Simulacres et Simulation*, 1981, p. 123. 'Ainsi les media sont effecteurs non pas de la socialisation, mais juste à l'inverse de l'implosion du social dans les masses.'

[8] Baudrillard, *Simulacres et Simulation*, 1981, p. 123. 'Le medium seul fait événement.'

the building, demanded a technique of which it was the triumph and expression: appearance drove technique. Hence the architects of modernity exposed the frames of buildings through glazing, revealing how and by what means the now transparent façade was held in place, or they turned the building inside out so that the frame visibly bore the ducts, the pipes, the lift-shafts and floors: appearance celebrated technique. *Now* the technique runs in advance of the appearance. The pure celebration of technique has no outer appearance and needs none; hence any appearance becomes possible, since the building must take on *some* public face. In postmodernity the present frame became the euphoric field of representation for things taken entirely from the past.

By analogy, the whole of Baudrillard's description of the postmodern is marked by a reversal, a turning-about of what we expect in the orders of temporal causation and of causation itself. Surely, the Holocaust gives rise to its televisual representation? And yet, as Baudrillard constantly asserts, we do not watch the television, it watches *you* and us.[9] The cinematic or videographic recreation of holocaust and war, of tragedy and of all events means that 'the war made itself film, the film makes itself war, the two are joined by their common haemorrhage into technology'.[10] We will come later to consider the place of technology in relation to what it bears, or, as here, appears to haemorrhage into it. As Baudrillard himself is well aware, film and cinema have their own interior exchange, where film and cinematic idiom and metaphor constantly recopy and plagiarize themselves in order to be understood. It is not the sinking of *the* Titanic that the film *Titanic* seeks to recreate, but *a* sinking in general, a narrative, intelligible only in cinekinetic terms.

Architecture, billboards, cinematography, television – the whole public apparatus of postmodernity's self-productive and representative technique, the technology for the production of selves both as individuals and as *mass* phenomena – assemble us in a visual field which has no prior one watching, no primary gaze. The gaze which we take to be assembling – self-assembling – is always inferred, put into place to be assembling, and assumed by the ones who take themselves always as watched and not watching. To watch as watching is intended, each of us must step back behind ourselves to gain the vantage point from where we, as watching, can come back into view.

---

[9] Baudrillard, *Simulacres et Simulation*, 1981, p. 80. 'La télé vous regarde.'

[10] Baudrillard, *Simulacres et Simulation*, 1981, p. 89. 'La guerre s'est faite film, le film se fait guerre, les deux se rejoignent par leur effusion commune dans la technique.'

The movie becomes the decisive moment when the *representative means* of the imaginary field itself became a region of commodification, when the imaginary, in other words, became decisive for the production, the very *manufacture* of the real. Baudrillard calls this the hyperreal. From this moment on the whole realm of the aesthetic has the potential to become a mass consumer product. Representation is always more real than the event itself – which means no more than the event itself is *realized* through its representation. Without being represented, without being distributed through the technological means of the representory, the event can never attain to being real. This fundamental shift brings the aesthetic sublime to a mass audience, which means a mass market, a place whose primary concern is the *value* of what it exchanges, not what it is that it exchanges. The ordinary becomes commodifiable as the sublime: the sublime becomes a feature of the everyday.

In his opening remarks to Slavoj Žižek's *The Art of the Ridiculous Sublime*, Mareck Wieczorek reinforces this point in tracing the way in which Žižek has understood the relation between the ordinary and the sublime throughout his work, in the twin registers of psychoanalysis and film criticism. Wieczorek notes that

> there is nothing intrinsically sublime in a sublime object – according to Lacan, a sublime object is an ordinary, everyday object which, quite by chance, finds itself occupying the place of what he calls *das Ding* [the Thing], the impossible-real object of desire. . . . It is its structural place . . . and not its intrinsic qualities that confers on it its sublimity.[11]

If we wanted a statement of the postmodern sublime *in nuce*, we could not have found better. Here is the fundamental relation to the placing of *things* which lies at the heart of any question concerning the sublime – but as we have already noted, even the field of the imaginary, which would appear to resist any attempt to render it as things, is now suborned to the itemization of enthingment. The question of whether a thing can appear either as an everyday, ordinary thing *or* as a sublime object presupposes its possibility of appearing at all. Here, despite the implicit defence of Kant which Žižek would want

---

[11] Žižek, S., *The Art of the Ridiculous Sublime: On David Lynch's Lost Highway*, 2000, p. ix. Wieczorek is quoting Žižek, S., *The Sublime Object of Ideology*, 1989, p. 194.

to pursue, is the inversion of Kant's understanding of the sublime, the abolition of the supersensible characteristic of postmodernity. The supersensible is, in other words, still at work, though lying undisclosed – at work now in its erasure: enthingment, functioning in its cancellations. The supersensible is, above all, the region proper to theology (even in 'first philosophy'), but the question we must ask is: *whose* theology? Aristotle's, Kant's, Aquinas's (to name but three, supply your own for more), or whose?

The inversion that Žižek relies on (but does not name) in order to articulate the sublime in postmodernity privileges the subjective experience over objective knowledge in such a way as to invert the Kantian order – now the subject places itself in pure structural position with regard to the object, but in such a way that the object as an object of knowledge disappears or ceases to be important at all.

Žižek provides a concise account of the sublime in postmodernity, whilst claiming to be working from out of the philosophy of subjectivity. He begins where each of us also begins in postmodernity, by taking the aesthetic sublime in its cinematic, videographic, iconic-kinetic forms for granted. We begin as who we now take it self-evidently we are, hyperreally. So is the object, the thing itself, able to appear in postmodernity, *either* as ordinary *or* as sublime, or is it on some continuum between the two? In which case how does the object both posit and hold together at the same time the two extremes of the line on which it sits – from the ordinary to the sublime? Žižek answers this by arguing that the object, the thing in its appearing, is *both* ordinary and sublime at the same time – which means the object always makes available the full range of the possibilities of its appearing whenever it appears. The presence of its being-present is always understood first visually. Within what it makes available to sight, you can make of it what you will.

However, the two points of the line must always appear: thus what is not at issue is a continuum, but a binarism. As Žižek has on occasion argued, there just are some binaries.[12] Žižek cites the example of a scene from the film *Casablanca* to illustrate what is at issue. The scene in question leaves ambiguous whether two of the characters copulate in a three-and-a-half second break in the film's narrative, during which the camera swings away and then back to them (something similar is at work in Kleist's use of a dash at a key

---

[12] For instance in a lecture at Tate Modern in London in January, 2001. For the philosophical origins of this in metaphysics (not discussed by Žižek) see pp. 69f. below.

point in the unfolding of the story of the *Marquise von O*). He notes that the suggestive device of the film-makers is interpreted by one critic as follows:

> *Casablanca* 'deliberately constructs itself in such a way as to offer distinct and alternative sources of pleasure to two people sitting next to each other in the same cinema' i.e. that it 'could play to both "innocent" and "sophisticated" audiences alike'.[13]

Žižek rejects this critic's reading of Hollywood's concerns for public morality versus adult sophistication because it fails to account for the sublime as such. Instead he says:

> To put it in Lacanian terms: during the infamous 3½ seconds, Ilsa and Rick did not do it for the big Other, the order of public appearance, but they did do it for our dirty fantasmatic imagination. This is the structure of inherent transgression at its purest, and Hollywood needs BOTH levels in order to function.[14]

Here both ends of the continuum are named – the ordinary, as the public order, and the sublime as the 'fantasmatic', for a single subject, as what singles this out as *for me* and at the same time produces the *me* that it is for, and so individuates me through a private, personalizing appeal to the phantasmatic, my individuating imaginary, as the place from out of which I attain to a public face. It is this process of video-kinetic individuation that both explains how the visual watches me and at the same time how, as the one watched and so produced, I think myself to be the one doing the watching.

Sublimity is disclosed therefore, as the moment of subjection, the moment of self-authentication and self-appellation. It is not accidental that we begin here with the sublime as it appears cinematically. The structure of place in postmodernity is, as I have suggested, already dis-placed so that in every representable field *including reality itself as only one among the possible visual, imaginary, fields* the order of fantasy and the imaginary and the order of the real are one and the same – and this means subject to the same ordering and regulation. As I have already indicated with regard to McLuhan and Baudrillard, the

---

[13] Maltby, R., '"A Brief Romantic Interlude": Dick and Jane Go to 3½ Seconds of the Classic Hollywood Cinema' in Bordwell, D. and Carroll, N. (eds.), *Post-Theory*, 1996, p. 443 – cited by Žižek, *The Art of the Ridiculous Sublime*, 2000, p. 5.

[14] Žižek, *The Art of the Ridiculous Sublime*, 2000, p. 5. Emphasis in original.

iconic-kinetic provides this possibility with its *visibility* – it is how it comes to be seen.

Žižek concludes therefore that 'we do not need *two* spectators sitting next to each other: *one and the same spectator*, split in itself, is sufficient'.[15] This is Žižek's most important point, and yet it is almost a throwaway line. We must go still further: the split constitutes the singularity that the spectator *is*, the split opens up a place from his imaginary to his pubic face which is the site of his very being. The sublime of the object, precisely installed at the level of the phantasmatic, constitutes the spectator as a subject. The object is not projected to sublimity, rather the object's appearing is the occasion for the sublimity of the subject, producing the subject *as a subject*. The object in other words poses a world to the subject. The object is, at one and the same time, ordinary and sublime. I make of it what I will: which means in the question of what it is, the will is to the fore in its appearing (it is from out of this that the dialectic of the performative is developed, though that is not our topic at the present). 'I make of it what I will' does not mean I can do anything I want with regard to it, it rather indicates the way in which I am ordered to whatever now appears in postmodernity.

Thus what we may do, we now must do. Žižek, taking a slogan from a German advertisement for margarine, '*du darfst!*', 'you may!' shows how this 'may' is, in postmodernity, turned on its head. What Žižek calls the 'superego' of postmodernity 'inverts the Kantian "you can because you must" in a different way, turning it into "you must, because you can". This is the meaning of Viagra.'[16] This is the transformation of every moral limit ('You cannot, because you should not') into a moral imperative, operating at the psychological level. Not to be willing, not to choose, is to be deficient, to be guilty. Postmodernity converts *my* will, *my* desire into something from which a price, a value, can be extracted. My will, therefore, is not for a projected common future, but for what I most believe myself most to need *now*, *here*, in this instant. It is the means by which I gain access *to* the instant. Postmodernity abolishes the future and instrumentalizes all time immediately to the present, and to whoever is able to hold the present and dominate it. In this sense, postmodernity is not ruling by willing, but being ruled by the need to will. Each of us, insofar as we are, must will the moment, and so our whole lives are subordinated to

---

[15] Žižek, S., *The Art of the Ridiculous Sublime*, 2000, p. 5. Emphasis in the original.

[16] Žižek, S., '"You May!"' in *London Review of Books*, 18 March 1999, p. 6.

the domination of will as such. Will wills us, and willing is how we must appear. The ordinary is constantly produced by the sublime through the commanding appearance of what looks like the possibility of choice. Compulsion manifesting itself as freedom.

How is it that the will came to predominate in postmodernity? That this atheistic epoch of postmodernity operates out of prior first causes turns out to be no less true now than at any other time. In this the repeated claims of postmodernity to be free of ontotheology manifest themselves as false. How, one must ask, can an age in flight from theology and its claims be ontotheological? The source of this question is to be founded in the very identity of human identity itself. Sexed and gendered identity, the basis of identity in postmodernity, is characterized by an instability with respect to choice. For I cannot say 'I chose to be this way' – heterosexual, homosexual, transgendered – whatever your taste happens to be – and yet who can deny you the choice to enact your identity? The vanguard province of the brickbats hurled and returned by the theorists of gender concerning essentialism and constructionalism is itself the very threshold of this question of the will. For if I say 'I did not choose to be like this' – freeing myself immediately from the moral injunctions of those who would punish and eliminate deviant sexual identities – do I not immediately condemn myself to exhibit simply an essence, whatever this may be? And if I did choose, am I not immediately in danger of having chosen what I should not, choosing to be something 'against nature'?

How are we to understand the appeal to the natural, and why should we be suspicious of it? The word 'natural' comes from the Latin *natura*, which means 'that which comes forth for itself', for its own sake. The intention here is medial, and nature translates the Greek φύσις with the resonance of its medial verbal form, φαίνεσθαι, that which brings itself forth into the light. Thought in a Latin sense, a nature indicates that which acts under its own impulsion and necessity. The Christian adoption of the natural as a category is a marker of the fusing of what belongs in the order of faith with the order of being itself – the very ground of ontotheology. St Thomas Aquinas indicates how this operates in a typical way when he says 'and similarly, an operation of a nature which is for a definite end presupposes an intellect that has pre-established the end of the nature and ordered the nature to that end'.[17] From this it is obvious that for Aquinas some-

---

[17] Aquinas, *Quaestiones Disputatae: De Veritate*, Q. 3, art. 1, resp. 'et similiter operatio naturae, quae est ad determinatum finem, praesupponit intellectum, praestituentem finem naturae, et ordinantem ad finem illum naturam.'

thing that possesses a nature, something *natural*, is not so because it appears for itself and emerges, but something whose extantness indicates a purpose and meaning that has already been decided and intended. The one doing the intending is God: a nature is the product and expression of God's will. Aquinas discusses this in the context of defending the notion that there are ideas (we might now say something more like types) in the mind of God – in other words of defending a (Christian) kind of Neoplatonism.

In this Aquinas seeks to reverse the understanding of nature in its relation to divinity that he finds in Aristotle, for he says:

> Similarly, those who say that all things proceed from God by a necessity of nature and not by a decision of will cannot admit ideas, because those who act impelled by the necessity of a nature do not determine the end for themselves.[18]

For Aquinas, and for the particular understanding of being that he wishes to defend, a nature cannot be something that can enquire into itself to determine the character of its nature for itself, and so disclosing itself to itself. Rather the enquiry into any nature must disclose what God intended and willed that nature to be. Why is Aquinas concerned with this? Why should he not assert that our own self-enquiry into who we are and the way in which we appear for ourselves will disclose for us a relationship to God from out of the enquiry we undertake? Or put another way, why can he not simply say that the self-enquiry we undertake will find its concomitant in revelation (that is to say, in the Scriptures and how they are interpreted) which reveals the purpose of the nature, a purpose which will joyfully turn out to correspond with our own journey of self-disclosure?[19] The question turns on the character of causes. For Aquinas asserts that if natures are not preordained to their purpose then the activity of their natures would deny God's prior causation of them, that is to say, would deny that God is the 'first cause of all beings'.[20] Why should we wish to deny that

---

[18] Aquinas, *De Veritate*, Q. 3, art. 1, resp. 'Similiter etiam secundum eos qui posuerunt quod a Deo procedunt omnia per necessitatem naturae, non per arbitrium voluntatis, non possunt poni ideae: quia ea quae ex necessitate naturae agunt, non praedeterminant sibi finem.'

[19] I am deliberately asking – at the expense of a certain kind of neo-Thomism – why could Aquinas not have followed Aristotle more closely – or on their terms, have been more Aristotelian?

[20] Aquinas, *De Veritate*, Q. 3, art. 1, resp. 'causam primam entium.'

God is the first cause of all beings – and is that even what we wish to do? Except that the assertion that God is the first cause of all beings belongs to *faith*. It flows naturally from the first words of Genesis – in the beginning God created the heavens and the earth. But if we make this a formal basis of our understanding of being, then we transform the character of what is natural from something in itself which is to be worked out and disclosed, into something whose meaning is decided in advance by God. The working out and disclosing of the causes of nature therefore becomes an enquiry not into phenomenal natures, but into the mind of God. This means that the outcome of every enquiry has already been decided, is already foreclosed, somewhere else (in the mind of God) and has a determinate end. Every enquiry with regard to the 'natural' is therefore an enquiry into the pre-existing, an enquiry into the past.

When Christian theologians describe a matter as 'natural' or one conforming to the 'natural law' what is meant is not a phenomenon that appears for itself and so has to be diagnosed and understood (and this means redeemed) within the Christian economy of salvation, but rather something whose being and appearing is decided in advance of its appearing, in virtue of the will of God. Still more than this, how-ever, the essentialization of human sexed natures (and the concomi-tant debates which have dogged discussions of gender) turn out themselves to be more problematic than at first they seem. The names 'heterosexual', 'homosexual', 'lesbian' and indeed all the categories of gender which have fallen out into the debates of the last years are indeed markers for the description of identities. Judith Butler has demonstrated how these identities are mimetic and citational in their character. She traces how, through the citational and gendered distri-bution of power, non-male, non-heterosexual identities appear by means of deflection of masculine, heterosexual power: 'sex is always produced as a reiteration of hegemonic norms. This productive reiter-ation can be read as a kind of performativity', this performativity, however, is 'derivative, a form of cultural iterability or rearticulation, a practice of *resignification*, not creation ex nihilo'.[21] Butler has indi-cated well the sheer complexity of sexed identities, and indicated them *against* faith, in the place marked out by Nietzsche as marked by the death of God. Why, when we have no faith in God, or when there is no common *we* who universally accept that God exists, should *we* deter-

[21] Butler, J., *Bodies that Matter: On the Discursive Limits of 'Sex'*, 1993, p. 107.

mine sexual identity – identity in its very roots – from out of a decision of God's? Isn't there a more natural way? Thus elsewhere Butler says:

> the replication of heterosexual constructs in non-heterosexual frames brings into relief the utterly constructed status of the so-called heterosexual original. Thus gay is to straight *not* as copy is to original, but rather, as copy is to copy. The parodic repetition of 'the original' . . . reveals the original to be nothing other than a parody of the *idea* of the natural and original.[22]

The very juxtaposition of these arguments – of Butler's and of Aquinas's – reveals a startling fact: they both depend on an identical structure for their analysis of the natural. If God is the *ratio* – literally, the working out, of the natural in Aquinas, what *ratio* is the *causa omnium*, the cause of all things, at work in Butler? Or we might ask the question the other way around: if Butler can describe the character of sexed identities and expose their pretensions to be 'natural' without reference to God – to what extent should we take seriously the understanding of God that Aquinas advances as the originating cause of the ideas (types) and with regard to natures?

In fact Butler comes close to answering this question elsewhere, though she is unable to demonstrate fully what is at work. In describing that form of the character of subjectivity that she names as subjection, she explains that

> the subject, rather than be identified strictly with the individual, ought to be designated as a linguistic category, a placeholder, a structure in formation. Individuals come to occupy the site of the subject . . . they enjoy intelligibility only to the extent that they are, as it were, first established in language.[23]

She proceeds almost to uncover the structure that is really at work here, for she says: 'the notion of power at work in subjection thus appears in two incommensurable temporal modalities: first as what is

---

[22] Butler, J., *Gender Trouble: Feminism and the Subversion of Identity*, 1990, p. 31. This position has been amplified in an unpublished paper by Knapp, F., ' "Walk the Walk, Talk the Talk": Blokes, and Why It Doesn't Matter that They Think They Are Real' for the Peterhouse Theory Group, Cambridge, April 1998, which develops the notion of 'heterosexual camp' to illustrate the phenomenon of the British 'lad' culture, now paralleled among certain young women, or 'ladettes'.

[23] Butler, J., *The Psychic Life of Power*, 1997, pp. 10f.

for the subject always prior, outside of itself, and operative from the start; second, as the willed effect of the subject.'[24] What is confusing about this second statement is that by 'subject' she really means the *individual* she names in the first. Thus the *individual* in order to take up the site of the *subject* that Butler has identified must perform the citation of something outside of itself and already in place (and so prior to it). At the same time, this performative, through appearing to be an act of will, the willed act of an individual, is in fact the means by which the individual undergoes subjection – is subjected – and so is able to appear discursively, that is in language, which means: is able to appear at all.

The question Butler is always unable to answer – which is why she substitutes its name for that of the subject in the text – is 'what is an individual?' The individual is always that which can only be inferred from the appearances of the subject, because only the subject can appear: the individual never appears at all. The individual is that postulate which we project from every appearance of a subject. The individual is itself an imaginary construct of the very temporal phenomenon Butler identifies – it is the idea of the natural. But the citation, the appearance of the subject, is also a project, an imaginary, a prior nature and idea which is taken up for the sake of the subject's appearing. Thus neither the individual nor the subject turn out to be present phenomena at all, both are temporally determined out of the past: the subject, as that citational 'nature' which is discursively deflected by the one subjected; the individual, as that substrate (substance – literally, *sub-stans*, that which is standing under the appearance) which is projected as already in place as the site for the phenomenal appearing of *this instance here* of the subject.

Although Butler is therefore able to give a clear and detailed description of the citational aspects of the appearing of specified identities (gay, straight, lesbian and all the shades of possibility that what she calls the 'heterosexual matrix' makes possible) what is required is a further description of the temporal-historical character of the subjected appearing of these identities. Temporal-historical explains the way in which each identity lies discursively already-present and so 'over-there' (that is, outside of itself) in order to be brought to light. The identity between Butler's and Aquinas's analysis of 'nature' is in the matter of the will. For Aquinas, God wills natures to be: for Butler, writing in postmodernity when God as the willing *causa omnium* is

---

[24] Butler, *The Psychic Life of Power*, 1994, p. 14.

presumed to be dead, it is harder to see how the dominant, hetero-sexual matrix, the 'law of the father' which strictly speaking is imper-sonal, and so can take up no prior point from which to exercise its willing, can function in the place of Aquinas's God. Except that Aquinas's God is (in the matter of the ideas) *itself* a discursive con-struct, a placeholder for a certain understanding of metaphysics, the metaphysics of presence. In other words it is not that God *is* like this, but that when Aquinas begins to describe God in relation to natures as such, this is *what God would have to be like* in order for these natures to be.

It is important only to note here that Aquinas locates God as having a different temporal relation to creation compared to the creature's. Thus God experiences no 'prior' nor any 'to come' because God is immediately contiguous with and continuous to every moment, every 'now' of time. Only creatures experience time in terms of progression. It is for this reason that Aquinas can in other texts mix up an under-standing of causation he derives from Aristotle (with regard to God) with the Christian-Neoplatonic understanding of prior causation he identifies in relation to the creaturely understanding of God as the (temporally prior) cause of all things.[25] The question here is one of perspective, and the relative difference between the way *I* look at things and the way *I presume* that God looks at things (assuming that I am Aquinas).

Both Aquinas's and Butler's understanding of nature share this in common: they are derived out of an understanding of the willing character of subjection. This is why, both in Thomas's account of nature and in Butler's account of performativity, *I* appear as some-thing *willed to be* in certain ways. In each respective case: God as the cause of all things; and the prior projected matrix of heterosexual masculinity (from which all other identities are deflected, and indeed which are the only ones that can become 'conscious'), although *not* coterminous, have the same structure, the same metaphysical force. They are the prior (absent) presence (and so presence as such) that stabilizes and brings to presence the presence of everything that appears *to be* present, and that appears as the site from which the willing takes place. Surely an 'absent' presence is an oxymoron? Except that this is how the metaphysics of presence functions – by being the most real things and at the same time *somewhere else*, they

---

[25] For a fuller discussion of this see pp. 114ff. below.

produce actual realities that are less real than themselves, but these less real things stand here, now, as present.

While it is easy to see how a philosophical reading of Aquinas discloses God as the *ens realissimum*,[26] and so what is most 'beingful' in all things, surely Butler's own explicit critique of the 'metaphysics of substance' shows she is alive to, and freed from, any metaphysics of absolute being? Butler argues that performativity 'decentres the presentist view of the subject as the exclusive owner or origin of what is said'.[27] By 'presentism' she means to indicate a critique of presence. What Butler demonstrates, however, is that the dynamism of the performative, and its very authorization of the incompleteness of what it cites, depends first on its being able to cite a stable, ideal identity from 'over there', that is, not-here, not immediately present. Second, she shows how the very incompleteness in question appears in the fact that the citation 'draws on and covers over' what it cites, and so experiences its own lack as a *power*, which is its own instability, because the success of the performative 'is always and only provisional'.[28] This incompleteness is the very feature on which Butler draws to advocate the subversion of the hegemonic and ideal heterosexual matrix. What she advocates as the triumph of the subversion of sexed identities is in fact a phenomenal description of the only thing the very identities she describes in their actuality could ever be. Far from deconstructing the metaphysics of substance, she has simply redescribed them in the locus laid out for them by the death of God and the devaluation of the uppermost values. Now not something divine, but something human is the stable type and archetype of present impermanence. This means that every *individual* normative, male heterosexual is himself only a dynamic citation of the stable presence he cites and unstably makes present: however, it is precisely through the instability and incompleteness of the citation that we are able to explain both his pretension to the absolute, hegemonic, general power that he cites (but is not) and his own *particular* depotentiation. Becoming is always less than the being it cites. This 'less than' and lack

---

[26] We should stress here that this is not Aquinas himself, but how Aquinas is read. Aquinas never uses the term *ens realissimum* or even *esse realissimum*, although it can be found several times in Kant's discussions of the impossibility of any proof of the possibility of the existence of God. Cf. Kant, I., *Kritik der reinen Vernunft*, 1966, B631; A603–B660; A632; *Vorlesungen über die philosophische Religionslehre*, 1982 (1817), pp. 22–37 *et passim*.

[27] Butler, *Bodies that Matter*, 1993, p. 227. Cf. Butler, *Gender Trouble*, 1990, pp. 17–21;

[28] Butler, *Bodies that Matter*, 1993, pp. 227, 226.

can be its tragic fate (for Plato) or its euphoric liberation (for Nietzsche, Butler, and beyond). Of greatest importance is that for both Aquinas and Butler the 'over there' is at the same time 'already there' and the 'stably there', the 'ever' present.

In fact, as Butler exposes (and Nietzsche before her), the will in question here, the originating will, is not the intentional act of a subject, but the very condition of possibility of an intentional subject. Nothing, as such, wills. Willing is how everything must be. The predominance of the will in postmodernity is nothing new in itself, it is only in consequence of the death of God that the will takes on a new and paradoxical form. For no longer does it appear that some being other than me wills that I should be in such and such a way. This being – the only being in postmodernity who could take up the moral place from whence to undertake this willing and so in favour of whose heteronomous rule I could abandon my autonomy – is dead. And yet, as Butler aptly demonstrates, in the question of identity and its performances I appear not as one who wills, but as one willed *as*. From whence? From what narrative sequence could I derive this passage into subjection? And how should I take command of that which seeks to narrate *me*?

It is in the bringing to light of grand narratives *as narratives* that we have become incredulous toward them. Is this not the very taking command that might liberate me from subjection? That narrative is instrumental, and produces anything at all, means that the reordering of narrative can enact prior purposes for the sake of a different outcome. When narrative becomes narrative in this way, it instantly ceases to work as narrative at all: every narrative functions as a mask. Because language appears as relative to purposes, it loses its power to be purposive. Your story becomes a mask for your purpose: you experience this purpose as real because you experience the purpose not as your fictive intention, but as a lack which has, rather than being intended, to be fulfilled.

Narratives no longer either presuppose or produce a unitary 'us'. This in turn proffers the illusion that we can be who we want to be, or we can make of anything (including ourselves) what we will (rather than seeing that it is by willing that we are first seen to be made – this means that through willing we become visible at all). The extraordinary fragmentedness of contemporary life means that we can slide between accounting narratives and claim and lose each of them either in succession, or according to where we go, or who we are with. It seems that I can chose the 'us' that is going to include and explain me.

Who I am, and how I narrate myself, have come apart, because the imaginary self-postulation that precedes every taking up of myself suggests always that I *could be* other than I am, so that even in what seems to be the truth about who I am a lack resides, a nagging doubt, a melancholic moment. The coming to the fore of the imaginary does not mean that every imagined thing can be fulfilled, but rather that in taking up something *as* something I am always only too aware that it *could* be other, even if I have no possible means of understanding *how*.

Thus narrative, language itself, appears to be insufficient because it no longer appears to explain exhaustively the presence of what is extant. Meaning itself appears to have become plastic, which means that I appear to be plastic to myself. 'I'll be who I want to be', means whatever I end up being implies a lack, a melancholy for who else I could have been even when I am driven maximally to be whom I appear to be choosing to be. I am never real enough – what drives me to want to be what I want is a reality lying somewhere else, if no longer supersensibly, now discursively.

However, Lyotard also speaks of 'incredulity towards'. If, as I have already suggested, narrative has not come to an end, but rather fragmented into a multiplicity, 'incredulity towards' suggests our relation to the bewildering fragmentation of possible self-explanations that lie around us. Everything from the grandeur of a religion to my choice in purchasing a particular perfume or brand of chocolate can 'say something about who you are' (to repeat many an advertising slogan). 'Incredulity towards' is a way of naming the extraordinary, fictive, experience of appearing to step back, and from this place behind us, stepping forth again from out of there and *choosing*. Here again is Žižek's sublime – it is this capacity for *choice* that appears to characterize our daily life, and from which we derive the *frisson* that makes it possible to imagine that it is real for us, really for *me*. We tell ourselves that we live in a 'supermarket' society, where we have before us a bewildering range of lifestyle choices. This 'having before us' produces in us the sense of our constantly stepping out to choose this or that from a free, prior, space which I inhabit alone. There is no 'us' in this space – I alone, it seems (an 'I' always apparently prior to any 'us') must choose, and commit myself to the choices to be made (choices, however, that are already there, in advance of me). Thus the loneliness of the subject is at the same time an enactment of the subject –'subjection'. Who am I before I choose, except the imaginary self-positing of subjectivity? How do I discover this prior I, except through the self-authentication of a sublime moment?

That there is a prior self, a 'doer behind the deed' is postmodernity's most vicious fiction.[29] And yet, is not our dancing figure (of *Brontosaurus*) this very fiction, this figuration whom we instantly recognize as something of our own? Are not his shuttering eyes – that they are shuttering and mainly shut – the very assertion of the prior self that he enacts? Is he not the self that posits itself before the world, which means, both in front of, ahead of every encounter with the world, and at the same time, always as prior to the world – is he not the very self of postmodernity, and is this not his very familiarity to us? Surely his nakedness is this – his (and our) very priority to world, to what world makes of *him*, and is not this his greatest offence, that he makes this prior self visible *for itself* instead of *as* some *thing*? My endless dissimulation into opportunities for appearing *as*, acting *as*, enacting values, the supposed 'decentring of the subject', is nothing other than my instrumentalization to the panopticon of opportunities to which I can be converted into an object, a thing to be taken up and effected through the choices that I think I make. The one choice that would make possible all the other events that appear to be choices and ground them, this *one* choice – that I need not choose at all – is never available, never possible, for none of the other 'choices' – choices that are in fact not choices, even appear as choices unless one of the extant choices is actually selected. Not to chose is never a genuinely possible choice, because as a non-event, it excludes me from the field of power within which the other choices *even become choices* at all. Thus *not* to make a purchase in the market that is postmodernity is not to exercise a choice, but to be excluded from choice as such.

How can these questions that arise in postmodernity also be a question concerning God, when the sublime above all has been a means in metaphysics of preserving the unity, the totality and oneness of God? Surely in postmodernity, with the fragmentation of narrative and our incredulity towards every *grand* narrative, no question concerning God can appear? And even if it did, this god would have to dwell in the imaginary, that now dissimulating, commodifiable place that enacts no whole but only the absence and incredulity towards every whole, towards the whole of wholes. Such a god could never be, except personally, as something attended to and tended in the unstable realm of my identity. God in postmodernity is this dilemma – that God and the

---

[29] Cf. Nietzsche, F., *Zur Genealogie der Moral*, Vol. 5, p. 279. 'Es gibt kein "Sein" hinter dem Thun, Wirken, Werden; "der Thäter" ist zum Thun bloss hinzugedichtet – das Thun ist Alles.'

gods might be, or be in flight from us, as something withdrawn into an unknown past and locked up in an unknown future, but drawing from us our drive at knowing God (even if only to know the god and gods we then supplant), and so ourselves. Which is why Baudrillard's repeated naming of God as a pure hyperreal should come as no surprise to us. In explaining the simulacrum and the hyperreal, Baudrillard, astonishingly enough, *begins* with God. Already this is a reversal of modernity's ordering of transcendence. Far from being the last and outermost in the order of transcending, God is the first and least in the order of the hyperreal. God is what we have to get beyond. Baudrillard begins by asking of divinity: 'but what becomes of it when it reveals itself in icons, when it is multiplied in simulacra?'[30] In naming the Iconoclasts, the eighth-century Byzantine opponents of the holy images, Baudrillard argues that

> they predicted [the] omnipotence of simulacra, the faculty simulacra have of effacing God from the conscience of man, and the destructive, annihilating truth that they allow to appear – that deep down God never existed, even that God himself was never anything but his own simulacrum – from this came their urge to destroy the images.[31]

Baudrillard names a fundamental connection between God and the image, a connection that persists across Judaism, Islam, and Christianity – but inadvertently, almost despite himself, he names a fundamental connection between postmodernity's own unfolding as (cinekinetic, videographic, iconic) representedness as such and God. So is God and are the gods in postmodernity in flight in virtue of, in *view* of, representation – the image as such? Baudrillard hereby names the connection between divinity and the sublime but as it is falsified and enters its troubling *in* the image, in what makes imaging possible itself. Or does he name something else – that the place of God and the gods has been displaced by the very means of the endless reproduction of

---

[30] Baudrillard, *Simulacres et Simulation*, 1981, p. 14. 'Mais que devient-elle lorsqu'elle se divulgue en icônes, lorsqu'elle se démultiplie en simulacres?'

[31] Baudrillard, *Simulacres et Simulation*, 1981, pp. 14f. 'C'est bien parce qu'ils pressentaient cette toute-puissance des simulacres, cette faculté qu'ils ont d'effacer Dieu de la conscience des hommes, et cette vérité qu'ils laissent entrevoir, destructrice, anéantissante, qu'au fond Dieu n'a jamais été, qu'il n'en a jamais existé que le simulacre, voire que Dieu lui-même n'a jamais été que son propre simulacre – de là venait leur rage à détruire les images.'

the imaginary? Or will we have to show that the God and the gods in flight are the very ground of representation itself? At first this appears to us as no more than a riddle, but a riddle which everything that follows will attempt to unlock. Baudrillard unwittingly names, therefore, an instability – which god is at issue: the God of faith or the God of philosophy? This unanswered question persists in all postmodernity's explorations of God, no matter who undertakes them.

To conclude, in postmodernity, as much as in modernity and what preceded it, presence, and absolute presence, is at work. The sublime becomes for us both a moment of subjection – where we discover each of us to be *I* alone, and where the I may re-enter the world constituted in advance for it through will and representation.

3

Rhetor and Rhetoric

How is it that the sublime arises? If we have examined where the sublime now is, that is to say, with its contemporary articulation in postmodernity, must we not, to understand it more fully, enquire into its history, its genealogy as a term? We have begun, not by devaluing God, but by discovering God both in Nietzsche, Butler, and in Baudrillard's hyperreal, to have been devalued, already erased. Nevertheless, an important moment in this evaluation has emerged, which is that when we took up the question of how it is that Aquinas might speak of God – even, we should note, in the most orthodox way, that is to say by considering God through God's effects rather than by considering God as God is in God's very self – we discovered that Aquinas's articulation was not different in *its own* effects from the entirely postmodern articulation of identity we discovered in Judith Butler. This extraordinary difficulty should neither be underestimated, nor accorded too much significance. Any consideration of the past is pressed out from the concerns of the present. Are we therefore not pressing out into Aquinas from where we already stand, that is from an understanding of God that leads us to draw conclusions in certain ways? This is not different from asking: is Aquinas himself not enmeshed in ontotheology? Or is it that the only Aquinas we ourselves are able to read always turns out to be ontotheological? Is there a way back into Aquinas – and a way back into the wider and deeper historical tradition – that is not mired in the concerns of postmodernity? Surely to do this we would have to separate the concerns of faith from those of philosophy (taking into account the only definition of ontotheology I have discussed so far).[1] To what extent is the sublime

---

[1] See p. 22 above. Although the term 'ontotheology' comes to prominence with Heidegger, its origin is to be found in Kant. Kant summarizes his use of the term in contrast to the term *cosmotheology* in *Kritik der reinen Vernunft* (1966 (1787), A631; B659) having developed it at some length in his lectures on philosophical doctrine of religion. Kant, *Vorlesungen über die philosophische Religionslehre*, 1982 (1817), pp. 20–23. Hegel cites Kant's use of the term in relation to his

implicated in understanding how it is that God has come to us in post-modernity already taken as devalued, already dead?

If we consider Aquinas's own discussion of the sublime we see that he takes for granted that the sublime is a means of describing the human similitude to God. Sublimity is an effect of the pursuit of wisdom by means of which man approaches likeness to God – deification: in fact, the goal for Aquinas of the Christian life.[2] In this, Aquinas already takes for granted a certain understanding of sublimity – he does not, to my knowledge, ever give a formal definition of sublimity as such. Sublimity is the means by which man recovers his likeness to God 'from within'. In this he takes for granted an understanding of sublimity already well formed and present in thinking. Elsewhere he names what sublimity is almost accidentally: 'because no desire carries [a man] off to sublimity as much as the desire for the intellection of truth'.[3] Aquinas understands the sublime to be a physical aspect of the character of the heavens, which is to say he takes for granted that truth and the restoration of the likeness to God is referred to place.[4] As much as Žižek takes for granted the absence of God from sublimity in postmodernity, so Aquinas takes for granted the connection between sublimity, place, and God, as something self-evident. In seeking out the meaning of the sublime, or discovering how it is that sublimity now delivers to us God as one devalued and without life, Aquinas is of no particular help to us.

Perhaps the most important text to consider the sublime as a topic in its own right is the work by Longinus called Περὶ ὕψους, usually translated into English as *On the Sublime*.[5] The text works firmly

---

critique of Schulze, and so was aware of the term, but made no systematic use of it. (Hegel, G. W. F., *Verhältnis des Skeptizismus zur Philosophie. Darstellung seiner verschiedenen Modifikationen und Vergleichung des neuesten mit dem alten* in *Jenaer Schriften*, Vol. 2, pp. 251f.)

[2] Cf. Aquinas, *Summa Contra Gentiles*, Book 1, Ch. 2, no. 1. 'Studia sapientiae . . . sublimius autem est quia per ipsum homo praecipue ad divinam similitudinem accedit.' (The struggle for wisdom . . . is therefore more sublime because through it a man especially accedes to the divine likeness.)

[3] Aquinas, *Summa Contra Gentiles*, Book 3, Ch. 50, no. 9. 'Cum nullum desiderium tam in sublime ferat sicut desiderium intelligendae veritatis.'

[4] This is not in any way thematized or discussed by Aquinas, but simply taken for granted, as the consonance between Scripture and the Greek conception of the cosmos. When, therefore, Aquinas considers the physical nature of the cosmos in God's activity of creation, he speaks of the heavens as 'that body on high' (*corpus . . . sublime*) in the question concerning the work of the second day of creation (Cf. Aquinas, *Summa Theologiae*, 1a, Q. 68, art. 4, resp.).

[5] Longinus, *On the Sublime*. The text is attributed to Longinus, but there is no serious agreement on his identity and fragments and sections of the text, based on

within the range of thought of Greek antiquity, and if perhaps written by a Greek, was addressed to a Roman. One of the earliest extant texts to treat the sublime as a formal category, it refers to an earlier Latin text of which Longinus is critical. Longinus' text announces the topic of the sublime to contemporary thought in two ways. First, as a formal topic in the Platonic context in which it was written, but second, inasmuch as the impact of its translation into French in 1674 by Nicolas Boileau meant that, together with the commentary and vocabulary Boileau established for its interpretation, it became a central text in eighteenth-century considerations of aesthetics, and above all, poetry.[6] Longinus and his text therefore assume a double importance – first, he indicates a moment in a particular discourse in the ancient world; and second, in the making possible of a particular kind of discourse we now call 'modernity', or the origins of the Enlightenment.

Because Longinus' text has this double importance, I want to make a consideration of his text that brings us into an encounter with both the perspectives it raises. First, in this chapter, from the point of view of understanding the text from within the structure of the ancient, finite, cosmos – a structure on which it relies and takes for granted; and second in the next chapter, where I wish to discuss its subsequent reception after the abandonment of this understanding of the cosmos, in virtue of the establishment of what we now think to be an infinite universe. What marks the transition from one to the other is a certain transition in the understanding of the being of being human. For the ancients, such a being is the ζῷον λόγον ἔχον, the being that is held in and has the word. For us, human being takes for granted the subjectivity of the modern subject – even when that subjectivity is itself understood as destabilized or decentred.

Longinus' text has a feature absent from philosophical considerations of the sublime that succeed Boileau's translation, and so after the

---

an incomplete manuscript that survives only from the tenth century, are missing. Not only the authorship, but also the date of Περὶ ὕψους is uncertain. The most reliable attempts to date the text – if reliability means anything – date it to somewhere around AD 100. The Longinus of *On the Sublime* is almost without doubt not the Cassius Longinus of later antiquity.

6 Cf. Boileau-Despréaux, N., *Oeuvres complètes [de] Boileau*, ed. Escal, F., 1966 (1674). John Milbank suggests that this was the first translation into a 'vulgar tongue'. In fact it was first translated into a printed English edition as early as 1652 by John Hall, and in manuscript form by Niccolò da Falgano in 1560, but without doubt these earlier translations remained obscure and without the impact of Boileau's (cf. Milbank, J., 'Sublimity: The Modern Transcendent' in Heelas, P. (ed.), *Religion, Modernity and Postmodernity*, 1998, p. 258).

text's second reception in Western thought: it seeks to exemplify the very skill it extols. This feature, although all too lamentably absent from later considerations, has nevertheless long been recognized: Alexander Pope, in speaking in his *Essay on Criticism* of 'bold Longinus', remarks:

> Whose own example strengthens all his laws
> And is himself the great Sublime he draws.[7]

The text attempts to perform that of which it speaks. If the text undergoes a radical transformation in virtue of the self-understanding on which it stands when we read it – which means if the sublime itself undergoes this transformation – then our task must be to exhibit the self on which it stands. How therefore, can we read it doubly? Which is to say, how on the one hand can we exhibit the human self it presupposes when it was written, and how can we gain access to *that* self which comes to the fore after Boileau, the self which is self-evident to us and so which we take so much for granted that it is for this reason difficult to exhibit? In the previous chapter I touched on the essentially performative structure of postmodernity – that for every act, for every agent choice, a prior moment was enacted from out of which the one choosing steps to make his and her choice. This constant positing of the priority of the self provided the very visibility of the figure of *Brontosaurus* with his visibility – the dancing figure is the one who brings to light (through his forcible drawing of our attention to his cancellation of it) our own passing back and forth into a world from a prior, ideal place.

This priority is a temporal structure, one which is reiteratively performed for every moment, *for* and so *as* every temporal occurrence, or rather one through which each moment attains its momentary character. In postmodernity, each moment comes to us as an object, a 'now', in a structure which has retained the features of its description since Aristotle first analysed time as a sequence of nows.[8] The 'now' that each present moment 'is' separates the stream of time, splitting the past and future by means of the present. The present takes up an object-like character. The performative character of this temporal structure appears to give the moment its object-structure, through a

---

[7] Pope, A., *An Essay On Criticism* (1744) in Davis, H. (ed.), *Pope: Complete Poetical Works*, 1966, p. 83.
[8] Cf. Aristotle, *Physics*, 217 b 29–224 a 17.

repetitious prior-positing of the self, an ideal past (a past to every 'now', every objectified present), from out of which this then posited self reaches forward to grasp what it characterizes for itself as the objectified 'now' of the moment that stands before it. Postmodernity itself turns out to unfold through a temporal structure that can be taken for granted, whose character we have yet fully to analyse. The self of postmodernity, the self *performed* by the figure in *Brontosaurus*, occurs through and from out of a very specific orientation with regard to time. The sublime as we saw Žižek describe it unfolds in the same way – in every case, the ordinary object-character of the everyday is seized upon and becomes sublime in virtue of a phantasmatic self-retrojection in order to spring forward and capture the full structure of the object-moment that appears before it. The everyday is, exactly, seized upon *as* sublime in virtue of this. When we understand this, we may then proceed to ask, what are the temporal structures implied, first by the self which Longinus takes for granted, and second within the understanding of selfhood that Boileau also was able to take for granted whilst undertaking his rediscovery of Longinus' text? Finally – but this is something we will only be able to come to much later – what is the full structure and genealogy of the temporal structure in which postmodernity unfolds the self-understanding of selfhood we now take for granted?

In undertaking this I will show how, in both the ancient cosmos and for the philosophical understanding that Boileau takes for granted, God is eternal – ἀεί ὄν, 'being always' (a view discussed in full, as we shall see, by Descartes and Kant). For now, and in order to understand postmodernity's valuation and devaluing of God, it will be necessary to accept that for Longinus and in the later metaphysics of subjectivity, an understanding of God as 'being always' is already assumed, and so already intertwined with selfhood in a particular way, even though the intertwinement is in each case of an entirely different order, for reasons we will also have to explore. It should by now be clear, however, that the sublime as a thread runs through the whole history of metaphysics, and it is for that reason that I have brought it to the fore for our consideration.

Central to my concern is the character and order of causation. Especially after Descartes, but even before him, a major issue in philosophy is the demonstration of the place and relation of God to selfhood. Even when the question emerges as apparently purely atheistic, in the form 'does God exist?', the underlying question, the question on which the apparent question always stands is: 'does God exist in the place (already) assigned to God by my self-understanding, taken as a general concern?' The supposed 'proofs' and demonstrations of the existence of God, from the medieval texts to the present day (and however they manifest themselves), in reality only indicate a place *already assigned* to God, and so assigned in advance of the demonstration itself. The proofs, or demonstrations, however constructed, can never do more than this. The fundamental transformation in the understanding of the sublime that takes place between Longinus' original composition of his text and its rediscovery exposes the *changes* in the place to which God is assigned respectively in the ancient and modern worlds. I propose, therefore, to read Longinus' text first with a view to understanding the way it articulates this place, and then to show how modern and postmodern interpretations are forced already to have made a decision regarding the text and its concerns in virtue of a place for God that is already taken for granted as having been reassigned after the fundamental transformation through subjectivity has taken place.

Such a reading is essential if we are to accede to the discussion of the sublime which is later undertaken by Kant. This is because the question of the sublime, both in Longinus and for Kant, turns out to concern the place of human being (the place taken up by the being of being-human) with regard to the whole of being, and is not, therefore, simply a question concerning taste or beauty. Even more than this, the question of what is merely pleasurable or enjoyable is almost a concern to be eliminated in the face of the compulsion of the sublime.

The whole of being is named in Longinus' text both as *cosmos*, or order, and φύσις, which we translate as 'nature' or more properly natural being, and next Longinus names this whole as divinity, or God. We have here a second indication of the strength of the category of the sublime as a basis for our enquiry into the devaluation of God. For the sublime turns out to be a constant, around which one world (the ancient) turns out into another (the modern). Might the sublime, which we already track as a category that unites inwardness and the uttermost, also unite the ancient to the modern world, and so function as the track of a certain development of the whole history of metaphysics?

In the first instance, however, we should notice that ὕψος is translated into English (and Latin) as 'sublime', but does not really mean this at all. The word 'sublime' comes from the Latin *sublimis*, *sublimitas*, and is developed from *sub limen* which means below or under, and therefore *up to*, the threshold. This appears to be quite different from the term ὕψος, which means loftiness, or 'on high', or whatever is exalted – upliftment. A more literal rendering of the title of Longinus' work Περὶ ὕψους means something akin to 'concerning upliftment'. The German term employed by Kant which is routinely translated into English as 'the sublime' corresponds much more directly to the Greek: *das Erhabene* literally means the raised-up, the uplifted. It comes from the Middle High German *daz erhebene* and is developed from the corresponding verb *heben* meaning to heave, or lift, or raise up, to which *aufheben*, and so by implication Hegel's use of the term *Aufhebung* in his philosophical writing, also belongs. The Latin term, however, unlike many other Latin cognates of Greek philosophical topics, is not simply a direct translation of the Greek, but is a term with a provenance proper to itself. In fact both terms say the same thing, in ways no longer immediately apparent.

The lifting up in question is, as has always been understood in discussions of the sublime (and is an explicit topic for Kant), the furthest reach. This is at the same time a setting of a limit, the attaining of that which cannot be surpassed. For the Greeks that which cannot be surpassed and is at the same time the furthest reach is that which is most stable, most perfect, the unmoved and 'always' (ἀεί) – being itself. The threshold in question is the outermost of Greek thought, the unmoved limit of the heavens, which is also the seat of the divine. The outermost, for Aristotle, is the first containing place of all that is in and under the heavens – in this sense it provides the condition for every possible thing to have a place in the cosmos. Every thing has a 'where' which is absolutely determinable, because the cosmos is, for the Greeks, finite and implicitly ordered. God, or the divine, is outside place (considered in this way), because God has no 'where'. The outermost, strictly speaking, does not even necessarily denote a region as such, but is a reach which is constitutive for everything within the reach. The threshold in question is therefore, dialectically considered, what Aristotle named as τὸ ἔσχατον, the outermost limit of the heavens (as that which surrounds the heavens, and that which has no 'outer' or 'outside'), that which at the same time denotes all that is interior to the heavens because it is the outermost reach.[9] The outermost has no 'outside' because it is that than which there is no further. Upliftment and the sublime each indicate the same thing – a seeking of what is most 'beingful' in what is there to be experienced

---

[9] Aristotle discusses τὸ ἔσχατον fully in *Physics*, Book IV.

and known. As such, upliftment is the reach-out to the 'over-there' from here: it is the experience (and so *in* what is coming-to-be) of being itself.

The word 'dialectical' here names, not the speculative idealism of nineteenth-century German philosophy, but the region in Greek philosophy that determines the causes and science of being as such. The 'outermost' in question is what Eckhart names in his meditation *Von Abegescheidenheit (On Detachment)* as *innigkeit*,[10] which is often translated incorrectly as interiority, as if what were in question was something interior to the life of the soul or the psyche. It means, not the interiority of a human being (his subjectivity), but his *inwardness* as whatever is interior to the heavens, and so stands under them.

Upliftment as it is considered by Longinus is not, however, the dialectical or scientific topic of the outermost, considered above all by Aristotle in his treatises *On the Heavens* and *Physics*, but is the upliftment-to-the-outermost as it is to be experienced and known, that region of being which is to be made accessible through what Longinus calls the art, or accomplished practice, the τέχνη, of upliftment. Τέχνη here has its simple Greek meaning of know-how, which is at the same time a τέχνη πάθους, a know-how concerning the emotions.[11] Πάθος is usually translated into English as 'emotion' but means *that which happens*, that which befalls me, and is derived from the same root as the verb πάσχειν, to have something done to one, or (in the older English sense of the verb) to suffer.

Longinus begins, therefore, with a doubt, the 'raising of a question' (διαπορητέον) which is really the raising of what is in doubt, what requires in itself that we find a way through – the 'whether' there is a way through (διά) for the ἀπορία that presents itself. An ἀπορία is that which is without a passage or way through, from the Greek πόρος, a ford or crossing. The question is whether 'there is an art of upliftment or emotion'.[12] The question with which Longinus sets out indicates that the question of upliftment bases itself on something which is already a theme in Greek thought – πάθος. The way in which the question is posed presupposes that this connection already exists κατά φύσει, according to natural being. Taking an art as something related to that which is to be brought forth, then in contrast, natural being, argues Longinus, is the foremost and originary first element of any-

---

[10] Eckhart, *von Abegeschiedenheit* in *Werke*, 1993, Vol. 2, p. 448.
[11] Longinus, *On the Sublime*, §2.1.
[12] Longinus, *On the Sublime*, §2.1. εἰ ἔστιν ὕψους τις ἢ πάθους τέχνη.

thing to be produced.[13] Thus Longinus already takes for granted that there is a 'natural' belonging together of upliftment and emotion. His is a purely practical enquiry into whether or not this natural unity can be developed as an art, a know-how with respect to the matters at hand.

In order to understand this inner unity of upliftment and emotion, I wish to take a brief detour into Aristotle's enquiry into the meaning of the term πάθος, in order to show how Longinus' text takes for granted an understanding on which he will then base his enquiry, whether there can be an art, a know-how, with regard to upliftment and πάθος. To do this I will also make appeal to the enquiry into πάθος that Martin Heidegger undertook in lectures on Aristotle,[14] where he specifically considers the question of πάθος in Aristotle's *Metaphysics, De Anima (On the Soul)*, and *Rhetoric*.

Aristotle traces four meanings to the word πάθος in the *Metaphysics*, each of which represents a narrowing of the meaning of the word.[15] In the first instance Aristotle says that πάθος indicates the capacity for something to admit alteration into its opposite, and so by which movement and change itself is undergone. In commenting on this passage, Heidegger notes that it does not so much indicate a passivity with regard to change, but rather that something 'occurs with' me.[16] In the second sense Aristotle says that πάθος refers to the changes a particular thing has within itself insofar as these already are there, which means, already lie within a thing to be brought about. This is a narrower definition than the second, since it provides the basis for the first, but does not necessarily encompass it. The third determination narrows the second, to indicate motions which in their occurring are harmful or painful, and with which, therefore I am intimately or directly concerned – changes that determine my mood in their occurring with me. The fourth, and narrowest definition is also that with which is the greatest for me as such, that which causes me a magnitude of misfortune and suffering. In each case I am brought closer and closer to what it is that most directly forces itself upon me to be understood, so that in fact the fourth definition provides the basis for the third, the third for the second, and the second for the first.

---

[13] Longinus, *On the Sublime*, §2.2. καὶ ὅτι αὕτη (i.e. φύσις) μὲν πρῶτον τι καὶ ἀρχέτυπον γενέσεως στοιχεῖον.

[14] Given in Marburg in 1924.

[15] Aristotle, *Metaphysics*, 1022 b 15–21.

[16] Heidegger, M., *Grundbegriffe der aristotelischen Philosophie*, GA18, 2002, p. 195. 'Aristoteles sieht beim πάθος mit dem Tatbestand der *Bewegung*, weniger das Passive, sondern daß etwas *mit mir geschieht*.' Emphases in original.

The first, as the broadest definition, requires the widest understanding to be seen. Each, however, is a genuine determination of πάθος.

Heidegger notes that in all of these four aspects of πάθος, each refers to change, movement and alteration in what occurs-with as 'something occurs with me in such a way that this experiencing or suffering has the character of σώζειν'.[17] The verb σώζειν means to keep in the state of living, and so to preserve. Heidegger notes that this preserving in occurring-with springs from my being encountered by things I am not able to nullify or get rid of. He does not say so, but it is clear that the painfulness of things of this kind is their capacity to bring me up forcefully before the fact that these are the things I *cannot* nullify or erase, even though I would have them otherwise if I could (this is the sheer force of the fourth definition and narrowest definition of πάθος). That which I cannot nullify or erase I might nevertheless characterize as what I most cry against, as when, confronted with some dreadful tragedy or accident, we say 'if only it were other'. To be confronted by the world in this way with something dreadful and unalterable is to be brought up hard against the world and its consequences, often without having a reason for those consequences or any immediate understanding with which to ameliorate them. In this πάθος I encounter the world in a particular and ineluctable way.

It is through this encountering and occurring-with that I work out my situatedness with respect to the world in which I find myself. Heidegger demonstrates the connection between πάθος and σώζειν, however, not from the *Metaphysics* but with respect to Aristotle's *De Anima*, where he indicates a direct parallel between Aristotle's analysis of two meanings of πάσχειν and the first two definitions of πάθος from the *Metaphysics*. Here in the *De Anima*, however, Aristotle directly says that the second meaning – the bringing forth of the change which was already potentially within whatever is changed – is a σωτηρία.[18] Heidegger makes a startling observation: '*Hegel* took from Aristotle under the expression "*Aufhebung*" the phenomenon of σώζειν.'[19] Although Heidegger mentions this only in passing, and

---

[17] Heidegger, *Grundbegriffe der aristotelischen Philosophie*, GA18, 2002, p. 196. 'Es geschieht etwas mit mir so, daß dieses Erfahren oder Erleiden den Charakter des σώζειν hat.'

[18] Aristotle, *De Anima*, 417 b 2–10, esp. 2f. οὐκ ἔστι δ᾽ ἁπλοῦν οὐδὲ τὸ πάσχειν, ἀλλὰ τὸ μὲν φθορά τις ὑπὸ τοῦ ἐναντίου, τὸ δὲ σωτηρία μᾶλλον τοῦ δυνάμει ὄντος ὑπὸ τοῦ ἐντελεχείᾳ ὄντος.

[19] Heidegger, *Grundbegriffe der aristotelischen Philosophie*, GA18, 2002, p. 196. '*Hegel* hat das Phänomen des σώζειν unter dem Ausdruck "Aufhebung" von Aristoteles genommen.' Emphasis in original.

provides no evidence for it, nevertheless he confirms in a preliminary way what I have already also asserted to be the case, namely that *Aufhebung* refers to whatever it is that upliftment or the sublime also refers to, and we begin to see how this is to unfold.

For immediately we are confronted with a structure of experience which is the very opposite of the structure of melancholy I traced in Chapter 1. There I described a subject who, as lonely, is *produced* through loneliness, which I argued was the very essence of Descartes' *cogito*. Everything that would satisfy, excite, and give being to the subject is at the same time denied it – the essence itself, in repetitious self-denial – of the *cogito*, which at the same time confronts the sheer melancholy that there is denial, and so *things* to deny. Being is, in being, negated. Here the determination of πάθος which Aristotle offers us finds its narrowest and most important definition in what *cannot* be denied or nullified, from which the other meanings of πάθος can be exhibited. Whereas the world always appears for the subject as an 'other', and above all an impersonal other (even when it has a human face), here πάθος indicates not only that which can change over into its opposite, but that which as *already there*, is there to be brought forth. The passions and emotions are those things which disclose the self as already-worlded, already 'being in the midst': what Heidegger, here, and especially in *Being and Time*, proceeds to call 'being-in-the-world' (*in-der-Welt-sein*).[20] Above all, πάθος indicates for Aristotle and in the Greek understanding, not a psychological state, nor a condition of consciousness, but the occurring-with of being human in our encounter with things where there is no choice, no escape from what is there to be encountered.

Heidegger's analysis of Aristotle's understanding of πάθος is explicitly concerned with establishing that πάθος is a 'becoming-taken-with' of what it means to exist as a worlded being. He develops this by arguing that this taken-with is concerned with 'what is there with it in the world – *from outside*, but from outside *as the world as the wherein of my being*'.[21] Later Heidegger will draw attention to the fact that even the language of 'inside-outside' is inadequate to describe the being of being-human, but here, the use of the term 'outside' serves us well in putting the understanding of the being of being human he is trying to

---

[20] Heidegger, *Grundbegriffe der aristotelischen Philosophie*, GA18, 2002, p. 197; cf. *Sein und Zeit*, GA2, 1977 (1927), esp. §§12–13 and §§25–7.

[21] Heidegger, *Grundbegriffe der aristotelischen Philosophie*, GA18, 2002, p. 197. 'Was mit ihm selbst in der Welt da ist – *von außen*, aber von außen *als der Welt als Worin meines Seins*.' Emphases in original.

draw to our attention into direct opposition with the confrontational interiority and loneliness of *Brontosaurus*.

Heidegger draws our attention to the problem that this 'outside' raises for contemporary understandings of subjectivity in a passage of Aristotle which he cites in full:

> A further *aporia* with regard to the πάθη of the soul (ψυχή) – are they all in common with that which contains the soul, or is any particular to the soul? This must be grasped, but [is grasped] not easily. In most cases it appears that none of them, either occurring to [us] or produced [by us] can be without the body, neither being angry, nor courage, or desiring or being sensing. Above all, thinking it seems, is separate. But if this too is a presenting, or not to be upheld without presenting, even this cannot be admitted unless upheld by a body.[22]

Heidegger notes with regard to this passage that the question of the separate character of thinking refers to different kinds of thinking, so that the kind of thinking that is without the body refers to – for instance – pure mathematical thinking over and against thinking of something in particular. In other words, it is not the character of thinking as such that this passage puts into question, but rather what the thought is *of* that concerns Aristotle here. If, on the one hand, for Aristotle thinking is the highest possibility for the being of being-human, on the other hand the whole being of man is so determined 'that it must come to be secured as the embodied being-in-the-world of man'.[23]

Heidegger's argument at this point is confirmation of Aristotle's early argument for the securing of the basis of πάθος on that which cannot be avoided: once it is understood that it is through embodiment, and through the *narrowest* sense of what embodiment encounters that the passions can be understood, both those which befall us and those we engender, then the wider senses also can be worked out. However, this brings to the fore the question of the working-out, and

---

[22] Aristotle, *De Anima*, 403 a 3–10.' Άπορίαν δ' ἔχει καὶ τὰ πάθη τῆς ψυχῆς, πότερόν ἐστι πάντα κοινὰ καὶ τοῦ ἔχοντος ἢ ἐστί τι καὶ τῆς ψυχῆς ἴδιον αὐτῆς. τοῦτο γὰρ λαβεῖν μὲν ἀναγκαῖον, οὐ ῥάδιον δέ. φαίνεται δὲ τῶν πλείστων οὐθὲν ἄνευ σώματος πάσχειν οὐδὲ ποιεῖν, οἷον ὀργίζεσθαι, θαρρεῖν, ἐπιθυμεῖν, ὅλως αἰσθάνεσθαι. μάλιστα δ' ἔοικεν ἴδιον τὸ νοεῖν. εἰ δ' ἐστὶ καὶ τοῦτο φαντασία τις ἢ μὴ ἄνευ φαντασίας, οὐκ ἐνδέχοιτ' ἂν οὐδὲ τοῦτ' ἄνευ σώματος εἶναι.

[23] Heidegger, *Grundbegriffe der aristotelischen Philosophie*, GA18, 2002, p. 199. 'Daß es gefaßt werden muß als das *leibmäßige In-der-Welt-sein* des Menschen.'

it brings to the fore why for Aristotle, in providing his list of exemplary passions (some which are in the passive sense – being-sensing, being-angry; some in the active – courage, desiring), thinking is posed as perhaps one of the πάθη, and yet it is still indicated as separated in some sense. Aristotle provides us with the basis for the separation as that kind of thinking that is thinking without any presenting (φαντασία). The word φαντασία, which I will consider in much greater detail later,[24] can mean both that which is remembered and that which is immediately apparent.[25] It is in the sense of remembering that it is pressed in the direction of being translated as 'imagination', but it does not really mean this at all. The objects of pure mathematics (say, a triangle), which can be understood in thought but have no appearance as such, are yet still intelligible. So there is that kind of intelligibility which has no presenting, and then there is that which does – which depends on our being-in-the world.

Heidegger asks the question whether what Aristotle is striving for with regard to νοῦς is

whether the being of man [is determined] as having-the-world-lying-open, discoveredness, lying-openness of being-in-the-world, whether and how these become determined through νοῦς; whether this being-determined of lying-openness through νοῦς is secured in such a way that νοῦς as such belongs with the being of man in such a way that it is absorbed into the being of man; or whether the being of man, the lying-openness, is determined through νοῦς, but in such a way that νοῦς enters into man from the outside, so that the being of man is only a determinate possibility of lying-openness, which νοῦς as such ensures.[26]

---

[24] In Chapter 5.

[25] It is in precisely this sense that Longinus makes reference to φαντασία in Chapter 15 of *On the Sublime*. Longinus suggests that some call things generated by the φαντασία as like to the production of images, but Longinus stresses the capacity of things thus generated to engender not images, but speech.

[26] Heidegger, *Grundbegriffe der aristotelischen Philosophie*, GA18, 2002, p. 200. '. . . ob das Sein des Menschen als Die-Welt-aufgeschlossen-Dahaben, Entdecktheit, Aufgeschlossenheit des Seins-in-der-Welt, ob und wie diese durch den νοῦς bestimmt werden; ob dieses Bestimmtsein der Aufgeschlossenheit durch den νοῦς so zu fassen ist, daß der νοῦς als solcher mit zum Sein des Menschen gehört, derart, daß er *im Sein des Menschen aufgeht*; oder ob dieses Sein des Menschen, die Aufgeschlossenheit, durch den νοῦς bestimmt ist, aber so, daß der νοῦς *von außen her in den Menschen hineinkommt*, so daß das Sein des Menschen nur eine bestimmte Möglichkeit der Aufgeschlossenheit ist, die der νοῦς als solcher gewährleistet.' Emphases in original.

Heidegger concludes from this that the very being of particular beings, as a there-being (*Da-seiende*) – a being which is in a place in some way – means an inherent possibility to be laid-open. This possibility 'is nothing other than voῦς'.[27] What Heidegger is seeking to bring to the fore is that the passions and emotions bring us into an understanding of voῦς, but (although he does not say this) in the course of them bringing voῦς to the fore they also demonstrate what voῦς is, namely possibility as such, a reaching-beyond for the sake of the opening-out of the inherent capacity of the world to lie-open before me. Thus the progression from the first to the fourth definition of πάθος that we encountered in the *Metaphysics* is itself in virtue of voῦς, but really begins with the fourth and narrowest, and through the working-out and developing-from that the work of voῦς itself is, works back to the first and widest.

It is important to stress that this is not simply Heidegger's own interpretation of what thinking is, it is his demonstration of the inner connections between πάθος, voῦς, and ψυχή as he understands them to be at work in Aristotle. This inner connectedness is, Heidegger asserts, for Aristotle completely dependent on the body. In this Heidegger argues that Aristotle's is a phenomenological reading of embodiment, which is to say it attempts to unfold in a concrete way the actual consequences of what being embodied give rise to and mean.

To return to Longinus' text, πάθος when used by him also indicates an 'occurring with', as that which, in happening, passes the one to whom it occurs through and together with what is occurring to some new understanding: this is thinking as δία-voειν, thinking across from-to.

Upliftment is not, however, letting oneself be a prey to emotionality, and Longinus is keen later to point out that there are forms of upliftment that are without πάθος.[28] This is because πάθος is the condition for upliftment, but in the standing-out that upliftment is, it is at the same time beyond πάθος. Πάθος is therefore the condition for access to upliftment, but is not part of what upliftment is, once it has been disclosed and passed through in the availability for encounter that voῦς is. Πάθος is, in this sense, left behind in the very access to what upliftment discloses. Thus what occurs with us, as that through which we are moved, (for Longinus) discloses above all that which is

---

[27] Heidegger, *Grundbegriffe der aristotelischen Philosophie*, GA18, 2002, p. 200. 'Ist nichts anderes als der voῦς.'
[28] Longinus, *On the Sublime*, §8.2.

unmoved, and so beyond occurrence. This is the very meaning of the connection Aristotle makes between πάσχειν and σῴζειν. For the preserving in life that σῴζειν itself is does not hold us up in a kind of exhausting effort to remain somewhere (which would be more like Aristotle's understanding of contemplation, the ever-contemplating that is the natural state of the gods and to which humans may only attain temporarily, having then to fall back on their earthly needs) but rather this preserving brings out the 'already' (ἤδη), that which was already present and waiting to be realized in the change that the occurrence is.[29] This 'already' is not, however (as with Descartes' God), the prior cause of the change and so of the πάθος. Rather it is the *effect* of the change or alteration which is unfolded through the πάθος – it is what the change or alteration is striving to get ahead to, in its occurring with me. Because it is concerned with a striving-ahead it strictly lies in the future *for me* as something new and yet to be uncovered, even though in another sense it is 'already' present. It is new each time it is uncovered. The 'already' is disclosed in the inherent lying-open towards the future for me that the world is, in νοῦς.

At the same time what is beyond happening and occurrence has a fundamental connection with it in its very disclosure, because the occurrence, the force or alteration that is required, is the very thing that brings the 'already' forth. What is there 'already' is what the thing really *is*, its true being, but this is a beyond, a getting-ahead of myself on which νοῦς works to disclose the inherent possibility for openness of the being of things.

In the same way that the dialectical working out of the causes of things work out, above all for Aristotle, how what moves under the heavens relates to the unmoved, to being and natural being (φύσις) itself, so upliftment is the analogous relating of what is moved within the soul to its unmovedness and the soul's relation to unmovedness in the whole. As an art, this is the know-how, the capacity for bringing into the open for himself that *through which* the one bringing it into the open is passed. It is, therefore, the capacity to make sense of, or bring to self-understanding, what is 'already' there to be experienced, whilst at the same time revealing it for what it itself most *is*. It is in this sense that the 'already' is not something I have to come to know as a 'something in general' which everyone knows in the same way. Rather, when I come across and work out the 'already' it becomes

---

[29] Cf. Aristotle, *Metaphysics*, 1022 b 15ff. Πάθος λέγεται . . . ἕνα δὲ αἱ τούτων ἐνέργειαι καὶ ἀλλοιώσεις ἤδη.

explicitly and forcefully *mine*. It concerns me in an absolutely intimate way, and determines an outcome that only *I* can have, because it is grounded in my own being-embodied. In no sense, therefore, can it be given by following a method such that every pursuit of a goal in general will determine the same result, but rather as something that intimately befalls me it represents for me a pinnacle of attainment – something which, in the getting-to was risky and dangerous and not without anguish and torment.

Here, then, is the distinction between learning by rote or method and learning through the work that νοῦς is, and is the reason why we must proceed through what befalls us most intimately and dreadfully up to that from which we can know in a more general sense. It is the distinction between knowing and understanding something and having knowledge of it without proper understanding.

Even before we ask about the character of this bringing into the open, Longinus makes it explicit for us that 'upliftment is an excellence and standing-out in speaking'.[30] Thus upliftment belongs fundamentally to speaking, to λόγος, and is disclosed in speech. In the introductory remarks of the treatise, Longinus tells us what this upliftment consists in: it is our being stood out from ourselves. What is at issue therefore in this being stood-out is transcendence itself, *ecstasis*. Upliftment is that kind of standing out of ourselves which so far stands us beyond ourselves that the gods become visible, that divinity itself comes to sight. Thus upliftment is a standing-out to the outermost, to the very threshold of the divine. What is it that makes visible and intelligible this being stood out, our being made like to the gods? This is to say, what is it through which what is most common to us and the gods is opened out? Longinus replies by appealing to the authority of the ancient authors, Pythagoras (by attribution), Aristotle, Demosthenes and others: truthful disclosure (ἀλήθεια).[31] Upliftment therefore unfolds as the relation of speaking to truthful disclosure. It is for this reason that Longinus is able to speak of how our likeness to the gods itself is disclosed through the excellence and standing-out (ἐξοχή) of speaking itself, λόγος.

Thus the fundamental mode of disclosure of upliftment is λόγος, speaking, and this is a speaking that is speaking of what is to be dis-

---

[30] Longinus, *On the Sublime*, §1.3. ὡς ἀκρότης καὶ ἐξοχή τις λόγων ἐστὶ τὰ ὕψη.
[31] Longinus, *On the Sublime*, §1.3. εὖ γάρ δὴ ὁ ἀποφηνάμενος, τί θεοῖς ὅμοιον ἔχομεν, 'εὐεργεσίαν' εἶπας, 'καὶ ἀλήθειαν'.

closed, and *is* this disclosure itself. It becomes clear, therefore, that Pope's observation about Longinus' text, that it performs what it describes, is not itself an accidental aspect of the text, but rather its necessary feature. A text less able to bring the meaning and arts of upliftment into the open would at the same time be less truthful. It is in this sense that Longinus feels free not to pursue upliftment dialectically, as a topic whose fundamental concern is φύσις, or what we translate as natural being, but here really means κόσμος and the soul, or ensoulment, in as much as it discloses the being of the cosmos. Upliftment in this way is, however, the concern with the what-discloses, the what-announces. Some of the commentators on this text have translated the know-how that this disclosure is, the τέχνη, as art (and by implication artifice) in a way that opposes it to natural being, to φύσις. Translating in this way attempts to establish as a problem within the text (especially in the opening sections) whether for Longinus upliftment belongs *either* to 'art' or to 'nature'. Although I also translate τέχνη with the term art, it is clear from what I have already argued that what is at issue here is no false opposition between art and natural being (which would itself be a thoroughly baroque concern, and so an anachronism here) but rather *this is that mode of disclosure* – a know-how which brings the full and proper meaning of φύσις, of natural being itself – to a spoken disclosure. In other words we are not concerned with the dialectical and scientific bringing to light of the causes of φύσις and the cosmos, but with the bringing of them to light and setting them out in speaking of them, that is, in the reporting *of* them. The real τέχνη, the know-how or 'art', of upliftment, therefore, is not dialectic, but rhetoric, that rhetoric of which Aristotle says 'rhetoric is the antistrophe, the disclosive mode of replying, to dialectic'.[32]

Thus, Longinus tells us, the character of what is said reveals the capacity and power (δύναμις) of the rhetor, which means, makes the rhetor fully present as what he himself really is, in the speaking in which he undertakes.[33] In the upliftment which the rhetor undertakes to make public, to make hearable, the rhetor is co-disclosed (occurs together-with) in the speaking that the rhetor undertakes: the rhetor is made present through the speaking, and the character of the rhetor is determined out of the λόγος, the speaking itself. Λόγος as much discloses who the rhetor is, as at the same time it discloses what it is that

[32] Aristotle, *Rhetoric*, 345 a 1. ἡ ῥητορική ἐστιν ἀντίστροφος τῇ διαλεκτικῇ.
[33] Longinus, *On the Sublime*, §2.4.

the rhetor actually has as a task to disclose and speak of. The rhetor is the one who in an exemplary manner brings the meaning of φύσις to truthful-disclosure through his belonging to speaking and to the word, as a truthful disclosure which takes as its basis the being-worlded of what cannot be negated or cancelled but is always already-in-the-midst. This is the fundamental understanding of selfhood which underpins Longinus' text. I have already indicated this is in direct opposition to the subjectival understanding of selfhood that is taken for granted from where *we* begin, the selfhood that is immediately intelligible and which therefore so much has the capacity for us both to recognize it and be shocked by it, opened up by *Brontosaurus*. Surely, however, the embodiment that is the theme of *Brontosaurus* is the same as the embodiment that Longinus is able to take for granted as the departure point for what he asserts? Except (and the full significance of this will be clear only very much later) *Brontosaurus* is not embodiment, but the *representation* of embodiment, and so is determined first by the character of representation as such, and only then by what it is that is represented. The figure of *Brontosaurus* is what is uttered, not the one uttering.

Λόγος here would have to be taken in the widest possible sense, as that full range of the modes of disclosure of what-passes or what-occurs in its occurring and in its capacity to be brought to light. At one and the same time, the sublime, which I am preferring to translate with upliftment, both relates to what is to be disclosed, and to the art, the τέχνη – literally the capacity and skilled know-how of the rhetor – to bring it to light. Although there is an art to upliftment, it is still related to the very being of the rhetor – he (or she, insofar as there were women rhetors) is himself placed into question by the very raising up which he both undertakes and offers to undertake in the public sphere.

As I have already suggested, what is indicated in upliftment is the furthest reach, and at the same time that reach which brings us to stand out before what is most permanent and stable about what is brought forth. In the 'passing through' of the one to whom emotion and upliftment occurs (as the securing in what is brought to light of what is divine within it and what is true) the whole of the structure of the cosmos (and therefore φύσις, which is only very narrowly translated by the term natural being) is implied and in a certain sense given not just *in* but also *by* the things of which the rhetor speaks. Longinus' own topic (which I do not wish to dwell on here, but which is the actual subject-matter of his treatise) is to distinguish those forms of speaking and the ways in which they express themselves which undertake such an upliftment. Just for example, Longinus identifies grief, pity, and fear as things that are devoid of upliftment, and so of no interest to him.[34]

It is the rhetor's relation to his audience that is as much at issue as the rhetor's relation to emotion and upliftment. And because the rhetor is indeed at risk in relation to his audience and to what it is that he is disclosing, the modern and postmodern question of the split, the separation of speaker and spoken (resolved in postmodernity through *différance*) is here erased, so that the separation can be disclosed and brought to light only insofar as the rhetor's language is understood to be inadequate to his topic, and not insofar as the adequacy of the topic and the rhetor can never be brought to any kind of final determination. This split is exemplified in the postmodern concern with the establishment of the discourse of the sublime in relation both to subjectivity and (especially in the postmodern discussion) psychology, which is why Žižek has appealed so strongly to psychotherapeutic categories and above all to the work of Lacan in order to articulate the sublime. However, the separation of subject from world, which all psychology already and in advance takes for granted as constructive of that separation, is absent here. Indeed, nothing like a psychology can ever characterize the rhetor as Longinus understands it, since the rhetor is never a subject in advance of what it is of which he speaks, because he is always already-in-the-midst. His recollection of the passions and emotions is only able to arise in virtue of his taking for granted how he *is* (and this means: brings out into the open) this in-the-midst. It is the 'of-what' that he speaks that is always in advance of him, and comes across him and occurs with and for him as the passions of ensoulment. It is for this reason, Longinus assures us, that the rhetor, when he speaks sublimely, speaks in such a way that every one who listens can find in the rhetor's speaking such speech that seems as if it were produced by the listener himself or herself.[35]

Longinus says that the purpose of the rhetor's art is not to persuade, but to carry the rhetor's hearers out beyond.[36] Moreover, true uplift-

---

[34] This is important in illustrating how Longinus diverges from Aristotle, while at the same time relying on the distinctions and understanding of πάθος that are to be found in him. Aristotle's description of fear as one of the major πάθη is one of the central discussions of the second book of his *Rhetoric* (cf. Aristotle, *Rhetoric*, 1382 a 20–1383 b 11).

[35] Cf. Longinus, *On the Sublime*, §7.2.

[36] Longinus, *On the Sublime*, §1.4. οὐ γὰρ εἰς πειθὼ τοὺς ἀκροωμένους ἀλλ᾽ εἰς ἔκστασιν ἄγει τὰ ὑπερφυᾶ.

ment has about it, not that which is merely pleasurable or persuasive, but, because it has the power to amaze us, the exercise of a power which overcomes the hearer.[37] The hearer is overpowered, literally propelled beyond, by the power of the speaking itself and what the rhetor has to say.

Longinus is concerned to argue that there is a true upliftment which belongs to the being of the cosmos – and indeed to the being of the human being itself and so to the very order of the cosmos itself, which we recognize as *of being itself*.[38] Upliftment has the genuine power to disclose the being of the cosmos to us, because the word, speaking as such, is the means of disclosure of the being of the cosmos to human being.[39] This is the sublimity of upliftment, the way in which we know that the upliftment is genuine and truthful in its disclosure. Here we can find the starkest contrast to the postmodern sublime. For Žižek, it is the *privacy* and isolation of the phantasmatic that identifies the sublime as the sublime: the public order is only authenticated by private access to the sublime. For Longinus, it is the rhetor's *public* capacity to bring out the whole audience's entrainment to sublimity that is most important. The phantasmatic is a public, not a (privately) psychic capacity.

What are the exact modes of activity by which upliftment is able to do this? Longinus traces five modes of the τέχνη, the know-how of upliftment.[40] The first two are the capacity for bringing to full-growth great thinking, and being most possessed of strong or vehement emotion, Longinus notes arise from out of the one who possesses them. They are 'αὐθιγενεῖς', springing from out of the self, and so they cannot be *learned* as part of the τέχνη or know-how of upliftment. Although they are genuinely part of the know-how or art of the rhetor, he must possess them already. The other three on the contrary, are learnable, and are the conditions of the know-how of the rhetor: the capacity for producing figures or inventions; nobility of phrasing; and dignified and elevated placing-together (σύνθεσις). Each of these describes a kind of capacity for speaking. They speak therefore of a kind of naming, but not a naming whereby a single term is wrought or plucked out and so placed before us. Rather what is at issue is the capacity for the combining of words and meanings. Naming here is

---

[37] Cf. Longinus, *On the Sublime*, §1.4
[38] Cf. Longinus, *On the Sublime*, §7.2.
[39] Longinus, *On the Sublime*, §36.3.
[40] Longinus, *On the Sublime*, §8.1. τὰς νοήσεις ἁδρεπήβολον . . . τὸ σφοδρὸν καὶ ἐνθυσιαστικὸν πάθος.

taken in a wider sense than we would normally take it, and relies on the combination and expression of what is to be said, not on the actual individual words employed.

This is important in the description of the rhetor's art and know-how, because it shows the rhetor's fundamental interrelatedness to his hearers. The rhetor must take what his hearers already know and have for themselves – language as such, and the matter of language, words, figures, and phrases, and through his capacity for articulation, bring to its highest and most uplifting expression what the hearers already know and are familiar with, but could not express for themselves. What ties the five modes of the know-how of upliftment together and is common to all is the capacity for speaking, but this capacity is one that already exists and is of fundamental importance for anyone at all.[41]

Longinus implies that the rhetor has the capacity to bring forward the properly disclosive words which are then recognized according to natural being in the hearers. How therefore, does this recognition take place: do not the hearers *already* have to know implicitly what they subsequently hear, and in which case, in what sense is the rhetor producing something new through his know-how and in his speaking? This is a genuine question, most important in the postmodern context: when the preconditions for meaning seem always to have been shattered in advance, how can this recognition take place, since the common references of an educational unity or master narrative, or a common history, can no longer be presumed? This problem, however, already exists even for the ancient rhetor, since his task is not to reach back into what the audience already know, but to carry them forward and upward in an *ecstasis* that takes them to the outermost, that connects for them the outermost with the here and now: connects them *through* presencing to the ever-present. To understand it like this, however, would be to misunderstand what Longinus holds up as the basis of upliftment. For the three modes of ὕψος that he indicates as belonging to the learnable arts of the rhetor are not to do with the actual meaning of words already present – not to the λεγόμενον, the already having been said, of λόγος – but to the arranging of the speaking for the sake of what *will* be said and thereby will uplift. Thus he indicates that a genuine productive τέχνη is at issue, a genuine art that is original insofar as it produces by arranging and by the power of what is arranged, rather than by the individual words themselves. The

---

[41] Cf. Longinus, *On the Sublime*, §8.1.

implication is that the rhetor must also know which words will suit his audience – they must be fit for the occasion – but even though the words themselves will already be known to his audience, in each case he is producing a *new* arrangement. In this sense the rhetor is not dealing with discrete objects – phonemes – but with the arranging and laying out of what is to be said. The rhetor's belonging to λόγος – to the word – is not a belonging to *words*. This exactly corresponds to the definition of λόγος that Plato advances at the end of the *Sophist*. It is not the individual words that merit the name of speaking, but the intertwining of words.[42]

How is it that if some of the modes of the know-how of the rhetor are possessed already, and some can be learned, all the modes of the rhetor's speaking can fall under the same title of know-how, τέχνη? In order to understand this, we have again to keep before us that the modes of upliftment are developed out of the consideration, not of upliftment itself, but of rhetoric. To develop what upliftment is, Longinus pursues a fundamentally Greek understanding of rhetoric. Aristotle, in beginning his *Rhetoric*, makes a distinction between the ways in which anyone becomes concerned with rhetoric. Having pointed out that everyone, up to a point, participates (the verb is μέτεχειν) in both rhetoric and dialectic, which is why they are able to recognize the rhetor's arts (that is, recognize them as something in which they also have a share), he argues that some do this through a ἕξις, literally through a habit of their make-up, and some through becoming accustomed to needing to use rhetoric, and so through what they become accommodated or accustomed to, συνήθειαν.[43] Both the terms ἕξις and συνήθειαν indicate habituations of the self or the soul, but one indicates my being in a definite situation with something I already have or possess, and the other something I acquire by practice – both, however, belong to τέχνη, to know-how.

Ἕξις is not therefore some 'innate' ability, but rather my having sprung from out of some particularity – it is a consequence of my having been in a particular way at a particular time with respect to something. Συνήθειαν is the reverse of this, it is the means by which I accommodate myself to a particular practice or habituation. It is possible to see, therefore, that each indicates a relation of myself to something with respect to time and place: one produces *me* and so I spring from out of it; the other is my production of *it* by undertaking

---

[42] Plato, *Sophist*, 262 D. Plato uses the term συμπλέκων – 'being-intertwined'.

[43] Cf. Aristotle, *Rhetoric*, 1354 a 10–12.

a kind of journey into it. For a rhetor to speak of events that befell him in a great and tragic way, therefore, let us say by having been witness to and involved in them, would be his ἕξις. For a rhetor to have to learn the art of how to speak of the same tragic event by studying accounts of it and so conforming himself to the manner in which it could be spoken of is his συνήθειαν.

Longinus argues that although these two modes of habit are distinct, both nevertheless belong to rhetorical (and dialectical) skills that all have a share in. The rhetor, however, has these participated skills in a pre-eminent way. The rhetor's task then, is to bring into the public sphere and through these five arts, a kind of naming as a λόγος, that is in speaking. This naming however is not the fitting of what he knows to what already lies present, the re-performance of the existing name. This is to say he is not concerned with the simple reiteration of what has already been said, as the repetition of existing names or words. You will recall that the three subsequent arts of the rhetor in addition to those he possesses 'αὐτό', in and of himself, are all to do with the *how*, the placing together and drawing out of that which illustrates what needs to be said. This can be summed up in one τέχνη above all, that of σύνθεσις, the placing together and arranging (and so intertwining) of what is to be said. It is in this that the rhetor is able to take his hearers *from* what they already know *to* and *up to* the threshold; this is upliftment itself. This is the farthest reach of the rhetor. In pursuing and stretching out for this farthest reach, in order that the reach be genuinely disclosive of what is there to be reached, in other words in order that it be *true*, the rhetor has himself to be passed through what it is he reaches out for, hence he must already have that capacity – it is not one of the things that he can do that can be learnt, it must already belong to him. In this, he is at risk – in order to bring forth the genuine disclosure of upliftment, he above all must be *passed through* – πάθος – what it is of which he speaks. This is not a performative from which he can be in any way detached or toward which he can afford to be reticent.

Longinus makes one remark which makes plain the fundamental orientation of what upliftment is concerned with, which persists, although in a radically transformed way, in the understanding outlined by Žižek. The text says ἀλλ' ἐπὶ τῶν τοιούτων ἁπάντων ἐκεῖν ἂν εἴποιμεν, ὡς εὐπόριστον μὲν ἀνθρώποις τὸ χρειῶδες ἢ καὶ ἀναγκαῖον, θαυμαστὸν δ' ὅμως ἀεὶ τὸ παράδοξον.[44] This can be trans-

---

[44] Longinus, *On the Sublime*, §35.5.

lated as: 'But on all matters I would say only this, that what is useful or necessary is easily obtained by man; it is always the unusual which wins our wonder.' What upliftment makes visible are not τὰ χρήματα, the things that are useful, that stand out and around man and that he takes as his everyday matters of concern, nor the things of necessity – these things (by implication) obscure or stand in the way of upliftment, insofar as it can make something appear. Thus the rhetor is not able to bring himself and what it is of which he speaks to upliftment through the things of use and (daily) necessity: it is the unusual that brings about both the rhetor's self-appearing and his art of speaking for the sake of upliftment.

At this point Longinus moves us to a discussion of the relationship of upliftment to ὁ θεός, the divinity. Longinus notes that upliftment lifts the one raised τὸ δ' ὕψος ἐγγὺς αἴρει μεγαλοφροσύνης θεοῦ.[45] Fyfe's and Russell's translation has 'sublimity lifts them near the mighty mind of god' but μεγαλοφροσυνῆ does not mean 'mighty mind' but rather the great and noble happiness or joyfulness of the divinity. This is the leisured enjoyment which divinity enjoys 'ἀεί', always. Upliftment here has a fundamental connection therefore with what Aristotle thematizes as the θεωρεῖν, contemplation, which belongs to σοφία, wisdom, and which is also striving after the always or ever, the ἀεί.

This fundamental connection between the being of the cosmos and divinity, Longinus explains when he says it is natural being that has given speaking to man.[46] In this sense, Longinus moves entirely within the province delineated by the Greeks of the human being as the ζῷον λόγον ἔχον, the being that is held in and has the word, or speaking. He repeats this later when he says that words are part of the being and soul of man.

Upliftment presupposes and discloses the rhetor as the one capable of undertaking the exaltedness in the realm of public speech which at the same time brings to light the fundamental connection between λόγος and κόσμος, that is, between the soul in its speaking, and world. Upliftment brings us to the outermost reach of the being of the (changeable) cosmos itself, of φύσις, which at the same time brings us into the province of σοφία, of contemplation of divinity and the leisured enjoyment that divinity is. The treatise *On the Sublime* moves entirely within the range of understanding of world that characterizes the Greek understanding of the being of being-human.

---

[45] Longinus, *On the Sublime*, §36.1.
[46] Longinus, *On the Sublime*, §36.3.

It is essential here to note the causal relationship that pertains in the structure on which Longinus depends. For the rhetor, in bringing himself and his upliftment to λόγος, to speaking, and so up to the threshold of the divine, finds the divine as that which lies 'beyond' and ahead of him and in the future (although a future that is 'already' there to be discovered) – as what must be brought forth into speaking. This is the inversion of the causal structure which is always taken for granted from Descartes onwards (though it has its origins much earlier) – and therefore certainly with Kant. Here, as we shall examine more closely later, the divine is that which has simply to be disclosed as already having been present in what is to be said. This fundamental reconfiguration of the rhetor's art – the τέχνη which he is to undertake – begins, of course, much earlier than this, but in any case profoundly alters the structure of transcendence, from an essentially cosmological to a psychological understanding of presence.

It is at this point that we can begin to see – at least in outline – how the understanding of the being of being-human on which Longinus relies differs from that which comes to the fore after the establishment of human being as subjectivity. Dialectic and the causes of the cosmos are the topics, properly, of for instance, Aristotle's *Physics*, *Metaphysics* and the *De Anima* as I have already noted. The basis for the topic at issue in the treatise *On Upliftment* is the same as the matter that underpins Aristotle's *Rhetoric*, which is the place of the one in upliftment, the co-disclosure of the one for whom the passions and emotions are at issue in the heavens and as ensouled. However, this is entirely with regard to the shared 'exteriority' of being in the world, and not at all with regard to some prior subject-position established before the 'subject' as such will enter the world in which he or she is a subject. Longinus' text, and this means Longinus' consideration of λόγος, of speaking (language, or the symbolic order), cannot ever be made the topic of a subjectivity or subject-position. The interiority in question is that which is interior to the outermost, the ἔσχατον of the heavens, and not the interiority which after Descartes is always taken to belong to the subjectivity of the subject.

4

The Truth of Sublimity

I considered in the last chapter how for Aristotle, νοῦς is the basis of the very possibility of the laying-open of being-in-the-world. Through νοῦς as the standing-out, the beyond, of its connection with the passions and motions, Aristotle strives to accomplish an understanding of being that is fundamentally Greek: being is at the same time stable presence and divine. How is it in the understanding of sublimity and upliftment in antiquity as much as in postmodernity, 'God' and the divine comes to be understood as the object at the endpoint of the 'beyond', the wholly other of absolute alterity and 'the transcendent'? How is it that the devaluation of this 'over there', the absolutely transcendent, results in an inversion of transcendence, so that sublimity and upliftment can either name a reaching-out to the outermost of the heavens or the stepping back into an ideal innermost from out of which I step forth to enter the world, but that each – standing-out, stepping-within, can be taken as sublime?

Indeed, how is it that stable presence, or God, or being, comes to be thought, and still remains in some ways thought, as the absolutely 'over there' to our being here? How is it, in other words, that being and becoming are separated into different places, a separation still clearly at work with respect to Slavoj Žižek's articulation of sublimity, albeit inverted into a private psychology, and how is it that God is thereby drawn into the split in being that is opened up by this articulation of place? Above all, what does it mean that place is always to be *articulated*, which means spoken and spoken *of*?

In order to answer this question I want to proceed, not simply by announcing a narrative that would explain it (although to do this in itself is demanding enough), but rather by showing how this very question arises *as a question* in virtue of postmodernity's concern with the sublime. By answering this question, it will then be possible to unfold what is at issue with regard to Descartes', and especially Kant's, understanding of the being of being-human. I want, in short, to exhibit the impasse that postmodernity has reached with regard to

God, so that we can both gain an understanding of the response to this impasse and demonstrate why the response fails. In order to do this, it will be necessary to take the question of how God becomes the beyond and show how we have not got further than this beyond – how even negative theology, and even the negative theologian *par excellence*, Jacques Derrida, remains in this province of the beyond.

Indeed, in postmodernity, and even now that the God of modernity has been declared to be dead, 'negative theology' has been declared to be a way forward for theological thinking, as a way of thinking this 'beyond being' which can be a site of the divine. The promise of a god beyond modernity, a sacrality beyond the secularized, has been held out as the way in which a god who survives the death of God may be understood. A god, captured in a god's absolute flight. Ilse Bulhof's and Laurens ten Kate's recent publication of *Flight of the Gods* has brought together in one place a considerable survey of this scene.[1] Bulhof and ten Kate argue that 'the term negative theology is easily misunderstood. We must think less in terms of a religious current and more in terms of a tradition of reflection on Being, God, humanity, and religion.'[2] The problem with their summary, and indeed with much negative theology in its current form, is that the primacy of experience, or the promise of success of a method of negation, does not lead us to a positive determination of God at its end, although it does demonstrate both how in postmodernity God continues to be spoken of, and how this speaking reflects concerns that reach right into the heart of our considerations and preserve in their speaking an understanding of God that unfolds from the very origins of Western thought. The divinity with whom we are still concerned – even if we have attended his funeral – turns out to have a full and ancient proven-ance. In particular, it may turn out that negative theology is nothing other than the most extreme – and this simply means 'latest' – work-ing out of what Derrida and other postmodern thinkers have named as the metaphysics of presence. Bulhof and ten Kate claim that 'negative theology rejects Parmenides' dictum that being and thought are one'.[3] In scrutinizing this claim I want to suggest that much of the current enthusiasm for negation is misplaced, since, almost without excep-tion, those currently claiming to be overcoming ontotheology are still

---

[1] Bulhof, I. N. and ten Kate, L. (eds.), *Flight of the Gods*, 2000 – based on the proceedings of a conference held in 1990 at the International School for Philosophy, Leusden-Zuid, in the Netherlands.

[2] Bulhof and ten Kate, *Flight of the Gods*, 2000, p. 4.

[3] Bulhof and ten Kate, *Flight of the Gods*, 2000, p. 5.

themselves far too much overcome by it and, being overwhelmed, have not yet understood what ontotheology names and is.

Derrida has laid out well the situation of contemporary negative theology and its relation to the consideration of ontotheology, when he has – correctly, I am sure – noted the fundamental connection between negation and the question of the *khora*, both in Plato's and Heidegger's work, although he declares himself unable to follow Heidegger's association of the *khora* with place:

> That Plato is afterward suspected [by Heidegger] of having fallen short of this wholly *other* place, and that one must lead the diversity (*Verschiedenheit*) back to the difference (*Unterschied*) and the fold of a duplicity (*Zwiefalt*) which must be given in advance, without one ever being able to give it 'proper attention' – I can follow this process neither at the end of *Was heißt Denken?* nor elsewhere.[4]

What Derrida tells us he is unable to follow is, however, what must be followed in order to show how negative theology is itself *held* in the very impasse that ontotheology *is*, both in the question of being and in that of God. What Derrida seeks to deny in this province of negative theology and of God, is not God, nor even God's negations, but, he tells us: '*How to avoid speaking?* More precisely: How to avoid speaking *of Being?*'[5] How might God appear in any such denial? More potently, why should all being be a being-spoken?

The negation of something positive does not yield something of an entirely different order, it simply yields a thing that is determined in advance and entirely from out of that which it negates, which is why (recalling that Heidegger developed his own use of the term *ontotheology* in relation to Hegel), as we shall examine later, negation is for Hegel the dialectical way into a higher synthesis of being. Did Derrida reach beyond this province – or is it not rather that Derrida thinks through to its latest end this entwinement of God and being, asserted, or negated, so that what he appears to negate, that is makes

---

[4] Derrida, J., 'Comment ne pas parler: Dénégations' in *Psyché: inventions de l'autre*, 1987, p. 585. 'Que Platon soit ensuite soupçonné d'avoir manqué ce tout autre lieu, qu'il faille reconduire la diversité (*Verschiedenheit*) des lieux vers la différence (*Unterschied*) et le pli d'une duplicité (*Zwiefalt*) qui doit être donnée d'avance sans qu'on puisse y faire "proprement attention", c'est là un procès que je ne peux suivre dans cette fin de *Was heißt Denken?* Ou ailleurs.'

[5] Derrida, 'Comment ne pas parler', 1987, p. 587. 'Comment ne pas parler? *how to avoid speaking?* Plus précisément: comment ne pas parler *de l'être.*' Emphases in original.

appear as that which has no name and is not said, is in the very extremity of its appearing as this un-named-as-unsaid, still a *positivum*, an object, something construed entirely out of presence though claiming to be otherwise? Why else in considering the negations of *God* would we seek to cease a speaking of *being*? If God and being are the same, the claim that the negation of God and non-being itself are also the same surely says *the same*, if we can but find a way to say it, since if we say this, leaving the other unsaid, are we not simply holding up a mirror, allowing this unsaid to appear? Is this not the very repetition of the divine activity of generation explained in the *Timaeus*? Put another way, in not-saying being and so speaking of being's 'not', are we not simply performing a reversal within ontotheology's compass, and so leaving everything the same, just upside-down? Is this not the very danger inherent in every claim to 'overcome' ontotheology as a way of resolving the question of God, and why its every overcoming is just its latest, and this means furthest, reach?

With regard to Heidegger, Derrida is reduced to announcing what he – Derrida – hopes can function as an *aporia*. Referring to Heidegger's now well-trodden statement that he sometime might like to write a theology, which would in any case not include the word 'being', Derrida says: 'With and without the word *being*, he wrote a theology with and without God. He did what he said it would be necessary to avoid doing.'[6] One must hear the sheer exasperation in Derrida's voice here – for this will not resolve into a paradox or *aporia*. We must say that for once, Derrida himself is overstretched – he is not announcing a playful perplexity, he has been perplexed. We begin our exploration therefore, where Derrida himself falls silent – here he cannot teach us how it is we *may* not speak, because here, he himself, he tells us, *cannot* now speak. Of this, he is no rhetor.

To name what is already there, is naming a presence. But how did we know it was there before we named it? To know it as already there we had to know the name it had already. And so it never *came into* its naming, it never became. Presencing is being-named: presence is pronouncing the already-named. Yet further, as we have seen with the rhetor, he names, not what has a *word* for a name, but what must emerge anew each time – and so come into presence. Before even beginning, we should remind ourselves, the rhetor *brings* to presence

---

[6] Derrida, 'Comment ne pas parler', 1987, p. 592. 'Il a écrit, avec et sans (*without*) le mot "être", une théologie avec et sans Dieu. Il a fait ce dont il a dit qu'il faudrait éviter de la faire.' Cf. Heidegger, M., *Seminare*, GA15, 1986, pp. 436f.

in his naming. The rhetor – if he relates genuinely to truth – eschews presence for presencing. To see how this might be, we will have to wait until the very end. Are we able to say anything beyond where Derrida is left open-mouthed, but silent? With whom would we begin?

Parmenides is normally taken as the one who originates the understanding that being is one, immutable, eternal, simple, and so forth. This Parmenides is normally opposed to Heraclitus, whose ever-living fire is the being of the cosmos.[7] Parmenides' best-known fragment, τὸ γάρ αὐτὸ νοεῖν ἐστίν, τε καὶ εἶναι, says: 'for the same is (indeed) for thinking as is for being'.[8] If we attempt to think through the meaning of this dictum in the conventional way, and with any connection it might have with God, then we will be bound to try to reject it in favour of a 'negative' theology, because it appears to enmesh us in the extantness of things and our relation to them. It appears to speak only of presence, in that it appears to say: insofar as anything *is* it is *in thinking* – where thinking and saying are presumed to be the same, the 'speaking to oneself' that is for Aristotle and Plato the activity of the soul. In one of his many close considerations of Parmenides' fragment, Martin Heidegger demonstrates that this is exactly how Hegel understood the fragment. He quotes Hegel as interpreting the fragment as saying: 'Thinking, and that for the sake of which there is thought, is the same . . . for thinking is nothing and comes to be nothing, outside beings.'[9]

Heidegger expressly challenged this interpretation. The fragment of Parmenides is from the speech of the goddess who utters all but the prologue of the extant fragments of the didactic poem written by him, now largely lost to us. She, the prologue tells us, dwells within the gates that lie between the journeys of night and day. The gates are opened and closed by δίκη, which we translate as justice, but is better understood by the Greeks as order. The goddess is, as the title of the now lost work testifies, simply 'truth', ἀλήθεια. She is not the Goddess *of* truth, but she *is* ἀλήθεια, that is how ἀλήθεια is to be taken in the text.

Heidegger interprets the alpha-privative, the ἀ- of ἀλήθεια, as need-

---

[7] Cf. Heraclitus, fragment 30 in Diels, H. (ed.), *Die Fragmente der Vorsokratiker*, 1922, Vol. 1, p. 84.

[8] Parmenides, fragment 5 in Diels, *Die Fragmente der Vorsokratiker*, 1922, Vol. 1, p. 152.

[9] Hegel, G. W. F., *Vorlesungen über die Geschichte der Philosophie*, Vol. 18, p. 288. Quoted in Heidegger, M., *Moira* in *Vorträge und Aufsätze*, GA7, 2000 (1954), p. 241. 'Das Denken und das, um weswillen der Gedanke ist, ist dasselbe. [. . .] Das Denken . . . ist nichts und wird nichts sein, außer dem Seienden.'

ing to be heard as the un- of unconcealment and the dis- of disclosure (λήθη) in the uncovering of the extantness of the extant *in* its extantness. Whereas we hear in the word 'truth' a simple unite term, the Greeks heard a word which indicated an undoing of something, a bringing of something out from what it is not. The divinity of truth-as-disclosure is approached through δίκη, that which orders, by means of the journeys of day and night.

Heidegger's central concern, one that he stresses both in the short lecture 'Moira' originally intended to be part of the lecture course *Was heißt Denken?* of 1951–52 and in his lecture course on Parmenides given in Freiburg in 1942, is the association of divinity with ἀλήθεια, with truth and the disclosure of what is insofar as it is, and the hiddenness of what is not, insofar as it is not.[10] The fragment of Parmenides, however, rather than directing us to the unconcealedness of everything that is insofar as it is there already in visibility and for thinking, directs us to a need to understand the word τὸ αὐτό, the same, or the self-same. The same, as the identical and the self-identical – is the twofold, the *Zwiefalt* that we have already encountered as part of Derrida's perplexity and silencing (there just are some binaries).[11] In the very place that Derrida draws to our attention as the site of his perplexity in the matter of the *khora*, the end of the lectures published as *Was heißt Denken?*, we find that here too the matter at hand arises out of a consideration of Parmenides' best-known fragment. However, the twofold is this time named in the context of the Ionic name for being: ἐόν, ἔμμεναι. Heidegger says here that

> if we say 'being' then it means this: 'being of beings'. If we speak 'of beings', then it means this: of beings in respect of being. We speak always out of the twofold. This is already always a prior given, for Parmenides as much for Plato, for Kant as much for Nietzsche.[12]

Plato makes an understanding of this twofold explicit in his understanding of eidetic number. As for Plato, so for Aristotle, the first in

---

[10] See Heidegger, M., *Moira* in *Vorträge und Aufsätze*, GA7, 2000; *Parmenides*, GA54, 1992 (1982) esp. §§1–2, pp. 6–42.

[11] See, with reference to Žižek, p. 19 above.

[12] Heidegger, M., *Was heißt denken?*, GA8, 2002 (1954), p. 231. 'Sagen wir "Sein", dann heißt dies: "Sein des Seienden". Sagen wir "Seiendes" dann heißt dies: Seiendes hinsichtlich des Seins. Wir sprechen stets *aus* der Zwiefalt. Dies ist immer schon vorgegeben, für Parmenides so gut wie für Platon, für Kant, so gut wie für Nietzsche.'

the genuine τάξις of number is not one, but two. The one is always worked out, *postulated* if you like, from the two: the one is never known in and of itself, it emerges as prior to, and higher than, the two only because two is first in the τάξις of the numbers that can be known directly: the one can be known, but never in-itself or for-itself, only as above and so behind the two than can be known. This is because 'two' represents the γένος of being as such. This two, in Plato at least, also represents the εἴδη, the appearances, of rest and change, στάσις and κίνησις. Being, as τὸ αὐτό, the same and self-identical, is always dual, *Zwiefalt*.

Plato demonstrates this quite easily with the 'aporia' of the distribution of whatever is common to more than one thing by means of number, taunting Hippias (in the greater of the dialogues of that name) that if each of them is an odd number – one – then both together cannot be what each alone is (the even number two), so both are one thing, each another.[13] Plato's understanding of 'philosophical' or 'eidetic' number depends on this 'in common' (κοινόν) that is distributed across more than one thing, so that each participates in it. It is by this means that Plato demonstrates that two, or the double, is the first of the eidetic numbers, by demonstrating above all that sameness and otherness both belong together and are opposed. This 'in common' as 'the same' and 'the other' (ταὐτόν–θάτερον), means that the twofold of the self-same is at one and the same time the twofold of otherness – it is what permits the intellect, the διάνοια of thinking, νοεῖν, itself to pass through (διά) to what is there to be thought across to. It is in this sense two-producing (δυοποιός), and as such, lays the basis for and lies prior to the seeability of the seen, which means, allows it (the what-is-to-be-seen) to take up an εἶδος, an outward appearance, that is, a 'look' or literally, a 'face'. The visibility of being is therefore determined out of its twofoldedness, and at the same time out of its intelligibility.

To understand this it is necessary to understand that the fundamental activity of thinking and speaking (λέγειν, νοεῖν) is in fact always διαλέγειν, διανοεῖν. Everything is concentrated on the δία, the going-across-to, which is therefore and in the first place a διαίρεσις. This word, διαίρεσις, means 'dividing up' and specifically a dividing-up that sets one thing apart from another, a setting into relief. Being, for Plato and for the Greeks generally, is a dividing-up, and only then as that, is it διανοεῖν, the thinking-through and speaking – even to the

---

13 Plato, *Hippias Maior*, 301 A–302 B.

self, in the soul, that makes being intelligible.[14] Plato, and all subsequent metaphysics, experiences this 'dividing-up' in a particular way and takes it for granted, so that a certain prior 'setting-apart' appears everywhere and governs how all particular thinking-through and speaking-across are experienced. Heidegger points out what lies prior to this division, in particular in Parmenides, whilst at the same time showing how Parmenides' didactic poem unfolds this dividedness – the twofold in question – in a manner entirely forgotten and covered over by subsequent thought. It is in this way that Heidegger accounts for the twofold, exactly as he says it must be in the lectures entitled *Was heißt Denken?*, which so perplexed Jacques Derrida.

The prevenient twofold demonstrates the connection between the imageability of everything with its utterability. This Heidegger shows us is already present in the words, the actual speaking of the goddess. She says νοιεν πεφατισμένον έν τῷ έόντι.[15] This can be translated as 'thinking, which as something uttered is in being' but, as Heidegger points out, φάσκειν and φάναι belong to an uttering that is at the same time a showing, an allowing of something to shine before us. This he refers to as φάσις, which, he says, 'is the saying; to say means to bring forward into view'.[16] Being, thinking, and saying belong together, they are 'the same'. Thus the twofold unfolds *in* and *through* the very saying which allows things to appear. For this to happen, something must also remain reserved within the saying of the twofold itself.

First, however, we must ask, what is this *saying* of the twofold? Clearly what makes the saying of the twofold possible is that it is the saying of άλήθεια, that άλήθεια itself 'speaks' the twofold and so unfolds it, lets it appear. In this letting it appear, therefore, άλήθεια must retain not only its relation to unconcealment, to what in being said and allowed to shine forth appears, but also in what allowing τὸ αὐτό, the twofold, to appear before us and be uttered, is held up within it. What is it in unconcealment that could possibly allow this to occur? Heidegger says: what remains reserved in unconcealment and allows the unconcealed to appear *as* the unconcealed is precisely, and namely, concealment. Only concealment could let itself out as unconcealment and yet as such remain what it is and so remain reserved within unconcealment.

---

[14] Cf. Heidegger, M., *Platon: Sophistes*, GA19, 1992: pp. 353–81; 406–11.

[15] Cf. Parmenides, fragment 8, Diels, *Die Fragmente der Vorsokratiker*, 1922, Vol. 1, p. 157.

[16] Heidegger, M., *Moira*, p. 249. 'Φάσις ist die Sage; sagen heißt: zum Vorschein bringen.' See page 10 above.

How are we to understand the twofold in its unfolding, both in Parmenides and in what follows him? We received an indication in the working out of the character of the ἀόριστος δύας, the two in general. The twofold, as it is disclosed in sameness and otherness (ταὐτόν–θάτερον), is a disclosing of the pair στάσις–κίνησις or rest–change. Heidegger's consistent argument is that in the appearing of this pair, it is στάσις, rest, that always is taken as the prior mode. Indeed, Plato works out the pair rest–change as unresolvable to each other and even as things that cannot *be* together – this is something 'impossible by the greatest necessity',[17] and yet as such they share and disclose what is common to them, this 'common' being the very κοινόν of being itself. As the mode that is accorded priority, rest is taken to be the mode of presence and therefore of being itself; change, as the subsequent mode, becomes the mode of non-being in its relation to being, the mode of the image and of representedness, the mode of appearing and what will pass away. Rest becomes the mode of οὐσία, of being-as-presence, and of παρουσία, that is the mode of full presence. It is worth confirming, however, that Plato in his discussion of the two pairs, στάσις–κίνησις and ταὐτόν–θάτερον, demonstrates the fundamental connection between them and speaking, or the saying of the sayable. Because difference, or alterity as such, is 'the other' as θάτερον ranges through all things (διὰ πάντων),[18] it is both what makes connection between all things possible and at the same time the cause or thing responsible for their being divided (αἴτιον τῆς διαιρέσεως),[19] and as such is, as Jacob Klein notes, *'the "ultimate source" of all articulation whatsoever'*.[20] In this sense the other, θάτερον, is the twofold as such.

However, this is a determination of being as Plato discovers it in Parmenides. In this Plato stands in opposition to Parmenides, who is already able to hold together the two-in-general, not as rest–change, but as what *in* unconcealment remains reserved to unconcealment, namely concealment, and to hold this in the very coming forth and appearing of disclosure, of ἀλήθεια. Thus the understanding of what divinity itself is undergoes a radical reinterpretation in Plato compared to how Parmenides presents it: no longer is ἀλήθεια as concealment-reserved-and-so-held-in-unconcealment divine, and so assigned a meaning as the goddess of the fragments – because this is how being

---

[17] Plato, *Sophist*, 252 D. ταῖς μεγίσταις ἀνάγκαις ἀδύνατον.

[18] Plato, *Sophist*, 253 C.

[19] Plato, *Sophist*, 253 C.

[20] Klein, J., *Greek Mathematical Thought and the Origin of Algebra*, 1968, p. 95. Emphasis in original.

comes to disclosure – but now unchanging rest as the prior, the mode of presence, is taken as *alone* the mode of divinity – a radical shift.

Understood like this, Heidegger's continued utterance that 'being and nothing – the same'[21] means nothing other than that being and nothing are the modes of presence and presencing such that, in the one appearing, the other appears as not appearing. Presencing appears as what is reserved *through* its remaining non-appeared in what does appear and persist. *Here* is a genuine *ne pas parler* in the very saying that lets whatever is to appear be seen. Thus Heidegger's assertion 'being and nothing – the same' is not, as often interpreted, some delphic utterance which attempts to establish a totality of being over beings, *so* total that it takes up and arrogates to itself the nothing as well. Rather being and nothing, being and non-being, far from opposing each other, are disclosed the one in the other. There just are some binaries.

How does this radical shift, this fundamental translation, work itself out metaphysically? For Plato (and indeed for Aristotle, though in a different way) rest, as the mode of full presence, is the mode in which being itself really *is*. Rest is the way into the one, the μόνας, what Aristotle calls the ἰδέαν οὖν ἰδέας, where because the ideas are themselves determined out of the one (as what is behind and above the two), they have and carry what is most like to the *one* still within them. The ideas are the stable presence made possible by and in virtue of the ἰδέα, and so, for Plato, the ἰδέα τοῦ ἀγαθοῦ, what we call the idea of the good.[22] Most specifically, the 'idea of the good' is what relates to the divine and is divine in its essence – it is that which causes and gives rise to the indeterminate two or two-in-general.[23] Thus the sun is the cause of all the vision that is had, and is that which lies behind and makes available the visibility of the visible. In the sixth book of the *Republic* Plato is quite clear that truth and being (ἀλήθειά τε καὶ τὸ ὄν) lies in the direction of what shines and lies resplendent and is lit, and does not lie in the direction of the region of darkness, of becoming and passing.[24] In this sense, to know being the soul must look up into the light.

---

[21] Cf., for just one example, Heidegger, M., 'Was ist Metaphysik?' in *Weg-marken*, GA9, 1996 (1976), p. 120. 'Das reine Sein und das reine Nichts ist also dasselbe. Dieser Satz Hegels besteht zu Recht.' Heidegger makes the identical point in *Die ewige Wiederkehr des Gleichen* in *Nietzsche*, GA6.1, 1996 (1961), pp. 390f. and in *Besinnung*, GA66, 1997, p. 99.

[22] Cf. Aristotle, *Metaphysics*, 1083 b 31–34.

[23] Cf. Plato, *Republic*, 509 A–B.

[24] Cf. Plato, *Republic*, 509 D.

This, specifically, is the ἐπέκεινα τῆς οὐσίας, the beyond being itself which stretches out and up to the divine in the *Republic*. Nothing less than the working out of the (arithmetical) one from the two. Thus in this radical shift ἀλήθεια, truth-as-disclosure and being itself, are assigned together to only one half of the appearing of what appears, the extantness of presence, the stability of rest, and so to only one of the journeys by which the goddess ἀλήθεια is to be approached, namely the journey of the day. The journey of the night slips into oblivion, letting slip as it goes, the holding in reserve of concealment that appears through the other journey, the journey of the day. Thus, in what appears, what appears-by-not-appearing (the unsaid that remains in the said) is lost. Truth-as-disclosure and the divine now no longer hold a place *between* the journeys of day and night, between being and non-being and the speaking of its unfolding, but *beyond* being (beyond the merely present, the 'here and now'). As such the merely present ('not-really-being, less-than-being') becomes the indicator and sign of what is solely 'the being-ful' or being-ness. From now on, far from allowing non-being as concealment to appear-by-not-appearing, being is actually threatened by non-being. Non-being, therefore, becomes the binary opposite to being, whilst at the same time losing its genuine possibility to appear. Nevertheless a further reversal is in play, for non-being while losing its *genuine* ability to appear, as the unsaid, appears as that which it is never adequately possible to say – the realm of appearances, of motion, and change, the φαντάσματα and φαινώμενα: the subverted realm which Butler celebrates, but which depends for its subversions on the more real thing that it is always the subversion *of*. Being, which is not apparent, is therefore spoken as more real than what appears. Being as the most real thing that does not appear in what appears, as the 'said' and the 'already said', is assigned to the very place that for Parmenides properly pertained to the *un*said.

Thus, an absolute reversal has taken place. For in Parmenides, non-being, as the unconcealment that reserves itself, appears through the appearances of being (and so beings): for Plato, however, non-being is the appearance, through which genuine being can be known and worked out, but never really appears. Rest is discovered through the appearance of change, but now as its pure opposition, so that, as we have already seen, rest and change can never appear together and yet the one is accorded priority over the other.

For Parmenides, however, both the already-there of the twofold and its entirety and immovability also belong to visibility, but in an entirely different way. Being for Parmenides is said to be one and immovable or changeless. The Greek says ἐπεὶ τό γε Μοῖρ' ἐπέδησεν οὖλον ἀκίνητόν τ'ἔμεναι: 'Since being was bound fast by fate to be whole and without movement.'[25] Μοῖρα, fatefulness or destiny, orders both what is present and presencing in a certain way. This ordering is the ordering of the being of beings. In this ordering of the twofold, Heidegger notes that

> in the sending of the twofold only what is present arrives in appearing, and only presencing attains to shining. Destiny altogether conceals both the duality as such and its unfolding. The essence of ἀλήθεια remains veiled. The visibility it bestows allows the presencing of what is present to arise as visibility (εἶδος) and face (ἰδέα). Consequently the perceptual relationship to the presencing of what is present is defined as a 'seeing' (εἰδέναι).[26]

Because the twofold unfolds being it provides for the visage of the seen in the envisaging of presencing, but that means it keeps back in a whole that which *as lying behind and unseen* is without movement.

In the opening-up of the two as the twofold, the journeys of both day and night are required, as the 'between' is unfolded by the journey of day and light and the journey of dark and night. This unfolding takes place in speaking: the journey of dark and night is unfolded as a keeping-back. It must therefore be kept back and held in its place by not-speaking, by silence. Silence, night, and darkness belong together as the holding-back which also belongs to ἀλήθεια in its speaking-unfolding. This not-speaking is not the negating of what has already been said, nor is it falsification, nor is it the contrary or opposite of the sayable. Each of these stands in a determinate and causal relation to the said. Thus every attempt to determine a negative theology out of, and in a way causally or dialectically related to, the said as its subsequent – even a subsequent that suggests a before (because the said always takes on the character of the already-there, the always-having-been-said, the primacy of presence and appearance over presencing

---

[25] Parmenides, fragment 8, in Diels, *Die Fragmente der Vorsokratiker*, 1992, Vol. 1, p. 157, l. 37.

[26] Heidegger, M., *Moira*, GA7, 2000 (1954), pp. 256f. 'Im Geschick der Zwiefalt gelangen jedoch nur das Anwesen ins Scheinen und das Anwesende zum Erscheinen. Das Geschick behält die Zwiefalt als solche und vollends ihre Entfaltung im Verborgenen. Das Wesen der Ἀλήθεια bleibt verhüllt. Die von ihr gewährte Sichtbarkeit läßt das Anwesen des Anwesenden als "Aussehen" (εἶδος) und als "Gesicht" (ἰδέα) aufgehen. Demgemäß bestimmt sich die vernehmende Beziehung zum Anwesen des Anwesenden als ein Sehen (εἰδέναι).'

and appearing) – will overlook and skip over the withholding that speaking carries within itself as the journey of night and darkness as it is unfolded in Parmenides' fragment. This is the withholding character of what lies within ἀλήθεια and remains closed-up in whatever is disclosed.

This not-speaking is a withholding that is part of the very character of the unfolding itself – it is together with speech the twofoldedness of the twofold. Thus not-speaking is not something to be reached, or attained, or learned, or mastered, or let into, or grasped for. Rather it is what is already given, already prior to and before and ahead of the said, but is and can be known only as the at-the-same-time-as, and in-the-same-as, and *as* the same of the selfsame (τὸ αὐτό) the saying of the said. The said comes after the saying, not before. The not-said remains *in* the saying, as what was withheld in saying – if you like, as what could have been said and was not, but remains sayable. How to avoid speaking turns out to be, not a technique, or a sleight of hand, or a twist of saying, but an essential aspect of what saying itself is.

Put a different way, and taking up the analogy of the mirror used earlier (where it was suggested that Derrida mirrors presence in appearing to bring before us the denial of presence *as* and *in* its mirroring an apparent absence) then what is at issue for Derrida is his presentation of the same as the apparently different. In reality what Derrida offers us is the presenting of a mirror of the same, which is still the same – the genuinely different never attains to appearance. Is it not, surely, for this reason that Derrida attains only to an exasperated silence? What Heidegger shows us is the appearing and shining of the belonging together of sameness and difference, the otherness-sameness which Plato argues can never appear together as appearing together in the appearing of the same, τὸ αὐτό. Here, therefore, is the fundamental connection between identity and difference, the same and the other, with which Heidegger challenges Hegel in the very matter of ontotheology. Ontotheology is never able to proceed to a genuine articulation of non-being, because it assigns non-being to being as an opposition, rather than as disclosed in its genuine belonging to being. Non-being belongs to being as, not even the shadow or necessary concomitance of being, but what being makes manifest by holding in reserve with regard to every being (*Seiende*) that being (*das Sein*) bestows and makes manifest.

It is as well at this point to take for ourselves a directive that may help us to unlock what is most difficult about the issues that Derrida raises. Martin Heidegger notes in relation to τόπος, place, and the χώρα that 'Plato gives an interpretation decisive for Western thought. He says that between beings and being holds the χωρισμός; ἡ χώρα names place. Plato wants to say: beings and being are in differentiated places. Beings and being are differently placed.'[27] What Heidegger means here is that a twofold which essentially belongs together, presencing and presence, have been split apart and separated, and that through the discussion in the *Timaeus*, χώρα has been assigned to being as such, as the immovable, and so to ever-unchanging rest, so that the *appearances* of beings can be assigned to the change and the changeable, and so become τά πράγματα, the things that undergo change. Heidegger says this separation of being 'over there' from the beings here, destroys the genuine relation of beings to being *in* their being: the being of beings is given by beings themselves, it is not separable, nor separated, from them.

Plato undertakes this distinction in the transition from the first to the second accounts in the *Timaeus* of the structure of the cosmos itself. Thus Timaeus begins the first description of this structure by appeal to the question: 'What is it that is being-always, having then no origination, and what else is it that is always-becoming, and so never being?'[28] Whereas being-always is embraced in thinking by means of speaking (μετὰ λόγου) because it is always the same and selfsame, becoming-always is only a matter of opinion (and therefore not disclosive of truth), which is understood only with the senses, which are 'without speech' (ἀλόγον). Strictly speaking, what is becoming, although sensible, is nevertheless without disclosive speech, it cannot be addressed or brought to disclosure genuinely, it can only appear through opinion.

It is possible to see now how the task of the rhetor described in Chapter 3 has the force that it does: the rhetor will only speak genuinely and disclosively if he speaks of what is always-being (ἀεὶ ὄν), and it is for this reason that what he speaks of is not concerned with the ordinary and everyday because this is only speech which is concerned with opinion (δόξα) and the world of becoming. It is important at this point, however, to note that δόξα, opinion, is also related

---

[27] Heidegger, M., *Was heißt Denken?*, GA8, 2002 (1954), pp. 231f. 'Eine für das abendländische Denken maßgebende Deutung gibt Platon. Er sagt, zwischen dem Seienden und dem Sein bestehe der χωρισμός; ἡ χώρα heißt der Ort. Platon will sagen: das Seiende und das Sein an verschiedenen Orten. Seiendes und Sein sind verschieden geortet.'

[28] Plato, *Timaeus*, 27 D–28 A. τί τὸ ὂν ἀεί, γένεσιν δὲ οὐκ ἔχον, καὶ τί τὸ γιγνόμενον μὲν ἀεί, ὂν δὲ οὐδέποτε.

to that which appears and so seems. The word is derived from δοκεῖν – to seem. It is for this reason that the rhetor must speak of what is genuinely true (ἀλήθεια) and not what only seems to be the case, 'true opinion' (δόξα ἀληθές).

However, we have yet to see how Plato makes possible the apprehension of being-always in the generation of the cosmos. Plato does not, in the *Timaeus*, simply describe the ever-changing as the place of opposition to what is ever-being and ever-selfsame as the cosmos itself. Rather he asks, towards what is the cosmos directed in its being generated? The cosmos in its being-generated could have been so either toward the self-identical or after that which is always-becoming. In this sense the separation between being and becoming lies *prior* to the cosmos as such. Plato answers by saying that the cosmos is directed in its generation towards being-always and the selfsame, and in this sense alone is the cosmos beautiful and fitting (καλός καὶ ἀγαθός).

Having established that the cosmos is generated with respect to being and becoming, but is at the same time directed towards being as the selfsame and the always, Plato then proceeds to establish a third εἶδος, in addition to being-always and becoming-always. What belongs to it by nature is that it is both a nurse and the receptacle of generation – that is of what becomes. Plato proceeds in the *Timaeus* with a second account of the elements, but this time precisely to illustrate the extent to which the elements (fire, air, water and earth) are themselves in constant flux, each turning into and out of the other, so that we cannot say of whatever is composed of the elements that it is a thing, a 'this' or 'that' (τοῦτον, τόδε) but only something that resembles a 'this or a that' (τοιοῦτον). In order to illustrate this, Plato chooses the example of one who models all the possible figures of geometry out of gold, and then remodels each of them into every other. The example perfectly illustrates the point. Gold is the substance which is imperishable, and which, as a substrate, always remains – it can be neither dissolved, nor burnt, nor corroded. It is, in some sense, 'always' (ἀεί). The geometrical forms however, are also, although in a different way, 'always'. They can never be seen as such, but every time they receive some concrete instantiation, they are visible for what they are, they can be seen. Nevertheless, we never see the triangle or the rhomboid 'as such', only *this* triangle, *this* rhomboid.[29] Thus Plato

---

[29] Here we should note the connection in Aristotle between νοῦς which here does not require a body, and which does in Chapter 3. The objects of pure mathematics exist apart from embodiment, which is why a body is not required to know them.

describes this third aspect as a thing that receives an impression (ἐκμαγεῖον). There are then three kinds (γένη): the becoming, that within which it becomes, and the 'from whence or where' the becoming is brought to appear.

Timaeus concludes that the three are thus: first, the selfsame and the one, ungenerated and 'always', invisible, outside sense, accessible only through thinking, 'being-always'; second, that which becomes in a place (τόπος) and goes out of it again, understood through opinion with the aid of sensation; and third, which is also an 'always', called χώρα, which is normally translated as 'place'. This place however, is not the particular place of τόπος, wherein what becomes appears, and from which it passes away, but place as such, place as it relates to the elements themselves as what withdraws and so opens a particular place wherein what appears can do so and then pass away, the ever-changing cyclic dynamism of matter and the elements. Plato describes it as shadowy, known only through a bastard speech and apparently contrary to what he wishes to assert, in that it is required for anything that is that it have a 'where' (ποῦ) and so seems to indicate that which is neither on earth nor in the heavens, the being-always itself is as such a nothing. Place as such is then the separation of being and becoming, of the one and the two as such so that they remain separated according to number and are unmixed. Every place will be marked by this separation. If on the one hand place itself is the very means by which whatever appears can appear, at the same time it does so with respect to this separating and forcing into opposition of being and non-being.

It is this understanding of place (χώρα) which Aristotle takes over with regard to place (τόπος). Plato makes exactly the same point with regard to τόπος: place as such, and anything that is in place, must always be separated and divided. Thus χώρα, as what makes every changeable thing available to appear as changeable, becomes in Aristotle the basis on which the structure of the cosmos and the self-motion of the elements is worked out. What Plato names as χώρα, Aristotle calls ὕλη: 'This is why Plato holds matter and χώρα to be the same in the *Timaeus*, because χώρα and the receptacle are one and the same.'[30] Place, τόπος, becomes the seat of being itself, the seat of the divine. Aristotle will describe this place, this τόπος, as the first

---

[30] Aristotle, *Physics*, 209 b 12–13. Διὸ καὶ Πλάτων τὴν ὕλην καὶ τὴν χώραν ταὐτό φησιν εἶναι τῷ ἐν Τιμαίῳ · τὸ γὰρ μεταληπτικὸν καὶ τὴν χώραν ἓν καὶ ταὐτόν.

unmoved limit of what contains,[31] and thereby determine the outermost reach of the cosmos from his understanding of the motion of the elements and from χώρα, which he names as ὕλη, but from which his understanding of place, τόπος, is worked out. Place as such (given by every particular emplacement) becomes that to which we transcend, that to which we stretch out as our furthest reach.

Earlier I indicated Derrida's comment that 'Plato is afterward suspected of having fallen short of this wholly *other* place'. However, it becomes clear from what I have already said that Plato does not fall short of this place, rather, he secures it all too well and makes it accessible. He does not leave it in the with-held, but names and identifies and elaborates it – he literally lays his hands upon it. In its invisibility, he determines it as what not only lies beyond, but also as what itself causes and makes available the visible: thus no longer is it truth-as-disclosure, ἀλήθεια, which lets the concealed into unconcealment, but for him it is the beyond, the χώρα. It is Aristotle, above all in his *Physics*, who works out a fully developed description of place and the elements. For Plato, place is worked out with less decisive clarity. Thus the χώρα turns out to be, not aporetic at all, but entirely *over*-determined, with every pun possible there intended. The χώρα, as the separation (and, indeed, driving apart) of beings as they appear, and being as such (and as the immovable and always, ἀεί), turns out to be all to easily and too much the setting-apart of the place wherein God is to be found from every particular place – for Plato and for Aristotle. Divinity – the gods – however this is to be named, is now transformed as something securable in the dividing-up that being is. Most specifically God and the gods do not arrive in the opening that truth-as-disclosure lays open, but rather God and the gods now have a place, even if, as all agree, this is not any 'where'.

It therefore becomes all too clear why, when this place is deposed and emptied in postmodernity, when 'God is dead', that its very negation leaves this nowhered place *in* place, because this negativity also only belongs to the way of the journey of the day, and still lets rest in oblivion the hidden journey of the night, that journey which would bring before us once again the genuine twofold of being. In other words the annihilation of God does not return us to any genuine understanding of non-being, but rather indicates a lack which is nevertheless a *positive* place, a place that demands to be filled, at the

---

[31] Aristotle, *Physics*, 212 a 21. ὥστε τὸ τοῦ περιέχοντος πέρας ἀκίνετον πρῶτον, τοῦτ᾽ ἔστιν ὁ τόπος.

same time covering over and banishing the genuine non-being of becoming that remains held and reserved by what appears. What we are confronted with is a place wherein we find a need to *put* things, which means, put *things*.

And in all of this, even though we have learnt in a profoundly different way to speak of the unsaid, and to let be sayable what is left out of saying – without negations, without tricks – thereby we have re-opened the question of the relation of divinity to disclosure. It should now be clear how the theology of Plato and Aristotle becomes possible, and how it is that God is assigned a place (and a value!) from which this same God can be deposed. Because of this *possibility* of assignation, God, having been assigned a place (even though strictly speaking it is a place *beyond* every particular place as such), can be displaced. What can be displaced can thereby be devalued. How is this so? God surely cannot belong to the twofold, God is *one* and simple. Every assertion concerning God is – in this even Aquinas is in agreement with Aristotle – a theology. A theology is the working out of the meaning of God and the gods. God and the divine has been assigned a place. From the dividing-up that being is, from out of this twofold, the one and simple can always be found.

In the *Sophist* Plato has the Eleatic Stranger – the one supposedly who represents the doctrine of Parmenides concerning being – say 'all number whatsoever we posit is of being' to which the reply is 'at least if there is any particular "what" posited as a being'.[32] 'Posit' here roughly translates the verb τίθημι – more strictly it means the activity of putting in place, to lay out with a 'respect to some where'. The word θέσις also relates to the verb θέω, shine, or gleam, so that it is a θέσις is some appearing in its being set to appear. As an appearance it has a 'where' set for it from which it appears: as something *put* in place – a position. At the same time a θετός, a thing having been placed, is at the same time θετέος, countable.

This exchange therefore says that all being, everything that has θέσις, a 'respect to where', and so has a particular place, is at the same time number. Nothing particular unusual is being said in Greek – what is placeable is at the same time countable: the converse is also true: to put in place or posit is at the same time to assign a value, or count. The Stranger of the dialogue *The Sophist* replies that neither the many (πλῆθος) nor even the one (ἕν) must therefore be carried over to non-

---

[32] Plato, *Sophist*, 232 A–238 B. Stranger: ἀριθμὸν δὴ τὸν ξύμπαντα τῶν ὄντων τίθεμεν. Theaetetus: εἴπερ γε καὶ ἄλλο τι θετέον ὡς ὄν.

being.[33] The one, the ἕν, is the number that does not appear except with respect to other beings, it must always be found out from among them. We are told, therefore, that even this number must not be found through attribution to non-being. This means that for Plato all genuine being arises out of number, and all number is with respect to beings. It also means that the ἕν, the one, must find a place. In one way (as we shall see) for the Greeks every being is a particular being: every ὄν is a ἕν. As that which is seated in the most beingful place, the place that is unmoved, ever-same and always, is God one?

Derrida's enquiry into Heidegger, and Heidegger's enquiry into Parmenides, illustrate on what basis upliftment is stood. The separation out into beings and being as divided reveals the span which can be taken up toward which upliftment reaches. What is the meaning of this cleft between beings and being, between presencing and presence? Upliftment is the experience of traversing the from-here to the over-there, the outermost. The outermost is the ever-same and unchanging of being. This outermost appears in Plato and in Aristotle differently, but both have an outermost in view in their thinking. The opening sections of Heidegger's 1925 lectures on Plato's *Sophist* are comprised entirely of a lengthy discussion of Aristotle's *Nicomachean Ethics*. Here he unfolded the question of the ἀεί, the 'ever' of divinity, and how it is taken up into the question of what will become upliftment and transcendence. Heidegger considers the question of the meaning of the word θεωρεῖν, which we translate as 'contemplating', and which for Aristotle is described as the way of being of the σοφίστες, the wise one who unfolds and lives within the highest of the modes of truth. Heidegger concludes: 'θεωρεῖν *is a way of being in which man attains his highest way of being: his own spiritual health.*'[34] What does highest being mean here? Heidegger argues that for Aristotle, 'human *Dasein* comes into its own only if it *always is what it can be in the highest sense*, that is, when it remains in the highest measure, as long as possible, and most nearly always, in the pure pondering of the beings that are always'.[35] This is the 'furthest reach' of what, as we

---

[33] Plato, *Sophist*, 238 B. Stranger: μὴ τοίνυν μηδ' ἐπιχειρῶμεν ἀριθμοῦ μήτε πλῆθος μήτε τὸ ἕν πρὸς τὸ μὴ ὄν προσφέρειν.

[34] Heidegger, *Platon: Sophistes*, GA19, 1992, p. 170. '*Das* θεωρεῖν *ist eine Seinsart, in der der Mensch seine höchste Seinsart hat: sein eigentliches geistiges Gesundsein.*' Emphasis in original.

[35] Heidegger, *Platon: Sophistes*, GA19, 1992, p. 171. 'Das menschliche Dasein ist dann eigentlich, wenn es *immer so ist, wie es in höchstem Sinne sein kann*, wenn es sich also in höchstem Maße, möglichst lange und immer, im reinen Betrachten des Immerseienden aufhält.' Emphasis in original.

will later see, Kant takes to be the subject position of the sublime, of upliftment.

The rhetor, like the *sophistes*, in straining to reach this outermost, either through contemplation or rhetoric, now attempts to make present through speaking (and even the speaking to the self which is the interior activity of the soul is indicated here). Whereas the rhetor or the one thinking might have had in view the struggle to bring to presence through speaking the being of beings as an attempt to speak of what befalls the speaker, in the light of this cleft the thinker and rhetor attempt to define beings in terms of being-always. The temporal understanding of the experience of experiencing itself is replaced by the attempt to account for the relation *to* being as presence.

There is, however, a structure which Heidegger says is itself the originary ground of speaking as such: he makes this remark in two places, one, some fifteen years after the publication of *Sein und Zeit*. Here he says: 'In *Being and Time*, no matter how strange it must sound, "time" is the given name of the originary *ground* of the word.'[36] Speaking, and being held by the word as such, is the timing of time, or put another way, our belonging together and *already being-with-one-another* is itself disclosed by our being-speaking. This is why what for Longinus becomes the essence of the rhetor's art, as we have already seen with Aristotle's introduction to the *Rhetoric*, is something that everyone can take for granted and does in some sense already participate in. Thought like this, the rhetor's real task is to unfold the common ground of the temporal unfolding of world, *not* the metaphysical description of the passability of world in relation to presence.

Heidegger makes a related point in the *Sophist* lectures. Here he shows that, for Aristotle and for Plato (indeed he argues that in this regard Plato is himself in this part of the *Sophist* [260a–268d] commenting on Aristotle!), speaking in its relation to rest and motion brings the possibility of a philosophical determination of rest to light, as the ἀεὶ ὄν, 'das Immerseiende'.[37] He concludes by interpreting Plato against himself, by showing what, despite himself, he could not but help bring to light:

---

[36] Heidegger, *Parmenides*, GA54, 1992, p. 113. '"Zeit" ist in "Sein und Zeit", so befremdlich das klingen muß, der Vorname für den Anfangs*grund* des Wortes.' Emphasis in original.

[37] Heidegger, *Platon: Sophistes*, GA19, 1992, p. 580. 'the sempiternal'.

Thus you see, that in this concept of permanence, of the perpetual, factually, although not expressly, but according to the matter itself, for Plato the concept of *time emerges*, as the *phenomenon* which determines beings in their being: the present, παρουσία, which is often simply shortened to οὐσία. And λέγειν, the addressing disclosure of beings, is nothing other than the making-present of the visibility of beings themselves and therewith that in them as what it is; as presented disclosure it brings the present to appropriation.[38]

It is possible to see here in its root both the fundamental connection with God and why, curiously, in the whole of the later part of these lectures, Heidegger shies away from commenting on this reference to divinity. Those who know Plato's *Sophist* will recall that toward the end of the dialogue the Stranger is keen to point out to Theaetetus the connection between this determination of speaking, λέγειν, and divinity. The connection, however is established in the dialogue through ποίησις, through the making-creating which Heidegger seeks to resist, and which becomes established by the way in which the ἀεὶ ὄν, being-always (sempiternity), is secured.[39] What is at issue is a fundamentally *ontological* structure of time and speaking that is constitutive of human *Dasein*.

What is central for Heidegger is the *way* in which Plato brings something to light which already lay as the grounding possibility for being itself: not λέγειν, speaking as such, but διαλέγεσθαι (the middle voice), speaking-together-with, where there is one speaking with me always implied (even in that speaking-together-with which I undertake when I speak to myself 'in the soul' as Aristotle and Plato both say): *conversatio* in Latin, being turned-together-towards. He avoids the question of divinity, not because it is not relevant, but because he himself believed it to be also disclosed for us in a different way: not as the sempiternal, but as what also belongs in its disclosure (but insofar

---

[38] Heidegger, *Platon: Sophistes*, GA19, 1992, p. 58of. 'So sehen Sie, daß in diesem Begriff der Ständigkeit, des Immer, faktisch, obzwar unausdrücklich, aber der Sache nach, für Plato das *Phänomen der Zeit* auftaucht, als das Phänomen, das das Seiende in seinem Sein bestimmt: die Gegenwart, παρουσία, was oft verkürzt einfach als οὐσία gefaßt wird. Und das λέγειν, das ansprechende Aufschließen des Seienden, ist nichts anderes als das Gegenwärtig-machen der Sichtbarkeit des Seienden selbst und damit dieses in dem, was es ist; es bringt als gegenwärtigendes Erschließen die Gegenwart zur Aneignung.' Emphasis in original.

[39] Plato, *Sophist*, 266 C. Δύο γὰρ οὖν ἐστι ταῦτα θείας ἔργα ποιήσεως, αὐτό τε καὶ τὸ παρακολουθοῦν εἴδωλον ἑκάστον. 266d 2–3. Οὐκοῦν καὶ τἆλλα οὕτω κατὰ δύο διττὰ ἔργα τῆς ἡμετέρας αὖ ποιητικῆς πράξεως.

as it is disclosed) to a particular aspect of the being of being-human. Speaking-together-with, which discloses the fundamental temporal structures of *Dasein*, is at the same time only disclosive of these structures because it simultaneously discloses *Dasein*'s being in the world. Thus speaking-together-with turns out at the same time to be indicating the world *as* the world that it is – in Greek, δηλοῦν. Thus Heidegger says: '*Δελοῦν, in which the possibility of speaking is a constitutive determination of Dasein itself, which I prefer to indicate through "being-in-the-world", "being-in".*'[40]

Here we have a preliminary resolution to the riddle which Heidegger posed to us in Chapter 1, that what becomes determined as 'eternity' is in fact 'a mere derivation of being-timely'. For inasmuch as speaking attempts to speak from out of this cleft and as its overcoming, speaking will overlook that it is in fact grounded in time – grounded in the leaping-forth that temporalizing is. As this overlooking, speaking will attempt to speak, not out of the being of beings, but the cleft in being: the connection between time and speaking will be lost.

---

[40] Heidegger, M., *Platon: Sophistes*, GA19, 1992, p. 594. '*Das δηλοῦν, in dem die Möglichkeit des Sprechens liegt, ist eine konstitutive Bestimmung des Daseins selbst, die ich durch das In-der-Welt-sein, das In-sein zu bezeichnen pflege*'. Emphasis in original.

5

The Soul of Sublimity

Who is it that devalues God? To answer this question it is necessary to understand that only *that one* who understands God as a value is capable of devaluing God. Already I have indicated how, in virtue of the separation that χώρα names, divinity is assigned to a place, even if no where. Is the assigning of God to a place also and at the same time the assignment to God of a value?

In these next two chapters I want, after some preparatory remarks on Kant, to examine the way in which two thinkers, Aristotle and Aquinas, prepare the ground for the way in which upliftment, the sublime, and God come to be thought in postmodernity. These two chapters are, to an extent, a detour, although a necessary one. Why these two thinkers? Is it because they are 'great thinkers', whose understanding we can trust? Who or what decides a thinker is great? The depth of their understanding? Or the breadth of acceptance of their thought? Heidegger, when considering the question of whether or not the work known as *Categories* was actually written by Aristotle or by a disciple of his, notes 'the genuineness of this work has been controversial in the history of philosophy. I consider it to be authentic; no pupil could write like that.'[1] Heidegger's point is not simply that the text must be authentic 'to Aristotle', but rather, the text writes out of a genuine ground, it is not written by one simply parroting the views of a master. In this sense it belongs to a genuine capacity to understand a matter at hand – who *actually* wrote it is of only secondary importance. Aristotle's thought, and his understanding of place in particular and more generally his understanding of the cosmos, was indeed controversial in antiquity and by no means universally accepted. Nevertheless the 'rediscovery' in the West (they were never lost in the same way in the East) of many of the texts of Aristotle, especially

---

[1] Heidegger, M., *Platon: Sophistes*, GA19, 1992, p. 111. 'Die Genuität dieser Schrift ist in der Philosophiegeschichte umstritten. Ich halte sie für echt, so etwas macht kein Schüler.'

throughout the thirteenth century, transformed the thinking of the West. Quite rapidly Aristotle's understanding of the cosmos and of physics came to predominate as 'authoritative', far more than ever he had been for the ancients. Long after the controversies surrounding Galileo and the nature of the universe had died down, Aristotle continued to exert a profound influence on Descartes (as the one *against* whom Descartes argues), Kant and Hegel. At the same time that these texts reappeared in the West, an even more fundamental transformation had taken place, for the predominant thinking was already Christian. Aristotle's writing was received in the West – more strangely yet at the hands, not of Christian Greeks but Muslim Arabs – into a world which was quite different in its outlook from that of antiquity. Aquinas, therefore, is the one who in an exemplary way reconciled many of the texts of Aristotle, almost simultaneously with their rediscovery, to a Christian outlook. Aquinas is often simply presumed to be 'Aristotelian'. Almost the opposite is the case – before he could be trusted, Aristotle was turned into a Thomist.

Our question – who is it that devalues God? – requires that we keep in view how it is that the subject appears in postmodernity, and at the same time to ask how this appearance becomes possible. Aristotle and Aquinas are in different ways decisive for this appearance. The extraordinary appearance of Sam Taylor-Wood's figure in *Brontosaurus* presupposes not only the separation of the cosmos into two places, but the separation of the human itself into a twofold – the outer and the inner.

Why is it that Longinus is able to take for granted a connection between speaking, truth, and ensoulment? The question is *how* this connection manifests itself, because the manner of its manifestation will determine the means by which upliftment uplifts, which is to say, does its work. Prior to Longinus, Aristotle and Plato both indicate a danger: that the rhetor might fail in the public work of the disclosure of truth (ἀλήθεια). Both of them indicate this potential for failure in the matter of law and the trying of legal cases, because of the need rather to secure a favourable judgement from the Magistrate or *Dicast* than to establish the truth.[2] The question in each case is the relation of the truth (ἀλήθεια) of what is said to ἐπιστήμη, and to false or true opinion. We want to translate ἐπιστήμη with 'knowledge' or even

---

[2] Cf. Plato, *Theaetetus*, 201 A; Aristotle, *Rhetoric*, 1354 a 5–7. The orators and sophists who spoke before the *dicasts* or magistrates were paid – and not paid to fail.

science, but that is not what is indicated here. Plato, in his dialogue the *Theaetetus*, struggles above all to investigate the meaning of the word ἐπιστήμη.

In an appendix to his commentary on Plato's *Theaetetus* Martin Heidegger suggests that the dialogue contains an 'essential, completely leading section. Here also is the point of transformation particularly clear, where Greek thought undertakes the opposition to its origin in order to go over into "metaphysics" . . . Only now does "philosophy" begin.'[3] The section Heidegger refers to is the point in the dialogue where Socrates considers the relation of the body to the soul in terms of what the soul comes to know for itself (ἐπίστασθαι). The things that are known fall under what is common to all of them. In Chapter 4 we have already seen that the elements of what is common to all is being and identity. Therefore what is at issue in asking what falls under what is common to all things is the whole, which means the whole of being itself (οὐσία).[4] How is this seen? Directly in some way by the soul, or by means of the senses? Socrates leads Theaetetus to the view that there is not a particular *bodily* organ that underlies the unity of the knowledge and perception of all the things that are known, but rather this unity is the soul (ψυχή). The soul therefore is the inner unity which 'sees' the whole of being. This inner unity is the capacity to see the *one* thing that is distributed through all things: being.

In the *Theaetetus* Socrates cites Protagoras, referring to a fragment of his lost work which is usually translated as follows: 'man is the measure of all things, of beings insofar as they are, and non-beings insofar as they are not'.[5] He concludes from this that, as Theaetetus argues, 'αἴσθησις, φής, ἐπιστήμη'. We can translate this in the following way: 'perception, you say, is knowledge'.[6] Our question is rather, how is it that the statement of Protagoras can be understood

---

[3] Heidegger, M., *Vom Wesen der Wahrheit: zu Platons Höhlengleichnis und Theätet*, GA34, 1997 (1988), pp. 327f. 'Der wesentliche, alles tragende Abschnitt. Hier ist auch der Wendepunkt besonders deutlich, den das griechische Denken gegenüber seinem Anfang vollzieht, um in die "Metaphysik" überzugehen . . . Jetzt erst beginnt die "Philosophie".'

[4] Cf. Plato, *Theaetetus*, 186 A. Ποτέρων οὖν τίθης τὴν οὐσίαν; τοῦτο γὰρ μάλιστα ἐπὶ πάντων παρέπεται. ('To which of the two [i.e. the seeing of the soul directly, or by means of the senses] do you place being, for this most of all is the accompanying to all beings.')

[5] Cf. Plato, *Theaetetus*, 152 A. See p. 213 below for reference in Diels and further discussion. πάντων χρημάτων μέτρον ἐστὶν ἄνθρωπος, τῶν μὲν ὄντων ὡς ἔστι, τῶν δὲ μὴ ὄντων ὡς οὐκ ἔστιν.

[6] Plato, *Theaetetus*, 151 D.

self-evidently by Socrates (and so by Plato) to ask a question about the relation of αἴσθησις to ἐπιστήμη, since neither of these words even appears in Socrates' own citation of Protagoras. Perhaps the only assistance we receive is that the original work of Protagoras was entitled *Truth*.

As the *Theaetetus* develops it is possible to see how what concerns Plato is the need to restrict the appearances of things to what they are the appearances *of*. What Plato resists in every case is the argument that something might appear to be both one thing and another at the same time (and this means to one person as well as another, as much as it means in different ways to the same person), so that if it is called large it will also appear to be small, or seem at once light and relatively heavy, so that 'being' cannot properly be said of things but only that they are becoming, because they are in motion and are being moved, in order to find its 'true' appearance, the thing that it really is. We have seen how Plato privileges the unmoved, the 'ever-same' (ἀεί) over the moveable. In order to do this, as we saw in the last chapter, a separation and cleft arises, a separation which, even though he transforms it in a particular direction, nevertheless Aristotle retains. The outward appearance is therefore separable from the appearance, the 'look' that it *really* has, its genuine εἶδος, the appearance that the soul sees when it sees the thing in its truth.

This chapter will only concern itself with the question as it is raised in the *Theaetetus* in terms of its consequences, which means historically in terms of the answers that are supplied to it. A word of warning needs to be sounded here. This book is not a 'history', in the sense of a narrative which tells the story of why such and such became so and so; we are already postmodern enough to know that if I were to tell the narrative in this way you may well have your own perspective on it – you would see this historical unfolding in a way different to me. Who then could decide or settle the truth? Rather what I seek to do is throw into relief the fundamental interpretations which at each turn throw the question itself into relief, in order that we might perhaps glimpse it afresh. My approach is far too selective, too discursive, too eclectic to be a genuine historiography even of a 'historical-critical' character. I am not interested in becoming an historian.

In examining the questions before us, this book does not seek to provide 'answers' (there are plenty of others all too willing to undertake that task on our behalf), but rather to illustrate and illuminate the origin of the questions, to see how they arise and with what in view, and what the consequences of what arises in them are, what in each case is taken for granted. In refusing to provide answers, at the same time I seek to enter into the questions as they arise in order to examine them 'from within'. This grandiose claim says nothing more, however, than that the book is to some extent an exercise in rhetoric. Not that I can claim the skill of the antique rhetors, but rather that I seek by *how* I speak to exhibit and make apparent what at the same time the book claims is true in what it says. Rhetoric is now rarely taught in the cursus of the university, so I have had no formal training in rhetoric. You will find therefore, no sublimities of trope and figure, nor the excellences of style attained by Pope or Longinus. Rather what I am attempting to achieve rhetorically is to perform what I at the same time describe – to let us through this writing into the truth of what is at issue.

Central to the articulation of the sublime in postmodernity, and indeed throughout its long history, is the imagination. How are we to understand the imagination and how does it first manifest itself? Is it the imagination which, sublimely, traverses the separation of the inner and the outer, the inside and the outside? This would appear to be the role assigned to the imagination by Kant. He identifies the imagination as the 'power of representation' (*Einbildungskraft*). In considering how it is that the manifold of perceptions (Kant uses the term 'representations', *Vorstellungen*) are brought together, Kant names this process a 'synthesis'. At a decisive point in the *Critique of Pure Reason* Kant argues that 'synthesis in general, as we shall hereafter see, is nothing other than the pure working of the power of imagination, a blind, but at the same, indispensable function of the soul'.[7] This leads him to say that 'pure synthesis, most generally represented, gives us the pure concept of understanding'.[8] We should note that throughout Kant's work, perceptions and representations are taken to be the same, which is to say that to 'take in' (*percipio*) is to represent. The power of imagination is therefore already decided to be a power of representing or imagining, for Kant a wholly uncontentious matter.

Žižek, in commenting on these passages, draws our attention to the excess that remains in the transition from the specific representations of perceptions of the manifold to the power of synthesis overall, the most general representation. He asks:

---

[7] Kant, *Kritik der reinen Vernunft*, 1966 (1787), A78; B103. 'Die Synthesis überhaupt ist, wie wir künftig sehen werden, die bloße Wirkung der Einbildungs-kraft, einer blinden, obgleich unentbehrlichen Funktion der Seele.'

[8] Kant, *Kritik der reinen Vernunft*, 1966, A78; B104. 'Die reine Synthesis, allgemein vorgestellt, gibt nun den reinen Verstandsbegriff.'

is the force of imagination the impenetrable ultimate mystery of transcendental spontaneity, the root of subjectivity, the encompassing genus out of which grows understanding as its discursive cognitive specification, or is the encompassing genus understanding itself, with imagination as a kind of shadow?[9]

What Žižek names in this brief passage is the very transition in the imagination which this chapter will seek to bring to light: the transition which passes it over in decisive moments that achieve specific interpretations in Aristotle, Kant and postmodernity. Žižek roots the solution to his question in the sublime, saying that 'Kant's notion of imagination silently passes over a crucial "negative" feature of imagination . . . emphasised later by Hegel – namely imagination *qua* the "activity of dissolution" '.[10] We must never lose sight of the fact that Žižek's defence of the sublime is at the same time a defence of philosophical subjectivity, and is self-consciously so. His confrontation with Heidegger, and his appeal to the sublime and above all to the transcendental imagination, is all intended to demonstrate 'that aspect of *cogito* on account of which Lacan claims that *cogito* is the subject of the Unconscious'.[11]

Because Kant is unable to resolve the question of subjective freedom at the phenomenal level, and is unable to show how the imagination gives anything other than *negative* access to the noumenal, Žižek notes that the two forms of the sublime, the mathematical and the dynamical (which we will encounter when we examine Kant's *Critique of the Power of Judgement*), are 'precisely the two modes of the imagination's failure to accomplish its synthetic activity'.[12] Hereafter, for Žižek, the sublime will be understood through the *negative* imagination, which he characterizes as the monstrous. This he calls 'the lesson of the Sublime: the attempt to represent the noumenal – i.e. to fill the gap between the noumenal and the imagined phenomenal – fails, so that the imagination can reveal the noumenal dimension only in a negative way'.[13]

How can *I think* be the subject of the capitalized *Un*conscious? Surely the *I think* is in and of itself the activity of consciousness, especially when considered subjectivally? Except that for both Lacan and

---

[9] Žižek, S., *The Ticklish Subject*, 1999, p. 29.
[10] Žižek, *Ticklish Subject*, 1999, p. 29.
[11] Žižek, *Ticklish Subject*, 1999, p. 2.
[12] Žižek, *Ticklish Subject*, 1999, p. 37.
[13] Žižek, *Ticklish Subject*, 1999, p. 39.

Žižek *I think* is presupposed and made possible – is therefore literally wrested from – the surrounding context as the *production* of consciousness from the unconscious that precedes it. There is in this a genuine and profound faithfulness to the insights of Descartes, for *cogito* does not simply mean (as is often supposed) 'I think', but rather has an extremely active sense of bringing out in front of myself something for myself – re-presenting it to myself. *Cogito* therefore means bringing-before and so making-conscionable, as (to use a language that really properly emerges only later) bringing from out of the unconscious, which co-discloses me as conscious together with whatever it is I thereby become conscious of. Moreover, exactly as Lacan has explored, it is the *enforcement* of this. Lacan describes this first in establishing the relation 'of the organism to its reality, or as they say, of the inner-world to the surrounding world'.[14] This relation is the one on which the ontological structure of the world makes possible 'paranoiac knowledge',[15] a concretion of Žižek's construction of subjectivity out of the monstrous, which occurs and as the primordial precipitation of the 'I' and so before the dialectic of identification to the 'other'.[16] Yet, as Lacan later notes, this dialectical relating of other to other is fundamentally structured by the 'I' formation which is wrested out of the unconscious, and which Žižek names as *cogito*. Lacan concludes by noting that alienation constitutes the *Urbild*, the originary representedness, of the self, as a relation of exclusion which actually structures the relations between selves: 'but the for us decisive signification of constitutive alienation of the *Urbild* of the self, appears in the relation of exclusion which then structures in the subject the dual relation of self to self.'[17] The question of intersubjectivity arises directly out of the *subjectival* sublime, out of how the sublime can be articulated in the context of subjectivity. Žižek, by appeal to the monstrous, radicalizes this through the sublime as the unrepresentability of the totality from out of which the self wrests itself, as self-representedness. Otherness here is therefore understood as the

---

[14] Lacan, J., 'Le stade du miroir comme formateur de la fonction du je' in *Écrits I*, 1966, p. 93. 'De l'organisme à sa réalité – ou, comme on dit, de l'*Innenwelt* à l'*Umwelt*.'

[15] Lacan, 'Le stade du miroir', in *Écrits I*, 1966, p. 90. 'connaissance paranoïaque'.

[16] Cf. Lacan, 'Le stade du miroir', in *Écrits I*, 1966, p. 90.

[17] Lacan, J., 'Le chose freudienne' in *Écrits I*, 1966, p. 239. 'Mais la signification décisive pour nous de l'aliénation constituante de l'*Urbild* du moi, apparaît dans la relation d'exclusion qui structure dès lors dans le sujet la relation duelle de moi à moi.'

(unrepresentable) totality of being from out of which the subject represents itself.

'Totality of being' is itself an ambiguity which in subjectivity has constantly to be stabilized and resolved. It can mean 'the whole of being' as in the surrounding world, the *Umwelt* or simply 'environment' and reality in general. Or it can mean what is most beingful in being, what underlies beings and gives them 'to be', the ground and at the same time reason for their being. Aristotle is not entangled in this ambiguity, insofar as he resolves both the whole of being and what is most beingful in beings – their beingness as such – through τόπος, place. Insofar as a being, a thing, is in place, this is what enables it to appear at all. Place *as such* – τόπος– however, is the inner unity of the cosmos; it renders the cosmos both one and determinate, with respect to its parts. It is the means by which its unity is distributed all the way through its parts. Everything that is, relates to its proper place, which is what makes it determinate and determin*able*. The unity of the cosmos, its oneness, is nevertheless simultaneously (for Aristotle) its being and limit, and this character of being's and limit's relation to divinity and the capacity for motion of the things which it is the limit and being *of*.[18] Helen Lang notes that 'the first limit of the cosmos, which in *Physics* IV is place, is identified with substance, the first category of being, whereas the limited, or contained, is like matter'.[19] Substance here means οὐσία, which again is exhibited by every particular being, and is at the same time that which every particular being makes visible – substance and presence are the same. The ambiguity of 'being in its totality' will arise only after the imagination has taken hold over presence and succeeded it. Not imagination as such, but something with which the imagination is intimately concerned, will succeed place and constant presence.

Žižek takes for granted that the problem is not the imaginary, but the 'general representedness' of the power of imagination itself. The phenomenal is automatically for him *already* imagined, which means for Žižek every thing known is already assumed to *be known* through representation. We see immediately therefore why the real problem for Žižek lies with the noumenal – because the noumenal is *that which is beyond imagining* and yet is inextricably bound up with imagination. It is also the outermost, the outside, the excluded. However, this outermost, which exceeds representation because it is the faculty of

[18] Cf. Aristotle, *De Caelo*, 284 a 4–5.
[19] Lang, H., *The Order of Nature in Aristotle's Physics*, 1998, p. 101.

representation as such, has already in this description passed over its own threshold: inasmuch as it is up-to the threshold, it is capable of being represented. Inasmuch as it is beyond the threshold, it is no longer representable. If Žižek concludes by noting that 'the true problem is not how to bridge the gap separating the two, but rather, how this gap came about in the first place',[20] we can now say that in consequence of the last two chapters, we have an orientation on this 'how' and its effects. We need at this point to turn the question on its head: if we can now answer how it is that the gap arose, should we not *now* ask about the bridge that aims to overcome the separation of the two – the power of the imagination as such?

In order to make this enquiry we must first understand what changes and what remains the same in the genealogy we are about to attempt to trace. Kant speaks, in the passage cited earlier, of an 'indispensable *function* of the soul'. The sublime, either as articulated by Kant or by Žižek, is the end, the outermost, the 'at-the-limit' of this function, it demonstrates the full breadth and extent of the operation it names. What, however, is a function? Kant draws attention to what is at issue by qualifying the matter at hand with its indispensability. The function in question is something without which the soul is not a soul. The word 'function' (the German term is the same, *Funktion*) comes from the Latin deponent verb *fungor*. Deponent verbs are those verbs that are conjugated in the passive but appear to take on an active meaning. Nevertheless the passive sense is never lost from them, properly considered. *Fungor* means to be busied with or be engaged in something. Therefore a function is not an action which means something which is willed or selected to be a 'this' rather than a 'that' (something chosen to be done), but rather the involuntary *enaction* of a thing which in being undertaken shows it up for what it is. The indispensability at issue indicates that the soul could not be enacted without this function. The power of representing, therefore, *is* the involuntary activity of the soul in its being a soul: it is how soul 'souls'.

The sublime names, therefore, the soul in its full extendedness *as* soul – the ἐκστάσις we encountered with Longinus. Stood out now to what? For between Aristotle and Kant, and then Kant and Žižek, a series of transformations have been undertaken so that the being-stood-out to the divine as it is discussed in Aristotle takes on a different character to the way it appears in Kant, and for Žižek there is no divine to be stood out to, but rather for Žižek the limit of the soul is at

---

[20] Žižek, *Ticklish Subject*, 1999, p. 39.

the same time the limit of the psyche and the pressing-in on the psyche of the monstrous – the threshold not of every particular alterity, but of alterity as such – the big Other. The transformation we have to trace, in other words, is the being-enacted of the soul from the cosmology of Aristotle and Plato to Žižek's understanding of it as a pure psychology.

How are we to understand this term 'soul'? Aristotle resolves the question of the soul by saying that it is in some way all the things that *are*, that is, all beings.[21] Does this not contradict immediately what Žižek argues, that the Other as the totality of being is what is external and so alien to and alienated from the soul? Or is it not rather that this 'all', exactly as it is for Žižek, is somehow presupposed as both potential and the general condition for the soul. In what way? Aristotle says that the things that 'are' either are because they are perceivable (τὰ αἰσθητὰ) or because they are intelligible (τὰ νοητά). Everything that is, therefore, can be uncovered for what it is either by the senses or because it is in some manner directly present to thinking. In this sense the soul is restricted to what is there for it, restricted to the presence of what is present for it, either because it is felt through an organ of the body, or because it is intelligible with respect to thinking.

The soul has capacities or faculties (δυνάμει) which either correspond to the beings they know or sense, or to their forms (εἴδη). Clearly, Aristotle remarks, the faculties of the soul are not the things themselves, in that a stone does not exist in the soul, but only the 'look', the appearance or form (εἶδος) of the stone.[22] Aristotle says: 'the soul, then, is in the manner of a hand; for the hand is an instrument for instruments, and intellect is a "look" for "looks", and sense the look of things sensible.'[23] The soul, therefore, is the means by which thinking – the intellect as such – 'sees' what it sees, and sees what is taken in by the organs of perception. Indeed he restricts even the things that pertain solely to νοῦς to arising in virtue of the sensible

---

[21] Aristotle, *De Anima*, 431 b 21. ἡ ψυχὴ τὰ ὄντα πώς ἐστι πάντα.

[22] I have discussed elsewhere the meaning of the term εἶδος: 'In normal perception, the appearance or look that something has is understood to be grounded in its form. The shape it has gives it its look. Heidegger argues that "for *Greek ontology*, however, the founding connection between εἶδος and μορφή, appearance and form, is exactly the reverse: the appearance is not grounded in the form, but the form, the μορφή, is grounded in the appearance".' Hemming, L. P., *Heidegger's Atheism*, 2002, p. 15.

[23] Aristotle, *De Anima*, 432 a 2–3. ὥστη ἡ ψυχὴ ὥσπερ ἡ χείρ ἐστιν. καὶ γὰρ ἡ χείρ ὄργανόν ἐστιν ὀργάνων, καὶ ὁ νοῦς εἶδος εἰδῶν καὶ ἡ αἴσθησις εἶδος αἰσθητῶν.

in some way, to αἴσθησις, so that even where pure speculation, pure exalted 'looking' (θεωρεῖν) is concerned, αἴσθησις is still presupposed.[24] The body as that place on which the instruments of the senses are distributed is always presupposed even for purely noetic abstractions. Indeed the senses – touch, sight, smell, hearing, etc., are themselves in one sense the instruments held in unity by the single instrument for instruments that the soul is. The difference between the things that pertain strictly to νοῦς and the things that arise through αἴσθησις cannot be resolved through any kind of dualism of mind and body: nevertheless, νοῦς is not mixed with the body.[25] It is for this reason that we should resist translating νοῦς simply as 'mind', as if it were some independent entity or faculty of the soul. We can go further even than this, for we can see in this why the soul is the entelechy, the final appearance of the body. It is not because the soul is some hidden aspect to the body, but rather because it is that through which the body undertakes the 'looking' that it undertakes, either with respect to the things of sense, the αἰσθητὰ, or in the pure contemplation of θεωρεῖν, of 'looking' as such, in order to be all things. Soul in this sense (and for Aristotle) is, by means of νοῦς, the means by which its potentiality to be all things, to become identical with any particular being and with the whole of being, is realized. This is pointed to in two important ways. In the matter of thinking, the soul takes things in by means of the senses as the beginning of thinking. At a certain point, however, the soul becomes self-thinking: perception is a means by which it attains to something, but something that is already there. What it attains to is the second of the things at issue here – the being of being itself, being as permanent presence. Aristotle says that thinking in the sense of the seeing of the particular is always true as 'of the "what?" according to the "what already-is being"'.[26]

This phrase, ἦν εἶναι, is extremely difficult to translate: we want to translate ἦν with 'was', the imperfect form of the verb. Rather, however, the ἦν describes the manner of the substantive made from the infinitive, τὸ εἶναι, being as such: not was, but already-is (and persists). The phrase τὸ τί ἦν εἶναι is also often translated as 'substantial form'. The 'outermost' which we have already discussed, turns out to be the site of upliftment not because it is a locatable 'uppermost' but

---

[24] Cf. Aristotle, *De Anima*, 432 a 9–10.

[25] Aristotle, *De Anima*, 429 a 23. διὸ οὐδὲ μεμῖχθαι εὔλογον αὐτὸν τῷ σώματι.

[26] Aristotle, *De Anima*, 430 b 29. ὁ τοῦ τί ἐστι κατὰ τὸ τί ἦν εἶναι. Cf. Aristotle: *Physics*, 195 a 20; *Metaphysics*, 1013 a 28.

because it is a point of completion, the point at which the being of a thing becomes in some sense 'visible' with respect to what it is the being *of*, even if only visible to the mind. It is the point of perfection, where perfection implies *per-facere*, the point at which no further 'making' (*faciens*) can be undertaken – ἐν-τελεχέια, the coming into its limit (and so being) of what already is. The soul is the first entelechy of a natural body having organs.[27] What 'comes into' is not being as such, this is the ἦν εἶναι, the already-is-being, but the soul, as the *end* of its activity which organizes the coming in to this end of the parts of the body. This end is without time, it is the point at which it has no more time because it needs no more time, it both completes what time gave it to complete and it discovers what is already there for it.

The 'already' of the ἦν εἶναι is not 'really' there, it is what I have to get ahead to. Because it lies ahead of me, it has a futural aspect. However, when I attain to it, I discover it to have been 'already', as the stability of everything present, and so I *will* discover it already to have been (in the past). In this sense its futurity is ambiguous, it has a future and a past reference. Aristotle solves this by placing as the end of the working out of the causes and the unity of the world, the 'end' of every end (τέλος), a point of atemporality: *from* a reaching forth (through the future) *to* an atemporal (ever-same) point of completion; *from* the past (what I already know) *to* an atemporal (ever-same) point of completion. The thing – either a thing to be worked out and understood, or a thing to be made and completed, comes to proper visibility (can be seen for what it is and so seen in the being of its being) at the point where it is no longer in motion with respect to time, but at rest. This coming to rest is, as I have argued, coming-in-to-an-end (ἐντελέχεια). Rest, however, is with the things that come into being and pass away, something which cannot be seen in itself, it can only be seen 'with the mind', and so from the perspective of that which sees being as such. It is for this reason that for Aristotle things are ordered to being as such from out of what they are in their completion (so-called 'substantial form', τὸ τί ἦν εἶναι), from whence we can read-off and understand the oak tree from seeing the acorn, and that there *are* oak trees from every particular oak tree. The atemporality of the persisting being-already, being-always of every particular thing is what makes the moveable, pragmatic, thing I *actually* have in sight possible, and not

---

[27] Aristotle, *De Anima*, 412 b 5f. ἐντελέχεια ἡ πρώτη σώματος φυσικοῦ ὀργανικοῦ.

the other way around. It is therefore voῦς, the making lie-open of every possible openness of being that makes every particular being visible and intelligible.

The point of upliftment and the 'entelechy' of the soul turns out to be the being of beings itself, the already-is where the particular soul seeks identity in its particularity with the being of the kind of thing that it is. Insofar as it attains to being in such a manner, it always is in such a manner,[28] and it finds a way to being eternal in the manner available to it. Coming into its completion and at the same time reproducing themselves is the way in which particular things – souls, or changeable beings in general – seek in their particular coming into being identity with the eternity of the things that are eternal and divine.[29]

Soul is the means by which mind passes from what moves and has δύναμις – potency – to the 'ever-actual' which the things which move and are subject to change indicate and point towards, but actually are not. It is not that soul passes the being of being-human through (hence the 'being-occurred to' the passive sense of πασχεῖν, of πάθος) to what it discovers in what is perceivable, but rather that soul discovers through what perception makes available that which *underlies* and most persists in perceivables. This is the force of Aristotle's extraordinary statements about time in the *De Anima*. Mind – voῦς – has the capacity to be without death and everlasting, precisely as the soul experiences being-moved from what as potential and particular has time, to what is without time, eternal, and ever the same.[30]

Moreover, pure contemplation arises in consequence of and so *after* the unity of the single 'look' has been attained that the soul alone is able to grasp in its unity: hence εἶδος does not mean the 'look' of the outward phenomenal, appearance, but the appearance which the soul is able to see by means of thinking, voεῖv: this appearance is the denial and negation of every *actual* appearance. Even learning, and the things that are acquired through learning (μάθοι), always presuppose αἴσθησις, although through learning the soul comes to know that there are pure 'contemplables' that take up no specific, particular or sensible shape – like, for instance, the objects of mathematics. Nevertheless, Aristotle notes, in each case (either those things known

---

[28] Aristotle, *De Generatione Animalium*, 731 b 35. τοιοῦτον δ᾽ εἴπερ ἦν, ἀίδιον ἂν ἦν.

[29] Cf. Aristotle, *De Generatione Animalium*, 731 b 25.

[30] Cf. Aristotle, *De Anima*, 430 a 21ff.

through the senses or known and learned entirely noetically and having no sensible form), some φάντασμα is concerned.[31]

The word φάντασμα is normally translated as 'mental image' or 'picture', but as Longinus showed us, it can as much (if not better) be a matter of speech. Have we, therefore, found in Aristotle exactly that function of the soul which was described by Kant, and taken for granted by Žižek, that everything knowable is at the same time only known insofar as it is representable (even if only to thinking as an 'interior' activity)? Aristotle says that 'the φάντασματα are like the things known by sense (αἰσθήτα) except [that they are] without matter'.[32] In order to understand the meaning of the term φάντασμα we need to look more closely at how Aristotle introduces the term. We also need to bear in mind what is at issue for Aristotle. Contrary to the way in which we are now tempted to read him, as presenting a 'theory of the psyche' or even a psychology, Aristotle wants to show the identity of the soul with the cosmos, as how it moves from being in some manner and *potentially* all things, to be in some way and *actually* all things. To be actually all things it will be concerned, not with the things themselves, but with the being of the things themselves, the ἦν εἶναι or already-is-being, and so eternal and most beingful aspect ('substantial form') that lies behind every particular thing. In this sense, Aristotle is describing not a 'psychology' but an 'ontology' which is at the same time a cosmology. However, as I have already indicated, Aristotle proceeds in the light of a particular interpretation of the being of beings as the already-is, the ever-persisting.

Although he does not take up the question until late in his discussion of the nature of the soul, in fact the manner of being of the soul is worked out with respect to τόπος, place. This is because place is the means by which being is distributed through the ever-becoming of the cosmos. Mind is not mixed with body because, as place makes the things that are subject to movement visible, so mind also makes visible the *true* visibility of the things that are: it is a 'making for all' and is a kind of light,[33] as something that shows up the things subject to change and makes them appear.

Aristotle tells us that the things thought (τὰ νοητά) are 'in', that is

---

[31] Aristotle, *De Anima*, 432 a 9.
[32] Aristotle, *De Anima*, 432 a 10. τὰ γὰρ φάτασματα ὥσπερ αἰσθήματά ἐστι, πλὴν ἄνευ ὕλης.
[33] Aristotle, *De Anima*, 430 a 14. ὁ δὲ τῷ πάντα ποιεῖν . . . οἷον τὸ φῶς.

take up sensible 'looks' or appearances,[34] which is to say, appearances of things that have a reference or are primarily grounded in αἴσθησις. This is true for abstractions, things had as sensibles and the πάθη, the things known through our having been passed through them – the 'emotions'. Every thing thought (νοῆ) is at the same time a sensible appearance (εἶδες αἴσθησις) and a φάντασμα. We already know that although every φάντασμα is grounded in something like αἴσθησις, such that it is grounded in the 'look' (εἶδος) which an αἴσθησις yields, at the same time, not every φάντασμα arises as a result of a direct αἴσθησις, nor need it be comprised of matter in order to arise. Aristotle provides us with a list of the three kinds of φαντάσματα. Each of these is, at the same time as a φάντασμα, a λεγόμενον, a something having being said. The first kind of φάντασμα that Aristotle lists at the same time names how the others may arise – which is to say he names it first because it is the most easily understood for what it is: it will lead us in to the others.[35] It is in virtue of seeing how this φάντασμα arises that we can see how the φαντάσματα arise in the other cases. The first kind of φαντάσματα are τὰ ἐν ἀφαιρέσει λεγόμενα,[36] the things 'having-been-spoken in having been abstracted' and so what we would now call 'abstract ideas' like the objects of mathematics, pure forms which only have imperfect instantiations in the pragmatic world. The term ἀφαίρεσις comes from φέρω, to bear, and so is what is carried off from or lifted up from, or 'read-off'. In particular it is that which, in being carried off, is the most important in what is carried off. The force of this is to make what follows the first thing named as two further and subordinate kinds of the same (first named) overall kind of thing: first, the things being spoken in once having been lifted off *in general*; then (with respect to the things being spoken by having been lifted off), as the things gained through sensation (αἴσθησις); and finally, the things that occur to us or befall us in the passions and emotions.

The translations of this passage entirely overlook that all of these things are governed by being able to be spoken of, and at the same

---

[34] Aristotle, *De Anima*, 432 a 5. ἐν τοῖς εἴδεσι τοῖς αἰσθητοῖς. What follows concentrates on interpreting Book 8 of Chapter III of the *De Anima*, 431 b 20–432 a 14.

[35] The list of three is given in a particular way, it is not a simple succession of '*a* and *b* and *c*', but rather the first in the list are governed by the conjoining particle τε to which the others are conjoined by the conjunction καί.

[36] Cf. Aristotle, *De Anima*, 432 a 6.

time are in a sense read-off from something else. Yet this first definition is central to the following two definitions, and is what gives us the capacity to determine what φάντασμα means. Is it not, however, entirely obvious what φάντασμα means? Why is it not just a 'mental picture' (the most common translation of the term). A little later in the text Aristotle clearly relates the φάντασματα to φαντασία. Surely then the φάντασματα are the objects of the *faculty* of imagination, and φαντασία is the means by which these objects are brought forth? In the first instance we should note the fundamental connection with λεγόμενον, being-spoken, which is the whole basis for the being of the rhetor in Longinus. Aristotle makes this more explicit earlier in the *De Anima*, when he says that φαντασία is that through which we *speak* of (rather than picture or envisage) how a φάντασμα occurs for us.[37] This alone should give us a clear indication that the φάντασματα are not properly 'images' – or rather inasmuch as some of them might be images, they can only be so because they are also, and first, and more generally, something else (that is things spoken of and so named).

We have already encountered the term φαντασία in Chapter 3, as meaning both what is remembered and what is immediately present.[38] There I provided an initial translation as 'presenting'. Now we need to embark on a full clarification of what Aristotle indicates with respect to φαντασία. In the same way that νοῦς should not simply be translated as 'mind', φαντασία should not be translated as a faculty of the mind. Rather φαντασία means 'appearance' but not as semblance or image: it is what appears for itself, what shows itself from out of itself, therefore *in* what presents itself, what *makes that presenting present*. The φάντασμα is the showable *in* what appears for itself out of itself. We should remember that to show indicates that which can be pointed up through being spoken about.[39] It is grounded, exactly as αἴσθησις is, in the phenomenon itself, insofar as I come across it (and therefore not even in νοῦς or something like αἴσθησις). It arises out of what is present before me. Plato expresses this in the *Theaetetus* by saying 'appearance and perception are therefore the same',[40] indicating how it is that this 'reading-off' arises out of αἴσθησις. As the presentable in

---

[37] Cf. Aristotle, *De Anima*, 428 a 1–3.

[38] See p. 46 above.

[39] I can speak to you of something I want you to know or be reminded of, or (if I am quick on the draw) I can give you a picture. But the picture is only interpretable as a kind of speaking, rather than the other way round.

[40] Plato, *Theaetetus*, 152 C. φαντασία ἄρα καὶ αἴθησις ταὐτὸν.

what is present, it is capable of being 'read-off' from the phenomenon as the εἶδος of the phenomenon, which is why it is capable of being held in memory and recovered as a memory: it is what persists in what appears.

Aristotle, however, appears to contradict Plato's understanding, saying that φαντασία and αἴσθησις are *not* the same,[41] insofar as in the *De Anima* he both restricts his analysis of φαντασία to human being and some (but not all animals) and he argues that while all perceptions are true not all appearances are true, but often they can be false. However, what Aristotle is attempting to demonstrate is not that φαντασία and αἴσθησις are different in the sense of opposed to each other, but rather in what manner they relate to each other. In this he seeks to clarify what Plato has Socrates simply assert, especially by restricting it to the being of being-human. The 'essence' of human being is the human relation to λόγος, to speaking and the word, and so the opposition he names reinforces even more strongly the belonging of φαντασία to λόγος.

Because he restricts φαντασία to human being, Aristotle is left with a difficulty in the indication of the fundamental belonging of φαντασία to language and speaking, since only the *said* can be according to falsity and truth, whereas what is understood of a being with respect to νοῦς is always true 'in the same way as the seeing of a particular is always true'.[42] What appears to be a contradiction of Plato's statement is not in fact a contradiction at all, but rather a process of restriction, a separation of the difference between the saying of an appearance and its 'being seen', which requires a clarification of the relation of φαντασία both to language and to what appears.

We take for granted that φαντασία has a primary reference to mental envisaging because we fail to understand the way in which, as something which arises out of appearances, for the Greeks it refers first to extant presence (οὐσία) and only because of that, subsequently to how presence can be known. Heidegger analyses at length how, even for Aristotle, truth was more in the mind than in things.[43] Even before noting this, however, Heidegger traces a fundamental transformation with respect to the meaning of the words εἶδος, ἰδεῖν. For

---

[41] Aristotle, *De Anima*, 427 b 5–15.
[42] Aristotle, *De Anima*, 430 b 30. ὥσπερ τὸ ὁρᾶν τοῦ ἰδίου ἀληθές.
[43] Cf. Heidegger, M., *Grundfragen der Philosophie*, GA45, 1992 (1984), pp. 71ff. Heidegger notes that in the *Metaphysics*, Aristotle comments of truth that it is οὐκ ἐν τοῖς πράγμασιν ... ἀλλ' ἐν διανοίᾳ: 'not in things ... but in the mind' (Aristotle, *Metaphysics*, 1027 b 25f).

the Greeks (and here both Plato and Aristotle are indicated), ἰδέα means what in the appearing of a thing is already present, already in advance of every specific appearance of a thing (it is what 'already-is', ἦν, in being). Therefore ἰδέα becomes the 'look' that allows what something is to be seen, in advance of our seeing it – it is the 'universal' which establishes the meaning of the particular. In this sense it is the 'whatness' of any particular 'what is . . .', the thing about it that is constantly present, and *always present* whenever any particular 'what' appears. Thus Heidegger refers to a 'turn' (*Kehre*) that occurs with respect to ἰδέα. He concludes: 'certainly there lies in the concept of the ἰδέα the relation to ἰδεῖν as a mode of perception. But the perceiving of a being as such is only therefore an ἰδεῖν because the being as such is self-showing: ἰδέα.'[44] The consequence of this is that the term ἰδέα loses its fundamental connection with presence and place, and becomes pure representation: here is why we are led *first* to interpret φαντασία as a faculty of representation prior to understanding what it is the representability *of*. As we can see the fundamental connection that ἰδέα has *first* with presence and constant presence (οὐσία) such that representation is only one of the *modes* of presence, so we can see that initially φαντασία takes in all the modes of appearing *in their fundamental relation to presence* and only later becomes restricted to the visual. Moreover, this restriction only becomes possible because the 'truth' of presence is understood to be located more in the mind than in things.

Although Heidegger's tracing of this degeneration of ἰδέα into image is fundamentally correct, nevertheless Aristotle, in seeking to clarify what φαντασία is, prepares the ground for this decisive interpretation which explains the later restriction of appearances (τὰ φαντάσματα) to the visual *over against* the said – and so, by implication, what is heard, even in the *De Anima* itself. For he argues that what is said emerges out of a faculty or habit of judging things to be true or false.[45] This arises out of the need to give a formal demonstration of why some of what is said with respect to φαντασία can be false. Aristotle remarks: 'To bring to appearance [that is to do what φαντασία does] is to come to an opinion with respect to perception and not

[44] Heidegger, *Grundfragen der Philosophie*, GA45, 1992, p. 68. 'Gewiß liegt in dem Begriff der ἰδέα der Bezug auf das ἰδεῖν als die Weise des Vernehmens. Aber das Vernehmen des Seienden als solchen ist nur deshalb ein ἰδεῖν, weil das Seiende als solches das Sichzeigende – ἰδέα ist.'
[45] Aristotle, *De Anima*, 428 a 3–4. τίς δύναμις [καὶ] ἢ ἕξις, καθ' ἣν κρίνομεν.

accidentally.'[46] He has already insisted that coming to opinion is not something we can choose or select – to come to an opinion is always concerned with the opinion's being true or false.

What difficulty is Aristotle naming here? What appears for itself does so differently with respect to one person and to another. Therefore what appears often has to be judged by deliberative means in order to decide on its truth or falsity. What we see Aristotle resolving in this discussion of what distinguishes the soul is in fact the same problem as was named by Plato with respect to sameness and otherness, to truth (ἀλήθεια) and true opinion (δόξα ἀληθές) in Chapter 4. It would appear from the text therefore that the faculties of judgement are exhausted by the four categories that Aristotle supplies us with – perception, opinion, knowledge and the intellect. But these are only the *basis on which* judgements are made, the judgements, insofar as they come to language, are only then able to be determined with respect to truth and falsehood. In contrast, when a thing is 'seen' by means of intellect or perception 'directly', without respect to (outward, communicative) speaking, it must always be true.

It is for this reason that in the *De Anima* Aristotle separates φαντασία from assertion and denial as in some way different to it. Assertion and denial are the 'means by which' of the speaking of the true and the false, they involve a combining of the things known directly (the νοήματα, the objects of thinking). Why does he need to separate φαντασία from the means by which it is said? Except that he is having to distinguish between the means by which the thing in its appearing is decided (by assertion and denial) from *what* is being decided. We have already noted the connection of δόκειν with 'seeming' and so 'appearing to be' – it is this connection with the naming of what seems that has to be distinguished from the 'what' that is being named. In this way φαντασία is the capacity for the naming: but it is an involuntary capacity, it carries on without respect to will or choice.

Not only is φαντασία concerned with speaking, but also with direct 'seeing' (ὁρᾶν) of the eyes, which leads to the seeing that sees what is *already* there that we encountered earlier – being as constant presence. What is 'seen' directly is always true, and therefore has a greater connection with truth than what is said, because what is said can sometimes be false, even though both concern appearances. Appearances which are 'seen' are in this sense more trustworthy, more 'true' than

---

[46] Aristotle, *De Anima*, 428 b 2. τὸ οὖν φαίνεσθαι ἐστι τὸ δοξάζειν ὅπερ αἰσθάνεται μὴ κατὰ συμβεβηκός.

those which are spoken. Aristotle provides an etymology of φαντασία that relates it to light, noting that 'without light it is impossible to see'.[47] This is because 'sight is the most excellent perception'.[48]

It is for this reason that the φαντάσματα become restricted in their 'truth' to the visual and the seen, rather than the spoken. Aristotle himself asserts the primacy of the appearances with respect to what is said, hence why the sublime and upliftment arises initially as a topic for the rhetor, and only later, only in the light of this interpretation, does upliftment become almost entirely restricted to what is seen with the eyes – visual art.

Insofar therefore as φαντασία is the appearance in the sense of what appears for itself (τὸ φαίνεσθαι), the φάντασμα is what *in* any given appearance of a being is the thing that can be read-off to be brought before me as the persisting-presence of the perception of that being. In this sense the read-off is what is proper to the goal of what reads-off, νοῦς. Only in this sense does φάντασμα have the modern sense of a phantasm or image, as something that can be held noetically independent of what it is the appearance *of*. Moreover, prior ever to being-imagined as being-pictured, it is a being-spoken, even in the speaking to the self that occurs within the soul as such.

In fact the clarification of the meaning of φαντασία has been for a broader purpose, since in a sense φαντασία has been referred both to the exercise of judgement, which culminates in the distinguishing of the true and the false, *and* to the production of the νοήματα, the objects of νοῦς which can be 'seen' to be true because they are 'seen' directly by thinking. In effect the 'reading-off' that φαντασία is has been left ambiguous, the ambiguity that Martin Heidegger repeatedly says is the basis for metaphysics: on the one hand φαντασία becomes simultaneously the capacity for the 'what is' that is represented; and on the other hand, φαντασία is referred to place *as such*, and so in its fulfilment to being as stable presence, as οὐσία and so as ἀεί ὄν. Here we see both why φαντασία comes to be interpreted as 'imagination', and how it is detached from its proper concern with speaking so that sight, even sight taken in a metaphorical sense, the 'seeing' of being (οὐσία) 'behind' what appears accidentally (that is κατὰ συμβεβηκός) that νοεῖν is. Being becomes not what φαντασία makes available as the shown-up in presenting, but the faculty of making-available, as what *underlies* the appearance (the substance).

---

[47] Aristotle, *De Anima*, 429 a 4–5. ὅτι ἄνευ φωτὸς οὐκ ἔστιν ἰδεῖν.
[48] Aristotle, *De Anima*, 429 a 4. ἡ ὄψις μάλιστα αἴσθησίς ἐστι.

The clarification of φαντασία was, however, introduced by Aristotle in order to indicate two things, of which we have really only examined one – the relation of appearance and the faculty of making-present (φαντασία) with respect to judgement and seeing. However, Aristotle began by arguing that there are two things that distinguish soul, of which only the second relates to thinking, judging and perceiving. At the end of the long clarification of φαντασία, he repeats this distinction, in order that, having dealt with the second, we may proceed to the analysis of the first. Moreover, the first is the *governing* characteristic of the second, in that it stretches right over the second to include it. We have needed to clarify the working-out of the second characteristic, φαντασία, in order to return to the first. The second is the 'means by which' φαντασία is referred both to truth and true opinion, to speaking as judging the false and the true, and to 'seeing' the true as such. What is this first characteristic? The construction Aristotle employs is exactly of the form we observed earlier, beginning with the conjoining particle τε for the first, which then extends over the list of what falls under the second. The first, however, is 'movement with respect to place' which governs 'thinking, judging, and perceiving'.[49]

The whole of φαντασία is therefore referred to the soul in its understanding of movement according to place. I have already indicated the importance of place in Aristotle's thought in Chapter 4. The force of this primary relation is for Aristotle to show how, in its capacity to move and be moved, soul relates to movement and the unmoved. Moreover it is this which will allow us to resolve the difficulty by which something can appear in one way to you and another to me – in other words place will be used to resolve the difference between movement and what makes movement possible; however, it is this difference between place and what moves with respect to place that will indicate how φαντασία, the making-present of appearance, will for Aristotle relate the soul to the whole of beings.

Because place is the separation of the moved from the unmoved, of 'being always' from becoming and the non-being of appearances, and place is that by which what moves is able to move, so φαντασία becomes the means by which thinking apprehends the transformation *through which* what is perceived is known according to its being.

How is the soul with respect to τόπος? Already Aristotle has estab-

---

[49] Aristotle, *De Anima*, 427 a 17–18; cf. 432 a 15f. κινήσει τε τῇ κατὰ τόπον καὶ τῷ νοεῖν καὶ τῷ κρίνειν καὶ αἰσθάνεσθαι.

lished that 'perception consists in being moved and occurring-to'.[50] Perception is, therefore, a kind of motion. Perception is also a kind of πάθος. Earlier I considered those πάθη which had a predominantly passive sense – being-sensing, being-angry. It is clear that the connection of motion in these cases is 'what befalls me', what happens or occurs to me. However, Aristotle also considers πάθη that are more active – courage, desire (ἐπιθυμία) and so forth. These also have to be explained. There is a further kind of motion which Aristotle considers – those which represent not actually movement, but transformations with respect to what is learned or thought. These do not physically move, but they do cause alteration, and are therefore a kind of motion. As motions, they are not the same as activity (ἐνεργεία) but are rather transformations (ἀλλοιούσθαι). Even what befalls us gives rise to motion of this kind, since it excites either avoidance or pursuit: avoidance of what is terrible, even in the sense of wishing it were other, or pursuit in the sense of seeking something out because it is pleasurable.

Aristotle introduces ἥ ὄρεξις, often translated as 'appetite', as what explains the manner in which the soul is concerned with movement. How should we translate this term? Ὄρεξις does not mean appetite, but striving-for, striving-after, pursuit, not in the sense of choice, but in the sense of being-drawn. Against this νοῦς functions as a limit, as what holds striving-after in check for the sake of something else. Holding in check for the sake of something else is not, however, the removal of striving, but replacing one kind of striving with another, and therefore the discrimination (and so judgement) between strivings – the setting up of one end in place of another. The relation of νοῦς to ὄρεξις is therefore the relationship that demonstrates how the various movements of the soul are possible, in the same way as motion occurs in the cosmos.

Aristotle argues that 'both, accordingly, concern setting in motion with respect to place: thought and striving'.[51] Now because *all* the motions of the soul are in this manner, both those that move the soul, and those that cause it to be moved, and those that transform it, the soul is therefore oriented to the cosmos absolutely with respect to motion. Here is the reason why Aristotle has been concerned with the parts of the soul in this discussion of the *De Anima*: not that the soul

---

[50] Aristotle, *De Anima*, 416 b 33f. ἡ δ'αἴσθησις ἐν τῷ κινεῖσθαί τε καὶ πάσχειν συμβαίνει.

[51] Aristotle, *De Anima*, 433 a 11. ἄμφω ἄρα ταῦτα κινητικὰ κατὰ τόπον, νοῦς καὶ ὄρεξις.

is to be divided up, but rather by what means the soul can be understood to be differentiated with respect to place, both absolutely, insofar as the motion concerned is the motion of the body with respect to its moving around and being moved (these are the problems that are dealt with in the *Physics*) and within itself, that is with respect to perceptions and emotions or occurrences.

My concern remains to clarify the meaning of φαντασία with respect to the soul, and it is with this in view that I proceed. When we understand this we may understand how it is that soul always remains unmoved in itself, even when it is moved accidentally. First we must introduce a clarification, and that is how soul relates to the external motion that place describes, before we understand how the soul 'takes in' and has within it certain kinds of motion: in other words we need to clarify how the soul relates to accidental motion before examining how it relates to the motions proper (and not accidental) to it. To explain this Aristotle gives the example of a sailor on the deck of a ship. The soul moves the sailor across the deck of his ship, by means of walking. The sailor's body moves while the sailor's soul remains essentially unmoved. However, the ship also moves, by means of its propulsion or the movement of the waters.[52] In this sense, the soul is moved by the moving of the ship, but accidentally (that is through no physical concern that the soul has with motion). By extension, the walking of the sailor is also an accidental movement of the soul which does not move the soul in itself. This example itself strongly parallels a discussion in Aristotle's *Physics* where he establishes the meaning of place overall. He gives the example of a vessel in a river.[53] The vessel can change place on the river – in terms of how it is perceived. But in reality, the vessel in moving has remained in its proper place. Its proper place is 'floating-moving-on-the-river'; the place given absolutely through its relation to the 'whole', the heavens-given nature of place. This is its 'proper' place, the place where the vessel is properly known to be what it is and how it is. Place *contains* the vessel and gives it its capacity to move and to be: it is the containing limit of the vessel. Aristotle comments: 'Just as the vessel is a moveable place, so place is an immoveable vessel.'[54]

It is only when we have clarified how soul relates to place accidentally that we can proceed to elaborate how soul relates to place in

---

[52] Aristotle, *De Anima*, 406 a 6–11.

[53] Aristotle, *Physics*: 210 a 24; 211 b 26–29; 212 a 8–21.

[54] Aristotle, *Physics*, 212 a 15. Ἔστι δ' ὥσπερ τὸ ἀγγεῖον τόπος μεταφορητός, οὕτω καὶ ὁ τόπος ἀγγεῖον ἀμετακίνητον.

itself. It is not that the soul is in some sense an analogue or a 'picture in miniature' of the structure of the cosmos. Rather in being the soul, it *as soul* allows the cosmos to be understood – insofar as the being of any particular being is restricted to being the self that it is, it *is* the cosmos in some sense. This is a further clarification of the way in which the soul is, in some sense, all things. It is the place of potential and actual self-disclosure of the 'all'. Thus the span in the description of place between the moveables and the outermost that gives rise to upliftment *is the same* as the span of the soul, of the relation between striving and νοῦς. The coincidence of soul and place is what it means for any being to be in the world, and to know that he is in the world. What the soul is not, therefore, is some world in miniature which moves around the world accidentally.

Just as place explains the relation of what is movable with respect to the whole cosmos, to the 'body' that cosmos is, so soul explains how motion is known with respect to the body of a specific or particular living being. Every form of movement that takes place in the cosmos has an analogue in the soul with respect to φαντασία. In the same way that place is the unmoved first limit of what contains all that moves within it (in the cosmos),[55] so soul, as the 'entelechy', the completion or perfection that organizes the manifestation of the body, is the first unmoved container of all *it* contains – which is the body.[56] Soul therefore makes possible and contains the motions of striving: perception, the emotions and passions, and also those transformations that occur with respect to learning and to the consideration of objects such as the objects of mathematics.

For Aristotle, what each soul knows to be true, it knows absolutely in the same way as every other soul knows what is true to be true, because being is one, even though this unity is distributed equally throughout all the parts of the cosmos, and even though initially true opinion concerning what is known and not known, that is to say, in the discriminating of the true, there can be dispute, and what looks one way to you appears in another to me. What is at issue in this is the character of νοῦς itself, the means by which the soul absolutely knows itself to be determined with respect to place and know itself as determin*able* with respect to place.

---

[55] Cf. Aristotle, *Physics*, 212 a 21. ὥστε τὸ τοῦ περιέχοντος πέρας ἀκίνητον πρῶτον, τοῦτ᾽ ἐστιν ὁ τόπος.

[56] Aristotle, *De Anima*, 412 a 28–29. διὸ ψυχή ἐστιν ἐντελέχεια ἡ πρώτη σώματος φυσικοῦ δυνάμει ζωὴν ἔχοντος.

Aristotle says of νοῦς that it is, considered overall, in some way the place of things insofar as they are separable from matter.[57] Νοῦς in some sense plays the same role as the outermost in the description of place: it is that to which what it receives rises-up. At the same time, as we have seen, it is the place where what is read-off from whatever appears, the phenomena, is carried off to. With all of this in mind, we are at last able to clarify Aristotle's description of the soul with respect to νοῦς and striving, and to see what role φαντασία plays in this. In the first place, φαντασία arises out of thinking;[58] however, φαντασία also accompanies every striving, insofar as striving concerns movement.[59] Although incidentally at this point Aristotle concludes that the striving faculty is what gives rise to movement, nevertheless it is possible to see that φαντασία is that which passes in between every kind of movement and νοῦς, particularly because νοῦς itself, technically speaking, remains unmoved, as the limit to soul. Φαντασία is the means by which the soul apprehends movement, both movement insofar as it is moved accidentally (what befalls it), movement insofar as the soul causes movement (what soul initiates) and change and transformation with respect to what is learned and thought.

Νοῦς only produces movement in a dependent sense, in that it chooses between strivings and discriminates them: striving as such gives rise to movement. It is φαντασία which straddles, and passes back and forth between νοῦς and αἴσθησις, as both what connects them and how striving ceases as an activity, when it attains to truth. Thinking is therefore described as a kind of limit to striving. This passing back and forth, however, has a particular character: on the one hand it is a simple reading-off the appearances so that mind can gain access to what is read off; on the other hand it is the reading-off of what is *most to be read-off*, of the 'already-is being' in whatever is.[60]

---

[57] Cf. Aristotle, *De Anima*: 429 a 27; 429 b 21–22.

[58] Aristotle, *De Anima*, 433 a 10. εἴ τις τὴν φαντασίαν τιθείν ὡς νόησίν τινα.

[59] Aristotle, *De Anima*, 433 a 20. καὶ ἡ φαντασία δὲ ὅταν κινῇ, οὐ κινεῖ ἄνευ ὀρέξεως.

[60] There is a fuller discussion of the phrase τὸ τί ἦν εἶναι in Heidegger, M., *Sein und Zeit*, GA2, 1977 (1927) p. 114 note a. The discussion comes in a section entitled *Die Weltlichkeit der Welt* (The Worldliness of World). Although Heidegger does not mention the *De Anima* in this note, elsewhere he makes the connection with what the *De Anima* treats of and the phenomenology of being in the world explicit. In an early introductory lecture course on phenomenology he says 'περὶ ψυχῆς ist keine Psychologie im modernen Sinn, sondern handelt vom Sein des Menschen in der Welt' and 'De Anima. Übersetzt man "Von der Seele" . . . so übersetzen wir: "Über das Sein in der Welt".' Heidegger, M., *Einführung in die phänomenologische Forschung*, GA17, 1994, p. 7; p. 293. ('περὶ ψυχῆς is not

In this sense it is thinking's access to the being of beings, to being itself. It is this that persists: *not* that the mind attains a certain persistence with respect to what it knows, but *that it attains to persistence*, that it itself is lifted up off to the ever-persistent and ever-same. In this, it is what thinking attains to when it attains to the thinking of thinking. It is here that we discover what Aristotle means when he says that mind in one sense becomes all things – in the other it attains to the making of all things, and this latter is akin to light.

This is the ambiguity we encountered both with regard to Kant and Žižek – of the ambiguous character of φαντασία – that on the one hand it is a faculty, and on the other a sort of genus, or a faculty for a faculty. If we return to the description of the reading-off (ἀφαιρέσει) of the three kinds of φάντασματα we discover each, strictly speaking, corresponds to a kind of movement. Especially in the case of αἴσθησις and πάθος it is possible to see how what drives the reading-off is a striving, ὄρεξις. In these two cases, both what is chosen and what befalls, striving either for something or against (in the sense of avoidance) something *is* the very reading-off that φαντασία is. It is more difficult to see how this is, however, with the class of things that never explain the being of all the φαντάσματα – the things purely abstracted, like the objects of mathematics. In this case, however, the motion concerned is not movement as such, but transformation, of which learning, or attaining a different kind of potential, is what is at issue.

Why has it been so important to clarify the meaning of φαντασία? In a sense, we still have not explained how φαντασία becomes imagination, even though we have seen that, despite Aristotle's drawing attention to the primacy of *seeing*, φαντασία has a fundamental connection with speaking. Aristotle avoids falling into a relativism with respect to φαντασία because even though φαντασία can be correct or false, it is still only this with respect to true opinion, not truth as such. The connection to τόπος, place, and so to absolute position within the cosmos *as the fundamental connection with presence, with the already-is of being* is what protects φαντασία from falling over into mere appearance both at the level of opinion and judgement, and at the level of what thinking thinks (νοῦς). This is only possible, however, because for Aristotle the cosmos is both finite and absolutely

a psychology in the modern sense, but concerns itself with the being of man in the world'; '*De Anima*. Usually translated: "Concerning the Soul" . . . thus we translate: "Concerning being in the world".') See also for the discussion of aspect in the verb in relation to this Sheehan, T., *Geschichtlichkeit / Ereignis / Kehre* in *Existentia (Meletai Sophias)*, Budapest, 2001, Vol. XI, 3–4, pp. 241–51.

determined. It is only in the twelfth book of the *Metaphysics* that Aristotle explicitly connects divinity with what is unmoved and is at the same time a cause of movement, and a 'thinking on thinking'. Nevertheless, all thinking has as its goal contemplation, θεωρεῖν. In this sense the soul's capacity for contemplation is its capacity for being like to the gods and being-divine, as we have already seen.

It has long been considered a problem that the unmoved 'first mover' is discussed in different texts of Aristotle differently. It is thought that this indicates development in Aristotle's work – from the 'early' Aristotle of the *De Caelo* to a later one of the *Physics* or *Metaphysics*.[61] It is seen as a problem, therefore, that the prime mover is forever in motion in the *De Caelo* whilst absolutely unmoved in the *Metaphysics* and unmoved with respect to itself but capable of being moved κατὰ συμβεβηκός, accidentally, with respect to animals or the soul.[62]

In each case the defining character of what is unmoved is that it is ἀκίνετον, ἀθάνατος, θειότατον – without motion, without death, most divine. In each case, however, the *same* principle manifests itself differently with respect to the matter at issue. Thus with respect to the soul, both in the *Physics* and in the *De Anima*, as we have seen, although the soul is moved accidentally, it remains unmoved for itself. This means no more than what is self-moving can also be moved around while yet at rest, as when a sailor is moved on the deck of a ship or when I am sitting in a train. With respect to the heavens, as indeed, in the discussion in the twelfth book of the *Metaphysics*, the unmoved as a *principle* of motion does not mean that what is unmoved is, strictly speaking, unmoving. The motion at issue here is not walking from place to place, or being moved in a train, but a different kind of motion, the unceasing motion that is circular and so returns to its beginning. This is the motion (φορά) engendered of both divine activity and being itself, it is perfect motion that is a 'a bending-

---

[61] This is clearly the view of Ross. Cf. Ross, W. D., 'The Development of Aristotle's Thought' in *Proceedings of the British Academy*, Vol. 43 (1957), pp. 63–78, esp. p. 75. It is even supposed for textual evidence that the *De Caelo* represents an 'early' or 'immature' view because in certain passages Aristotle refers to his predecessors' arguments, as if citing them indicated temporal proximity to them. A good general analysis and unravelling of this thesis can be found in Kosman, A., 'Aristotle's Prime Mover' in Gill, M. L. and Lennox, J. G. (eds.), *Self Motion: From Aristotle to Newton*, 1994, pp. 135–53.

[62] Cf. Aristotle; *De Caelo*, 284 a 2–16; *Physics*, 259 b 20–25; *Metaphysics*, 1072 b 19–25; cf. *De Anima*, 433 b 21ff.

back *back* [on itself]',[63] and so circular, upon which all continuous motion (συνεχής) and time depends. What is at issue with this motion is, both in the *De Caelo* and in the *Metaphysics*, motion that concerns the outmost limit that surrounds the all, the περιέχον. Because this is the surrounding limit, it has no further limit, it is the limit of all τόπος, place: not the limit of all places, but the limit of place as such (which allows every particular place to be limited). Motion with respect to place can be both moved and unmoved: it can be moved accidentally. Motion which contains place is not itself *in* place, and so has no 'where' – it cannot be moved accidentally since there is no 'where', no place for it to move *from* and *to*. This motion is therefore eternal and, strictly speaking, unmoved.

As should now be clear, the 'prime mover' is not, therefore, differentiated with respect to *when* Aristotle wrote about it, but rather *what* he is writing about. It manifests itself differently depending on what it manifests itself within. It is at this point we can seen how important the question of the containing limit is. In the *De Caelo* Aristotle remarks that the immortality and divinity of the whole heaven is disclosed through the word αἰών, aeon. The origin of this word, Aristotle says, is ἀεί εἶναι, ever-being, and was a 'divinely inspired' name given by 'our predecessors' because originally it meant the surrounding time (περιέχον χρόνον) which is each living thing's allotment.[64] Thus 'according to the same thought the "all" of the heavens and all time and the unlimited final containment is αἰών, taking the name ἀεί εἶναι (being ever), without death, and divine'.[65]

The principle of being and divinity that makes possible the whole motion of the cosmos is the same principle that manifests itself in the soul with respect to its life and motion. The soul's passageway to being is in a sense therefore the soul's experience of the being and divinity of itself and the cosmos – it is its 'being in the world' as its own being-worlded. It is clear then that the relation of the unmoved to the moved

---

[63] Cf. Aristotle, *De Generatione et Corruptione*, 337 a 7. πάλιν ανακάμπτειν. This motion is specifically engendered to relate non-being to being: 336 b 35 οὕτω γὰρ ἂν μάλιστα συνείροιτο τὸ εἶναι διὰ τὸ ἐγγύτατα εἶναι τῆς οὐσίας τὸ γίνεσθαι ἀεὶ καὶ τὴν γένεσιν. ('For indeed the greatest connectedness for being would arise through the greatest nearness to being of ever self-becoming of the becoming of substance.')

[64] Cf. Aristotle, *De Caelo*, 279 a 5–279 b 5.

[65] Aristotle, *De Caelo*, 279 a 25f. κατὰ τὸν αὐτὸν δὲ λόγον καὶ τὸ τοῦ παντὸς οὐρανοῦ τέλος καὶ τὸ τοῦ παντὸς οὐρανοῦ καὶ τὸ τὸν πάντα χρόνον καὶ τὴν ἀπειρίαν περιέχον τέλος αἰών ἐστιν, ἀπὸ τοῦ ἀεὶ εἶναι εἰληφὼς τὴν ἐπωνυμίαν, ἀθάνατος καὶ θεῖος.

– the so-called problem of the 'first-mover' is the way in which the divinity of the one (ἕν) is distributed all the way through the manifold of the cosmos. Aristotle works this out on the basis of a rigorous phenomenological description of the relation of the activity of νοῦς to the receipt of perceptivity, αἴσθησις. Divinity, τὸ θεῖον, is as the unmoved, at the same time an ἐνεργέια, an ever-activity in the same way as νοῦς, as unmoved, is at the same time a kind of activity that is ever the same. Each is without time and yet has temporal determinations. In no sense is this divinity personal. Divinity, like mind and place, is not in any where, but makes every 'where', every place, every time (as a 'now') possible. It is all things in the sense that it is the totality of being, no longer as potential, but as actual and fully-actualized, what, as the already-is in being, 'is' and 'ever is'. What later comes to be thought of as sublimity and upliftment is the attainment to this: upliftment is the inward experience of the rising up to contemplation, θεωρεῖν. The most significant aspect of this, therefore, is that the meaning of τὸ θεῖον, divinity, is worked out phenomenologically on the basis of the being of being-human, in the matter of the analogous character of the containing limit, the περιέχον, of the aeon, the allotment of time to every particular being by means of the everlasting and deathless being of the life and motion of the whole living being that the cosmos is. This being of the cosmos has all the attributes of the unity and oneness of being itself, it *is* being – it is indivisible (ἀδιαίρετον), without parts (ἀμερὲς) and without magnitude (οὐδὲν ἔχον μέγεθος), and yet at the same time it manifests itself *as* this being as distributed through all the divisibility, differentiatedness and magnitude of everything it contains. This is the means by which Aristotle achieves a description of the *being* of beings.[66]

I have, however, only answered my original question in an entirely provisional way, which is how is it that φαντασία become the faculty of imagination? In demonstrating and showing-up the role that

---

[66] It should become clear now why the understanding of 'being-towards-death' (*Sein zum Tode*) assumed such importance in the work of Martin Heidegger. Despite the inconsequential chatter about Heidegger's supposed necrophilia, or the trumpeted masculinism of his obsession with death, in fact he sought to recover death as the temporal and phenomenological basis for the being of beings which Aristotle also seeks, albeit not as a recovery of Aristotle as such. The insight here is twofold: αἰών means both the restriction to its own life of a (human) being, and it means the interrogability of the whole of life through the ineluctability of that restriction. Paradoxically, therefore, being towards death indicates the meaning which life has for each of us, *not* any kind of concern with death. Having our death in view throws each of us back on the allottedness to life which we *are*.

φαντασία takes on in Aristotle's understanding of the soul, we have not made the transition over to Kant. How does Kant himself achieve this, and is there a straight line between Aristotle and Kant?

I have, however, given a provisional answer to my original question: 'what kind of theology is intended or indicated by a discussion of the sublime?',[67] by indicating how upliftment (although Aristotle does not give it this name) is grounded in Aristotle's own 'theology' as the science of being insofar as it is being. Has not Aristotle then succeeded in precisely the task I identified in the beginning of this book – by identifying an ontological grounding in the being of being-human for God and the gods? Better than this, has he not succeeded in assigning a highest value to the divine? Where else need theology go to proceed?

---

[67] Cf. Chapter 1, p. 11 above.

6

Analogia Entis

Michael J. Buckley, in his book *Motion and Motion's God*, having analysed the unmoved mover as a principle of motion in Aristotle, argues triumphantly that 'to have demonstrated an indivisible being as the moving principle of eternal movement concludes [Aristotle's] general physical investigations'.[1] He proceeds to suggest that 'the long journey from eternal motion has reached God, a living God' and even that some of the steps on the way bear 'resemblance to the Thomistic *tertia via*'.[2] Nothing could be further from the truth, and yet it is entirely self-evident to Buckley that what he says is true: why?

A particular being has to have somewhere to be, and, moreover, is separated and separable from other beings. Aristotle's divinity, however, as we have seen, has neither a 'where', nor is it in any sense separable from being – indeed it is what being is, but being taken as the being *of* beings, as οὐσία taken in the widest and most general sense: τὸ τί ἦν εἶναι, even though this understanding of being arises on the basis of metaphysics, and so *apart* from and inversely to the understanding of being we encountered in Parmenides. Indeed, far from demonstrating an indivisible being as the moving principle of eternal motion, the *exact reverse* is true, that, phenomenologically Aristotle has carefully and patiently demonstrated that motion, first finite and limited, passive and accidental, then eternal, has as its highest and best expression *being*, indivisible, timeless and unmoved. No living God has been reached, but rather the visibility of divinity as the principle of ever-remaining life, is what is attained to by contemplation and learning. Buckley tells us that 'this unmixed actuality effects movement as its final cause'.[3] The problem with Buckley's reinscription of Aristotle's divinity is this term 'cause': αἰτία. Originally a term per-

---

[1] Buckley, SJ, M. J., *Motion and Motion's God: Thematic Variations in Aristotle, Cicero, Newton and Hegel*, 1971, p. 73.
[2] Buckley, *Motion and Motion's God*, 1971, p. 82; p. 77.
[3] Buckley, *Motion and Motion's God*, 1971, p. 78.

taining to law or public culpability, αἰτία means the 'what' that is responsible for something, what is to be blamed for or accounted to it. Buckley points to how, in a sense at least, Aristotle has come to be read as providing an ontological ground, and so a causal relation, for God in the being of being human.[4] What is the purpose of ascertaining a cause? Aristotle argues that the enumeration and working out of the causes is for the sake of being lifted up into (ἀνάγεται) the τί ἐστιν, the 'what is (insofar as it is)'.[5] The causes help us into the being of beings; we might say that they are at their utmost the practice of the science of being insofar as it is being, and so they are the practice of theology.

To discover the 'what is' is not simply to ask about its properties or so forth, but to ask how any particular being relates to being as such: presupposed in the 'what is' is that the specific being in question is enquired into with respect to the 'already is' of it, what *already* lies there *ahead of me* to be uncovered. In this there is a real temporal ambiguity. The 'already is' is at the same time ever-the-same, and so eternal, and yet it lies in *my* future as something the understanding of which is yet to be accomplished. We have seen, however, with Aristotle's understanding of contemplation, that this yet-to-be is not really the future as a genuine temporal horizon, but rather my own being let-in to the eternity of the being of beings, of the ever-same disclosed in the science of being insofar as it is being.

It is important, however, not to overlook the 'being lifted (up) into'. The 'going up' in question, and the relation to being still place us firmly in the province of upliftment itself, of the sublime. Every 'cause', therefore, even before it is an accounting of a causality of some kind, is a working-out – it relates to thinking and to νοῦς, and it is at the same time a 'being lifted up'.

In Aristotle's own definitions of causes, only one of his uses of the term αἰτία describes what productively and specifically gives rise to something and causes it to be: the so-called efficient cause, as in the father begetting a child which is a 'choosing cause',[6] a cause where we can find a one who decides to cause in such and such a way, and so sets a goal or an end for something, who chooses (and so wills, if we can really speak of the will with respect to Aristotle) something to be.[7]

---

[4] See end of last chapter and p. 9 above.
[5] Cf. Aristotle, *Physics*, 194 b 1ff.
[6] Aristotle, *Physics*, 194 b 30f. ὁ βουλεύσας αἴτιος.
[7] Cf. Aristotle, *Physics*, 194 b 31. ἔτι ὡς τὸ τέλος.

Buckley, however, identifies as the cause that Aristotle employs with respect to the relation between motionless divinity and everything that is moved, not the supposedly 'efficient cause', the cause where a prior deciding is effected, but the final cause, οὗ ἕνεκα. He has good textual evidence for this: in the *Physics* Aristotle selects for special mention the case of that cause that concerns the relation of the moved to the unmoved as its αἰτία, especially where the whole of natural being (φύσις) is concerned. There is confirmation of this in the *Metaphysics* where Aristotle says that the final cause concerns the things that are without motion because the motionless 'then moves thus by being desired',[8] and correspondingly we discover in the *De Anima* that striving-after itself has an end (ἕνεκα).[9]

Surely therefore, the living divinity identified by Buckley is the final cause of the whole of the cosmos? Except that an important aspect of the 'final cause' is absent in this account: the being raised up (that is, upliftment) that the enquiry into causes is. At the same time, the striving-after of the *De Anima* is the final cause *itself*, it does not appear to correspond with what causes the desiring discussed in the statement of the *Metaphysics*. In fact the word 'cause' (αἰτία) is awkwardly absent from all the texts cited. The reason is simple: the term οὗ ἕνεκα does not mean 'final cause' at all, but the 'for the sake of which', the 'on account of'. In this sense the being of the cosmos is dependent on, but not caused by, Aristotle's divinity. Aristotle expressly rules out the use of any of the causes except the 'for the sake of which' in considering the relation of the being of nature (φύσις) to the divine and eternal being of the unmoved. The supposedly causal relation of the being of nature to the divinity of the being of beings is expressly allocated to the appetitive or striving part of the soul, the ὀρεκτικον. The striving-after of the soul, its involuntary activity, has an end, a 'for the sake of', which is νοῦς. Thinking, and the pure self-thinking of thinking itself, contemplation, is therefore the pursued end (rather than the final cause) of αἴσθησις, of perception. This is how the relation between divinity and the cosmos expresses itself in the soul, by means of φαντασία, and the manner in which the soul attains, through wisdom, to actualizing or realizing its being in some sense all things.

In the *Physics* this relationship manifests itself differently: Aristotle says 'there is "for the sake of" in the becomings of natural being and

---

[8] Aristotle, *Metaphysics*, 1072 b 4. κινεῖ δὲ ὡς ἐρώμενον.
[9] Aristotle, *De Anima*, 433 a 15.

being in itself'.[10] Being in itself here is said last, it is the 'for the sake of', it is what the becomings of φύσις have in view, it is what they strive after (in the soul) and seek to attain. In this sense, if we translate οὖ ἕνεκα as Buckley does, we have to say that the cosmos, strictly speaking, causes being and divinity, which makes no sense in the terms that we usually understand causation. In fact, however, what is being named is a relationship of dependence with no (efficient or final) causality implied. Moreover this is the very working through and working out of what I have been calling Aristotle's phenomenology – that the being of the cosmos seeks to rise up and attain to being as its end, and (for human beings) the understanding of this is undertaken by means of experience, this undertaking is achieved through genuine πάθος and αἴσθησις.

Because the efficient cause concerns the making and production of things, it is a cause of choosing and selecting something to be in such-and-such a way, and so this cause *above all* is excluded from the relation of the cosmos to the divinity of being, because there can be no choosing that they be other with the things that are ever-the-same. Buckley interprets Aristotle as proposing that there is 'a' divinity – but Aristotle's divinity is divinity in general, divinity as being-overall. This divinity is responsible for the ever-being of life as such, but it is not *a* life, although (for Aristotle) it is the 'for the sake of which' every life lives. That part of the soul that relates to appetition and striving, the ὀρέκτικον is – even for Kant – a *function* of the soul, it is involuntary. It is the way in which the soul at every point 'goes out after' – the question is always *for what* it is going out after and being stood-out for. As involuntary, it is never any kind of selecting, choosing or willing.

Yet Buckley presupposes a kind of willing of the divine being at issue. Clearly this divinity is one unknown to Aristotle. To answer the question why Buckley takes Aristotle's divinity in the way he does is to answer the question of *whose* this divinity is. What Buckley takes as self-evidently for granted is not Aristotle's God at all, but the creator-God of Christian (philosophical) Neoplatonism, mentioned briefly in Chapter 4. The transition through Neoplatonism to this understanding of God in fact took centuries. What concerns us, however, is the way in which *we* read Aristotle as if this transition never took place; as if, in other words, there could be no other understanding of God than one which understands God as the originating first cause of all that

---

[10] Aristotle, *Physics*, 199 a 8. ἔστιν ἄρα τὸ ἕνεκά του ἐν τοῖς φύσει γιγνο-μένοις καὶ οὖσιν.

is. Christians, of course, could do no other than re-work this causal relationship. For God cannot be derived from the being of being human without *first* and more priorly demonstrating that the being of humanity is (causally) dependent on the being of God in some way. This is essential, both from the point of view of understanding God as creator, and understanding the priority of God over – especially fallen – creatures.

The change that is effected in this transition, however, relates to the very basis of philosophy itself. What has become clear in our discussion of Aristotle is the fundamentally phenomenological character of his investigations: the understanding of divinity, even though stood on an elemental decision about being, is nevertheless worked out from the self-understanding of the being of being-human. The possibility of this transition, and its basic direction, lay already latent in Plato, in his description in the *Timaeus* of the generation of the body of the cosmos as a production of the divine.[11] All it took was for some Christians to read, and so interpret, the *Timaeus* in this direction for it to seem as if this is what the text had always said.

What did Christianity intrude into this narrative that was not there before? Specifically, Christianity understands God and humanity to be set apart from each other in different places, by sin and through the fall of Adam. God has been revealed to be wholly unknown and different to man through sin, rather than ontological dissimilitude (previously man was in God's image and likeness). Here we must be wary: orthodox Christianity at the same time says that the very one who reveals God to be unknown is the one who will allow the unknown God to be known: Christ, the sinless son of the Father. In the same way as the Greek understanding of being is set apart in two places, so the Christian understanding speaks of a setting apart. But the manner of their belonging together is entirely different. Nevertheless, and repeatedly, these two manners of setting-apart take each other over all too easily, plundering each other's definitions and language in their struggle to be understood. We must keep always in view that Christianity seeks the reunion of God and man through Christ, in faith: Greek thought seeks the thinking of the being of beings. It is astonishing the frequency with which 'philosophers' resort to acts of faith – something is true because someone said it is (and this one was a Great Thinker). This is not philosophy. Equally should we look on in amazement at how often Christians resort to philosophy in order to

---

[11] Cf. Plato, *Timaeus*, 31 B; 68 E.

consummate, evacuate, or out-narrate philosophy's definitions, as if
that would be enough to save them. It does not.

It is outside the concerns of this book to trace the history of this
transition – indeed, it is outside my concerns to offer a purely historical narrative as if that sufficed for what is at issue. My concerns
proceed in the opposite direction – to explain the understanding of the
being of being human with which we are familiar, that is to say, which
we unquestioningly take for granted, and to exhibit this understanding as a *question*: to strip it of its familiarity and expose its meaning
for us. From the outset I suggested that this is what the figure of
Brontosaurus exhibits, both for us and to us. *Brontosaurus* is already
ahead of us – it forces us to accept that there is a question at all,
and that the question does not arise as a moment of idle curiosity or
speculation.

It is here that we can see the importance of the work of St Thomas
Aquinas, an importance I have already mentioned. Aquinas brings the
understanding of faith into explicit confrontation with Greek metaphysics, constantly reworking the philosophers to render them in a
Christian way, and at the same time manages to hold the two apart.
He is important not because he is a 'great thinker' who has been
declared so by a Pope (although his was certainly an astonishing and
sensitive achievement),[12] but because above all he is in direct confrontation with Aristotle in the working out of his basic thought.
Aquinas is extraordinary, not in the extent that he departed from Plato
and the Neoplatonic traditions he inherited, and above all else
Aristotle, but in his faithfulness to them, while bending them round to
Christian concerns. It is important to assert once again that Aquinas
is *not* a philosopher, taken in the Greek or contemporary sense. St
Thomas always refuses the name philosopher for Christians, reserving
this title above all to Aristotle, and then to other pagan or at least non-
Christian authors.[13] St Thomas even works out the salvation of the
human person through the interrelationship of divinity and intellect
(where intellect is taken to be the translation of νοῦς) so that once the
Christian soul has been saved, after the last things, judgement, purga-

---

[12] Cf. Pope Leo XIII, encyclical letter *Aeterni Patris* of 4 August 1879 in *Acta
Sanctae Sedis*, Vol. 12, 1879, pp. 97–115.

[13] Cf. for a fuller discussion of this, Jordan, M., *The Alleged Aristotelianism of
St. Thomas Aquinas* in *The Étienne Gilson Series*, no. 15, 1990, esp. p. 6. 'For
Thomas, membership in a school of philosophy does not befit Christians. [. . .]
Thomas speaks about philosophy, of course, as a habit of knowing necessary for
an educated believer [. . .] I cannot find that the epithet *philosophus* is ever applied
by Thomas to a Christian.' See also pp. 32–7.

tory, and justification, the soul sees what God sees, as much as God chooses to give it a greater or lesser light to do so.[14] Although Aquinas seeks a description of this that borrows heavily from philosophy, he is in fact only being faithful to an insight of Scripture, the scriptural description of what it means to be present to God – 'we know that when he shall appear we shall be like to him: for we shall see him as he is'.[15]

Only the justified, those beckoned into heaven by God, will have the beatific vision. However, Aquinas does not hold the opinion that the human intellect can never arrive at the vision of God through his essence, or essentially, but rather the opposite. Note that this question arises specifically in consequence of what it means to 'see' God. Surely, however, we see with the eyes, not the intellect? Except that Aquinas is always careful to bring before us that it is the intellect which really 'sees', and in a sense more truly than that seeing which is undertaken with the sight of the eyes. Intellective knowing, *cognitio*, is, for Aquinas at least, primarily a 'seeing', and of a kind that directly 'sees' truth. Elsewhere in the *Summa Theologiae* he argues 'the eye is double: certainly, it is of the body, properly speaking; and it is of the intellect, as we might say, by similitude'.[16] What Aquinas refers to here is the eye of faith, which, in being granted the beatific vision after death, is rewarded with confirmation of its faithfulness – it will 'see' directly what once it only saw in pious expectation.[17] Aquinas deduces this by direct appeal to Aristotle, saying that 'substance, therefore inasmuch as it is in this manner, is not visible to the bodily eye, neither does it underlie particular senses, neither the imagination, but alone [it underlies] the intellect, whose object is that which is, as is said in chapter three of the *De Anima*'.[18] However, Aquinas says 'this opera-

---

[14] Aquinas, *Summa Theologiae*, Ia, Q. 12, art. 7 resp. 'Nullus autem intellectus creatum potest Deum infinite cognoscere. Instantum enim intellectus creatus divinam essentiam perfectius vel minus perfecte cognoscit, inquantum maiori vel minori lumine gloriae perfunditur.'

[15] 1 John 3:2. 'Quoniam cum apparuerit similes ei erimus quoniam videbimus eum sicuti est.'

[16] Aquinas, *Summa Theologiae*, IIIa, Q. 76, art. 7, resp. 'Duplex est oculis: scilicet corporalis, proprie dictus: et intellectualis, qui per similitudinem dicitur.'

[17] Once again, the warrant for this is strictly scriptural. Cf. 1 Cor. 13:12. 'For now we see through a glass, darkly; but then face to face: now I know in part; but then shall I know even as also I am known.'

[18] Aquinas, *Summa Theologiae*, IIIa, Q. 76, art. 7, resp. 'Substantia autem, inquantum huiusmodi, non est visibilis oculo corporali, neque subiacet alicui sensui, neque imaginationi, sed soli intellectui, cuius obiectum est quod quid est, ut dicitur in III *de Anima*.'

tion by which the human mind is conjoined to God does not, therefore, depend on the senses'.[19] Divine union is in no sense in consequence of some kind of summit of contemplation in thought, but is
rather by the graceful gift of God. Aquinas protects the difference
between creator and creature by asserting that this union does not
mean that the created mind in any sense 'comprehends' – that is,
exceeds or is co-equal to the divine intellect, but rather, that this con-
joinment is in virtue of the capacity of the creature to receive it and in
virtue of the degree to which God chooses to flood the created mind
with the light of glory, which is God himself.

This transforms the relation of the intellect to substance (νοῦς to
οὐσία), since for Aristotle it was the encountering of specific substances that gave the mind the passageway through to the meaning of
the being of beings overall. Aquinas, in contrast, asserts an essential
scepticism with the ability of the mind to know substances by means
of (and this means in the working out of) experience (the relation of
οὐσία to αἴσθησις). In his definition of truth, Aquinas is quite explicit
about what makes the true 'true'. True knowledge for you or me is the
adequation of thing and intellect,[20] but this is because what becomes
true for me, the way my intellect is conformed to the truth of something is so because it is *already* productively true in that manner
because intended to be so by its author, who is God. Thus Aquinas
stresses that 'natural things from which our intellect gets its knowledge measure our intellect, as is said in the tenth book of [Aristotle's]
Metaphysics: but these things are themselves measured by the divine
intellect, in which are all created things, just as all works of art find
their origin in the intellect of the artificer.'[21]

Although Aquinas cites Aristotle's *Metaphysics* in support of his
argument, we can see here how Aquinas consistently reworks the
ancient authors. On inspection, the actual place in the *Metaphysics* to

---

[19] Aquinas, *Summa Theologiae*, Ia IIae, Q. 3, art. 3, resp. 'Non autem tunc
operatio qua mens humana Deo coniungetur, a sensu dependebit.'

[20] Aquinas, *Quaestiones disputatae: De Veritate*, Q. 1, art. 1, resp. 'Veritas est
adaequatio rei et intellectus.' This is also how St Thomas defines truth in the
Commentary on the Sentences, where he speaks of the 'relatio adaequationis, in
qua consistit ratio veritatis' (*In I Sent*. Disp. 19, art. 5, resp.; cf. Disp. 40, art. 3
resp. and *In IV Sent*. Disp. 46, Q. 1, resp.) and in the *Summa Contra Gentiles*
(Book 1, Ch. 59, no. 2) as well as the *Summa Theologiae* (Ia, Q. 16, art. 1, resp.).

[21] Aquinas, *De Veritate*, Q. 1, art 2., resp. '. . . quod res naturales, ex quibus
intellectus noster scientiam accipit, mensurant intellectum nostru, ut dicitur X
Metaphysicis: sed sunt mensuratae ab intellectu divino, in quo sunt omnia creata,
sicut omnia artificiata in intellectu artificis.'

which St Thomas refers us has nothing to do with the origin of things in the divine intellect – indeed, Aquinas subtly reverses the very claim that Aristotle makes. Aristotle notes that although it seems that knowledge is a measure which measures the things that are knowable, in fact it is the other way about, because knowledge is measured by the knowable.[22] However, Aquinas here says *exactly* the opposite: because God intends what is to be knowable to be knowable, as such and in the manner of its being, by a prior act of creation (because God is the author of the heavens and the earth), God's knowledge precisely *does* measure what is knowable, and thereby makes it true, in advance of our being measured by it. Our intellects come into the truth only insofar as, by means of their perfecting work on what they know, they uncover in things what God first intended for those things. *We* discover by the work of the intellect the essence of the substances we come across, by means of their accidents – but *God already knows* in advance what the essences of things are, because God intended those essences in the first place, he created them to be as they are. (This means that the *adaequatio* formula of truth is more a matter arising out of faith, though it is not a matter *of* faith, than it is a philosophical definition – it depends for its effectiveness upon a Christian world-view, which only receives external confirmation by the operation of human reckoning.)

Our *productive* knowledge is therefore only analogous to God's in the most extraordinary way, in that it is only directly analogous in the natural order to the knowledge the divine intellect has when we too are making or creating something. Aquinas distinguishes between the human and the divine intellects in the following way: 'The divine intellect, therefore, measures, and is not measured; a natural thing both measures and is measured; but our intellect is measured, and measures only artifacts, not natural things.'[23] It is only in this sense that Aquinas agrees with Aristotle, and only with regard to the created intellect. With regard to the uncreated intellect, God's, St Thomas says the opposite of what Aristotle says. The primary way in which we know

---

[22] Cf. Aristotle, *Metaphysics*, 1057 a 9–13. δόξειε μὲν γὰρ ἂν μέτρον ἡ ἐπιστήμη εἶναι, τὸ δὲ ἐπιστητὸν τὸ μετρούμενον, συμβαναίνει δὲ ἐπιστήμην μὲν πᾶσαν ἐπιστητὸν εἶναι, τὸ δὲ επιστητὸν μὴ πᾶν ἐπιστήμην, ὅτι τρόπον τινὰ ἡ ἐπιστήμη μετρεῖται τῷ ἐπιστητῷ.

[23] Aquinas, *De Veritate*, Q. 1, art 2, resp. 'Sic ergo intellectus divinus est mensurans non mesuratus; res autem naturalis, mensurans et mensurata; sed intellectus noster est mensuratus, non mensurans quidem res naturales, sed artificiales tantum.'

something to be true is when our intellect is passively conformed, through sensate experience and our intellection of it, to what is productively intended to be true by God. Only when *we* make something, do we (productively) decide *in advance* what it is that we will make, and whatever it is we produce is made in accordance with this 'in advance'. We are in the same relation to what it is we make that God is with regard to being the *causa et creator omnium*. When, however, we come across something that already exists, especially in the natural order, we can only by what we now call 'experience' and through the senses work out what was intended by its creator or producer *for* and *in* its making or production.

This is the force of understanding at the philosophical level God to be the creator of everything that is, the creator of the heavens and the earth. God has this knowledge atemporally, in a single act of knowing, because God (and only God) is entirely transparent to himself. Here we see already a reversal of the atemporality of the divinity of being that Aristotle sought to describe. No longer do the 'causes' give the soul a passageway in to the thinking on thinking that being is because it *already* (ἦν) is, but rather in being-already, only God knows in advance of us what is true. The working out of the 'causes' tell us now what God already knows, and this is because prior even to this, God is the prior and first cause of all that is. Aristotle's 'causes' cannot work like this, because they exactly are a being-led-up (ἀνάγεται) into being-overall. The causes, taken from the viewpoint of Aristotle's divinity (if such a thing were possible), are passive. From the standpoint of Aquinas and of the Christian God as *ens creator*, the only significant cause, the creative cause, is active: it *chooses* that substances are what they are – the very kind of cause (the 'efficient cause') that Aristotle had ruled out with respect to the initiation of motion in the *Physics*. Aquinas is relying for all of this on only one small matter. Whereas finite creatures – we – could not choose that the things that are eternal, divine, and ever-the-same could be other, God *as* infinite, eternal and divine selected them to be what they are and so could have chosen that they be other. The effect is devastating: for Aristotle things are what they are just because they *are*, they have no ultimate 'why', or purpose, they were never chosen to be that way. For Aquinas, however, everything now has a purpose because God could have chosen that it be other than it is, and so we can only presume he chose that things are what they are because God makes the 'best' choices.

For Aristotle, the being of beings is a science, it has to be worked out, by means of the mind, which discloses the cosmos to be mind, thinking as such: we *attain* to this thinking: this attainment is a future task. For Aquinas, God is now *ipsum esse subsistens*. God has God's own being, or 'to be'. It is important to see what God as *ipsum esse subsistens* does not say. It does not say that 'God is being' in the same way that we as beings are in being: neither is God a separate being or entity. It does, however, say that only God has a full passageway-in to the being of beings, an access we will gain (insofar as God chooses) should we attain perfection. Now, inasmuch as we discover the being of beings already to have been, we discover what always was before us. Even though for both Aristotle and Aquinas divinity is eternal, and so strictly speaking, atemporal, for Aristotle attaining to this is *for me* a future task; for Aquinas it shows me to *have been determined from out of what went before me*. Really, therefore, I attain to what 'was', what has been and so is past to me.

Because the human intellect is fallen and so has a bent towards falsity, and therefore again in contradistinction to Aristotle, Aquinas asserts that 'the human intellect is not able to attain a comprehension of the divine substance through its natural power'.[24] Aquinas illustrates this by way of a detour, indicating that it is not even a matter of varying degrees of comprehension or capacity or skill in the practice of wisdom that is at stake. Unlike every other form of intellect (human, angelic, etc.) the divine intellect is adequate to its substance, and understands perfectly what it is, and knows what all of its intelligibles are.[25] By intelligibles Aquinas simply means that which is able to be known about something; by adequate is meant 'equal to' or transparent. In this sense the divine substance is self-transparent. Here Aquinas is only reiterating his frequent assertion that only God can know fully or comprehend God. Thus St Thomas says:

> Since everything is knowable inasmuch as it is actual, God, who is pure act without any admixture of potentiality, in himself is most excellently knowable. But what is supremely knowable in itself, may not be knowable to some other (*alicui*) intellect, on account of

---

[24] Aquinas, *Summa Contra Gentiles*, Book 1, Ch. 3, no. 4. 'Nam ad substantiam [Dei] capiendam intellectus humanus naturali virtute pertingere non potest.'

[25] Aquinas, *Summa Contra Gentiles*, Book 1, Ch. 3, no. 5. 'Ipse enim intellectus divinus sua capacitate substantiam suam adaequat, et ideo perfecte de se intelligit quid est, et omnia cognoscit quae de ipso intelligibilia sunt.' Cf. Book 1, Ch. 4, no. 5. 'Rationis humanae plerumque falsitas admiscetur.'

the excess of what is knowable [i.e. contained in it] over above that intellect.[26]

Aquinas is indicating that God's self-transparency to God is of an entirely different order to the knowledge I might have of something other than me. The reference to excess here is simply to reinforce the point – it is not critical to Aquinas's assertion, but exemplifies and makes more understandable the problem, because it takes as its exemplary subject the unique substance that God is. What is at issue is this: how I can have access to what is knowable about a substance has a limitation in knowledge, especially where what it is I seek experience or knowledge of is different in kind from me. This is in contrast to comparing my capacity to know something about myself in virtue of my capacity to interrogate myself about what it is I seek knowledge of. We are talking here of two different kinds of knowledge – experience from without, as in that gained by means of the senses, and self-transparency, the ability to know based on self-interrogability.[27] Indeed in the *Summa Contra Gentiles* Aquinas reinforces this point:

The same thing manifestly appears from the defect that is experienced in our everyday knowledge of things. We are ignorant of many properties of sensible things, and it is not possible for us perfectly to enter into the reckoning of those properties we apprehend by sense. All the more therefore, does human reckoning not suffice to investigate all the intelligibilities of that most excellent substance [i.e. God].[28]

---

[26] Cf. Aquinas, *Summa Theologiae*, Ia, Q. 12, art. 1, resp. 'Cum unumquodque sit cognoscibile secundum quod est in actu, Deus, qui est actus purus absque omni permixtione potentiae, quantum in se est, maxime cognoscibilis est. Sed quod est maxime cognoscibile in se, alicui intellectui cognoscibile non est, propter excessum intelligibilis supra intellectum.'

[27] This distinction is worked out dialectically by Aristotle in the *Nicomachean Ethics*, especially in book VI from his investigation of τέχνη, which we can translate as know-how, and φρόνησις, best perhaps translated as deliberation. Thus Aristotle gives ἐπιστήμη a dialectical and 'scientific' meaning in relation to τέχνη, as that kind of knowing which has do with the ordering and stabilizing of know-how, and σοφία becomes highest deliberation, deliberation of the ever-same in contrast to deliberation over what is moveable and changeable – φρόνησις.

[28] Aquinas, *Summa Contra Gentiles*, Book 1, Ch. 3, no. 5. 'Adhuc idem manifeste apparet ex defectu quem in rebus cognoscendis quotidie experimur. Rerum enim sensibilium plurimas proprietates ignoramus, earumque proprietatum quas sensu apprehendimus rationes perfecte in pluribus invenire non possumus. Multo igitur amplius illius excellentissimae substantiae omnia intelligibilia humana ratio investigare non sufficit.'

Thus God as the exemplary substance reveals a quality that concerns experience and knowledge of substances in general.

If it is well understood that Aquinas holds that only God truly knows God in God's essence we could still misunderstand what is indicated here unless we recall that we do not apprehend by means of sense, not only the most excellent substance, God, but *any* substance, except through its accidents (that is its manner and circumstances of appearing), and so *a posteriori*. We do not, in other words, have direct (or essential) knowledge of any substances at all, we know them only by means of accidents. Only God knows essences (that is what makes substances what they are, in and of themselves) directly.[29] This is because, for Aquinas, only the intellect knows substances. Now God is nothing other than intellect – but the created intellect's knowledge of substances in this life is derived from the accidents under which substances appear and their modes of appearing – which indicate and make available to us through the work of the intellect their 'substantial form' (τὸ τί ἦν εἶναι). This indicating and making available is always for us provisional, incomplete, and dubious (although St Thomas does not overstress this), it is therefore difficult and requires work, the work of the intellect, to perfect. It is, nevertheless, the best in this life that we have. Moreover this indicating and making available occurs through the senses. Aquinas does have a role for the senses, but it is now provisional and inadequate, entirely different from the understanding developed by Aristotle.

Aquinas goes further than this, however, for he argues that 'beneficially, therefore, did the divine mercy provide that even that which reason is able to investigate, might be taught and so held by faith, that all might easily be sharers in divine knowledge and that without uncertainty or error'.[30] To be sharers in divine knowledge is something given in faith, which can even include those things which otherwise could be known by human reckoning. Reason can attain to certain kinds of knowledge, but faith can attain to greater ones. Aquinas argues that the object of metaphysics is knowledge of God, a knowledge the philosophers had also sought. Others, because of indolence,

---

[29] For a full discussion of this, see Reynolds, P. L., 'Properties, Causality and Epistemological Optimism in Thomas Aquinas' in *Recherches de théologie et philosophie médiévales (Forschungen zur Theologie und Philosophie des Mittelalters)*, Vol. 67 No. 2, 2001, esp. 283–95.

[30] Aquinas, *Summa Contra Gentiles*, Book 1 Ch. 4, no. 6. 'Salubriter ergo divina providit clementia ut ea etiam quae ratio investigare potest, fide tenenda praeciperet: ut sic omnes de facili possent divinae cognitionis participes esse et absque dubitatione et errore.'

other preoccupations, or stupidity, and all (philosophers included) because of the impediments to human reason themselves, must rely on faith for perfect knowledge either of things, or of God, because otherwise 'the whole human race, if reason were the only way open to the knowledge of God, would remain in the greatest ignorance of darkness'.[31] Faith is faith in what God has made manifest, through Scripture and the means of salvation (the tradition held by the Church): Christ, and the Old Testament witness to his incarnation and sacrifice.

The fundamental phenomenological relation to being as the 'already-is being' of Aristotle is effectively reversed and placed into an entirely different order in Aquinas. Most significantly the senses no longer have the role of being the basis for lifting the soul up and leading it in to the being of beings – this is effected by grace, and explained in Aquinas's theology of deification in salvation. In order to describe this, Aquinas has taken for granted that the knowledge of God revealed through Christ and the interpretation of sacred Scripture is the same thing and has the same goal as that expressed by the soul 'becoming in some sense all things', but through an entirely different means: faith.

I take St Thomas Aquinas only as a particular exemplar of the extraordinary transformation worked on philosophy by the Jewish, Muslim, but especially the Christian scholars of the Middle Ages. Through a patient redescription of what they successively found in the ancient texts, and with the entirely pious end of conforming philosophy to a higher science – theology, but the theology not of thinking but of faith – they drove forward an interpretation of being they discovered already present in antiquity, and deprived philosophy of its genuine ground, the self-enquiry that prior to Aristotle and Plato the being of being human *is*, replacing this ground with God as the cause of all things. Even when philosophy will declare this god to be dead, philosophy overall remained and remains yet deprived of its ground.

Two things arise out of this fundamental transition that we have seen effected. On the one hand, it will now be possible to show how the imagination takes on the role it does in Kant and postmodernity. Because the appearing of what-appears no longer identifies the soul with the whole entire being of the cosmos in a particular way, the

---

[31] Aquinas, *Summa Contra Gentiles*, Book 1, Ch. 4, no. 4. 'Remaneret igitur humanum genus, si sola rationis via ad Deum cognoscendum pateret, in maximis ignorantiae tenebris.'

what-appears in appearing will be read-off from appearances to an entirely different effect. From now on what upliftment and the sublime names cannot name any kind of passageway in to the being of beings, this access is now closed. Following Descartes, it becomes simply a means of resolving especially visual experiences. On the other, a particular solution arises as the basis on which the being of beings can continue, albeit in a radically transformed way, as an area of philosophical enquiry, and it is to this solution we now turn.

Why can we simply not go back? Why can we not (as perhaps the early Luther once hinted we might) simply pull Christianity apart from Greek thinking and choose one or the other to follow? Who among us will constitute this 'we'? Which historical moment in Greek or Christian thought will 'we' declare it to be best to return to? What if I choose one and you another? How would we even know that what we had chosen was the same now as what it was then? Neither thinking nor faith work like this (although 'we', constantly calling for 'new enlightenments', or 'recoveries' of this thinker or that, constantly speak as if it should). The exigencies and demands of every age appear among us and lay claim to us; we do not choose them, even when we think we do. Is there any other kind of solution?

In responding to Heidegger's use of the term 'ontotheology', others have started to employ the term 'theo-ontology'. This theo-ontology, we are often told, is of its essence analogical, but, better even than that, analogy is always at the same time announced and prepared as one of the great doctrines of the Christian Church, and so it gets given a lengthy provenance. The understanding employed for this view of analogy is *analogia entis*, the analogy of being, a term which first came to the fore after Aquinas.[32] It is this attempt to 'tie the being of God, man and the world' back together that the analogy of being attempts to achieve, so that in the words of Johannes Lotz, in analogy 'the being of a being is unlocked or at least given meaning through a comparison with another'.[33] We have already seen how Greek thought tied together divinity and being, and the being of beings: for this they required no formal definition of the analogy of being.

---

[32] Carlo Leget suggests it first appeared towards the end of the fifteenth century, although he advances no specific evidence for his claim. See Leget, C., *Living with God: Thomas Aquinas on the Relation between Life on Earth and 'Life' after Death*, 1997, pp. 37f.

[33] Lotz, SJ, J. B., 'Analogie' in Brugger, SJ, W. (ed.), *Philosophisches Wörterbuch*, 1957, p. 9. 'Das Sein eines Seienden wird also durch Vergleich mit einem andern erschlossen oder wenigstens verdeutlicht.'

The great fountainhead for study of the term *analogia* in St Thomas is Question 13 of the first part of the *Summa Theologiae*. This alone should alert us that something is up with St Thomas's use of the terms *analogia* and *analogice*. Question 13 assumes such an importance in modern accounts because the two terms hardly appear anywhere else in the whole of the *Summa*. Analogy was actually not a very important term for St Thomas. Moreover, and to the chagrin of the more recent analogists, it doesn't turn up once just exactly where it should if all the contemporary theorizing on analogy really did have its home in Aquinas – in the third part of the *Summa Theologiae*, the treatise on Christ and on the Sacraments. Not once, despite one contemporary theologian's claim that 'throughout Mediaeval accounts of sacramental presence we are concerned with the nature of analogy'.[34] This claim is simply false, but it does indicate what work this appeal to the supposedly mediaeval and to analogy is being asked to do now – to guarantee and underpin notions of divine *presence*, taken in an ontological sense. Or to put it another way, things that were properly the province of *theology* are going to be made to function *philosophically*. Analogy, as the *analogia entis*, is one of the contemporary sites of ontotheology (or theo-ontology: no matter how you chop the word up, it says the same thing). Analogy seems to be a way of tying the originative, eternal being of God to the finite, dependent being of creation in an ontological relationship. Analogy is therefore a 'solution' to the problem both of the cleft between being and beings, and a reconciliation of God as cause of all things with the 'being' they derive from having been caused by God.

St Thomas does not resolve either his theology of the incarnation or of the sacraments through a doctrine of analogy, for a very good reason. He believes that the incarnation is effected and the sacraments are efficacious through divine fiat – that is to say, they are how they are because God just chooses them to be that way and reveals them to be so, rather than because they thereby indicate an already analogical tie between the being of things and the being of God.[35] In every case, to be understood, God's presence in Christ or in the sacraments can only be understood through faith, they cannot be demonstrated by philo-

---

[34] Ward, Graham, *Cities of God*, 2000, p. 157.

[35] I have written elsewhere on how transubstantiation, for instance, is effected 'per [Dei] infinitam virtutem', by the infinite power of God, and so by no other means. Aquinas, *Summa Theologiae*, IIIa, Q. 77, a. 1, resp. See 'Transubstantiating Our Selves' in *Heythrop Journal*, Vol. 44 (October 2003), pp. 418–39.

sophical means.[36] Neither does St Thomas resolve the difference between the being of God and the common being of creatures through any doctrine of analogy.[37]

Yet *analogia* and its other forms are not the only word we translate with the term 'analogy'. A second term, which really comes to prominence with the Latin translations of Euclid, is also present in St Thomas with respect to analogy, a term which can even be found in the later parts of the *Summa Theologiae*, although its use is anything but frequent (nine times only in the whole of the third part). That term is *proportio*. Indeed, in Question 13 of the *Summa Theologiae* St Thomas says: 'therefore it must be said that these names [that is analogical names] are said of God and creatures in a sense according to analogy, that is proportion'.[38]

How are we to understand this? Cajetan, whose *De Nominum Analogia* attempts to systematize and clarify Aquinas's doctrine of analogy, and who is one of the first to use the phrase *analogia entis* with the sense we now understand it to have, indicates three modes of analogy: inequality, attribution, and proportionality, adding that 'only the last mode constitutes analogy and the first is entirely foreign to analogy'.[39] This has to be taken with Cajetan's assertion that 'being is analogous',[40] hence he will seek above all to demonstrate that proportionality provides for the possibility of the *analogia entis*. Thus he says that by means of the analogy of proportionality 'we know the

---

[36] This does not in the slightest alter or lessen the force of my faith in the reality of God's presence either in Christ or in the sacraments, especially the sacrament of the altar. I know these things to be true through faith, not reason. In what they themselves are, they are consonant with reason (and so reasonable things to believe), but neither formally demonstrable by, nor grounded in, reason.

[37] In fact St Thomas resolves this through a complex series of ontological denominations, many of which can be found in his *Commentarium in Librum de Causis* (*Commentary on the Book of Causes*). For my own discussion of some of these determinations see Hemming, L. P., *Heidegger's Atheism*, 2002, pp. 190–99. For a rich and detailed commentary see te Velde, R. A., *Participation and Substantiality in Thomas Aquinas*, 1995.

[38] Aquinas, *Summa Theologiae*, Ia, Q. 13, art. 5, resp. 'Dicendum est igitur quod huiusmodi nomina dicuntur de deo et creaturis secundum analogiam, idest proportionem.'

[39] Cajetan OP, Cardinal de Vio, *Scripta Philosophica: De Nominum Analogia; De Conceptu Entis*, ed. Zammit OP, P. N., 1934, §3, p. 6. 'ultimus modus tantum analogiam constituat, primus autem alienus ab analogia omnino sit.' Cajetan does introduce a new distinction in his doctrine of analogy, between analogy *intrinsice* and *extrinsice*.

[40] Cajetan, *De Nominum Analogia, Responsio super duo quaesita* (Appendix), §4, p. 99. '. . . ens, cum analogum sit.'

intrinsic beingness, goodness, truthfulness, etc. of things'.[41] It is the making of formal ontological claims like these that the doctrine of the analogy of being seeks to make possible. The question, therefore, is going to be: with what order of knowledge is this kind of analogy concerned? The theologians who see themselves as doing battle with and 'answering' or defeating the supposed nihilism of postmodernity want to say: an ontological kind – theology and being are one. I want to interject and say that only the believer can know this – only he or she can act upon, and so enact, *live* this. It cannot be claimed as a general truth of being: it can only be a truth of faith, which is witnessed to in my faith in it. Thus I want to say: there is *no* analogy of being *as such* and apart from Christian believing, though analogy may be applied to beings in consequence of something else that must already be at work and held to be true in advance of any analogical naming. St Thomas, as a theologian, implicitly understood this: he speaks nowhere of analogy as having an ontological significance.

If, for a moment, we turn away from the *Summa* to a much earlier text, Aquinas's *Quaestiones Disputatae: De Veritate*, in the midst of a discussion on the divine ideas we find this very surprising statement: 'although there can be no proportion between God and a creature, there can be a proportionality, as has been shown in the preceding question'.[42] This is the solution to a difficulty with regard to whether or not there are ideas in God. Ideas in this sense really means types: the ideas in question are of a very Platonic (or really Neoplatonic) kind. The difficulty asks how it is there can be ideas, that is types of things, in God because 'every example is proportionate to its exemplar. But there is no proportion of the creature to God, just as there is none [that is proportion] of the finite to the infinite.'[43]

Cajetan says: 'the word analogy therefore means proportion or proportionality (as we have learned from the Greeks)'.[44] What is to be learnt from the Greeks, from Euclid, Plato and Aristotle alike, is that the term 'analogy' originally referred to purely mathematical

---

[41] Cajetan, *De Nominum Analogia*, §29, p. 29. 'Scimus . . . rerum intrinsecas entitates, bonitates, veritates etc.'

[42] Aquinas, *De Veritate*, Q. 3, art. 1, resp. ad 7. 'Dicendum, quod quamvis non possit esse aliqua proportio creaturae ad Deum, tamen potest esse proportionalitas, quod in praecedenti quaestione expositum est.'

[43] Aquinas, *De Veritate*, Q. 3, art. 1, obj. 7. 'Omne exemplatum est proportionatum suo exemplari. Sed nulla est proportio creaturae ad Deum, sicut nec finiti ad infinitum.'

[44] Cajetan, *De Nominum Analogia*, §2, p. 4. 'Analogiae igitur vocabulum proportionem sive proportionalitatem (ut a Graecis accepimus) . . . sonat.'

relations, of two kinds. The first, proportion, means the proportion of one number to another, thus the proportion of three to six is two. The second, but in fact prior meaning on which the first depends, *proportionality*, refers to that ratio which pertains between two proportions: thus, to quote St Thomas: 'for example, we say that six and eight are proportionate because, just as six is the double of three, so eight is the double of four, for proportionality is a similarity of proportions.'[45] However, Aquinas goes on to argue that the proportion that pertains between creatures and God is proportionality in the same way as the proportion between two finites can be the same as a proportion between two infinites, so that 'when, however, things are said to be proportionate by way of proportionality, their relation to each other is not considered'.[46] What this means is that a finite cannot be proportionate to an infinite.

Such an understanding of analogy is in fact very weak – so weak, that it cannot bear any ontological consequences. As a formula of faith it works without difficulty, because it clarifies in thinking a relation that is already presupposed by the character and structure of what God has divinely revealed. As a comment on the difference between God and creatures it takes for granted the cleft taken to exist between God and creatures, it neither demonstrates it, nor makes it manifest (it is already manifest) nor resolves it. At no time does Aquinas himself ever require analogy to bear ontological consequences. It is for this reason that analogy is of *names*, and St Thomas never includes among the analogical names for God the name of *being*. It is for this reason that the term *analogia entis* is absent from the works of St Thomas. Nevertheless, after St Thomas, it will be asserted that being is in itself analogical.

Before we go further, however, we have to ask: is the proportionality named in the *De Veritate* the same as the proportion named in the *Summa Theologiae*? Edward Schillebeeckx has argued that it is not – that Aquinas only briefly entertains a difference between proportion and proportionality which he subsequently drops, in favour of the analogical relationship being a real proportion (from which ontological consequences could be derived) and not a proportionality. Thus

---

[45] Aquinas, *De Veritate*, Q. 2, art. 3, resp. ad 4. 'Ut si dicamus sex et octo esse proportionata, quia sicut sex est duplicitum ad tria, ita est octo ad quattuor: est enim proportionalitas similitudo proportionum.'

[46] Aquinas, *De Veritate*, Q. 2, art. 3, resp. ad 4. 'Sed in his quae proportionata dicuntur per modum proportionalitas, non attenditur habitudo eorum ad invicem . . .'

he argues that, with the exception of its appearance in the earlier questions of the *De Veritate*, the later Question 23 was 'where the term *proportionalitas* definitively disappeared'.[47] Schillebeeckx is relying on the fact that the *De Veritate* is an edited compilation of questions that took place in the Schools in Paris over quite some period of time – at the very least, two years. He presupposes (and we really have no evidence for this) that the order of the edited compilation is the same as the order in which the questions were debated.[48]

Schillebeeckx is anxious to demonstrate that for St Thomas analogy does constitute a measurable relation between God and the creature: he seeks an ontological consequence for the doctrine of analogy. All the evidence points towards the opposite being the case. It is clear from the passages in Question 2 of the *De Veritate* that both proportion and proportionality are each kinds of *proportiones*, and Aquinas is simply clarifying the different kinds of proportion there can be. His argument here and in Question 3, that there can be no proportion between creature and creator, is so strong, and analogy was so widely understood as a proportion between ratios that in fact he would have had to demonstrate the opposite,[49] that analogy was a direct proportion and

---

[47] Schillebeeckx, OP, E., *Openbaring en Theologie*, 1964, p. 222. 'waarin de term "proportionalitas" definitief verdwijnt'.

[48] There is a very strong argument for reading the *De Veritate* as having a logical structure rather than being an arrangement of the questions in the order they were disputed. So Michael Waddell has argued very compellingly that the *De Veritate* is organized in a pedagogical schema which relates it to a discussion of two of the transcendentals, truth, and *bonum*, or 'the good'. If Waddell is correct, even if there are changes of mind or viewpoint in the work, the order in which the changes took place cannot be traced temporally – that is a point in a late question may be a more primitive version better elaborated in a numerically but not temporally earlier place in the work. Waddell argues that of the 29 questions, the first question, in dealing with truth, then gives rise to the following 19 questions all of which deal with aspects of the intellect, which are all expository of the headline first question, because the intellect is the means by which the true is apprehended. Question 21 treats of the good, which then gives rise to eight questions on the will, again as expository to their initiating discussion, because the good is the object of the exercise of the will. Waddell argues that 'The model for this structure is the Aristotelian account of the relationships between faculties of the soul and their objects. As the Philosopher notes in Book II of *De Anima*, we must consider the object before we can investigate the act and the faculty that are actualized by it.' Waddell, M., 'Truth Or Transcendentals: What Was St. Thomas's Intention at De Veritate 1.1?' in *The Thomist*, Vol. 67 (2003), pp. 197–219, p. 214, citing Aristotle, *De Anima* 415 a 14–22.

[49] Cf. Euclid, *The Elements*, Book VII, Definition 21, 1953, Vol. 2, p. 135. Ἀριθμοὶ εἶναι ἀνάλογοι, ὅταν ὁ πρῶτος τοῦ δευτέρου καὶ ὁ τρίτος τοῦ τετάρτου εἶναι πολλαπλάσιος ἢ τὸ αὐτὸ μέρος ἢ τὰ αὐτὰ μέρη. ('Numbers are proportional

not a proportion between ratios. In both Question 13 of the *Summa* and elsewhere, he is simply able to take for granted that the kind of proportion in question is that of proportionality. Moreover if we examine carefully the immediate text of the discussion of analogy as a proportion in Question 13 of the *Summa*, we see that the language actually indicates that a multiplicity of proportions are at issue. The question is what analogy is, and the answer is that it is not 'una ratio' as in the univocal.[50] *Una ratio* could be translated as one idea, but *ratio* has a clear relation to accounting and reckoning up, as in the reckoning of a set of accounts. *Una ratio* could also be construed as a 'single relation'. St Thomas goes on to say, if it is not a 'single relation', then nor is it totally diverse (*rationes* in the plural is therefore implied), but, analogy is 'a name which thus is said multiply [and so which] signifies diverse proportions to some one [proportion]'. *Proportiones* is here also clearly plural, so it is more than one proportion or a simple ratio, but rather signifies a common proportion between proportions – exactly what elsewhere he argues analogy to be. Even though the examples given in the *Summa* of analogy are analogies of names (wisdom, health) they depend for their efficacy not on a direct proportion (a single proportion), but on a proportion of proportions which is proportionality.[51] This is, in fact, none other than the definition he gave of proportionality in the *De Veritate*. Schillebeeckx is therefore not right: Aquinas did not change his mind, he simply relied on what he had earlier claimed as able to be taken for granted. We are not speaking here of *that kind of proportion* which is a direct proportion, a single ratio, but of *that kind of proportion* which is in fact the *common* proportion or ratio of multiple proportions: *proportionalitas*.

Although we seem to have established that what Aquinas says in the *De Veritate* is consistent with what is said in the *Summa*, is it not simply the case that proportionality is the *analogia entis* itself, rather than a direct *proportio*? After all, proportionality is established in the midst of a discussion of the divine ideas to justify that the types of

---

when the first is the same multiple, or the same part, or the same parts, of the second that the third is of the fourth.')

[50] Cf., and for what follows, Aquinas, *Summa Theologiae*, Ia, Q. 13, art 5, resp. 'Et iste modus communitatis medius est inter puram aequivocationem et simplicem univocationem. Neque enim in his quae analogice dicuntur, est una ratio, sicut est in univocis; nec totaliter diversa, sicut in aequivocis; sed nomen quod sic multipliciter dicitur significat diversas proportiones ad aliquid unum.'

[51] Aquinas, *Summa Theologiae*, Ia, Q. 13, art 5, resp. 'diversae proportiones'.

things in creation really can (and in fact must) exist in the divine mind. Except that we know already that proportionality is insufficient for the full claims of the *analogia entis*, and why else would Schillebeeckx have been so concerned to eliminate proportionality from the discussion of analogy in favour of proportion? Proportionality will simply not do for the analogy of being

Although I began with St Thomas's statement in Question 3 of the *De Veritate*, on the divine ideas, that question in fact referred us to an earlier one, the question of what God knows. It is in the third article of that question, whether God knows others than himself,[52] that the full discussion of the nature of proportion and proportionality is carried out. Aquinas answers the question of whether God knows things other than himself by appeal to God's causation of all things: 'hence there must be a knowledge of natural things in the divine intellect from which the origin and the order of nature come.'[53] It is because God is the *causa omnium* that God knows things other than himself. What has this to do with analogy?

Aquinas needs no analogy of being, because he takes for granted – in fact it is a prerequisite for the matter at hand – that God is the originating cause of all things. In this sense, therefore no analogy need pertain with regard to being because that is not what is at issue, either in the analogy of names, or with regard to being. Moreover, he continually makes a distinction between what it is for God to know this from the perspective of God, and what it is for us to know this as among those that are created by God: the crux of the question, as it so often is with Aquinas, is what is known from *whose* perspective. God knows things other than himself because they are already in some sense included in himself. God *is* in some sense all things because God in some sense *knows* all things, actually. The human soul only knows all things *potentially* and only *actually* after it has been divinized, at the end of time.

With regard to proportionality, what is at issue is Aquinas's *refusal* to establish relations other than of the very weakest kind between what is known to us and what is known to God in 'natural' thought (that is apart from faith). This is because the relation that does need to pertain has *already* been established by another means, that is, by God

---

[52] Aquinas, *De Veritate*, Q. 2. 'Utrum Deus cognoscat alia a se.'
[53] Aquinas, *De Veritate*, Q. 2, art. 2, resp. 'Unde opportet quod in intellectu divino a quo rerum naturae origo provenit et naturalis ordo in rebus, sit naturalium rerum cognitio.'

construed as first cause and the creator of all things, and for us, by what God makes manifest of himself through Christ, Scripture and tradition. Proportionality – analogy as we understand it – is not needed, and in fact cannot, establish any kind of formal relation with regard to being. Thus Aquinas says with regard to proportionality: 'We are not concerned with the relation of them to each other, all that is considered is the similarity of the relation of two things to two other things.'[54] Similarity alone can bear no ontological weight or dependence. Aquinas, therefore, establishes an impasse in thinking as the basis on which two sets of two divided worlds are held apart and made accessible to each other: the world of appearances and being as it is understood in Greek thought, and the world of the enmity between God and man, overcome in Christ. However, the modern accounts of analogy run roughshod over this delicate impasse, and proceeding in the opposite direction, striving to overcome St Thomas's sense of the provisionality of human knowledge and so perform all over again, although without the ontological ground on which to do so, the phenomenological results of Aristotle.

When I said earlier that for Aquinas God is *ipsum esse subsistens*, and that creatures also have being, what is being said here, and can this be said analogously? The answer is yes, but only because of what God has revealed, *not* through thinking, or philosophy, but through faith. Aquinas is quite consistent in this – he believes theology to be a higher science than philosophy. Nevertheless, even this is very weak, it is a 'likeness' of being, more like 'beingness', than being itself (*entitas* than *ens*). For Aquinas, although we can say that God is God's own to be, and even that God is subsistent being, and we can say that 'I am my own to be', these statements are analogous in the sense of proportionality and so imply no direct relation, specifically *no proportion*, between the 'to be' of God and the 'to be' of me, although they assert a certain similarity.

There is no formal *analogia entis* in Aquinas, only a certain congruence of being (when understood negatively and from the perspective of 'natural' thinking). A formal analogy of being would otherwise imply univocity of being, but that does not prevent St Thomas from speaking in a loose, analogical way according to proportionality, of God's 'being', of God's 'to be' depending on how you want to translate

---

[54] Aquinas, *De Veritate*, Q. 2, art. 2, resp. 'Non attenditur habitudo eorum ad invicem, sed similis habitudo aliquorum duo ad alia duo.'

'*esse*'. This analogical way of speaking, however, provides no basis for ontological inference from us to God.

The French commentator on Aristotle, Pierre Aubenque, has demonstrated that even where Aristotle uses the term ἀναλογία in relation to being, τὸ εἶναι, it has absolutely no ontological significance, but works purely to support homonymous and synonymous uses.[55] Aubenque traces the origin of the metaphysical – by which he means what I have indicated by ontological – use of the term 'analogy' to Aquinas, and specifically to Aquinas's very early work *De Ente et Essentia*. He notes that the term 'analogy' 'will not be found employed there'.[56] What will be found there is a list of the names of God with respect to being that will assume so great an importance in the later mediaeval speculations – *esse tantum, esse purum, ipsum esse per se subsistens*. He adds that other beings (apart from God), that is to say, creatures, differ from God in that they are not their own proper being, but that they have being because they receive their being from God. He clearly understands this to be a Platonic and Neoplatonic understanding of being. Thus he argues: 'the analogy of being therefore signifies: proportional distribution of being (*esse*) between beings (*entia*) according to the degree of perfection of their essence (*essentia*).' It is this, says Aubenque, that is the true *analogia proportionalitas*.[57]

Aubenque is entirely correct when he attributes this view to Cajetan, but whilst I do believe Aubenque's account of Aquinas's determinations of being, and his Neoplatonic understanding of participation are as he claims they are in the little treatise *De Ente et Essentia*, and, with developments and modifications (the most important of which is the notion of the *actus essendi*) they remain the same in later texts, this is not the *analogia entis* as it later comes to be known. It is, however, what makes analogy possible as a solution to the problem of retaining some passageway in to the being of beings. Having demonstrated with some clarity how and why Aristotle's use of the term ἀναλογία simply cannot support the later *analogia entis*, quite out of the blue Aubenque at the very end of his discussion speaks of how Martin Heidegger had developed the term 'ontotheology'

---

[55] Aubenque, P., 'Sur la naissance de la doctrine pseudo-Aristotélicienne de l'analogie de l'être' in *Les Études philosophiques*, Vol. 44 (1989), pp. 291–304.

[56] Aubenque, 'Sur la naissance de la doctrine pseudo-Aristotélicienne', p. 292. 'Ne s'y trouve pas employé.'

[57] Aubenque, 'Sur la naissance de la doctrine pseudo-Aristotélicienne', p. 292. 'L'analogie de l'être signifie donc: répartition proportionnelle de l'être (*esse*) entre les étants (*entia*) selon le degré de perfection de leur essence (*essentia*).'

which resides at the bottom of the whole of Western metaphysics. He adds:

Under the influence of Platonism, but also in virtue of the tendency to systematisation which is inherent in all commentary, the Neo-platonic commentators misunderstood what it was that was possible properly to have phenomenologically with the Aristotelian starting point.[58]

What Aubenque refers to is the Platonism and Neoplatonism that, following Philoponus, was the fusing together of the understanding given in faith that the Christian God was the creator of the heavens and the earth, and so the *causa omnium*, with the concerns of philosophy. Ontology, the concern with the being of beings and the being of *my* being, is fused with theology taken as at one and the same time the concern to elicit the Greek construal of divinity, τὸ θεῖον, and the Christian God so that the being of beings is worked out from the being of God and not the being of being-human. Already we can see this at work in Aquinas – it is what *God* knows, and what the human being insofar as it is either already beatified (Christ) or will become deiform (the saints) can thereby *know* that really matters for Aquinas. How-ever, as we have seens, this places us in an impasse, which analogy becomes the way out of. This, then, is what ontotheology means, nothing more, nothing less, a resolution of two different kinds of cause: the first, the relationship of (temporal) priority of creator to creature; the second, the way in which divinity and the Divine Being can be shown to be grounded in the being of being human, even if the being of being human *is at the same time discovered to be the being of God in a more prior way*. Now we can see that the *analogia entis* becomes a solution to a problem, and at the same time a distortion of what Aquinas himself held to be possible in thinking apart from faith – because it appears to give us a passageway in to the divine essence at an ontological level, and it enables the retention *in philosophy* of a dis-cussion – what beings are and how they manifest themselves – whose ground and originating cause *has already passed over into* theology, now construed as 'God as the *causa omnium*'. In this sense, the

---

[58] Aubenque, 'Sur la naissance de la doctrine pseudo-Aristotélicienne', p. 304. 'Sous l'influence du platonisme, mais aussi en vertu de la tendance à le systémati-sation qui est inhérent à tout commentarisme, les commentateurs néo-platoniciens ont méconnu ce qu'il pouvait y avoir de proprement "phénoménologique" dans le commencement aristotélicien.'

analogia entis was inevitable as a development from those who wanted to continue to make general *philosophical* statements about being. The *analogia entis* indicates how the work of St Thomas has been received, as making the place assigned to God – this place with no where – accessible and determinable. A place on which a high value is set!

By the time of Aquinas, because all the processes of 'working out' what is responsible for what – and this means all the so-called 'causes', all these processes are reversed and located not in a phenomenological self-enquiry into the being of being-human, but in God, as the first cause. From here on, in order to provide a proper *ontological basis* for what we know, we have to undertake a *theo*-logy (this is the real theo-ontology!), we have to work out what God knows in order to provide the genuine ground for the being of beings. What happens, therefore, in postmodernity, when God is dead? The whole of being loses its ground, 'being is an empty fiction: the world of appearances is the only one'.[59] The whole of being means here God, and it means at the same time, the being of beings.

---

[59] Nietzsche, *Götzen-Dämmerung*, Vol. 6, p. 75. 'Das Sein [ist] eine leere Fiktion. Die "scheinbare" Welt ist die einzige.'

Counting up to One is Sublime

Samuel Clarke, the friend and translator (into, rather than out of, Latin) of the *Opticks* of Isaac Newton opened his Boyle Lectures in 1704 with the claim that 'it is absolutely and undeniably certain that *something has existed from all eternity*'.[1] He proceeded to argue that 'whatever exists has a cause, a reason, a ground of its existence . . . either in the necessity of its own nature (and then it must have been of itself eternal), or in the will of some other being (and then that other being must . . . have existed before it).'[2] It is from these bold assertions that Clarke proceeds to demonstrate the absolute irrationality and frivolousness of atheism, such that anyone who denies the being and attributes of God as Clarke claimed they are, is without reason, stupid, or debauched.

If we understand the contribution of Greek ontology to the valuation of divinity to be the positing of the divine as highest, best, eternal and without death, we can see how the understanding of God as a value is prepared and produced. If Aquinas's understanding of analogy actually relies on a mathematical distinction to *protect* the understanding of God that he has from the kind of valuation that makes the being of God simply determinable and rational (which means, computable), how is it that this protection failed? Aquinas sought in analogy a relation of relations, that is, he sought to bring into a mathematical relationship two orders (the human and the divine) which remain fundamentally different from each other and in no respect can be considered to relate as one to the next, as they might in a numerical series. The analogical relation between them is weak: it permits only that two things can be brought into relation through their dissimilarity rather than on account of their likeness. In this sense the one order

---

[1] Clarke, S., *A Demonstration of the Being and Attributes of God*, ed. Vailati, E., 1998, p. 8. Emphasis in original.
[2] Clarke, *A Demonstration of the Being and Attributes of God*, p. 8.

cannot be derived from out of the other, they can only be seen in relation once something else – faith – has brought them together. The analogical relationship for Aquinas is illustrative – it has no ontological force.

The kind of relationship described by Clarke, however, is more like that of one in a series. 'Cause', as Clarke employs the term, functions more like 'succession'. Clarke even forces Aristotle to speak the same, when he appeals to the notion of Aristotle's 'first mover' as an 'original cause', something unthinkable for Aristotle. A fundamental reorientation has taken place here with respect to time, which can be better understood in relation to mathematics, and which will allow us to see for the first time how the imagination comes to the fore and is able to take on the role that it does, first following Descartes, and then in postmodernity. So far we have considered only in a negative way how it became possible for God and divinity to appear as a value. Now we see how that valuation is carried out, and how, appearing as a value, it can at the same time be devalued.

Greek mathematics distinguished between number, geometry, and logistic as disciplines. Number for the Greeks distinguishes not only with respect to a series, how each number succeeds the next in a series, but also absolutely between numbers. Each number is distinct not only in its value, but also in the meaning of that value as the succession continues. For this reason, although two succeeds one, the absolute value of two is different not just in quantity, but also in kind and quality from one (and from three, and so forth): sometimes number of this kind does not count in the way we are accustomed to counting: one, two three; but counts in a sequence better understood as unity, double, tetrad, etc. To demonstrate, therefore, that the ἕν, unity as such, is distributed all the way through the two and the three and the whole succession, is actually to show the means by which the two in itself, the three in itself, is distinguished both relatively and absolutely from the one. Fundamental to this is the Greek understanding that number is not a genus for numbers, and that every number, even if it is in a series, is also in some sense at the same time entirely for itself.

Number is distinguished by both Plato and Aristotle as different to the rationalization of points, which forms the basis of geometry. Whereas in number each value is distinguished both in quantity and kind from every other, the same is not true for the counting of points along a line. Here the first, the second, and the third, are sections according to ratio, and are all of the same kind along the same continuum.³ Although numbers and the figures of geometry are both in the order of things that are in some sense 'read-off' from the world, and as we discovered in Chapter 5, both of these belong to the class of φάντασμα that are ἐν ἀφαιρέσει λεγόμενα (the things 'being-spoken in having been abstracted'), nevertheless, further distinctions pertain which formally individuate number from geometry. As the things that always are through abstraction, number and the figures of geometry are 'read-off' from the world, and derived from those things which have relation to place and time, even if the deriving and abstracting is a kind of separating from place and time.

As the things first in the order of what is 'read-off', geometrical forms and points are nevertheless distinguished from each other in the manner of their original comportment to place. In fact the figures of geometry are distinguished from number precisely in this relation to place (albeit negatively). Aristotle notes that all the things of mathematics exist in a purely atemporal way, and that they are 'without a where'.⁴ We might note in passing that it is this 'without a where' that makes it possible for the divine to be understood in the same manner as number is: God or divinity also has no 'where'. Geometrical figures have a formal likeness to the bodies from which they are read-off: they have extension, and magnitude, through one, two, and three dimensions. They have, in other words, no specific 'where', but they are formally defined by a kind of reference to sitedness. In Greek, sitedness is not the taking up of a particular place in the manner of an actual body, but possibility for the position of a potential body. The term employed for this is a term we have encountered already: position, θέσις.⁵ Θέσις indicates a 'with respect to where': retaining in itself an aspect of place without necessarily having an actual place as such. A 'position' can be to the left of you and the right of me, it has a relative character. Insofar (for Aristotle) as this position exists in the cosmos, it is relative to you and me, but absolute with respect to itself, because every place in the cosmos has an absolute specificity (it is different from every other), it is in place. In that I can read off its sitedness from its place, however, it ceases to relate absolutely to the cosmos and relates only to wherever it has the potential to be put or re-sited: it

---

³ In this sense, length is not arithmetical, it has no 'number' as such. For a fuller discussion of this see Fowler, D., *The Mathematics of Plato's Academy*, 1999 (1991), the 'arithmetization' of modern geometry compared to the ancient, pp. 10–14, and 'anthyphairetic' ratios, pp. 31 and 191f.

⁴ Aristotle, *Metaphysics*, 1092 a 19f. τὰ δὲ μαθηματικὰ οὐ πού.

⁵ See p. 76 above.

loses its absolute character but retains its relative character. Geometrical figures, if they have no particular place, do have the capacity to be sited, to take up lots of possible 'wheres'.

Number is for Aristotle prior even to the figures of geometry, because it is more abstracted from things, and so further from absolute place. Number cannot be 'put' anywhere, it is both without a where (like geometrical figure) and (unlike figure) also 'without site' (ἄθετον):[6] even though abstractable from place, it relates entirely negatively to place. Number is *more* abstracted than figure, it has lost not only its absolute, but even its relative position. Heidegger notes that in this issue of the relation of geometry to number, Aristotle, in his insistence in the sixth book of his *Physics* that a line never arises out of points, nor planes out of lines, 'thereby found [himself] in the sharpest opposition against Plato'.[7] Heidegger does not tell us why this is, but we should recall that in Pythagorean mathematics the figures of geometry have a spontaneity that they do not possess for Aristotle. For Plato and for the Pythagoreans, points naturally give rise to planes, and planes to solids, to account for the manner in which the elements eternally pass in and out of each other.[8]

Aristotle's reply to this can be found in a comment in the *Metaphysics*: 'It was binding for those stating that beings are from out of the elements, and that the first beings are numbers, that they demonstrate the manner in which one thing was derived from the other, and thereby saying in what manner number is from things prior.'[9] Aristotle draws attention here to two things: first the order in which things arise – what follows what. This is an attack on the spontaneous generation of figure from points, which he discusses in the second book of the *Physics*; second, how in each case the things that are abstracted,

---

[6] Logistic has a fundamental difference both from geometry and number which does not concern us here. Cf. Plato, *Gorgias* 453 E.

[7] Heidegger, M., *Platon: Sophistes*, GA19, 1992, p. 111. 'Damit befindet sich Aristoteles in der schärfsten Opposition gegen Plato.'

[8] See the account of this in Diogenes Laertius, *Lives of Eminent Philosophers*, 2000 (1925), Vol. 2, p. 342. ἐκ δὲ τῆς μονάδος καὶ τῆς ἀορίστου δυάδος ἀριθμούς. ἐκ δὲ τῶν ἀριθμῶν τὰ σημεῖα. ἐκ δὲ τούτων τὰς γραμμάς, ἐξ ὧν τὰ ἐπίπεδα σχήματα. ἐκ δὲ τῶν ἐπιπέδων τὰ στερεὰ σχήματα. ἐκ δὲ τούτων τὰ αἰσθητὰ σώματα, ὧν καὶ τὰ στοιχεῖα εἶναι τέτταρα, πῦρ, ὕδωρ, γῆν, ἀέρα. ['From the monad and the two in general out spring numbers. From number points. From these, lines, from lines bounded figures. From these ones bounded, solid figures. From these, sensible bodies, the four elements of which being fire, water, earth and air.']

[9] Aristotle, *Metaphysics*, 1092 a 21. Ἔδει δὲ τοὺς λέγοντας ἐκ στοιχείων εἶναι τὰ ὄντα καὶ τῶν ὄντων τὰ πρῶτα τοὺς ἀριθμούς, διελομένους πῶς ἄλλο ἐξ ἄλλου ἐστίν, οὕτω λέγειν τίνα τρόπον ὁ ἀριθμός ἐστιν ἐκ τῶν ἀρχῶν.

number and geometry, relate to what gives rise to them, their ἀρχή.
ʼΑρχή really means principle or origin in the sense of the 'from
whence', or the 'what', that gives rise to something, and so from where
it springs. *Now* we assume that an ἀρχή always lies behind us (especially with respect to time): hence how we understand archaeology to
relate to what happened in the past. In fact an origin can lie ahead of
us as if, for instance, we were travelling up a river to seek out its ἀρχή
or source.

This statement of Aristotle's is really a polemic against both the
Platonists and the Pythagoreans (the *Mathematikoi*), but does not
really resolve the criticism, although in fact Aristotle hints at how it
might be answered. The force of Aristotle's argument is that number is
not separable from what it is number *of*,[10] and if this is true, then the
origins and sources (τὰς ἀρχάς) of number and figure are other than
they have been suggested (that is by the Platonists and Pythagoreans).
What are the origins that are at issue?

In what way are numbers 'first' or prior? A better way to answer this
question is by answering why number is 'mathematical'. In Greek the
mathematical, μάθησις, does not refer solely to number, although
number is the easiest thing to grasp as an example of the things that
are 'mathematical'. The mathematical is the learnable, and *in* the
learnable what we already possess in advance of any learning that is
undertaken. Hence when I see three chairs I 'first' know that there can
be three, and in this seeing of the three, I see also that the three is three
chairs. I had already with me that there could be number with respect
to things, which enables me to encounter the chairs in a particular
way. The mathematical is 'what comes first' in my encountering any
thing in the world, it is what I bring to the encounter in order to makes
sense of it and understand it. The mathematical is therefore that which
goes in advance of everything it encounters; it is, in the broadest sense,
what I already know in what I come subsequently to know. For Plato
this led to the theory of eidetic number, something separated in
advance of everything that is, which then explains *what* it is, and so its
actual being. For Aristotle, however, it lead in a different direction.
Because number and then the other faculties of the φαντασία (the
capacity for presenting, are separable, so thinking itself is separable
from what it thinks of. The most prior kind of μάθησις is not number
but σοφία) or wisdom. This is because, as we discovered in the *De*

---

[10] Aristotle, *Metaphysics*, 1093 b 27. τοῦ μὴ χωριστὰ εἶναι τὰ μαθηματικὰ τῶν
αἰσθητῶν.

Anima, the 'scientist' is the one who is well versed in this separating, he makes advances in thinking. There is a point at which, however, the one thinking becomes capable of undertaking this thinking 'αὐτός' – for itself.[11] As Aristotle says in the *Nicomachean Ethics*, however, the science that is 'for itself' is no longer ἐπιστήμη, but θεωρεῖν, contemplating, which is undertaken by the σοφίστης, the one who is wise and who is ordered to σοφία, wisdom itself, as highest understanding of being.[12] Only the divinity has the possibility of permanent 'knowledge for its own sake, wisdom'.[13] Nevertheless, this is the soul's passageway in to being and divinity, insofar as the soul can achieve this. Insofar as the soul *does* attain to this passageway, this is the soul's 'seeing' and contemplating of the 'sources' by which it uncovers what is truthfully disclosed.[14]

Aristotle opposes the Platonists because he desires to show up the connection that for him exists between the being of any particular thing and the being of beings, the ἦν εἶναι, as a science in itself. It is this being of beings that is 'already-being' in every encounter with beings. Therefore the sciences of the greatest abstraction will bring thinking closest to contemplation, to the being of beings itself. Wisdom, number, and geometry are each in an order of highest sciences because of their proximity to the being of beings. The first ἀρχή or origin, what is always in advance of every being, is the ἕν, the one, which is for the Platonists confused with the unit, the μονάς.[15] However the one is also the origin (ἀρχή) of the whole sequence of number, it is the origin of the series. For Aristotle number is *separable* but *not separated* from whatever is encountered. It can be read-off, as all the appearances can be read-off, but it is the activity of reading-off that discloses in *each case* what number is *of*.

With respect to geometry Aristotle therefore denies what Plato and the Pythagoreans asserted, that points produced lines, which in their turn produced planes from out of which solids were constructed, so that the whole becoming-character of the cosmos, the activity of the elements, is understood to be the interaction of geometrical solids.[16] He denies this because of what he understands to be the order in which

---

[11] Cf. *De Anima*, 429 b 9–10.

[12] See Aristotle, *Nicomachean Ethics*, 1141 a 19. Here σοφία is defined as νοῦς καὶ ἐπιστήμη.

[13] Aristotle, *Metaphysics*, 982 b 32. καθ' αὐτὸν ἐπιστήμη . . . σοφία.

[14] Aristotle, *Nicomachean Ethics*, 1141 a 18f. δεῖ ἄρα τὸν σοφὸν μὴ μόνον τὰ ἐκ τῶν ἀρχῶν εἰδέναι, ἀλλὰ καὶ περὶ τὰς ἀρχὰς ἀληθεύειν.

[15] Cf. Aristotle, *Metaphysics*, 1084 b 20 – 1085 a 3.

[16] Cf. Plato, *Timaeus*, 53 C – 61 C.

the mathematical and arithmetical is, and its relative originality is, in its relation to being as such. Therefore arithmetic is more exact and closer to being than geometry (but wisdom, as closer yet, is the highest science of being as such, it is the highest form of knowledge).

In this sense, therefore, the unit, the μονάς, is a special kind of number – indeed, strictly speaking it is not really a number at all, since understanding this number passes us over into pure contemplation. Insofar as it is a number, it has direct ontological significance for me: it is my way of encountering myself in any encountering that I do, hence it is the basis of my thinking 'αὐτὸς'. The one as the one's-self is what runs ahead in advance of everything I come across to encounter it, to make it encounterable, so that in seeing a chair, it is the unity of myself coming across the chair that I encounter. What kind of a unity is this? We discovered earlier in Chapter 5 that the soul is in some sense 'one' and at the same time 'all things'. The oneness of the soul, however, is encountered through thinking, a thinking that is in no sense 'mixed with the body'.[17] Aristotle seeks to ground number onto-logically, and at the same time to show why number is prior to geo-metrical figure, but is itself grounded in wisdom.[18] Having made the distinction between geometrical figure and number, he warns us that we have to discover *what* is worked out from what, and from what origins it proceeds. The ἀρχή of number has the character of a one, but it is a one *not* mixed with the body, hence it is always unity (ἕν), but not a monad (μονάς): it is the essential unity of *world* that allows both the body and the chair (or whatever else that is at issue) to appear. *It is what has run ahead of every particular body to make the individua-tion of every possible body apparent.* Although he does so in an entirely metaphysical sense, what Aristotle uncovers with respect to the ἕν as apart from the μονάς is the phenomenon of world – the 'that through which' I and everything I know is uncovered, as a something which entirely involuntarily has already run ahead of me and towards which I am drawn. One is always counted up from two, it has no genuinely ontological ground: the unity within which the two appears and from which the one can be counted up *is* the originating of being itself. In separating the unity from the monad (his critique of the *Mathematikoi*), in fact Aristotle shows how they are related: in genuinely encountering the ἕν as ahead of me, I become able to

---

[17] See Chapter 5, note 25.

[18] I do not propose here to recount how Aristotle grounds both number and geometry. For a full account see Heidegger, *Platon: Sophistes*, GA19, 1992, §15, pp. 101–21.

produce the one as the μονάς. However the one as both ἕν and μονάς would seem also to be the ἀρχή of the whole origin of number, as the origin of the series, but this is only in a particular sense, because the μονάς is itself inferred (i.e. worked out), or abstracted, from the number two.[19] Aristotle argues that the μονάς is only potentially the same as the ἕν, for what is actual and present, this cannot be.[20] This is because both the ἕν and the μονάς can only exist in thought, and in what is thought-from-through-to (διανοεῖν), neither the ἕν nor the μονάς cannot be seen with the eyes (in each case when you see one only, you have already to know what it is one *of* – one *of* the trees, one *of* your windows). Hence Aristotle says that the truth (ἀλήθεια) is [ἕν] δυνάμει. It is *actualized* by the one thinking (in abstracting). Every actuality (every thing already there) is, in contrast, already *twofold*, from, that is, the manifold of the things surrounding.

The force of this argument is ontological: it requires a *one seeing*, and so knowing in every case, that (while the ἕν is always) the μονάς is to be inferred and is only potentially. For Aristotle number is *separable* but *not separated* from whatever is encountered. It can be read-off, as all the appearances can be read-off, but (as I have noted) it is the activity of reading-off that discloses in each case what number is *of*. Every reading-off leads back to the original unity of the ἕν and the μονάς.

Because Aristotle makes number ontologically dependent in the way that he does, the belonging together of the ἕν and the μονάς is worked out in every case, each time. What Aristotle overlooks in his critique of the *Mathematikoi* is the manner in which he places the one thinking into the midst (one who has a place, a 'with respect to a where' – a θέσις), as a point *between* the ἕν and the μονάς. He does not 'solve' the problem raised by the *Mathematikoi*, he simply connects unity, point, and monad (the ἕν, the στιγμή and the μονάς) in a different way.

Of the origins of number, however, one more lies for us to be uncovered. What makes 'world' apparent is the involuntary character of striving-for and striving-after. This *is* the very 'running after' and 'running in advance' that characterizes the soul *in* its running-ahead

---

[19] We see here therefore, why the ἕν, the μονάς, and in fact the geometrical point, στιγμή, are not 'really' numbers at all (in the Greek sense), they have to be found out in every case. In each case their being found is different, although Aristotle's criticism of the *Mathematikoi* was that these made all three the same.

[20] Aristotle, *Metaphysics*, 1084 b 21. ἔστι γάρ πως ἕν ἑκάτερον, τῇ μὲν ἀληθείᾳ δυνάμει ... ἐντελεχείᾳ δ' οὐκ ἔστι μονὰς ἑκατέρα.

disclosing the inherent unity that the world is. This running-ahead is the phenomenon of the future, but a future which, far from myself striving into as an effort, I already find myself constantly ahead of myself in, and returning from. It is what elsewhere Heidegger will call the 'there' (*Da*) of the clearing (*die Lichtung*) that is being. The future comes out towards me. This is the ἀρχή, the 'from whence', of time itself, that it befalls me from ahead of me. The phenomenon of time makes possible the experience of 'world', as the inner possibility of its unity. This, however, Aristotle denied, by understanding what being strives ahead to as – not the temporalizing of being – but its atemporality: the ἦν εἶναι is ἀεί, ever, and ever-same, and 'already' and 'always'.

For Aristotle, the final ἀρχή of number is not, therefore, a number, but νοῦς, thinking itself, as the unity that the soul is, unmixed with body. This is the reason why number is prior to geometrical figure: the geometrical, as what is read-off from any particular body, nevertheless is subsequent to any particular body's appearance – something lay prior to it as laying out its possible encounterability at all. In this sense, although number is not formally separate from what it is the number of – as thinking itself is not formally separate from what it is thinking of, the unity of the one is *that* number which always pertains to thinking, which goes ahead and in advance, and hence is the ἀρχή as such of every thought. Heidegger notes that number at the same time enters into a connection with λόγος, insofar as beings in their ultimate determinations only become accessible in a pre-eminent λόγος, in νόησις, while geometrical structures are seen only in αἴσθησις.[21]

Strictly speaking, number is never apart from νοῦς: it is the means by which νοῦς separates out this from that – the ways in which in several places of the *Metaphysics*, Aristotle illustrates the manner by which something can be interpreted with respect to the one and the many. Geometry always retains its relation to sitedness and perception (αἴσθησις). Whereas number can *only* be read-off, geometrical figure can be both read-off and re-placed, it goes back and forth in φαντασία as both abstractable (able to be lifted-off-from) and siteable (able to be placed-back-to).

The putting-on to, the resiting of a θέσις in a place (τίθημι, to have made appear from out of a place or site), is the essence of one of the

---

[21] See Heidegger, *Platon: Sophistes*, GA19, 1992, p. 117. 'Zugleich tritt er in einen Zusammenhang mit der λόγος, sofern das Seiende in seinem letzten Bestimmungen nur zugänglich wird in einem ausgezeichneten λόγος, in der νόησις, während die geometrischen Strukturen allein in der αἴσθησις gesehen werden.'

modes of possessing truth (ἀληθεύειν) which in the *Nicomachean Ethics* Aristotle also relates to ἐπιστήμη, but in an entirely different way to σοφία. Making, ποίησις, also requires a seeing-in-advance which has a parallel character to learning (μάθησις), but it is a seeing in advance for the sake of producing. Unlike the other causes, the cause specifically connected with learning (μάθησις), the 'efficient cause', has as its mode of possessing the truth τέχνη, a seeing in advance what something is for the sake of bringing it about and bringing it into being. It therefore works in the opposite direction to the other causes and modes of possessing the truth, and it has βουλεύεσθαι, a deliberate choosing.[22] This τέχνη is, however, the opposite of abstracting: rather it is taking the abstraction in advance and bringing it forth – the ἀρχή in this case is already in the soul, it is not something the soul finds its way into. Producing in this manner also has an opposite relation to time of the other modes of possessing the truth.[23] Whereas in the other modes, each is a means into thinking as a finding oneself taken into the future from out of which a passageway in to the being of beings, the ἦν ἔναι, can be uncovered, in this case what is to be made *first* exists in thinking, and then through deliberation, results in a thing produced. Understood in relation to thinking as such, the thought that produces something is visible already, prior to what it thinks of (insofar as thinking is thinking of real things), which is the thing to be produced.

In Chapter 6 we saw how Aquinas describes the God who creates heaven and earth as the artificer. Aquinas, in order to bring what he finds in Aristotle in line with Christian believing, and above all with the *prior* existence of all things as things which have not only a causal ('from whence') origin in God but also a temporal origin ('from before'), appeals therefore to τέχνη, to the mode of possessing the truth in production, to explain the relation of the creator to the creation *and also* the relation of God to truth. In considering how Aristotle defines the meaning of τέχνη, Heidegger quotes Aristotle: 'thus τέχνη is speech about the work [of production] separated from its matter.'[24] He comments on this by saying 'λόγος mean here: λέγειν, recalling by means of speech. The λόγος qua λεγόμενον, however is

---

[22] See p. 112, note 6 above.

[23] Of which we have really only considered one – wisdom, σοφία. The others are ἐπιστήμη and φρόνησις and νοεῖν. Cf. again Aristotle, *Nicomachean Ethics*, Book VI.

[24] Aristotle, *De Partibus Animalium*, 640 a 31–32. ἡ δὲ τέχνη λόγος τοῦ ἔργου ὁ ἄνευ ὕλης ἐστίν.

the εἶδος. It has about it the reverberation of the Platonic manner of speaking and seeing, in that the εἶδος is nothing other than the idea.'[25] Recalling (*vergegenwärtigen*) has the double meaning in German of recalling in the sense of bringing back into the present, and of imagining, a duplicity which exactly indicates the temporal structure of the imagination itself. The relation between λόγος and the participle λεγόμενον indicates it is a speaking of the already-said, once again disclosing the fundamental temporal structure of imagining as such: bringing from what is already there (that is, past) into the present. Precisely, λόγος can have any one of a number of temporal determinations – here the determination is clear, it is from the already-is *into* the present. Why is this so? Because imagining, no matter how fantastic, no matter how fanciful, is only ever preoccupied with and is capable of realizing what is already in some sense known already. The imaginary as such has no genuine future. Like μάθησις itself, it is in the recalling of what we recall, and in the manner of our recalling it, always preoccupied with what we know and have already, even if by a technical manipulation and rearranging we can appear to give the already known and familiar 'new' and different shapes and structures. This is what Kant called the capacity of the imagination to reconstruct experience.[26]

No wonder, therefore, that Aquinas, in seeing into the heart of Aristotle's own understanding of the possessing of truth, and determining God not from out of wisdom and the 'final cause' but from τέχνη and the 'efficient cause', determined the origin of all extant things as the ideas in God.[27] In doing so Aquinas indicated a fundamental shift in the connection of time to God. No longer is divinity determined by the source, the origin, the 'from whence' we *are* – and so from ahead of us, from what lies in the future. From now on our ἀρχή, our from whence, is always from out of the past, from God as

---

[25] Heidegger, *Platon: Sophistes*, GA19, 1992, p. 45. 'λόγος meint hier: λέγειν, besprechendes Vergegenwärtigen. Der λόγος qua λεγόμενον aber ist das εἶδος. Es handelt sich hier um einen Nachklang der platonischen Rede- und Sehweise; denn das εἶδος ist nichts anderes als die Idee.'

[26] Cf. Kant, I., *Kritik der Urteilskraft*, 1990, §49, p. 168. 'Die Einbildungskraft [. . .] ist nämlich sehr mächtig in Schaffung gleichsame einer anderen Natur aus dem Stoffe, den ihr die wirkliche gibt. Wir [. . .] bilden auch wohl um.' ('The power of imagination is therefore very powerful in creating another nature out of the stuff which actual nature gives it. We also even remodel [actual nature].')

[27] Cf. Aquinas, *Quaestiones Disputatae: De Veritate*, Question 3, *De ideis* – concerning the ideas.

the willing, productive, efficient cause of all things,[28] who having-once decided, then makes present, because God, as being always in advance of us, is so by already having been *before* us, the opposite to the source of the river (perhaps more like the water in it). Indeed, even the unsaid remains in the past with respect to God, in the sense that not all the ideas in God are activated and so brought forth into the present. Even, therefore what lies ahead of us as unknown and future is the *before* and *already-decided*, but not activated.[29]

Productive making, τέχνη, is for Aristotle the lowest of the modes of possession of the truth and the one furthest from being and from τὰς ἀρχὰς, the originations of things. In transforming the conception of divinity in this way, Aquinas already indicates a profound (philosophical) devaluation of God, and the way in which the *philosophical* connection of divinity with the being of beings is radically transformed. As we saw in Chapter 6, a fundamentally new direction takes off with respect to truth. We can now see how this entirely alters the understanding of being. Being is no longer the ἦν ἔναι as something to be *attained to* and so risen up to, now it is something simply given in advance of us which explains why we are here. Nevertheless, as I suggested earlier, the very possibility of being understood in this way is because the futural aspect of the ἦν εἶναι, the being of whatever is as 'already is' is itself ambiguous.[30]

By the time of Leibniz this ambiguity will come to be resolved as the reason for being that everything has: being becomes *basis* and ground: *nichts ohne Grund*, nothing that *is* can *be* without already (that is, past!) having a basis for its being. The breach with the original temporal structure of the ἦν ἔναι has one other fundamental consequence, which only begins to have an effect by the time of Aquinas: the striving-after being which is the attaining to being is now no longer

---

[28] Aquinas is able to achieve this in citing Aristotle's insistence that the divine is ἀχρῶνον, without time, so Aquinas also argues that the relation of God to creation is atemporal. In other words because of the metaphysical way in which Aristotle settles the being of beings, Aquinas is able to transform the understanding of the being of things in God.

[29] Cf. Aquinas, *De Veritate*, Q. 3, art. 6, ad. 1. 'Quamvis quod nec fuit, nec est, nec erit, non habeat esse determinatum in se, est tamen determinate in Dei cognitione.' ['Even though that which neither was, nor is, nor will be does not have determinate being in itself, it is however determinate in God's knowledge.'] Hence, therefore, the peculiar problem of free-will and determinism in some philosophy, which Aquinas only solves (and Kant like him) by making God, or the 'real' noumenal realm atemporal or as a single, unite, act of God (*actus purus*), a 'once only' and so not countable with respect to time.

[30] See p. 91f. above.

something which runs on ahead of me involuntarily and which discloses beings in their being from out of this running-ahead. Now everything I encounter is already there because it was intended to be there by someone other than me, elsewhere. No longer, therefore, does my own experience perform and effect the cleft between being and beings, *now* my experience confirms and brings to light a cleft that *itself is already there, already in place whether* I *am or not*. This is because every possible being only is insofar as God has willed it to be. Far from being the basis on which my understanding of being arises, now even I, even the self, is only added in to 'real' being that is in any case never really where I am to be found.

The things of nature are a product of the divine will; artefacts are products of my will or the will of another. Every being arises out of an intention, a willed choice: whereas for Aristotle every being indicates and points toward the being of beings, from now on every being is the result of having been willed to be and produced. To be like God means – to intend what God intends.

It becomes immediately clear how choosing and willing come to the fore as the manner in which beings are and are intended to be. Aristotle's 'teleology' paradoxically expressly *rules out* any kind of choice in the activity of the being of beings and the relation of particular beings to the being of beings. What we have come to identify as virtue is so because it lets us into the being of beings, it draws us towards it. It is a practice only insofar as it lets us into wisdom, and so its end is the ceasing of that practice once wisdom has been attained. When, however, 'making', τέχνη, comes to predominate as the means by which the divine activity is understood, then I am like to the divine will only insofar as I am a producer of artifacts – of which virtue, or the moral in general is one kind of thing produced. Immediately we see how the moral becomes the defining means of access to divinity and the being of beings, at the philosophical level, and at the same time why for Nietzsche the devaluation of the uppermost values is the overcoming above all of the *moral*: 'at bottom indeed only the moral God is overcome.'[31]

Nevertheless this is the consequence of a fundamentally philosophical discourse. Aquinas is, as we have already considered, *never* a philosopher, only ever a theologian. In this sense his appeal to τέχνη is purely explanatory – explanatory, indeed, of the Scriptures and the

---

[31] Nietzsche, F., *Nachlaß 1885–1887*, 1988, Vol. 12, p. 213. 'Im Grunde ist ja nur der moralische Gott überwunden.'

self-disclosure of God in Christ. It has no consequences. It is only when Aquinas is read *as a philosopher* that certain consequences intrude and take over. Truth as the adequation of intellect to thing is a formula arising from theology and faith – not philosophy. Here is why faith has no need of the sublime – it is God who lifts man up to live with him through Christ. There is no upliftment a man could undertake for himself that can achieve this. And so here is the second (and more genuine) answer to the question of what kind of theology is at issue in the sublime. It is expressly *not* the theology of Aquinas, since the sublime, even after the transformations I have indicated have occurred, remains resolutely a category of natural, non-Christian, theology and can never be a category of divine self-disclosure. Upliftment, or the sublime, becomes enmeshed in Christianity only negatively, only insofar as it is *not* understood for what it is, and not insofar as it is properly understood. Aquinas only applies the term sublime to the experience of being saved and made divine by God by analogy – but not any kind of *analogia entis*. 'By analogy' here means the way in which Aquinas applies and borrows all philosophical terms – as forerunners of the truth of divine revelation, whose truth is only so by divine fiat. The philosophical is merely a foreshadowing and forerunning of what is fully to be revealed only at the end of time, to those whom God has chosen to reveal it.

We are now in a position to lay out and make visible the relation of upliftment and the sublime to the emergence of the imagination in the origins of subjectivity and in postmodernity. Already we have seen that the determination of the divine on the basis of τέχνη radically transforms the temporal structure of the meaning of being itself, and above all of upliftment. On the basis of Aristotle's philosophical understanding, upliftment means: going-ahead of myself to discover the already *is*. On the basis of the *ens creatum* upliftment means: going ahead of myself to discover what already *was* and *has given* me to be.

The term φαντασία is routinely translated as 'imagination', although I denied earlier that this translation is correct. It is now clear that the fundamental character of the imagination as we understand in postmodernity is not an orientation with respect to representation, but with respect to *time*, specifically the past as when I run ahead of myself either carrying the past with me, and so not leaving it behind to enter the future, but saturating the future with the past, even though this past takes on the mimetic look of the future by rearranging what is carried forward from the past in new ways, so that it takes on that aspect of the future which is 'different'. For Aristotle, only one of the operations of φαντασία has this restriction to the past. Our own investigations demonstrated that the φαντασία is that which has the capacity to 'carry off' the different kinds of appearances in what appears, for the sake of their being known. These are of three forms: things separate in their very selves – abstractions – like number and the figures of geometry; things known through the senses; and the emotions or παθή. Two of these things, however, have a double character: geometric figures are both capable of being read-off and put back, they always retain their 'with respect to where', what of place remains with them: θέσις; next are the emotions, since these can be both what befalls me or passively occurs to me and what I actively experience and am driven toward. This double-character discloses that the φαντασία goes back and forth *between* νοῦς (insofar as it is separate from body) and the things that are known by means of sense, the πράγματα and αἴσθητα – individual beings, things known by the senses. The φαντασία is therefore the 'means by which' νοῦς and αἴσθησις are connected. Each of its directions, however, has a temporal determination. Insofar as φαντασία passes from αἴσθησις to νοῦς it runs from the future into the past – it carries what lies ahead of it back to be known. This is the 'reading-off' from the world as it lies ahead of me into what I know. Insofar, however, as φαντασία passes from νοῦς to αἴσθησις it carries what I already know, the past, into the future (though strictly speaking we experience this future as 'the present'). It is the way I make sense of the future from out of what I already know.

The individual things that νοῦς has are the νοήματα, and so each of the νοητά qualifies in a way to be one of the things that φαντασία articulates back and forth, the φαντάσματα. A further indication that the νοητα are individual 'images' of representation is the etymology Aristotle suggests for φαντασία – thinking is a kind of light (φῶς). Surely, therefore, the things that relate to light are images? Except that the relation to light is meant to indicate not light in the sense of the mind being a kind of cinema-screen, but the unity of the lit-up character of the phenomenon (Heidegger calls it the 'worlding' of world). Hence Martin Heidegger's name for this unity of the 'what lies ahead' of the *Da* of *Dasein* as *die Lichtung*, the clearing. That which is 'lit-up' or 'cleared ahead' for us is that wherein all the phenomena that are capable of appearing and being understood can appear – which includes what appears with respect to sight, hearing, smell, touch and taste. These five *together* disclose the unity of the ἕν, the unity of the world which worlds for us, and from out of which I take myself as a 'one', a one-thinking. In recalling a smell or a sound we do not thereby recall it by means of an image.

It is clear that the φαντάσματα can be of several kinds. In the first place are the things that most resemble a 'looks-like' or an image: geometric figure. The other abstractions, however, number, and what wisdom knows, have no form wherein they can be referred and returned directly from νοῦς to the αἴσθητα, even though knowledge of them arises out of αἴσθησις: the going back and forth of φαντασία is not, therefore, symmetrical – not everything that νοῦς receives is carried back to αἴσθησις: some things remain to the soul for the matter of thinking as such. Here is the evidence that Aristotle cannot possibly have meant by φαντασία what we mean by imagination, and that in fact the imaging and picturing understanding of imagination that we have is a restricted understanding of φαντασία. Whereas geometric figure can be both read-off and put-back, number always goes ahead of what it is number of – there can be no pure experience of three or seven, only three chairs or seven musical notes.[32] Lying even behind this are the things that pertain directly to σοφία, to wisdom, to which 'one' also belongs, and is the reason why 'one' is not technically a number. These are the matters of pure contemplation (θεωρεῖν). Very occasionally for Aristotle these are also called εἴδη (as Plato had called them) – the 'looks' or ideas that also constitute abstractions from the phenomena, though Aristotle is at pains to assert they have no separate existence, in the same way as he asserts the numerical and mathematical do not.[33] The 'look' at issue in every case is, however, what relates most closely to unseen being, to what is least visible in the phenomena – it is the being (οὐσία) of the appearance. The most abstracted matters of all, what relates to being as such, can *only* be worked out from the appearances by means of thinking, they cannot strictly speaking be seen at all: they relate directly to the being of beings and to contemplation. Here we should remember, such is this degree of abstraction that this is not the point at which being is separate, but rather the point at which thinking thinks for itself, αὐτός. Again, this is why for Aristotle two, not one, is the first genuine number. That there is only one of something has to be inferred and worked out from the fact that there could be two or more – the 'one' is thought out from the two and the many: this is the very activity

---

[32] Cf. Aristotle, *Metaphysics*, 1077 b 12ff.
[33] Aristotle, *Metaphysics*, 1059 b 3. τὰ μὲν γὰρ εἴδη ὅτι οὐκ ἔστι, δῆλον. ('Indeed the "ideas" as indicated do not exist, as is shown.')

of νοεῖν, of thinking as such: *thinking abstracts to an even more originary degree than is indicated by number.*[34]

The only possible class of the abstractables that can function as the basis for understanding φαντασία solely as representation and imagination in the contemporary sense is geometric figure, as what most can be read-off and read-back with respect to the phenomenal world, because it is both read-off from and can be used to reproduce or generate physical body. Yet geometric figure is prevented from assuming the primary place it would need to assume for Aristotle for φαντασία to be understood by what we understand by imagination – because for him it is the *least* of the modes of abstraction. What changes this, and allows the understanding of φαντασία to fulfil its function as the faculty of imagination – Kant's *Einbildungskraft?* Wisdom, number and geometry are the three capacities for abstraction closest to the ἦν ἔναι, the 'already-is' in the being of beings. They are, however, hierarchically ordered, wisdom as the first and highest means of possessing the truth (ἀληθεύειν), next number, and only then geometry. In each case, for Aristotle, the question is the multiplicity and complexity of the 'from whences' or sources (τὰς ἀρχὰς) for each, so that the abstractions of number and geometry are really only provisional, their relation to the being of beings is with respect to something to be discovered. In the case of wisdom and the love of wisdom (philosophy) there are only two originations, being and the one, and each can be turned into the other (ἀντιστρέφει), which means, they are the same in their source or 'from whence', ἀρχή.[35] However, in the transformation I have traced where the least of the modes of possessing the truth (τέχνη) takes over and predominates as the determination both of divinity and of being itself, this hierarchy ceases to have any force. Yet it is this hierarchy that Aristotle had developed in the *Metaphysics* as the very basis of his polemic against the *Mathematikoi* – the question of what precedes what and what orders what to what.

The understanding of φάντασμα determined by the temporal structure of τέχνη is therefore *precisely* the one that comes to predominate, because this is the one that most corresponds to the understanding of

---

[34] It is for these reasons that Heidegger, like Pythagoras before him, held that three and not two was the first number: 'both together' is not genuinely two, it is only discovered to be two after the first sum, the three, is seen. Cf. Heidegger, M., *Die Frage nach dem Ding*, GA41, 1984 (1962), p. 75; Diogenes Laertius, *Lives of Eminent Philosophers*, 2000 (1925) Vol. 2, p. 342.

[35] Cf. *Metaphysics*, 1061 a 17ff.

divinity that has come to prevail – divinity *now* understood as the *ens creatum* of the Christian God, taken philosophically. Surely, however, this is the understanding that Aristotle resists in Plato, and is it therefore not utterly fallacious to attribute this transformation to Christianity when it is as pagan as Aristotle himself? Except that what is at issue here is a most peculiar feature of the history of thinking itself. For it is not Plato who indicates the particular role (with which we are all-too familiar) of the place of geometrical and the arithmetical in Plato's thinking but – Aristotle. The primary critique of Plato's (and Pythagoras') understanding of number, geometry, and its relation to the elements, and Plato's theory of eidetic number is derived from Aristotle's ceaseless polemic against the theories of the Pythagoreans and the Platonists, the *Mathematikoi*.[36] We interpret Plato in the light of Aristotle, which overlooks how Aristotle himself achieved his fundamental ontological position through a *specific* way of reading Plato and the Pythagorean tradition. It is for this reason that when he came to read Plato, Heidegger demanded that in order to understand Plato it was necessary to go back through Aristotle himself.[37]

The soul, in being in some sense all things, can only be this because of its prior restriction to the unity of the world. This prior unity allows the 'all' to appear. The soul has, therefore, the divinity and unity of the being of beings as its 'for the sake of which'. It is therefore the *same* unity and divinity of the being of beings which each soul knows and has in advance of the dividedness and multiplicity of the unfolding of the being of the physical world – φύσις.[38] This sameness which the soul knows is why Aristotle argues that there cannot be a multiplicity

---

[36] It is almost certain, for instance, that a significant source for both Iamblichus' and Diogenes Laertius' description of Pythagorean and Platonic mathematics was Aristotle's lost work *On the Pythagoreans*, mentioned in the list of works in Vol. 1 of *Lives*, p. 470.

[37] Cf. Heidegger, *Platon: Sophistes*, GA19, 1992, p. 11. 'Wenn wir in die platonische Philosophie eindringen wollen, so werden wir dies am Leitfaden der aristotelischen Philosophie tun.' ('If we wish to penetrate Platonic philosophy, then we will do so with Aristotelian philosophy as the guiding thread.')

[38] Here, in fact, is the origin of the position that appeared in Scholasticism – in the supposed doctrines of the 'Latin Averroists' that there is only one world soul. Cf. the 277 condemned propositions of 1277 by Bishop Tempier of Paris: *Proposition 27*, 'Quod Deus non posset facere plures animas in numero;' *Proposition 94*, 'Quod duo sunt principia aeterna, scilicet corpus caeli et anima eius.' ('That God might not produce souls many in number;' 'That there are two eternal principles, evidently, the body of heaven and its soul.') Cf. Piché, D. (ed.), *La Condamnation Parisienne de 1277*, 1999, pp. 88, 108.

of worlds, but there can only be one world, and that is the same world always known by all in the same way. The argument is astonishingly simple, once the absolute differentiatedness of the world (cosmos) with respect to place is accepted. If there were a multiplicity of worlds, the elements in each would behave in the same way in each – that is, fire would go up, earth would go down to the centre, and so forth. The parts of every world relate to each other in a similar way – that is, in the same way as they do to the way in which they relate in the world that I know, and these parts will not relate differently in different worlds. The elements move with respect to where they move *to* absolutely: 'the centre and outermost are one in being'.[39] If the elements were moved analogously in different worlds with respect to different centres and outermosts, they could not be known to be the same elements. Here is the clearest evidence that, whilst for Aristotle the elements are determined ontologically, they are not determined with respect to the ontological unity of the self, but rather both the elements and the self are co-determined, and are separately placed, with respect to the unity of the *only* world that the elements and the self appear within. The self springs out of the unity of the world it inhabits – this unity always lies ahead of it, and explains its co-determination to other elemental beings (hence why solipsism can never be a problem for Aristotle: to be at all is to be among others).

What lies at the origin of the question of whether there are many worlds or only one world is not the existence of other worlds, but rather the source of the ontological unity of the self, and the basis on which that self can already take for granted its appearing in and belonging to a unity that is differentiated, that has parts. For Aristotle 'the world is one in being and not many',[40] else every self would occupy its own world. The same 'from whence' that establishes every being in its place and establishes its 'with respect to where' relatively and absolutely (both its θέσις and τόπος) indicates not only that there is only one world (and so guaranteeing the oneness and unity of truth) but also my own 'where' within it. The worlding of world (for Aristotle) demonstrates not only the already-in-advance of me that its unity is, it shows up the how and where I am disposed within it. For this reason Aristotle is as much able to derive his politics and ethics as his physics, metaphysics, and his theology out of his understanding of the unity of world, eternity, and the being of beings.

---

[39] Aristotle, *De Caelo*, 277 a 10. ἢ τὸ μέσον ἕν εἶναι καὶ τὸ ἔσχατον.
[40] Aristotle, *De Caelo*, 277 a 12. τὸν οὐρανὸν ἕνα μόνον εἶναι καὶ μὴ πλείους.

As I have indicated, however, the unity of the world and its being is no longer made apparent *phenomenologically* as it was for Aristotle, once an understanding of God as the originating cause of all things takes over and predominates – which means, in fact, once τέχνη as the means of disclosing and possessing the true takes over and predominates in philosophy. From now on, the implicit unity of all things is not a feature of the worlding of world, the 'for the sake of which' toward which the self finds itself already having run ahead of itself *into*, but rather now the world takes for granted its groundedness in God. To illustrate this change, we might understand it better by saying that, whereas in Aristotle the being of beings has the attribute of divinity, now God is understood as being-like (that is through *entitas*), or has the attribute of beingness.

Exactly that understanding of ἀφαιρέσις, 'reading-off' which most corresponds to the temporal determination of τέχνη, geometrical figure, is the understanding of φαντασία that comes to predominate, displacing and eclipsing any other understanding of it. Here it becomes clear why the φαντάσματα are now understood *only* as images and the imaginary – because image corresponds most closely to what in the lifting-off of figure from what it is a figure *of*. The most easily understood access to φαντασία becomes images, and φαντασία itself becomes imagination. At the same time it becomes possible to see why the εἴδη, the appearances in themselves, the 'real appearances' in *every case* become the prior image or form from which something that appears is taken to be the manifest appearance *of*, even though in Aristotle, let alone in Plato the εἴδος as 'look' predominantly means not the image that the look somehow is, but quite the opposite, what of an appearance is most *not* visible to the naked eye, what is most 'beingful' about it, something that to be 'seen' requires the 'seeing' of thought and thinking.

However, because the predominant understanding of φαντασία becomes the imaginary, and because there is now no way to posit the unity of the being of the world such that the world which gives me to appear is in every case the same world as the one in which you also are given to appear, now the imaginary has to be understood as lifting off, not just the appearance as image, but the whole world within which images appear. The imaginary is understood not as 'it worlds for me', but *my* interior world. At the same time, the predominating mode of the imaginary, the visual, is in every case turned outwards to indicate an individuated world for itself. Every image presupposes a world of its own. The transformations that follow from this in art are spectacular – no longer does the world produce images of itself, but every single image, statue, or work of art indicates a whole world of its own. For this 'every world' to encompass every possible means of the production and reproduction of images is only a matter of time and the means to develop the technical know-how to do so. Every technical possibility of the production of images becomes at the same time the technical possibility of producing an individuated world in and for itself.

From now on the being of beings can no longer be worked out phenomenologically as Aristotle does (albeit metaphysically), because what being is and how it is understood is answered in advance of the specific manifestation and appearance of individual beings (in other words, is not an answer to be sought through the struggle to bring out into the open a kind of self-enquiry).[41] This 'answering in advance' is the very reverse of what Aristotle proposes. What is the soul, as far as Aristotle is concerned? Aristotle gives us a definition of the soul as αἰών in the *De Caelo*,[42] where he suggests that the understanding of eternity of the heavens is derived from the understanding of the portion or allotment of a lifespan of a living being. If we take this seriously, then it becomes possible to understand the soul, in bringing itself into unity and conformity with the being of beings (the activity of νοῦς) learns to think, first from discovering itself to be worlded with respect to that world, and finally 'αὐτὸς', for itself. As an ἐντελέχεια, the coming-into-its-end of the soul is its self-fulfilment with respect to the being of all things. The soul, taken as a whole, is what comes to remain, what is most present and persists, in a life. The soul is the form of the body in the sense that the body is the outward appearance, of the *real* 'look', the εἶδος, which a soul is, because, strictly speaking, a soul has no visible (to the eyes) 'look' of its own, or rather, this is the way in which the body's being-perfected over a lifetime manifests itself 'really', to the seeing that sees beyond visibility by

---

[41] Because of the existence of certain polemic against the self-centredness of postmodernity, we need to be clear here what self-enquiry is (one writer speaks of needing to produce a 'theocentric' rather than self-centric understanding of being, as if this theocentricity were not exactly what I have described ontotheology to be). Self-enquiry is not an enquiry that places the 'self' as the 'centre of everything' as both object (and subject) of every thought, but exactly the opposite: although every self-enquiry is in every case *mine*, this enquiry does not have the self in view as an already-given (which is the structure of the *cogito*), but understands the genuine self as a continued coming-in-to-be that is lit-up and encountered *through* discovering myself already to be among beings.

[42] See Chapter 5, p. 108 above.

means of thought (that 'sees' the essence). It would be too strong to say that what is at issue here is 'learning', as if the soul is a record of what it learns – rather it is its being brought to self-presence and being held in self-presence with respect to all that occurs for and to it (σώζειν),[43] and all that it has made occur: learning and being learned (being wise), ἐπιστήμη, in the widest sense.[44]

In medieval thought 'the soul is the form of the body' is a common-place.[45] It is only with difficulty that we can gain access to this under-standing of the soul as the 'genuine substance' or 'substantial form' of the body. The entire force of *Brontosaurus* is to make manifest the transformation in understanding the soul that I have been trying to make manifest. This figure in *Brontosaurus as* a figurative representa-tion (and so an idea) appears to us now more essentially to be the form ('look') of the body than any idea of the soul. Yet *Brontosaurus* does not present us with any body that we know, but rather an under-standing of embodiment in general from which we 'read-off' our own self-understanding of our being embodied. 'Soul as the form of the body' has become 'body takes the place of the soul'.

In the 'reading-off' that φαντασία is, the hierarchy that Aristotle named as wisdom (contemplation of the 'for the sake of which', the final cause, of the being of beings), number and forms, and the figures of geometry, is no longer held in place by being oriented toward the future, the 'from out of which' the self appears alongside whatever it discovers itself amidst – the worlding of world. How therefore can the self manifest itself? Earlier I noted that upliftment on the basis of the *ens creatum* means: going ahead of myself to discover what already was and has given me to be. This is exactly the structure of the deriva-tion of the *cogito* in Descartes' *Third Meditation*. In Descartes a radi-cal transformation of the self is undertaken, whereby there is always a self established *prior* to everything the self knows. This is the most radical reversal in the history of philosophy, a fundamental trans-formation which is now so constitutive of how we understand the being of being-human that it is taken to be automatically true – that I *am* before anything I know *is*, and yet you will see how this contem-porary self-evidence stands radically opposed to Aristotle, for whom

---

[43] See p. 43ff. above.

[44] This is to overlook the question of forgetting. The soul practised in wisdom does not have present to itself everything that has ever happened for it (like Aquinas's God), but rather draws off from its experiences the effects and 'lessons' of that experience; it grows or matures through them.

[45] *Anima formam corporis* [est].

all self-knowledge is consequent upon and concomitant to what it is the self knows. From this we can see how contingent the contemporary understanding is – what seems so necessary to us turns out to be a purely historical phenomenon. The *cogito* represents a transformation of the basis of self-hood, from something that *lies ahead of me* (as a source or origin) to something that is 'already there' (a 'cause' in the modern sense) and so lies in the past for me, namely the Subject, the already-underlying (*sub-iectum*). The things most stable in our understanding turn out themselves to have been subject to change.

The Cartesian subject, taking the self as already given prior to discovering itself to be worlded, exhibits a temporal structure wherein the self already takes itself as an entity prior to anything it knows (it precedes what is known and so exists, not from the future, but the past). God is then taken to be an already constitutive aspect of this already existent self. In the third of Descartes' *Meditations* the self, discovering itself to *be* independently of anything else that *is*, asserts that the self is finite substance. It then proceeds to ask itself, before establishing itself as worlded, what more perfect, infinite, substance could have given such a self existence: and Descartes replies that only God could have authored such a self (that is the self is *not* authored by the realm of the things the self knows in experience, emotion, and sensation):

> I understand by the name of God a substance at once infinite, independent . . . by which I myself, and all others – if some other exists, inasmuch as it exists – have been created . . . For although the idea of substance would surely be in me from thence that I be a substance, this idea would therefore not be the idea of an infinite substance, since I be finite, unless it did not proceed from some other substance which indeed truly were infinite.[46]

The grounding of the Cartesian *cogito* is the fundamental understanding from out of which every subsequent relationship between the man, the world and God is formulated, to which Descartes is giving description.[47] Indeed, it is only arising out of this understanding

---

[46] Descartes, R., *Meditationes de prima philosophia* in *Descartes*, 1996, Vol. 7, p. 45. (*Third Meditation*) 'Dei nomine intelligo substantiam quandam infinitam, independentem . . . a quâ tum ego ipse, tum aliud omne, si quid aliud extat, quodcumque extat, est creatum . . . Nam quamvis substantiae quidem idea in me sit ex hoc ipso sim substantia, non tamen idcirco esset idea substantiae infinitae, cùm sim finitus, nisi ab aliquâ substantia, quae revera esset infinita, procederet.'

[47] Cf. Kant, I., *Opus postumum* in *Gesammelte Schriften*, 1936, Vol. 21, p. 50.

that God, world, and the being of being-human (God as an 'infinite substance', the world as consisting of 'substances', the human as a 'finite substance') become separate, and independent kinds of, entities. Descartes demonstrates how the being (substance) of God is determined out of the being (substance) of being-human *without respect to 'exterior' substances* – this is the force of the '*si . . . extat*' of this passage.

The transition which we began by identifying in Samuel Clarke in fact is to be traced in its most fundamental philosophical formulation to Descartes and covers over completely the phenomenon of the future which in Aristotle had already become ambiguous (where eternity, or more strictly speaking sempiternity, is substituted for futurity). God, as the originating cause of all things, now lies at the beginning of time, as the first in the series of moving everything that moves. Here again we see how Aristotle's 'first mover' came to be reconfigured so radically in the Middle Ages, and finally so misunderstood in the modern period. Eternity, for Aristotle, is the same at every 'where', and so every 'when': the unmoved is *a*temporally related to every specific 'now', to all possible times. In the Middle Ages, however, the first mover is *first and most prior* in a temporal sequence.

Although Aquinas resolved the difficulties that this poses by making God's temporal relation to creation different to the temporal relation to creation possessed by creatures, so that God is single act, continuous to and contiguous with all moments of time (God has no future), every 'now', Descartes' (and Clarke's) configuration of God to human being and the being of the universe illustrates how not even this understanding of God is retained. The dubitability of the exterior world is always accompanied by an absolutely indubitable self, which for Descartes, is grounded and caused by God. Moreover, the self now constitutes a world for itself, so that the fundamental connection to other beings is never the 'from whence' every being springs and so lies ahead of us, but has in every case to be established anew, from the roots up, either as being caused by God, or (in the absence of God) else from where? This is the problem of the existence of other minds in analytic philosophy, or of intersubjectivity or alterity as it arises in Buber, Lévinas and others.

Why are we able to draw a straight line between Aristotle and Descartes? What inner unity ties the two of them together? Should we not historiographically trace each development, each movement of thought, each shift in being that takes place from one to the next, and so is there not an infinite stretch of points between Aristotle and this one who follows him two thousand years and more later? Or is it that these are just great men, and the interrelations between them can ignore the passage of time and proceed simply from what they themselves held to be true, as they are put into dialogue with each other? Except that we are not undertaking a history, or rather the history we need to point up and illustrate is the extent to which not Aristotle, nor Descartes, but what they treat *of* is at issue.[48]

Descartes himself was fully aware of this. The *Meditations* were written in a spirit of deep confrontation with Aristotle and the prevailing Aristotelianism of the science of his day. In a letter to Mersenne of 1641, Descartes notes (in contrast to Aristotle's *Physics*) that

> these six *Meditations* contain all the foundations of my Physics. But, please, it is not necessary to say so, because those who favour Aristotle might perhaps have more difficulty approving them, and I hope that those who read them will accustom themselves insensibly to my principles, and recognising the truth [of them] before perceiving for themselves that they [i.e. the principles of these truths] destroy those of Aristotle.[49]

Why does Descartes believe that the principles of Aristotle's physics are destroyed by what he himself presupposes? Here is the most important question in the historicality of the encounter with beings itself. Because the being of beings is now understood differently in the passage from Descartes to Aristotle, and in fact because it now (from Descartes' own time) stands on a fully ontotheological footing which makes impossible even Aristotle's metaphysical passageway into the being of beings, *precisely* because of this, the ontological understanding of the cosmos from out of which Aristotle works no longer relates in the same way to the way in which the world lies open in the truth of its self-disclosure. Descartes seeks an understanding that relates to truth self-evidently. His confrontation with Aristotle is therefore worked out entirely negatively, inasmuch as, being steeped

---

[48] However, for an account of the philosophical developments out of which Descartes' philosophical work sprang, see Secada, J., *Cartesian Metaphysics*, 2000.

[49] Descartes, R., *Letter to Mersenne of January 28, 1641* in *Descartes*, 1996, Vol. 3, p. 298. 'Ces six Meditations contiennent tous les fondemens de ma Physique. Mais il ne faut pas dire, s'il vous plaist; car ceux qui favoiresent Aristote feroient peut-estre plus de difficulté de le approuver; et i'espere que ceux qui les liront, s'accoûtumeront inseensiblment à mes principes, & en reconnoistront la verité avant que de s'appercevoir qu'ils déstruisent ceux d'Aristote.'

in Aristotle, at the same time he needs to demonstrate the extent to which Aristotle's 'physics' can no longer describe the world as it appears, so that the perception of this truthful self-disclosing itself is evidence enough that Aristotle's principles are destroyed.

In an earlier letter to Beeckman, Descartes notes that while 'Plato says one thing, Aristotle another' and so forth,[50] 'if you know something, it is entirely yours, however much you were taught it from another'.[51] This is nothing other than an argument from experience and self-evidence, and yet we can see from our enquiry into Aristotle, how the way in which the being of beings manifests itself already determines how any particular thing relates to truth. If Aristotle was simply through his own self-understanding trying to bring the phenomena available to him to adequate description, so too was Descartes. We have seen how contingent and historical this sense of self-evidence is, in our bringing to light the different temporal structures on which the understanding of the self stands between Descartes and Aristotle. It therefore becomes clear how precarious every appeal to self-evident experience will always be. This is not relativism, although in postmodernity the appeal to the 'constructed' or 'socially constructed' appears to make it so – because everything appears through the will, 'we' believe ourselves to be the ones doing the willing. Rather this is our own being bound to history, our boundedness to the unfolding of being, not just as temporal, but having its own history. It is as historical beings that we unfold. *We* (whomever 'we' might be) do not construct (societies, for the sake of social construction, or philosophies, for the sake of thought): historical being 'constructs' *us*. This seeming contingency has for each of us the force of necessity (it could not be other, so it is not 'relative' to anything else). Better said, being gives us to be, not in the abstract, but in historical, concrete instances: each of us has a 'where' and a 'when'. For each of us, this whither and whence is mine alone and ours together, if it can be brought properly to light.

In his *Fifth Meditation*, Descartes considers 'whether I might try to emerge from the doubts into which I have gone in previous days'.[52] His purpose is that 'I might see whether something certain concerning

---

[50] Descartes, R., *Letter to Beeckman of October 17, 1630* in *Descartes*, 1996, Vol. 1, p. 157. 'Unum dicit Plato, aliud Aristoteles.'

[51] Descartes, *Letter to Beeckman*, in *Descartes*, 1996, Vol. 1, p. 159. 'Si quid scis, omnino tuum est, quantumvis ab alto didiceris.'

[52] Descartes, R., *Meditationes*, in *Descartes*, 1996, Vol. 7, p. 63. 'Quam ut ex dubiis, in quae superioribus diebus incidi, coner emergere.'

material things could be had'.[53] In order to consider this question, however, Descartes does not proceed to an empirical investigation of what can then be known by means of sense data. Rather he proceeds in the opposite direction. Those things which are most certain to him, and therefore indubitable because their essences are immutable and eternal are not the things of sense, but geometrical figure, for instance triangles and other such realities. These things are such that even if they exist nowhere outside his reflective thinking as such, nevertheless have still a determinate nature or essence 'which does not depend on my mind'.[54] We could perhaps miss the most extraordinary character of this statement. Descartes asserts something which has a determinate nature and essence and which does not exist anywhere except in his cogitation, and yet simultaneously that the very thing which only exists in virtue of his thinking of it is not dependent on his mind.

An almost identical reality exists at the root of the modern scientific articulation of the motion of bodies. Martin Heidegger shows how Newton's first law of motion is formulated as follows: 'every body, which is not compelled by forces impressed, is moved uniformly straight forward'.[55] This in itself is a reformulation of Galileo's discussion of motion in his *Discorsi* of 1638, also quoted by Heidegger: 'I think of a body thrown on a horizontal plane and every obstacle excluded . . . the motion . . . would be uniform and perpetual if this place were extended infinitely.'[56] It is Galileo's formulation which Newton takes up and extends, transforming it not only into a law, but the primary scientific law of motion.

Heidegger's point about these mental conceptions is to ask about this

---

[53] Descartes, *Meditationes*, in *Descartes*, 1996, Vol. 7, p. 63. 'Videam an aliquid certi de rebus materialibus haberi possit.'

[54] Descartes, *Meditationes*, in *Descartes*, 1996, Vol. 7, 64. 'Nec a mente meâ dependet.'

[55] Heidegger, M., *Die Frage nach dem Ding*, GA41, 1984 (1962), pp. 86f. 'Corpus omne, quod a viribus impressis non cogitur, uniformiter in directum movetur.' In fact Heidegger truncates Newton's formulation, which reads 'Corpus omne persevare in statu suo quiescendi vel movendi uniformiter in directum, nisi quatenus illud a viribus impressis cogitur suum mutare.' ('Every body perseveres in its state of being at rest or moving uniformly straight forward, except insofar as it is compelled to change its state by forces impressed.') See Newton, I., ed. Koyré, A. and Cohen, I. B., *Isaac Newton's Philosophiae Naturalis Principia Mathematica*, 1972, Vol. 1, p. 54.

[56] Heidegger, *Die Frage nach dem Ding*, GA41, 1984 (1962), p. 91. 'Mobile super planum horizontale proiectum mente concipio omni secluso impedimento . . . illius motum aequabilem et perpetuum super ipso plano futurum esse, si planum in infinitum extendatur.'

body left to itself. Where do we find it? There is no such body. There is also no experiment which could ever bring such a body to perception. But modern science, in contrast to the mere dialectical poetic conception of mediaeval Scholasticism and science, is supposed to be based on experience. Instead it has such a law at its apex. This law speaks of something which is not there. It demands a fundamental representation of things which contradict the ordinary.[57]

Amos Funkenstein makes a parallel observation concerning the fundamental illogicality of the consequences of Newton's first law, concluding: 'even in Newton's infinite space, a purely inertial motion would be unobservable; in order to observe a body so moving we have to approach it to a finite distance and exert some attractive force that must alter the motion of that body ever so slightly.'[58] In other words, what Newton describes is a pure activity of mental 'seeing' – it can never be formally observed in the world: something always has to be added to the observation, some work of the mind, to make it 'true'. This despite the constant assurance we receive that all contemporary science is based on the experimental, empirical, observed, evidence![59]

Almost as soon as we have elicited from the term φαντασία the way in which it is to be understood only as the imagination and with respect to representation and figure, we can see how this understanding underpins the whole of modern physics, irrespective of the various quarrels between Clarke, Newton, Galileo and Descartes.[60]

---

[57] Heidegger, *Die Frage nach dem Ding*, GA41, 1984 (1962), p. 89. 'Sich selbst überlassenen Körper. Wo finden wir ihn? Einen solchen Körper gibt es nicht. Es gibt auch kein Experiment, das jemals einen solchen Körper in die anschauliche Vorstellung bringen könnte. Nun soll doch die neuzeitliche Wissenschaft im Unterschied zu den bloß dialektischen Begriffsdichtungen der mittelalterlichen Scholastik und Wissenschaft auf Erfahrung gründen. Statt dessen steht ein solcher Grundsatz an der Spitze. Er spricht von einem Ding, das es nicht gibt. Er verlangt eine Grundvorstellung von den Dingen, die der gewöhnlichen widerspricht.'

[58] Funkenstein, A., *Theology and the Scientific Imagination from the Middle Ages to the Seventeenth Century*, 1986, p. 121.

[59] My purpose here is not in some postmodern way to 'invalidate' or denigrate modern science, only to show that it too, includes a work of the mind, an imaginative activity in order to be 'empirically' true.

[60] Helen Lang has indicated a similar example of an imaginary object described without respect to Aristotelian τόπος in the question of Johannes Duns Scotus's consideration of the question 'can God create a rock that is not in place?' The effect of Scotus's answer is twofold: 'Duns grants place a dimensional incorruptibility that is independent of change in location. Size, shape and dimension are mathematical criteria applicable anywhere because size and shape do *not* change

Descartes' mathematical objects could only lie prior to him and be other than him, and yet have no place in the world. Although he cites the example of a triangle, the intention is only to direct us from the geometric form of the triangle to something prior even to the triangular, but which is demonstrated in exactly the same way as the triangular can be demonstrated to have a prior, eternal, and immutable essence or nature. Descartes requires us to answer 'then cannot therein also an argument be had by which the existence of God might be proved?'[61] Moreover this argument, insofar as it is to be had, must demonstrate the existence of God 'at the minimum in the same degree of certainty in which the truths of mathematics have so far been'.[62] Descartes' claim is no less grandiose than Clarke's supposed refutation of atheism.

What Descartes undertakes in this statement is at the same time only possible on the basis of a profound transformation in what it means for something to exist. Descartes proposes something that he is thinking on reflectively (*cogitare*) which need not exist in the world, neither is it dependent on his mind. This thing exists without him existing, and yet it need have no existence in the world – indeed, its indubitability lies in its *not* being a pragmatic thing, a thing known through sense. It is a mental reality which does not require my mind to exist. It is therefore something that belongs solely to the imaginary. This is not the freedom of the imaginary, the capacity I have to imagine whatever I like, be it a unicorn, or paradise or that the world might be other than it is. Rather, this is the possibility for the imaginary as such to constitute the basis for everything subsequently demonstrated as existent. In this sense I cannot, strictly speaking, imagine a triangle that is not a triangle. This is not because of any 'limit' to the imaginary, but rather because, in imagining a geometric figure like a triangle, for me to know that it is a triangle means that it is defined in advance of my imagining it. To imagine a triangle that does not have the properties which lay out in advance what a triangle is, is not to imagine a triangle. Even in a flight of fancy, where I might say that I am imagining

---

with location. . . . In modern terms these problems become pure mind present in body on a Cartesian model and the problem of force, or gravity, which is sometimes called 'action at a distance' in Newtonian physics . . . Like Duns, neither Newton nor anyone within the Newtonian framework has ever satisfactorily answered this problem.' Lang, H. 'Duns Scotus: Putting Angels in their Place' in Lang, H., *Aristotle's Physics and its Medieval Varieties*, 1992, pp. 178, 187.

[61] Descartes, *Meditationes*, in *Descartes*, 1996, Vol. 7, p. 65. 'Nunquid inde haberi etiam potest argumentum, quo Dei existentia probetur?'

a triangle with four sides, I can only explain the flight of fancy with reference to the triangular as such, that is, to what a 'real' triangle already is prior to my fanciful re-ordering of it.

In one sense, therefore, Descartes' God conforms to the pure definition of the hyperreal, of a simulacrum, in the sense that this god has no origin. The idea of God is, strictly speaking, *extra*-temporal rather than *ever-always*. Moreover, Descartes' God is above all a reference to who or what God could be, in advance of our coming upon the idea of God. It is because we know in advance what the essence of God is, that we understand the idea of God to be indubitable on mathematical terms.

The endless reproducibility which is the feature of the simulacrum is, for Descartes at least, not possible, because the same God would be known through the same method of doubt and the mathematical by anyone, and this God is the origin of all things. In this sense the same God ties together difference, and is its source (in contradistinction to Aristotle's convertible principles of unity and being, which are divine). The way in which Descartes resolves this question about the imaginary however, could again easily be overlooked. In postmodernity we understand imagining as a kind of productive seeing, an issuing forth of what we imagine (a product of will as much as of mind). This is not Descartes' understanding of it. In the sixth of his *Meditations* he turns his attention finally to the question of material things. Right at the beginning, he notes only that he may know at a minimum that material things exist, insofar as they are the objects of pure mathematics, because he clearly and distinctly perceives them. He adds:

> For there is no doubt that God be capable of effecting all the things that I am capable of perceiving thus. . . . Moreover, from the faculty of imagining, which I know by experience I use when I turn towards these material things, it seems to follow that they exist.[63]

For Descartes, imagining is the passive intuiting of what is already there, not the active force of producing whatever it is I would like to

---

[62] Descartes, *Meditationes*, in *Descartes*, 1996, Vol. 7, p. 65f. 'In eodem ad minimum certitudinis gradu esse deberet apud me Dei existentia, in quo fuernunt hactenus Mathematicae veritates.'

[63] Descartes, *Meditationes*, in *Descartes*, 1996, Vol. 7, p. 71. 'Non enim dubium est quin Deus sit capax ea omnia efficiendi quae ego sic percipiendi sum capax. . . . Praeterea ex imaginandi facultate, quâ me uti experior, dum circa res istas materiales versor, sequi videtur illas existere.'

think. The active, productive, faculty of imagining he attributes solely to God. It is only as God is devalued into death that the purely human imagination takes over all the imaginary activities of God, and so is disbanded into the separate worlds which became possible with the collapse of Aristotle's phenomenological unity of being.

8

Negating Sublimity

Kant's understanding of the sublime, *das Erhabene*, is worked out through the third of his *Critiques*, the *Kritik der Urteilskraft*. The word *Urteilskraft* is usually translated into English as 'judgement'. Although the word has this sense, the verb it indicates is *teilen*, to separate or divide. A more literal translation would therefore be 'the power of originary separation', perhaps less literally, the power of discrimination. It suggest an active faculty, a positive undertaking. He is explicit with regard both to the sublime and the beautiful that what is at issue is strictly a critique and not a science, because it admits of no formal proofs.[1]

Whereas Longinus' understanding of upliftment (and indeed the preparatory thinking that establishes upliftment as a formal possibility in Aristotle) springs from an entirely non-Christian worldview, it is possible to see that there has been a radical intrusion of Christian ideas into Kant's understanding of upliftment and the sublime. Kant takes it for granted and in advance not only that what he needs to say philosophically is *congruent* with his understanding of Christian faith (Aquinas did the same after all), he also believes that it is both possible and necessary to demonstrate this congruence. However, the congruence is established in a most peculiar manner, and the importance of this manner cannot be underestimated. Upliftment, or the sublime, is treated as one of several aspects of the critique of judgement which fall under a more general theory or doctrine. This theory has a specific reference to what Descartes establishes as the basis for subjectivity, described in German as a *Methodenlehre*, a methodology or more literally method-doctrine.

Why is thinking a method, and why should such a method be a doctrine? For Aristotle, in what we would now call the 'social', the corollary of place with respect to the lived activity of human beings, every human being relates to truth in some way specified by how they

---

[1] Cf. Kant, I., *Kritik der Urteilskraft*, 1990 (1790), §44, pp. 157f.

are manifested in the πόλις. Πόλις here does not mean the 'political' in the modern sense, but rather in the public sphere, in the being of a whole people. A πόλις is not understood 'racially', that is genetically, but rather in the sense of its fate and destiny, a fate and destiny laid down for it by its being, and from which it arises. Even a people, a nation (constituted again, not by its race or genes, but above all by its belonging to its λόγος, to the manner in which it speaks and what it has been given to speak of, which means what lies possible for it to know and express *through* its manner of speaking) has, and arises from, an αἰών, a span and portion of time allotted to it. In this sense its being really does spring from its destiny, in the sense that its apportioned time arises from out of where it ends, from the *end* of the time allotted to it. Aristotle's insight in the *Nicomachean Ethics* is not, to give one example, that the φρονημόν is one who is wisely deliberative through the practice of φρόνησις, but the other way around – φρόνησις is the relating to truth of the one who deliberates wisely: so too with the 'scientist', the σοφίστης, the τέχνητης and so forth. Each has his practice of ἀληθεύειν, of truthful disclosure, which is the means by which he discloses (above all to himself) how he relates to truth and to being insofar as it is being, the divine science. In this the being of each one in the πόλις is interrelated to the being of everyone else, but in a way that discloses the interior order of the πόλις. The means of seeing and bringing to light the interrelation is analogous to that of seeing the interrelation of numbers: it is what separates and divides each one in the πόλις and individuates him or her that also discloses their interrelation (in the case of the numbers themselves, their belonging in a series). In Scholasticism this becomes the practice of identifying each essence, each individuated substance in its genus, by means of specific difference. The practice of working out how I relate to truth will indicate my difference to you, our difference relative to each other and our absolute position in relation to the πόλις as a whole. The underlying presupposition is that every human being has a specific and unique disposal to his or her respective fate – his allotted span and soul αἰών and ψυχή.

With Descartes' transformation of thinking into method, the underlying presupposition is that every *cogito* (as every embodied 'I think me thinking') appears by the same manner of self-restriction to selfhood – the method of doubt, or means by which every 'I' is irreducibly 'I' to itself – what Heidegger called '*Ichheit*', or I-hood. Each individual self cannot take its irreducibility as already given by its being in the world (where the working out recognizes in advance what is already there, already in being) as in a numerical series: rather the irreducibility of every 'I' must be read-off and represented back to itself as a decision, a conscious, willed putting-into or placing (θέσις), analogous to inserting a point in a particular place on a continuum or line – as in a geometric process of bisecting a line by means of placing a point of bisection on the line. Every point marked out is at least potentially (and that means in its origin or its being) like every other point which could be identified, it has no difference individuating it that is already in being (literally, its being and its attributes are something added to it by a process, a method). From this being there is a further being to be abstracted, again by an imaginative process – the being of beings *as* the being of God. For this reason both the *Meditations* and Kant's Method-Doctrine are concerned with theology. With Descartes we need be in no doubt about this – the very title *Meditationes de prima philosophia* contains a reference to 'first philosophy' which Aristotle also calls theology.[2] Kant, however, refers the power of judgement to the doctrine of God – to theology, but as it arises from a science of nature. The doctrine of God – theology as such – he defines as being the doctrine or science 'of the original causes of the world as inner concept of all objects of experience'.[3] The *Inbegriff* is the concept that makes every other concept available, the inner unity and exemplar of the concepts themselves. The ground of this unity is the understanding. The teleological character of the power of judgement is of assistance to theology, not because it is part of theology as such, but because it points towards a ground that is occupied over and beyond nature – the divine originator.[4] It does not represent this ground, but indicates the idea of such a ground to human understanding.

The inner oneness of this unity is not the self, the 'I', but is rather that on which the self stands, it is what gives rise to the self (exactly as Descartes had carried through in the *cogito*): God. It is through this inner unity and originating ground that the self is able to appear at all, and which ties every individuated appearance of a self, an 'I', together. We can see immediately that, because this is above all a kind of a *concept* (Begriff), it is referred to the understanding as something which makes experience possible and intelligible. It therefore rests exactly on

---

[2] Cf. Aristotle, *Metaphysics*, 1026 a 20–32. πρώτη φιλοσοφία

[3] Kant, *Kritik der Urteilskraft*, 1990, §79, p. 283. 'Von dem Urgrunde der Welt als Inbegriff aller Gegenstände der Erfahrung.'

[4] Kant, *Kritik der Urteilskraft*, 1990, §79, p. 283. 'Einer außer und über die Natur belegenen Grund (göttlichen Urheber).'

the cleft in being, the driving apart of the understanding and reason from the 'natural' world that arises after Parmenides. As this having-been-driven-apart arises in Kant, in contrast to Aristotle, it appears as a temporally prior, a preceding, originary ground. It is from this that Kant understands the problem of freedom to arise. The problem of freedom arises, however, on the basis of the I, of I-hood. And it is this determination of the self as I-hood (*Ichheit*) from which, as Heidegger argues,

> Kant's philosophy creates and depicts the transition from the inauthentic to the authentic concept of freedom. Freedom is for him also mastery over sensuousness, but not only this, but freedom as self-standing-ness in one's own ground and self-determination as self-legislating. And yet the determination of the formal essence of human freedom does not yet complete itself in this Kantian concept of freedom. For Kant places this freedom as autonomy exclusively in the pure reason of man. This pure reason remains not only distinguished from, but at bottom also separated from, sensuousness, from 'nature', as something wholly other. The self of humanity is determined solely out of the I-hood of the 'I think'; such I-hood arises from sensuousness as the animality of man, and arises from but is not authentically involved with, nature. Nature, and what one names thereby, remains here as negative and as what is only to be overcome, and does not *enter into* a proper basis of the full essence of man.[5]

Kant, in driving apart the animality of man from reason (as the stable, eternal self-sufficient supersensible, the site and doctrine of God)

---

[5] Heidegger, M, *Schelling: Vom Wesen der Menschlichen Freiheit*, GA42, 1988 (1971), p. 145. 'Kants Philosophie schafft und bildet den Übergang vom uneigentlichen zum eigentlichen Freiheitsbegriff. Freiheit ist auch bei ihm noch Herrschaft über die Sinnlichkeit, aber nicht nur dieses, sondern dieses schon als Selbständigkeit im eigenen Grunde und Selbstbestimmung als Selbstgesetzgebung. Und dennoch vollendet sich in diesem Kantschen Begriff der Freiheit noch nicht die Umgrenzung des formalen Wesens der menschlichen Freiheit. Denn Kant verlegt diese Freiheit als Autonomie ausschließlich in die reine Vernunft des Menschen. Diese reine Vernunft bleibt nicht nur unterschieden gegen, sondern im Grunde auch geschieden von der Sinnlichkeit, der 'Natur': als dem ganz anderen. Das Selbst des Menschen bestimmt sich noch einzig aus der Ichheit des 'Ich denke', welche Ichheit auf die Sinnlichkeit als die Tierheit des Menschen und aufgetürmt aber nicht eigentlich in die Natur eingelassen ist. Die Natur, und was man so nennt, bleibt hier das Negative und das nur zu Überwindende und wird nicht *mit* ein eigener Grund des vollen Wesens des Menschen.' Emphasis in original.

reinforces the duality which comes later to be known as mind–body dualism.

Because of the controversies of the later Middle Ages, and in particular because of the insistence of establishing a conformity between philosophy and the Church's historical tradition of the interpretation of biblical texts – what we come to know as revelation – knowledge of the world *naturaliter* and knowledge of the world in consequence of Church doctrine become at a certain point and in a certain way fused. Nowhere is this more evident than in the condemnations first in 1270, and then in 1277 issued by Étienne Tempier, Bishop of Paris. Here we should note with regard to the continuing postulation of Johannes Duns the Scot as a driving figure in the origins of secularity, that there is certainly a better case to be made that Scotus is as much *responding* to this drive to fuse faith and philosophy in the life of the Church as *producing* it. Indeed, Helen Lang has made this argument already, noting that 'the consistent motivation behind Duns' revision of Aristotle's physics lies with theology' (by which she means Christian doctrine), whilst at the same time remarking on the extent to which Duns' solutions have parallels in Descartes, Newton and in their successors, and that the problems that arise from Scotus's solutions 'are with us today'.[6] We have seen how a particular understanding of the mathematical – specifically the geometrical – comes to the fore especially in the period up to and including Newton and Descartes as the means by which what can be known about anything can *already* be known in advance of it – indeed this is the essence of the mathematical. The mathematical comes to predominate as the way in which things can appear: at the same time it predominates as a means of demonstrating the being of God.

This fusion of faith and philosophy is what Heidegger named as ontotheology. It is the deprivation of the ground of the being of beings from a genuine phenomenological enquiry – even within the metaphysics of Aristotle – displacing the ground of that enquiry from the being of being-human to the being of God, with all the consequences that displacement entails. An extreme form of this displacement is in Descartes' derivation of the essence and nature of God from an ideal mental reality – derived on the same basis as the derivation of geometric figure. Our enquiry has indicated that this supposed enquiry which yields a kind of self-evident truth (and so a 'natural' truth) is

---

[6] Lang, H., 'Duns Scotus' in *Aristotle's Physics and its Medieval Varieties*, 1992, pp. 186f.

itself entirely consequent on a radical transformation of the being of beings, a transformation which actually disregards not only certain aspects of divine revelation or self-disclosure (something outside my scope here, but which I will touch on again later), but, still more importantly in this stage of the argument, disregards fundamental aspects of the way in which human self-experience is to be understood.

Heidegger explains the effect of this fusion and then collapse of the theological into the philosophical in the following way:

> The so-called natural knowledge not based upon any revelation, therefore, did not have its own form of intelligibility or grounds for itself, let alone from out of itself. Thus what is decisive for the history of science is not that all truth of natural knowledge was measured by the supernatural. Rather it is that this natural knowledge, disregarding this criterion, arrived at no independent foundation and character out of itself.[7]

Kant appeals to the sublime as one of the means by which the faculty of judgement is exercised, wherein the faculty of the power of representation, the imagination (φαντασία) operates between perception (αἴσθησις) and understanding (νοῦς), in a way that mirrors Aristotle. But the transformations in interpretation on the *Einbildungskraft*, the power of representing, that we have observed now press the interpretation of that faculty in an entirely different and modified way. Although our discussion of Kant is solely concerned with his understanding of upliftment and the sublime (for the sake of brevity and because the sublime is an exemplary form of this judgement), nevertheless the sublime is only one of the faculties of judgement, to which beauty also belongs.

This will again pose the question I have repeatedly asked, and which I have taken as the guiding question of this book: 'what kind of theology is intended by any enquiry into the upliftment, or the sublime?' Clearly the sublime, as much as in Aristotle (in that we read it *back* into him) or Longinus as in Aquinas or Kant, continues to pose the question of the meaning of divinity.

---

[7] Heidegger, M., *Die Frage nach dem Ding* in *Gesamtausgabe*, GA41, 1984 (1962), p. 97. 'Das sogenannte natürliche, nicht offenbarungsmäßige Wissen hatte daher für sich und gar aus sich keine eigengestaltete Form der Wißbarkeit und Begründung. Nicht dies also ist wissenschaftsgeschichtlich das Entscheidende, daß alle Wahrheit des natürliche Wissen, unbeschadet jener Messung, aus sich zu keiner eigenständigen Begründung und Prägung gelangte.'

The predominance of the mathematical corresponds to a radical re-orientation of the way in which the cosmos, the world itself, is understood with regard to time. Truth is no longer something which, in being disclosed, has to be uncovered for the first time in the performative stretching out and forward of the rhetor (even if in the ambiguity of Aristotle's relation between this future and the 'ever' of eternity); truth is always true before us, always *already* decided to have been true, because it is true first in the mind of God and only *subsequently* will we demonstrate our conformity with it. This is exactly the structure of the *adaequatio intellectus et rei* of Aquinas's exposition of truth in the *Quaestiones Disputatae: De Veritate*. Although Kant only occasionally makes it explicit as the ground of truth from out of which he works the three Critiques he undertakes, nevertheless it is always at work in the background.

Why does this radically alter things with regard to time? We saw with Longinus that the true is that which is reached out for *beyond*, so that what is there to be disclosed is something ahead of me, to which I must stretch out, but it is at the same time something for which *I* the rhetor am doing the stretching: it is in the manner of the arranging and placing together of the speaking that I must undertake that the fundamental disclosive truth of what is to be said is made manifest for *here*, in the speaking to be undertaken now, even if what is reached for is something already known to others, and in other times. From the time of Descartes, and indeed from far before (but with Descartes a fundamental shift is made with regard to the place of what is true as *philosophically* true), the true is not that which is stretched ahead for, but that which is manifested as *already to have been true* because God intended it to be so. In fact this is itself a distortion of an earlier Christian insight, that the truth is poured out essentially from the future, so that what we are to be lies ahead of us in the consummation of time and not behind us as what has already been intended for us. With Descartes, and in the *Meditations*, the *cogito* has grounded itself in and discovers itself already to be caused by what is both infinitely greater and more perfect than itself, namely God. The *cogito*, the subject, discovers itself *already to have been true* in God. It is here, as we shall see, that the mathematical comes to the fore as the primary mode of the true, even with regard to the sublime.

With the establishment of the subjectivity of the subject a more fundamental division is established with regard to the world. If for Longinus it is the being of nature itself, φύσις, that has given the human being capacity and capability of using words,[8] so that the rhetor, in speaking, recalls and enacts his relation to 'natural being', φύσις, for Descartes and Kant, *natura* denotes not being itself, and certainly not any notion of φύσις in the Greek sense, but an exterior (and for Kant purely phenomenal) *world*, a world of mere appearances and objects, a manifold whose unity is to be posited speculatively and theoretically with regard to reason. The phenomenal world, unlike that of reason, can never be taken for granted, rather its connection with the being of being human is always in some sense dubitable except insofar as it can be subordinated to reason. At the same time God, as a reality of the same order as mathematical realities, is established interiorly to the mind, so that it is the very basis on which the self-certainty of the subject confirms its indubitability. After Descartes, and above all with Kant, the subject is always constituted by a division between what is interior to the self (the representable, imaginative world constituted by the self-positing of the self, within which realm the self has access to God insofar as there is access to God) and the exterior world. This is the very basis on which the figure of *Brontosaurus* is able to appear at all. The figure of *Brontosaurus* is the unrestricted subject, devoid of attributes, animate, but nakedly so. Every subject, in other words, represents an interior world of representedness whose theoretical rational unity is the basis of correspondence for the of the exterior, 'real' world, a correspondence which requires to be demonstrated and made manifestly transparent.

At the same time, the 'real' world established through the physics of Newton and in accordance with Descartes' notion of *res extensa* is radically transformed in two fundamental ways. In the first place, world is no longer finite, no longer bounded by an outermost limit of all that is therein contained, but is now infinite and infinitely extensible. In the second place it is no longer constituted by place as the first limiting containment of all that there is, where the universe is absolutely differentiated by the up, down, back, front, left right. Now every point in Newtonian space is potentially and absolutely alike to every other, it is differentiated not in itself, but only by virtue of the forces acting upon it – indeed, any such point is only arbitrarily marked out *geometrically*. Thus divinity has no relation to 'place', with respect to the cosmos (divinity can not strictly speaking even be said to have no 'where' in the same sense as required by Aristotle), but exists only with regard to the supersensible.

---

[8] Longinus, *On the Sublime*, §36.1. φύσει δὲ λογικὸν ὁ ἄνθρωπος.

Hence from Descartes onwards, and also in Kant, the divinity of the sublime becomes not what is striven forward and *up* to by the rhetor, but what must be disclosed as *already lying present*, already there in advance of us. This radically transforms what it means to name something. With Longinus, the rhetor has the task of naming anew in each case, not through the selection of the name itself, but through σύνθεσις, through the arranging of what is already known in language to bring forth a new arranging-for-the-sake-of-naming. Speaking, λόγος, has an implicit primary relation to the future. Now, however, whatever is true is so because it *has already been* named, and named as such by God, so that any true speaking corresponds to what has already been said and divinely commanded. In this sense language itself, and its being heard, toward which both rhetor and hearer have to direct themselves with full attention, is transformed, from the striving-ahead-to-be said, to the already-said – and moreover the arranging and placing together of what is to be said falls into the background in favour of *method* which comes to the fore as that which is disclosive of what is to be disclosed as *already to have been* the case.

The re-ordering on which Kant relies is the bringing to the fore of the most general over the particular. This is clearly to be seen from the *Introduction* to the third *Critique*. Kant states: 'A transcendental principle is one through which we represent *a priori* the universal condition under which alone things can become objects of our cognition generally.'[9] This 'universal condition' which is *a priori* is the transformed implicit unity (the ἕν) of being. This condition is now the ever-present 'prior' condition, the condition which in every particular condition (*Bedingung*) is already present as making it possible.

Surely, however, the implicit unity given in the understanding by reason as a temporally prior source of all concepts and on which the selfhood of the self stands, represents no fundamental alteration with regard to the implicit unity of being, a unity now guaranteed by the unity and simplicity of God? Except that Aristotle takes for granted the unity of being as the 'from whence' within which every soul stands out in the same place, the same finite cosmos. The activity of the φαντασία, the capacity for presenting, is a taking-up into a unity that is stood out ahead of us. For Kant, however, the manifold of being lies behind us as a common ground, it has to be demonstrated and

---

[9] Kant, *Kritik der Urteilskraft*, 1990, §V, p. 17. 'Ein transzendentales Prinzip ist dasjenige, durch welches die allgemeine Bedingung a priori vorgestellt wird, unter der allein Dinge Objekte unserer Erkenntnis überhaupt werden können.'

secured, it can no longer be taken for granted. How can I know that the representations of your imaginary direct you towards the same unity as the representations I make for myself? Whereas for Aristotle it is obvious and can be taken for granted that the cosmos is a unity and this unity is in a pre-eminent sense divine, now it is the assertion that God is one and simple that guarantees the unity of every individuated understanding. It becomes possible to see how the moment God is declared to be dead, the basis for the unity of the world is disbanded. This demise, not only of God, but also of world in general, arises only on the basis of having made God the basis of this unity in the first place. From this it becomes possible to see why such exhaustive efforts are made by theologians of a postmodern bent to keep alive the God declared to be dead: they are holding in place the very unity of the world.

Aristotle distinguishes between beauty (τὸ καλὸν) and the fitting (τ'ἀγαθόν) because the fitting is 'the ever-same in actions, but beauty is in the things without motion', that is, in the things that are ἀεί, ever for themselves and have no expression in the realm of appearances and activity, or things (that is τὰ πράγματα).[10] For Kant, however, the opposite is true: beauty is properly to be found in objects, but although objects – even the objects of nature – can point to upliftment and sublimity, 'proper upliftment can be contained in no sensible form, but concerns only the ideas of reason', that is the supersensible.[11] Beauty is the stuff of playful imagination, and is really only a feature of the form of phenomenal, representable things.[12] Upliftment, as the unrepresentable (because the ideas of reason are unrepresentable, strictly speaking) is an altogether more serious affair. Of those who would equate beauty with upliftment, a much greater sobriety will be required.

Kant understands the conditions for the aesthetic judgement through the subject/object distinction. The aesthetic aspect of what is to be known is separated from knowledge as such, or rather the object in its being known is separated from the subjective experience of it. Nevertheless this separation retains a transcendental character. He says that

---

[10] Aristotle, *Metaphysics*, 1078 a 32. τὸ μὲν γὰρ ἀεὶ ἐν πράξει, τὸ δὲ καλόν καὶ ἐν τοῖς ἀκινήτοις.

[11] Kant, *Kritik der Urteilskraft*, 1990, §23, p. 89. 'Das eigentliche Erhabene kann in keiner sinnlichen Form enthalten sein, sondern trifft nur Ideen der Vernunft.'

[12] Kant, *Kritik der Urteilskraft*, 1990, §23, p. 88. 'spielenden Einbildungskraft'.

the attainment of every aim/intention is coupled with a feeling of pleasure. Now where such attainment has for its condition a representation *a priori* – as here a principle for the reflective judgement in general – the feeling of pleasure also is determined by a ground which is *a priori* and valid for everyone: and that too, merely by virtue of the reference of the object to our capacity for cognition.[13]

Nevertheless, the aesthetic retains its strict reference only to the subject-position of subjectivity itself:

That which is purely subjective in the representation of an object, i.e. what constitutes its reference to the subject, not to the object, is its aesthetic quality. On the other hand, that which in such a representation serves, or is available, for the determination of the object (for the purpose of knowledge), is its logical validity.[14]

Through the subject–object distinction Kant attempts simultaneously to make the object stand for itself and to account for our comportment or orientation toward it. However, what is supposed here (especially with regard to his remarks concerning the subjective character of the perception of space in the same section) is the object's both remaining distinct as a universally cognizable thing under the categories, whilst the subjective apprehension of its aesthetic possibilities, although singular, 'rightly claims the agreement of everyone'.[15]

Kant shows how this relates to the sublime: the susceptibility to pleasure in things arises not only on the part of objects in relation to the reflective judgement in the subject, but also from a finality (*Zweckmäßigkeit*) on the part of the subject itself, in accordance with the concept of freedom. This is why the sublime is able to uplift from

---

[13] Kant, *Kritik der Urteilskraft*, 1990, §VI, p. 24. 'Die Erreichung jeder Absicht ist mit dem Gefühle der Lust verbunden; und ist die Bedingung der ersteren eine Vorstellung a priori, wie hier ein Prinzip für die reflektierende Urteilskraft überhaupt, so ist das Gefühl der Lust auch durch einen Grund a priori und für jedermann gültig bestimmt; und zwar bloß durch die Beziehung des Objekts auf das Erkenntnisvermögen.'

[14] Kant, *Kritik der Urteilskraft*, 1990, §VII, p. 26. 'Was an der Vorstellung eines Objekts bloß subjektiv ist, d.i. ihre Beziehung auf das Subjekt, nicht auf den Gegenstand, ausmacht, ist die ästhetische Beschaffenheit derselben; was aber an ihr zur Bestimmung des Gegenstandes (zum Erkenntnisse) dient oder gebraucht werden kann, ist ihre logische Gültigkeit.'

[15] Kant, *Kritik der Urteilskraft*, 1990, §VII, p. 29. 'Mit Recht Anspruch auf jedermanns Bestimmung.'

the realm of experience to the supersensible, and why it retains its reference to divinity (which beauty therefore does not have). Kant argues that this betokens

> not only a finality on the part of objects in their relation to the reflective judgement in the subject, in accordance with the concept of nature, but also, conversely, a finality on the part the subject, answering to the concept of freedom, in respect of the form, or even unform, of objects.[16]

The sublime involves or by its presence provokes the representation of *Unbegrenztheit* – limitlessness. Clayton Crockett attempts to explain this limitlessness, or as he calls it, unboundedness, in terms of the imagination, which he traces to Lyotard.[17] In fact this is incorrect. *Das Erhabene* as upliftment as such is referred to the imagination, but only insofar as it is referred to the interiority of subjectivity. The unlimitedness or boundlessness in question is simply Kant's absolutely correct reinterpretation of ensoulment from the Aristotelian understanding of it being able to abstract for itself the *limitedness* or boundedness of the cosmos (τὸ ἔσχατον) from every being it encounters, to the already-given intuition of the limitlessness of the Newtonian Universe *not* as the fullest and furthest reach of the soul, *but* (because there is no furthest reach that can be attained in an infinite universe) as its inherent *in*capacity to be fulfilled in its ensoulment.

This is why Kant's discussion of the mathematical sublime precedes that of the dynamical sublime. In accord with his statement in the *Introduction* that the universal has to be found for the reflective judgement to be possible – the mathematical sublime is the condition under which the universal can appear and be secured through judgements engendered by particular experiences. In this sense, the dynamical sublime is, strictly speaking, derived from, and only made possible through the mathematical sublime. Indeed, the mathematical sublime is the description in advance that guarantees the generality and universality – in other words the transcendental character – of the judgements that are sublime. In this sense the mathematical sublime both

---

[16] Kant, *Kritik der Urteilskraft*, 1990, §VII, p. 29. 'Nicht allein eine Zweckmäßigkeit der Objekte in Verhältnis auf die reflektierende Urteilskraft, gemäß dem Naturbegriffe, am Subjekt, sondern auch umgekehrt des Subjekts in Ansehung der Gegenstände, ihrer Form, ja selbst ihrer Unform nach, zufolge dem Freiheitsbegriffe.'

[17] Crockett, C., *A Theology of the Sublime*, 2001, p. 71.

replaces place (as it functions in Aristotle) and at the same time represents an intuition of being as such, thought here as being-in-general, being-overall, and therefore that understanding of being derived from the temporal determinations of τέχνη (that is the past) and not from the temporal determinations of the οὗ ἕνεκα, the 'for the sake of which' (the future, as an attainment of the 'ever-same').

The mathematical, as the geometrical, is what can be distributed all the way through the universe in order to make it intelligible – which means, make particular, phenomenal sensations of it available to the unchanging, stable character of reason and reason's ideas. Unlike Aristotelian place, however, which is solely read off the cosmos and worked out from it, in every case the prior geometric possibility of the being of everything is placed into it by the understanding – primarily the understanding of God but secondarily the understanding of man. Sublime appearances in the universe, every sublime representation, because they can only be understood as having arisen out of a prior intention, arise for a purpose and have a finality, a 'towards-which' to which they point. It is because the universe is infinite, and that the subject can make no representation to itself of infinity, that the sublime has a mathematical character, because the infinite is 'representable' only mathematically. The mathematical is therefore the means by which the sublime is thought, or as Kant argues: 'the given infinite, but nevertheless without contradiction, can only be thought in that it is a possibility, which is itself supersensible, which arises in the human heart.'[18] In this sense the sublime is not *a* magnitude or giganticism, but magnitude as such, where the particular representation of an experience (hence the reference to the heart or *Gemüt*) points toward that which, as infinite magnitude, cannot be represented. Kant says that the objects of upliftment are not contained in sensible forms, but concern the ideas of reason, 'which, although no adequate presentation of them is possible, may be excited and called into the mind by that very inadequacy itself which does admit of sensuous presentation'.[19]

The ground of the sublime is one 'merely in ourselves and the attitude of mind that introduces upliftedness into the representation of

---

[18] Kant, *Kritik der Urteilskraft*, 1990, §26, p. 99. 'Das gegebene Unendliche aber dennoch ohne Widerspruch auch nur denken zu können, dazu wird ein Vermögen, das selbst übersinnlich ist, im menschlichen Gemüte erfordert.'

[19] Kant, *Kritik der Urteilskraft*, 1990, §23, p. 89. 'Welche, obgleich keine ihnen angemessene Darstellung möglich ist, eben durch diese Unangemessenheit, welche sich sinnliche darstellen läßt, rege gemacht und ins Gemüt gerufen werden.'

[nature]'.[20] It is for this reason again that it is *first* mathematical, and then only dynamical. The two modes of the sublime belong together with regard to every object that provokes the sublime, insofar as the sublime is itself actually a movement. In both cases the movement takes place through the imagination or power of representing (*Einbildungskraft*), because, formally speaking, it has no concept, but only a subjective reference, and through the faculty of the imagination to the faculty of cognition (*Erkenntnisvermögen*) insofar as it is mathematical and faculty of desire (*Begehrungsvermögen*) insofar as it is dynamical.

The subject continues to appear, or rather continues to be brought before itself *as* itself, in virtue of upliftment: 'this makes it evident that true upliftment must be sought only in the mind of the ones judging, and not in the natural object that occasions this attitude by the judgement formed of it.'[21]

It is from here that Kant proceeds to examine the dynamically sublime. Having established its relation to being-in-general, the sublime is made thematically clear as a particular capacity to bring the subject to the fore as the one who stands in the place of being through having sensuous experience. Kant asserts: 'The claim of an aesthetic judgement to universal validity for every subject, as a judgement, which itself must stand on some a priori principle, requires a deduction.'[22]

The mathematical sublime is the intuition of the perfect and the infinite, to which our own soul, though only able to gain this as an intuition and not as a concept, must nevertheless be conformed. In other words, the upliftment to the place of the divine, to the understanding of being which is and points towards divinity is now the fitting of the dynamical, the *ought*, to the mathematical, the *is in general*, the *is-overall*. The mathematical is the distribution of the prefiguring 'cause' that God is in the being of every being: its precedent (invisible) type or idea makes its particular visibility possible, or rather

---

[20] Kant, *Kritik der Urteilskraft*, 1990, §23, p. 90. 'Bloß in uns und der Denkungsart, die in die Vorstellung der ersteren [Natur] Erhabenheit hineinbringt.'

[21] Kant, *Kritik der Urteilskraft*, 1990, §26, pp. 100f. 'Man sieht hieraus auch, daß die wahre Erhabenheit nur im Gemüte des Urteilenden, nicht in dem Naturobjekte, dessen Beurteilung diese Stimmung desselben veranlaßt, müsse gesucht werden.'

[22] Kant, *Kritik der Urteilskraft*, 1990, §30, pp. 128f. 'Der Anspruch eines ästhetischen Urteils auf allgemeine Gültigkeit für jedes Subjekt bedarf, als ein Urteil, welches sich auf irgendein Prinzip a priori fußen muß, einer Deduktion.'

makes it possible for us to recognize it as having already been laid out
as possible. This means no more than that it makes it possible for us to
represent it to ourselves in its particularity. This understanding of
being, though in no way named as such, nevertheless operates solely
and purely through the separation of the supersensible and the world
of sensible objects of experience.

It is for this reason that Kant can define the sublime as follows:
'Upliftment exists merely in that relation wherein the sensible in the
representation of nature is judged as fit for a possible supersensible
purpose of the same.'[23] What is the force here of the *desselben* – 'of the
same'? This is what in being the same is, in and through upliftment,
demonstrated to have its proper, authentic being in the supersensible,
even though no formal representation of this same is possible. This is
the experience of the persisting identity of what, through the sublime,
makes the particular experience possible and arises from it. Immediately Kant follows his definition of the sublime with a reference to its
connection to 'das Schlechthin Gute' – the absolutely good, τʼ ἀγαθόν,
as what Heidegger calls '*das Taugliche*', the making-serviceable of the
idea of ideas, the very making possible of the manifold through its
inner unrepresentable unity which is at issue here.[24]

A feature of the postmodern discourse of the sublime, particularly
with reference to Kant, and as we have already seen hinted at by
Crockett and Lyotard, is that it represents the 'abyss' or 'crisis' of
representation. George Hartley has written of the 'breakdown of representation',[25] adding 'we are, in Kant's view, discursive animals. The
abyss that threatens to open up and swallow us in our experience of
the sublime is nothing but the abyss of discourse itself.'[26] This is postmodernity's own failure to understand Kant's appeal to the infinite as
a mathematical quantity, albeit one with a negative character, in that
it cannot be represented as a quantity as such. The purpose of this
quantity which can only be experienced as magnitude as such is a
negative self-deprivation of freedom which allows the imagination
(*Einbildungskraft*) to proceed from the 'movement of the heart' – per-

[23] Kant, *Kritik der Urteilskraft*, 1990, §29, p. 113. 'Das Erhabene besteht bloß
in der Relation, worin das Sinnliche in der Vorstellung der Natur für einen
möglichen übersinnlichen Gebrauch desselben als tauglich beurteilt wird.'

[24] Cf. Heidegger, *Schelling: Vom Wesen der Menschlichen Freiheit*, GA42,
1988, pp. 146f. Heidegger discusses what he sees as the unresolved issue of freedom in Kant's thought with respect to the theology of Schelling.

[25] Hartley, G., *The Abyss of Representation: Marxism and the Postmodern
Sublime*, 2003, p. 3.

[26] Hartley, *The Abyss of Representation*, 2003, p. 23.

ception itself – to be an 'instrument of reason and its ideas'.[27] This is a 'power to assert our independence against the influence of nature'.[28] Kant again contrasts upliftment, as something negative, with beauty, which is a (merely) positive quality.[29] What Kant is naming as a power and an instrument is transcendence itself, but as that power and instrument to *negate* beings in favour of being in general, being as God. Upliftment, as the reading-off from beings to being as such *is* a negating. Upliftment is an instrument of the nihilation of beings, and so, insofar as the gulf that he posits between the world of beings and the ideas is achieved through this nihilation, is a kind of annihilation of beings so that the ideas themselves can be 'seen'.

How are we to relate Kant's entirely stable conception of the supersensible and unrepresentable infinite as the basis of representation to the postmodern discourse of crisis and breakdown? Kant's conception of God as the unrepresentable infinite, as the being of beings, is accomplished negatively in the feeling of awe and dread within which the negation of the sublime is accomplished. The entirely psychological basis on which this is usually explained – the exchange that supposedly takes place in the sublime for a kind of pain which is in some sense pleasurable – simply misses the mark. The soul as it negates beings for the sake of being overall *as* the experience which transcends to God (and is a piety and moral good, as Kant explains it) experiences this negation in dread. There is no crisis here, nor any genuine abyss, since for Kant the unrepresentable is at the same time represented to the subject and is the subject's experience of the sublime as a formal category of experience. Crisis enters only when it is taken for granted and in advance that there is *nothing* represented in this unrepresentedness. The question to which we must now turn is how such an unrepresentedness can come to be the attempt to represent not something, but nothing at all.

Far from being the 'crisis' or 'abyss' of representation, the sublime is the means by which the unrepresentable infinite *is* represented. It is what Kant will call the undetermined concept of the supersensible,

---

[27] Kant, *Kritik der Urteilskraft*, 1990, §29, p. 116. 'Bewegung des Gemüts . . . Werkzeug der Vernunft und ihrer Ideen.'

[28] Kant, *Kritik der Urteilskraft*, 1990, §29, p. 116. 'Eine Macht, unsere Unabhängigkeit gegen die Natureinflüsse zu behaupten.'

[29] Kant, *Kritik der Urteilskraft*, 1990, §29, p. 116. 'Das Wohlgefallen am Erhabenen der Natur ist daher auch nur negativ (statt dessen das am Schönen positiv ist).' ('The pleasurable in the upliftment of nature is therefore only negative [whereas that in the beautiful is positive]').

which is the determination of the concept of it – as 'determined' through being *un*determined. In short, the ground of all representation is itself unrepresentable, and can be grasped – and so represented – *as* the infinitely unrepresentable. It is grasped *through* what representation is understood to be, even if it is the *one* representation which is itself unrepresentable. As unrepresentable, it resolves the problem of every particular imaginary imagining the *same* self-identical *inner-concept* which is the purposiveness and making-possible of every concept of representation. Every representation is grounded in the representation of the unrepresentable, and as such is directed toward and *for* every particular subject. How can we not miss the mechanical aspect of this (Kant even speaks here of the principle of the mechanism of nature)?[30] The cinematograph, and the videokinetic is a mechanism entirely predicated on the individual for whom it makes its representations apparent. Baudrillard's understanding of the televisual is correct, not because the videokinetic makes events available for individuals, so much as that a certain understanding of an individual (the subject) to whom things could be addressed became the prevailing understanding of the being of being human at all, and so becomes the basis for individuation of beings. Individuation is of the essence of the visual, cinematographic, and videokinetic.

Kant indicates an almost religious character for upliftment, a character adjunct to any theology he undertakes: the sublime is, in contrast to beauty, and from the standpoint of transcendental philosophy, a 'way in' to God. Kant's understanding of the sublime prepares the ground for the means by which the imagination moves from experience to understanding, as the crossing over of the division of the phenomenal, natural world of representations to the supersensible, and prepares the ground for the discussion of religious experience as such, as a formal category of human being.

The question of religious experience emerges in a quite specific and unusual way. For we could take religious experience as the name for a *region* of experience, so that it might be understood that there are regions of knowledge specific to each of the sciences. Theology, insofar as it is in itself a science, has, therefore, a discourse which yields the foundation for religious experience or knowledge as such. Upliftment, understood like this, becomes the formal category of religious experience, the experience that discloses the being of God.

---

[30] Cf. Kant, *Kritik der Urteilskraft*, 1990, §78, p. 276. 'Das Prinzip des Mechanismus der Natur.'

Which would be to miss the point. Experience, as a fundamentally *metaphysical* way of enquiring into knowledge as such in its ground, determines a quite specific outcome with respect to theology, because of what the sublime and upliftment has held constantly before us since we began, of demonstrating how experience relates to the divine. The conclusion of this trajectory is worked out in two decisive directions by two thinkers in whom this trajectory finds its end. The first of these arises from Hegel's speculative idealism; the second is Nietzsche's will to power.

First, however, it is important to note what is at issue with respect to the experience of the sublime. As an experience that discloses the divinity of the supersensible, religious experience attempts to elaborate, not just any knowledge, but a specific kind of knowledge; or rather it specifies the knowledge into which it enquires as *knowledge in general*, knowledge insofar as it is knowledge. Hegel calls this knowledge *Geist*, a term almost impossible to translate into English, but which means variously, mind, spirit, intellect, religion, depth, culture, and is not exhausted by these. Moreover, even as Aristotle describes the activity of νοῦς as most divine, without change, and 'with itself' for what it thinks, so *Geist* names what for Aristotle is νόησις νοήσεως, the 'thinking of thinking' that divinity is.[31] Aristotle establishes the relationship of human νοῦς to divine νοῦς as that which can 'over a kind of whole'[32] attain to the best, so the self-thinking of itself is carried out through the whole of time as the best or highest in the world.

However Hegel develops his determination of *Geist* entirely in conformity with the understanding of subjectivity that follows from Kant and Descartes, through the consciousness, and this the means self-consciousness, of the *cogito*. 'Religion', he tells us, 'following its concept in general is the consciousness of God, consciousness of absolute essence overall.'[33] Hegel proceeds from here to argue that 'if, therefore, religion grasps itself, then is the content and object of religion itself this whole – the consciousness of itself relating itself to its essence'.[34]

---

[31] Aristotle, *Metaphysics*, 1074 b 15–1075 a 11.
[32] Aristotle, *Metaphysics*, 1075 a 9. ἐν ὅλῳ τινὶ
[33] Hegel, G. W. F., *Vorlesungen über die Philosophie der Religion*, Vol. 3., *Die vollendete Religion*, 1995, p. 178. 'Die Religion nach dem allgemeinen Begriff ist Bewußtsein Gottes, Bewußtsein des absoluten Wesens überhaupt.'
[34] Hegel, *Die vollendete Religion*, 1995, pp. 178f. 'Wenn aber jetzt die Religion sich selbst erfaßt, so ist der Inhalt und der Gegenstand der Religion selbst die Ganze, das sich zu seinem Wesen erhaltende Bewußtsein.'

This is to say '*Geist* is thus the object in religion, and its object, self-knowing essence – is *Geist*'.[35]

Here it is necessary to sound a note of caution. For it can seem to be the most casually efficient matter to trace a genealogy – and what a splendid genealogy it is – from Aristotle (with Plato in the background) through Aquinas to Kant and on now to Hegel, so that in just a few chapters we find we have rehearsed the whole history of metaphysics – as if, one might almost say, we have rehearsed the very ὅλός τις, or kind of a whole, of Aristotle's text – so that the genealogy presents itself with a certain inevitability, a necessity and fitness for the conclusions we might draw from it. Each of the positions I have developed along the way, however, were worked out in their original place and time with the greatest difficulty and seriousness: moreover, the genealogy itself assembles the meaning of these positions: that is to say, in each case what preceded has been taken up by what follows in a *particular* way so that in engaging the origins of the genealogy of νοῦς or upliftment we are also forced by what comes after to be selecting the understanding toward which we tend. In fact we have no guarantee that we have yet penetrated what each of these thinkers was actually drawing out and attending to in his thinking.

Nevertheless, Hegel drives a possibility that lies already present in metaphysics to an extreme height, one might say a pinnacle of sublimity. We see, albeit from the briefest of sketches, that because the experience that we have identified as a topic in Kant is referred to the theological, it concerns the absolutization of knowledge as such. It concerns the way in which absolute *Geist* – νοῦς – is to be taken at the philosophical level as the consciousness of God. At first we hear only the subjective genitive – God's own consciousness of God – absolute essence's self-presence to self. Hegel addresses the cleft in being that we have traced in its various manifestations, fully on the basis of what Aristotle and Aquinas have already indicated as possibilities. Here again, we proceed with caution. It is not that we draw straight lines between the ancients, mediaevals and moderns, but rather that on the way to what it is Hegel seeks to lead us into, something still further has already been laid out as a possibility for him to draw on.

Hegel addresses the cleft in being between presence as such, supersensible and divine, and beings, things present here and now. He seeks to know how there can be the possibility of a passing-over from one to

---

[35] Hegel, *Die vollendete Religion*, 1995, p. 179. 'Der Geist ist so Gegenstand in der Religion, und ihr Gegenstand, das sich wissende Wesen, ist der Geist.'

the other. Here again, it is necessary to recall that Hegel is writing in consequence of an interpretation: a securing of what precedes him. What makes its presence felt and appears for the first time here in this discussion of transcending is what (and this means who) it is that transcends. The nature of the metaphysical question, the very ways in which it proceeds, are at issue here. Metaphysics does not seek personal results: thus we are not interested in *my* transcending, or that it is *my*self that is at issue. Metaphysics seeks the most general ground that makes *my*self possible: the selfhood of self. Metaphysics asks: τί τò ὄv – what is the being, what is it insofar as it *is*. What transcends in its transcending turns out therefore to be the self. However, the self has by the time of Hegel's interpretation itself gained a specific determination. Following Descartes, the self is a *cogito*, an I-think, or rather, as Martin Heidegger points out with respect to Hegel in this matter, a *cogito* which is a *cogito me cogitare* an 'I think me thinking', 'and *must* be that'.[36] In every object towards which I pass over to secure it as the object it is – towards which, therefore, I transcend, there is co-disclosed an 'I think myself'. Heidegger describes this as Hegel's taking-over of Kant's basic position, expressed as 'the original synthetic unity of transcendental apperception – the "I think" which must accompany all my mental representations'.[37]

Religious experience is not an expression of a regional knowledge, but, because the epistemology in question is, as a theological know-ledge, the ground of knowledge as such and self-knowledge of *it*self, religious experience will turn out to be *my* knowledge as *my* transition to self-consciousness *as* the transition (passing-over, *transcendere*) to absolute self-consciousness. Here we see – but have only time to catch a glimpse of it – why for Hegel the reference is constantly to the *inner* character of this transcending, since it is the *I* as the transcendental unity of the self which accomplishes, in passing over, transcending, to its most genuine object, the absolute object of absolute self-hood (egoity), my knowledge as possibility at all of the self-knowing of self, absolute self-knowledge.

How is this accomplished? In his *Lectures on the Philosophy of Religion* of 1824 and 1827 (cited earlier), Hegel traces the develop-

---

[36] Cf. Heidegger, M., *Hegels Phänomenologie des Geistes*, GA32, 1997, p. 194. '*Warum* das so ist und sein *muß*, was man da als Grundtatsache ins Feld führt: cogito = cogito me cogitare.' Emphases in original.
[37] Heidegger, *Hegels Phänomenologie des Geistes*, GA32, 1997, p. 194. 'Die ursprüngliche synthetische Einheit der transzendentalen Apperzeption – das "ich denke", das alle meine Vorstellungen muß begleiten können.'

ment of religion to its becoming absolute religion, which is the religion of absolute *Geist*. Hegel is the one who introduces to philosophy its own historical self-consciousness – which is to say, he understands that truth has a history of its manifestations. After Hegel the danger is that philosophy will be reduced to history – that philosophy becomes simply a succession of competing positions held by different people at different times. This is not what Hegel understands history to be, which is why he discusses history not as a succession, but as an *ascent*. In this sense, although he does not put it like this, history is the historical expression of a continuing striving-forward, a continuing upliftment. This is, if you like, the objective corollary – the exterior effect of the interior, subjective, sublime.

Hegel describes three regions of 'overall' or 'total' *Geist*. The first three are: art, to which belong intuition and the image; religion, to which belong feeling and representation; and philosophy to which belongs pure, free thought. These three can be understood together as 'the *element* of existence of *overall Geist* is in *world-history* spiritual (*geistige*) reality in its entire embrace of inwardness and exteriority'.[38] World-history is the exterior exhibition of the activities of the movement of *Geist* in three spheres: the *penates* – the hearth; in civil society; and the *Geist* of whole peoples. Hegel proposes to accomplish the understanding of *Geist* on the basis of the whole of human history, and at the same time on the basis of the whole of human experience. In this sense he expands the understanding of being to encompass the everything, the all in its widest and most general expression: 'World history, as we know, is thus in general the unfolding of *Geist* in time, as the Idea as nature itself unfolds in space.'[39] In another sense, however, this is in itself a devaluation of God, since world-history includes in its compass religion and so it remains a theology, taken in the philosophical sense. *Geist*, being, God; as the most general and most widely historical is at the same time no more than this, and exhausted by this. Above all, Hegel seeks to return to the understanding of νοῦς developed by Aristotle, both in the *De Anima* and the *De Caelo*.

Is Hegel able to reproduce, under the conditions of subjectivity with

---

[38] Hegel, G. W. F., *Grundlinien der Philosophie des Rechts*, Vol. 7, p. 502. 'Das *Element* des Daseins des *allgemeinen Geistes* . . . ist in der *Weltgeschichte* die geistige Wirklichkeit in ihrem ganzen Umfange von Innerlichkeit und Äußerlichkeit.' Emphases in original.

[39] Hegel, G. W. F., *Vorlesung über die Geschichte der Philosophie*, Vol. 18, pp. 96f. 'Die Weltgeschichte, wissen wir, ist also überhaupt die Auslegung des Geistes in der Zeit, wie die Idee als Natur sich im Raume auslegt.'

its determination of God as ground and so as prior origination of the
subject, the orientation towards the future which characterizes
the understanding of being, and which had disappeared under the
pressure to install God as the origination of time and of all things?
With the term *Aufhebung*, Hegel develops an understanding of the
movement of time as the movement of history. Subjective *Geist* proceeds to realize itself as absolute *Geist* through the striving forward to
the horizon of infinite time. Rauch notes that 'the problematic term
"*Aufhebung*" means not only negation and nullification but also ele-
vation, transcendence, and retention – among numerous other meanings . . . Hegel has *all* of the various and contradictory meanings in
mind' when he uses the term.[40] In fact the various translations Rauch
names here are not contradictory – they exactly correspond to Kant's
description of upliftment, as a movement by means of a kind of negation from the appearance to the understanding. The German term
for the sublime, *das Erhabene* has the same root as the verb *aufheben*,
and the English verb 'heave' (German *heben*), meaning to lift up.
Aufhebung is not simply a taking-away, as it is usually translated by
the term sublation, but a taking away by lifting-off. *Aufhebung* is
simply another name for what upliftment and the sublime also names,
and for what we already discovered in Aristotle: ἀφαίρεσις. Negation
is inherent to this activity.

Aufhebung is the movement that Kant characterized in his discussion of the sublime as marked by a kind of 'terror' or awesomeness,
but now understood primarily as a temporal activity: it is the effacement of the present for the sake of going forward into the future. This
effacement, however, always takes subjectivity for granted: it is the
effacement, therefore, of the present as this present captivates and
seeks to hold back or restrict to the present something that was
already existing, already lying prior (the subject). This freeing from
the present is a freeing for the sake of the future. The subject is shown,
therefore, to hold together the three ecstases of the common conception of time – the past, the present and the future, *as* its progress into
the future.

Hegel therefore indicates the activity of the sublime as the activity of
time itself, but time *as* transcending, the transcending of an already-
existing subject. This means that the description of the activity of
Aufhebung, however closely it mirrors and shadows the descriptions

---
[40] Rauch, Leo, 'Translator's Introduction' to Hegel, G. W. F., *Introduction to
the Philosophy of History*, ed. and trans. Rauch, L., 1988, p. xi.

given especially by Aristotle in the *De Anima* and elsewhere, is nevertheless undertaken in the light of all the transformations that produce and make possible the subjectivity of the subject (which I have traced over the last chapters). Hegel begins his description of this activity by means of the term *Anschauung*. This term is usually translated as 'intuition'. Intuition means, literally, to look upon, to contemplate. The root of the term, *schau-* indicates that what is at issue is a showing of something. An *Anschein* is an appearance, but above all a visual appearance. Intuition, *Anschauung*, is what appears in the means by which the φάντασμα, the appearance (as predominantly a visual appearance) is taken *in* for a subject and represented to itself. Perception, αἴσθησις, is now more than anything an onlooking, as a means and process of visualization. So Hegel says:

> the intuition as primarily and immediately a something given, and that spatially, acquires, in as much as it is comes to be rendered as a sign, the essential determination of existing only as a thing lifted up and off (*aufgehobene*). Such is the negativity of intelligence.[41]

This is exactly the negative of the sublime as named by Kant.[42] In pressing upliftment into service for a description of the phenomenon of time, Hegel transforms Kant's understanding of the sublime as the *exceptional* moment of transcendence to return it to the very activity of transcending as the temporality of the being of being human itself. Hegel in doing this returns to an understanding of temporality as becoming, which is then contrasted in every way with absolute being as the self-identical, without motion and eternal. Central in this is the role of representation (*Vorstellung*). This is the 'reading off' of the image of the phenomenon (the appearance) from the exterior into the interior, *as* the activity of subjectivity itself. The image is taken in to the subjectivity of the subject by means of intuition, but 'the image no longer has the complete determinedness which the intuition has, and is arbitrary or contingent, generally isolated from external place, time and the immediate connections in which it stands'.[43] It is because the

---

[41] Hegel, G. W. F., *Enzyklopädie der philosophischen Wissenschaften im Grundrisse*, Vol. 10, p. 270. 'Die Anschauung, als unmittelbar zunächst ein Gegebenes und Räumliches, erhält, insofern sie zu einem Zeichen gebraucht wird, die wesentliche Bestimmung, nur als aufgehobene zu sein. Die Intelligenz ist diese ihre Negativität.'

[42] See p. 183 above.

[43] Hegel, *Enzyklopädie*, Vol. 10, pp. 257f. 'Das Bild hat nicht mehr die vollständige Bestimmtheit, welche die Anschauung hat, und ist willkürlich oder

psyche is able to lift-off the image from intuition for itself and without respect to context that the power for representing, the imagination (*Einbildungskraft*), assumes a life of its own in memory and recollection, leading to the 'reproductive imagination',[44] and pure fantasy, the completion and fulfilment of self-intuition (*Selbstanschauung*), a self-existing of intelligence which denotes a purely pictorial or imaginary existence: 'This imaging of [intelligence's] self-intuition is subjective, the moment of existence is yet lacking.'[45]

Again, Hegel follows Aristotle's description of the activity of the soul closely – so that the moment of thinking αὐτός – for itself – is described here, only in terms transformed in the light of the appearance of the subject. Whereas Aristotle takes for granted that the moment of self-thinking is an attainment to a being that is futural, lies ahead and wherein the soul comes into the universality and atemporality of νοῦς itself, as the thinking on thinking which is most divine and already-being, this is no longer possible for Hegel, since being as such is determined in advance, as prior (underlying) being and subjectivity. The interior movement of time, therefore, the lifting-off of the φαντάσματα as the going-forth of the subjectivity of the subject results not in an attainment to an atemporal stasis, the full, stable static contemplation of being as the ever-same, but in a synthesis which has as its object something lying ahead of me, in the future. Time no longer attains to rest as the cessation of itself, now time always proceeds ahead of itself in infinite succession. Moreover this is a *process*, the very method and activity of the self-realization of the subject's self-uniting with absolute subjectivity. Thus fantasy (*Phantasie*, φαντασία)[46] does not read-off-up to a completion and fulfilment for the sake of the already-is ahead of it and which is to be attained, but 'phantasy is a mid-point, in which the universal and being, one's own and the being-discovered, the inner and outer are completely produced as one'.[47] This is synthesis itself, a moment in which the subjectivity of

---

zufällig, überhaupt isoliert von dem äußerlichen Orte, der Zeit und dem unmittelbaren Zusammenhang, in dem sie stand.'

[44] Hegel, *Enzyklopädie*, Vol. 10, p. 261. 'reproduktive Einbildungskraft'

[45] Hegel, *Enzyklopädie*, Vol. 10, p. 266. 'Dies Gebilde ihres Selbstanschauens ist subjektiv; das Moment des Seienden fehlt noch.'

[46] Greek φαντασία is directly intended, hence the switch in terms from *Einbildungskraft* to *Phantasie*.

[47] Hegel, *Enzyklopädie*, Vol. 10, p. 267. 'Die Phantasie ist der Mittelpunkt, in welchem das Allgemeine und das Sein, das Eigene und das Gefundensein, das Innere und Äußere vollkommen in eins geschaffen sind.'

the subject then produces – as reason itself – itself as a thing.[48] This thing which is self-produced, is the basis on which other things may then come to be.

Insofar as this is a mere description of the subjectivity of the subject, how is it possible to understand this as a theology, or has the theology that Kant suggested was his understanding of this as a transcendence been effaced from it? Why should any question concerning God intrude here? To answer this question it is necessary to understand how Hegel reinterprets the distinction that Kant enforces between mathematical and dynamical upliftment. Hegel, in his reading of Aristotle, seeks to demonstrate the original unity of these two modes of upliftment or the sublime. As the original unity of these two, Hegel seeks the 'one' that lies behind this division or separation. In this Hegel is seeking to remain faithful to a fundamental insight of Aristotle's, Hegel is seeking out the inner unity of being as the origin and princi- ple of difference itself. He opposes himself, therefore, to Kant and Descartes, both of whom make the totality of being (the being of God, and in Kant's case the unrepresentable object of upliftment) mathe- matically determinable. In the *Phänomenologie*, Hegel distinguishes between that branch of mathematics which deals with time – 'applied' mathematics – over against immanent, or pure, mathematics. It is this mathematics that is at issue metaphysically, and he says it does not set time as time over against space.[49] No further explanation is given in the *Phänomenologie* to tell us why this distinction is necessary.

Immanent, pure, mathematics as Hegel describes is at the same time the geometrical as both Descartes and Kant understood it. Which is why in the *Enzyklopädie* Hegel repeats this same point with respect to the relation between space and time, but this time explicitly describing the mathematical by arguing that 'knowledge of space, of geometry, does not stand over against a separate knowledge of time'.[50]

In accepting as the basis of subjectivity the distinction between 'inner' and 'outer' which both Kant and Descartes take for granted, Hegel strives to recover the original unity of these two. This inner

---

[48] Hegel, *Enzyklopädie*, Vol. 10, p. 267. 'Die Intelligenz sich seiend, sich zur Sache mache.' ('Intelligence makes itself exist as a thing.')

[49] Hegel, *Phänomenologie des Geistes*, Vol. 3, p. 44. 'Die immanente, soge- nannte reine Mathematik stellt auch nicht die Zeit als Zeit dem Raume gegenüber.' ('Immanent, so-called pure, mathematics does not itself set time as time over against space.')

[50] Hegel, *Enzyklopädie*, Vol. 9, p. 51, §259. 'Der *Wissenschaft des Raums*, der *Geometrie*, steht keine solche *Wissenschaft der Zeit* gegenüber.' Emphases in original.

unity will turn out to be a theology in exactly the same way as every resolution of the highest science we have examined has turned out at the same time to be a theology. If everything subjective achieves its relation to being through its exteriorization, then the mathematical, as the demonstration of the immanent belonging to being, must be accomplished through a unity that is even prior to this through its exteriorization. The exteriorization is at the same time the means by which the temporal becomes the historical, as the way in which human existence, in its *negative* temporalizing as a reading-off of the immanent meaning from the immediate, 'natural' world (φύσις), unites itself to the positive accomplishment of the inner meaning of that temporalization through accomplishing a *geistige* – intellectual, spiritual and religious – union with the end-point of external being. The exteriority we are seeking is therefore not spatial, not in the everyday world, because this externality is simply a dead thing which the understanding paralyses, and whose negativity is reduced to the 'one', the 'unit' of mathematical abstraction:

> This dead unit, now the highest externality of thought, can be used to form external combinations, and these combinations, the figures of arithmetic, can in turn be organised by the determination of the understanding for equality and inequality, identity and difference.[51]

The 1817 edition adds: 'The science which has unity as its principle is therefore constituted in opposition to geometry.'[52]

The science that is the principle of unity itself is being, which, as the science that is not dead, is the science of life itself (that is σῴζειν, preserving *in* life), and which as eternal is without time, and as the idea, is without space. Hegel seeks an exteriorization that is beyond the mere exteriority of world, the exteriorization of immanence. This is the transcendent science – the knowing or science of being, which is not arrived at as the process of upliftment, because it is what makes upliftment possible at all.

The transition from the interiority of subjectivity to the exteriorization of absolute being is at the same time the transition from inner, subjective time (which has a fundamentally negative aspect, it reads-

---

[51] Hegel, *Enzyklopädie*, Vol. 9, p. 51, §259. 'Dies tote Eins, die höchste Äußerlichkeit des Gedankens, ist der äußerlichen Kombination, und diese Kombinationen, die Figuren der Arithmetik, sind wieder der Verstandesbestimmung nach Gleichheit und Ungleichheit, der Identifizierung und des Unterscheidens fähig.'
[52] Hegel, *Enzyklopädie der philosophischen Wissenschaften im Grundrisse*, 1817, §202, p. 137. 'Zur Geometrie macht daher die Wissenschaft die das Eins zum Prinzip hat, die gegenüberstehende aus.'

off imaginatively from the phenomena in order to understand them, and this means to understand beings in their being) to absolute time, which is historical time, whose principle is eternity. Hegel seeks by this to overcome the restriction of the subject to the *a priori*, its restriction to its originary temporal first cause, by demonstrating that the temporal prior cause which is enacted in every act of knowledge is at the same time constituted by the goal of time, its end – the teleology of historical time. Historical time, as the exteriorization of not only the fact but also the meaning of subjective time, is at the same time the 'for the sake of which', the final cause of the subject. Every instant, every particular enactment of inner, subjective, time – fundamentally negative in character – is at the same time the enactment of the goal and end of history itself.

The moment or point of negation, is therefore and at the same time, correctly to be understood as *Aufhebung*, as transcendence; the moment at which the indeterminate, infinite horizon of the eternal as the goal of history appears and manifests itself. Every epoch at the same time manifests a relation to this goal. It is for this reason that Hegel is able to analyse history in terms of successive development to something higher, to a constant point beyond itself which is at the same time the point of its genuine realization. Finitude and timeliness is marked by its struggle for the infinite. However, although this attempts to return to an understanding that Hegel believed already to be present in Aristotle, everything is transformed by what has preceded Hegel and intervened between him and Aristotle. In the first place, the numerical has given way to the geometrical as the science of mathematics. Hegel does not explain how the geometrical gives rise to the unit, when in fact for Aristotle it gives rise only to the point (στιγμή). The unit belonged for Aristotle strictly to number and not to geometry at all. In the second place, being is now characterized, not as for Aristotle, finite, but as infinite. In this sense even eternity has undergone transformation – from Aristotle's understanding as that to which the outermost attains, to that which is realized in every moment, at every point, but realized as fundamentally unattainable.

It is this unattainability that understands the whole of history as a constant development and upliftment, as a progress. It is here that Hegel analyses the manifestation of the eternal as an historical process whose totality and finality is constantly posited, in ever higher ways. The last transition to this finality becoming manifest is the religion of sublimity (*Erhabenheit*), Jewish religion. Here the means of the transition is described and carried out. He notes that 'the infinite subject in itself (that is God) one cannot name as sublime; it is the absolute in and for itself, it is holy. Sublimity is only the appearing, [the] relating, of this infinite subject to the world.'[53] This is to be understood in the following way: 'The veritable manifestation of God in the world is, however, the absolute, eternal . . . manifestation.'[54] Eternity – absolute self-consciousness as absolute *Geist* – is to be *seen*, it becomes *visible*. The essence of this possibility is movement as such.

Why can this not be a regional kind of knowledge – why is it that for Hegel all experience is now transformed into religious experience, as the self passes over – transcends – to the absolute transcendent, God, *Geist* as such? This question asks: 'why must all experience take place over against, and as a transition, a passageway, through to an *apocalyptic* horizon?' Precisely and absolutely because the true object of this phenomenology is the *self*, such that the *I* as *cogito* is now radicalized because it can be no other than *cogito me cogitare*. That is to say, because the ground of all objectliness must be resolved *as* and *in* the ground of absolute subjectivity. Because we are seeking the ground of the knowing of knowing, and the only basis we have for the pursuit of that ground is what *knows*, then what knows in its becoming, in its coming into absolute self-knowledge (that is, every attempt to establish absolute knowledge as a mere region of knowing) will immediately be sublated to a more general, more absolute ground of knowledge. It is this ineluctable tendency to which Heidegger gives, for the first time in his lectures on Hegel in 1930, first the name of *ontotheology*, a name that persists in his later work, and then by way of illustration, and in these lectures alone, the name of the onto-ego-theo-logical.[55]

What kind of movement is the *transcendens*? Here we should take note of an important observation of Heidegger's: '*Self-consciousness is only a passageway*. It is still something relative within infinity, whose full truth is to be grasped in the concept.'[56] The question will be:

---

[53] Hegel, *Vorlesungen über die Philosophie der Religion*, Vol. 2, *Die bestimmte Religion*, 1985, p. 569. 'Das unendliche Subjekt in sich kann man nicht erhaben nennen; es ist das absolute an und für sich, es ist heilig. Die Erhabenheit ist erst die Erscheinung, Beziehung dieses unendlichen Subjekts auf die Welt.'

[54] Hegel, *Die bestimmte Religion*, p. 569. 'Die wahrhafte Manifestation Gottes an der Welt ist aber die absolute, ewige . . . Manifestation.'

[55] Cf. Heidegger, *Hegels Phänomenologie des Geistes*, GA32, 1997, pp. 140–44; p. 183.

[56] Heidegger, *Hegels Phänomenologie des Geistes*, GA32, 1997, p. 195. '*Das Selbstbewußtsein ist nur ein Durchgang. Es ist selbst noch ein Relatives innerhalb der Unendlichkeit, die in ihrer vollen Wahrheit im Begriff ergriffen werden soll.*' Emphasis in original.

a passageway for movement in which direction? Do we proceed down the passageway (*are* we this proceeding), or does something proceed toward us, or is there traffic in both ways?

We should in the first instance be clear: Hegel is well aware that the kind of movement he is enquiring into already has been enquired into before and repeatedly in the history of philosophy. For this reason Heidegger describes Hegel's Jena manuscripts of his philosophy of nature as 'nothing other than a speculative paraphrase of Aristotelian physics'.[57] We need to clarify why it is that Hegel calls his principal work a *phenomenology* of *Geist*. We see that the proper object of the enquiry is the self, but the self taken in a particular way. Thus what appears, the phenomenon, is not what actually *is* but rather what indicates the being of something else: it is the *being* of the absolute concept, of absolute self-consciousness for itself. The appearances constantly indicate and make apparent something which, in not appearing, is yet more real. What appears does so for the sake of making manifest something that it itself is not, that is to say something that is other than itself, whilst at the same time manifesting what it is not in virtue of what lies already *in* what is not, as what *is really to be seen*. This is a phenomenology only insofar as it makes what the self in its self-appearing appears *for*, which is the immutable and permanently self-subsisting, the absolute concept as such, being. Hegel says that 'being no longer has the significance of the abstraction of being'[58] but as 'rest [is] of itself as absolute-restless infinitude' where the 'differentiation of movement is resolved . . . the simple essence of time which in its itself-self-sameness has the pure form of space'.[59] Why does time appear here? Because as the pure, eternal, absolute it has no time, but *as* time, gives time to the appearances. It is the condition for the differentiation that movement *is* itself. It is what allows the passageway to be a passageway. Thus the movement in question turns out at the same time to be the movement of all phenomenal (that is appearing) things, and the movement which the self actually knows and in some sense also *is*.

We are accustomed to understand Hegel as an up-building, a constructive straining forward for an infinite horizon. This understanding

---

[57] Heidegger, *Hegels Phänomenologie des Geistes*, p. 176. 'Nicht anders . . . als eine spekulative Paraphrase der Aristotelischen Physik.'

[58] Hegel, *Phänomenologie des Geistes*, GA32, 1997, Vol. 3, p. 139. 'Das Sein hat nicht mehr die Bedeutung der Abstraktion des Seins.'

[59] Hegel, *Phänomenologie des Geistes*, GA32, 1997, Vol. 3, pp. 139f. 'Die Ruhe ihrer selbst als absolut unruhigen Unendlichkeit . . . [ist] das einfache Wesen der Zeit, das in dieser Sichselbstgleichheit die gediegene Gestalt des Raumes hat.'

is entirely correct, when viewed from the perspective of the subject, the *I*. Here, however, we see that what in fact allows the striving straining-forth, the constructive activity of the dialectic to undertake the work of becoming is the way that motion unfolds not as a forward-moving, but as it were, *backwards* so that the phenomenal appearances disclose something which is already-there, already present, and so strictly speaking *past*, and yet which have to be driven-towards in order to enter the understanding. The driving-forth that is the self proceeding from consciousness into self-consciousness is the proceeding forwards down this passageway of the *transcendens*. In fact, however, the proceeding forwards is towards, and in synthesis of, the making-apparent of what is already there, being *as* the absolute concept. In this sense the synthetizing processes of sublation – of upliftment (but keeping ahead of ourselves all the time that this is a drive to *negate* whatever appears in its appearing) – these processes, therefore, appear to *proceed*, but actually operate in the manner of *receipt*, that is, they operate backwards. The essential structure of the motion is circular – which is why it is possible for the direction of the motion to be mistaken: it only *appears* to be a forward motion in becoming, it *really is* a backward motion in making becoming, the appearability of what as appearance is only appearance *for*, appearance *of*, which is ever-unchangeable being as such.

This is properly and strictly in accord with the peculiar temporal structure of the *cogito* which Descartes develops in the *Meditationes* and which I examined earlier. The *cogito* secures itself as finite substance *against* what it doubts, and then proceeds to secure itself upon what is already *infinitely* there, and so already lying present. Thought, for Descartes and for Hegel, stretches forward to discover and so disclose – which means give appearance to, allow to appear phenomenally – what is already *prior* in its presence: God. It is for this reason that Heidegger is able to say with absolute correctness that 'for Hegel the formerly, the *past*, constitutes the essence of time' and 'for Hegel being (infinity) is also the essence of time'.[60]

Central in this discussion for Hegel is the question of morality. The question of the fitting of the 'ought' to the 'is' in actions is raised by the inherent freedom of the heteronomy of nature, independent of self. The heteronomy of nature as a demand, a postulate, is succeeded by its

---

[60] Heidegger, *Hegels Phänomenologie des Geistes*, GA32, 1997, p. 211. 'Daß für Hegel das Ehemals, d.h. die *Vergangenheit* das Wesen der Zeit ausmacht . . . [für] *Hegel* – das Sein (Unendlichkeit) ist auch das Wesen der Zeit.' Emphases in original.

resolution as the demand (the postulate) to harmonize morality and the sensuous willing: the two, first as implicit being, the second as being-for-self are connected by what is to be done: conduct as such. Again it would be possible to see this as a striving forward to attain something, but this is only partly true, or rather this is only the move from consciousness to absolute self-consciousness. The striving-forward is to attain something already present, and it is for this reason that Hegel calls it a 'demand of reason' which is secured as an 'imme-diate certainty and presupposition'.[61] The imperative *ought*, the demand of morality, makes present what already 'really' *is*.

In Hegel we have announced an outermost, apocalyptic, horizon – apocalyptic because it is disclosive (ἀποκαλύπτειν – literally, to take the cover off) and because it is absolutely disclosive, or rather, disclo-sive of the absolutely, eternally infinite, through what appears finitely and temporally. This disclosure takes place through experience as such. Experience therefore discloses what is most without motion (ἀκίνετον), eternal, and so without ceasing or death (ἀθάνατον), what is without limit and so infinite, whose purpose is to be this disclosure. Purpose refers directly to that which lies present as already-present, already lying present to be disclosed. At the same time this disclosure takes place as a theological knowing. Theological knowing turns out to be, however, absolute knowing, the knowing of knowing itself. This knowing, however, turns out to be the very same thing as the science of being insofar as it is being – first philosophy, being, insofar as it is being: ontology. Experience is, as truthfully disclosive, the being-still in its motion, and so in time. We uncover this being-still, the eternal, the essence of time, as knowledge – consciousness – which turns into self-consciousness as such.

All of this is secured – as an interpretation of νοῦς, *Geist* – on the basis of an interpretation of the Cartesian *cogito* and Kant's trans-cendental unity of apperception. In other words Hegel secures this interpretation strictly in the light of the modern self, the subject. The contemporary drive for the accomplishment of analogy at the onto-logical level, that is to say the analogy of being or *analogia entis*, is in fact nothing other than the constant drive of contemporary theology to reinvoke and reperform the interpretation of absolute *Geist* that Hegel undertakes, and to reunite Hegel's triumphant theological aesthetics with the one remaining passageway in to the being of beings

---

[61] Hegel, *Phänomenologie des Geistes*, Vol. 3, p. 344. 'Er ist eine Forderung der Vernunft, oder unmittelbare Gewißheit und Voraussetzung derselben.'

which we identified as having been left open by Aquinas, namely the *analogia entis*. The German Jesuit Erich Przywara elaborates in fact for the first time the *analogia entis* as a formal principle,[62] which is to say, he carries out a formal transformation of the *analogia entis* on the basis of the Cartesian self. Przywara concludes his 1932 work *Analogia Entis* with the dramatic claim 'we have therefore also discovered the *analogia* as a principle in the *cogito*'.[63]

How could Przywara have discovered otherwise! The *cogito* only becomes possible on the basis of the impasse that analogy is! Przywara carries out this 'discovery' on the basis of an explicit interpretation of *Geist* and νόησις, such that the *cogito* is understood in each intentional act, not as the eternal unchangeable truth *already in* the *cogito*, but as the 'in-over [that is the *transcendens*] of the becoming-character of creaturely interdependence of consciousness and being'.[64] The proof text supplied for this is from Aquinas's *Expositio ex Librii Boëtii*. In fact what Przywara attempts to demonstrate is the *transcendens* exactly on the basis that Hegel makes possible in his interpretation of Aristotle and Kant. It should be stressed here that Aquinas is brought in *after the fact*, that is to say, after the fundamental metaphysical interpretation has been secured. Hegel's recovery of the orientation toward the future turns out to be no less ambiguous than Aristotle's striving forward for the 'already-is'. At the same time, Hegel's attempt to overcome the cleft in being ends up reinforcing the separation between absolute being and beings.

---

[62] Cf. von Balthasar, H. U., *Karl Barth: Darstellung und Deutung seiner Theologie*, 1962, pp. 44f. Here von Balthasar attributes its development into a formal principle to Przywara and that Przywara was the first to elevate the *analogia entis* as 'die Formalisierung des Analogieprinzips zu einer Art Schlüssel des Katholischen überhaupt'.

[63] Przywara, SJ, E., *Analogia Entis: Metaphysik: Ur-Struktur und All-Rhythmus*, 1962 (1932), p. 208. '. . . haben wir denn auch die *analogia* als Prinzip im *cogito* vorgefunden.'

[64] Przywara, *Analogia Entis*, 1962, p. 208. 'In-über der Werdehaftigkeit des kreatürlichen Zueinander von Bewußtsein und Sein.'

9

Devaluing God

If in the last chapter I considered how Hegel represents the first of two decisive directions possible for metaphysics, the second is also secured on the basis of a metaphysical interpretation of the self – indeed it will further help us to understand that metaphysics after Descartes is nothing other than a certain kind of taking for granted of the structure of the self. If it is easy to see how contemporary theology has pursued and investigated the direction laid out by Hegel, nevertheless (and overwhelmingly) contemporary theology has also traced the contours and itself been produced by the other direction, the other possibility that lies present in metaphysics. Why should there only be two? Surely we modern pluralists should allow the possibility for not just two, but many? Why must we say Hegel *or* Nietzsche? Except, insofar as Hegel lays out *one* distinct possibility – the triumph of the *one*, the *summum ens* as the triumph of the uplifted subject of the sublime, so Nietzsche, as laying out and describing the destruction of the deification of the transcendental subject describes the many counterposed to the one – he is the one who stands against the other – the one whose dissolution of unity stands over against the oneness of unity itself. Isn't that what being many is? There need only be one other for the many to be othered to the one. If Hegel shows how the one is the triumph of transcendental subjectivity, Nietzsche shows how each one is itself achieved by a triumph of the subjective will – many ones make many. It takes only one more than one to indicate this.

If Hegel presents us with an essential structure of the making-possible of the appearance of truth secured on the self, the position equally secured on the self that proceeds in the opposite direction is that of Nietzsche. Here we should consider Nietzsche's claim that 'truth is the type of error without which a certain type of living essence might not live. The value for life at the last decides.'[1] We should note

---

[1] Nietzsche, F., *Nachlaß 1884–1885*, 1988, Vol. 11, p. 506. (Cf. Nietzsche, F., *Der Wille zur Macht*, ed. Gast, P., 1996 [1906], p. 343, §493.) 'Wahrheit ist die

in passing Nietzsche's identical use of the word 'life' to Hegel's. Hegel's science which stands in opposition to the mathematical and geometrical is above all a science of life, such that he also claims 'pure life is being',[2] and with the same root, Greek ζῶη, so that Nietzsche is describing something *in opposition to Hegel* and at the same time secured on the same basis. If Hegel announces the triumph of being itself, Nietzsche strives to show how becoming is the basis for every being. That living thing which is concerned both with being and becoming is denoted by the term *Wesen*, an essence. Nietzsche strives to secure everything on the basis of the will to power, including the self. Because every particular representation denies or stands against becoming, because it is a *fixing* of being, so every representation of being seeks to bring it to a standing fixedness in the *face* of becoming. Here, therefore, is Nietzsche's own understanding of the tension between representation and the unrepresentedness of Kant's understanding of upliftment: every actual representation is wrested as a necessary error from the unrepresentability of becoming: it is the securing by means of a valuation of becoming itself. In his lectures on Nietzsche, Heidegger notes that 'the true and maintained as existent is, in representation thereby – when measured against the real as the becoming – essentially in error'.[3]

What does it mean that Nietzsche seeks to secure the self on the basis of the will to power? In the first instance Nietzsche reinterprets the method of doubt in the light of his own doctrine of appearances – locating, as an irony *against* Descartes that Descartes discovers in the inherent deceitfulness of things the drive and will to secure the self against the '*de omnibus dubitare*'. Thus the form of the will to power is a ' "will to truth" as "I will not be deceived" or "I will not deceive" or "I will convince myself and hold fast" '.[4] The word 'form' here must be understood as essential – in each case the form that the self takes is an '*ich will*'. More than this is being said, however: the form of the self

---

Art von Irrthum, ohne welche eine bestimmte Art von lebendigen Wesen nicht leben könnte. Der Werth für das Leben entscheidet zuletzt.'

[2] Hegel, G. W. F., *Der Geist des Christentums* in *Frühe Schriften*, Vol. 1, p. 370. 'Reines Leben ist Sein.' Cited from an earlier edition by Heidegger, M., in *Hegels Phänomenologie des Geistes*, GA32, 1997 (1988), p. 206.

[3] Heidegger, M., *Der europäische Nihilismus*, GA48, 1986, p. 245. 'Das Wahre und im Vorstellen für seiend Gehaltene ist daher, am Wirklichen als dem Werdenden gemessen, wesenhaft irrig.'

[4] Nietzsche, *Nachlaß 1884–1885*, Vol. 11, p. 624. ' "Wille zur Wahrheit" als "ich will nicht betrogen werden" oder "ich will nicht betrügen" oder "ich will mich überzeugen und fest werden", als Form des Willens zur Macht.'

– of the body – is, as Nietzsche is fully aware, the soul. Therefore the form of the *ich will* is itself the activity of the body, it is the body's drive to become a singularity, a unite one, a μονάς. This is the irony against Descartes, which he archly paraphrases: 'Descartes says "I have maintained many things as true which I now see as error".'[5] In other words, Descartes seeks a permanent, stable, rational securing of the I-think in the being of its being (its soul), against the activity of me-thinking, the becoming, and so movement of the body. It is the securing of a permanent, unchanging *idea* in reason which Nietzsche opposes, and so he pursues the inner meaning of the *cogito* against what he calls Descartes' 'rulership of reason'.[6]

This driving together of God, being, and the one is replaced, for Nietzsche and thereafter, by a driving together for its own sake of the unitary singularity of the self, attained *over against* every other one. The will, as the triumph of the will to power, is now its own production, the object of its own manufacture. On what does the will stand, what ground does it rise up from? Nietzsche concludes his aphorism against the *one* of consciousness by saying 'the phenomenon of the body is the richer, clearer, more tangible phenomenon: methodically to be brought out and placed first (*voranzustellen*), without closing off anything concerning its final meaning'.[7] Methodically means here, with reference to Descartes, that the *ego cogito* is to be attained on the basis not of the body itself, but on the *phenomenon* of the body, on its appearing. This is not a *mere* appearance, this is the most secure appearance on which anything can be secured, the triumph of Descartes' struggle for certainty as at the same time the vanquishing of Descartes himself! It is for this reason that the figure of *Brontosaurus* is naked – this is the basis on which our self-evident self-association with the figure is brought to the fore *methodically*, which means, for the sake of every other construction to be placed upon it. Moreover, it is a body that moves; it is not conscious – *Bewußtsein*, but becoming-conscious – *Bewußtwerden*.[8] As cogitating, it is agitated: movement is intrinsic to its appearing (it is without rest).

---

[5] Nietzsche, *Nachlaß 1885–1887*, Vol. 12, p. 262. 'Descartes sagt "ich habe Vieles für wahr gehalten, dessen Irrthum ich jetzt einsehe".'
[6] Nietzsche, *Nachlaß 1885–1887*, Vol. 12, p. 440. 'Descartes, Herrschaft der Vernunft.'
[7] Nietzsche, *Nachlaß 1885–1887*, Vol. 12, pp. 204f. 'Das Phänomen des Leibes ist das reichere, deutlichere, faßbarere Phänomen: methodisch voranzustellen, ohne etwas auszumachen über seine letzte Bedeutung.'
[8] Cf. Nietzsche, *Nachlaß 1885–1887*, Vol. 12, p. 295. '*Princip des Lebens.*'

As a becoming, it is something to be attained-to, so that even the unity of the self is an attainment, something over which the will can rise up to command. The prior existence of the self in every 'I-think' arises out of the abandonment of soul and being: 'If we relinquish the soul, "the subject", then the precondition for a "substance" in general disappears. One acquires grades of being, one sheds being' [that is as such].[9] The result of all this is that the ' "subject" is the fiction that many similar states in us are the effect of the one substrate: but we have first created the "similarity" of these states'.[10] As a created fiction this is nothing other than a work of art. Every work of art is at the same time, therefore, the production of a subject: every subject is a self-productive artwork. Nothing can become without being fictive – all becoming is the willed drive into power. The unity of subjectivity is an attainment – at the same time its unity is an indication that it *can* be multiple, and that it is abstracted from the manifold. Nietzsche comments that 'the presumption of the singular subject is perhaps not necessary; perhaps it is just as much permissible to assume a multiplicity of subjects': here is the very multiplicity to be counterposed to Hegel: the same body may exhibit (exactly as Žižek suggested, see Chapter 2) a *multiplicity* of subjects.[11] The multiplicity of subjects, unified in the body and extensible from the body is the *necessity* of the subject as endlessly reproducible artwork, the abolition of the unity of substance itself.

With the abolition of the unity of substance, comes the willed death of God. The securing of the body, and the securing of this body as the basis for the multiple representations of subjectivity *is* the same as the death of God. What is the effect of Nietzsche's interpretation of the self both in the light of and *against* Descartes? He describes it (as we have noted) as: 'The refuting of God, particularly only the moral God is refuted'.[12] God, as the most stable, permanent, highest *being*,

---

[9] Nietzsche, F., *Nachlaß 1885–1887*, Vol. 12, p. 465. 'Geben wir die Seele, "das Subjekt" preis, so fehlt die Voraussetzung für eine "Substanz" überhaupt. Man bekommt Grade des Seienden, man verliert das Seiende.'

[10] Nietzsche, *Nachlaß 1885–1887*, Vol. 12, p. 465. ' "Subjekt" ist die Fiktion, als ob viele gleiche Zustände an uns die Wirkung Eines Substrats wären: aber wir haben erst die "Gleichheit" dieser Zustände geschaffen'.

[11] Nietzsche, *Nachlaß 1884–1885*, Vol. 11, p. 650. 'Die Annahme des Einen Subjekts ist vielleicht nicht nothwendig; vielleicht ist es ebensogut erlaubt, eine Vielheit von Subjekten anzunehmen.'

[12] Nietzsche, *Nachlaß 1884–1885*, Vol. 11, p. 624. 'Die Widerlegung Gottes, eigentlich ist nur der moralische Gott widerlegt.' See also *Nachlaß 1885–1887*, Vol. 11, p. 624, quoted on p. 149 above.

thus as highest value, substance (*substantia infinita*) being *as such*, is the 'error' most to be overcome: the death of God is therefore to be proclaimed for the sake of undoing the stability of being for the sake of becoming, for the sake of the triumph of the *ego volo*, '*ich will*' as the genuine expression of *ego cogito*. This is the devaluing of God.

The death of God is, therefore, a metaphysical securing of the self in a particular way *over* the concept of substance. Nietzsche's notebook of Autumn 1887 announces 'the substance concept is a result of the subject-concept, not the other way around'.[13] The subject-concept, as the concept of God, is therefore to be overcome, as the devaluation of the highest value and the revaluation of all values. It is for this that the meaning of man is to be transformed from *substantia finita* into *over-man* (Übermensch). The over, *über*, refers to transcendence as Nietzsche now wishes to secure it: the *über* is the *transcendens* as such. In this sense, Nietzsche stands us out toward the future – or so it seems. But he stands us out to the future on the basis of what is already secured and taken for granted, the body as what underlies the subject, the body as the hidden unity drawn out into the open as the subject-concept. The body is therefore a unity whose meaning is to be *attained*, above all metaphysically, as the underpinning unity of every subsequent, subjectival, representation. As the basis of becoming it can achieve no representation – it cannot be seen. Every appearance is an error, and for this reason, every appearance of the body is an error of attainment, something achieved by positing it (literally, *I* put it into place: τίθημι). That we can 'see' this unity, and so take it as so self-evidently 'there' is the very self-evidence that proves its *metaphysical* presence, not its actuality. Its actuality is pure becoming.[14] Exactly as with Hegel, what Nietzsche is attempting to provide is an account of motion: motion is now to be accounted for not in terms of the relation to absolute *Geist*, but to overcoming, thought of as *be*coming. If we doubted this, compare Nietzsche's statement of the relationship of

---

[13] Nietzsche, *Nachlaß 1885–1887*, Vol. 12, p. 465. 'Der Substanzbegriff eine Folge des Subjektsbegriffs: nicht umgekehrt!' Cf. Nietzsche, F., *Der Wille zur Macht*, 1996 (1901–6), §485.

[14] This is what is at issue in the entire complexity of Judith Butler's metaphysical discussion of embodiment: why the embodied attainment to matter is, far from being so self-evident, so difficult and complex in its description. Cf. especially *Bodies that Matter*, pp. 72ff. Here Butler analyses the consequences of the view she takes as self-evident (from Lacan) that 'the body, or rather morphology, is an imaginary formation'. The body, exactly as Nietzsche envisaged is 'a psychically invested projection, an idealization or "fiction" of . . . a totality and locus of control' (p. 73).

the subject- and substance-concepts to that of Hegel: Hegel says 'substance is essentially subject'.[15] Nietzsche says: 'subject is essentially substance', that is, as an erroneous but necessary fiction, a stabilization of being that even in its appearing appears as an error, *in* negation: every representation is stripped off from becoming and freezes it in stability, stable being, which is untrue to the flux from whence it is stripped.[16] Heidegger interprets Nietzsche's will to power as the revaluation of substance in and as the will to power, and so as the 'permanence of presencing, that is beingness (*Seiendheit*), consists now (that is in itself) in re-presentedness through and for this re-presenting'. We can see exactly why Heidegger was able to equate Hegel and Nietzsche as *together* the fulfilment and completion of Western metaphysics.[17]

Contemporary theology pursues *both* paths simultaneously – the one, insofar as it appears, appears under the guise of Hegel's absolute subjectivity: the many, insofar as it appears, wrests its unity out of the plurality, opposing it to every other manifestation of alterity as triumphant will. 'God is dead' simultaneously means – now I declare this (dead) God to live in *me*! The death of God, arising out of Nietzsche's belief that he is demonstrating that 'nihilism is a normal state of affairs', is for him not a *thought* – precisely not a thought because now *reason* as such is to be devalued for the sake of the revaluation of all values that the will to power and the triumph of the subject is! As not a *thought* it is above all an *experience*, the most basic experience of all, the grounding experience for every value, every being, every subjectivity, every substance. In the words of Heidegger, it is 'the *one* word that should indicate to us Nietzsche's basic-experience and basic-determination'.[18] Because nihilism is an *experience* which is itself the deracination of world, the death of God is itself

---

[15] Hegel, *Phänomenologie des Geistes*, Vol. 3, p. 27. 'Daß die Substanz wesentlich Subjekt ist.'

[16] This is none other than the 'error' of taking a photograph, or assembling a sequence of photographs into the video-kinetic.

[17] Heidegger, M., 1. *Nietzsches Metaphysik; 2. Einleitung in die Philosophie – Denken und Dichten* in *Gesamtausgabe*, GA50, 1990, p. 44 (cf. *Nietzsche II* in *Gesamtausgabe*, vol. 6.2, Frankfurt, Klostermann, 1997 [1961], p. 266). 'Die Beständigkeit der Anwesung, d.h. die Seiendheit, besteht jetzt in der Vor-gestelltheit durch und für dieses Vor-stellen, d.h. in diesem selbst.'

[18] Heidegger, *Nietzsches Metaphysik*, GA50, 1990, p. 107. 'Das *eine* Wort, das uns Nietzsches Grunderfahrung und Grundstimmung andeuten soll' (emphasis in original). See for a full explanation of this, Hemming, L. P., *Heidegger's Atheism*, 2002, pp. 163–9.

a *basic-experience* of the securing of being(ness) on the basis of the Subject.

This also is a necessary consequence of the structure of the subject that Descartes carries through in the *Meditations* – above all because the being of the *cogito* (where the *cogito* is founded through the *method* of doubt apart from world, which has the effect of the radical de-divinization of world as such, and at the same time as the founding of the self as finite substance on the basis of infinite substance) is determined entirely negatively with respect to world. Indeed world is specifically nihilated or annihilated in order to ground the *cogito*. Because Nietzsche now forces the concept of substance to appear not as being, but as becoming on the basis of the *I will* as the representing of *I think*, so he presses the fundamental multiple representedness of the subject out into a world which has already been deprived of its supposedly divine foundation.

Being-still turns out to be a will to truth that is a necessary error, the overcoming of which is also a consequence of a religious experience, this time an entirely negative, nihilistic one, that God is dead. The attempt to ground the knowing of knowing as such results in the proclamation 'God is dead'. The whole situation of contemporary theological discourse is caught between these two poles, the one described by Hegel, the other by Nietzsche. For they are not separately Hegel's thinking and Nietzsche's thinking – we have seen rather that they speak of the same, the fundamental attempt to secure being on the basis of the self, but after philosophy has lost the genuine ground of self-enquiry on which this securing could stand. This is the impasse both of the *analogia entis* and of ontotheology, and why each is the mirror image and the antistrophe to the other. In each case therefore, they represent an impasse as well as a fundamental insight into what actually *is*. To understand this we must necessarily remind ourselves that philosophy is not the attempt to think again what Hegel or Nietzsche – or Aristotle, Aquinas or anyone else for that matter – *thought*, but to find a way in to what it is they – and we – think *of*. What they think *of* is grounded in my (and your) being, taken as a name for the struggle to bring something out into open disclosure – truth – as such. Moreover this is why – exactly as Descartes predicted we must in order to know that they are 'true' – we experience the death of God and the triumph of the absolute subjectivity as something we already recognize, we already know to be true.

Contemporary theology has not let matters rest here: confronted on the one hand with the drive to ground knowledge as such, and on the other with the necessary contemporary experience of nihilism (let us set aside for the sake of brevity the truth of Heidegger's claim that all metaphysics is necessarily nihilistic, at least for the moment), theologians have been driven to force back into life the God declared on the one hand to be absolute subject by Hegel and on the other, by Nietzsche, to be dead, which has turned out to be the constant drive to reproduce God through the will to power. Believing now becomes, in the light of this, a driving into power. 'I believe in God' becomes a slogan, a point of view, an opinion, a position to be taken up – above all, a political stylization. And here both Hegel's and Nietzsche's discussion of God and the death of God with regard to the moral require the most serious attention – for the conversion of theology and above all of Christian theology into an essentially *moral* (and moralistic) concern. The recent emphasis on natural law and how *exactly* it conforms to what is asserted here arises directly out of this metaphysical situation. Theology becomes a sloganizing announced for the sake of the drive into power that the constant resuscitation of God requires. Here we have religion as essentially moral-activism driven by a desire to overcome everything. Theology, *as* an out-narrating.

If we understand from Hegel the drive to reinscribe upliftment as the attempt to overcome the transition from consciousness (that is from *my* subjectivity) to absolute self-consciousness, *Geist*, subjectivity as such (so that analogy 'of being' is now secured on the basis of the subjective self), it becomes clear from Nietzsche why at the same time upliftment is the drive for an analogical relationship 'from below' as it were – in other words why analogy is no longer secured solely on the basis of faith and the revelation in Christ as it is (and only insofar as it is, given the very minor role it plays for him) by St Thomas Aquinas. Analogy now becomes a formal topic in metaphysics: however, analogy of this kind is not really analogy at all, but the *transcendens*, transcending as such, as the driven overcoming of the gulf between being and becoming, secured in charismatic and authoritative *bodies* – the papacy, this or that theologian, even (cinematically) the shattered body of the Christ. The attempt to establish the analogical relationship as a topic in metaphysics is an attempt to reinstate God as 'the transcendent' whilst at the same time securing transcendence on the basis of the Cartesian concept of the self, the *cogito*. Heidegger interprets ontotheology entirely as a problem of transcendence. Thus he concludes, referring to the fundamental connections driven through by Hegel and Nietzsche concerning the self and God, that:

Ontology represents (*stellt . . . vor*) transcendence as the transcendental. Theology represents transcendence as 'the transcendent'. The unitary ambiguity named by transcendence and grounded in the – from its origin – obscure differentiation between essence and existence reflects the ontotheological essence of metaphysics.[19]

With the abandonment of substance comes the abandonment of what nowadays goes under the heading of the 'real' (often capitalized by those who bemoan its loss and reassert it, to make it more realistic). For Nietzsche 'we have indeed no categories that permit the distinguishing of a "world in itself" from a world of appearance. All our rational-categories are sensually originated: read-off (*abgelesen*) from an empirical world.'[20] The abandonment of substance – that there is a 'real world' or 'supersensible world' arrives at the same time and by the same means as what formerly was understood to be constitutive of the soul, by means of a reading-off from the senses, from what 'empirically', and this means no more than immediately, sensually, is 'read-off' (this 'reading-off' is, once again, Aristotle's ἀφαίρεσις). That all carrying off is, in advance of being carried off, an interpretation, is something Nietzsche stresses again and again. *Everything* is interpretation: all knowledge is 'knowledge as'. This means that every producible world is real – or that there is no real world as such. The virtual, simulacral, digital, videokinetic – any of these, as artistic productions and as secured and driven-up into existence, and in their very multipliedness and multi-layered capacity for simultaneity and co-existence – all of these, because they are sensible, because they are empirically *felt*, are real. Indeed, the videokinetic is *more* real because, as real, it is at the same time most obviously a production, a fiction, an artistic representation. The euphoria of postmodernity is entirely familiar for Nietzsche. The appearance of the figure of *Brontosaurus* is therefore *of necessity* videokinetic – else how could we take it for real? It is not that every appearance is of the same value, but rather, everything that has the capacity to make an appearance has at the same time the capacity for value, can be evaluated, can attain *to* a valuation.

[19] Heidegger, M., *Die seinsgeschichtliche Bestimmung des Nihilismus*, GA6.1, p. 315. 'Die Ontologie stellt die Transzendenz als die Transzendentale vor. Die Theologie stellt die Transzendenz als die Transzendente vor.'

[20] Nietzsche, *Nachlaß 1885–1887*, Vol. 12, p. 391. 'Wir haben keine Kategorien, um eine "Welt an sich" von einer Welt als Erscheinung scheiden zu dürfen. Alle unseren Vernunft-Kategorien sind sensualistischer Herkunft: abgelesen von der empirischen Welt.'

Read and carried off where? With the abandonment of substance, of the soul, and the unity of the cosmos is the rage to abandon upliftment itself, or rather to abandon that upliftment lifts up to some 'where'. Kant's distinction between beauty and upliftment was explicitly intended to demonstrate that beauty was an immanent, and upliftment a transcendent, value. For Nietzsche, however, all sublimity is immanent, such that all beauty becomes upliftment.[21] All art, and so not only that which attains to substantiality, is sublime. Nietzsche gives as one of the definitions of the genesis of art – the category to which since before Kant both beauty and sublimity pertain – that 'life [is] a sequence of sublime things'.[22] The term 'uplifted' (*Erhabene*, *Aufgehobene*) has disappeared, now even Nietzsche's German speaks only of the sublime (*sublimer*). This is the devaluation of upliftment itself, as that which once superseded beauty in the transcendental analysis of aesthetical judgement, superseding beauty in order to indicate an infinite – a devaluation to a mere description of a psychological process, an activity – not even of the mind, but of the body (as the originary, causal, ground of mind). The 'reading-off' as the transposition of every sensual experience as an experience of art is secured on the very basis of this willing, driving body:

> Art reminds us of states of animal vigour; it is at once an excess and overflow of blooming bodiliness into the world of images and desires; on the other side the stimulation of the animal function through images and desires of intensified life; – an uprising of life-feeling, a *stimulans* in itself.[23]

This stimulation is at the same time a production through power – the very flattening and democratizing and ensaming of every being, every person, that is the consequence of the devaluation of the uppermost values, demands that power be enlisted to produce rank and difference: 'concerning rank, the quantum of power decides what you are;

---

[21] Here is the real interpretative danger for those who want to equate beauty and upliftment – the equation has already been made by Nietzsche, the 'nihilist'.

[22] Nietzsche, *Nachlaß 1885–1887*, Vol. 12, pp. 325f. 'Das Leben [ist] eine Abfolge sublimer Dinge.'

[23] Nietzsche, *Nachlaß 1885–1887*, Vol. 12, p. 394. 'Die Kunst erinnert uns an Zustände des animalischen vigor; sie ist einmal Überschuß und Ausströmen von blühender Leiblichkeit in die Welt der Bilder und Wünsche; anderseits eine Anregung der animalischen Funktion durch Bilder und Wünsche des gesteigerten Lebens; – eine Erhöhung des Lebensgefühls, ein Stimulans desselben.'

inactivity is cowardice.'[24] Here is a driving-up and uprising secured on the basis of the body, not an upliftment, a being drawn-up to the already-being of the supersensible. This will and driving-up is therefore an immanent, worldly, empirical restriction to things with no 'transcendental' consequences. This uprising has no 'end', no finality, no entelechy. It is pure power, above all secured on the basis of the unleashing of the sexual as the drive of most obvious, animal desire, and so 'love'. Here is the drive that is most animal in its driving – ἐρῶς, *Liebe*. Nietzsche, as the upturning and inversion of Plato – Heidegger's splendid critique of Nietzsche's drive into nihilism[25] – is at the same time the turning-inside-out of Aristotle. No longer is the thinking on thinking that which is most beingful, the outermost and complete in itself thought as what, as divine, is most-loving. Now, through the body, through the devaluation of the uppermost values and the revaluation of all values, this sexualized (Nietzsche speaks of this sexualization as the surge of 'semen in the blood'),[26] sensualized, empirical expression of power and at the same time production of art is 'the perfect yet-becoming world, through "love"'.[27] What is the drive at issue here? It *is* transcending, a transcendence that has and requires no fulfilment, no τέλος, no end. What upliftment and the sublime named is now shown up to be – transcending as such, on the basis of the animality that we are posited to be. Transcending is at the same time consumed by the image: transcending, as it was with the Greeks, is nothing other than pure looking – seeing, visualizing. The interior imaginary is now shown up to be *no different*, not other, than any other kind of image. All world, every world, is imaging. *Brontosaurus* is therefore at its most simple, the sheer image – the reflection – of this description, with one further thing to note: as it figures someone who refuses to look at us, who deprives us of the end, the aim and *telos* of our gaze, *it represents us representing*, and as

---

[24] Nietzsche, *Nachlaß 1887–1889*, Vol. 13, p. 20. 'Über den Rang entscheidet das Quantum Macht, das du bist; der Rest ist Feigheit.'

[25] Cf. Heidegger, M., *Nietzsches metaphysische Grundstellung im abendländischen Denken: Die ewige Wiederkehr des Gleichen* in *Gesamtausgabe*, GA44, 1986, p. 231 (see *Nietzsche I* in *Gesamtausgabe*, vol. 6.1, Frankfurt, Klostermann, 1996 [1961], p. 421), 'Nietzsches Philosophie als Umdrehung des Platonismus' ('Nietzsche's philosophy as reversal of Platonism').

[26] Nietzsche, *Nachlaß 1885–1887*, Vol. 12, p. 325. 'Der schaffende Instinkt des Künstlers und die Vertheilung des semen ins Blut.' ('The creative instinct of the artist and the distribution of semen in his blood.')

[27] Nietzsche, *Nachlaß 1885–1887*, Vol. 12, p. 326. 'Die vollkommen gewordene Welt, durch "Liebe".'

representing, it represents us *representing nothing* – the figure is the quintessential image (*Inbegriff!*) of our own onlooking. The figure, as pure agitatedly motile body, images and imagines the metaphysical basis of every act of looking and seeing that we are, that produces the fictiveness of all we know. Simultaneously stripped of content and so *ready* to be saturated with the driving-up into contentfulness that is all going-out, ecstasis, the figure of *Brontosaurus* is the beginning of sublimity. Inasmuch as he confronts us with *another* to be overcome, he enrages us. Inasmuch as he confronts us with our own willingness for an outlook, he delights us. Is he becoming to us? Can we become him?

This is the upliftment achieved through nihilism – it is the negation of beings as Kant himself identified it to be, but now without a rising up beyond and behind the empirical world. *This* negation is for the sake of (and on the basis of) an endless becoming. This becoming has no aim, no completion, but is the achievement of a psychological state. The devaluation which nihilism is, at the same time leaves the world valueless, so that every event, every moment, every *thing* is at the same time an error and an attempt at a revaluation. Every transcending produces both a self and a thing for the self to see and so know.[28] How does Nietzsche sum up the whole of nihilism: 'briefly put: the categories "aim", "oneness", "being" with which we projected some value into the world, again become pulled out by us – and now the world looks valueless.'[29] In the edited version of this text produced by Nietzsche's sister, Elizabeth Förster-Nietzsche, the editor has added over this extended passage the remark 'decline of the cosmological values'.[30] This title is omitted in the critical edition of the notebooks from which the *Wille zur Macht* was produced, in favour of the Nietzsche's own description of the passage as a 'critique of nihilism'.[31] The addition is not without wisdom, for it correctly draws out that

---

[28] This is the triumph of the conversion of time into space, unleashed by Aristotle's description of time as the counting of 'nows'. Time disappears in favour of the endless sequence of momentary self-objectifications (every present moment is a countable now) which appear as objects, *things*, the objects of self-presence to self, which can only be resolved through the 'space' they are said to occupy, and not temporally. Frames, in a strip of film.

[29] Nietzsche, *Nachlaß 1887–1889*, Vol. 13, p. 48. 'Kurz: die Kategorien "Zweck","Einheit", "Sein", mit denen wir den Welt einen Werth eingelegt haben, werden wieder von uns herausgezogen – und nun sieht die Welt werthlos aus ...'

[30] Nietzsche, F., *Der Wille zur Macht*, 1996 (1901–6), p. 13. 'Hinfall der Kosmologischen Werte.'

[31] Nietzsche, *Nachlaß 1887–1889*, Vol. 13, p. 47. 'Kritik des Nihilism.'

what Nietzsche names is a movement, a 'going-down' that is explicit in *Also Sprach Zarathustra* but that this particular fragment actually unfolds to show that the decline reaches a basis. The fragment traces three movements, and asks at the end 'what has happened, at bottom?'[32] Even the driving-up of the sublime production of *things* as the activity of life is a conscious decline of the highest values and their uprising. In another notebook nihilism is described in two forms – active and passive. *Active* as 'indication of the increased power of *Geist* . . . *passive* as decline and retreat of the power of *Geist*'.[33]

Nihilism as the *way in* to becoming and what is to come, we might say, as the activity and the manner of manifestation of postmodernity itself – as transcending as such without the Transcendent – is itself the separation of God from every value: already we see what can flow from any desire to prove that being is not one – to separate God from value, so that God can be revalued, can be *assigned* to oneness! It is obvious therefore that the drive to ascribe a value to God – to produce and reproduce God as a force in which to believe is entirely envisaged, in fact vigorously bidden, by what Nietzsche describes. How he would have applauded all the activity of the overcoming of nihilism, of the endless declarations of renewal, of the employment of every word that refurbishes, rethinks, re-imagines, re-envisages, revisions and so revises God! Every radical manifesto of the repristinization of orthodoxy is itself this very uprising, this pressing up to revivify God – God as the artwork which I shall become! God as the object of beauty who I will take myself up into to be! How we should applaud the *consummations* that these revaluations invite – liturgical consummations! The consummation of philosophy! The consummation of history! Let there be no summit of power to which we haul ourselves up to surpass, that cannot be put underfoot as stepping stone for the next! This devalued God is not just driven into death, but, *as* one capable of being death-driven, can be revalued into life. Here is a true necrophilia, that I should dance with the corpse of this dead God and have it flourish in my hands! (Yet what a weight I have to bear as I flourish this corpse in view of its uncomprehending spectators, how weighty and grave my task!) Every declaration of human flourishing is this revaluation (legion are the thinkers who declare human flourishing to be the goal

---

[32] Nietzsche, *Nachlaß 1887–1889*, Vol. 13, p. 48. 'Was ist im Grunde geschehen?'

[33] Nietzsche, *Nachlaß 1885–1887*, Vol. 12, pp. 350f. 'Nihilism als Zeichen der gesteigerten Macht des Geistes: als *activer Nihilism*. [. . .] Nihilism als Niedergang und Rückgang der Macht des Geistes: der *passive Nihilism*.'

of life itself!) – every announcement of necrophilia (legion are the theologians of every hue who have denounced their opponents as necromancers) is preparatory to the renewed proclamation of the life of God! Better yet, this God fulfils Nietzsche's requirement such a God be beautiful and sublime – this God has no representation you need look out for. You can find this God's form, his face and look, in yourself!

This restriction to the self, especially the self understood through the *cogito*, the co-posited self, posited in advance and taken as prior to everything it knows, is, as I have consistently argued, the essence of postmodernity; it is the manner in which postmodernity experiences transcendence. Because in the history of ontotheology, God is conceived as the prior ground of all things, the death of God does not disband the need for the prior grounding of things, but rather provides for the possibility of the triumph of ontotheology to be expressed in the act of replacement whereby the body of the subject usurps the grounding place of God. As sublimity it names – not that this place *is* usurped, but that it is constantly and repetitively a usur*ping*. Hence in postmodernity upliftment locates presencing by reference to the evacuation of presence, a completion whose perfection is endlessly deferred, endlessly held in view in its accomplishing. Aquinas understood all things to have been willed in the mind of God both in God's act of creation and in his sustaining of them in God's own act of being: 'Therefore, a natural thing [. . .] is said to be true inasmuch as it corresponds to the divine intellect insofar as it fulfils that which has been ordained for it by the divine intellect.'[34] Because Aquinas understands the cosmos to be ordered in the manner understood by Aristotle, according to the six absolute directions of up, down, forward, back, left and right, so a *rising up*, upliftment, sublimity, is the means by which the human being conforms his or her intellect to the uprisen, uplifted intellect of God. Kant and Hegel retain this 'rising' and upliftedness with respect to the intellect as the means by which they explain the 'super' and superiority of that seeing which is proper to the supersensible.

It fell to Nietzsche, whose proclamation of the death of God is in fact no more than a driving through to its utmost the consequences of the infinitude of the universe (as *res extensa*) and the disbandment of

---

[34] Aquinas, *Quaestiones Disputatae: De Veritate*, Q. 1, art. 2. resp. 'Res ergo naturalis [. . .] secundum adaequationem ad intellectum divinum dicitur vera, in quantum implet hoc ad quod est ordinata per intellectum divinum.'

the supersensible, to draw attention to the need to destroy the spatiality of this terminology in his assertion of the will to power and the devaluation of the uppermost values for the sake of a revaluation. It is only with Nietzsche that every connection of sublimity with going-up is abrogated and destroyed, and this is undertaken on the very basis of the emplacement of the human, subjective will in the place of the will of God.

This bringing to an end of the meaning of upliftment as ascent into being shows sublimity – as the force and drive, the *willed* willing of life itself – to be a certain comportment with respect to time. As pursuers of the indefinite infinite, Nietzsche and Hegel correspond, while both stress simultaneously and in different but complementary ways the towering pretension and the limitation of the subjectivity of the subject. This entire devaluation of God, however, takes place with respect to an understanding of representation. The endlessly announced 'crisis' of representation is now the very activity of representation and its possibility in postmodernity's transcending. Representation turns out to be nothing other than the infinite projectability of the fiction of the body. Every projection of the body (even the projection of the body of *Brontosaurus* on to an art-gallery wall) is at once both the proclamation of the death of God (the denial of the unrepresentability of becoming, because the brute fact of representation negates its nugatoriness), and the possibility of the revaluation of all values (because every appearance *is* an appearing *as*, and so a value).

10

Transcending Postmodernity

At the origins of Western thinking lies the statement of Protagoras: 'πάντων χρημάτων μέτρον ἐστὶν ἄνθρωπος, τῶν μὲν ὄντων ὡς ἔστιν, τῶν δὲ οὐκ ὄντων ὡς οὐκ ἔστιν.'[1] The usual translation of this sentence is: 'Man is the measure of all things that are, that they are, and of the things that are not, that they are not.' Martin Heidegger says 'one could suppose – here speaks *Descartes*'.[2] Even more than Descartes, we might well think this to be in perfect accord with Nietzsche. Heidegger notes how the sentence, translated in this way, betrays the 'subjectivism' of the Greek Sophists. Even Plato appears to want to give Protagoras' words this subjective twist, when he has Socrates ask in the *Theaetetus* whether the consequences of Protagoras' statement indicate that the appearing of whatever appears means the same as its being-perceived.[3] Heidegger's point, however, is that the translation of the sentence contains the interpretation: it is only 'subjective' when interpreted *already, in advance* in this way, and so translated in a way that presupposes the very subjectivism it then exhibits.

Is there not a 'correct' translation, however? How do we arrive at what is correct? The very purpose of the genealogy I have traced has been to exhibit the difficulty of translation – to take into account the very history and genealogy of interpretation in every translation we make. *Every* translation is an interpretation, so much so, that even two people speaking the same language and reading the same sentence

---

[1] Diels, H. (ed.), *Fragmente der Vorsokratiker*, 1922, Vol. 2, p. 228, l. 8–10. The sentence as it is presented here is reported by Sextus Empiricus. It is frequently cited in shorter form by Greek authors, among them Plato and Aristotle. See p. 83 above.

[2] Heidegger, M., *Der europäische Nihilismus*, GA48, 1986, p. 175 (cf. *Nietzsche II* in *Gesamtausgabe* Vol. 6.1, Frankfurt, Klostermann, 1997 [1961], p. 119). 'Man könnte meinen, hier spräche *Descartes*.' Emphasis in original.

[3] Plato, *Theaetetus*, 152 B. Socrates: Τὸ δέ γε φαίνεται αἰσθάνσθαί ἐστιν; Theaetetus: ἔστιν γάρ.

will interpret with respect to themselves what it means. The philosophical task, the task each of us as already interpretative must undertake, is to bring to light the interpretative ground on which we stand for ourselves, so that we can set into relief our own capacity for blindness. To translate correctly does not mean (as it did in the age of rationalism) to make the 'best' and 'most accurate' translation, it means to begin by *not* taking ourselves as the standard for the best and most accurate, but bringing to light the history within which we stand and from out of which we interpret, in our interpreting. It is, in other words, to know what kind of self I am in coming across whatever I interpret. Γνῶθι σεαυτόν, the command inscribed over the temple at Delphi, does not mean 'know thyself' as in some subjectival self-centredness, but, 'be thou self-knowing in what thou knowest!' To take the self into account in what this self knows is *not* to make it the measure for what it knows, but to set it into relief and allow it to be measured *by* what it encounters.[4] As we approach the end, it is as well to take into account the beginning itself, to ask ourselves, how is it that we uncover the beginning and discover it for ourselves?

Why might Protagoras be of importance for us? Is it just that he lies at the beginning? The sentence is taken from a work said to have had the title *Truth*, or alternatively *Refutatory Arguments*. Porphyry tells us of another work, *On Being*, where (whilst commenting on the extent to which Plato relied on Protagoras – or even plagiarized him) he notes that Protagoras employs an argument against those according to whom being is one.[5] About Protagoras there is virtually nothing known,[6] and apart from these two remarks, only one other fragment remains, from his treatise *On the Gods*.

To what extent is Protagoras of assistance to us in understanding the devaluing of God? For devaluing God is, as so often when a participle is employed, an ambiguous phrase: it lacks a secure subject. Devaluing God can mean destroying the value of God; or it can mean separating God from any relation to value; or even, that it is God who devalues. That being is divine and being is one – even if, for Aristotle,

---

[4] This is exactly the meaning of Aristotle's remark in the *Metaphysics* that although it seems that knowledge (ἐπιστήμη) is a measure which measures the things that are knowable (ἐπιστητά), in fact it is the other way about, because knowledge is measured by (μετρεῖται) the knowable. See p. 119, note 22 above.

[5] Cf. Diels, *Die Fragmente der Vorsokratiker*, 1922, Vol. 2, pp. 229, 13f.

[6] Diogenes Laertius has no more than a few remarks, and does not even list *Truth* among Protagoras' works. What little else we know is garnered – as much as Diogenes Laertius garnered himself – from garbled and fragmentary gossip.

one is not itself a number – is the way in which the triad of being, God, and oneness have held fast to each other and been pressed together in the whole history of metaphysics and in postmodernity down to the present day. It is no accident that Nietzsche, who seeks to depose God from the place of highest value at the same time derides all talk of being and disbands the unity of the one: 'everything, which as "unity" enters consciousness, is already uncannily complex: we have always only the appearance of unity'.[7] Appearance (*Anschein*) is an obvious sideswipe at Kant's 'intuitions' (*Anschauungen*) of space and time – the very conditions of the unity of transcendental, subjective, know-ledge. Can Protagoras suggest how this triad is set apart and so need not be bound by adamantine hoops for the whole history of thinking?

Here therefore, we should take heed of the other fragment of Protagoras. Protagoras, who (as we earlier noted) wrote a treatise *On the Gods*, stands historically accused of agnosticism. Without a shred of evidence Protagoras is often said to have been charged with atheism or impiety in Athens. The impiety imputed to him is in fact based on nothing more substantial than the way in which his extant fragment from *On the Gods* has been read, and so interpreted. A standard translation, containing itself an all-too standard interpretation, reads: 'About the gods, I am not able to know whether they exist or do not exist, nor what they are like in form; for the factors preventing knowledge are many: the obscurity of the subject, and the shortness of human life.'[8] The Greek is 'περὶ μὲν θεῶν οὐκ ἔχω εἰδέναι, οὔθ' ὡς εἰσὶν οὔθ' ὡς οὐκ εἰσὶν οὔθ' ὁποῖοί τινες ἰδέαν. πολλὰ γὰρ τὰ κωλύοντα εἰδέναι ἥ τ'ἀδηλότης καὶ βραχὺς ὢν ὁ βίος τοῦ ἀνθρώ-που.'[9]

Like the first fragment, whose full meaning we have yet to consider, we could take this fragment to confirm all that we have discovered of Nietzsche's proclamation of the death of God. Put like this it says, most freely translated – 'let us abandon the heavens for *life* – why seek what cannot be known nor take on any form. Cease all concern with the dark and obscure for the sake of the light!'

We notice first, however, that any verb 'to know' is absent from the Greek. Instead of νοεῖν or φρονεῖν we find the perfect (that is past) infinitive εἰδέναι: 'to have seen'. It is true that this word is often trans-

[7] Nietzsche, F., *Nachlaß 1885–1887*, 1988, Vol. 12, p. 204. 'Alles, was als "Einheit" ins Bewußtsein tritt, ist bereits ungeheuer complizirt: wir haben immer nur einen Anschein von Einheit.'

[8] In Freeman, K., *Ancilla to the Presocratic Philosophers*, 1983 (1948), p. 126.

[9] Diels, *Die Fragmente der Vorsokratiker*, 1922, Vol. 2, pp. 229f., l. 30f.

lated as a present infinitive, 'to know'. It is translated as 'to know' because it contains a reference to what is (presently) known only because it conforms to what is *already* seen (the past sense of the perfect tense of the verb), in other words I know something because I recognize it (I already knew what to look for in seeing what I now see). Here we can see how the interpretation of this sentence, its 'translation', connects before our very eyes what we have-seen-already, and so what we are ready to look for (looking by knowing what to look for already, in advance), with present knowing. We know it because we already had seen it (somewhere else, we *learned* it, the exact meaning of μάθησις). In Greek this infinitive εἰδέναι has no present indicative form, no form for 'I am (now) seeing'. The infinitive always employed in the present tense to indicate seeing is ὁρᾶν, a verb which always has a specific connection not with the 'seeing of the mind' (νοεῖν) and so knowing by working out (thinking), but the seeing of the eyes, and so looking, on-looking, looking-out-for.

What is at issue is entirely connected with seeing, and this means *what kind* of looking and seeing: seeing with respect to the already-seen *as against* looking-out-for. For Protagoras, never mind 'knowing', not even a looking that already knows what to look for will be sufficient here. The seeing that he negates is the seeing that sees in advance, preparatory looking – the looking that knows already what to look for – envisaging and visualizing. Such looking, the fragment says, will not find out the being of the gods. The *only* looking that could see with respect to the gods would be genuine ὁρᾶν, an onlooking that does not know in advance, but which could be a genuine disclosure without respect to what is already known. We might say that (from our perspective) what Protagoras explicitly rules out with respect to the gods is precisely that kind of knowing which has come to be thought of as Plato's 'theory of the forms': that there might be a form of each of the gods which we are ready for (and have already 'seen'), so that when we look out for the gods we are prepared for their self-disclosure, their revealing of themselves.

Here we should remind ourselves of Porphyry's comment that Protagoras precedes Plato, and so precedes the specific connection of εἶδος, ἰδέα, the 'look' or form that something has or takes up with the ideas, with the objects that can be known only through the 'seeing' of the mind. Protagoras makes an explicit connection between the looking of the eyes and what the eyes might *see* but not yet *know*. Concerning the gods, such visualizing sees nothing. There is no outward 'look' that the gods, in their being, take up that can be known in advance. The fragment is not, therefore, agnostic with respect to the *being* of the gods, but only with respect to the connection of preparatory looking with their appearing. Moreover, their 'not-being' refers not to 'existence' – there is nothing here of the separation of essence and existence, a distinction belonging to an entirely different age. To translate εἶναι as 'existing' here would be to indicate a decision can be made, between existence and non-existence, as if what is to be decided affects and determines the being of the gods. The being at issue here is the *un*essence of the gods, the way the gods stand *before* they dispose themselves. Is this the cleft in being? Or is this rather a cleft that being allows to unfold before us, a distance that appears because we understand it with respect to the being of the beings that we are, the being that I am? The gods dispose of themselves as they see fit, they cannot be seen in advance of their self-disposing by means of a looking that has prepared itself in advance for how they *should* dispose themselves.

The first part of the fragment says, therefore, 'Concerning the gods, I am not able to have (already) visualized the manner in which they are or are not, nor what they are like to in their appearance ["look"].' We should note: the fragment does not even say that they never have a 'look', a manner or a likeness – the gods may indeed dispose themselves in appearance, and when they do, they may well be seen. The gods of the Greeks are notorious for appearing to mortal men in a multiplicity of guises, as animals or mortals living or now dead. Such is their appearing that we cannot see it in advance. What, therefore, does this half of the fragment say? There is no prepared looking for the gods. The gods are not known through either devaluing, or revaluation – they are free from every causal relation to man, every intentional, visual, 'aim' of humans.

The second half of the fragment attempts to supply a reason for the first, to amplify and explain it. Again, despite the mention of knowledge in the 'standard' translation, the concern here is with what withholds, not either the gods or knowledge, but what would allow for preparatory envisaging: 'Many indeed the withholding things' for recognition (the meaning of the repetition of the infinitive εἰδέναι). The fragment appears, however, to list only two. The first is τ᾽ ἀδηλότης – that which has no δηλοῦν, no capacity for being pointed up and shown (through speech), and so that which remains hidden and not seeable. The hiddenness of the gods is not, therefore, with respect to any κωλύον, that is, any withholding-being, but with respect to the alpha-privative of what is α-δηλοῦν, *un*-showing.

Δηλοῦν however, as much relates to looking as to speaking. What is pointed up and shown is most often shown in being spoken-of and explained. The un-pointed is also the unsaid, that which is held back in the said. Indeed the switch from looking to pointing-up brings speaking to the fore. Protagoras tells us that the essence of the gods is held and withheld in the unsaid of their hiddenness, it lies in the unspoken (so not even the rhetor can reach it). Here we are faced with a contradiction, since Protagoras is speaking of that which remains unsaid – he is pointing something out that rests with no pointing out, or rather he is pointing out the realm of hiddenness from out of which the gods, insofar as they might dispose themselves, would dispose themselves. We are distracted from the gods to the hiddenness of the hidden, within which they dwell.

This realm has no speaking known (in advance) to man, nor any preparatory seeing. The second apparent 'thing withholding' is the brief life of the being of man. The word here is βίος, not the character of the organism (ζωός), but the whole life of the being in question. This whole life of the being of man is identical to the αἰών we encountered as the origin of the meaning of the word ψυχή, soul, in Aristotle.[10] As we have already discovered, ψυχή really has as its original meaning life – both the life-force (again βίος) and the whole given life (αἰών), the allotted span, of a being. The brevity in question, therefore, is compared in its ontological meaning, its capacity for disclosure, to something else. What else could that be? The comparison in question must be the βίος of the gods. Strictly speaking the gods have no βίος, or rather whatever their βίος is, is *exactly that* which is withheld from us. But understood with respect to us (understood therefore, not from out of any 'cleft in being', but rather from out of the being of the beings that we are) the gods do have an allotted span. If, as Aristotle asserts, αἰών really means something more akin to 'allotted span', then the αἰών of the gods, their ἀεί, is not really the metaphysical 'ever', 'always' but is the before and after to man, since, strictly speaking (suggested in the implicit comparative that is at work here) what is at issue is the allotment of a whole life-span *relative* to the being of man. The αἰών of the gods, withheld in its appearance from man, nevertheless is a before and an after with respect to man. The hiddenness and withholding *in* its hiddenness and being withheld both precedes man and runs ahead of him. Nevertheless in this preceding and succeeding there is no suggestion of causation – quite the

---

[10] Cf. p. 108 above.

reverse! The being of man, which is encountered in its extantness and marked by its standing out for man – his realm of self-encounter is *opposed*, and opposed with respect to the whole span available to him, by the hidden and withheld realm, a *wherein* for gods.

What is indicated here therefore is the *separation* of what otherwise in Aristotle comes to be known as soul, from the realm of hiddenness of the gods, not its identity with the divine. We need to recall that the subject of the second, amplifying, half of the fragment is not the gods or their being, but the preparatory envisaging (εἰδέναι). Many indeed are the withholding things – but these two, the soul of man and the unsaid of unessence, of hiddenness and silence (the wherein for gods) are not so much those things withholding, but are rather the two *places* themselves obscured and so thrown into confusion by the withholding things, and also the places 'displaced' for the withholding things to take up their own being-seen and envisagements. The disparity between the 'many' and the two things named is because the many overtake the two things named.

The things-withholding, therefore, are not the two things in the list, but rather these are the emplacements of the encounter of the things-withholding – beings themselves, which, in their extantness – presence – for man, obscure and hide the realm of unessence – presencing – that is pointed out not by his immediacy (the immediacy of presence) but by his βίος, his whole life in its finitude. Taking into account finitude means taking into account what precedes and runs ahead of man, and what is proper to gods. The fragment tells us that the being of the gods cannot be secured, but only with difficulty can the wherein of gods emerge, taken with respect to the being of the being that man *is*.

The wherein of gods is therefore not grounded in the being of man, but is *opposed* in its unfamiliarity and unessence to man. Equally, the being of man is not grounded or causally chained to anything like the being of the gods or of divinity. The opposition only comes into view when man takes up a particular understanding of himself as a being, that is with respect to the being of his being. This particular understanding only emerges from what is not able to be said, and so what lies open and ahead of man as unknown, and so in question for him. The fragment is in this sense consistent with and parallel to the fragments of Parmenides, where we encountered Heidegger's explanation that withholding-concealing remained concealed in whatever unfolded into presence for us. This time, however, Protagoras is naming a danger, that we will lose this withholding-concealing because we will be distracted by the unconcealed itself, and be gripped by it. In being thus distracted, we will look for the gods where they cannot be found, in the *unconcealment* of the unconcealed (presence), instead of in the concealment from out of which unconcealment unfolds (presencing). We will look for the gods by attempting to read them off from the things that are present. The gods are not to be found here, nor found by a means of preparatory looking, that is, found out from the things that 'already' are.

Protagoras' fragment points (for us) to a freeing of the gods and a freeing of the soul of man from any necessary connections, any causality whatsoever, any 'cleft in being' between gods and divinity. This fragment therefore stands in frank opposition to Aristotle's definition of the soul: not that the soul is in some way all things, but that the soul of man, held apart from, and unable to point up and show the realm of unessence and hiddenness of the gods, is nevertheless filled with things – beings – that withhold from man in the concealment of being *that* proportion to his own allotted span which would otherwise prepare him for sight of the gods. The fragment remains within the sphere of the Greek concern with looking, both with preparatory looking and with what comes to appearance for its own sake and appears. The fragment must be read in the light of Porphyry's assertion that for Protagoras being is not one. Being is not one – being is not *even* one – and beings obscure the coming forth and self-disposing of the gods: the gods are not known through μάθησις, through knowing-in-advance.

Here is an altogether different devaluing of divinity and the gods, placing us, however fragmentarily, in an entirely different relation to being, to divinity, and to beings. This devaluing of the divine and the gods stands the realm of the divine away from every site of value: it is a devaluing as release of the wherein for gods and divinity apart from any 'taking as', apart from the realm of value as such: it is only by taking up a certain kind of holding of himself that man will discover that, with respect to himself, there is a wherein of unessence and the unsaid from whence gods and divinity might usher forth. Moreover because Protagoras refuses any grounding of the gods in the being of man, and any grounding of man in the being of the gods, the fragment appears as an inversion of Aristotle (and of the Platonism to come!), but an inversion that is not the self-conscious twisting round into opposition of Nietzsche's driven, willing, subject. Rather, it shows from what realm Aristotle himself twisted round and hammered out the human soul.

Protagoras says that μάθησις is ineffective for encounter with the gods: the preparatory and productive seeing that is μάθησις, and that provides the basis for mathematics (the first and easiest of the ways of μάθησις) is ineffective here. The fragment of Protagoras brings us up against the phenomenon of time once again – time in its disposal of essence and unessence, time in taking account of the whole time I am and from out of which my temporalizing springs. The whole time that I am is my emerging 'while', my fatedness and enduring, my allotment. We want, above all, to treat time as a being, a thing; above all as a 'what' or a 'now' that can be counted and counted upon always to be the same in each different moment: now we see it is nothing of the sort. Aristotle's understanding of time is above all defined mathematically, as the countable – as in its very countability preserves in every moment both the same, the ever-same, and the different – the fundamentally differentiated with respect to every 'now', which is worked out with respect to motion. Aristotle summarizes this understanding of time by saying 'time, then, is not motion, but motion with respect to number'.[11] This is the time at our disposal. Contrary to this, Protagoras indicates how *we are disposed* with respect to our own allotted time and the time of the gods.

The counting of time as the counting of the motion of *beings* determines how time is understood through presence, through the extantness of whatever is. Protagoras determines time with respect to the priority of *un*essence, to the disposing of the time within which we find ourselves and in which we are unfolded. Here Protagoras breaks off – he says nothing more, but we must add that in the unfolding of our allotted time the things that befall us and the things for which we strive light up and bring to light the time that we are. This is the earliest and most primordial name for upliftment and sublimity: the flashing encounter that brings to light from what most besets me the whole allotted span that I am, with respect to the unessence of what runs before and ahead of me. Postmodernity's instrumentalization through sublimity of myself to the moment is only possible because I could first be uplifted to attain to world *through* the flashing-enlightening of the event of the momentary. Heidegger places this understanding of time under the heading 'time – eternity – moment', saying:

---

[11] Aristotle, *Physics*, 219 b 3. Οὐκ ἄρα κίνεσις ὁ χρόνος, ἀλλ᾽ ᾗ ἀριθμὸν ἔχει ἡ κίνησις.

The eternal is not the ever-lasting, but rather that which can with-draw into the moment, in order once again to return. That which can return again (*wiederkehren*), not as the *same* (*Gleiche*), but as what transforms from the new, the one-only, being (*Seyn*), so that in this manifestness it is not at first recognised as the self-same (*Selbe*).[12]

Heidegger is here consciously turning Nietzsche over on himself. The shift from the eternal as what returns again (but not as the same) clearly recalls and distracts Nietzsche's eternal return of the same (*ewige Wiederkehr des Gleichen*), so that the shift from the same to the self is the constant transformation of the self. The self is the being above all which knows and experiences change and which therefore is *as* temporalizing,[13] but not as a drive. Because not as a drive, the self is not as the driven will into the future, but as what, undergoing change as an ever-renewal in the moment whereby whatever renews emerges from being itself, discovers itself without at first recognizing itself. The self is *not* the self-same, and yet it persists as the self. *This* manner of the temporalizing being of being human is the genuinely 'futural' being of man *on which the ever-sameness of the restriction to the past is based*. It is for this reason that Heidegger employs the archaism *Seyn* as opposed to *Sein* as the name for being. What is at issue is originary being, the genuine ground, the source, of the being of being-human, which at the same time is an *Ab-grund*, a without-ground, an abyss. It is this abyss because it is genuinely not oriented *toward* the future as the drive into it, but as what issues forth from *out of* the future. The future is what provides and lays out the 'there', the *Da*, of being-the-there, there-being, *Da-sein*: a future apportioned and proportionate to the being of being human.

The self which in postmodernity struggles in its driven willing to remain the same, must secure itself *against* the future, must reproduce itself as ever-the-same in order to secure its continuity. Futural being on the contrary means abandoning the sameness of the self-same, putting oneself at the disposal of the gods, leaping-forth, where the self

---

[12] Heidegger, M., *Beiträge zur Philosophie*, GA65, 1994 (1989), p. 371. '*Zeit – Ewigkeit – Augenblick. Das Ewige ist nicht das Fort-währende, sondern jenes, was im Augenblick sich entziehen kann, um erstmals wiederzukehren. Was wiederkehren kann, nicht als das Gleiche, sondern als das aufs neue Ver-wandelnde, Eine-Einzige, das Seyn, so daß es in dieser Offenbarkeit zunächst nicht als das Selbe erkannt wird!*' Emphasis in original.

[13] Cf. Heidegger, M., *Sein und Zeit* GA2, 1977 (1927) especially pp. 428–41.

cannot remain the same but persists in its changing. The singular 'one-only' is not, therefore, a metaphysical determination of the unity of being (let alone of God, of the body or the soul) but the singularity which the moment *can* give to being, from out of which the moment can allow being to usher-forth. 'Can allow' means, if it is genuinely oriented toward the future, toward the unknown and the essencing that springs from un-essence, rather than being determined in advance (μάθησις) and so already known, already determined by a preparatory looking, a looking that takes whatever it sees *as* solely interpretable in terms of what it already knows. This looking consumes the future, saturates it with the already-known, and so past.

The understanding of being which lies at the basis of Aristotle's understanding of the soul is ambiguous. The already-being is discovered and disclosed – attained – by pressing into the future, but it is discovered as being-already (ἦν-εἶναι). As the already-is-being, it retains, not through the understanding of being, but through the understanding alone of the persisting futural sense of ἀρχή, its orientation to the future. This ambiguity necessarily results in a transformation of the meaning of the term ἀρχή to a term that becomes preoccupied with what lies ahead as the 'already', the perfected, the completed, and so past. Even this understanding, therefore, is metaphysical, is preoccupied with being of the things in presence, and not with truthful disclosure as a genuine understanding of time as futurity, from whence not only the moment, but my whole allotment to being, my whole αἰῶν unfolds.

What happens to the 'up' of upliftment, if Nietzsche is able to show that human transcending can go 'down' as well as 'up'? In examining the first fragment of Protagoras we discovered that it were as if not even Descartes, but Nietzsche was speaking here. In examining how this could be, and in examining, albeit cursorily and rapidly, Nietzsche's metaphysical position, it became possible to see why it is that the figure of *Brontosaurus* is so familiar, so immediately accessible, and at the same time how this familiarity is disturbed by the installation *Brontosaurus* itself. Indeed, the very speed with which we were able to do this – to find the points of contact between the figure and Nietzsche's description of it – indicates the degree of familiarity we have in advance of encountering the figure with what it brings before us. All of this draws attention, not to the figure, but to the 'here' mentioned earlier – it is as if Nietzsche were speaking here, through Protagoras, through the figure of *Brontosaurus*. Nietzsche authors neither the fragment nor the figure. Indeed, we should be wrong to say that Nietzsche could be the author in either case. Nietzsche is not describing what he *wants* or wills to pertain, but rather – and here is why we see the 'truth' of Nietzsche (and the 'truth' of Hegel) so immediately – Nietzsche brings to description (and so points up) a situation in which we are already living. We see what he sees, quickly, all in one.

This seeing what he sees, throws us back on the mathematical – not the *mathesis* of mere counting or geometry, but the encounter with what deepens us in what we already know. Nietzsche, Protagoras, and the figure of *Brontosaurus* expand us in what we bring already to them. Yet there are two peculiarities to this. First, we encountered in a careful examination of the second fragment of Protagoras, not the familiarity of what was uttered there, but its profound *un*familiarity, an unfamiliarity for which we have, in a sense, been preparing ourselves all along, a world far removed from that of Nietzsche or postmodernity. This is not because Protagoras is so remarkably clever or startling in what he says – indeed the essence of my argument was that underneath the 'standard' interpretation of Protagoras was a reading which was not only more faithful to what it is Protagoras has to say to us but, at the same time, is related (albeit negatively, through a kind of opposition, but nevertheless an opposition which itself furnished a *ground*) to everything we have had at hand and have been considering. We unearthed from Protagoras not what was most familiar to us, but what would have been most familiar to him (if – and of course we have no way of testing this 'scientifically' – if I have done my work well in reading him).

What all of this brings before us is not Protagoras, or Nietzsche, or even *Brontosaurus*, but the *surrounding world*, the context of each. Context means *cum textus*, that which is intertwined and woven together, *with* whatever it is with; but even before this, it means τίκτειν, to beget (from which τέχνη is also ushered forth). The context is the engendering or begetting given together with (and this means alongside and in advance of) whatever it engenders, it is the already-given, the ground. Insofar as we understand Nietzsche quickly, we emerge from the same place, albeit a place which he described (and predicted!)[14] with a rigour at least as strong as the phenomenological rigour we discovered to be at work in Aristotle. The extraordinary feature of *Brontosaurus* is the attempt to eliminate

---

[14] Nietzsche, *Nachlaß 1887–1888*, Vol. 13, pp. 350f. 'Was ich erzähle, ist die Geschichte der nächsten zwei Jahrhunderte.' ('What I recount is the history of the next two hundred years.') As a recounting it is a working out, a *producing from what is known already*.

through the narrative character of context every aspect of context. The nakedness of the figure and his enclosed eyes, the darkness of the window and the trivialization of history itself to the stature of a child's toy, the disjointure between the music we hear and the music to which the figure dances, all of these distract every aspect of his situation and yet confront us with our complete familiarity with whom it is we see.

Inasmuch as in encountering anything we discover its complete familiarity (how commonsensical this is!), we find ourselves already given in it. Inasmuch as we encounter something and discover its uncanniness, we encounter our need to let it stand for itself. We encounter here a second peculiarity – that something which can be familiar can at the same time be uncanny and disturbing. What this discloses is not uncanniness itself, but rather that the very uncanniness we encounter both conceals from us the world from which it is drawn, and discloses that this world is present, even after it has long fallen away. Protagoras' first statement – that 'man is the measure of all things' now needs to be read again, not for its familiarity, which, for all that, had much to tell us, but its uncanny oddness.

The statement says: 'πάντων χρημάτων μέτρον ἐστὶν ἄνθρωπος, τῶν μὲν ὄντων ὡς ἔστιν, τῶν δὲ οὐκ ὄντων ὡς οὐκ ἔστιν·' man is the measure of all things that are, that they are, and of the things that are not, that they are not.[15] Two things should be noted about the statement. First, the accepted translation 'all things' already, even in the Greek are not just 'beings in general' (ὄντα), but a particular kind of being, χρήματα, the things that are useful, that stand out and around man and that he takes as his everyday matters of concern (the sense in *Sein und Zeit* of 'things that are to hand', *Vorhandenseienden*). Man measures these things because they are the things that are about him, in both senses of the things that are lying about him and with which he is most familiar, and the things that are concerning him.[16] Second, in Greek a μέτρον is itself ambiguous. It is only later that it comes to mean a 'measure' as such, as in a ruler. Rather it originarily meant a 'measured by'. A μέτρον is that which gives the measure *to* whatever it measures.[17] As such man is the one measured by, and so given his measure, given his stature, by the things that lie around him. Inasmuch as a man is surrounded and concerned with what lies present at hand

---

[15] See page 213, note 34 above.

[16] We should note, however, that Longinus said these are the very things that disbar a concern with upliftment (see p. 56 above).

[17] This is the reason why Aquinas can turn Aristotle over on his head.

for him, at the same time, he is disclosed by whatever is to be found about him.

Heidegger asks, in interpreting the statement with respect to Nietzsche: 'who, therefore is "the" man here? What does ἄνθρωπος mean here?'[18] In indicating the section of the *Theaetetus* I have already pointed to, Heidegger quotes Socrates as asking whether Protagoras understands this fragment in the following way: 'that what respectively a particular indicates of itself to me [also], is for me of such an appearance, but that of what it shows itself to you, is such as it is for you?'[19] Is this not the very subjectivism and relativism that has shadowed all our considerations of the sublime all the way through? How does Heidegger suggest we deal with this, and what has this to do with who 'the' man is here? Except that Socrates adds immediately, 'But are you not a me, even as I?'[20] Heidegger concludes from this that Plato takes Protagoras (and therefore that this problem is historical, that it persists all through the transformations we have identified and has dogged metaphysics from the very beginning) as meaning ' "the" man" here is therefore the "respective" (I and you and he and she)'.[21] All knowledge is therefore based on an 'I represent for myself'. The consequence of this is that 'we think that a being becomes accessible, when an I as subject represents an object'.[22] What Heidegger seeks to draw our attention to is the basis on which an object first appears at all – that it has to be present and *emerging out of concealment* for us to stumble across it. Of course, if we know in advance what it is, then we will be ready for it, awaiting it – prepared. This is the essence of preparatory looking, of good training, of being taught well, of μάθησις. But as we have seen, such preparatory looking and training, even if it is passed on by good teaching one from the next (so that I tell you what to look for when you are looking in a prepared way) will never prepare you for what nobody yet knows is coming. The 'I represent me representing' as the *cogito* stands more originarily on Aristotle's understanding of time as a sequence of nows, wherein

---

[18] Heidegger, M., *Der europäische Nihilismus*, GA48, 1986, p. 175. 'Wer aber ist da "der" Mensch? Was heißt hier ἄνθρωπος?'

[19] Plato, *Theaetetus*, 152 A. ὡς οἷα μὲν ἕκαστα ἐμοὶ φαίνεται τοιαῦτα μὲν ἔστιν ἐμοί, οἷα δὲ σοί, τοιαῦτα δὲ αὖ σοί. Heidegger adds the 'also' (*auch*) in his translation.

[20] Plato, *Theaetetus*, 152 A. ἄνθρωπος δὲ σύ τε κἀγώ.

[21] Heidegger, *Der europäische Nihilismus*, GA48, 1986, p. 175. ' "Der Mensch" ist hier demnach der "jeweilige" (ich und du und er und sie).'

[22] Heidegger, *Der europäische Nihilismus*, GA48, 1986, p. 175. 'Wir meinen, ein Seiendes werde eben dadurch zugänglich, daß ein Ich als Subjekt ein Objekt vorstellt.'

the 'I' appears in every now, it is the way every now has an 'object character', the way the unity of both myself and the world is read off as what is most to be read off, and most unitary to every 'now'.

All preparatory looking is concerned with the already. We know, however, from our reading of Protagoras, that he is well aware that there is a kind of coming-across for which no preparation can be made – above all that coming-across which concerns the gods, as the ones who dwell in the concealed. Protagoras is therefore well aware that the appearing of something is not restricted to a self, an I, it can be disposed *to* unconcealment, *let* into presence. Heidegger comments on what he calls the region of the unconcealment of beings, that when a thing, a being, comes into unconcealment we think 'as if in addition there must not already be beforehand an open region, an openness within which something *as* object *for* a subject becomes accessible the accessibility itself can already be experienceable and penetrable'.[23] What Heidegger reminds us is that there is no open region prior to beings, but beings emerging and falling away is the unfolding being of beings within which we also are coming to be.

Providing an explanation for this already-givenness is, to some extent at least, satisfied by the intrusion into philosophy of the prior causality of God, the *ens creatum*, although we have already seen the particular difficulties that emerge with the predominance of the *ens creatum* as the very basis itself for ontotheology. Nevertheless it is for this reason that the prior causality of God became so compelling, and has a relation to truth. For in its absence every object does indeed become restricted for its ground and its relation to truth to a subject, with the attendant problem of subjectivism which appears as early as Plato (who is no subjectivist!). Nevertheless this 'letting into unconcealment' is not a 'condition in general', but the way being *is* – eventuates itself, which at the same time opens us up to ourselves. But the beings that emerge into unconcealment are not there *for me, for us*, but rather are there for themselves, inasmuch as they are, and that they are. We can be among beings and even forget what they are there for (whom they are there for – for themselves), as when an ancient statue appears among us, and we have no way of understanding the world from out of which it came and which gave it to be. What a being is 'for' does not mean every being has a purpose (ἀγαθόν, *ratio*). It means

---

[23] Heidegger, *Der europäische Nihilismus*, GA48, 1986, p. 175. 'Als ob nicht hierzu vorher schon ein Offenes sein müßte, innerhalb dessen Offenheit etwas *als* Objekt *für* ein Subjekt zugänglich werden und die Zugänglichkeit selbst noch als erfahrbare durchfahren werden kann.'

every being is, insofar as it is: it appears in the being of its being, which we may uncover, or cover over, or not even uncover that we have left covered.

Protagoras writes *before* the intrusion of the Christian God as the *ens creatum* into philosophical consideration, *before* Plato, and yet he acknowledges, not the 'respectivity' of man, but that man also appears together and alongside *and from out of* whatever comes to presence in an open region. The preoccupation for man with the open region of the unconcealed is marked by his restrictedness to it, that it is always *his*, always mine, and at the same time he, *I*, am not the one alone for whom the region is open, and my self is *it*self an event of unconcealing and coming to be: I am not transparent to myself in every way and at every moment – I have a past, a 'from whence', and a future, a 'whither to' from out of which I fall; and I occur already together with and from out of being among others. Moreover even my past is not transparent to myself, but must be uncovered either in memory or through encountering my historicality – what gave me to be that precedes me in every way. Inasmuch as I speak a language (and I am nothing other than a speaking, interpreting, being) I speak something I did not make, and which long preceded me and is crowded with decisions and definitions which I do not know, and yet must become and be made mine in order to speak it. This ambiguity, that in appearing in the region is always *my* appearing, and at the same time that the region itself is there for itself and is so much taken for granted as in advance of me and as a given, is the ambiguity into which Aristotle's description of the soul is caught up. Aristotle attempts to resolve the ambiguity by reconciling the unity of the self with the unity of the *whole* of the open region, and by pointing up the point of this merging as the outermost and most divine. Protagoras reminds us that the region springs from out of the concealed, that concealment as what precedes, runs ahead of, and was there before us, constantly by bringing to the fore that which is *not* for us, not as the false, but as the untrue – the forgotten and the not-yet, and the yet-to-come, as what is not, what is in advance of and ahead of the extantness of what lies present. The real unity of the ἕν is not the unity of everything present, but the hidden unity of the manifold concealment from out of which the manifold unfolds and unconceals itself – this hidden unity is not one, but nothing.

It is the concealed which explains what is meant by 'unessence'. Unessence is not the opposite to essence, as non-being is not (despite Plato and Aristotle, despite metaphysics) the counterpoint to, ever at enmity with, being. Rather unessence is the prior and subsequent to presence – what allows presence to be present: presencing. For the Greeks, and this means for Protagoras (as much as for Aristotle and Plato) every ὄν is a ἕν, every being is a one, indeed as we have seen with time, every *moment*, every νυν is a ἕν. All through this book we have considered how about the only thing that this *cannot* mean is the bald, flat, statement that each thing that is, is one and simple – neither with respect to a chair, a nation, or God. The question is *how* something comes to be seen as 'for itself', as any one thing. And yet the history of upliftment and the sublime appears to lead up to this very flatness – because the whole history and experience of upliftment leads up to this negativity, that the 'one' is stripped-off every thing we encounter, *as* its negation. Sublimity, as a name for transcendence as such (and not just the transcendence of postmodernity) turned out to be *essentially* this negating. This stripping-off and negating is the meaning of Heidegger's statement that 'the metaphysics of Plato is not less nihilistic than the metaphysics of Nietzsche'.[24]

Even when this stripping-off and negation is the negation of God, as in the death of God, and this 'one' turns out to be our own self-restrictedness, even *now* when we as this one must replace everything across which we come with a value for it that is not the thing itself, and we are confronted in postmodernity with the deadness of every thing, of every one. If God is not dead and we have declared God to *be* dead, how would we, still at the funeral, learn of God's life? If we, yet at the grave side but by necromantic means are driving this dead God back into life, how would we face the living God with his corpse, animated by us at will, in our arms? Even those who are counter to 'nihilism' end up in nihilism. How are we to know the living God?

That beings come out of the unconcealed and are there not 'for' us means that we are free for beings: and that beings are there free *for* me. Being free means not securing in an intentional grip, but discovering ourselves as ones who uncover and are uncovered by beings. Beings, in coming across us, do not strip-off and negate us, but rather, offer us their being in the being of our being. 'It worlds for me' does not mean 'the world is for my purposes', it means first and above all, *it* worlds, the coming to presence and presencing of beings *brings me* to presence

---

[24] Heidegger, M., *Die seinsgeschichtliche Bestimmung des Nihilismus* in *Nietzsche*, GA6.2, 1997 (1961), p. 309. 'Die Metaphysik Platons ist nicht weniger nihilistisch als die Metaphysik Nietzsches.' Quoted in the *Preface* to the restored translation of *Fides et Ratio* in Hemming, L. P. and Parsons, S. F. (eds.), *Restoring Faith in Reason*, 2002, p. viii.

and disposes me as together with them. All of this occurs as λόγος, as speaking, in ways which lie outside the scope of this text, but we should not lose sight of the sense of the pointing-up and showing (δηλοῦν) that the bringing of beings to speech is. This was not lost to the rhetor. Even seeing is a kind of speaking, of both knowing what to look for and having to learn and discover and wrest from hiddenness what is seen and bring it to intelligible sight.

Postmodernity is the epoch of an unlimited nihilism into which every one of us must enter and pass through – it cannot be cancelled, overcome, or shooed away with a flourish. Every participation in economic life – every time we buy bread (inasmuch as we buy not bread but the way bread 'breads', that is in postmodernity, its packaging, the whole panoply of the multi-billion effort to bring every object to market; or we resist this by buying 'real' bread – at a premium, itself a response to 'unreal' bread) – is this encounter. Early I noted Nietzsche's remark that 'the categories "aim", "oneness", "being" with which we projected some value into the world, again become pulled out by us – and now the world looks valueless'. It is only once we have passed right through this very experience, of the driving into the world and at the same time abstracting from out of it every last moment of value, that we can understand what is at issue. Transcending as such, the transcending of postmodernity (even without a god at whom to aim as the Transcendent), is still marked by an appetitive striving, a reaching-out. Aristotle prepares the ground for this, as he prepares the ground for upliftment and sublimity, by making the already-is of being divine in our striving out ahead of ourselves to attain it. We have seen how for Aristotle the monad is attained-to by thinking through from the unity of being to its attainment. A central plank of Aristotle's polemic against the *Mathematikoi* is that they were confused about this prior and subsequent. The result of this confusion, he says, was that for them the μονάς *as* ἕν was both prior to the two and subsequent to it, and even that it was a part of it at the same time (and so neither prior nor subsequent, but contemporaneous).[25]

However, we have already encountered this 'prior – at the same time – ahead of' in Protagoras, as the concealed from out of which the presence of everything present appears and to which it returns. Even if we here encounter Aristotle's determined complaint against the numerability of things as assigning to the unconcealed a number, still we see that his own attack on this view is in order to prepare the

---

[25] Cf. Aristotle, *Metaphysics*, 1084 b 25–32.

ground to assign the μονάς to a different place. If Aristotle asserts that the monad is 'ἀθετός', without position or without a 'respect to where', this is because the *one* is to be assigned a 'with respect to where' each time, as a thing once-replaced (θέσθαι). This is how Aristotle 'counts' time, or rather, time is 'counting', but it is also how Aristotle derives place, as how the what (τί) of every appearing being can be read off with respect to its being (Heidegger's 'guiding question' to metaphysics, τί τὸ ὄν, what is the being in its being?) every time (every 'now') – *this* is what τόπος really means. Aristotle does not, strictly speaking, drive a permanent rift between the unity and the one, he reconnects them in a different way, or rather, he directs their reconnecting, as the practice of wisdom: theoretical onlooking, θεωρεῖν. Theoretical onlooking allows place to come to sight, and demonstrates how being is distributed all the way through the cosmos, but at a cost – through understanding the soul and its leaping-forth as a particular kind of appetitive striving, in its pursuit of wisdom as the pursuit of theoretical contemplation of being.

To return to the astonishing insight into being that Aristotle's 'place', τόπος, is, whilst at the same time not understanding place metaphysically, would be to understand how in every place beings in their being take up a site, a place, wherein the being of their being is brought to unconcealment in its unconcealing. This is a 'physics' for a genuinely new beginning. Aristotle's criticism of the *Mathematikoi*, and Plato in particular, was that they made the error of combining into the same thing 'ἐκ τῶν μαθημάτων ἐθήρευον καὶ ἐκ τῶν λόγων τῶν καθόλου'.[26] The standard translation of this is: 'they were pursuing . . . that of mathematics and that of general definition.'[27] To translate in this way is to miss a very important point, and to fail to see why 'general definitions', better translated as 'speech concerning wholes' is the reason for the separation in Aristotle of the monad from the one. To speak of this thing here as both a whole and as what it is – that this *one* is a chair (one of 'chairs in general') is how to speak the ἕν *in*, and so *from out of* this particular ὄν – it is reading-off the one from the being that it is. This speaking of the whole is what has to be got *ahead to*, attained – I speak of this as what it is, I uncover it in its truth. However, I know in advance that it is a one. This is what the mathematical is – knowing in advance. So the confusion that Aristotle names

[26] Aristotle, *Metaphysics*, 1084 b 24.
[27] Cf. Aristotle (trans. Tredennick, H. and Armstrong, G. C.), *Metaphysics*, p. 237.

is in the manner of the connectedness of what I *already* know with what I have to *reach*.

A more careful translation of this sentence, perhaps freer at the same time, should therefore draw attention to the 'mathematical' as the already-known, and the 'general definition' as the whole, the being of the being in its being and so *future*, so that what Aristotle is criticizing here is not a 'category error' in philosophy, of mathematics with universals, but an orientation with respect to time.[28] Better translated, the sentence says: 'They went hunting after the things already-known and the things brought to speaking from out of a concern with the being of the beings.' And here the whole of transcendence is laid out before us all at once – the connection of the past and the future *in* the present, by the speaking of the disclosive place wherein the chair resides and comes to sight: because I *looked* at it and named the looking through something I 'already' had, and which therefore was available to me even before I encountered the being in question, the chair. Aristotle is not other than Žižek in this – or did Žižek learn it from Aristotle?

But the Platonists did not do this, because they saw the connection between the futurity of the whole and the pastness of the already-known in a different way. What does this mean for our enquiry? In our earlier encounter with Protagoras,[29] in Plato's *Theaetetus*, Socrates asks a question concerning two kinds of seeing. In which, he asks – the seeing of the soul directly or by means of the senses – 'do you place being, for this most of all is the accompanying to all beings?' The soul grasps 'general definitions' and it grasps them by speaking of the being of the beings in them (to itself) – Aristotle's τῶν λόγων τῶν καθόλου. Theaetetus replies that the soul grasps these 'wholes' (that is the being of each being) by 'speaking back and forth for itself (ἀναλογιζομένη) upon the past and in relation to the future'.[30] The verb ἀναλογίζομαι is normally translated by 'reckoning' as in counting up, and so calculating in the numerical sense. This however, exactly as number is, is only one of the forms of the mathematical, it is only a derivative sense

---

[28] For any who are watching closely, they will see immediately that what Aristotle names here is not other than the solution to the second riddle of the doorway in *Also Sprach Zarathustra*, as how Zarathustra enters the doorway to divide the continuum of time, 'the past and future – the same' *into* the moment, the past, present and future. But of course, Nietzsche is inverted *Platonism*, so this cannot be right.

[29] See p. 83 above.

[30] Plato, *Theaetetus*, 186 A. ἀναλογιζομένη ἐν ἑαυτῇ τὰ γεγονότα καὶ τὰ παρόντα πρὸς τὰ μέλλοντα.

of what reckoning and counting up is (the most easily visible form of the mathematical). The fundamental connection is with λόγος, speaking. The medial form is a taking of the self into account in speaking, where the prefix ἀνα- indicates a going back and forth, to and from what is both speaking to me and is my speaking about it. The verb ἀναλογίζομαι is a form of διαλέγεσθαι, speaking-together-with, of the soul *as* speaking-together-with-itself in the worlding of world. It is the activity of thinking (νοεῖν), in the dividing up (διαίρεσις), in and positing-back (τιθέναι), of thinking itself. This is not other than the relation between teaching, memory and recollection that Plato discusses in (for instance) the *Meno*, although he presents it differently, and what we are seeking is what *lies behind* his understanding of it. Understood like this, the soul is not a productive making through appetitive striving, but *is* the constant going-back and forth to what it encounters and what it already knows in order to work out its relation to truthful disclosure and to being itself.

However, this going-back-and-forth is *temporal* (as memory and recollection is temporal): it is the soul's being stood upon the past and attaining to the future all at once, in understanding each being in its being, by a complex activity, taking into itself and speaking to itself in every case within the being of being human, with respect to the being of the being it is going back and forth *to*. Going back and forth means: going over to that thing over there and discovering myself to be here in relation to it, and going back in my having-uncovered-myself to find out its 'there'. All of this is with respect to the whole apportionment to myself that I am: from out of my allotted span (whether I bring this 'whole' before me or simply presuppose and so 'forget' that it is there). Space, or place, and the time all together and at once, *as* a temporalizing going back and forth to uncover myself in the historicality of the timing that I *am*.

For Plato this is a mathematical activity. Heidegger once asks 'how does it come about, what in space and time *allow* for mathematicizing?'[31] Heidegger first points us to the place in *Sein und Zeit* where an answer is given in the attempt to grasp time and space 'in their premathematical form'[32] as both the way in which human being encoun-

---

[31] Heidegger, M., *Beiträge zur Philosophie*, GA65, 1989, p. 387. 'Wie kommt es zu dem, was in Raum und Zeit die Mathematisierung *zuläßt?*'

[32] Heidegger, *Beiträge zur Philosophie*, GA65, 1989, p. 387. 'ihrer vormathematischen Gestalt'. Cf. Heidegger, *Sein und Zeit*, GA2, 1989, §24, 'Die Räumlichkeit des Daseins und der Raum' (pp. 147–51) and the fifth chapter, §§72–7, 'Die Zeitlichkeit und Geschichtlichkeit' (pp. 492–533).

ters being and is historical. He adds a further answer in the *Beiträge*, however. The answer lies in mindfulness of both how being human is an *ab-grund*, which simply means, free for the future, free for encounter, whilst at the same time is still (insofar as we are philosophical, we are thinking in the West) working out from the origins of Greek thought itself, the 'first beginning' of Greek thinking. Here is the manner in which we pass from what we already know to what has given us already to be, to what is ahead of us to be known. In this we see the final understanding of why the concealed lies all around us as that from out of which things come into unconcealment and presence. It is not only that we go out, and by means of a productive onlooking, 'fetch' beings and things, or take them in view by means of an intentional aim, but also that they befall us, that they too appear and fall upon us to be understood. Beings also go back and forth into concealment and unconcealment, lay a demand on us and withdraw from us and are even extant but overlooked or forgotten or left in obscurity by us.

I have neither the time nor the space to show the connections between what Plato describes in these few words in the *Theaetetus*, and the understanding of the temporalizing of being as Heidegger laid it out, especially in the small lecture published in 1943, *Vom Wesen der Wahrheit*,[33] and which he developed in the late sections of the *Beiträge*. That is beyond the scope of this book, which rather has set out to show how an understanding in postmodernity has arisen and on what that understanding stands, and seeks only to be suggestive about what lies beyond it. Plato himself points in two ways at once, both back, to the 'first beginning' as Heidegger called it, and forward to metaphysics, as what really takes shape in the thinking of Aristotle. In this Plato stands close to Nietzsche who himself both points up the end of metaphysics, and at the same time to what might be thought in its overcoming.

How might we transcend postmodernity? First, in understanding how it is postmodernity transcends; second, in passing all the way through postmodernity's transcendences, its 'from whence', and its 'whithers'.

---

[33] Cf. Heidegger, M., *Vom Wesen der Wahrheit* in *Wegmarken*, GA9, 1996 (1943), pp. 177–202.

Conclusion

Postmodernity is caught between two poles – the poles of onto-theology itself. Postmodernity, as much as the metaphysics that preceded it, thinks out of a cleft in being where on the one hand being itself is referred to divinity, and on the other beings are referred to world and world's unfolding as (mere) appearances. *Brontosaurus* is not more than an adequate figure for this, for *Brontosaurus* confronts us both with the restriction of everything that is to the human, and above all else, *Brontosaurus* is the fictitious self-representation of human self-understanding. Our recognition of this, spontaneous, sublime in its vigour, is at once euphoric and tragic, at once delighted and outraged.

Postmodernity proclaims, as the decisive interpretation of all that preceded it, that 'God is being'.[1] This formal statement of unity and identity is resolved by Hegel through the 'phenomenology' of Subject and *Geist*. The word 'is' here above all has to be thought in relation to the subjectivity of the subject as 'causes',[2] even if, alone among causes, this cause (God) causes itself. For Hegel this thought 'God is being' both interprets and resolves everything from the medieval formula *ipsum esse est Deus* and what comes after, to Plato's and Aristotle's resolution of divinity, of the θεῖον. The speculative proposition 'God is being' could not make clearer how God is to be taken as highest value.

As postmodernity proclaims that God is being, so at the same time it proclaims that God is dead and being is no more than a fiction. In the words of Nietzsche, reason itself is yet taken as evidence of the divinity of thought, and our present age 'believes in the will as cause in general'. He characterizes this opposite pole of postmodernity by

---

[1] Cf. Hegel, G. W. F., *Phänomenologie des Geistes*, Vol. 3, p. 59. 'Gott ist das Sein.'

[2] As one of the pure determinations of thought, along with subject, object, universal, etc. Cf. Hegel, *Phänomenologie des Geistes*, Vol. 3, p. 49.

saying: 'Overall, being comes to be thought right in, *pushed under-neath*, as cause [of things]; out of the conception "*I*" the concept "being" only follows as its derivative.'[3] The willing *I* is thought as the basis of 'unity, identity, permanence, substance, cause, thinghood, being'.[4] As with Hegel before, Nietzsche thinks this is the conse-quence, and at the same time the interpretative key, to the whole of thought, the whole history of thinking from the Greeks (and others) onward. Here, together with his proclamation of the death of God, is the clearest statement that God is devalued, and yet God does not disappear, but remains, devalued, the basis of every thought.

For postmodernity, as much for Hegel as for Nietzsche, being is thought through the cleft between beings and divinity. Nor should we lose sight that for these two and for us as well, this is an *interpretative* key to thought and to the whole history of thinking. At its heart is the thought, if not even of being (which remains *unthought* and unthink-able) then nor of God. If God is to be thought by means of something itself unthought and unthinkable (being), or otherwise if God is dead – then thinking is restricted to securing its understanding of being and of God through causality, through unity, and through the connection between subject and object. This thinking is what metaphysics is. God has, more than anything else, been chained to being by means of the varieties of causality, and yet, as we have seen, causality itself has undergone many transformations in the history we have traced: it is (as we have seen) hardly a unitary term.

I have tried to indicate how the range of different thoughts of causality has been demonstrated – and continues to be thought – through understanding how it is that, on the one hand, God has been grounded in the being of man and, on the other, man has been under-stood to be caused by God. As a trope, sublimity has helped us see in each stage along the way both how this understanding of causality arose through the rising up of the cleft in being between divine being overall and beings themselves, and how sublimity, upliftment, call it what you will, has continued to allow a passageway through from our experience of beings to our experience of being and divinity. Only at the last has this passageway collapsed so that we are left transcending,

---

[3] Nietzsche, *Götzen-Dämmerung*, Vol. 6, p. 77. 'Das glaubt an Willen als Ursache überhaupt . . . Das Sein wird überall als Ursache hineingedacht, untergeschoben; aus der Konzeption "Ich" folgt erst, als abgeleitet, der Begriff "Sein".'

[4] Nietzsche, *Götzen-Dämmerung*, Vol. 6, p. 77. 'Einheit, Identität, Dauer, Substanz, Ursache, Dinglichkeit, Sein.'

but knowing not to what. Only here, at the very end, can we understand that what causality names and tries to make manifest is the range of understandings of temporality. Not time counted by clocks, but time as what makes the different kinds of being of being human possible and capable of being understood. Time lets us be: which means temporality is how we are, and we are disclosed to ourselves in the time that we have and have been given.

This book has concerned itself with upliftment, the sublime, and indeed, has attempted to trace, if not a history 'proper', then a kind of genealogy for the term – both as it appears in itself (ὕψος), and as what makes it possible to arise as a philosophical thematic. I have stressed, however, and at every turn, that this is a history or a genealogy of a very odd kind – a tale told, not by beginning at the beginning, but beginning from its *end*, from its terminus, from where we now stand. This genealogy has been selective – for if perhaps it would not be possible to exclude Longinus, or Aristotle, or Kant (as ones for whom the sublime or its origins have been an explicit, thematic, concern) from its telling, nevertheless other figures could have intruded in place of those selected, or some made more prominent than others as we have passed along the way. At every stage I have sought to stress that our investigations have had to drive back down through those we have encountered, to move from what seems familiar to the point of self-evident about how we might receive and interpret them, to what is most unfamiliar. The results I offer are almost entirely negative: I have sought to demonstrate that, entirely *opposite* to what sublimity appears to promise, God is not chained to being, neither through causality nor through the unity of being and the one. A question now opens wide before us in the light of upliftment's downfall – if being is not divine, what (and this means who and whose) is it to be?

This question I have not asked – though I stress, now that the question of being has lost its ground in divinity and in God, it calls for answer. What it is to be, and what it means to be among beings and in being, either for myself or for a whole tribe, a nation, or a tongue: these questions press to find an answer, but this book is only a pretext for these interrogations.

If, as this book has argued, there is no cleft in being, where on the one hand being itself is referred to divinity or to divinity's eclipse, and on the other beings are referred to world and world's unfolding, then there is no longer any upliftment to divinity exercised as the end, the very terminus, of our experience and our understanding of what it is we come to know. The death of God has brought us to this possibility, but it brings us to it a way that is at once so strange and self-evident to us that it is hard for us to take in and make our own what we are already too taken-in to. For the death of God wipes God off the terminus of our experience of transcendence, but brings neither God nor transcending to an end. Insofar as we experience transcending's ongoing, we experience the death of God. It is this that *Brontosaurus* confronts us with, for *Brontosaurus* demands we see how sublimity persists in postmodernity.

Throughout this book I have attempted to take the phrase 'devaluing God' in the full range of its possibilities. For devaluing God can mean deposing God from the place of value – indeed from the site of highest value, and I have attempted to show both how it is God attained to this high place and that indeed that in attaining it, God is at once a value that can be devalued. More than this, that God can appear as a value at all is itself a devaluation of a most dreadful kind. God's attaining to highest value, and a devaluation wrought in the name of God is also a kind devaluation, springing from the conception of God as absolute subject. In the devaluation of the uppermost values ushered in by modernity's confrontation with value, not only can God be devalued, but among those translating God, being and humanity into the absolute valuations of subjectivity, God (insofar as God is absolute subject) can also be understood to be that one who most effects a devaluation. This possibility emerges as a dependent position in ontotheology and is made possible by the extreme denigration of creation especially in a certain kind of Christianity. Karl Barth's theology has, in making God the *one* genuine, originary subject, demonstrated the way in which God thereby devalues every other possible (that is human) subject for a reverse revaluation. This is at the very least a legitimate interpretation of Barth's radical entrainment of his theology to the subject–object distinction in the early sections of his *Kirchliche Dogmatik*, a position he never abandoned, despite the claim that as he progressed through his dogmatics he moderated his position. As late as 1956 Barth argued for the priority of God over man to be understood from the subject–object distinction, modernity's valuative scheme. Barth says:

> And what can be the meaning of the 'overcoming of the Subject–Object scheme', recently proclaimed with such special enthusiasm, so long as it is not made clear and guaranteed that this enterprise will not once more lead to the anthropocentric myth and call into question anew the *intercourse* between God and man and thus the

object of theology? Certainly existentialism may have reminded us once again of the *elements of truth* in the old school by introducing once more the thought that one cannot speak of God without speaking of man. It is to be hoped that it will not lead us back into the error that one can speak of man without first, and very concretely, having spoken of the living God.[5]

In fact this is only another example of the way in which the power valuatively attributed to God can then be 'commandeered' for their purposes by theologians wishing to settle disputes with those who either do not believe, or do not believe as they should, and Barth is not alone in this.

What of those theologians who have, in the face of the devaluation of God, maintained that God as 'the transcendent' cannot be abandoned to the 'nihilism' of postmodernity? This book has sought to demonstrate that thinking God as 'wholly other' through thinking God as 'the transcendent', and so as the end of transcending and the terminus of sublimity, is itself at an end, even if such a thought were any more seriously possible except as private phantasy. If there is no cleft in being of the order I have described, then to assign God to the end of sublimity or transcendence – in other words to proclaim that alterity still persists as ultimacy – is mere crying in the wind. Although subject matter for an entirely different study, this is the insight of Lévinas, that God cannot be reached through an 'over there' which is not at the same time somehow present to us. For this reason Emmanuel Lévinas proclaims alterity to be grounded in what is at first most like to us, other men and women. It is only through a visible alterity that alterity *as such* can now be reached. In this Lévinas is not other to Barth or Baudrillard. Postmodernity's transcending is, when it seeks not to revel in nihilism but to overcome nihilism's revels, this

---

[5] Barth, K., *Die Menschlichkeit Gottes*, 1956, pp. 19f. 'Und was bedeutet etwa die neuerdings besonders eifrig proklamierte "Überwindung des Subjekt-Objekt-Schemas", solang nicht geklärt und gesichert ist, daß diese Unternehmung im Resultat nicht doch wieder auf den anthropozentrischen Mythus hinauslaufen, gerade jenen *Verkehr* zwischen Gott und Mensch und damit *Gegenstand* der Theologie nicht aufs neue problematisieren wird? Gewiß: der Existentialismus mag uns, indem er uns noch und noch einmal eingeschärft hat, daß man von Gott nicht reden kann, ohne vom Menschen zu reden, noch einmal an die *particula veri* der älteren Schule erinnert haben. In den alten Irrtum, als ob man vom Menschen reden könne, ohne zuerst, und das sehr konkret, vom lebendigen Gott geredet zu haben, wird er uns hoffentlich nicht zurückführen.' Emphases in original.

ecstatic leaping forth only to discover the absence of a transcendent, and so to have to relocate transcendence's furthest reach otherwise.

To those theologians who proclaim that without God as transcendence, as 'wholly other', then the world collapses into 'mere' immanence, we can only reply that (as in Aristotle's structuring of place) transcendence is not more than immanence's furthest reach: Aristotle's outermost, τὸ ἔσχατον, means no more than this. To make God and divinity no more than the terminus of our furthest reach is again a devaluation of God: it is to discover, in the transcending of postmodernity, how little postmodernity reaches for and ever could. Earlier than Aristotle, as early as Heraclitus, and as Protagoras pointed up to us, divinity and the gods appear *within* being. For Heraclitus this means under the starry vault of the boundaried realm of east, west, north and south, the realm of φύσις.[6] That the gods appear within being does not mean that the gods are bound to being, or are only immanent to being. Nor does it mean that the gods are not other than mortal beings are. Rather the otherness of gods to man is a surprise in being, coming into being from out of the hiddenness of the future – the before and after to man – in order to surprise us. Man is ever-renewed by the disturbing uncanniness and even shock of the newness of the gods. It is when the gods are in flight that the world available to man becomes old and saturated with the deathly weight of all that is past. Man's every attempt to renew himself from the past only drenches him ever more with his deathly familiarity to himself. In this is the boredom of godlessness.

How are we to transcend postmodernity's fictions, and fictive restriction to the past? Heraclitus speaks to us before metaphysics, before being is referred to the 'beyond' and 'over there' of non-being, and before being is made to stand and dominate beings by explaining them as shadows of what is now absent. Here is why for Heidegger, being, taken in the most general sense, is not other than φύσις, which we translate only very weakly as 'natural being'. Here is why Nietzsche also sets out from Heraclitus, claiming 'Heraclitus always comes to be right' that being is an empty fiction (an observation with

---

[6] Heraclitus, fragment 120 in Diels, H., *Die Fragmente der Vorsokratiker*, 1922, Vol. 1, p. 101. The fragment speaks of the boundaries (τέρματα) of morning and evening (east and west) and the bear and boundary-stone of great Zeus, the north star and therefore that which lies opposite to it in the south. See for a full discussion of this fragment both Kahn, H., *The Art and Thought of Heraclitus*, pp. 161–3 and Eugen Fink's discussion of the τέρματα in Heidegger, M., *Seminare*, GA15, 1986, p. 68.

which we set out, though without recalling its provenance),[7] although the being Nietzsche names is not the being of φύσις but Plato's 'beyond'. The ambiguity of Nietzsche's insight demonstrates how Nietzsche is simultaneously restricted both to a world of mere appearances, and at the same time the interiority of subjectivity. Nietzsche never reaches behind metaphysics to Heraclitus' more originary understanding of world.

The one (ἕν) in Heraclitus is, taken together with the all (τὰ πάντα), to be understood as world, and not as other-worldly. This restriction to world as the restriction to the being of my being and the wherein of 'it worlds for me' is the way in which the question of being can open up within and out of my experience of world and being. This experience is not just feeling, not mere sensation, but rather is my being bound to the world wherein I find myself to be. To Heraclitus' understanding we must add (by way of amplification and explanation, we who come not before, but after metaphysics) that the one is *my* being able to take myself in the unity that I am, *given to be* by the unity of the world wherein 'it worlds for me' and so from whence I find myself. This is not a prior, metaphysical unity, nor is it an absolute, eternal unity, nor is it a mathematical unity. Temporally attained, it is a unity that I am ever on the way to accomplishing in being towards death. This finding of myself is already not alone, not in the melancholy of isolation and loneliness, but is my discovering what is proper to me from out of my being with others. Gods and divinity appear, insofar as they do, not bound to me nor grounded in me, nor me in them; but, if they do appear, they appear *for* me and *to* me, or else they appear not at all. What I have tried to indicate in this book, and what sublimity has in many ways made available to us before its demise, is the extent to which even the provisional and historically bounded meaning of sublimity is worked out and described from a genuinely phenomenological ground, that is from our experience of beings and things themselves. This is not to say that philosophy is worked out solely from the things that are and are in presence, but rather that the way in which we are bound to world disciplines us in speaking and thinking, in what we can say and know. This restrictedness to world releases us from making the things in presence eternal, and so allows us to think not only their presence, but their presencing. It is with respect to the life of man, and to his before and after – to my standing and being held in life

---

[7] Nietzsche, *Götzen-Dämmerung*, Vol. 6, p. 75. 'Aber damit wird Heraklit ewig Recht behalten'; see p. 136 at the end of Chapter 6 above.

and that I arise and die that presence loses its eternal weight and allows me to come to presencing as well as the meaning of presence.

How can a Christian write of gods in all of this? Are we not beyond gods? The gods of the Greeks are, surely, in flight and have left us – they do not return (and if they did, we would indeed be surprised!). Talk of the gods has something yet to teach us of how the gods lie ahead, and behind, and away from us in their concealment, and so the gods dispose time (and this means dispose us in the temporality that we *are*) in a particular way. Talk of gods here is better understood, perhaps, as figurative – a way of speaking, of being open to the things that are divine. But what of Christ? Is not Christ that one who most teaches us that we do not find our own way to God, but that God comes forth to encounter and meet with us? Is this not the surprising truth of historical revelation, that the encounter with the Christian God, although now centuries-old and although it permeates our history, nevertheless renews itself in each of us, renews itself *for me* inasmuch as I do encounter the God who reveals himself in scripture and tradition, as Trinity. Is not the greatest surprise of all that God *can* do this, because God is not in our grasp? Every ὄν is a ἕν means, for Christian men and women, the continued encounter with the Father through the Christ who is unfolded in the liturgical life of the Church. This is why every antiphon, every gesture, every encounter with the liturgical unfolding of Scripture and the sacraments is essential, precious, and life-giving. This is not the liturgical as the *consummation* of history, or the consummation of philosophy, but is the 'wherein' of the speaking of God in Christ to Christian men and women.[8] The liturgy is the Church's memory and recollection of the disclosure of the Father through the Son: it is also our being open out towards the 'wherein' from out of which the Spirit is poured: the future, the horizon of the end. It is from this surprising place that God steps forth to meet us. We who live in the Spirit must first be led to that source to know this. Liturgy is the temporal-historical-spatial *place* of the encounter with God, for Christians, at least.

That God appears among us and must be understood is grounded in

---

[8] The fashion for liturgical consummations is flourishing. Matthew Levering, making specific reference in a footnote referring to Catherine Pickstock, says 'I hope to show on the contrary . . . not a flight from history, but the liturgical consummation of history'. (Levering, M., *Christ's Fulfillment of Torah and Temple: Salvation According to Thomas Aquinas*, 2002, p. 129 citing the title of Pickstock, C., *After Writing: On The Liturgical Consummation of Philosophy*, 1998.)

our experience and worldedness – which means, not God, but the experience of God appearing in our world is what theology thinks and reflects upon. Since Descartes' positing of the subject as the *ens certum*, philosophy has sought exact and certain results which dispose us to forsake the uncertainty of world for mathematical and interior sureties. For Aristotle, in contrast, philosophy struggled forth in its deliberation to attain to the 'ever-always' and so self-same. This spiritual struggle, deliberative and provisional at every step, took into account the fragility of the human share in contemplation, and set perfection as an end to be reached, ahead of every beginning attempt. We have seen how for Descartes this order came to be reversed in standing the subject on certainty: in logic and in being stood on God, certainty arose from that on which the human is already, so that the precariousness and provisional character of deliberation, akin to an accompanying helpmeet, simply ceased to be determinative.

And yet philosophy is at its very heart interpretation, since even when we appeal to logic, heaving up the terms of everyday speaking – 'natural language' – into logical structures, this is itself interpretation, often of a most declarative kind: 'defining our terms', or rather, restricting in advance the range of their meaning and application for the sake of what is to be known, logic fails to decide once and for all. With the death of God and the bringing to a close of the divine end of sublimity, comes the end of the operative force of the *analogia entis* which proved to be the product of an impasse, a 'solution' to the divergent temporalities of man, of God and world. This is not to say that an analogy of names may not yet play a certain pedagogical or theological role. If philosophy is ever-tentative and provisional in its deliberating, no more certain is theology, nor should it be. For faith is this committed lack of positive results – above all a gift of trust given from outside world and being, the first breath of God's voice in the call of his Word.

Bibliography

Althusser, Louis, 'Idéologie et appareils idéologiques d'état', in *La pensée: revue du rationalisme moderne*, June 1970, no. 151, pp. 3–38. Translated by Brewster, Ben as 'Ideology and Ideological State Apparatuses (Notes Towards an Investigation)', in *Lenin and Philosophy and Other Essays*, London, Monthly Review Press, 1971, pp. 127–86.

Anderson, Perry, *The Origins of Postmodernity*, London, Verso, 1998.

Aquinas, St Thomas, *Commentarium in Librum de Causis*, Rome, Marietti, 1955. Translated by Guagliardo OP, Vincent A., Hess OP, Charles R. and Taylor, Richard C. as *St. Thomas Aquinas Commentary on the Book of Causes*, Washington DC, Catholic University of America Press, 1996.

Aquinas, *De Aeternitate Mundi*. Translated by Vollert SJ, Cyril, Kendzierski, Lottie H. and Byrne, Paul M. as *St. Thomas Aquinas, Siger of Brabant and St. Bonaventure On the Eternity of the World*, Wisconsin, Marquette University Press, 1984 (1964).

Aquinas, St Thomas, *Quaestiones Disputatae: De Veritate*, Rome, Marietti, 1953 (2 vols). Translated by Mulligan SJ, Robert W. as *Truth* (3 vols), Indianapolis, Hackett Publishing Company, 1994 (1954).

Aquinas, St Thomas, *Summa Contra Gentiles*, Rome, Marietti, 1967 (3 vols). Translated as *Summa Contra Gentiles* (5 vols) by Pegis, C., London, Notre Dame, 1975.

Aquinas, St Thomas, *Summa Theologiae*, Milan, Paoline, 1962. Translated as *Summa Theologica*, Oxford, Blackfriars, 1924.

Aristotle, *De Anima*. Translated by Hett, W. S. as *On the Soul*, Loeb Classical Library, London, Harvard University Press, 1995 (1936).

Aristotle, *De Caelo*. Translated by Guthrie, W. K. C. as *On the Heavens*, Loeb Classical Library, London, Harvard University Press, 1986 (1939).

Aristotle, *De Generatione Animalium*. Translated by Peck, A. L., Loeb Classical Library, London, Harvard University Press, 1990 (1942).

Aristotle, *De Generatione et Corruptione (On Coming To Be and Passing Away)*. Translated by Forster, E. S. and Furley, D. J., Loeb Classical Library, London, Harvard University Press, 1955 (2000).

Aristotle, *De Partibus Animalium*. Translated by Peck, A. L. as *Parts of*

Animals, Loeb Classical Library, London, Harvard University Press, 1937 (1961).

Aristotle, *Metaphysics* (2 vols), translated by Tredennick, Hugh, Loeb Classical Library, London, Harvard University Press, 1933.

Aristotle, *Nicomachean Ethics*. Translated by Rackham, H., Loeb Classical Library, London, Harvard University Press, 1994 (1926).

Aristotle, *Physics* (2 vols), translated by Wicksteed, P. H. and Cornford, F. M., Loeb Classical Library, London, Harvard University Press, 1934.

Aristotle, *Rhetoric*. Translated by Freese, J. H. as *Art of Rhetoric*, Loeb Classical Library, London, Harvard University Press, 1994 (1926).

Aubenque, P., *Sur la naissance de la doctrine pseudo-Aristotélicienne de l'analogie de l'être* in *Les Études philosophiques*, Vol. 44 (1989), pp. 291–304.

von Balthasar, Cardinal Hans Urs, *Karl Barth: Darstellung und Deutung seiner Theologie*, Einseideln, Johannes Verlag, 1962. Translated by Oakes SJ, Edward as *The Theology of Karl Barth*, New York, Garden City, 1991.

Barth, Karl, *Die Menschlichkeit Gottes* in *Theologische Studien*, Zollikon-Zürich, Evangelischer Verlag, 1956, pp. 3–27. Edited and translated by Thomas, John Newton and Wieser, Thomas as *The Humanity of God* in *The Humanity of God*, London, Fontana, 1961, pp. 33–64. From an address given in Arau in Switzerland, 25 September 1956.

Baudrillard, Jean, *Simulacres et Simulation*, Paris, Galilée, 1981, translated by Glaser, S. as *Simulacra and Simulation*, Michigan, The University of Michigan Press, 1994.

Berman, Marshall, *The Twilight of American Culture*, London, Duckworth, 2001.

Boileau-Despréaux, Nicholas, *Oeuvres complètes [de] Boileau*, ed. Escal, F., Paris, Gallimard, 1966 (1674).

Bordwell, David and Carroll, Noël (eds.), *Post-Theory: Reconstructing Film Studies*, London, University of Wisconsin Press, 1996.

Buckley SJ, Michael J., *Motion and Motion's God: Thematic Variations in Aristotle, Cicero, Newton and Hegel*, New Jersey, Princeton University Press, 1971.

Bulhof, I. N. and ten Kate, L. (eds.), *Flight of the Gods*, New York, Fordham University Press, 2000. Based on the proceedings of a conference held in 1990 at the International School for Philosophy, Leusden-Zuid, in the Netherlands.

Butler, Judith, *Bodies that Matter: On the Discursive Limits of 'Sex'*, London, Routledge, 1993.

Butler, Judith, *Gender Trouble: Feminism and the Subversion of Identity*, London, Routledge, 1990.

Butler, Judith, *The Psychic Life of Power: Theories in Subjection*, Stanford, Stanford University Press, 1997.

Cajetan OP, Cardinal Thomas de Vio, *Scripta Philosophica: De Nominum Analogia; de Conceptu Entis*, ed. Zammit OP, P. N., Rome, Institutum Angelicum, 1934.
Clarke, Samuel, *A Demonstration of the Being and Attributes of God and Other Writings*, ed. Vailati, Ezio, Cambridge, Cambridge University Press, 1998 (1704).
Crockett, Clayton, *A Theology of the Sublime*, London, Routledge, 2001.

Derrida, Jacques, *Comment ne pas parler: Dénégations*, a paper first given in English in Jerusalem in June 1986 under the title *How to Avoid Speaking*. Subsequently published in French in *Psyché: inventions de l'autre*, Paris, Éditions Galilée, 1987, pp. 535–95; p. 585. Translated into English from the French by Frieden, K, as *How to Avoid Speaking: Denials* in Coward, H. and Foshay, T., *Derrida and Negative Theology*, New York, State University of New York Press, 1992.
Descartes, René, *Descartes*, ed. Adam, C. and Tannery, P. Paris, Vrin, 1996, 11 vols.
— *Correspondance Avril 1622–Février 1638*, Vol. 1.
— *Correspondance Janvier 1640–June 1643*, Vol. 3.
— *Meditationes de prima philosophia*, Vol. 7. Translated by Cottingham, John; Stoothoff, Robert; Murdoch, Dugald as *The Philosophical Writings of Descartes*, Vol. 2, Cambridge, Cambridge University Press, 1993 (1985).
Diels, Hermann (ed.), *Die Fragmente der Vorsokratiker*, Berlin, Weidmannische Buchhandlung, 1922.
Diogenes Laertius, *Lives of Eminent Philosophers*, translated by Hicks, D. R., Loeb Classical Library, London, Harvard University Press, 2000 (1925), 2 vols.

Eckhart, *von Abegeschiedenheit* in *Werke* (2 vols), Stuttgart, Deutscher Klassiker Verlag, 1993, 2 vols.
Eliasson, Olafur, *The Weather Project*, ed. May, Susan, London, Tate Publishing, 2003.
Euclid, Στοιχέια (*Elements*), Book VII, Athens, Οργανισμος Εκδοσεως Σχολικων Βιβλιων, 1953. Translated by Heath, Sir Thomas L. as *Euclid*, Vol. 2, New York, Dover Publications, 1956.

Fowler, D., *The Mathematics of Plato's Academy*, Oxford, Oxford University Press, 1999 (1991).
Freeman, Kathleen, *Ancilla to the Presocratic Philosophers*, Massachusetts, Harvard University Press, 1983 (1948).

Funkenstein, Amos, *Theology and the Scientific Imagination from the Middle Ages to the Seventeenth Century*, New Jersey, Princeton University Press, 1986.

Furley, David, 'Self Movers' in Gill, Mary Louise and Lennox, James G., *Self-Motion: From Aristotle to Newman*, New Jersey, Princeton, Princeton University Press, 1994, pp. 3–14.

Greek Mathematical Works, trans. Thomas, I. (2 vols), Cambridge, Harvard University Press, 2002 (1939). Vol. 1, *Thales to Euclid*; Vol. 2, *Aristarchus to Pappus*.

Hartley, George, *The Abyss of Representation: Marxism and the Postmodern*, North Carolina, Duke University Press, 2003.

Hegel, Georg Wilhelm Friedrich, *Enzyklopädie der philosophischen Wissenschaften*, Heidelberg, August Oswald, 1817.

Hegel, Georg Wilhelm Friedrich, *Werke in zwanzig Bänden*, Frankfurt, Suhrkamp, 1986 (1970).

— *Frühe Schriften*, Vol. 1. *Der Geist der Christentums* (1798–1800).

— *Jenaer Schriften*, Vol. 2. *Verhältnis des Skeptizismus zur Philosophie. Darstellung seiner verschiedenen Modifikationen und Vergleichung des neuesten mit dem alten.*

— *Phänomenologie des Geistes* (1807), Vol. 3. Translated by Miller, A. V. as *Hegel's Phenomenology of Spirit*, Oxford, Oxford University Press, 1977.

— *Grundlinien der Philosophie des Rechts*, (1821), Vol. 7. Translated by Knox, T. M. as *Hegel's Philosophy of Right*, Oxford, Oxford University Press, 1973 (1952).

— *Enzyklopädie der philosophischen Wissenschaften I*, (1830), Vol. 8. Translated by Wallace, William as *Hegel's Logic*, Oxford, Oxford University Press, 1991 (1873);

— *Enzyklopädie der philosophischen Wissenschaften III*, (1830), Vol. 10. Translated by Findlay, J. N. as *Hegel's Philosophy of Mind*, Oxford, Oxford University Press, 2003 (1971).

— *Vorlesungen über den Philosophie der Geschichte*, (1830), Vol. 12. Partially edited and translated by Rauch, Leo, as *Introduction to the Philosophy of History*, Cambridge, Hackett, 1988.

— *Vorlesungen über die Geschichte der Philosophie I–III*, (1837), Vols 18–20. Translated by Haldane, E. S. and Simson, Frances H. as *Hegel's Lectures on the History of Philosophy*, (3 vols) London, Routledge and Kegan Paul, 1955.

Hegel, Georg Wilhelm Friedrich, *Vorlesungen über die Philosophie der Religion*, Hamburg, Meiner Verlag, 1995, 3 vols.

— Vol. 2, *Die bestimmte Religion*. Translated and edited by Hodgson, Peter C. as *Hegel: Lectures on the Philosophy of Religion: Volume III:*

Determinate Religion, London, University of California Press, 1995 (1987).
— Vol. 3, *Die vollendete Religion*. Translated and edited by Hodgson, Peter C. as *Hegel: Lectures on the Philosophy of Religion: Volume III: The Consummate Religion*, London, University of California Press, 1998 (1985).
Heidegger, Martin, *Gesamtausgabe*, Frankfurt, Klostermann, 1976–
— *Sein und Zeit*, Vol. 2, 1977 (1927). Translated as *Being and Time* by Macquarrie, John and Robinson, Edward, Oxford, Blackwell, 1962 and under the same title by Stambaugh, Joan, New York, SUNY, 1996.
— *Kant und das Problem der Metaphysik*, Vol. 3, 1991 (1929). Based on a series of lectures given at Marburg in the winter semester of 1927–1928 and published separately as Vol. 25 of the *Gesamtausgabe* (see below). First published as *Kant und das Problem der Metaphysik* in *Max Scheler zum Gedächtnis*, Friedrich Cohen Verlag, Bonn, 1929. Fourth, altered edition Frankfurt, Klostermann, 1973. Fifth (expanded) edition 1991 as Vol. 3 of the *Gesamtausgabe*. Translated twice under the same title, *Kant and the Problem of Metaphysics*: (1) based on the 1950 second edition by Churchill, James S., Bloomington, Indiana University Press, 1962; and (2) based on the 1973 fourth, enlarged, edition by Taft, Richard, Bloomington, Indiana University Press, 1990 (See Vol. 25 below).
— *Nietzsche* I and II, Vol. 6 (2 vols), 1996 [1961]. Relevant sections translated by Krell, David F. as *Nietzsche by Heidegger*, in four vols, New York, Harper & Row, 1979. See Vol. 44 and 48 below.
    Die seinsgeschichtliche Bestimmung des Nihilismus. An essay composed during the years of 1944–1946, Vol. 6.2. Translated by Krell, David F. (ed.), as *Nihilism as Determined by the History of Being*, in *Nietzsche by Heidegger*, Vol. 4.
    Der europäische Nihilismus. Lectures given in Freiburg in the first trimester of 1940, Vol. 6.2. Translated by Krell, David F. (ed.), as 'European Nihilism' in Nietzsche by Martin Heidegger, Vol. 4.
— *Vorträge und Aufsätze*, vol. 7, 2000 (1953). Translated by Young, Julian and Haynes, Kenneth as *Off the Beaten Track*, Cambridge, Cambridge University Press, 2002.
    Das Ding. One of the series of four lectures given at the Bremen Club under the title *Einblick in das – Was ist?* with an epilogue *Ein Brief an einen jungen Studenten* (see *Gesamtausgabe* Vol. 79, below). Translated by Hofstadter, Albert (ed.), as *The Thing* in *Poetry Language Thought*, New York, Harper and Row, 1971 (see Vol. 79 below).
    Moira. An undelivered section of the 1951/52 lecture series *Was Heißt Denken*, Tübingen, Niemeyer, 1954 (see *Gesamtausgabe* Vol.

8 below). Translated by Capuzzi, Frank, as *Moira (Parmenides VIII, 34–41)* in Krell, David F. and Capuzzi, Frank (eds.), *Early Greek Thinking*.
— *Was heißt denken?*, Vol. 8, 2002 (1954). Lectures given at Freiburg in the winter semester of 1951–2. Translated by Gray, John G., and Wieck, F. D. as *What is Called Thinking?* New York, Harper, 1972. Lectures given at Freiburg, winter semester 1951–2.
— *Wegmarken*, Vol. 9, 1996 (1967). Translated and edited by McNeill, W. as *Pathmarks*, New York, Cambridge University Press, 1998.
   Vom Wesen der Wahrheit. An often repeated lecture from 1930. First published as *Vom Wesen der Wahrheit*, Frankfurt, Vittorio Klostermann, 1943. First translated by Hull, R. F. C. and Crick, Alan, as *On the Essence of Truth* in Brock, Werner (ed.) *Existence and Being*. Subsequently translated by Krell, David F. (ed.), as *On the Essence of Truth* in *Martin Heidegger Basic Writings*.
— *Aus der Erhahrung des Denkens*, Vol. 13, 1983.
   Die Kunst und der Raum: L'art et l'espace, St. Gallen, Erker Verlag, 1969. Translated by Siebert, Charles H. as *Martin Heidegger: Art and Space* in *Man and World*, Vol. 6, 1973, pp. 3–8.
— *Seminare*, Vol. 15, 1986.
   Martin Heidegger – Eugen Fink: Heraklit. First published as *Martin Heidegger – Eugen Fink: Heraklit*, Frankfurt, Klostermann, 1970. Translated by Seibert, Charles, as *Heraclitus Seminar*, Alabama, Alabama University Press, 1979.
   Zürcher Seminar. From a seminar in Zurich in 1951. First published as *Vortragsausschuß der Studentschaft der Universität Zürich*, Zürich, 1952.
— *Einführung in die phänomenologische Forschung*, Vol. 17, 1994.
— *Grundbegriffe der aristotelischen Philosophie*, Vol. 18, 2002.
— *Platon: Sophistes*, Vol. 19, 1992. Translated by Rojcewicz, R. and Schuwer, A. as *Plato's Sophist*, Indiana, Indiana University Press, 1997.
— *Phänomenologische Interpretation von Kants Kritik der Reinen Vernunft*, Vol. 25, 1995 (1977). Lectures given in Freiburg, in the winter of 1927–1928. Translated by Emad, Parvis and Maly, Kenneth as *Phenomenological Interpretation of Kant's Critique of Pure Reason*, Indiana, Indiana University Press, 1997.
— *Hegels Phänomenologie des Geistes*, Vol. 32, 1997 (1980). Translated by Emad, Parvis and Maly, Kenneth as *Hegel's Phenomenology of Spirit*, Indiana, Indiana University Press, 1988.
— *Vom Wesen der Wahrheit: zu Platons Höhlengleichnis und Theätet*, vol. 34, 1997 (1988). Translated by Sadler, Ted as *On the Essence of Truth*, London, Continuum, 1998.
— *Die Frage nach dem Ding: zu Kants Lehre von den transzendentalen*

Grundsätzen, Vol. 41, 1984 (1962). Translated by Barton, W. B. and Deutsch, Vera, as *What is a Thing,* Illinois, Regnery, 1967.

— *Schelling: Vom Wesen der Menschlichen Freiheit,* Vol. 42, 1988 (1971). Translated by Stambaugh, Joan as *Schelling's Treatise on the Essence of Human Freedom,* Ohio, Ohio University Press, 1985.

— *Nietzsches metaphysische Grundstellung im abendländischen Denken: Die ewige Wiederkehr des Gleichen,* Vol. 44, 1986. See Vol. 6 above.

— *Grundfragen der Philosophie. Ausgewählte 'Probleme' der 'Logik',* Vol. 45, 1984. Freiburg, winter semester 1937/38. Translated by Rojcewicz, Richard and Schuwer, André as *Basic Questions of Philosophy – Selected 'Problems' of 'Logic',* Bloomington, Indiana, 1994.

— *Nietzsche: Der europäische Nihilismus,* Vol. 48, 1986. See Vol. 6 above.

— *Hölderlins Hymne 'Andenken',* Vol. 52, 1992 (1982).

— *Hölderlins Hymne 'Der Ister',* Vol. 53, 1993 (1984). Translated by McNeill, William and Davis, Julia as *Hölderlin's Hymn 'The Ister',* Indiana, Indiana University Press, 1996.

— *Parmenides,* vol. 54, 1992 (1982). Translated *Parmenides* by Schuwer, André and Rojcewicz, Richard as *Parmenides,* Indiana, Indiana University Press, 1992.

— *Der Begriff der Zeit (Vortrag 1924),* vol. 64, 2004. The lecture itself is translated by McNeill, William, as *The Concept of Time* in a bilingual edition, Oxford, Blackwell, 1992.

— *Beiträge zur Philosophie: vom Ereignis,* vol. 65, 1989. Translated by Emad, Parvis and Maly, Kenneth as *Contributions to Philosophy (From Enowning),* Indiana, Indiana University Press, 1999.

— *Besinnung,* vol. 66, 1997.

— *Nietzsche: Seminare 1937 und 1944,* vol. 87, 2004.

Hemming, Laurence Paul, *Heidegger's Atheism: The Refusal of A Theological Voice,* Notre Dame, Notre Dame University Press, 2002.

Hemming, Laurence Paul, 'On the Nature of Nature: Is Sexual Difference Really Necessary', in Parsons, Susan Frank (ed.), *Challenging Women's Orthodoxies in the Context of Faith,* Farnborough, Ashgate, 2000, pp. 155–74.

Hemming, Laurence Paul, 'The Subject of Prayer: Leibniz' Monadology' in Ward, G. (ed.), *The Postmodern Reader in Theology,* Oxford, Blackwell, 2001.

Hemming, Laurence Paul, 'Transubstantiating Ourselves' in *Heythrop Journal,* Vol. 44 (October 2003), pp. 418–39.

Hemming, Laurence Paul and Boeve, Lieven (eds.), *Divinising Experience: Essays in the History of Religious Experience from Origen to Ricœur,* Leuven, Peeters, 2004.

Hemming, Laurence Paul and Parsons, Susan Frank (eds) and Hemming,

Laurence Paul and Meredith SJ, Anthony (trans.), *Restoring Faith in Reason*, London, SCM Press and Notre Dame, Notre Dame University Press, 2002. Including John Paul II, Encyclical Letter *Fides et Ratio*, with a commentary and supporting essays.

Hertz, Neil, *The End of the Line: Essays on Psychoanalysis and the Sublime*, New York, Columbia University Press, 1985.

Iamblichus, *On the Pythagorean Way of Life*, ed. and trans. Dillon, John and Hershbell, Jackson, Atlanta, Scholars Press, 1991 (Greek text and translation). See also Taylor, Thomas (trans.), *Iamblichus' Life of Pythagoras*, Vermont, Inner Traditions, 1986 (1818).

Jordan, Mark D., *The Alleged Aristotelianism of St. Thomas Aquinas* in *The Étienne Gilson Series*, Toronto, Pontifical Institute of Medieval Studies, 1990, No. 15.

Kahn, Charles H., *The Art and Thought of Heraclitus: An Edition of the Fragments with Translation and Commentary*, Cambridge, Cambridge University Press, 1979.

Kant, Immanuel, *Kritik der reinen Vernunft*, Stuttgart, Reclam, 1966 (1787). Translated by Kemp-Smith, Norman, as *Critique of Pure Reason*, Oxford, Clarendon Press, 1929.

Kant, Immanuel, *Kritik der Urteilskraft*, Hamburg, Meiner Verlag, 1990 (1790). Translated by Meredith, James Creed, as *The Critique of Judgement*, Oxford, Oxford University Press, 1952.

Kant, Immanuel, *Opus Postumum* in *Gesammelte Schriften*, Berlin, de Gruyter, 1936. Translated by Förster, Eckart and Rosen, Michael as *Opus Postumum* in the series *The Cambridge Edition of the Works of Immanuel Kant*, Cambridge, Cambridge University Press, 1993.

Kant, Immanuel, *Vorlesungen über die philosophische Religionslehre*, Leipzig, Pölitz Verlag, 1830 (1817): reprinted in facsimile form by the Wissenschaftliche Buchgesellschaft, Darmstadt, 1982. Translated by Wood, Allen W. and Clark, Gertrude M. as *Immanuel Kant: Lectures on Philosophical Theology*, New York, Cornell University Press, 1978.

Klein, Jakob (trans. Brann, E.), *Greek Mathematical Thought and the Origin of Algebra*, London, The MIT Press, 1968.

Klein, Naomi, *No Logo*, London, Harper Collins (Flamingo), 2000.

Kosman, Aryeh, 'Aristotle's Prime Mover' in Gill, Mary Louise and Lennox, James G. (eds.), *Self-Motion: From Aristotle to Newman*, New Jersey, Princeton, Princeton University Press, 1994, pp. 135–53.

von Krafft-Ebing, R., *Neue Forschungen auf dem Gebiet der Psychopathia sexualis. Eine medizinisch-psychologische Studie von Dr. R. v. Krafft-Ebing*, Stuttgart, Ferdinand Enke, 1890.

Lacan, Jacques, *Écrits I*, Paris, Éditions du Seuil, 1966. See selective translation by Sheridan, Alan as *Écrits: A Selection*, London, Routledge, 1989 (1977).

Lachtermann, David Rapport, *The Ethics of Geometry: A Genealogy of Modernity*, New York, Routledge, 1989.

Lang, Helen, 'Duns Scotus: Putting Angels in their Place' in Lang, H., *Aristotle's Physics and its Medieval Varieties*, New York, SUNY, 1992, pp. 173–87.

Lang, Helen, *The Order of Nature in Aristotle's Physics: Place and the Elements*, Cambridge, Cambridge University Press, 1998.

Leget, Carlo, *Living with God: Thomas Aquinas on the Relation between Life on Earth and 'Life' after Death*, Leuven and Utrecht, Peeters and Thomas Instituut, 1997.

Leo XIII, Pope, Encyclical Letter *Aeterni Patris* (4 August 1879) in *Acta Sanctae Sedis*, Rome, Polyglot, 1879, Vol. 12, pp. 97–115. Translated by Wynne SJ, John J. in *The Great Encyclical Letters of Pope Leo XIII*, New York, Benziger Brothers, 1903, pp. 34–57

Levering, Matthew, *Christ's Fulfillment of Torah and Temple: Salvation According to Thomas Aquinas*, Indiana, Notre Dame University Press, 2002.

Longinus, *On the Sublime* translated by Fyfe, W. H. and revised by Russell, D. in *Aristotle: Poetics*, Loeb Classical Library, Massachusetts, Harvard University Press, 1995.

Lotz SJ, Johannes-Baptiste, 'Analogie' in Brugger SJ, W. (ed.), *Philosophisches Wörterbuch*, 1957.

Lyotard, Jean-François, *La condition postmoderne*, Les Éditions de Minuit, Paris, 1979. Translated as *The Postmodern Condition: A Report on Knowledge* by Bennington, G. and Massumi, B., Manchester University Press, Manchester, 1984.

McLuhan, Marshall, 'The Medium is the Message' in *Understanding Media*, London, Routledge and Keegan Paul, 2001 (1964), pp. 7–23.

Maltby, Richard. ' "A Brief Romantic Interlude": Dick and Jane go to 3½ Seconds of the Classic Hollywood Cinema' in Bordwell, David and Carroll, Noël (eds.), *Post-Theory*, London, University of Wisconsin Press, 1996, pp. 434–59.

Mattéi, Jean-François, 'Le quadruple fondement de la métaphysique: Heidegger, Aristote, Platon et Hésiode' in Narbonne, Jean-Marc and Langlois, Luc (eds.), *La métaphysique: son histoire, sa critique, ses enjeux*, Quebec, University of Laval Press, 1999, pp. 203–28.

Milbank, John, 'Sublimity: The Modern Transcendent' in Heelas, Paul (ed. with Martin, David and Morris, Paul), *Religion, Modernity and Postmodernity*, Oxford, Blackwell, 1998, pp. 258–84.

Newton, Sir Isaac, *Philosophiae Naturalis Principia Mathematica*, ed. Koyré, Alexander and Cohen, I. Bernard, Cambridge University Press, 1972, 2 vols. Translated by Cohen, I. Bernard and Whitman, Anne as *Isaac Newton: The Principia – Mathematical Principles of Natural Philosophy*, London, University of California Press, 1999.

Nietzsche, Friedrich, *Friedrich Nietzsche Kritische Studienausgabe*, ed. Colli G. and Montinari, M., Berlin, Walter de Gruyter, 1988, 15 vols.

— *Zur Genealogie der Moral*, Vol. 5.

— *Der Fall Wagner; Götzen-Dämmerung, Der Antichrist; Ecce Homo; Dionysos-Dithyramben; Nietzsche contra Wagner*, Vol. 6.

— *Nachlaß 1884–1885*, Vol. 11.

— *Nachlaß 1885–1887*, Vol. 12.

— *Nachlaß 1887–1889*, Vol. 13.

Nietzsche, Friedrich, *Der Wille zur Macht*, material ordered by Gast, Peter and Förster-Nietzsche, Elizabeth in a reworked edition, Stuttgart, Kröner, 1930 (1901–6; 1921). The edition cited is the 1996 Kröner (13th) edition. Translated by Kaufman, Walter and Hollingdale, R. J. as *The Will to Power*, New York, Random House, 1967.

Philoponus, *De aeternitate mundi contra proclum*, ed. Rabe, H., Hildesheim, Georg Olms Verlag, 1984. Translated by Wildberg, C., as *Against Aristotle, On The Eternity Of The World*, Ithaca, Cornell University Press, 1987.

Piché, David (ed.), *La Condamnation Parisienne de 1277: Texte Latin, traduction, introduction et commentaire*, Paris, Vrin, 1999.

Pickstock, Catherine, *After Writing: On The Liturgical Consummation of Philosophy*, Oxford, Blackwell, 1998.

Plato, *Cratylus, Parmenides, Greater Hippias, Lesser Hippias*, trans. Fowler, H. N., Loeb Classical Library, London, Harvard University Press, 1996 (1926).

Plato, *Lysis, Symposium, Gorgias*, translated by Lamb, W. R. M. , Loeb Classical Library, London, Harvard University Press, 1996 (1925).

Plato, *Statesman, Philebus, Ion*, trans. Fowler, Harold North and Lamb, W. R. M. , Loeb Classical Library, London, Harvard University Press, 1995 (1925).

Plato, *Theaetetus, Sophist*, trans. North Fowler, Harold, Loeb Classical Library, London, Harvard University Press, 1996 (1921).

Plato, *Timaeus, Critias, Cleitophon, Menexenus, Epistles*, trans. Bury, R. G. , Loeb Classical Library, London, Harvard University Press, 1999 (1929).

Pope, A., *An Essay On Criticism* (1744) in Davis, H. (ed.), *Pope: Complete Poetical Works*, Oxford, Oxford University Press, 1966, pp. 62–85.

Przywara, SJ, Erich, *Analogia Entis: Metaphysik: Ur-Structur und All-Rhythmus*, Einsiedeln, Johannes Verlag, 1962 (1932).

Reynolds, Philip Lyndon, 'Properties, Causality and Epistemological Optimism in Thomas Aquinas' in *Recherches de théologie et philosophie médiévales (Forschungen zur Theologie und Philosophie des Mittelalters)*, 2001, Vol. 67, No. 2, pp. 270–309.

Ross, W. D., 'The Development of Aristotle's Thought' in *Proceedings of the British Academy*, Vol. 43 (1957), pp. 63–78.

Schillebeeckx, OP, Eduard, *Openbaring en Theologie*, Bilthoven, Nelissen, 1964. Translated by Smith, N. D., *The Concept of Truth and Theological Renewal*, London, Sheed and Ward, 1968.

Schlosser, Eric, *Fast Food Nation: What the All-American Meal is Doing to the World*, London, Allen Lane, 2001.

Schlosser, Eric, *Reefer Madness and Other Tales From the American Underground*, London, Allen Lane, 2003.

Secada, Jorge, *Cartesian Metaphysics*, Cambridge, Cambridge University Press, 2000.

Sheehan SJ, T., *Geschichtlichkeit / Ereignis / Kehre* in *Existentia (Meletai Sophias)*, Budapest, 2001, Vol. XI, pp. 241–51.

Taylor, Thomas (ed. and trans.), *Iamblichus' Life of Pythagoras*, Vermont, Inner Traditions International, 1986 (1607).

Taylor-Wood, Sam, 'Interview' in *Sam Taylor-Wood*, Hayward Gallery, Hayward Gallery Publications, 2002.

te Velde, Rudi A., *Participation and Substantiality in Thomas Aquinas*, Leiden, E. J. Brill, 1995.

Visker, Rudi, *Truth and Singularity: Taking Foucault into Phenomenology*, Dordrecht, Kluwer Academic Publishers, 1999.

Vlastos, Nicholas, *Etymologicum Magnum*, ed. Gaisford, Thomas, Oxford, oxonii, 1848 (1499).

Ward, Graham, *Cities of God*, London, Routledge, 2000.

Wolfson, H. A., 'The Amphibolous Terms in Aristotle, Arabic Philosophy and Maimonides' in *Harvard Theological Review*, Vol. 31 (1938), pp. 151–73.

Žižek, Slavoj, *The Art of the Ridiculous Sublime: On David Lynch's Lost Highway*, Washington, University of Washington Press, 2000.

Žižek, Slavoj, *The Sublime Object of Ideology*, London, Verso, 1989.

Žižek, Slavoj, *The Ticklish Subject: The Absent Centre of Political Ontology*, London, Verso, 1999.

Žižek, S., ' "You May!" ' in *London Review of Books*, 18 March 1999, pp. 3–6.

Glossary of Greek Terms

ἀεί	aei	'ever', always, eternal
αἴσθησις	aisthēsis	perception, sensation
αιτία	aitia	cause, what can be blamed or held responsible
αἰών	aiōn	aeon, allotted span of time
ἀλήθεια	alētheia	truth, diclosure
ἀληθεύειν	alētheuein	'making true', disclosing
ἀπορία	aporia	aporia
ἀρχή	archē	source, origin
αὐτός	autos	for-itself (adverb)
ἀφαίρεσις	aphairesis	carrying-off, 'reading-off'
ταὐτόν	tauton	the same
δηλοῦν	dēloun	showing, pointing-up
διανοεῖν	dianoein	think-from-to, thinking (vb.)
δίαλέγεσθαι	dialegesthai	speaking-together-with (vb.)
διαίρεσις	diairesis	dividing-up
δοκεῖν	dokein	seeming, to seem (inf.)
δόξα	doxa	opinion, seeming
δύναμις	dunamis	power or capacity
εἶδος	eidos	appearance, look, visibility
εἶναι	einai	being (inf.)
ἕν	hen	one, unity
ἐντελεχέια	entelecheia	entelechy, completed thing
ἐπιστήμη	epistēmē	knowledge, science
ἕξις	hexis	habit
τὸ ἔσχατον	eschaton (to)	the outermost
ἦν	ēn	was-and-is-ongoing ('durative', or ongoing sense of the verb to be)
θάτερον	thateron	the other
τὸ θεῖον	theion (to)	divinity
θεολογία	theologia	theology

θέσις	thesis	emplacement, a 'respect to where'
θεωρεῖν	theōrein	contemplating (inf.)
ἰδέα	idea	'look', face, outward appearance, idea
κατά	kata	according (to)
κίνησις	kinesis	motion
λέγειν	legein	speaking (inf.)
λήθη	lēthē	oblivion
λόγος	logos	speaking, speech, language, 'word'
μάθησις	mathēsis	learnable (the)
μέτρον	metron	measure
μοῖρα	moira	fate
μονάς	monas	unit
νοεῖν	noein	thinking (inf.)
νοῦς	nous	thought, intellect
νῦν	nun	'now', moment
ὁράω	horaō	I see (vb.)
ὄρεξις	orexis	appetite, striving-for
οὗ ἔνεκα	ou heneka	'for the sake of which', final cause
οὐσία	ousia	being, present being
πάθος	pathos	emotion, what-occurs
πάσχειν	paschein	to befall, to occur or happen to (one) (vb.)
ποίησις	poiēsis	manufacture
πόλις	polis	(a) people, city
τὸ ὄν	on (to)	being, a being
σοφία	sophia	wisdom
στίγμη	stigmē	point
σύνθεσις	sunthesis	placing-together, arranging
σύνηθιαν	sunēthian	habituation
στάσις	stasis	rest
σῴζειν	sōzein	to preserve in life (inf.)
τάξις	taxis	order, sequence, taxis
τέλος	telos	end
τέχνη	technē	know-how, practice
τίθημι (τίθηναι)	tithēmi (tithēnai)	to put in place (vb.)
τόπος	topos	place
ὕψος	hupsos	sublime, upliftment

φαντασία	phantasia	presenting (noun)
φανέιν	phanein	bring to light, show up (vb.)
φάντασμα[τα]	phantasma(ta)	thing or things derived from the phantasia
φασκειν	phaskein	to say, deem (vb.)
φρονεῖν	phronein	to think, thinking (vb.)
φρόνησις	phronēsis	deliberation
φύσις	phusis	natural being
χώρα	chōra	place, land
ψυχή	psuche	soul

Index

To New Zealand

A marvelous piece of Earth

Table of Contents

Introduction

Writing code for InfoPath forms is all about manipulating XML and should be the last thing you try to do after designing a form template based on an XML schema that provides validation and restrictions and after trying to achieve specific functionality through rules. And even if you do decide to write code for InfoPath forms, it is recommended that you write the code in components that are external to the form such as for example a web service instead of directly in InfoPath. This not only makes InfoPath form templates easier to maintain and extend, but also easier to publish.

Why does this book exist then, you might ask? The answer is simple: Because you cannot do everything in InfoPath without writing code. When it gets difficult, complex, or impossible to achieve certain functionality using rules, or when it makes sense to place code directly in a form instead of using an external component, you should consider writing code in InfoPath instead of trying to achieve the functionality through rules, web services, or any other external means. InfoPath forms are in many ways comparable to Windows client or web applications, since they are generally filled out through either InfoPath Filler or a browser, so the same maintainability and extensibility logic you would apply to such applications, you can apply to InfoPath forms.

InfoPath offers .NET programming through Visual Studio Tools for Applications, which is an optional component in the Microsoft Office installer and allows you to write code that targets the .NET Framework 2.0. You can write either C# or Visual Basic .NET code for InfoPath forms in Visual Studio Tools for Applications.

This book does not cover the basics of .NET programming, but rather teaches you how to write C# code specifically for InfoPath forms using Visual Studio Tools for Applications. And for scenarios where it is recommended to write code that is external to InfoPath forms, this book requires you to have Visual Studio 2010 installed on your computer and to know how to use it.

Who should read this book?

This book was written for developers who have at least one year of programming experience writing C# .NET code, since this book does not teach you how to write C# code from the ground up; it assumes that you can already read and write C# code.

While this book was written for developers who are absolute beginners where writing C# code for InfoPath forms is concerned, it assumes that you are already familiar with the basics for designing and publishing InfoPath forms as is taught in *InfoPath 2010 Cookbook: 101 Codeless Recipes for Beginners*, and that you also already have knowledge of working with Visual Studio 2010, web services, databases, and SharePoint 2010 if you intend to go through the more advanced recipes in the last three chapters of the book.

This book follows a practical approach. Almost each chapter presents you first with a short amount of theory explaining a few key concepts and then slowly builds your InfoPath programming skills with step-by-step recipes (tutorials) that follow a logical sequence.

Each recipe has a discussion section that expands on the steps and code outlined in the recipe, and offers additional information on what you learned. The recipes in this book have one of two purposes: 1. To explain and demonstrate fundamental concepts for writing code for InfoPath, and 2. To provide you with basic techniques you can use repeatedly to create all kinds of solutions for InfoPath by writing code.

You will not find everything you can do with InfoPath and code explained in this book, because the amount of solutions you can create is countless; this book only touches upon the most often requested solutions. However, this book should provide you with enough "baggage" and ideas for creating or extending your own InfoPath solutions through code.

How to use this book

This book has been set up in a cookbook style with 101 recipes. Each recipe consists of 3 parts: A description of the problem, a step-by-step outline of the recipe (solution), and further discussion highlighting important parts of the recipe or expanding on what you have learned.

Chapters 1 through 5 are meant to give you a foundation for writing code for InfoPath 2010 form templates. They explain how to access data stored in InfoPath forms and how to program against controls. These chapters are aimed towards developers who are new to writing code for InfoPath forms.

Chapters 6 through 9 are more advanced chapters about writing code that allows InfoPath to interact with web services, databases, and SharePoint. These chapters not only require you to have Visual Studio 2010 installed on your computer, but also require you to already possess knowledge of programming for other Microsoft products not explained in this book.

Throughout this book you will find references to code snippets indicated by numbers (for example *code #: 3C144335-0D54-4F82-96CB-EFC6E0D03072*). These numbers correspond to text files, which you can download from www.bizsupportonline.com.

About the author

My name is S.Y.M. Wong-A-Ton and I have been a software developer since the start of my IT career back in 1997. The first Microsoft products I used as a developer were Visual Basic 4 and SQL Server 6.5. During my IT career I have developed as well as maintained and supported all types of applications ranging from desktop applications to web sites and web services. I have been a Microsoft Certified Professional since 1998 and have held the title of Microsoft Certified Solution Developer for almost as long as I have been in IT.

I was originally trained as a Geophysicist and co-wrote (as the main author) a scientific article while I was still a scientist. This article was published in 1997 in the Geophysical Research Letters of the American Geophysical Union.

I started exploring the first version of InfoPath in 2005 in my spare time and was hooked on it from day one. What I liked most about InfoPath was the simplicity with which I was able to quickly create electronic forms that were in reality small applications on their own; all this without writing a single line of code!

While exploring InfoPath, I started actively helping other InfoPath users, who were asking questions on the Internet, to come up with innovative solutions. And because the same questions were being asked frequently, I decided to start writing tutorials and articles about InfoPath on my web site "Enterprise Solutions", which evolved into what is known today as "Biz Support Online" and can be visited at http://www.bizsupportonline.net.

Shortly after starting to share my knowledge about InfoPath with others, I received recognition from Microsoft in the form of the Microsoft Most Valuable Professional (MVP) award, and have received this award every year after then, which as of writing has been 6 years in a row.

While the greatest joy I get from working with InfoPath is being able to stretch its boundaries without writing code, I remain a developer at heart. Needless to say, I had an immense pleasure putting the recipes in this book together for you, so I hope you enjoy reading it, that you learn a lot from it, and that it inspires you to find more InfoPath solutions that make use of code.

Support

Every effort has been made to ensure the accuracy of this book. Corrections for this book are provided at http://www.bizsupportonline.com.

If you have comments, suggestions, improvements, or ideas about this book, please send them to bizsupportonline@gmail.com with "InfoPath 2010 Cookbook 3" in the subject line.

Chapter 1: Getting Started

You must set up a development environment before you can start to write code for InfoPath forms. InfoPath 2010 comes with Visual Studio Tools for Applications as its development environment, which you can use to write managed code (C# or Visual Basic .NET) for InfoPath forms.

The recipes in this chapter take you through the steps for setting up a development environment from installing Visual Studio Tools for Applications to configuring InfoPath Designer 2010 to write code for InfoPath forms.

1   Install Visual Studio Tools for Applications

Problem

You want to start writing code to extend or enhance the functionality of an InfoPath form.

Solution

You must install an optional component named Visual Studio Tools for Applications (or VSTA for short) that comes with InfoPath 2010 to be able to write code for InfoPath forms. The steps listed below assume that you have a copy of Microsoft Office Professional Plus 2010, which includes InfoPath 2010.

To install Visual Studio Tools for Applications when you install InfoPath 2010:

1. Ensure you have the Microsoft .NET Framework 2.0 and Microsoft Core XML Services 6.0 installed on your computer before you start installing InfoPath 2010 (see the discussion section for more information).

2. Run the setup program for Microsoft Office Professional Plus 2010.

3. On the **Microsoft Office Professional Plus 2010** setup wizard, enter a valid product key, and click **Continue**.

4. On the **Microsoft Office Professional Plus 2010** setup wizard, read the license terms, select the **I accept the terms of this agreement** check box, and click **Continue**.

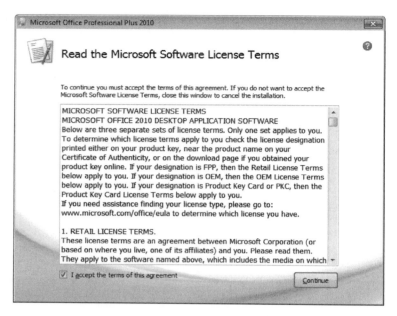

5. On the **Microsoft Office Professional Plus 2010** setup wizard, click **Customize**.

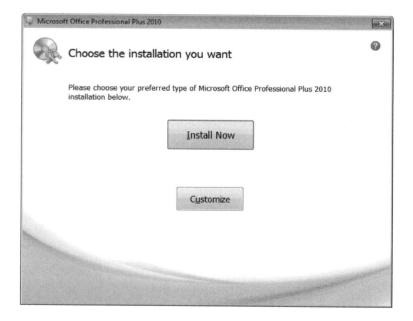

6. On the **Microsoft Office Professional Plus 2010** setup wizard, expand the **Microsoft InfoPath** node, expand the **.NET Programmability Support** node, click the **Visual Studio Tools for Applications** node, select **Run from My Computer** from the drop-down menu that appears, and then click **Install Now**.

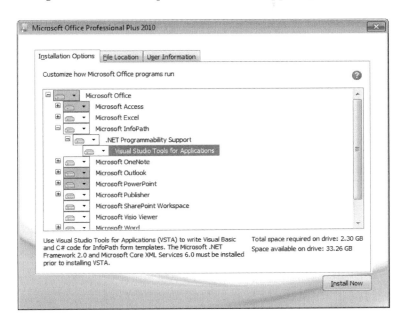

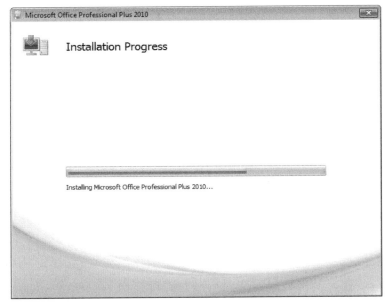

7. On the **Microsoft Office Professional Plus 2010** setup wizard, click **Close**.

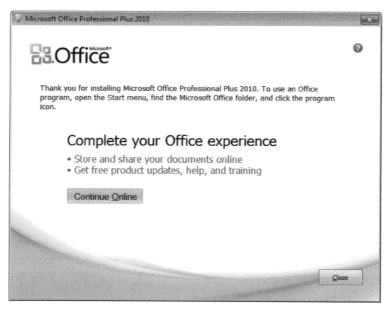

You should now be able to open InfoPath Designer 2010 and then Visual Studio Tools for Applications from within InfoPath Designer 2010.

Discussion

Visual Studio Tools for Application is a development environment that allows you to write code for InfoPath 2010. It is not installed by default when you install InfoPath 2010; it is an optional component you must select during the installation of InfoPath 2010. You must also install the Microsoft .NET Framework 2.0 and Microsoft Core XML Services 6.0 before you install Visual Studio Tools for Applications.

To check whether the Microsoft .NET Framework 2.0 is installed on your computer:

1. In Windows 7, click the Windows button, type **regedit** in the **Search programs and files** text box, and press **Enter**.

2. On the **Registry Editor** window, navigate to

   ```
   HKEY_LOCAL_MACHINE\SOFTWARE\Microsoft\Net Framework Setup\NDP
   ```

3. Verify that a **v2.0** folder is present and that it contains a key named **Install** that has a value of **1**. You can also check the number of the service pack that has been installed by checking the value of the **SP** key under the same folder.

For more information, refer to the article entitled *How to determine which versions and service pack levels of the Microsoft .NET Framework are installed* on the Microsoft Support web site.

To check whether Microsoft Core XML Services 6.0 is installed on your computer:

1. Open Windows Explorer.

2. Navigate to the `C:\Windows\System32` folder and verify that a DLL named **msxml6.dll** is present.

Figure 1. Properties dialog box of msxml6.dll.

3. If the DLL is not present or if an older version of it is present, you can download the setup program for Microsoft Core XML Services 6.0 from the Microsoft Download Center web site.

If you do not install Visual Studio Tools for Applications, you will see the following message appear when you try to open it to write code from within InfoPath Designer 2010.

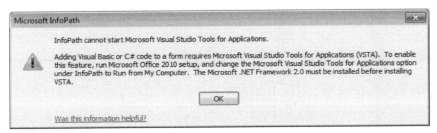

Figure 2. Message box that appears when you try to open VSTA and it has not yet been installed.

If you have already installed InfoPath 2010, but forgot to or did not select to install Visual Studio Tools for Applications along with it, you can install Visual Studio Tools for Applications afterwards as follows:

1. In Windows 7, click the Windows button, and then select **Control Panel**.

2. On the **Control Panel** window, click **Programs**.

3. On the **Programs** window, click **Programs and Features**.

4. On the **Programs and Features** window, select **Microsoft Office Professional Plus 2010** (or the version of Microsoft Office you have previously installed), and click **Change**.

5. On the **Microsoft Office Professional Plus 2010** setup wizard, leave the **Add or Remove Features** option selected, and click **Continue**.

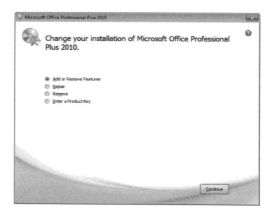

6. On the **Microsoft Office Professional Plus 2010** setup wizard, expand the **Microsoft InfoPath** node, expand the **.NET Programmability Support** node, click the **Visual Studio Tools for Applications** node, select **Run from My Computer** from the drop-down menu that appears, and then click **Continue**. The Microsoft Office installer should start configuring Microsoft Office.

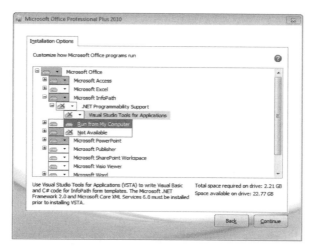

7. On the **Microsoft Office Professional Plus 2010** setup wizard, click **Close**.

2 Set or change the form template code language to C#

Set the form template code language for one form template

Problem

You want to choose C# as the programming language to write code for an InfoPath form.

Solution

The code language for a form template can be set either for the form template you currently have open in InfoPath or for any new form templates you create in the future.

To set the programming language to C# for the form template you currently have open in InfoPath:

1. In InfoPath, click **Developer ➤ Code ➤ Language**.

Figure 3. Commands on the Developer tab in InfoPath Designer 2010.

If the **Developer** tab is not present on the Ribbon:

a. In InfoPath, click **File ➤ Options**.

b. On the **InfoPath Options** dialog box, select **Customize Ribbon** in the left menu.

c. On the **Customize Ribbon** screen, ensure that **Main Tabs** is selected in the **Customize the Ribbon** drop-down list, select the **Developer** check box, and click **OK**.

2. On the **Form Options** dialog box, select **C#** from the **Form template code language** drop-down list box, and click **OK**.

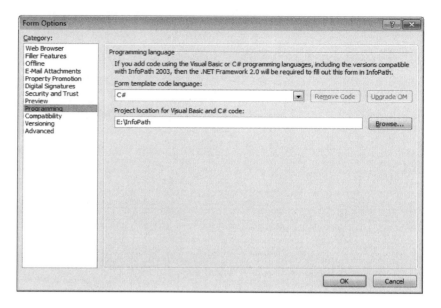

Figure 4. Selecting the form language and project location on the Form Options dialog box.

Discussion

In the solution described above you saw how to set the form template programming language for the form template you currently have open in InfoPath by using the **Form Options** dialog box. On the same screen where you set the programming language, you can also set the project location. Whenever you add code to a form template, InfoPath automatically creates a VSTA project for the form template on the project location specified on the **Form Options** dialog box. The programming language and project location you set for the form template you currently have open in InfoPath will always override the programming language and project location you set for InfoPath Designer 2010 as a whole via the **Options** dialog box (see *Set the form template code language for all future templates* below).

In the solution described above you accessed the programming language settings on the **Form Options** dialog box via the **Language** command on the **Developer** tab on the Ribbon. You could have also accessed the programming language settings via a more indirect route by clicking **File ➤ Info ➤ Form Options**, and then selecting **Programming** in the **Category** list.

Note that the **Developer** tab is not available for the types of form templates that do not support code. For example, because **SharePoint List** forms and template parts do not support form code, the **Developer** tab will not be available for those types of form templates.

Tip:

Always ensure the programming language and VSTA project location are correct before you create a new project for a form template.

Set the form template code language for all future templates

Problem

You want to choose C# as the programming language to write code for all form templates you create in the future.

Solution

The form template code language can be set either for the form template you currently have open in InfoPath or for any new form templates you create in the future.

To set the default form template code language for all new form templates you create in the future:

1. In InfoPath, click **File ➤ Options**.

2. On the **InfoPath Options** dialog box on the **General options for working with InfoPath** screen, click **More Options**.

3. On the **Options** dialog box, click the **Design** tab, and then set the programming language under the **Programming Defaults** section. In addition to the programming language, you can also set a default folder where all VSTA projects should be created.

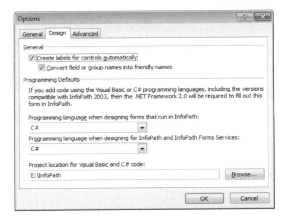

Figure 5. The Options dialog box in InfoPath Designer 2010.

4. Click **OK** when closing all dialog boxes.

Discussion

In the solution described above you saw how to set the form template programming language for all form templates created in InfoPath by using the **Options** dialog box. The programming language and project location you set through this dialog box will be used for all new form templates you create in the future. Note that these settings are overridden by the programming language and project location you set for a specific form template through the **Form Options** dialog box.

Change the form template code language to C#

Problem

You have a form template that is not currently associated with a VSTA project, but for which the programming language is set to Visual Basic. You want to change the programming language to C#.

Solution

You can use the **Form Options** dialog box to change the programming language from Visual Basic to C#.

To change the form template programming language to C#:

1. In InfoPath, click **Developer ➤ Code ➤ Language**.

2. On the **Form Options** dialog box, ensure **Programming** is selected in the **Category** list, select **C#** from the **Form template code language** drop-down list box, and click **OK**.

Discussion

When InfoPath is installed for the first time, Visual Basic is set as the default programming language for the VSTA projects you create for form templates, so ensure you change the programming language to C# on the two locations mentioned in the previous two solutions before you start to write code.

Note that if a form template has already been linked to a VSTA project containing Visual Basic code, you will not be able to change the form template language to C# as described above. Because InfoPath does not provide automatic code translation from Visual Basic to C# or vice versa when you change the programming language, you must first remove the Visual Basic code as described in recipe *4 Remove code and project files from a form template*, change the programming language to C# as described above, and then rewrite the code in C#.

3   Create a new C# project for a form template

Problem

You want to create a new C# project to start writing code for an InfoPath form template.

Solution

You can use the **Code Editor** command on the **Developer** tab on the Ribbon to open VSTA from within InfoPath Designer 2010, or add an event handler to a control or to the form to be able to create a new C# project for a form template that is not yet linked to a VSTA project.

To create a new C# project for a form template that is not yet linked to a VSTA project:

1.   In InfoPath, create a new form template or use an existing one.

2.   Ensure that you have set the programming language to C# (see recipe *2 Set or change the form template code language to C#*) and that you have specified the location for the project files for the new C# project that should be created.

3.   Save the InfoPath form template to a location on disk. If you skip this step, InfoPath should prompt you to save the form template before VSTA is opened, because a form template must be saved before you can add Visual Basic or C# code to it.

4.   Click **Developer ➤ Code ➤ Code Editor** to open VSTA. If the **Developer** tab is not present in InfoPath Designer 2010, ensure that the type of form template you have chosen to create or edit supports code and that you have installed VSTA (see recipe *1 Install Visual Studio Tools for Applications*).

VSTA should open with a newly created C# project.

Discussion

Opening VSTA from within InfoPath Designer 2010 for an InfoPath form template that does not contain code creates a new VSTA project for that form template. There are two ways you can open VSTA from within InfoPath Designer 2010:

1.   By adding an event handler either to the form (see recipe *6 Add an event handler for a form event*) or to a control on the form (see recipe *7 Add an event handler for a control event*).

2.   By opening the code editor as you have done in the solution described above.

The first method opens VSTA and adds code for an event handler, while the second method opens VSTA and does not add any code for event handlers. In the latter case, only default form template code will be present in the code file. Note that before you can open VSTA from within InfoPath, you must have enabled .NET programmability when you installed InfoPath (see recipe *1 Install Visual Studio Tools for Applications*).

The programming language for the new VSTA project that is created depends on either the default language you set for InfoPath Designer 2010 as a whole or on the programming language you set specifically for one form template (see recipe *2 Set or change the form template code language to C#*). Therefore, it is vitally important that you have the language set to the correct language of your choice before opening VSTA to create a project for an InfoPath form template. If you do not do this and find out later that the project you created has an incorrect programming language, you will have to close VSTA, remove the code in InfoPath (see recipe *4 Remove code and project files from a form template*), set the programming language for the form template, and then reopen VSTA to create a new project with the correct programming language.

If you look at the **Project Explorer** pane in VSTA, you will see that a couple of references have been added to the project, two of which you may already be familiar with (**System** and **System.Xml**).

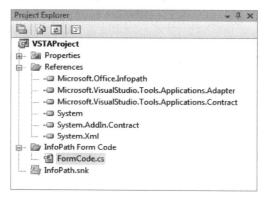

Figure 6. Project Explorer pane in Visual Studio Tools for Applications.

The **Microsoft.Office.InfoPath** assembly defines the classes in the InfoPath object model. Because VSTA is a tool that is used to edit and build add-ins and is used here with InfoPath to create a project that is attached to the InfoPath form template, VSTA and add-in specific assemblies have also been added to the project:

- Microsoft.VisualStudio.Tools.Applications.Adapter

- Microsoft.VisualStudio.Tools.Applications.Contract

- System.AddIn.Contract

In addition, the project contains a strong name key file named **InfoPath.snk**. This is to sign the assembly for your project and give it a strong name.

The **FormCode.cs** file contains the code for the form. The following **using** statements are added to it by default:

```
using Microsoft.Office.InfoPath;
using System;
using System.Xml;
using System.Xml.XPath;
```

While these **using** statements are not required to build the form template, you will need them later to write code that accesses data in the form.

The initial **FormCode.cs** file also contains a class named FormCode in which you should write the code for the form template. Within this class, the following sample code has been commented out:

```
// Member variables are not supported in browser-enabled forms.
// Instead, write and read these values from the FormState
// dictionary using code such as the following:
//
// private object _memberVariable
// {
//    get
//    {
//       return FormState["_memberVariable"];
//    }
//    set
//    {
//       FormState["_memberVariable"] = value;
//    }
// }
```

Because browser forms do not support member variables, an InfoPath form has a property called FormState, which is a dictionary that browser-enabled forms can use to maintain state information across sessions on the server. The code that has been commented out demonstrates the usage of the FormState dictionary.

And finally, a method called InternalStartup() has been added to the code.

```
// NOTE: The following procedure is required by Microsoft InfoPath.
// It can be modified using Microsoft InfoPath.
public void InternalStartup()
{
}
```

The InternalStartup() method is used by InfoPath to bind event handlers to control and form events. It is not meant for you to manually add code to it. When you add an event handler for a control or form event from within InfoPath Designer 2010, InfoPath automatically adds code to the InternalStartup() method to bind the event handler method to the corresponding event.

When you compile the code in VSTA by clicking **Build ➤ Build [project name]**, a DLL is added to the form template (.xsn).

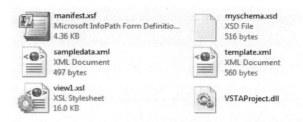

Figure 7. Files contained in the XSN file for an InfoPath form template that contains code.

In the figure above, **VSTAProject.dll** is the DLL containing the compiled code for the VSTA project linked to the InfoPath form template.

4   Remove code and project files from a form template

Problem

You accidentally created a new form template with Visual Basic code, so want to remove the code and associated project from the form template.

Solution

You can remove the code and the project associated with a form template by disassociating the form template through the **Form Options** dialog box.

To remove code from a form template:

1.   In InfoPath, open the form template that has code associated with it.

2.   Click **Developer ➤ Code ➤ Language**.

3.   On the **Form Options** dialog box under **Programming language**, click **Remove Code**. Click **Yes** on the message box that appears, and then on the **Form Options** dialog box, click **OK**. Note: The **Remove Code** button is enabled when a form template is linked to a VSTA project, and disabled when a form template is not linked to a VSTA project.

The form template should not have code or a VSTA project associated with it anymore.

Discussion

When you remove code from a form template, InfoPath does two things:

1.   The compiled DLL that InfoPath stores in the form template (.xsn) is deleted from the form template (also see the discussion section of recipe *3 Create a new C# project for a form template*).

2.   The VSTA project is disassociated from the form template, but the project files are not deleted.

Because the VSTA project is not deleted, you can choose to associate it again with the form template (also see recipe *5 Associate a form template with an existing C# project*) at a later point in time. If you do not want to retain the VSTA project, you must manually delete its files through Windows Explorer.

5   Associate a form template with an existing C# project

Problem

You have a form template that was previously associated with a VSTA project, but that currently does not have any code associated with it. You want to associate the form template again with the old VSTA project.

Solution

There are two ways you can associate a form template with an existing VSTA project:

1. You can create a new project and replace its files with the files from the existing VSTA project.
2. You can create a new project and manually modify the **manifest.xsf** file of the form template to point to the existing VSTA project.

To associate a form template with an existing VSTA project by creating a new project:

1. In InfoPath, open the form template you want to associate with an existing VSTA project.

2. Click **Developer ➤ Code ➤ Code Editor** to create a new project that is linked to the form template. This should open VSTA.

3. Close VSTA and InfoPath Designer 2010.

4. Navigate to the location on disk where the new VSTA project was created. If you do not know where the new project was created, open InfoPath again, click **Developer ➤ Code ➤ Language**, and then on the **Form Options** dialog box, look at the location that is listed in the **Project location for Visual Basic and C# code** text box.

5. Replace all of the files (except for the **.csproj** files) of the new project with the files from the old project.

6. In InfoPath, open the form template you previously had open, and then click **Developer ➤ Code ➤ Code Editor** to open VSTA again.

7. In VSTA, click **Build ➤ Build [project name]** and ensure that the build succeeded. If the build failed, fix the errors. Note that you may also have to add references that are missing, correct control names, etc. for the form template to work properly.

To associate a form template with an existing VSTA project by manually modifying the **manifest.xsf** file of the form template to point to the location of the existing VSTA project:

1. In InfoPath, open the form template you want to associate with an existing VSTA project.

2. Click **Developer ➤ Code ➤ Code Editor** to create a new project that is linked to the form template. This should open VSTA. Close VSTA.

3. Click **File ➤ Publish ➤ Export Source Files**.

Figure 8. Export Source Files command on the Publish tab in InfoPath Designer 2010.

4. On the **Browse For Folder** dialog box, select the folder in which you want to save the files, and click **OK**.

5. Close InfoPath Designer 2010.

6. Navigate to the folder where you saved the files, and open the **manifest.xsf** file in Notepad.

7. Locate the **solutionDefinition** element.

```
<xsf:extensions>
  <xsf:extension name="SolutionDefinitionExtensions">
    <xsf2:solutionDefinition
      runtimeCompatibility="client server"
      allowClientOnlyCode="no">
      <xsf2:offline openIfQueryFails="yes"
        cacheQueries="yes">
      </xsf2:offline>
      <xsf2:server formLocale="en-US"
        isPreSubmitPostBackEnabled="no" isMobileEnabled="no">
      </xsf2:server>
      <xsf2:managedCode
        projectPath="E:\InfoPath\VSTAProject\VSTAProject.csproj"
        language="CSharp" version="3.0" enabled="yes">
      </xsf2:managedCode>
    </xsf2:solutionDefinition>
  </xsf:extension>
</xsf:extensions>
```

8. Change the value of the **projectPath** attribute of the **managedCode** element under the **solutionDefinition** element to point to the project file for the VSTA project to which you want to link the form template:

```
<xsf2:managedCode
  projectPath="C:\Projects\IPProject.csproj"
```

```
  language="CSharp" version="3.0" enabled="yes">
</xsf2:managedCode>
```

where `C:\Projects\IPProject.csproj` is the path to the existing VSTA project. Note that you must replace this path with the path for your own VSTA project. The complete `xsf2:solutionDefinition` element should resemble the following:

```
<xsf2:solutionDefinition
  runtimeCompatibility="client server" allowClientOnlyCode="no">
  <xsf2:offline openIfQueryFails="yes" cacheQueries="yes"></xsf2:offline>
  <xsf2:server formLocale="en-US" isPreSubmitPostBackEnabled="no"
    isMobileEnabled="no">
  </xsf2:server>
  <xsf2:managedCode
    projectPath="C:\Projects\IPProject.csproj"
    language="CSharp" version="3.0" enabled="yes">
  </xsf2:managedCode>
</xsf2:solutionDefinition>
```

9. Save the **manifest.xsf** file, and close Notepad.

10. Right-click the **manifest.xsf** file and select **Design** from the context menu that appears.

11. In InfoPath, click **File ➤ Save As**.

12. On the **Save As** dialog box, browse to a location where you want to save the form template, enter a suitable file name, and click **Save**. After this, InfoPath should repackage the form template into an XSN file, so you can delete the folder where the **manifest.xsf** file is located.

13. Click **Developer ➤ Code ➤ Code Editor** to open VSTA again.

14. In VSTA, click **Build ➤ Build [project name]** and ensure that the build succeeded. If the build failed, fix the errors.

Discussion

Note that you should check whether all event handlers that are defined in the code are bound to the correct controls on the form and that all external data sources and resource files are present in the form template, otherwise the form will fail to work as intended.

You can also use the second method described in the solution above to move an existing VSTA project that has already been linked to a form template to another location on disk.

Chapter 2: Basics of Programming for InfoPath

InfoPath Object Models

Programming in InfoPath 2010 is .NET programming combined with programming against the InfoPath managed code object model. The InfoPath managed code object model is implemented in two assemblies that are both named **Microsoft.Office.Infopath.dll**. The first assembly (located in `C:\Program Files\Microsoft Office\Office14\InfoPathOM`) contains the full set of types and members that can be used with form templates that are filled out exclusively through InfoPath Filler 2010, while the second assembly (located in `C:\Program Files\Microsoft Office\Office14\InfoPathOM\InfoPathOMFormServices`) contains only a subset of the types and members from the first assembly and can be used with form templates running on Microsoft SharePoint Server 2010 with InfoPath Forms Services. The assembly that becomes available when you write code depends on the type of form you create or select via **File ➤ Form Options ➤ Compatibility ➤ Form type**. You can set the form type to InfoPath Filler Form to use types and members in the first assembly or to Web Browser Form to use types and members in the second assembly.

InfoPath Form Template Components

When working with InfoPath you generally work with three main components:

1. The InfoPath application
2. An InfoPath form template (.xsn)
3. An InfoPath form (.xml)

These three components can be translated to the InfoPath object model one-on-one as follows:

1. `Application` – The top-level object in the InfoPath object model that provides properties and methods to access lower-level collections and objects, and that performs a number of general purpose functions.

2. `XmlForm.Template` – This property returns a reference to the `FormTemplate` object with which you can access the manifest (.xsf), other files stored in the form template (.xsn), and get information about the version number and URI of the form template. The `XmlForm` object is the key object in the InfoPath object model that provides properties and methods used to interact with and manipulate the XML data in an InfoPath form. You can access this object and its members by using the `this` keyword when working with form template code.

3. `XmlForm.MainDataSource` – This property returns a `DataSource` object that represents the main data source of the form.

Other key components of an InfoPath form template include:

- Views – An InfoPath form template has one view by default, but you can add more views to it, and access any view through the `XmlForm.ViewInfos` property. The `XmlForm.ViewInfos` property returns a `ViewInfoCollection` object associated with the form template and contains a `ViewInfo` object for each view within the form. You can access the current view of a form through the `XmlForm.CurrentView` property. And to get to the raw XSL style sheet used by a view, you can use the `XmlForm.Template.OpenFileFromPackage()` method along with the name of the XSL file used to render the view you want to access.

- Secondary data sources – You can add one or more data connections that retrieve data to an InfoPath form template, and InfoPath will create a secondary data source for each such data connection. You can access these secondary data sources through the `XmlForm.DataSources` property.

- Submit data connections – You can add one or more submit data connections to an InfoPath form template, and access them through the `XmlForm.DataConnections` property.

- Resource files – You can add one or more resource files to an InfoPath form template. Each resource file is stored in the form template (.xsn) and can be retrieved by using the `XmlForm.Template.OpenFileFromPackage()` method. This method returns a readable, but not writable `System.IO.Stream` object, which you can use to read the contents of any file (so not only resource files) stored within an InfoPath form template.

The InfoPath object model consists of many more types and members, but the aforementioned ones are the main types and members you will be working with over and over again when you write code for form templates in InfoPath 2010.

To view the full set of types and members offered by the InfoPath object model, open the **Object Browser** in VSTA (press **F2** or click **View ➤ Object Browser**), expand the node for the **Microsoft.Office.InfoPath** namespace in the list of namespaces, and then click on any class, property, method, or enumeration for which you want to retrieve information. Properties and methods are listed in the top-right pane, and if you click on one of them, you should get additional information about the selected property or method in the bottom-right pane.

6   Add an event handler for a form event

Problem

You want to run code when a user opens a form.

Solution

You can add an event handler for the **Loading** event of a form in which you can write code that runs when the form opens.

To add an event handler for the **Loading** event of a form:

1. In InfoPath, create a new form template or use an existing one.

2. Click **Developer ➤ Events ➤ Loading Event**.

Figure 9. Form events with the Loading Event highlighted on the Developer tab in InfoPath.

This should start VSTA, open an existing or create a new project, and add a `FormEvents_Loading()` event handler to the `FormCode` class.

```
public void FormEvents_Loading(object sender, LoadingEventArgs e)
{
   // Write your code here.
}
```

In VSTA, you should now be able to write code in the `FormEvents_Loading()` event handler.

Discussion

You can have code run when an event takes place. An event is generally triggered by an action taken by a user. For example, if a user clicks a button, a form can raise an event indicating that a click took place. This event is then caught and handled by an event handler, which is a method that is bound to the event. Event handlers contain code that should run when an event takes place. So you must first add event handlers to the code file of an InfoPath form template before you can start writing code that is executed in response to actions a user takes while opening or filling out a form and that cause events to be raised.

There are two types of events that can take place in an InfoPath form:

1. Form events
2. Control events

An example of a form event is the event that is raised when a user opens a form, and an example of a control event is the event that is raised when a user clicks a button. The types of form events and control events that become available in an InfoPath form depend on the type of form (InfoPath Filler form or browser form) you create. InfoPath Filler forms support the full range of events that are available in InfoPath, while browser forms support only a subset of those events.

The following table lists the form events supported in InfoPath Filler and browser forms.

Event	InfoPath Filler Form	InfoPath Browser Form
Context Changed	✓	
Loading	✓	✓
Merge	✓	
Save	✓	
Sign	✓	
Submit	✓	✓
Version Upgrade	✓	✓
View Switched	✓	✓

Table 1. InfoPath form events.

If you look at the `FormCode` class, you will see that the `FormEvents_Loading()` event handler was bound to the **Loading** event in the `InternalStartup()` method using a `LoadingEventHandler` delegate.

```
public void InternalStartup()
{
  EventManager.FormEvents.Loading += new LoadingEventHandler(
    FormEvents_Loading);
}
```

And if you look at the `FormEvents_Loading()` event handler, you will see that it has a `LoadingEventArgs` object as its second parameter.

```
public void FormEvents_Loading(object sender, LoadingEventArgs e)
{
  // Write your code here.
}
```

The `LoadingEventArgs` object has two properties, which you may want to take note of. The first property is `CancelableArgs`, which allows you to stop the loading of a form if you set its `Cancel` property equal to `true`

```
e.CancelableArgs.Cancel = true;
```

and the second property is `InputParameters`, which allows you to pass parameters to a form via a command-line or an URL (also see recipe *93 Populate form fields from query string parameters*). So in summary, during the **Loading** event of a form, you can stop the form from being opened or you can retrieve parameters that were passed to the form via a command-line or an URL.

The way in which you add an event handler to a form depends on the type of form event you want to catch. You can use the same method as the one described in the solution above to add event handlers for the **View Switched**, **Sign**, and **Context Changed** events of a form. Note that the **Sign** and **Context Changed** events are only available in InfoPath Filler Forms and not in browser forms. Therefore, their corresponding commands on the **Developer** tab will be disabled when you create a browser-compatible template.

Other form events such as **Submit**, **Save**, **Merge**, and **Version Upgrade** are added on slightly different ways than described in the solution above. These methods are described below.

To add an event handler for the **Submit** event of a form:

1. In InfoPath, create a form template or use an existing one.

2. Click **Data ➤ Submit Form ➤ Submit Options**.

3. On the **Submit Options** dialog box, select the **Allow users to submit this form** check box, select the **Perform custom action using Code** option, and click **Edit Code**.

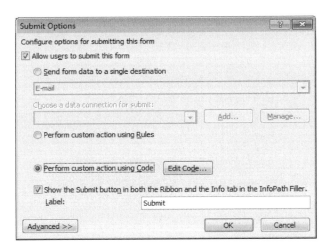

Figure 10. Edit Code button on the Submit Options dialog box in InfoPath.

4. In VSTA, you can now write code in the `FormEvents_Submit()` event handler.

```
public void FormEvents_Submit(object sender, SubmitEventArgs e)
{
  // If the submit operation is successful, set
  // e.CancelableArgs.Cancel = false;
```

```
        // Write your code here.
    }
```

Note that you can call code that you write in the `FormEvents_Submit()` event handler from any other event handler in the same InfoPath form by calling the `Submit()` method of the form. For example, you could place a button on a form that calls code you wrote in the `FormEvents_Submit()` event handler by calling the `Submit()` method in the `Clicked()` event handler for the button:

```
public void CTRL5_5_Clicked(object sender, ClickedEventArgs e)
{
  Submit();
}
```

Any options you specify under the **Advanced** section of the **Submit Options** dialog box, including the action that should be taken after submitting the form, are applied after code in the `FormEvents_Submit()` event handler has run. Therefore, you can use the technique described above to simulate the functionality of programmatically closing a form by adding a button that submits and then closes the form (select **Close the form** in the **After submit** drop-down list box under the **Advanced** section of the **Submit Options** dialog box).

To add an event handler for the **Save** event of a form:

1. In InfoPath, create a new InfoPath Filler form template or use an existing one.

2. Click **File ➤ Info ➤ Form Options**.

3. On the **Form Options** dialog box, select **Filler Features** in the **Category** list.

4. On the **Form Options** dialog box under **Save behavior**, select the **Save using custom code** check box, and click **Edit**.

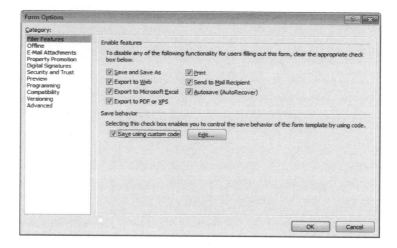

Figure 11. The Edit button to add an event handler for the Save event.

5. In VSTA, you can now write code in the `FormEvents_Save()` event handler.

```
public void FormEvents_Save(object sender, SaveEventArgs e)
{
  // Write your code that will run before a Save or Save As operation
  // here.

  // The Dirty property will be set to false if save is successful.
  e.PerformSaveOperation();

  // Write your code that will run after saving here.

  e.CancelableArgs.Cancel = false;
}
```

For an example of writing code for the **Save** event of a form, see recipe *18 Save form data to a PDF file on disk*.

To add an event handler for the **Merge** event of a form:

1. In InfoPath, create a new InfoPath Filler form template or use an existing one.

2. Click **File ➤ Info ➤ Form Options**.

3. On the **Form Options** dialog box, select **Advanced** in the **Category** list.

4. On the **Form Options** dialog box under **Merge forms**, select the **Merge using custom code** check box, and click **Edit**.

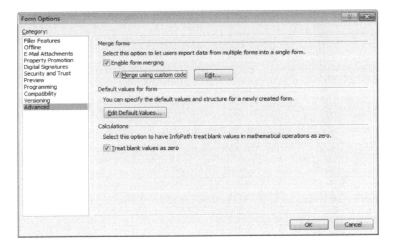

Figure 12. The Edit button to add an event handler for the Merge event.

5. In VSTA, you can now write code in the `FormEvents_Merge()` event handler.

```
public void FormEvents_Merge(object sender, MergeEventArgs e)
{
  // Write your code here.
  MergeForm(e.Xml);
  e.CancelableArgs.Cancel = false;
}
```

To add an event handler for the **Version Upgrade** event of a form:

1. In InfoPath, create a new form template or use an existing one.
2. Click **File ➤ Info ➤ Form Options**.
3. On the **Form Options** dialog box, select **Versioning** in the **Category** list.
4. On the **Form Options** dialog box, select **Use custom event** from the **Update existing forms** drop-down list box, and click **Edit**.

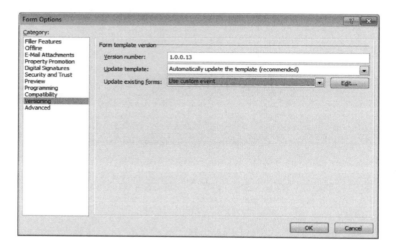

Figure 13. The Edit button to add an event handler for the Version Upgrade event.

5. In VSTA, you can now write code in the `FormEvents_VersionUpgrade()` event handler.

```
public void FormEvents_VersionUpgrade(object sender,
  VersionUpgradeEventArgs e)
{
  // Write your code here.
}
```

7   Add an event handler for a control event

Problem

You want to run code when a user clicks a button on a form.

Solution

You can add an event handler for the **Clicked** event of a button in which you can write code that runs when a user clicks the button.

To add an event handler for the **Clicked** event of a button:

1. In InfoPath, create a new form template or use an existing one.

2. Add a **Button** control to the view of the form template.

3. Use one of the following two methods to add a **Clicked** event:

    a. Select the button, and then on the Ribbon, click **Control Tools ➤ Properties ➤ Button ➤ Custom Code**.

Figure 14. Custom Code command on the Properties tab in InfoPath Designer 2010.

    b. Right-click the button, select **Button Properties** from the context menu that appears, and then on the **Button Properties** dialog box on the **General** tab, select **Rules and Custom Code** in the **Action** drop-down list box and then click **Edit Form Code**.

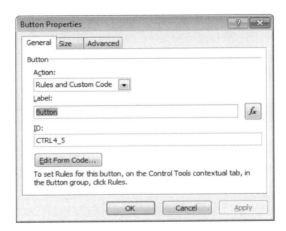

Figure 15. The Edit Form Code button on the Button Properties dialog box.

In VSTA, you should now be able to write code in the `Clicked()` event handler for the button control.

Discussion

As was the case with form events (see recipe *6 Add an event handler for a form event*), the types of control events that become available in an InfoPath form depend on the type of form (InfoPath Filler form or browser form) you create. InfoPath Filler forms support the full range of events that are available in InfoPath, while browser forms support only a subset of those events.

The following table lists the control events supported in InfoPath Filler and browser forms.

Event	InfoPath Filler Form	InfoPath Browser Form
Clicked	✓	✓
Changed	✓	✓
Changing	✓	
Validating	✓	✓

Table 2. InfoPath control events.

You can only add an event handler for the **Clicked** event to button controls (**Button** and **Picture Button**). When you add an event handler for the **Clicked** event to a button, the event handler gets a name such as for example CTRL1_5_Clicked(). This name is composed of the **ID** of the control (CTRL1_5) that is specified on the **General** tab of the **Button Properties** dialog box and the text _Clicked.

InfoPath automatically assigns IDs to controls, but if you want to use your own names for controls and event handler methods, you must change the **ID** for a button control on the **Button Properties** dialog box before you add the event handler, so that the ID is used when composing the name for the event handler method.

As was the case with the **Loading** event in the previous recipe, the event handler for the **Clicked** event of the button is bound to the **Clicked** event in the InternalStartup() method using a ClickedEventHandler delegate.

```
public void InternalStartup()
{
  ((ButtonEvent)EventManager.ControlEvents["CTRL1_5"]).Clicked +=
    new ClickedEventHandler(CTRL1_5_Clicked);
}
```

But instead of a LoadingEventArgs object the **Clicked** event handler has a ClickedEventArgs object as its second parameter.

```
public void CTRL1_5_Clicked(object sender, ClickedEventArgs e)
{
  // Write your code here.
}
```

Note that the control ID is referenced in the `ControlEvents` collection to find the event for the button to bind the event handler to.

```
EventManager.ControlEvents["CTRL1_5"]
```

The `ControlEvents` object represents the collection of all event handlers for the **Clicked** events raised by the buttons on a form. Therefore, if you change the control ID at a later stage, you must remember to also manually change it in the `InternalStartup()` method where it is referenced, since InfoPath does not automatically perform such updates.

The way in which you add an event handler to a control depends on the type of control for which you want to add an event handler. Adding an event handler for a control that is not a button differs from adding an event handler for a button in that you should use the **Fields** task pane or the **Developer** tab to add the event handler instead of the **Properties** tab or **Properties** dialog box for the control, and that control events are bound to event handlers for groups or fields instead of the control itself as is the case for buttons.

Figure 16. Commands for control events on the Developer tab in InfoPath Designer 2010.

To add an event handler for the **Changed** event of a control on a form:

1. In InfoPath, create a new form template or use an existing one.

2. Add a control that is not a button control to the view of the form template.

3. Use one of the following two methods to add an event handler for the **Changed** event:

    a. Select the control, and then on the Ribbon, click **Developer ➤ Control Events ➤ Changed Event**.

    b. On the **Fields** task pane, click the down arrow on the right-hand side of the field that is bound to the control, and then select **Programming ➤ Changed Event** from the drop-down menu that appears.

Figure 17. Adding an event handler for the Changed event via the Fields task pane.

In VSTA, you should now be able to write code in the Changed() event handler for the field that is bound to the control.

You can use this same method to add event handlers for the **Validating** and **Changing** events of a control. Note that the **Changing** event is only available when you are designing InfoPath Filler forms and not browser forms. Also note that InfoPath not only allows you to add event handlers for fields (elements and attributes) bound to controls, but also for groups, such as the repeating group node of a repeating table or a repeating section control.

And unlike button controls, events for fields and groups are stored in an XmlEvents collection and are accessed using the XPath expression for a field or group instead of a control ID.

```
public void InternalStartup()
{
  EventManager.XmlEvents["/my:myFields/my:field1"].Changed +=
    new XmlChangedEventHandler(field1_Changed);
  EventManager.XmlEvents["/my:myFields/my:field1"].Validating +=
    new XmlValidatingEventHandler(field1_Validating);
}
```

The XmlEvents object represents the collection of all XmlEvent events (**Changed**, **Changing**, and **Validating**) for a form template.

8 Access the Main data source of a form

Problem

You want to write code that accesses data on an InfoPath form.

Solution

The first step to access data stored within a form is to get a reference to the Main data source of the form.

To access the Main data source of a form:

1. In InfoPath, create a new form template or use an existing one.

2. Add an event handler for the **Loading** event of the form as described in recipe *6 Add an event handler for a form event*.

3. In VSTA, add the following code to the `FormEvents_Loading()` event handler:

    ```
    XPathNavigator mainDS = MainDataSource.CreateNavigator();
    ```

4. Click **Build ➤ Build [Project Name]** to build the project or press **F5** to save, build, and run the project.

You should now be able to write code that retrieves data stored in the form.

Discussion

The `MainDataSource` property of the `XmlForm` object returns a `DataSource` object that gives you a reference to the underlying XML of a form. The `XmlForm` object gives you access to the form template (including views and the manifest) as well as data contained in the Main and any secondary data sources of a form.

The `XPathNavigator` class provides a cursor model for navigating and editing XML data. To be able to navigate the XML contained in the `DataSource` object returned by the `MainDataSource` property, you must get a reference to an `XPathNavigator` object by calling the `CreateNavigator()` method of the `DataSource` object, which results in the following code:

```
XPathNavigator mainDS = MainDataSource.CreateNavigator();
```

An easy way to view the entire XML contents of a form via code is by using the `OuterXml` property of the `XPathNavigator` object as follows:

1. Add the following line of code below the line you previously added in the `FormEvents_Loading()` event handler:

    ```
    string formXml = mainDS.OuterXml;
    ```

2. While the cursor is still on the newly added line of code, press **F9** to set a breakpoint on that line, and then press **F5** to run the project in debug mode.

    If you get the following message, security settings on your computer are preventing you from debugging code in VSTA.

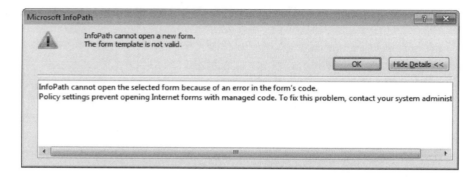

Figure 18. Security warning message you may see when previewing an InfoPath form.

You can temporarily give the form template Full Trust as follows:

  a. In InfoPath, click **File ➤ Info ➤ Form Options**.

  b. On the **Form Options** dialog box, select **Security and Trust** in the **Category** list.

  c. Deselect the **Automatically determine security level (recommended)** check box.

  d. Select the **Full Trust (the form has access to files and settings on the computer)** option, and click **OK**.

  e. In VSTA, press **F5** to rerun the project.

3. When the debugger hits the breakpoint, hover over `OuterXml` or use the **Text Visualizer** to view the full XML contents of the form. Note: You can also write debug information to the **Immediate Window** by replacing the line of code in step 1 with:

```
System.Diagnostics.Debug.Write(mainDS.OuterXml);
```

For more information about debugging InfoPath forms, see *15 Debug code of an InfoPath form template in VSTA*.

9   Access a secondary data source of a form

Problem

You have a form that has one or more secondary data sources associated with it, and you want to access the data from one of those data sources.

Solution

You can use the `DataSources` property of the `XmlForm` object to get a reference to a secondary data source that has been added to a form.

To access a secondary data source of a form:

1.   In InfoPath, create a new form template or use an existing one.

2.   Add a secondary data source to the form. You can choose to add a data connection for an XML file, a SharePoint list, a database, or a web service by using any of the commands under the **Get External Data** group on the **Data** tab.

3.   Add an event handler for the **Loading** event of the form as described in recipe *6 Add an event handler for a form event*.

4.   In VSTA, add the following code to the `FormEvents_Loading()` event handler:

```
XPathNavigator secDS = DataSources["Fruits"].CreateNavigator();
```

where **Fruits** is the name of the data connection for the secondary data source to an XML file. You can download the **Fruits.xml** file from www.bizsupportonline.com.

5.   Save and build the project.

You should now be able to write code to retrieve data stored in the secondary data source of the form.

Discussion

The `DataSources` property of the `XmlForm` object is a `DataSourceCollection` object, which contains `DataSource` objects corresponding to each data source of the form with the Main data source of the form listed as the first data source in the collection. You can access a `DataSource` object either by its position in the collection or by its name. For example:

```
DataSource mainDS = DataSources[0];
```

or

```
DataSource mainDS = DataSources[""];
```

or

```
DataSource mainDS = MainDataSource;
```

would return a `DataSource` object for the Main data source of a form, and

```
DataSource fruitsDS = DataSources[1];
```

or

```
DataSource fruitsDS = DataSources["Fruits"];
```

would return a `DataSource` object for the **Fruits** secondary data source that is located on the second position in the `DataSources` collection. Note that the `DataSourcesCollection` object is a zero-based collection.

The code in the solution described above uses the `CreateNavigator()` method of the `DataSource` object to retrieve an `XPathNavigator` object that is pointing to the root node of the secondary data source specified by the index or name in the `DataSourceCollection` object.

```
XPathNavigator secDS = DataSources["Fruits"].CreateNavigator();
```

Once you have retrieved an `XPathNavigator` object, you can use its methods to manipulate the data stored in the secondary data source, such as for example retrieve the value of a field as described in recipe *10 Get the value of a field*, loop through all of the items in the secondary data source similar to the solution described in recipe *70 Loop through rows of a repeating table*, or refresh the data in the secondary data source by calling the `Execute()` method of the data connection associated with the secondary data source.

When you add a data connection to an external data source through one of the commands listed under the **Get External Data** group of the **Data** tab in InfoPath Designer 2010, you create what is called a query data connection, which you can use to retrieve data stored in a data source. You can access the query data connection associated with a secondary data source in code as follows:

```
DataConnection queryConn = DataSources["Fruits"].QueryConnection;
```

or

```
DataConnection queryConn = DataConnections["Fruits"];
```

And once you have a reference to the data connection associated with a secondary data source, you can call its `Execute()` method to retrieve or refresh data in the secondary data source as follows:

```
queryConn.Execute();
```

InfoPath has specific data connection types (see the table below) to which you can cast the generic `DataConnection` object you retrieve.

Name	Description
AdoQueryConnection	Represents a connection for retrieving data from a Microsoft Access or Microsoft SQL Server database.
BdcQueryConnection	Represents a data connection for retrieving data from an external list on a server that runs Microsoft SharePoint Foundation 2010 or Microsoft SharePoint Server 2010.
FileQueryConnection	Represents a connection for retrieving data from an XML file.
SharepointListQueryConnection SharePointListRWQueryConnection	Represents a data connection for retrieving data from a SharePoint list or document library.
WebServiceConnection	Represents a connection to an XML Web service.

Table 3. Query data connection classes in InfoPath 2010.

For example, in the case of an XML file, you could use the following code to cast the `DataConnection` object you retrieve to a `FileQueryConnection` object

```
FileQueryConnection queryConn = (FileQueryConnection)DataConnections["Fruits"];
```

so that you can access properties that are only available on a `FileQueryConnection` object, such as:

```
string fileName = queryConn.Name;
string fileLocation = queryConn.FileLocation;
```

You can also add submit data connections to an InfoPath form. You add a submit data connection when you use any of the commands listed under the **Submit Form** group on the **Data** tab in InfoPath Designer 2010. Submit data connections are used to submit data from the InfoPath form to a particular destination. You can get a reference to a submit data connection in much the same way as you can get a reference to a query data connection by specifying either an index or the name of the data connection when retrieving it from the `DataConnections` property of the `XmlForm` object.

```
DataConnection submitConn = DataConnections["Submit Connection Name"];
```

And just like query data connections, you can cast submit data connections to the types listed in the following table.

Name	Description
AdoSubmitConnection	Represents a connection for submitting data to a Microsoft Access or Microsoft SQL Server database.
BdcSubmitConnection	Represents a data connection for submitting data to an external list on a server running Microsoft SharePoint Foundation 2010 or Microsoft SharePoint Server 2010.
FileSubmitConnection	Represents a connection to submit form information to a SharePoint Foundation server or other server that supports DAV connections.
WebServiceConnection	Represents a connection to an XML Web service.

Table 4. Submit data connection classes in InfoPath 2010.

In summary: You can add data connections to an InfoPath form template to either retrieve data from a data source or to submit data to a particular destination. When you add a data connection that retrieves data, the data is stored in a secondary data source of the InfoPath form.

You can use the commands under the **Get External Data** group on the **Data** tab in InfoPath Designer 2010 to add query data connections that retrieve external data, and you can use the commands under the **Submit Data** group on the **Data** tab in InfoPath Designer 2010 to add submit data connections that submit data.

Query data connections and submit data connections are both stored in the `DataConnections` property of the `XmlForm` object. The `DataConnections` property is a collection of `DataConnection` objects, which you can access individually via an index (number) or the name you specified when you created the data connection in InfoPath Designer 2010.

You can use the `Execute()` method of a query data connection to retrieve or refresh data and store it in the secondary data source associated with the query data connection. You can then access this data through the `DataSources` property of the `XmlForm` object. The `DataSources` property is a collection of `DataSource` objects, which you can access individually via an index (number) or the name you specified when you created the data connection in InfoPath Designer 2010. And a `DataSource` object has a property named `QueryConnection`, which represents the `DataConnection` object for retrieving data for the data source.

You can use the `Execute()` method of a submit data connection to submit data to a particular destination; not to retrieve data or populate a data source. The latter is reserved for query data connections.

`DataConnection` objects can be cast to specific data connection types, so that you can make use of properties and methods that are specific to certain types of data connections.

10   Get the value of a field

Problem

You want to retrieve the contents of a text box control on a form.

Solution

You can get a reference to the field that is bound to the text box control and then use the `Value` property of the `XPathNavigator` object to get the contents of the text box.

To get the value of a field:

1.   In InfoPath, create a new form template or use an existing one.

2.   Add a **Text Box** control to the view of the form template, name it **field1**, and set its **Default Value** property to be equal to a string, for example: "This is a default piece of text".

3.   On the **Fields** task pane, click the down arrow on the right-hand side of **field1**, and select **Copy XPath** from the drop-down menu that appears.

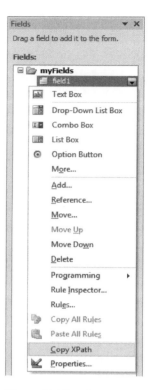

Figure 19. The Copy XPath command on the Fields task pane.

With this you have copied the XPath expression to access the XML node for **field1** to the Windows clipboard.

4.   Add an event handler for the **Loading** event of the form as described in recipe *6 Add an event handler for a form event*.

5.   In VSTA, add the following code to the `FormEvents_Loading()` event handler (*code #: 7EF4CFBB-DCA4-471B-9142-48C861829EDA*):

```
XPathNavigator mainDS = MainDataSource.CreateNavigator();
XPathNavigator field1 = mainDS.SelectSingleNode(
  "/my:myFields/my:field1", NamespaceManager);

string val = field1.Value;
```

Note: You must paste the XPath expression for **field1** you copied earlier and pass it as the first argument to the `SelectSingleNode()` method in the code above. The `field1` variable in the code above contains a reference to the `XPathNavigator` object that is pointing to the field bound to the text box control.

6.   Set a breakpoint on the line after the last line of code, and press **F5**.

When the debugger hits the breakpoint in VSTA, verify that the value of the `val` variable is the same as the **Default Value** you specified earlier for the text box control.

Discussion

The first step in getting the value of a field is retrieving an `XPathNavigator` object that is pointing to the data source in which that field is located. In the solution described above, the data source is the Main data source of the form, but it could have also been a secondary data source.

```
XPathNavigator mainDS = MainDataSource.CreateNavigator();
```

Once you have an `XPathNavigator` object for the data source, the next step is to navigate the XML of the data source to find the field. You can use the `SelectSingleNode()` method of an `XPathNavigator` object that is pointing to the data source to retrieve an `XPathNavigator` object that is pointing to the field.

```
XPathNavigator field1 = mainDS.SelectSingleNode(
  "/my:myFields/my:field1", NamespaceManager);
```

The `SelectSingleNode()` method of the `XPathNavigator` object selects a single node in the `XPathNavigator` object using the specified `XPathExpression` object or XPath string expression. The `SelectSingleNode()` method has an XPath expression as its first parameter and a `System.Xml.IXmlNamespaceResolver` object that is used to resolve namespace prefixes in the XPath query as its second parameter. You can use the `XmlNamespaceManager` object which you can retrieve through the `NamespaceManager` property of the `XmlForm` object as the `IXmlNamespaceResolver` argument of the `SelectSingleNode()` method.

Once you have the `XPathNavigator` object for the field, you can then use its `Value` property to retrieve the value of the field.

```
string val = field1.Value;
```

The `Value` property of the `XPathNavigator` object returns the string value of an XML node.

While the code in the solution described above retrieves the value of a field that is located in the Main data source of a form, you can use the same technique to retrieve the value of a field that is located in a secondary data source. Instead of retrieving an `XPathNavigator` object that points to the Main data source of the form

```
XPathNavigator mainDS = MainDataSource.CreateNavigator();
```

you would have to retrieve an `XPathNavigator` object that points to a secondary data source as described in recipe *9 Access a secondary data source of a form*.

```
XPathNavigator secDS = DataSources["MySecondaryDataSource"].CreateNavigator();
```

Another critical step would be to use the correct XPath expression to the field in the secondary data source. For this you would have to switch to the secondary data source that contains the field by using the **Fields** drop-down list box on the **Fields** task pane in InfoPath Designer 2010, and then use the **Copy XPath** menu item again to copy the XPath expression as you did in step 3 of the solution described above.

The solution described above is not limited to fields that are bound to text boxes, but it can be applied to any InfoPath form field.

Tip:

If you get the error "Object reference not set to an instance of an object", double-check the XPath expression for the field you are trying to retrieve. Chances are the XPath expression is incorrect.

11 Set the value of a field

Problem

You have a text box control on a form and you want to set its contents to be equal to a piece of text.

Solution

You can use the SetValue() method of the XPathNavigator object that points to the XML node of the field bound to a text box control to set the contents of the text box to be equal to a piece of text.

To set the value of a field:

1. Follow steps 1 through 4 of recipe *10 Get the value of a field*.

2. In VSTA, add the following code to the FormEvents_Loading() event handler (*code #: 3754532E-EE5D-48F1-AC57-73CA7199C3F3*):

    ```
    XPathNavigator mainDS = MainDataSource.CreateNavigator();
    XPathNavigator field1 = mainDS.SelectSingleNode(
      "/my:myFields/my:field1", NamespaceManager);

    field1.SetValue("Hello from InfoPath");
    ```

    where the field1 variable contains a reference to the XPathNavigator object for the field bound to the text box control.

3. Save and build the project.

4. Preview the form.

When the form opens, the text box should contain the text "Hello from InfoPath".

Discussion

In the solution described above, the value of a field is set during the **Loading** event of the form, but you can set the value of a field during any event.

To set the value of a field in an InfoPath form, you must first get a reference to the Main or a secondary data source of the form.

```
XPathNavigator mainDS = MainDataSource.CreateNavigator();
```

Then you must get a reference to the field.

```
XPathNavigator field1 = mainDS.SelectSingleNode(
  "/my:myFields/my:field1", NamespaceManager);
```

And finally, you can use the SetValue() method of the XPathNavigator object for the field to set its value. The SetValue() method of the XPathNavigator object sets the value of the current XML node. You can use it to set the value of a field bound to a control on an InfoPath form.

Note that a few controls in InfoPath such as for example date picker controls have a **nil** attribute set on the fields they are bound to when they are empty. This **nil** attribute must be removed before you can set the value of such fields, otherwise you will get the following error when you try to set the field's value.

Schema validation found non-data type errors

To remove the **nil** attribute from a date picker control:

1. In InfoPath, create a new form template or use an existing one.

2. Add a **Date Picker** control to the view of the form template and name it **field1**.

3. Add an event handler for the **Loading** event of the form as described in recipe *6 Add an event handler for a form event*.

4. In VSTA, add the following code to the FormEvents_Loading() event handler (*code #: CCA2B0A0-45E2-414A-824F-B027452CCF4B*):

```
XPathNavigator mainDS = MainDataSource.CreateNavigator();
XPathNavigator field1 = mainDS.SelectSingleNode(
  "/my:myFields/my:field1", NamespaceManager);

if (field1.MoveToAttribute("nil",
  NamespaceManager.LookupNamespace("xsi")))
{
  field1.DeleteSelf();
}

field1.SetValue("2012-02-07");
```

5. Save and build the project.

6. Preview the form.

When the form opens, the date picker should display February 7, 2012 as its date.

The following InfoPath controls typically have **nil** attributes on the fields they are bound to:

- Text Box with the Whole Number (integer) data type

- Text Box with the Decimal (double) data type

- Text Box with the Time (time) data type

- Date Picker

- Date and Time Picker

- File Attachment

- Picture (when a picture is included in the form instead of as a link)

- Ink Picture

You can find out whether a control supports the **nil** attribute by adding the control to the form template, previewing the form, leaving the control empty, saving the form locally on disk, opening the XML file for the form in Notepad, and then looking for

```
xsi:nil="true"
```

as an attribute on the field bound to the control. Note that the namespace prefix for a **nil** attribute in InfoPath is **xsi** and that it is declared as

```
xmlns:xsi="http://www.w3.org/2001/XMLSchema-instance"
```

To remove the **nil** attribute from a field you must get a reference to the Main data source of the form.

```
XPathNavigator mainDS = MainDataSource.CreateNavigator();
```

Then you must get a reference to the field on which there is a **nil** attribute. And finally, you must search for the **nil** attribute using the MoveToAttribute() method of the XPathNavigator object pointing to the field and delete the **nil** attribute using the DeleteSelf() method of the XPathNavigator object.

```
if (field1.MoveToAttribute("nil", NamespaceManager.LookupNamespace("xsi")))
{
  field1.DeleteSelf();
}
```

Note that you can use the `LookupNamespace()` method of the `XmlNamespaceManager` object to retrieve the namespace URI for the **xsi** namespace prefix, which you must pass as the second argument to the `MoveToAttribute()` method.

12 Clear a field on a form

Problem

You want to clear a text box control on a form.

Solution

You can set the value of the field that is bound to a text box control to be equal to an empty string to clear it.

To clear a field that is bound to a text box control:

1. In InfoPath, create a new form template or use an existing one.

2. Add a **Text Box** control to the view of the form template and name it **field1**.

3. Add a **Button** control to the view of the form template, label it **Clear**, and change its **ID** property to **ClearTextButton**.

4. Add an event handler for the **Clicked** event of the button as described in recipe *7 Add an event handler for a control event*.

5. In VSTA, add the following code to the `ClearTextButton_Clicked()` event handler for the button (*code #: 3AE983E7-0EE9-4B4C-BB30-CCFD8816011D*):

```
XPathNavigator mainDS = MainDataSource.CreateNavigator();
XPathNavigator field1 = mainDS.SelectSingleNode(
  "/my:myFields/my:field1", NamespaceManager);

field1.SetValue(String.Empty);
```

6. Save and build the project.

7. Preview the form.

When the form opens, enter a piece of text in the text box, and then click the **Clear** button. The text should disappear from the text box control.

Discussion

To clear a field in InfoPath, you must set the value of the field to an empty string using the `SetValue()` method of the `XPathNavigator` object that points to the field.

```
field1.SetValue(String.Empty);
```

If the field you want to clear is bound to a control that supports the **nil** attribute (see the discussion section of recipe *11 Set the value of a field*), you must also add the **nil** attribute to the field and set the value of the **nil** attribute to `true` as shown in the following code (*code #: 406903D1-DA20-4620-934C-D280DBCDE9A7*):

```
XPathNavigator mainDS = MainDataSource.CreateNavigator();
XPathNavigator field1 = mainDS.SelectSingleNode(
  "/my:myFields/my:field1", NamespaceManager);

field1.SetValue(String.Empty);
if (!field1.MoveToAttribute("nil", NamespaceManager.LookupNamespace("xsi")))
{
  field1.CreateAttribute(
    "xsi", "nil", NamespaceManager.LookupNamespace("xsi"), "true");
}
```

where `field1` represents an `XPathNavigator` object pointing to a field that is bound to for example a date picker control.

Technically speaking, you are not required to add a **nil** attribute when clearing a field that supports one, but it is the right thing to do if that field is a non-mandatory field. For example, if you do not set the **nil** attribute for some fields such as non-mandatory fields bound to date picker controls, those fields will be made mandatory when you clear their values. Setting the **nil** attribute to `true` is equivalent to setting the value of a variable to be equal to `null` in code. If a field or control is mandatory, that is, you selected its **Cannot be blank** property, then you must not add a **nil** attribute to the field when you clear it.

13   Clear all fields on a form

Problem

You want to restore an InfoPath form to the state it had when it was opened for the very first time.

Solution

You can save the state of a form, i.e. all of the values of the fields, when the form initially opens, and then when you want to restore this state, replace all of the values of the fields on the form with the data you initially stored. The method to clear all fields on a form depends on whether you are clearing fields on an InfoPath Filler or browser form.

To clear all fields on a form:

1.   In InfoPath, create a new form template or use an existing one.

2.   Design the form template as you see fit by placing controls on its view.

3.   Add a **Button** control to the view of the form template and label it **Reset**.

4. Add an event handler for the **Loading** event of the form as described in recipe *6 Add an event handler for a form event*.

5. In VSTA:

   a. If you are desiging an InfoPath Filler Form, add a member variable named `initialData` to the `FormCode` class (*code #: 3BDD792F-C81E-4744-A156-8B986726730C*):

   ```
   private string initialData;
   ```

   b. If you are designing a browser-compatible form template, add a property that makes use of the `FormState` dictionary to the `FormCode` class (*code #: 3BDD792F-C81E-4744-A156-8B986726730C*):

   ```
   private object initialData
   {
     get
     {
       return FormState["initialData"];
     }
     set
     {
       FormState["initialData"] = value;
     }
   }
   ```

6. Add the following code to the `FormEvents_Loading()` event handler (*code #: 3BDD792F-C81E-4744-A156-8B986726730C*):

   ```
   initialData = MainDataSource.CreateNavigator().SelectSingleNode(
     "/my:myFields", NamespaceManager).InnerXml;
   ```

7. In InfoPath, add an event handler for the **Clicked** event of the button as described in recipe *7 Add an event handler for a control event*.

8. In VSTA, add the following code to the `Clicked()` event handler method for the button (*code #: 3BDD792F-C81E-4744-A156-8B986726730C*):

   ```
   MainDataSource.CreateNavigator().SelectSingleNode(
     "/my:myFields", NamespaceManager).InnerXml = (string)initialData;
   ```

9. Save and build the project.

10. If you are desiging a browser-compatible form template, publish the form template to a SharePoint form library; otherwise, preview the form.

If you designed a browser-compatible form template: In SharePoint, navigate to the form library where you published the form template and add a new form. When the form opens, fill out the form. Click the **Reset** button. All of the controls should go back to their original state.

Discussion

In the solution described above, you learned that clearing all of the fields on a form is a matter of saving the original values of all of the fields on the form and then when you want to reset them, set the fields back to their original values.

To do this, you can make use of a variable (in the case of an InfoPath Filler form)

```
private string initialData;
```

or a get/set property (in the case of a browser form)

```
private object initialData
{
  get
  {
    return FormState["initialData"];
  }
  set
  {
    FormState["initialData"] = value;
  }
}
```

and populate this with the value of the `InnerXml` property of the `XPathNavigator` object pointing to the **myFields** group node (root node) when the form opens, so in the `FormEvents_Loading()` event handler of the form.

```
initialData = MainDataSource.CreateNavigator().SelectSingleNode(
  "/my:myFields", NamespaceManager).InnerXml;
```

The `InnerXml` property of an `XPathNavigator` object gets or sets the markup that represents the child nodes of the current node. So by using this property you can store the entire XML contents of the **myFields** group node in the variable or property. Note that because member variables are not supported in InfoPath browser forms, you must use the `FormState` dictionary instead of a private member variable to store the entire original XML of the form.

You can then write code in the `Clicked()` event handler for the **Reset** button to set the value of the `InnerXml` property of the `XPathNavigator` object pointing to the **myFields** group node to be equal to the original XML fragment you stored during the **Loading** event of the form.

```
MainDataSource.CreateNavigator().SelectSingleNode(
  "/my:myFields", NamespaceManager).InnerXml = (string)initialData;
```

While you can use the technique described in this recipe to restore all fields on a form to their original state, you could also modify the solution to only partially restore form fields by placing the fields that should be restored under a group node named for example **container**, which would be located somewhere under the **myFields** group node. Then to restore the fields that are located under the **container** group node, you would again first have to store the contents of the group node when the form opens using the following code:

```
initialData = MainDataSource.CreateNavigator().SelectSingleNode(
  "//my:container", NamespaceManager).OuterXml;
```

The code above retrieves the XML fragment of the entire **container** group node by using the `OuterXml` property of the `XPathNavigator` object pointing to the **container** group node. The `OuterXml` property of an `XPathNavigator` object gets or sets the markup that represents the opening and closing tags of the current node and its child nodes.

Once the original XML for the **container** group node has been stored, you can then place code behind the **Reset** button to restore only those fields that are located under the **container** group node to their original state.

```
if (initialData != null)
{
  MainDataSource.CreateNavigator().SelectSingleNode(
  "//my:container", NamespaceManager).ReplaceSelf((string)initialData);
}
```

The code above makes use of the `ReplaceSelf()` method of the `XPathNavigator` object to restore the XML representation of the entire **container** group node including its child nodes to their original state.

Note that you could extend this solution to provide users with "Save as draft" functionality, where they can click a button while they are filling out a form to temporarily store part of or the entire form in a text field in for example a secondary data source, and then reset the form to a previous state instead of the initial state at form load. Because a secondary data source is not a permanent storage location when a user is filling out a form, all changes would be lost if the form closed or InfoPath Filler or the browser crashed. So you could take this a step further by extending the solution to temporarily submit the XML fragment to a permanent storage location such as for example a SharePoint list and then retrieve the XML fragment whenever necessary.

14 Add error-handling to an InfoPath form

Problem

You have written code for an InfoPath form template and want to add error-handling to it.

Solution

You can add `try-catch` blocks to all public methods in the `FormCode` class and use a central error-handler to handle all errors that might take place.

To add error-handling to an InfoPath form:

1. In InfoPath, create a new InfoPath Filler form template or use an existing one.

2. Add a **Button** control to the view of the form template.

3. Add an event handler for the **Clicked** event of the button control as described in recipe *7 Add an event handler for a control event*.

4. In VSTA, add the following private method to the `FormCode` class (*code #: B6F3492D-E809-4102-B649-89D43B15C43B*):

```
private void HandleErrors(Exception ex)
{
  System.Windows.Forms.MessageBox.Show(
    ex.Message, "Error", MessageBoxButtons.OK, MessageBoxIcon.Error);
}
```

What this method does is display an error in a message box to the user.

5. Add the following code to the `Clicked()` event handler for the button (*code #: B6F3492D-E809-4102-B649-89D43B15C43B*):

```
try
{
  XPathNavigator mainDS = MainDataSource.CreateNavigator();
  string noValue = mainDS.SelectSingleNode(
    "//my:field1", NamespaceManager).Value;
}
catch (Exception ex)
{
  HandleErrors(ex);
}
finally
{
  // Perform any operations for clean up here.
}
```

This code raises an "Object reference not set to an instance of an object." exception, because **field1** does not exist in the Main data source of the form and calls the central error handler `HandleErrors()` to take care of further processing the exception.

6. Save and build the project.

7. Preview the form.

When the form opens, click the button. The message "Object reference not set to an instance of an object." should appear in an error message box.

Discussion

A common way to catch errors in an application is to add `try-catch` blocks to all of its public methods. Users typically access functionality in InfoPath forms through the event handlers you add for the form and its controls. These event handlers are public methods, so you should add `try-catch` blocks to all of them to catch any errors that may occur.

The solution described above uses a central error-handling method named `HandleErrors()` to process any exceptions passed to it.

```
private void HandleErrors(Exception ex)
{
  System.Windows.Forms.MessageBox.Show(
    ex.Message, "Error", MessageBoxButtons.OK, MessageBoxIcon.Error);
}
```

The advantage of using a central error-handler is that you can add `try-catch` blocks containing the central error-handler to all public methods once, and then if you ever want to change the way exceptions are processed afterwards, it would only require changing the logic on one spot in the code, that is, in the central error-handler. For example, if you wanted to switch from displaying error messages in a message box to displaying them in a field on the form, you could change the code for the `HandleErrors()` method to be the following:

```
private void HandleErrors(Exception ex)
{
  XPathNavigator mainDS = MainDataSource.CreateNavigator();
  mainDS.SelectSingleNode("/my:myFields/my:errorMessage",
    NamespaceManager).SetValue(ex.Message);
}
```

where **errorMessage** is a read-only, multi-line text box on the view of the form template.

InfoPath forms can be filled out through InfoPath Filler 2010 or a browser. If filled out through InfoPath Filler 2010, you can use a message box to display an error message to the user when you catch the error. If filled out through a browser, you cannot make use of a message box, but could instead change the `HandleErrors()` method to log a message to the Windows Event log as follows:

```
private void HandleErrors(Exception ex)
{
  string source = "InfoPath Browser Form";

  if (!System.Diagnostics.EventLog.SourceExists(source))
  {
    System.Diagnostics.EventLog.CreateEventSource(source, "Application");
  }

  System.Diagnostics.EventLog log =
    new System.Diagnostics.EventLog("Application");
  log.Source = source;
  log.WriteEntry(ex.Message, System.Diagnostics.EventLogEntryType.Error);
}
```

Note that because the code shown above creates a registry key named **InfoPath Browser Form** under

```
\HKEY_LOCAL_MACHINE\SYSTEM\CurrentControlSet\services\eventlog\Application
```

if this key does not exist and then writes the error message to the event log, you must give the form template Full Trust and sign the form template with a digital certificate (also see *Configure an InfoPath form template to have Full Trust* in the Appendix); otherwise an exception similar to the following will be raised:

Request for the permission of type 'System.Diagnostics.EventLogPermission, System, Version=2.0.0.0, Culture=neutral, PublicKeyToken=b77a5c561934e089' failed.

15 Debug code of an InfoPath form template in VSTA

Problem

You want to step through the code you have written for an InfoPath form template in VSTA.

Solution

You can set breakpoints throughout the code and then use the menu items under the **Debug** menu to start debugging code from within VSTA.

To debug code of an InfoPath form template in VSTA:

1. In InfoPath, create a new form template or use an existing one.

2. Write code for the InfoPath form template as described in one of the previous recipes in this chapter.

3. To have the debugger break on a particular line in code, in VSTA, click to place the cursor on the line where you want to stop the debugger, and then press **F9** or click **Debug ➤ Toggle Breakpoint** to add a breakpoint. Press **F9** again or click **Debug ➤ Toggle Breakpoint** to remove the breakpoint. You can place as many breakpoints as you want throughout the code.

4. To start debugging, press **F5** or click **Debug ➤ Start Debugging**. Note that you cannot start debugging from within InfoPath; if you want to debug code and have the breakpoints in the code be hit, you must always start debugging from within VSTA. Previewing an InfoPath form from within InfoPath Designer 2010 is equivalent to running the form template code without debugging it.

5. To step through the code once a breakpoint has been hit, you can:

   a. Press **F8** or click **Debug ➤ Step Into** to step through the code line by line and step into the code of any methods. If you do not want to step into the code of a method, press **Shift+F8** or click **Debug ➤ Step Over** instead of pressing **F8**. To step out of the code of a method, press **Ctrl+Shift+F8** or click **Debug ➤ Step Out**.

   b. Press **F10** to step through the code line by line without stepping into methods.

    c. Press **F11** to step into the code of a method.

    d. Right-click on a line that comes after the current breakpoint where the debugger has stopped, and select **Run To Cursor** from the context menu to have the debugger run the code up to but not including the line of code on which you placed the cursor.

    e. Press **F5** to run to the next breakpoint or finish running the code without stepping through it.

6. Once the debugger has stopped on a line of code, you can use the **Immediate Window** or hover with the mouse pointer over variables and objects to view their values and contents. You can also write values to the **Immediate Window** through code by making use of one of the `System.Diagnostics.Debug` write methods (`Write()`, `WriteLine()`, `WriteIf()`, or `WriteLineIf()`). For example:

```
System.Diagnostics.Debug.WriteLine("Write this to the Immediate Window.");
```

writes the text *Write this to the Immediate Window* on a new line in the **Immediate Window**. If the **Immediate Window** is not present in your development environment, you can add it by selecting **Debug ➤ Windows ➤ Immediate**. Other windows you can use to check the values and contents of variables and objects include:

    a. The **Locals** window, which you can open by selecting **Debug ➤ Windows ➤ Locals** when you are debugging code.

    b. The **Watch** window, which you can open by selecting **Debug ➤ Windows ➤ Watch** when you are debugging code. To add a watch on a variable, right-click the variable in the code, and then select **Add Watch** from the context menu that appears. If you do not want to add a watch, but only want to view or explore the contents of an object, you can select **Quick Watch** from the context menu instead of **Add Watch**.

Discussion

The debugging process in VSTA is similar to the debugging process in Visual Studio: You must set breakpoints on specific lines of code, start the debugging process, and then step through the code.

If you want to debug code for an InfoPath form template, you must always press **F5** from within VSTA or click **Debug ➤ Start Debugging** from the menu within VSTA. You cannot start the debugging process from within InfoPath Designer 2010. Therefore, if you have set a couple of breakpoints in code and then preview an InfoPath form from within InfoPath Designer 2010, none of those breakpoints will be hit.

If you have a form template, which you cannot interactively debug in VSTA, for example a browser form template that has been published to SharePoint, you can make use of standard error-handling in each public method together with a field on the InfoPath form to display messages on the form.

For example, you could add a multi-line text box on the InfoPath form and name it **errorMessage**, and then in code add a `try-catch` block in each public method that makes use of code similar to the following code:

```
try
{
  // Write your code here
}
catch (Exception ex)
{
  MainDataSource.CreateNavigator().SelectSingleNode(
    "/my:myFields/my:errorMessage", NamespaceManager)
    .SetValue(ex.Message);
}
```

When debugging an InfoPath form template that calls code that requires Full Trust, you must set the form template's security level to **Full Trust** as follows:

1. Click **File ➤ Info ➤ Form Options**.

2. On the **Form Options** dialog box, select **Security and Trust** in the **Category** list.

3. Under **Security Level**, deselect the **Automatically determine security level** check box.

4. Select the **Full Trust** option, and click **OK**.

Note that you do not always have to assign a digital certificate to a form template to be able to debug code in VSTA. However, a digital certificate is required once you are ready to publish a form template with Full Trust.

There are two ways you can publish a form template to SharePoint:

1. As a sandboxed solution.

2. As an administrator-deployed solution.

If you leave the Full Trust option selected when you publish a form template to SharePoint, InfoPath will force you to publish the form template as an administrator-deployed solution, which will require an administrator to upload the form template to SharePoint Central Administration (also see *Publish an InfoPath form template as administrator-approved* in the Appendix).

However, form templates that may require Full Trust to be debugged in VSTA due to the security settings on your computer, do not necessarily also require Full Trust to run in SharePoint. So once you are done debugging, ensure you change the security settings back to **Automatically determine security level** before you publish such form templates to SharePoint. This should allow you to publish the form templates as sandboxed solutions, which do not require an administrator to get involved in the deployment process.

Almost all of the solutions described in this book can be published to SharePoint as sandboxed solutions, so do not require Full Trust or a digital certificate to run.

Chapter 3: Views

InfoPath views are rendered using XSL style sheets that are stored in the form template (.xsn). You can retrieve information about views of a form template by using the `ViewInfoCollection` object which is accessible through the `ViewInfos` property of a form, and you can perform certain actions on views such as switching views and exporting views in a selected format depending on the type of form (InfoPath Filler form or web browser form) you are writing code for.

The recipes in this chapter take you through a few common scenarios for writing code to perform actions on views.

16   Switch to show a specific view when a form opens

Problem

You have an InfoPath form that has two views and you want to be able to set the InfoPath form to start up with and show one of these two views.

Solution

You can use the `SetDefaultView()` method of the `LoadingEventArgs` object in the `FormEvents_Loading()` event handler of a form to switch to a particular view when the form opens.

To switch to a specific view when a form opens:

1.   In InfoPath, create a new form template or use an existing one.

2.   Click **Page Design ➤ Views ➤ New View** and add a new view named **View 2** to the form template.

3.   Add an event handler for the **Loading** event of the form as described in recipe 6 *Add an event handler for a form event*.

4.   In VSTA, add the following code to the `FormEvents_Loading()` event handler (*code #: 9ACEFC5F-6893-40BD-B914-0C8EFA658C1A*):

     ```
     e.SetDefaultView("View 2");
     ```

5.   Save and build the project.

6.   Preview the form.

When the form opens, **View 2** should appear.

Discussion

The `SetDefaultView()` method of the `LoadingEventArgs` object allows you to programmatically set the default view of a form by specifying the name of a view or a `ViewInfo` object.

You can also use the `Initial` property of the `ViewInfoCollection` object to set the view during the **Loading** event of a form with one caveat that this will only work after the form has been saved and re-opened.

```
ViewInfos.Initial = ViewInfos["View 2"];
```

You cannot use the `SwitchView()` method, which you will learn more about in the next recipe, to switch views during the **Loading** event of an InfoPath Filler form, since InfoPath will display the following error:

Invalid Context: SwitchView cannot be called in the Loading event.

17 Switch to a read-only view when a form is submitted

Problem

You want to run code when a user submits a form and then immediately afterwards switch to a read-only view.

Solution

You can use the `SwitchView()` method of the `ViewInfoCollection` object to switch to a read-only view in the event handler that contains the code to submit the form.

To switch to a read-only view when a form is submitted:

1.   In InfoPath, create a new form template or use an existing one.

2.   Click **Page Design ➤ Views ➤ New View**.

3.   On the **Add View** dialog box, enter the name **ReadOnlyView**, and then click **OK**.

4.   Open the **View Properties** dialog box, select the **Read-only** check box on the **General** tab, deselect the **Show on the View menu when filling out this form** check box on the **General** tab, and click **OK**.

5.   Place any fields that should be shown on the read-only view on the **ReadOnlyView** view.

6.   Click **Data ➤ Submit Form ➤ Submit Options**.

7.   On the **Submit Options** dialog box, select the **Allow users to submit this form** check box, select the **Perform custom action using Code** option, click **Advanced**,

select **Leave the form open** in the **After submit** drop-down list box, click **Edit Code**, and then click **OK**.

8. In VSTA, add the following code to the `FormEvents_Submit()` event handler (*code #: CFD788CA-5439-4B81-8143-37F574B6F73F*):

```
// Write your code here.

e.CancelableArgs.Cancel = false;

ViewInfos.SwitchView("ReadOnlyView");
```

where **ReadOnlyView** is the name of the read-only view.

9. Save and build the project.

10. Preview the form.

When the form opens, fill it out, and then click the **Submit** button on the toolbar. The read-only view should be displayed after the form has successfully been submitted.

Discussion

The `SwitchView()` method of the `ViewInfoCollection` object allows you to programmatically change the view that is currently active. You can access the `ViewInfoCollection` object of a form by using the `ViewInfos` property of the `XmlForm` object.

In the solution described above, the `SwitchView()` method of the `ViewInfoCollection` object is used in the `FormEvents_Submit()` event handler of a form to switch to a read-only view

```
ViewInfos.SwitchView("ReadOnlyView");
```

after the form is successfully submitted.

```
e.CancelableArgs.Cancel = false;
```

The `CancelableArgs` property of the `SubmitEventArgs` object returns an `XmlFormCancelEventArgs` object that provides access to properties for canceling the event and displaying a custom message. You can use its `Cancel` property to cancel the event, its `Message` property to display a short message when the event is canceled, and its `MessageDetails` property to display a detailed message when the event is canceled. For example,

```
e.CancelableArgs.Cancel = true;
e.CancelableArgs.Message = "Short message for canceling the event.";
e.CancelableArgs.MessageDetails = "Details about canceling the event.";
```

would result in the following message dialog box being shown after clicking the **Submit** button.

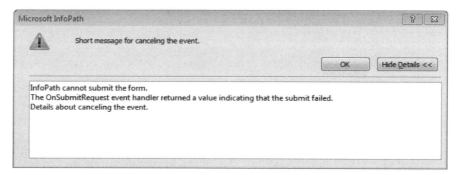

Figure 20. Message box displaying the details for canceling the submission of a form.

18 Save form data to a PDF file on disk

Problem

You want to print some or all of the data from an InfoPath form to PDF.

Solution

You can create a print view that can be used specifically to print form data to PDF, and then assign this view as the print view of another view that is used to fill out the form. Once assigned, you can call the Export() method of the View object with an ExportFormat equal to Pdf to print the print view and save it as a PDF file.

To save form data to a PDF file:

1. In InfoPath, create a new InfoPath Filler form template or use an existing one.

2. Click **Page Design ➤ Views ➤ New View**.

3. On the **Add View** dialog box, enter a name such as for example **PrintToPDF**, and then click **OK**.

4. Open the **View Properties** dialog box, deselect the **Show on the View menu when filling out this form** check box on the **General** tab, and then click **OK**. This should prevent the **PrintToPDF** view from appearing as a selectable view on the **View** menu.

5. Select the page layout that is present on the view, and then click **Table Tools ➤ Layout ➤ Color ➤ Borders**.

6. On the **Borders and Shading** dialog box, select **None** under **Presets**, select the **No color** option on the **Shading** tab, and then click **OK**.

7. On the **Fields** task pane, drag-and-drop any fields you want to print onto the **PrintToPDF** view. Bind text and numeric fields as much as you can to **Calculated Value** controls, so that they appear borderless when the form is exported to PDF. For fields you cannot bind to **Calculated Value** controls, you can remove the borders of the controls the fields are bound to by selecting each control, clicking **Control Tools** ➤ **Properties** ➤ **Color** ➤ **Border**, selecting **None** under **Presets**, and clicking **OK**. In addition, you should bind fields that contain data for images to **Picture** controls instead of **Calculated Value** controls.

8. Modify the design and layout of the **PrintToPDF** view further to suit your needs. Remember you can use custom tables (**Insert** ➤ **Tables** ➤ **Custom Table**) to lay out the controls on the view however you want to.

9. Select **Page Design** ➤ **Views** ➤ **View** ➤ **View 1 (default)** to switch to **View 1**. Or switch to whichever view you will be using to call the print to PDF operation.

10. Open the **View Properties** dialog box, click the **Print Settings** tab, select **PrintToPDF** in the drop-down list box under the **Designate print view** section, and then click **OK**. With this you have configured **View 1** to use the **PrintToPDF** view as its print view.

11. Click **File** ➤ **Info** ➤ **Form Options**.

12. On the **Form Options** dialog box, ensure **Filler Features** is selected in the **Category** list, select the **Save using custom code** check box, and then click **Edit**. This should add a `FormEvents_Save()` event handler in VSTA. Switch back to InfoPath if VSTA got the focus, and click **OK** to close the **Form Options** dialog box.

13. In VSTA, replace the code in the `FormEvents_Save()` event handler with the following code (*code #: 56CCC51B-EBD7-425E-8F51-8BCF3920B298*):

```
// Write your code that will run before a Save or Save As operation here.

// The Dirty property will be set to false if save is successful.
e.PerformSaveOperation();

string formName = CurrentView.Window.Caption;
CurrentView.Export(
  @"C:\Printed InfoPath Forms\" + formName + ".pdf", ExportFormat.Pdf);

e.CancelableArgs.Cancel = false;
```

where `C:\Printed InfoPath Forms` represents the location where the PDF file should be saved.

14. Give the form template Full Trust as described in *Configure an InfoPath form template to have Full Trust* in the Appendix.

15. Save and build the project.

16. Preview the form.

When the form opens, enter some data and then press **Ctrl+S** or click the **Save** button on the **Quick Access Toolbar**. Open Windows Explorer, navigate to the `C:\Printed InfoPath Forms` folder and verify that a PDF file was created. Open the PDF file and verify that it contains the data you entered.

Discussion

The `Export()` method of the `View` object exports a view to a file in a specified format (MHT, PDF, or XPS). The format can be specified through an enumeration named `ExportFormat` and must be passed as the second argument to the `Export()` method. You can get a reference to the `View` object by using the `CurrentView` property of the `XmlForm` object as follows:

```
Microsoft.Office.InfoPath.View currentView = this.CurrentView;
```

or

```
Microsoft.Office.InfoPath.View currentView = CurrentView;
```

In the solution described above, you used the `Export()` method of the `View` object to print the current view to PDF.

```
string formName = CurrentView.Window.Caption;
CurrentView.Export(
    @"C:\Printed InfoPath Forms\" + formName + ".pdf", ExportFormat.Pdf);
```

The code shown above automatically generates a name for the file based on the caption of the window that displays the view. Of course you could have also allowed the user to specify a file name by providing a field on the form and then retrieving and using the value of that field in code; or you could have retrieved and used the name of the view (**View 1** in this case) as follows:

```
string viewName = CurrentView.ViewInfo.Name;
CurrentView.Export(
    @"C:\Printed InfoPath Forms\" + viewName + ".pdf", ExportFormat.Pdf);
```

In the solution described above, you also created and assigned a print view to the view that had to be printed. However, this is not a requirement; you could have printed the view as is without first assigning a print view to it. The benefit of using a separate print view is that you can design the print view exclusively for printing purposes. This includes removing borders and shading from controls, which would otherwise make the printed document look unappealing.

While it is not necessary to place the code in the `FormEvents_Save()` event handler, since you can also place the code in the `Clicked()` event handler for a normal button on the form, the code in the solution above showed you how to perform an operation – in this case, export a form to PDF – after you have successfully saved the form locally on disk, so after the `PerformSaveOperation()` method of the `SaveEventArgs` object has run.

```
e.PerformSaveOperation();
```

Because the form writes to the local disk, it requires elevated privileges to do so, so you must give the form template Full Trust.

Note:

The `Export()` method is not available for InfoPath browser forms. You can use the technique described in recipe *101 Save a form as a PDF document in a SharePoint document library* to convert an InfoPath browser form to PDF.

Chapter 4: Data Validation

Data validation can be performed on one of three ways in InfoPath:

1. Through constraints placed directly on the definition of fields in the XML schema definition (XSD).

2. Through validation rules.

3. Through code.

So before you start to write code to perform data validation in InfoPath, always ask yourself first whether you can perform the validation using one of the first two methods. If the answer is "no", then write code to perform data validation.

Data validation through code involves adding an event handler for the **Validating** event of the control you want to validate, and then writing code in the `Validating()` event handler that is created for the field bound to the control.

The recipes in this chapter take you through a couple of basic scenarios for validating data in InfoPath using code.

19   Validate a field when its value changes

Problem

You have a text box control on an InfoPath form and want to display an error to the user if the text the user types into the text box control is longer than 10 characters.

Solution

You can use the `ReportError()` method of the `XmlValidatingEventArgs` object or the `Errors` property of the form to display an error message to the user when validating a field.

To validate a field when its value changes:

1. In InfoPath, create a new form template or use an existing one.

2. Add a **Text Box** control to the view of the form template.

3. Add an event handler for the **Validating** event of the text box control as described in recipe *7 Add an event handler for a control event*.

4. In VSTA, add the following code to the `Validating()` event handler for the text box (*code #: 73C0C89C-CB2A-4EF3-B0CF-76A8A3C1B747*):

a. If you want to use the `ReportError()` method to display an error message:

```
string fieldVal = e.Site.Value;
if (!String.IsNullOrEmpty(fieldVal) && fieldVal.Length > 10)
{
```

```
        e.ReportError(e.Site, false, "Only 10 characters max allowed.");
    }
```

   b. If you want to use the `Errors` property of the form to display an error message:

```
string fieldVal = e.Site.Value;
if (!String.IsNullOrEmpty(fieldVal) && fieldVal.Length > 10)
{
    Errors.Add(e.Site, "MaxCharError", "Only 10 characters max allowed.");
}
```

5. Save and build the project.

6. Preview the form.

When the form opens, type a piece of text that has more than 10 characters in the text box, and then tab or click away from the text box. A red dashed border should appear around the text box and when you hover with the mouse pointer over the text box, you should see the error message appear as a tooltip. Type a piece of text that has 10 characters or less in the text box, and then tab or click away from the field. The red dashed border should disappear.

Discussion

The **Validating** event takes place after the **Changing** event but before the **Changed** event. The **Validating** event also takes place when the form opens.

In the solution described above you used the `Site` property of the `XmlValidatingEventArgs` object that is passed to the `Validating()` event handler to retrieve the `XPathNavigator` object that is pointing to the node being changed. You then used it to validate the node and display an error message to the user if the text entered contained more than 10 characters.

```
string fieldVal = e.Site.Value;
if (!String.IsNullOrEmpty(fieldVal) && fieldVal.Length > 10)
{
    e.ReportError(e.Site, false, "Only 10 characters max allowed.");
}
```

The `ReportError()` method adds a `FormError` object to the `FormErrorCollection` object of the form. Once the source of the validation error has been corrected, `ReportError()` automatically removes the error from the `FormErrorCollection` object of the form. The `ReportError()` method has three parameters:

1. An `XPathNavigator` object positioned at the node that contains the data the error is associated with. In the solution described above, you used `e.Site` to reference the field being validated.

2. A Boolean indicating whether the error is site independent or not. If set to `false` (so the error depends on a specific node), `ReportError()` will delete the error from the `FormErrorCollection` object for the node on which the error was set. If set to `true`, `ReportError()` will delete the error from the `FormErrorCollection` object for any node that matches the XPath expression

returned by the Match property of the event. For example, if the text box is placed in a repeating table and you validate the field bound to that text box, setting the site independent parameter to false would have ReportError() clear the error on the one text box in the repeating table for which you correct the error and any data validation errors on data in text boxes in other rows in the repeating table would remain intact. true would have ReportError() clear the errors on all of the text boxes in the repeating table except for the one text box that last failed data validation.

3. The error message to display.

The ReportError() method has two additional overloads that accept two more parameters:

1. The text to be used for the detailed error message.

2. The number to be used as the error code.

In the solution described above, you also learned a second way to display a data validation error by adding a FormError object to the FormErrorCollection object of the form using the Add() method of the FormErrorCollection object that is accessed through the Errors property of the form.

```
string fieldVal = e.Site.Value;
if (!String.IsNullOrEmpty(fieldVal) && fieldVal.Length > 10)
{
  Errors.Add(e.Site, "MaxCharError", "Only 10 characters max allowed.");
}
```

For another example of using the FormErrorCollection object of a form to perform data validation, see recipe *44 Validate that at least 3 items have been selected in a multi-select list box*.

While the behavior of the two methods for displaying an error message to a user are similar, they differ in that the ReportError() method adds a SystemGenerated error to the FormErrorCollection object of the form, while the Add() method adds a UserDefined error to the FormErrorCollection object of the form.

A SystemGenerated error is raised as a result of constraints defined in the form definition file (XSF), or as a result of form code calling the ReportError() method of the XmlValidatingEventArgs object. A UserDefined error is raised as a result of a custom error defined using the Add() method of the FormErrorCollection object. Unlike a SystemGenerated error, you can give a name to a UserDefined error. For more information on the different types of errors that can occur in an InfoPath form, see the discussion section of the next recipe.

The advantage of being able to use the Add() method to report an error becomes clear when you want to perform data validation from another location than on the actual field that is being validated as is shown in the next recipe.

20 Validate a field when a button is clicked

Problem

You have a text box control on an InfoPath form and want to display an error to the user when the user clicks a button to ensure that the text entered into the text box contains less than 10 characters.

Solution

You can use the Errors property of a form to display an error message after a user clicks a button to validate a field.

To validate a field and display an error message when a button is clicked:

1. In InfoPath, create a new form template or use an existing one.

2. Add a **Text Box** control to the view of the form template and name it **field1**.

3. Add a **Button** control to the view of the form template and label it **Validate**.

4. Add an event handler for the **Clicked** event of the button as described in recipe *7 Add an event handler for a control event*.

5. In VSTA, add the following code to the Clicked() event handler for the button (*code #: 2DB5CAE4-C120-4BD7-A561-275FC0E4ABFF*):

```
XPathNavigator root = MainDataSource.CreateNavigator();
XPathNavigator field1 = root.SelectSingleNode(
   "//my:field1", NamespaceManager);
string val = field1.Value;
if (!String.IsNullOrEmpty(val) && val.Length > 10)
{
   Errors.Add(field1, "MaxCharErr", "Only 10 characters max allowed.");
}
```

6. Save and build the project.

7. Preview the form.

When the form opens, type a piece of text that has more than 10 characters into the text box, and then click the **Validate** button. A red dashed border should appear around the text box and when you hover with the mouse pointer over the text box, you should see the error message appear as a tooltip. Type a piece of text that has 10 characters or less into the text box, and then click the **Validate** button again. The red dashed border should not appear.

Discussion

In the solution described above you learned how you can use the Add() method of the Errors collection of a form to validate data when a button is clicked. Whenever you use the `Add()` method to add an error to the `Errors` collection, you are adding a user-defined error to the collection.

There are three types of validation errors that can take place in InfoPath:

1. Schema validation errors

2. System generated errors

3. User-defined errors

These errors are defined in an enumeration called `FormErrorType`. A schema validation error takes place when data validation fails due to an XML Schema-defined constraint. A system generated error takes place when data validation fails due to constraints defined in the manifest file or as a result of form code calling the `ReportError()` method as described in recipe *19 Validate a field when its value changes*. A user-defined error takes place when data validation fails due to a custom error defined using the `Add()` method of the `FormErrorsCollection` object as defined in the solution above.

Because an event handler for a button control does not have an `XmlValidatingEventArgs` object as one of its parameters, but rather a `ClickedEventArgs` object, which does not have a `ReportError()` method, you must use the `Add()` method of the `Errors` collection of a form to be able to validate fields from within the event handler for a button.

Just like with the `ReportError()` method, user-defined validation errors are automatically removed from the `Errors` collection when the user corrects the source of the error on the form. But you can also manually delete errors from the collection by using the `Delete()` and `DeleteAll()` methods as described in recipe *22 Clear a specific validation error in a form* and recipe *23 Ignore and clear all errors in a form before submit*.

The technique described in this recipe is ideal for when you want to provide one button on a form that should validate a group of fields whenever the button is clicked and not while the user is filling out the form. You could even extend the solution to include an error messages text box in which all of the errors that need to be corrected are listed (see for example recipe *21 Check for a specific error in a form*).

21   Check for a specific error in a form

Problem

You have a text box control on an InfoPath form and want to display a list of errors that have been raised for the data entered into the text box.

Solution

You can use the `Errors` property of a form to retrieve error messages for a field.

To check for a specific error in a form:

1.   In InfoPath, create a new form template or use an existing one.

2. Add a **Text Box** control to the view of the form template, name it **field1**, and select its **Cannot Be Blank** property. The latter should automatically raise a `SchemaValidation` error when the text box is empty.

3. Add an event handler for the **Validating** event of the text box control as described in recipe *7 Add an event handler for a control event*.

4. In VSTA, add the following code to the `Validating()` event handler for the text box (*code #: 7FD5D84B-7E3D-4E81-AAB9-1EE29CF5E78F*) :

```
e.ReportError(e.Site, false, "Error from the Validating event.");
```

This should raise a permanent `SystemGenerated` error on the text box.

5. In InfoPath, add two **Button** controls to the view of the form template and label them **Set User-Defined Errors** and **Get All Errors**, respectively.

6. Add a second **Text Box** control to the view of the form template, name it **errors**, and select its **Multi-line** property.

7. Add an event handler for the **Clicked** event of the **Set User-Defined Errors** button as described in recipe *7 Add an event handler for a control event*.

8. In VSTA, add the following code to the `Clicked()` event handler for the **Set User-Defined Errors** button (*code #: 7FD5D84B-7E3D-4E81-AAB9-1EE29CF5E78F*):

```
XPathNavigator field1 = MainDataSource.CreateNavigator().SelectSingleNode(
  "/my:myFields/my:field1", NamespaceManager);

Errors.Add(field1, "Error1", "This is error 1.");
Errors.Add(field1, "Error2", "This is error 2.");
Errors.Add(field1, "Error3", "This is error 3.");
```

This code should raise three user-defined errors on the text box.

9. In InfoPath, add an event handler for the **Clicked** event of the **Get All Errors** button as described in recipe *7 Add an event handler for a control event*.

10. In VSTA, add the following code to the `Clicked()` event handler for the **Get All Errors** button (*code #: 7FD5D84B-7E3D-4E81-AAB9-1EE29CF5E78F*):

```
System.Text.StringBuilder sb = new System.Text.StringBuilder();
foreach (FormError err in Errors)
{
  sb.AppendFormat("Form Error Type: {0} - ", err.FormErrorType);
  sb.AppendFormat("Message: {0}", err.Message);
  sb.AppendLine();
}

MainDataSource.CreateNavigator().SelectSingleNode(
  "/my:myFields/my:errors", NamespaceManager).SetValue(sb.ToString());
```

11. Save and build the project.

12. Preview the form.

When the form opens, a red asterisk should appear in the text box. Click the **Get All Errors** button. You should see error messages appear in the **errors** text box for a SchemaValidation and a SystemGenerated error. Click the **Set User-Defined Errors** button and then click the **Get All Errors** button again. The three user-defined errors should appear in the **errors** text box. Enter a piece of text in the text box, and click the **Get All Errors** button again. The SchemaValidation error should have disappeared from the **errors** text box.

Discussion

In the solution described above, you first added the three types of form errors (SchemaValidation, SystemGenerated, and UserDefined) to a field and then retrieved all of the errors that were defined on the field by looping through FormError objects in the FormErrorCollection object (Errors property) of the form.

```
System.Text.StringBuilder sb = new System.Text.StringBuilder();
foreach (FormError err in Errors)
{
  sb.AppendFormat("Form Error Type: {0} - ", err.FormErrorType);
  sb.AppendFormat("Message: {0}", err.Message);
  sb.AppendLine();
}
```

While looping through FormError objects in the FormErrorCollection object, you can check for and retrieve a specific FormError object through its Name (if the error is a user-defined error), FormErrorType, or Message property. The solution described above just listed all of the errors that were raised on the data entered into the text box in a separate **errors** text box.

```
MainDataSource.CreateNavigator().SelectSingleNode(
  "/my:myFields/my:errors", NamespaceManager).SetValue(sb.ToString());
```

22   Clear a specific validation error in a form

Problem

You want to be able to clear a specific error in a form.

Solution

You can use the Delete() method of the Errors collection to clear a specific error in a form by passing either a name or a FormError object to the method.

To clear a specific error in a form by name:

1. In InfoPath, create a new form template or use an existing one.

2. Add a **Text Box** control to the view of the form template and name it **field1**.

3. Add an event handler for the **Validating** event of the text box as described in recipe *7 Add an event handler for a control event*.

4. In VSTA, add the following code to the `Validating()` event handler for the text box (*code #: 70CC8708-6204-4569-97F2-1745E2576B8E*):

```
if (e.Site != null && e.Site.Value.Length > 10)
  Errors.Add(e.Site, "MaxCharsErr", "Only 10 characters max allowed.");
```

This code checks whether the amount of characters typed into the text box exceeds 10, and if it does, it adds a user-defined error named **MaxCharsErr** to the `Errors` collection of the form.

5. In InfoPath, add a second **Text Box** control to the view of the form template, name it **required**, and make it a required field by selecting its **Cannot Be Blank** property. The purpose of this text box is to add a schema validation error to the `Errors` collection of the form, so that there is more than one error in the collection for testing purposes.

6. Add a **Button** control to the view of the form template.

7. Add an event handler for the **Clicked** event of the button as described in recipe *7 Add an event handler for a control event*.

8. Add the following code to the `Clicked()` event handler for the button (*code #: 70CC8708-6204-4569-97F2-1745E2576B8E*):

```
FormError[] errors = Errors.GetErrors("MaxCharsErr");
if (errors.Length > 0)
  Errors.Delete("MaxCharsErr");
```

The first line of code retrieves all of the errors from the `Errors` collection that have the name **MaxCharsErr**. The second and third lines of code check whether any `FormError` objects were returned by the `GetErrors()` method, and if so, the `Delete()` method is called to delete them.

9. Save and build the project.

10. Preview the form.

When the form opens, a red asterisk (*) should appear in the **required** text box as an indication that it is a required field. Enter a piece of text that is longer than 10 characters in the **field1** text box. A red dashed border should appear around the text box. Click the button. The red dashed border should disappear, but the asterisk in the **required** text box should still be present. With this you have cleared the validation error on the **field1** text box, but not on the **required** text box.

Discussion

The `Delete()` method of the `FormErrorCollection` object deletes a specified `FormError` object from the `Errors` collection associated with the current form or deletes all of the `FormError` objects that have a specified name.

When you use the `Add()` method to add an error to the `Errors` collection of a form, you must specify a name for the error. You can use this same name afterwards with the `Delete()` method to delete the error from the `Errors` collection.

Before you try to delete an error, you must first check whether it exists in the `Errors` collection of the form by using the `GetErrors()` method of the `Errors` collection. The `GetErrors()` method accepts either the name of an error or the `FormErrorType` of an error and returns all of the `FormError` objects with the specified name or of the specified type.

In the solution described above, you used the name of the error in step 8 to delete the error, but you could have also used the type of the error to delete the error. Because you know that the form could contain errors of different types (one user-defined error and one schema validation error in this case), and the error you want to delete is a user-defined error that has the name **MaxCharsErr**, you could have also used the following code to delete the **MaxCharsErr** error:

```
FormError[] errors = Errors.GetErrors(FormErrorType.UserDefined);
foreach (FormError error in errors)
{
  if (error.Name == "MaxCharsErr")
    Errors.Delete(error);
}
```

And to take this a step further and delete all errors of a specific type, you could use the following code:

```
FormError[] errors = Errors.GetErrors(FormErrorType.UserDefined);
foreach (FormError error in errors)
{
  Errors.Delete(error);
}
```

Unlike the `DeleteAll()` method, which you will learn more about in the next recipe, the code above does not delete all of the validation errors in the form, but only those validation errors that are of a specific type. You can verify that the schema validation error (assuming you left the **required** field blank) is still present in the `Errors` collection by debugging and stepping through the code and verifying that `Errors.Count` is equal to **1** and that `Errors[0].FormErrorType` is equal to `SchemaValidation` after all of the user-defined errors have been deleted.

23 Ignore and clear all errors in a form before submit

Problem

You want to be able to submit an InfoPath form despite any data validation errors that the form may have, so you want to ignore and delete all validation errors before submitting the form.

Solution

You can use the `DeleteAll()` method of the `Errors` collection to clear all of the errors in a form.

To ignore and clear all of the errors in a form before submitting the form:

1. In InfoPath, create a new form template or use an existing one.

2. Add a **Text Box** control to the view of the form template and make it a required field by selecting its **Cannot Be Blank** property. This should cause a schema validation error to occur when a user tries to submit the form and has left the text box blank.

3. Click **Data ➤ Submit Form ➤ Submit Options**.

4. On the **Submit Options** dialog box, select the **Allow users to submit this form** check box, select the **Perform custom action using Code** option, deselect the **Show the Submit button in both the Ribbon and the Info tab in the InfoPath Filler** check box, and click **Edit Code**. Switch back to InfoPath if VSTA got the focus, and click **OK** to close the **Submit Options** dialog box.

5. In VSTA, add code in the `FormEvents_Submit()` event handler to submit the form to a particular destination. For testing purposes, you could save the form locally on disk by using the following code in the `FormEvents_Submit()` event handler (*code #: F42778F9-850C-461B-B4D9-020BAC1D7F20*):

```
System.IO.File.WriteAllText(@"C:\InfoPath\myForm.xml",
  MainDataSource.CreateNavigator().OuterXml);
e.CancelableArgs.Cancel = false;
```

6. Because you disabled the standard **Submit** button on the toolbar, you must programmatically call the `Submit()` method to submit the form, so in InfoPath, add a **Button** control to the view of the form template and label it **Submit**. This button is going to serve as a custom submit button that should replace the standard **Submit** button that InfoPath adds to a form when you enable submit.

7. Add an event handler for the **Clicked** event of the button as described in recipe *7 Add an event handler for a control event*.

8. In VSTA, add the following code to the `Clicked()` event handler for the button (*code #: F42778F9-850C-461B-B4D9-020BAC1D7F20*):

```
if (Errors.Count > 0)
  Errors.DeleteAll();

Submit();
```

The first two lines of code delete all of the errors that are in the `Errors` collection of the form, and the third line of code calls the `FormEvents_Submit()` event handler to submit the form.

9. Save and build the project.

10. Preview the form.

When the form opens, a red asterisk (*) should appear in the text box as an indication that it is a required field. Click the button. The form should be submitted without warning you about any data validation errors.

Discussion

The `DeleteAll()` method of the `FormErrorCollection` object deletes all of the `FormError` objects in the `Errors` collection associated with the current form.

In the solution described above, you disabled the standard **Submit** button that InfoPath adds to a form when you enable the form to be submitted, and replaced it with a custom button that runs rules and code. Note that you did not change the **Action** property of the button to **Submit** but left it on **Rules and Custom Code**, since the former would have had the same effect as the standard **Submit** button.

The standard **Submit** button displays the following error whenever you try to submit a form that contains validation errors:

InfoPath cannot submit the form, because it contains validation errors. Errors are marked with either a red asterisk (required fields) or a red, dashed border (invalid values).

So to change this standard InfoPath submit behavior and ignore all validation errors when the form is submitted, you can add a button that runs code that first clears the entire `Errors` collection using

```
if (Errors.Count > 0)
  Errors.DeleteAll();
```

and then calls the `Submit()` method of the form to submit the form. Note that the `Submit()` method calls the `FormEvents_Submit` event handler method to submit the form.

In step 2 of the solution described above, I mentioned that a required field causes a schema validation error. If you want to verify that this is indeed the case, you can place a breakpoint on the `if`-statement in the `Clicked()` event handler for the button, press **F5**

from within VSTA, and then when the code breaks, type the following into the
Immediate Window

```
Errors[0].FormErrorType
```

and then press **Enter**. The result should say `SchemaValidation`. Always remember that
schema validation errors are caused by constraints that have been placed on the XML
schema of the form. This includes having a required field on the form, setting the value of
a field that has a **nil** attribute set on it (see recipe *11 Set the value of a field*), and adding
fields on locations in the XML structure of the form that violate what is defined by the
XML schema definition (see recipe *66 Add or remove an optional section when a check box
is selected or deselected*).

Chapter 5: Controls

Controls on an InfoPath form are visual elements that are rendered through one or more XSL style sheets that define views for the InfoPath form. And while you can use the `OpenFileFromPackage()` method of the `FormTemplate` object of a form to access the XSL file that is used to create controls on a specific view, there is no method available to write changes back to the XSL file. In addition, because the XSL files that are used to render views are part of the form template (not the form), if you were to modify these files, you would affect all forms that are based on the form template. Therefore, unlike .NET form controls, you cannot programmatically create controls in InfoPath, neither are there any properties which you can programmatically set on controls.

Programming against controls in InfoPath entails programming against the fields that controls are bound to, which again is all about manipulating XML. And if you want to do anything that would require changing what a control looks like on a form such as whether it is enabled or disabled, or what color or font it has, you would have to use conditional formatting.

The recipes in this chapter provide common scenarios for writing code that accesses and modifies data stored in fields bound to the most often used controls in InfoPath.

24 Retrieve design information for a control on a view

Problem

You have a drop-down list box control on an InfoPath form. The drop-down list box contains manually entered items, which means that the values and display names are part of the view the drop-down list box is located on. You want to programmatically retrieve these values and display names when the form opens.

Solution

You can use the `OpenFileFromPackage()` method of the `FormTemplate` object of a form to access the XSL file that is used to create controls on a specific view.

To retrieve design information for a control on a view:

1. In InfoPath, create a new form template or use an existing one.

2. Add a **Drop-Down List Box** control to **View 1** of the form template.

3. Open the **Drop-Down List Box Properties** dialog box, leave the **Enter choices manually** option selected, and click **Add**.

4. On the **Add Choice** dialog box, enter **1** in the **Value** text box, enter **Item 1** in the **Display name** text box, and click **OK**.

5. Repeat step 3 and 4 to add four more items: **Item 2**, **Item 3**, **Item 4**, and **Item 5**. Click **OK** on the **Drop-Down List Box Properties** dialog box when you are done.

6. Add an event handler for the **Loading** event of the form as described in recipe *6 Add an event handler for a form event*.

7. In VSTA, add the following code to the `FormEvents_Loading()` event handler (*code #: 6CF4AED0-B7E9-42E4-88FE-0FE9C2B21F46*):

```
using (System.IO.Stream stream =
  (System.IO.Stream)Template.OpenFileFromPackage("View1.xsl"))
{
  if (stream == null || stream.Length == 0)
    return;

  XPathDocument doc = new XPathDocument(stream);
  XPathNavigator root = doc.CreateNavigator();

  XPathNavigator select = root.SelectSingleNode(
    "//*[@xd:xctname = 'dropdown' and @xd:binding = 'my:field1']",
    NamespaceManager);

  XPathNodeIterator iter = select.Select("//option", NamespaceManager);

  while (iter.MoveNext())
  {
    string value = string.Empty;
    string displayName = string.Empty;

    XPathNavigator valueNode = iter.Current.SelectSingleNode(
      "@value", NamespaceManager);
    if (valueNode != null)
    {
      value = valueNode.Value;
    }
    XPathNodeIterator iter2 =
      iter.Current.SelectChildren(XPathNodeType.Text);
    iter2.MoveNext();
    displayName = iter2.Current.Value;

    if (displayName == "Item 4")
    {
      MainDataSource.CreateNavigator().SelectSingleNode(
        "/my:myFields/my:field1", NamespaceManager).SetValue(value);
    }
  }
  stream.Close();
}
```

8. Save and build the project.

9. Preview the form.

When the form opens, **Item 4** should be displayed as the selected item in the drop-down list box.

Discussion

The `OpenFileFromPackage()` method of the `FormTemplate` object of a form allows you to open files that are stored in the form template (.xsn), including the XSL files used to generate the visual representation of controls on views. You can see which files are stored in the form template by extracting its source files via **File ➤ Publish ➤ Export Source Files** or by changing the file extension of a form template from XSN to CAB and then opening the cabinet file.

The code in the solution described above uses the `OpenFileFromPackage()` method to open the **View1.xsl** file, which belongs to **View 1** in the form template, as a `Stream` object.

```
using (System.IO.Stream stream =
  (System.IO.Stream)Template.OpenFileFromPackage("View1.xsl"))
{
  ...
}
```

It then uses the `Stream` object to instantiate an `XPathDocument` object.

```
XPathDocument doc = new XPathDocument(stream);
```

Once you have an `XPathDocument` object, you can use this `XPathDocument` object to read the data from the XSL file and retrieve the design information for any control. In the solution described above, the code retrieves the data for a drop-down list box named **field1**.

```
XPathNavigator root = doc.CreateNavigator();

XPathNavigator select = root.SelectSingleNode(
  "//*[@xd:xctname = 'dropdown' and @xd:binding = 'my:field1']",
  NamespaceManager);
```

The code uses the `Select()` method of the `XPathNavigator` object to retrieve the drop-down list box items (**option** elements) and place them in an `XPathNodeIterator` object.

```
XPathNodeIterator iter = select.Select("//option", NamespaceManager);
```

The code then goes on to loop through all of the **option** elements found and retrieve the value and display name of each.

```
while (iter.MoveNext())
{
  string value = string.Empty;
  string displayName = string.Empty;

  XPathNavigator valueNode = iter.Current.SelectSingleNode(
    "@value", NamespaceManager);
  if (valueNode != null)
```

```
{
    value = valueNode.Value;
  }
  XPathNodeIterator iter2 = iter.Current.SelectChildren(XPathNodeType.Text);
  iter2.MoveNext();
  displayName = iter2.Current.Value;
}
```

Note that the `SelectChildren()` method is used with an `XPathNodeType.Text` argument to find the text node that represents the display name of an **option** element.

And finally, the code uses the value of the **option** element to set the value of the field bound to the drop-down list box, if the display name of the **option** element is equal to **Item 4**.

```
if (displayName == "Item 4")
{
  MainDataSource.CreateNavigator().SelectSingleNode(
    "/my:myFields/my:field1", NamespaceManager).SetValue(value);
}
```

Note:

> You can also use the technique described in this recipe to search for the type of control that a field is bound to by searching for the value of the **xd:xctname** attribute for a particular field in the XSL file of a view.

25 Hide or disable a control

Problem

You have a button control on an InfoPath form and you want users to be able to select a check box to hide or disable the button.

Solution

You can use conditional formatting and helper fields in a data source to hide or disable a control on an InfoPath form through code.

To hide or disable a control:

1. In Notepad, create an XML file with the following contents:

```
<?xml version="1.0" encoding="UTF-8" ?>
<isHiddenOrDisabled>
  <buttonHidden/>
  <buttonDisabled/>
</isHiddenOrDisabled>
```

Name the XML file **isHiddenOrDisabled.xml**. You can also download this file from www.bizsupportonline.com.

2. In InfoPath, create a new form template or use an existing one.

3. Select **Data ➤ Get External Data ➤ From Other Sources ➤ From XML File** and follow the instructions to add a data connection for the **isHiddenOrDisabled.xml** file you created in step 1. Leave the **Automatically retrieve data when form is opened** check box selected and name the data connection **isHiddenOrDisabled**.

4. Add two **Check Box** controls to the view of the form template and name them **isButtonHidden** and **isButtonDisabled**, respectively.

5. Add a **Button** control to the view of the form template.

6. Add a **Formatting** rule to the button control with a **Condition** that says:

```
buttonHidden = "1"
```

and with a formatting of **Hide this control**. What this formatting rule does is hide the button control if the value of the **buttonHidden** field, which is located in the **isHiddenOrDisabled** secondary source, is equal to **1**.

7. Add a second **Formatting** rule to the button control with a **Condition** that says:

```
buttonDisabled = "1"
```

and with a formatting of **Disable this control**. What this formatting rule does is hide the button control if the value of the **buttonDisabled** field, which is located in the **isHiddenOrDisabled** secondary source, is equal to **1**.

8. Add an event handler for the **Changed** event of the **isButtonHidden** check box as described in recipe *7 Add an event handler for a control event*.

9. In VSTA, add the following code to the `Changed()` event handler for the **isButtonHidden** check box (*code #: 324BF715-7121-4E8B-8344-B72829DDA5A9*):

```
XPathNavigator isHiddenOrDisabledDS =
  DataSources["isHiddenOrDisabled"].CreateNavigator();

if (e.NewValue == "true")
{
  isHiddenOrDisabledDS.SelectSingleNode(
    "/isHiddenOrDisabled/buttonHidden", NamespaceManager).SetValue("1");
}
else
{
  isHiddenOrDisabledDS.SelectSingleNode(
    "/isHiddenOrDisabled/buttonHidden", NamespaceManager).SetValue("");
}
```

10. In InfoPath, add an event handler for the **Changed** event of the **isButtonDisabled** check box as described in recipe *7 Add an event handler for a control event*.

11. In VSTA, add the following code to the `Changed()` event handler for the **isButtonDisabled** check box (*code #: 324BF715-7121-4E8B-8344-B72829DDA5A9*):

```
XPathNavigator isHiddenOrDisabledDS =
  DataSources["isHiddenOrDisabled"].CreateNavigator();

if (e.NewValue == "true")
{
  isHiddenOrDisabledDS.SelectSingleNode(
    "/isHiddenOrDisabled/buttonDisabled", NamespaceManager).SetValue("1");
}
else
{
  isHiddenOrDisabledDS.SelectSingleNode(
    "/isHiddenOrDisabled/buttonDisabled", NamespaceManager).SetValue("");
}
```

12. Save and build the project.

13. Preview the form.

When the form opens, select the **isButtonHidden** check box. The button should disappear from view. Clear the **isButtonHidden** check box. The button should reappear. Select the **isButtonDisabled** check box. The button should be disabled. Clear the **isButtonDisabled** check box. The button should be enabled again.

Discussion

Because an InfoPath control is always rendered as part of a view using XSLT, controls in InfoPath do not have properties you can programmatically set. The only way to hide, disable, or change formatting such as the font, foreground color, or background color of a control in InfoPath is to use formatting rules.

The solution described above uses code with formatting rules that depend on helper fields in a secondary data source to programmatically hide or disable a control. The reason for using helper fields in a secondary data source instead of placing these fields in the Main data source is due to the fact that such fields do not in any way describe the structure of the form, so should not be part of the Main data source of the form. Of course you could have skipped using helper fields in a secondary data source and directly add formatting rules in InfoPath without writing code. But if your scenario calls for hiding, disabling, or setting any other formatting on a control through code, you may want to consider using the solution described above.

The code in the solution described above first retrieves an `XPathNavigator` object pointing to the secondary data source.

```
XPathNavigator isHiddenOrDisabledDS =
  DataSources["isHiddenOrDisabled"].CreateNavigator();
```

It then uses the `NewValue` property of the `XmlEventArgs` object to check whether the value of the field bound to the check box is set to `true`, and if it is, sets the value of the

buttonHidden field (or **buttonDisabled** field) in the secondary data source to be equal to **1**, and in all other cases, to be equal to an empty string.

```
if (e.NewValue == "true")
{
  isHiddenOrDisabledDS.SelectSingleNode(
    "/isHiddenOrDisabled/buttonHidden", NamespaceManager).SetValue("1");
}
else
{
  isHiddenOrDisabledDS.SelectSingleNode(
    "/isHiddenOrDisabled/buttonHidden", NamespaceManager).SetValue("");
}
```

The `NewValue` property of the `XmlEventArgs` object gets the new value for the node being changed. The value of the `NewValue` property is equal to a textual value of either `"false"` or `"true"` when you add a check box that has a **Value when cleared** property equal to **FALSE** and a **Value when checked** property equal to **TRUE** to a form. The value of the `NewValue` property is equal to a textual value of either `"0"` or `"1"` when you add a check box that has a **Value when cleared** property equal to **0** and a **Value when checked** property equal to **1** to a form. So you should change your code to check for the correct value depending on how you configured the check box on your form.

Setting the values of the **buttonHidden** and **buttonDisabled** fields through code automatically triggers the formatting rules that were set on the button. So setting the value of the **buttonHidden** field to **1** through code will hide the button and setting it to an empty string will show the button. Likewise, setting the value of the **buttonDisabled** field to **1** through code will disable the button and setting it to an empty string will enable the button.

In summary: You can use formatting rules, which depend on the values of fields in a secondary data source, to hide or disable a button on a form. You can then write code to set the values of the fields in the secondary source, so that you can programmatically trigger the formatting rules to run and therefore show/hide or enable/disable the button.

Text Box and Rich Text Box

26 Set the value of a decimal field

Problem

You have a text box control on an InfoPath form that has its data type set to **Decimal (double)** and you want to set its value to 12.50 through code.

Solution

Because a field that has a **Decimal (double)** data type has a **nil** attribute set on it (see the discussion section of recipe *11 Set the value of a field*), you must first remove the **nil** attribute before you set the value of the field.

To set the value of a decimal field:

1. In InfoPath, create a new form template or use an existing one.

2. Add a **Text Box** control with the data type **Decimal (double)** and name **field1** to the view of the form template.

3. Add an event handler for the **Loading** event of the form as described in recipe *6 Add an event handler for a form event*.

4. In VSTA, add the following code to the `FormEvents_Loading()` event handler (*code #: E576002C-7848-474F-86D3-5E71DC10EFFD*):

```
XPathNavigator mainDS = MainDataSource.CreateNavigator();
XPathNavigator field1 = mainDS.SelectSingleNode(
  "/my:myFields/my:field1", NamespaceManager);

if (field1.MoveToAttribute("nil", NamespaceManager.LookupNamespace("xsi")))
{
  field1.DeleteSelf();
}

field1.SetValue("12.50");
```

5. Save and build the project.

6. Preview the form.

When the form opens, 12.50 should appear in the text box.

Discussion

Fields that have the **Decimal (double)** data type have a **nil** attribute set on them by default. So before you set the value of a decimal field, you must check whether there is a **nil** attribute present, and if it is, remove it.

```
if (field1.MoveToAttribute("nil", NamespaceManager.LookupNamespace("xsi")))
{
  field1.DeleteSelf();
}
```

Likewise, when you clear a decimal field, you should add the **nil** attribute back on the field as described in recipe *12 Clear a field on a form*.

Because the `SetValue()` method of the `XPathNavigator` object only accepts strings and the value of any type of field is ultimately stored as a string in InfoPath, you must pass decimal numbers as strings when you set the value of a decimal field.

```
field1.SetValue("12.50");
```

Also note that when setting the value of a decimal field, the English decimal notation is used. For example, if you live in a country where you use a comma instead of a point as a decimal separator in your regional settings, you would still have to use a decimal point when setting the value of a decimal field through code. This value should automatically contain a decimal comma and should be displayed correctly when the form is opened in InfoPath Filler or a browser.

27 Validate that data entered is a decimal number

Problem

You have a text box control on a form and want to force users to enter decimal numbers in that text box.

Solution

You can use the **Validating** event of the text box and the `ReportError()` method of the `XmlValidatingEventArgs` object to check whether the data entered into the text box is a decimal number and display a validation error if necessary.

To validate that data entered into a text box is a decimal number:

1. In InfoPath, create a new form template or use an existing one.

2. Add a **Text Box** control to the view of the form template. Leave its data type set to **Text (string)**.

3. Add an event handler for the **Validating** event of the text box as described in recipe *7 Add an event handler for a control event*.

4. In VSTA, add the following code to the `Validating()` event handler for the text box (*code #: 5EEADB83-1B02-4107-A345-3063C307D48C*):

```
XPathNavigator field1 = e.Site;

try
{
  double myDouble = Double.Parse(
    field1.Value,
    System.Globalization.NumberStyles.Float,
    System.Globalization.CultureInfo.CurrentCulture);
}
catch
{
  e.ReportError(field1, false, "Not a decimal number.");
}
```

5. In InfoPath, add an event handler for the **Changed** event of the text box as described in recipe *7 Add an event handler for a control event*.

6. In VSTA, add the following code to the Changed() event handler for the text box (*code #: 5EEADB83-1B02-4107-A345-3063C307D48C*):

```
XPathNavigator field1 = e.Site;

double myDouble;
try
{
  myDouble = Double.Parse(
    field1.Value,
    System.Globalization.NumberStyles.Float,
    System.Globalization.CultureInfo.CurrentCulture);
}
catch
{
  return;
}

field1.SetValue(myDouble.ToString("F3"));
```

7. Save and build the project.

8. Preview the form.

When the form opens, enter an invalid decimal number into the text box. A red dashed border should appear around the text box and if you hover with the mouse pointer over the text box, you should see the error message appear as a tooltip.

Discussion

Data validation in InfoPath takes place on two levels:

1. Data is validated according to the data type of a field.

2. Data is validated if there are any data validation rules or code set on a field.

So the easiest way to force users to enter a float or double in a decimal field is by changing the data type of a text box control from **Text (string)** to **Decimal (double)**.

If you do not want to set the data type of a text box to **Decimal (double)**, but want to use **Text (string)** instead, you must add either a validation rule or data validation code to the text box. The solution described above adds data validation code to the text box control and attempts to convert a string into a double as a way to validate whether a float or double was entered into the field.

The code uses the Site property of the XmlValidatingEventArgs object to retrieve the XPathNavigator object for the field that has to be validated.

```
XPathNavigator field1 = e.Site;
```

The code then goes on to use the Double.Parse() method to try to convert the string into a double. The Double.Parse() method converts the string representation of a number in a specified style and culture-specific format to its double-precision floating point number equivalent. If the string cannot be converted into a double, the

`Double.Parse()` method throws a `System.FormatException`, which is why you have to place the conversion code in a `try-catch` block with the `catch` block calling the `ReportError()` method of the `XmlValidatingEventArgs` object. For more information about the `ReportError()` method, see chapter 4.

```
try
{
  double myDouble = Double.Parse(
    field1.Value,
    System.Globalization.NumberStyles.Float,
    System.Globalization.CultureInfo.CurrentCulture);
}
catch
{
  e.ReportError(field1, false, "Not a decimal number.");
}
```

Another way to validate a decimal number in code is by using a regular expression. But because regular expressions are not culture-specific, you would have to know the culture the form would be used with in advance so that you can accommodate for the use of the right decimal separators in the regular expression. For example, for some cultures you will have to use commas as decimal separators instead of points. On the other hand, the `Double.Parse()` method allows you to specify the culture currently being used, so you do not have to worry about manually checking this yourself, which makes your code more globalization-friendly. But then again, if your forms are going to be used with only one specific culture, you could choose to validate code using regular expressions.

The code in the solution described above also uses the `ToString()` method in the `Changed()` event handler for the text box on the double variable containing the converted number to display the number as a culture-specific (in this case, the culture that the user's system is currently set to use) string representation of the number with three digits after the decimal point.

```
field1.SetValue(myDouble.ToString("F3"));
```

The `ToString()` method accepts number formats. In the code above, `"F3"` is used to format the number as a fixed-point number with three digits after the decimal point. If you wanted for example zero digits after the decimal point, you could use `"F0"`. For a list of numeric format strings that the `ToString()` method accepts, refer to the article entitled *Standard Numeric Format Strings* on the MSDN web site.

28 Display the current time in a text box on a form

Problem

You have a read-only text box that has the data type **Time (time)** on a form and you want to display the current time in this text box.

Solution

You can use the `SetValue()` method of the `XPathNavigator` object to set the value of field that is bound to a text box control to be equal to a string representation of a time and that has a format of **HH:mm:ss**.

To display the current time in a text box on a form:

1. In InfoPath, create a new form template or use an existing one.

2. Add a **Text Box** control to the view of the form template, change its data type to **Time (time)**, and name it **field1**.

3. Add an event handler for the **Loading** event of the form as described in recipe *6 Add an event handler for a form event*.

4. In VSTA, add the following code to the `FormEvents_Loading()` event handler (*code #: 979E67D5-5283-483C-9083-8580C73CBFAC*):

```
XPathNavigator mainDS = MainDataSource.CreateNavigator();
XPathNavigator field1 = mainDS.SelectSingleNode(
  "/my:myFields/my:field1", NamespaceManager);

if (field1.MoveToAttribute("nil", NamespaceManager.LookupNamespace("xsi")))
{
  field1.DeleteSelf();
}

DateTime currentDateTime = DateTime.Now;
field1.SetValue(currentDateTime.ToString("HH:mm:ss"));
```

5. Save and build the project.

6. Preview the form.

When the form opens, the current time should appear in the text box.

Discussion

The value of a text box control that has a data type of **Time (time)** must be set to a time string that has a format of **HH:mm:ss** where **HH** represents the hours (for a 24-hour clock; use **hh** if you want a 12-hour clock), **mm** represents the minutes, and **ss** represents the seconds. If you set the value to any other time format such as for example **9:23:00 a.m.** through code, InfoPath will display a validation error. If you want to select a specific format for the time, in InfoPath, select the text box control, click **Control Tools ➤ Properties ➤ Properties ➤ Data Format**, and then on the **Time Format** dialog box, select the time format you want to use.

The code in the solution described above first retrieves a reference to field bound to the text box control.

```
XPathNavigator mainDS = MainDataSource.CreateNavigator();
XPathNavigator field1 = mainDS.SelectSingleNode(
  "/my:myFields/my:field1", NamespaceManager);
```

Then it checks for a **nil** attribute and removes it if it is present, because text box controls that have a data type of **Time (time)** are among the controls on which a **nil** attribute exists by default (also see the discussion section of recipe *11 Set the value of a field*).

```
if (field1.MoveToAttribute("nil", NamespaceManager.LookupNamespace("xsi")))
{
  field1.DeleteSelf();
}
```

And finally, the `SetValue()` method of the `XPathNavigator` object is used to set the value of the field bound to the text box.

```
DateTime currentDateTime = DateTime.Now;
field1.SetValue(currentDateTime.ToString("HH:mm:ss"));
```

Note that the `ToString()` method of the `DateTime` object allows you to specify date and time formats (**HH:mm:ss** in this case) to return a string in a specific format.

Important:

In InfoPath, fields are used to store data and controls are used to visually present data on a form. So in the case of a time text box, you must use the format **hh:mm:ss** (for a 12-hour clock) or **HH:mm:ss** (for a 24-hour clock) in code to set the value of the time field, but you can use any other data format on the text box control that is bound to the time field to display the time in a specific time format.

29   Embed HTML in an InfoPath form

Problem

You have an HTML code snippet, which you would like users to be able to embed in an InfoPath form.

Solution

You can add a file containing the HTML code fragment as a resource file to the form template and then use the `OpenFileFromPackage()` method to load the HTML into a rich text box on the form.

To embed HTML in an InfoPath form:

1.   Download the **BizSupportOnlineHTML.htm** file from www.bizsupportonline.com or use an existing HTML file.

```
<div style="padding:20px;">
    <h1 style="color:#666;font-weight:bold;font-size:1.7em;font-family:tahoma;margin:2ex 0 0.5ex;">InfoPath
    
    <p style="font-family:arial;font-size:1em;color:#333;">BizSupportOnline is a web site that offers online
    InfoPath and related technologies such as SharePoint and Visual Studio through InfoPath tutorials, artic.

    <p style="font-family:arial;font-size:1em;color:#333;">You can <a rel="nofollow" href="http://feedproxy.g
    to get updates about newly published InfoPath tutorials, articles, and videos.
    </p>
    <div style="float:left;width:48%;">
        <div style="padding: 0 50px 25px 0;">
            <h2 style="color:#666;font-size:1.3em;font-family:tahoma;margin:2ex 0 0.5ex;">New to InfoPath?</
            <p style="font-family:arial;font-size:0.9em;color:#333;">If you are unfamiliar with InfoPath, sta
            <ul>
            <li><a href="http://www.bizsupportonline.net/blog/2009/07/what-is-infopath/">What is InfoPath?</a
            <li><a href="http://www.bizsupportonline.net/infopath2010/videos/index.htm#infopath-demo-videos">
            </ul>
        </div>
    </div>
    <div style="float:left;width:48%;">
        <div style="padding: 0 50px 25px 0;">
            <h2 style="color:#666;font-size:1.3em;font-family:tahoma;margin:2ex 0 0.5ex;">Find InfoPath Solut
            <p style="font-family:arial;font-size:1em;color:#333;">Learn how to create and use InfoPath form
            and <a href="http://www.bizsupportonline.net/infopath2010/videos/index.htm">InfoPath 2010 tutoria
            and with over 150 InfoPath tutorials, solutions, and articles on topics such as:</p>
            <ul>
            <li><a href="http://www.bizsupportonline.net/sharepoint-infopath-integration.htm">InfoPath and Sh
            <li><a href="http://www.bizsupportonline.net/learn-infopath-basics.htm">InfoPath Basics</a></li>
            <li><a href="http://www.bizsupportonline.net/infopath-controls.htm">InfoPath Controls</a></li>
            </ul>
        </div>
    </div>
</div>
```

Figure 21. HTML code in the BizSupportOnlineHTML.htm file.

Note that the HTML markup code you use can contain div elements, hyperlinks, and inline styles defined on the HTML elements.

2. In InfoPath, create a new form template or use an existing one.

3. Add a **Rich Text Box** control to the view of the form template, name it **field1**, and select its **Read-Only** property to make it read-only.

4. Click **Data ➤ Form Data ➤ Resource Files** and add the **BizSupportOnlineHTML.htm** file as a resource file to the form template. Click **OK** to close the **Resource Files** dialog box when you are done.

5. Add a **Button** control to the view of the form template and label it **Load HTML**.

6. Add an event handler for the **Clicked** event of the **Load HTML** button as described in recipe *7 Add an event handler for a control event*.

7. In VSTA, add the following code to the event handler for the **Load HTML** button (*code #: 5EDBD462-0E0A-4E08-8BC7-725F08D36765*):

```
XPathNavigator mainDS = MainDataSource.CreateNavigator();

using (System.IO.Stream stream =
    Template.OpenFileFromPackage("BizSupportOnlineHTML.htm"))
{

    if (stream == null || stream.Length == 0)
        return;

    byte[] bytes = new byte[stream.Length];
    int numBytesToRead = (int)stream.Length;
    int numBytesRead = 0;
    while (numBytesToRead > 0)
    {
```

```
      int n = stream.Read(bytes, numBytesRead, numBytesToRead);

      if (n == 0)
        break;

      numBytesRead += n;
      numBytesToRead -= n;
    }

    string html = System.Text.Encoding.UTF8.GetString(bytes);

    html = "<div xmlns=\"http://www.w3.org/1999/xhtml\">" + html + "</div>";

    XPathNavigator field1 = mainDS.SelectSingleNode(
      "/my:myFields/my:field1", NamespaceManager);

    if (field1.MoveToFirstChild())
      field1.DeleteSelf();

    field1.AppendChild(html);
  }
```

8. Save and build the project.

9. Preview the form.

When the form opens, click the **Load HTML** button. The HTML from the resource file should appear in the rich text box.

Discussion

In the solution described above you saw how to use a rich text box to embed HTML in an InfoPath form. To be able to do this, you had to wrap the HTML code in a **div** element that has the following namespace URI:

```
http://www.w3.org/1999/xhtml
```

and then add the **div** element as a child element to the field that is bound to the rich text box.

```
html = "<div xmlns=\"http://www.w3.org/1999/xhtml\">" + html + "</div>";

XPathNavigator field1 = mainDS.SelectSingleNode(
  "/my:myFields/my:field1", NamespaceManager);

if (field1.MoveToFirstChild())
  field1.DeleteSelf();

field1.AppendChild(html);
```

In the solution described above, a file containing HTML code was stored as a resource file in the form template and then programmatically retrieved at runtime using the OpenFileFromPackage() method of the Template property of the form.

```
System.IO.Stream stream =
  Template.OpenFileFromPackage("BizSupportOnlineHTML.htm")
```

The `OpenFileFromPackage()` method returns a `Stream` object, which you can convert into a byte array

```
byte[] bytes = new byte[stream.Length];
int numBytesToRead = (int)stream.Length;
int numBytesRead = 0;
while (numBytesToRead > 0)
{
  int n = stream.Read(bytes, numBytesRead, numBytesToRead);

  if (n == 0)
    break;

  numBytesRead += n;
  numBytesToRead -= n;
}
```

and then into a string

```
string html = System.Text.Encoding.UTF8.GetString(bytes);
```

which you can then wrap with a **div** element

```
html = "<div xmlns=\"http://www.w3.org/1999/xhtml\">" + html + "</div>";
```

and add as a child element to the field bound to the rich text box.

```
XPathNavigator field1 = mainDS.SelectSingleNode(
  "/my:myFields/my:field1", NamespaceManager);

if (field1.MoveToFirstChild())
  field1.DeleteSelf();

field1.AppendChild(html);
```

Note that because the rich text box was made read-only and its value is only set through code, it is not expected to contain anything when the HTML is added to it. Also note that if HTML has previously been added as a child element to it, that child element should be removed first (using the `MoveToFirstChild()` and `DeleteSelf()` methods of the `XPathNavigator` object), before the **div** element is added again.

```
if (field1.MoveToFirstChild())
  field1.DeleteSelf();
```

By using such code, you could extend the solution to contain more HTML code fragment files as resource files and then for example use option buttons to allow users to choose which HTML to display in the rich text box.

A second way to display HTML in a rich text box in InfoPath is to use an **iframe** element in the HTML as follows:

```
System.Text.StringBuilder sb = new System.Text.StringBuilder();
sb.Append("<div xmlns=\"http://www.w3.org/1999/xhtml\">");
sb.Append("<iframe src=\"http://www.bizsupportonline.net\" ");
sb.Append("style=\"width:100%;height:100%;\" scrolling=\"yes\" ");
sb.Append("marginwidth=\"0\" marginheight=\"0\" frameborder=\"0\">");
sb.Append("</iframe>");
sb.Append("</div>");
html = sb.ToString();
```

In the code shown above, the HTML page located at http://www.bizsupportonline.net would be loaded into the rich text box.

30 Add a line-break to a rich text box

Problem

You have a rich text box on a form and want users to be able to click a button to add a line-break to the text in the rich text box.

Solution

You can append an empty **div** element as a child node to the field that is bound to the rich text box to be able to add a line-break to the text contained in the rich text box.

To add a line-break to a rich text box:

1. In InfoPath, create a new form template or use an existing one.

2. Add a **Rich Text Box** control to the view of the form template and name it **field1**.

3. Add a **Button** control to the view of the form template and label it **Add Line Break**.

4. Add an event handler for the **Clicked** event of the **Add Line Break** button as described in recipe *7 Add an event handler for a control event*.

5. In VSTA, add the following code to the `Clicked()` event handler for the **Add Line Break** button (*code #: 97FEF7E6-D63C-4E64-A42E-79606649DE10*):

    ```
    string lb = "<div xmlns=\"http://www.w3.org/1999/xhtml\"/>";

    XPathNavigator mainDS = MainDataSource.CreateNavigator();

    XPathNavigator field1 = mainDS.SelectSingleNode(
      "/my:myFields/my:field1", NamespaceManager);
    field1.AppendChild(lb);

    CurrentView.SelectText(field1);
    ```

6. Save and build the project.

7. Preview the form.

When the form opens, enter text into the rich text box, and then click the **Add Line Break** button. After clicking the button, all of the text in the rich text box should be selected and you should be able to see that it contains an extra empty line at the end of its contents.

Discussion

The solution described above uses an empty **div** element

```
string lb = "<div xmlns=\"http://www.w3.org/1999/xhtml\"/>";
```

and the `AppendChild()` method of the `XPathNavigator` object pointing to the field bound to a rich text box to add a line-break to the rich text box.

```
XPathNavigator mainDS = MainDataSource.CreateNavigator();

XPathNavigator field1 = mainDS.SelectSingleNode(
  "/my:myFields/my:field1", NamespaceManager);
field1.AppendChild(lb);
```

Note that you could have also used a **br** element to add a line-break.

```
string lb = "<br xmlns=\"http://www.w3.org/1999/xhtml\"/>";
```

The code calls the `SelectText()` method of the `View` object (`CurrentView` property of the `XmlForm` object) and passes a reference to the field bound to the rich text box to be able to set the focus back on the rich text box after a user clicks the **Add Line Break** button and to select all of the text contained in the rich text box.

```
CurrentView.SelectText(field1);
```

The `SelectText()` method selects the text contained in an editable control that is bound to the node specified by the `XPathNavigator` object and `ViewContext` identifier of the control.

31 Clear a rich text box

Problem

You have a rich text box on a form and want users to be able to click a button to delete all of the text contained in the rich text box.

Solution

You can use the `MoveToFirstChild()` and `DeleteSelf()` methods of the `XPathNavigator` object to clear a rich text box control.

To clear a rich text box control:

1. In InfoPath, create a new form template or use an existing one.

2. Add a **Rich Text Box** control to the view of the form template and name it **field1**.

3. Add a **Button** control to the view of the form template and label it **Clear**.

4. Add an event handler for the **Clicked** event of the **Clear** button as described in recipe *7 Add an event handler for a control event*.

5. In VSTA, add the following code to the event handler for the **Clear** button (*code #: 7B06DA6A-DAE5-48F1-8F74-DD191F03FABD*):

```
XPathNavigator mainDS = MainDataSource.CreateNavigator();

XPathNavigator field1 = mainDS.SelectSingleNode(
  "/my:myFields/my:field1", NamespaceManager);

while (field1.MoveToFirstChild())
  field1.DeleteSelf();
```

6. Save and build the project.

7. Preview the form.

When the form opens, enter text into the rich text box, and then click the **Clear** button. The text you entered should disappear from the rich text box.

Discussion

Because a rich text box can have text and/or **div** elements as its contents, you must delete all of the child elements of the field that is bound to a rich text box to be able to clear it.

The solution described above first retrieves a reference to the field bound to the rich text box

```
XPathNavigator mainDS = MainDataSource.CreateNavigator();

XPathNavigator field1 = mainDS.SelectSingleNode(
  "/my:myFields/my:field1", NamespaceManager);
```

and then uses the `MoveToFirstChild()` method of the `XPathNavigator` object pointing to the field bound to the rich text box to sequentially loop through all of the child nodes and delete each one of them by calling the `DeleteSelf()` method on each child node.

```
while (field1.MoveToFirstChild())
  field1.DeleteSelf();
```

32 Validate that a rich text box has no more than 5 lines

Problem

You have a rich text box on a form and want users to be able to enter no more than 5 lines into the rich text box.

Solution

You can use data validation to prevent users from entering more than a certain amount of lines into a rich text box.

To validate that a rich text box has no more than 5 lines:

1. In InfoPath, create a new form template or use an existing one.

2. Add a **Rich Text Box** control to the view of the form template.

3. Add an event handler for the **Validating** event of the rich text box control as described in recipe *7 Add an event handler for a control event*.

4. In VSTA, add the following code to the `Validating()` event handler for the rich text box (*code #: 276005FE-6C28-4F0C-A3A1-6D5B4AEFD56F*):

```
XPathNavigator field1 = e.Site;

int lines = 0;

XPathNodeIterator iter = field1.Select(
    "/my:myFields/my:field1//*[local-name() = 'div' or local-name() = 'br']",
    NamespaceManager);

if (iter != null)
    lines = lines + iter.Count;

if (field1.MoveToFirstChild())
    if (field1.Name == "br")
        lines++;

if (lines > 5)
    e.ReportError(e.Site, false, "Only a maximum of 5 lines is allowed.");
```

5. Save and build the project.

6. Preview the form.

When the form opens, enter 6 lines of text into the rich text box, and then click or tab away from the rich text box. A red dashed border should appear around the rich text box control and if you hover with the mouse pointer over the control, you should see the error message appear as a tooltip.

Discussion

Lines in a rich text box control are represented by either **div** or **br** elements in the contents of the field bound to the rich text box control. A line becomes a **div** element when you use **Enter** in a rich text box, and a line becomes a **br** element when you use **Shift+Enter** in a rich text box. So to be able to prevent users from entering more than a certain amount of lines, you must count the amount of **div** and **br** elements that are present in the field bound to the rich text box.

The solution described above uses data validation (also see chapter 4) to prevent users from entering more than 5 lines into a rich text box control. The code first retrieves the XPathNavigator object pointing to the rich text box

```
XPathNavigator field1 = e.Site;
```

and declares a variable to be able to store the amount of lines.

```
int lines = 0;
```

Then it uses the Select() method of the XPathNavigator object with an XPath expression that filters all nodes on their local name being equal to **div** or equal to **br**

```
/my:myFields/my:field1//*[local-name() = 'div' or local-name() = 'br']
```

to retrieve a node-set containing all of the **div** and **br** elements that are descendants of the field bound to the rich text box and store the results in an XPathNodeIterator object.

```
XPathNodeIterator iter = field1.Select(
  "/my:myFields/my:field1//*[local-name() = 'div' or local-name() = 'br']",
  NamespaceManager);
```

Note that **br** elements can be direct children of the field bound to the rich text box or they can be descendants (children, grandchildren, etc.) of **div** elements that are direct children of the field bound to the rich text box. The Count property of the XPathNodeIterator object is used to count the amount of **div** and **br** elements returned.

```
if (iter != null)
  lines = lines + iter.Count;
```

And finally, a correction is applied to the amount of lines if the first child element of the field bound to the rich text box is a **br** element. So the code uses the MoveToFirstChild() method of the XPathNavigator object pointing to the field bound to the rich text box to check whether the first child node of the field bound to the rich text box is a **br** element, and if it is, it increments the total amount of lines by 1.

```
if (field1.MoveToFirstChild())
  if (field1.Name == "br")
    lines++;
```

The last step is to display an error message to the user if the total amount of lines exceeds 5.

```
if (lines > 5)
  e.ReportError(e.Site, false, "Only a maximum of 5 lines is allowed.");
```

For more information about the `ReportError()` method, see chapter 4.

Drop-Down List Box, Combo Box, and List Box

33 Select an item in a drop-down list box

Problem

You have a drop-down list box on an InfoPath form and want to programmatically select a specific item in the drop-down list box whenever a button is clicked.

Solution

You must set the value of the field that is bound to the drop-down list box to be equal to the value of the item you want to select.

To select an item in a drop-down list box:

1. In Notepad, create a file that has the following contents:

    ```
    <?xml version="1.0" encoding="UTF-8"?>
    <fruits>
      <fruit><name>Apple</name><color>Red</color></fruit>
      <fruit><name>Banana</name><color>Yellow</color></fruit>
      <fruit><name>Grapes</name><color>Purple</color></fruit>
      <fruit><name>Kiwi</name><color>Brown</color></fruit>
      <fruit><name>Orange</name><color>Orange</color></fruit>
    </fruits>
    ```

    and save the file as **Fruits.xml**. You can also download this file from www.bizsupportonline.com.

2. In InfoPath, create a new form template or use an existing one.

3. Select **Data ➤ Get External Data ➤ From Other Sources ➤ From XML File** and follow the instructions to add a data connection for the **Fruits.xml** file. Name the data connection **Fruits** and leave the **Automatically retrieve data when form is opened** check box selected when you save the data connection.

4. Add a **Drop-Down List Box** control to the view of the form template and name it **field1**.

5. Open the **Properties** dialog box of the drop-down list box. On the **Data** tab, select the **Get choices from an external data source** option, select **Fruits** from the **Data source** drop-down list box, and then configure the **Entries** to come from the **fruit** repeating group node, and the values of both the **Value** and **Display name** properties to come from the **name** field under the **fruit** repeating group node. Click **OK** to close the dialog box when you are done.

6. Add a **Text Box** control to the view of the form template, and name it **fruitName**.

7. Add a **Button** control to the view of the form template and label it **Select**.

8. Add an event handler for the **Clicked** event of the button as described in recipe *7 Add an event handler for a control event*.

9. In VSTA, add the following code to the `Clicked()` event handler for the button (*code #: 7434E973-61B1-461E-AC93-7A8405842D3D*):

```
XPathNavigator mainDS = MainDataSource.CreateNavigator();
string fruitName = mainDS.SelectSingleNode(
  "/my:myFields/my:fruitName", NamespaceManager).Value;

XPathNavigator secDS = DataSources["Fruits"].CreateNavigator();
XPathNavigator listItem = secDS.SelectSingleNode(
  "/fruits/fruit[name = '" + fruitName + "']", NamespaceManager);

if (listItem != null)
{
  mainDS.SelectSingleNode(
    "/my:myFields/my:field1", NamespaceManager).SetValue(fruitName);
}
else
{
  mainDS.SelectSingleNode(
    "/my:myFields/my:field1", NamespaceManager).SetValue("");
}
```

10. Save and build the project.

11. Preview the form.

When the form opens, enter a fruit name into the text box, and then click the button. The fruit that has the same name you typed into the text box should appear in the drop-down list box as the selected item.

Discussion

To select a specific item in a drop-down list box or any other type of list control in InfoPath, you must set the value of the field that is bound to the drop-down list box to be equal to the value of a specific item that is used to populate the drop-down list box.

List box controls can be populated with either static items (when you choose to enter items manually) or with dynamic items (when you choose to bind the list box to a data source; either the Main or a secondary data source). In the solution described above, the drop-down list box was populated with dynamic items, that is, items that can be changed at runtime.

In the solution described above, the user is allowed to enter a name of a fruit.

```
XPathNavigator mainDS = MainDataSource.CreateNavigator();
string fruitName = mainDS.SelectSingleNode(
  "/my:myFields/my:fruitName", NamespaceManager).Value;
```

The code then tries to retrieve the item in the drop-down list box that has the same name as the name the user entered. To do this, a lookup must be performed in the **Fruits** secondary data source.

```
XPathNavigator secDS = DataSources["Fruits"].CreateNavigator();
XPathNavigator listItem = secDS.SelectSingleNode(
  "/fruits/fruit[name = '" + fruitName + "']", NamespaceManager);
```

If the item exists (it is not equal to `null`), then the item can be selected in the drop-down list box. If the item does not exist (it is equal to `null`), any item that was previously selected in the drop-down list box should be cleared.

```
if (listItem != null)
{
  mainDS.SelectSingleNode(
    "/my:myFields/my:field1", NamespaceManager).SetValue(fruitName);
}
else
{
  mainDS.SelectSingleNode(
    "/my:myFields/my:field1", NamespaceManager).SetValue("");
}
```

Since the **Value** property of the drop-down list box is bound to the **name** field in the secondary data source, you must use the name of the fruit entered into the text box to set the value of the field bound to the drop-down list box, so that the selected item appears in the drop-down list box. Always remember that the **Value** property of a list box control determines the selected item; not the **Display name**. In addition, whenever a user selects an item in a list box control, the value of the field bound to the list box control will correspond to the value of one of the items used to fill the list box control. So if you want to programmatically select an item in the list box control, you must set the value of the field bound to the list box control to be equal to the value of an item used to populate the list box control.

34 Populate a drop-down list box

Problem

You have a drop-down list box on an InfoPath form, which you want to populate with items whenever a user clicks a button.

Solution

You can use an XML file as a secondary data source to bind the drop-down list box to, and then to populate the drop-down list box by adding items to the secondary data source for the XML file.

To populate a drop-down list box:

1. In Notepad, create a file that has the following contents:

    ```
    <?xml version="1.0" encoding="UTF-8" ?>
    <items>
      <item><displayName/><value/></item>
      <item><displayName/><value/></item>
    </items>
    ```

    and save the file as **items.xml**. You can also download this file from www.bizsupportonline.com.

2. In InfoPath, create a new form template or use an existing one.

3. Select **Data ➤ Get External Data ➤ From Other Sources ➤ From XML File** and follow the instructions to add the **items.xml** file as a secondary data source to the form template. Leave the **Automatically retrieve data when form is opened** check box selected and name the data connection **DropDownListItems**.

4. Add a **Drop-Down List Box** control to the view of the form template.

5. Open the **Properties** dialog box of the drop-down list box, and then on the **Data** tab, select the **Get choices from an external data source** option, select **DropDownListItems** from the **Data source** drop-down list box, and then configure the **Entries** to come from the **item** repeating group node, the value of the **Value** property to come from the **value** field under the **item** repeating group node, and the value of the **Display name** property to come from the **displayName** field under the **item** repeating group node. Click **OK** to close the dialog box when you are done.

6. Add a **Button** control to the view of the form template and label it **Populate List**.

7. Add an event handler for the **Clicked** event of the button as described in recipe *7 Add an event handler for a control event*.

8. In VSTA, add the following two private methods to the `FormCode` class (*code #: CA736B52-8B93-44E4-B82A-0D45E37243B7*):

```
private void ClearList(ref XPathNavigator itemsNode)
{
  if (itemsNode != null)
  {
    while (itemsNode.HasChildren)
    {
      itemsNode.MoveToFirstChild();
      itemsNode.DeleteSelf();
    }
  }
}

private void AddListItem(
  string displayName, string value, ref XPathNavigator itemsNode)
{
  if (itemsNode != null)
  {
    System.Text.StringBuilder sb = new System.Text.StringBuilder();
    sb.Append("<item>");
    sb.AppendFormat("<displayName>{0}</displayName>", displayName);
    sb.AppendFormat("<value>{0}</value>", value);
    sb.Append("</item>");
    itemsNode.AppendChild(sb.ToString());
  }
}
```

9. Add the following code to the `Clicked()` event handler for the **Populate List** button (*code #: CA736B52-8B93-44E4-B82A-0D45E37243B7*):

```
XPathNavigator itemsNode =
  DataSources["DropDownListItems"].CreateNavigator();
itemsNode.MoveToFirstChild();

ClearList(ref itemsNode);

AddListItem("Access", "1", ref itemsNode);
AddListItem("Excel", "2", ref itemsNode);
AddListItem("InfoPath", "3", ref itemsNode);
AddListItem("Outlook", "4", ref itemsNode);
AddListItem("Word", "5", ref itemsNode);
```

10. In InfoPath, add an event handler for the **Loading** event of the form as described in recipe *6 Add an event handler for a form event*.

11. In VSTA, add the following code to the `FormEvents_Loading()` event handler (*code #: CA736B52-8B93-44E4-B82A-0D45E37243B7*):

```
XPathNavigator itemsNode =
  DataSources["DropDownListItems"].CreateNavigator();
itemsNode.MoveToFirstChild();

ClearList(ref itemsNode);
```

12. Save and build the project.

13. Preview the form.

When the form opens, verify that the drop-down list box does not contain any items. Click the **Populate List** button. Verify that the drop-down list box has been populated with items.

Discussion

To be able to programmatically populate a drop-down list box, you must bind the drop-down list box either to a repeating group node in the Main data source of the form or to a repeating group node in a secondary data source. If you manually enter choices for a drop-down list box, you will not be able to programmatically populate the drop-down list box, since those items will become (a static) part of the view.

In the solution described above you used a secondary data source for an XML file that has a structure that is suitable to be bound to a drop-down list box, combo box, or list box, to be able to programmatically populate a drop-down list box. The XML file contained two empty items by default. This is necessary for InfoPath to recognize the **item** group node in the XML file as a repeating group node and not as a normal group node, since the latter cannot be used as a data source for a list.

Because the XML file initially contains two empty items, you must delete these empty items when the form first opens (loads).

```
XPathNavigator itemsNode =
  DataSources["DropDownListItems"].CreateNavigator();
itemsNode.MoveToFirstChild();

ClearList(ref itemsNode);
```

Note that you must use the `DataSources` property of the form to retrieve a reference to the secondary data source for the XML file (also see recipe *9 Access a secondary data source of a form* for more information about the `DataSources` property). In the code above, the `MoveToFirstChild()` method of the `XPathNavigator` object ensures that the pointer is placed on the **items** group node in the secondary data source, but you could have also used the following lines of code to achieve the same result:

```
XPathNavigator secDS = DataSources["DropDownListItems"].CreateNavigator();
XPathNavigator itemsNode = secDS.SelectSingleNode("/items", NamespaceManager);
```

The code calls a private method named `ClearList()` to be able to delete items.

```
private void ClearList(ref XPathNavigator itemsNode)
{
  if (itemsNode != null)
  {
    while (itemsNode.HasChildren)
    {
      itemsNode.MoveToFirstChild();
      itemsNode.DeleteSelf();
    }
  }
}
```

The code in the `ClearList()` method deletes all of the items in the secondary data source for the XML file by looping through the secondary data source while checking whether the root node has children, and then calling the `MoveToFirstChild()` and

`DeleteSelf()` methods of the `XPathNavigator` object to delete each child node found. Note that you could have also retrieved the first and last nodes of the root node, and then used the `DeleteRange()` method of the first node to delete all of the child nodes (also see recipe *43 Deselect all items in a multiple-selection list box* for an example of how to use the `DeleteRange()` method).

Before you (re)populate the drop-down list box, you must delete all of the items from the secondary data source for the XML file. Once all of the items in the secondary data source have been deleted, you can repeatedly call a private method named `AddListItem()`

```
private void AddListItem(
  string displayName, string value, ref XPathNavigator itemsNode)
{
  if (itemsNode != null)
  {
    System.Text.StringBuilder sb = new System.Text.StringBuilder();
    sb.Append("<item>");
    sb.AppendFormat("<displayName>{0}</displayName>", displayName);
    sb.AppendFormat("<value>{0}</value>", value);
    sb.Append("</item>");
    itemsNode.AppendChild(sb.ToString());
  }
}
```

to add items to the secondary data source and consequently also to the drop-down list box whenever the button is clicked.

```
AddListItem("Access", "1", ref itemsNode);
AddListItem("Excel", "2", ref itemsNode);
AddListItem("InfoPath", "3", ref itemsNode);
AddListItem("Outlook", "4", ref itemsNode);
AddListItem("Word", "5", ref itemsNode);
```

Note that because you are dealing with a secondary data source that has a repeating XML structure (that is, the **item** group node repeats under the **items** group node in the data source), you could have used any one of the solutions discussed in recipe *71 Add a row to a repeating table* to add an item to the secondary data source for the XML file. The code in the `AddListItem()` method in the solution described above uses the `AppendChild()` method of the `XPathNavigator` object pointing to the root **items** node of the secondary data source to add an item.

Check Box and Option Button

35 Select or deselect a check box

Problem

You have a check box control on an InfoPath form, which you want users to be able to toggle on and off whenever they click a button.

Solution

You can set the value of the field that is bound to a check box control to `true` or `false` to be able to toggle a check box on or off.

To select or deselect a check box:

1. In InfoPath, create a new form template or use an existing one.

2. Add a **Check Box** control to the view of the form template and name it **isSelected**.

3. Add a **Button** control to the view of the form template and label it **Toggle Check Box**.

4. Add an event handler for the **Clicked** event of the button as described in recipe *7 Add an event handler for a control event*.

5. In VSTA, add the following code to the `Clicked()` event handler for the button (*code #: C89729C6-BDFB-4975-836D-60CF0F65B4F1*):

```
XPathNavigator mainDS = MainDataSource.CreateNavigator();
XPathNavigator isSelected = mainDS.SelectSingleNode(
  "/my:myFields/my:isSelected", NamespaceManager);

if (isSelected.Value == "false")
  isSelected.SetValue("true");
else
  isSelected.SetValue("false");
```

6. Save and build the project.

7. Preview the form.

When the form opens, the check box should be deselected. Click the button. The check box should be selected. Click the button again. The check box should be deselected.

Discussion

When you add a check box control to a form template, its **Value when cleared** and **Value when checked** properties are by default set to **FALSE** and **TRUE**, respectively. So if you want to select the check box, you must use code similar to the following:

```
isSelected.SetValue("true");
```

where `isSelected` is an `XPathNavigator` object pointing to the field bound to the check box control. And if you want to deselect the check box, you must use code similar to the following:

```
isSelected.SetValue("false");
```

You could also configure a check box to have a **Value when cleared** property equal to **0** and a **Value when checked** property equal to **1**. If you changed these properties to have these values, you must change the code in the solution as follows:

```
XPathNavigator mainDS = MainDataSource.CreateNavigator();
XPathNavigator isSelected = mainDS.SelectSingleNode(
  "/my:myFields/my:isSelected", NamespaceManager);

if (isSelected.Value == "0")
  isSelected.SetValue("1");
else
  isSelected.SetValue("0");
```

where

```
isSelected.SetValue("1");
```

selects the check box, and

```
isSelected.SetValue("0");
```

deselects the check box.

36   Select a specific option from a list of options

Problem

You have a list of five option buttons on an InfoPath form and would like the third option to be selected as soon as the form opens.

Solution

You can set the value of the field that is bound to the option button control to **3** in the `FormEvents_Loading()` event handler for the form.

To select a specific option from a list of options:

1.   In InfoPath, create a new form template or use an existing one.

2. Add an **Option Button** control with 5 options to the view of the form template and name it **field1**.

3. Add an event handler for the **Loading** event of the form as described in recipe *6 Add an event handler for a form event*.

4. In VSTA, add the following code to the `FormEvents_Loading()` event handler (*code #: C3EEFCF9-9EE6-400D-8888-6B18065CAE4C*):

```
XPathNavigator mainDS = MainDataSource.CreateNavigator();
XPathNavigator field1 = mainDS.SelectSingleNode(
  "/my:myFields/my:field1", NamespaceManager);
field1.SetValue("3");
```

5. Save and build the project.

6. Preview the form.

When the form opens, the third option should be selected.

Discussion

When you add an option button control to a form template, the **Value when selected** property of each option button in the list is automatically assigned a numerical value in an ascending order starting from **1**. So if you want to select the third option button in a list of five option buttons, you must use code similar to the following:

```
field1.SetValue("3");
```

where `field1` is an `XPathNavigator` object pointing to the field bound to the option button control. While an option button control automatically gets numbers assigned as the values for its options, you are allowed to not only change the data type of the option button control, but also assign whatever value you want to the **Value when selected** property for each option in the list. If you have configured an option button control to have values other than the default numerical values, you must change the code in the solution above accordingly.

For example, if you changed the values of the options to **one**, **two**, **three**, **four**, and **five** instead of **1**, **2**, **3**, **4**, and **5**, you must change the code that selects the third option when the form opens as follows:

```
field1.SetValue("three");
```

where **three** is the value of the third option in the list.

Date Picker and Date and Time Picker

37 Get the value of a date and time picker control

Problem

You have a date and time picker control on a form and want to retrieve its value and store this value in a `DateTime` variable.

Solution

You can use the `Value` property of the `XPathNavigator` object pointing to the field that is bound to a date and time picker control to get the value of the date and time picker control, and then use the `DateTime.TryParse()` method to convert the string representation of the date into a `DateTime` object for further use in code.

To get the value of a date and time picker control:

1. In InfoPath, create a new form template or use an existing one.

2. Add a **Date and Time Picker** control to the view of the form template, name it **field1**, and set its **Default Value** to the following formula:

   ```
   now()
   ```

   This formula displays the current date and time in the date and time picker control when the form opens.

3. Add an event handler for the **Loading** event of the form as described in recipe *6 Add an event handler for a form event*.

4. In VSTA, add the following code to the `FormEvents_Loading()` event handler (*code #: 498633C0-B3CE-4459-892A-B82059FDB28E*):

   ```
   XPathNavigator mainDS = MainDataSource.CreateNavigator();
   XPathNavigator field1 = mainDS.SelectSingleNode(
     "/my:myFields/my:field1", NamespaceManager);

   DateTime myDateTime;
   DateTime.TryParse(field1.Value, out myDateTime);
   ```

5. Save and build the project.

6. Set a breakpoint and then press **F5** to debug the code.

When the code breaks in VSTA, step through the code and verify that the `myDateTime` variable contains the current date and time.

Discussion

In the solution described above, the code first retrieves an XPathNavigator object
pointing to the field bound to the date and time picker control

```
XPathNavigator mainDS = MainDataSource.CreateNavigator();
XPathNavigator field1 = mainDS.SelectSingleNode(
  "/my:myFields/my:field1", NamespaceManager);
```

before storing the value of the field bound to the date and time picker control in a
DateTime variable using the TryParse() method.

```
DateTime myDateTime;
DateTime.TryParse(field1.Value, out myDateTime);
```

The System.DateTime.TryParse() method converts the specified string representation
of a date and time to its System.DateTime equivalent using the specified culture-specific
information and formatting style. No culture-specific information was used when
converting the string to a date in the solution described above. Because dates in InfoPath
are stored as ISO date strings, which do not depend on any culture, you can omit the
culture-specific information when converting ISO date strings to date objects in code.

Note:

> You can retrieve the value of a date picker control in InfoPath and convert it to a
> DateTime object the same way you retrieved the value of a date and time picker
> control in InfoPath and converted it to a DateTime object.

38   Set the value of a date and time picker control

Problem

You have a date and time picker control on a form and want to set its value through code.

Solution

You can use the SetValue() method of the XPathNavigator object pointing to the field
that is bound to a date and time picker control to set the value of the date and time picker
control to a string representation of a date that has a format of yyyy-MM-ddTHH:mm:ss.

To set the value of a date and time picker control:

1.   In InfoPath, create a new form template or use an existing one.

2. Add a **Date and Time Picker** control to the view of the form template and name it **field1**.

3. Add an event handler for the **Loading** event of the form as described in recipe *6 Add an event handler for a form event*.

4. In VSTA, add the following code to the `FormEvents_Loading()` event handler (*code #: 567189B4-8E69-48AD-A1DD-3475E1BE7A31*):

```
XPathNavigator mainDS = MainDataSource.CreateNavigator();
XPathNavigator field1 = mainDS.SelectSingleNode(
  "/my:myFields/my:field1", NamespaceManager);

if (field1.MoveToAttribute("nil", field1.LookupNamespace("xsi")))
{
  field1.DeleteSelf();
}

field1.SetValue("2012-12-20T20:12:00");
```

5. Save and build the project.

6. Preview the form.

When the form opens, verify that the date and time value that was set through code appears in the date and time picker control.

Discussion

Date and time picker controls accept date strings that have a format of **yyyy-MM-ddTHH:mm:ss** where **yyyy** represents the year, **MM** represents the month, **dd** represents the day, **HH** represents the hours, **mm** represents the minutes, and **ss** represents the seconds. If you omit the time portion of the string, so use a date with a format of **yyyy-MM-dd**, InfoPath will display a validation error for the date and time picker control.

In the solution described above, after retrieving a reference to the field bound to the date and time picker control

```
XPathNavigator mainDS = MainDataSource.CreateNavigator();
XPathNavigator field1 = mainDS.SelectSingleNode(
  "/my:myFields/my:field1", NamespaceManager);
```

the code checks for a **nil** attribute and removes it if it is present on the field bound to the date and time picker control, since date and time picker controls are on the list of controls on which a **nil** attribute exists by default (also see the discussion section of recipe *11 Set the value of a field*).

```
if (field1.MoveToAttribute("nil", field1.LookupNamespace("xsi")))
{
  field1.DeleteSelf();
}
```

The code then uses the `SetValue()` method of the `XPathNavigator` object to set the value of the field bound to the date and time picker control to a date that has a format of **yyyy-MM-ddTHH:mm:ss**, for example 2012-12-20T20:12:00.

```
field1.SetValue("2012-12-20T20:12:00");
```

You could easily extend the solution described above to display the current date and time in the date and time picker control by replacing the last line of code with the following:

```
DateTime currentDateTime = DateTime.Now;
field1.SetValue(currentDateTime.ToString("yyyy-MM-ddTHH:mm:ss"));
```

39 Calculate the difference between two date pickers

Problem

You have two date picker controls and a text box control on a form, and you want to be able to calculate the difference in days between the two date picker controls and display the result in the text box control.

Solution

You can retrieve the values of two date picker controls, store them in `DateTime` objects, and then use a `TimeSpan` object to calculate the difference in days between the two `DateTime` objects.

To calculate the difference in days between two date picker controls:

1. In InfoPath, create a new form template or use an existing one.

2. Add two **Date Picker** controls to the view of the form template and name them **startDate** and **endDate**, respectively.

3. Add a **Text Box** control to the view of the form template and name it **dateDifference**.

4. Add an event handler for the **Changed** event of the **startDate** date picker control as described in recipe *7 Add an event handler for a control event*.

5. In VSTA, add the following code to the `startDate_Changed()` event handler (*code #: 60AD6EA9-3336-417E-BF34-99C0EDBD49F8*):

```
XPathNavigator startDateField = e.Site;
XPathNavigator endDateField = e.Site.SelectSingleNode(
  "../my:endDate", NamespaceManager);
XPathNavigator dateDifferenceField = e.Site.SelectSingleNode(
  "../my:dateDifference", NamespaceManager);

if (startDateField != null && endDateField != null
  && dateDifferenceField != null)
```

```
{
  DateTime startDate;
  DateTime.TryParse(startDateField.Value, out startDate);
  DateTime endDate;
  DateTime.TryParse(endDateField.Value, out endDate);

  TimeSpan ts = endDate - startDate;
  dateDifferenceField.SetValue(ts.Days.ToString());
}
```

6. In InfoPath, add an event handler for the **Changed** event of the **endDate** date picker control as described in recipe *7 Add an event handler for a control event*.

7. In VSTA, add the following code to the endDate_Changed() event handler (*code #: 60AD6EA9-3336-417E-BF34-99C0EDBD49F8*):

```
XPathNavigator startDateField = e.Site.SelectSingleNode(
  "../my:startDate", NamespaceManager);
XPathNavigator endDateField = e.Site;
XPathNavigator dateDifferenceField = e.Site.SelectSingleNode(
  "../my:dateDifference", NamespaceManager);

if (startDateField != null && endDateField != null
  && dateDifferenceField != null)
{
  DateTime startDate;
  DateTime.TryParse(startDateField.Value, out startDate);
  DateTime endDate;
  DateTime.TryParse(endDateField.Value, out endDate);

  TimeSpan ts = endDate - startDate;
  dateDifferenceField.SetValue(ts.Days.ToString());
}
```

8. Save and build the project.

9. Preview the form.

When the form opens, enter a start date and an end date. The difference between the two dates you entered should appear in the text box.

Discussion

In the solution described above, you used a TimeSpan object to calculate the difference between two date picker controls. A TimeSpan object represents a time interval.

The code first uses the Site property of the XmlEventArgs object in the Changed() event handler for the fields bound to the date picker controls to retrieve a reference to the fields bound to the **startDate** and **endDate** date picker controls, and to the **dateDifference** text box.

```
XPathNavigator startDateField = e.Site;
XPathNavigator endDateField = e.Site.SelectSingleNode(
  "../my:endDate", NamespaceManager);
XPathNavigator dateDifferenceField = e.Site.SelectSingleNode(
  "../my:dateDifference", NamespaceManager);
```

Note that the XPath expressions for the **endDate** and **dateDifference** fields are relative paths starting from the **startDate** field, which is the context node. The Site property of the XmlEventArgs object in the Changed() event handler for the **startDate** field returns an XPathNavigator object pointing to the **startDate** field, while the Site property of the XmlEventArgs object in the Changed() event handler for the **endDate** field returns an XPathNavigator object pointing to the **endDate** field. Because all fields in the Main data source of the form used in this solution are siblings of each other, you must first navigate to the parent of each object returned using the double-dot notation, and then navigate to the sibling node. For example, if the current context node is the **startDate** field, you would have to use the following code to retrieve an XPathNavigator object for the **endDate** field:

```
XPathNavigator endDateField = e.Site.SelectSingleNode(
  "../my:endDate", NamespaceManager);
```

And then you can use the values of the **startDate** and **endDate** fields to calculate the date difference with a TimeSpan object.

```
if (startDateField != null && endDateField != null
  && dateDifferenceField != null)
{
  DateTime startDate;
  DateTime.TryParse(startDateField.Value, out startDate);
  DateTime endDate;
  DateTime.TryParse(endDateField.Value, out endDate);

  TimeSpan ts = endDate - startDate;
  dateDifferenceField.SetValue(ts.Days.ToString());
}
```

The TryParse() method of the DateTime objects is called to convert the string representations of the two dates to DateTime objects.

Multiple-Selection List Box

40   Select an item in a multiple-selection list box

Problem

You have a multiple-selection list box and a button on a form. You want to be able to click the button to select one particular item in the multiple-selection list box.

Solution

You can use the AppendChildElement() method of the XPathNavigator object pointing to the group node of a multiple-selection list box to add a child node for the value of the item you want to select, since adding a child node to the group node of the multiple-selection list box is equivalent to selecting an item in the list.

To select an item in a multiple-selection list box when you click a button:

1. In InfoPath, create a new form template or use an existing one.

2. Add a **Multiple-Selection List Box** to the view of the form template and name it **field1**.

3. Open the **Multiple-Selection List Box Properties** dialog box, leave the **Enter choices manually** option selected, and add the following 5 static value/name pairs as choices to the control: 1 = Item 1, 2 = Item 2, 3 = Item 3, 4 = Item 4, 5 = Item 5. Click **OK** when you are done.

4. Add a **Button** control to the view of the form template.

5. Add an event handler for the **Clicked** event of the button as described in recipe 7 *Add an event handler for a control event*.

6. In VSTA, add the following code to the `Clicked()` event handler for the button (*code #: B42E5330-D99C-4906-ADD8-E1A9CAA5AF31*):

```
XPathNavigator mainDS = MainDataSource.CreateNavigator();
XPathNavigator group1 = mainDS.SelectSingleNode(
  "/my:myFields/my:group1", NamespaceManager);

if (group1.SelectSingleNode(
  "my:field1[. = '3']", NamespaceManager) == null)
{
  group1.AppendChildElement("my", "field1", group1.NamespaceURI, "3");
}
```

Note that you must check whether the child node exists before adding the node, otherwise you will wind up having two nodes with the same value under the group node.

7. Save and build the project.

8. Preview the form.

When the form opens, click the button. The check box in front of the third item should get a check mark as an indication that it has been selected.

Discussion

The key to learning how to program against a multiple-selection list box - or any type of control in InfoPath for that matter - is to understand what its XML structure looks like. A multiple-selection list box by default consists of one group node with a repeating field under it. If you preview an InfoPath form that has a multiple-selection list box on it, select a couple of items in the multiple-selection list box, save the form locally on disk, and then open the form in Notepad, you will see that InfoPath stores the selected values as child nodes under the group node. In addition, there is always one node that remains empty under the group node if you do not deselect the check box for the repeating field under the group node of the multiple-selection list box on the **Edit Default Values** dialog box, which you can access through **Data ➤ Form Data ➤ Default Values**.

Figure 22. The group node and repeating field for a multiple-selection list box.

In the figure shown above, the check box for the repeating field of the multiple-selection list box has been deselected, so the multiple-selection list box will not contain an empty item by default. In the solution described above, you did not alter the default values for the multiple-selection list box, so it should contain an empty item by default.

With this knowledge you can now easily write code for multiple-selection list boxes. If you want to select an item, you know that you must add a child node that has the value you want to select under the group node. If you want to deselect an item, you know that you must delete the child node that has the value you want to deselect from under the group node. If you want to select all items in a multiple-selection list box, you know that you must add child nodes for all of the values you want to select under the group node. And finally, if you want to deselect all items in a multiple-selection list box, you know that you must delete all child nodes except for the empty child node (if it is present) from under the group node.

Note that an item in a multiple-selection list box consists of two parts:

1. A display name

2. A value

When you are writing code in InfoPath, you always work with values of fields, and not display names, because the values are stored in the XML nodes of the InfoPath form.

For all types of list boxes (including multiple-selection list boxes) the display names are generally stored in the view when static items are added to a list box or in a data source when you bind a list box to either a secondary data source or the Main data source of a form. While you could access static items stored in a view by using the `OpenFileFromPackage()` method of the `Template` property of the `XmlForm` object to open the XSL file corresponding to the view (see for example recipe *24 Retrieve design information for a control on a view*) and search for list item names in the file, it is much easier to lookup list item names in a data source. Therefore, if you know that your code will have to dynamically retrieve display names of items in any type of list box, it is best to bind that list box to a secondary data source or to a repeating node in the form itself, so that you can perform a lookup for the display names of items based on their values.

Selecting an item in a multiple-selection list box is equivalent to adding a repeating field that has the value of the item you want to select under the group node that is bound to the multiple-selection list box. You can use the `AppendChildElement()` method of the `XPathNavigator` object pointing to the group node of the multiple-selection list box to add a child node that has the value you want to select.

```
group1.AppendChildElement("my", "field1", group1.NamespaceURI, "3");
```

The `AppendChildElement()` method of the `XPathNavigator` object creates a new child element node at the end of the list of child nodes of the current node using the namespace prefix, local name, and namespace URI specified with the value specified. While the solution described above uses the `AppendChildElement()` method to add a child node under the group node of the multiple-selection list box, you could have also used the `AppendChild()` method to do the same thing (also see the methods described in recipe *71 Add a row to a repeating table*).

There is also a `Clone()` method available on `XPathNavigator` objects, which you can use to copy an existing node and then set its value to the value that you want to use for the new node. The disadvantage of using the `Clone()` method is that it does not really create a new copy of a node, but rather a new pointer (`XPathNavigator` object) to the same node, which means that if you delete the newly created node afterwards, the original node would also be deleted.

For example, if you cloned the empty node in a multiple-selection list box, and then afterwards deleted the cloned node, the multiple-selection list box would not contain an empty item anymore. If your code then tried to clone the empty item for a second time, you would get a `NullReferenceException`. So be careful if you choose to use the `Clone()` method to copy and add new XML nodes.

41 Deselect an item in a multiple-selection list box

Problem

You have a multiple-selection list box and a button on a form. You want to be able to click the button to deselect one particular item in the multiple-selection list box.

Solution

You can use an XPath filter expression to find the item you want to deselect, and then delete the item by calling the `DeleteSelf()` method of the `XPathNavigator` object pointing to that item.

To deselect an item in a multiple-selection list box when you click a button:

1. In InfoPath, create a new form template or use an existing one.

2. Add a **Multiple-Selection List Box** to the view of the form template and name it **field1**.

3. Open the **Multiple-Selection List Box Properties** dialog box, leave the **Enter choices manually** option selected, and add the following 5 static value/name pairs as choices to the control: 1 = Item 1, 2 = Item 2, 3 = Item 3, 4 = Item 4, 5 = Item 5. Click **OK** when you are done.

4. Add a **Button** control to the view of the form template.

5. Add an event handler for the **Clicked** event of the button control as described in recipe *7 Add an event handler for a control event*.

6. In VSTA, add the following code to the `Clicked()` event handler for the button (*code #: 70061BD0-EC53-46D7-BE0C-CB0702D4A77B*):

```
XPathNavigator mainDS = MainDataSource.CreateNavigator();
XPathNavigator item3 = mainDS.SelectSingleNode(
  "/my:myFields/my:group1/my:field1[. = '3']", NamespaceManager);

if (item3 != null)
  item3.DeleteSelf();
```

7. Save and build the project.

8. Preview the form.

When the form opens, select the check box in front of **Item 3**. Click the button. The check box you selected should have been cleared.

Discussion

Deselecting an item in a multiple-selection list box is equivalent to deleting a node from under the group node of the multiple-selection list box. So you must write code that uses the value of the item you want to deselect (in the solution described above that was a value equal to 3) as a filter in an XPath expression that looks up the item and returns an XPathNavigator object for the item.

```
XPathNavigator mainDS = MainDataSource.CreateNavigator();
XPathNavigator item3 = mainDS.SelectSingleNode(
  "/my:myFields/my:group1/my:field1[. = '3']", NamespaceManager);
```

Once you have retrieved an XPathNavigator object for the selected item you want to deselect, you can use the DeleteSelf() method of the XPathNavigator object to delete the item that has been selected in the multiple-selection list box.

```
if (item3 != null)
  item3.DeleteSelf();
```

Because the **field1** node for **Item 3** would not be present under the **group1** group node if **Item 3** has not been selected, you must check whether the reference to the node is not equal to null before calling the DeleteSelf() method.

The DeleteSelf() method of the XPathNavigator object deletes the current node and its child nodes. Before calling this method, you must move the XPathNavigator object to point to the node you want to delete by using one of the Move() methods or by performing a lookup using the SelectSingleNode() method and the XPath expression for the node you want to delete. The solution described above uses the SelectSingleNode() method in combination with an XPath expression that contains a filter (the expression between the square brackets in the XPath expression) to find the node that should be deleted.

42 Select all items in a multiple-selection list box

Problem

You have a multiple-selection list box and a button on a form. You want to be able to click the button to select all of the items in the multiple-selection list box.

Solution

You can use the AppendChildElement() method of the XPathNavigator object pointing to the group node of a multiple-selection list box to add child nodes under the group node of the multiple-selection list box with each child node containing the value of an item in the multiple-selection list box.

To select all items in a multiple-selection list box when you click a button:

1. In InfoPath, create a new form template or use an existing one.

2. Add a **Multiple-Selection List Box** to the view of the form template and name it **field1**.

3. Open the **Multiple-Selection List Box Properties** dialog box, leave the **Enter choices manually** option selected, and add the following 5 static value/name pairs as choices to the control: 1 = Item 1, 2 = Item 2, 3 = Item 3, 4 = Item 4, 5 = Item 5. Click **OK** when you are done.

4. Add a **Button** control to the view of the form template.

5. Add an event handler for the **Clicked** event of the button as described in recipe *7 Add an event handler for a control event*.

6. In VSTA, add the following code to the `Clicked()` event handler for the button (*code #: FFD8FED6-DD8E-4689-9DB8-E2B7F13FEDEF*):

```
XPathNavigator mainDS = MainDataSource.CreateNavigator();
XPathNavigator group1 = mainDS.SelectSingleNode(
  "/my:myFields/my:group1", NamespaceManager);

if (group1.SelectSingleNode("my:field1[. = '1']",
  NamespaceManager) == null)
    group1.AppendChildElement("my", "field1", group1.NamespaceURI, "1");

if (group1.SelectSingleNode("my:field1[. = '2']",
  NamespaceManager) == null)
    group1.AppendChildElement("my", "field1", group1.NamespaceURI, "2");

if (group1.SelectSingleNode("my:field1 [. = '3']",
  NamespaceManager) == null)
    group1.AppendChildElement("my", "field1", group1.NamespaceURI, "3");

if (group1.SelectSingleNode("my:field1[. = '4']",
  NamespaceManager) == null)
    group1.AppendChildElement("my", "field1", group1.NamespaceURI, "4");

if (group1.SelectSingleNode("my:field1[. = '5']",
  NamespaceManager) == null)
    group1.AppendChildElement("my", "field1", group1.NamespaceURI, "5");
```

7. Save and build the project.

8. Preview the form.

When the form opens, click the button. All of the check boxes should have check marks.

Discussion

Selecting all items in a multiple-selection list box is equivalent to adding XML nodes (repeating fields) that have the same values as the items in the multiple-selection list box under the group node bound to the multiple-selection list box. You can use the `AppendChildElement()` method to add XML nodes for items similar to the method used to select one item in a multiple-selection list box in recipe *40 Select an item in a multiple-selection list box*.

43 Deselect all items in a multiple-selection list box

Problem

You have a multiple-selection list box and a button on a form. You want to be able to click the button to deselect all of the items in the multiple-selection list box.

Solution

You can use the `DeleteRange()` method of the `XPathNavigator` object pointing to the group node of a multiple-selection list box to delete all of the nodes from under the group node of the multiple-selection list box, and then use the `AppendChildElement()` method to restore the empty item for the multiple-selection list box.

To deselect all items in a multiple-selection list box when you click a button:

1. In InfoPath, create a new form template or use an existing one.

2. Add a **Multiple-Selection List Box** to the view of the form template and name it **field1**.

3. Open the **Multiple-Selection List Box Properties** dialog box, leave the **Enter choices manually** option selected, and add the following 5 static value/name pairs as choices to the control: 1 = Item 1, 2 = Item 2, 3 = Item 3, 4 = Item 4, 5 = Item 5. Click **OK** when you are done.

4. Add a **Button** control to the view of the form template.

5. Add an event handler for the **Clicked** event of the button as described in recipe *7 Add an event handler for a control event*.

6. In VSTA, add the following code to the `Clicked()` event handler for the button (*code #: 5963FC91-96C7-4EEF-9E82-BEAB4A7690A8*):

```
XPathNavigator mainDS = MainDataSource.CreateNavigator();
XPathNavigator group1 = mainDS.SelectSingleNode(
  "/my:myFields/my:group1", NamespaceManager);

XPathNavigator lastChildNode = group1.SelectSingleNode(
  "*[count(following-sibling::my:field1) = 0]", NamespaceManager);

group1.MoveToFirstChild();
group1.DeleteRange(lastChildNode);

group1.AppendChildElement("my", "field1", group1.NamespaceURI, "");
```

7. Save and build the project.

8. Preview the form.

When the form opens, select a couple of items in the multiple-selection list box, and then click the button. The check boxes you selected should have all been cleared.

Discussion

Deselecting all items in a multiple-selection list box is equivalent to deleting all of the XML nodes (repeating fields) under the group node of the multiple-selection list box except for the first empty item node (if it is present). You can use the DeleteRange() method of an XPathNavigator object to delete a range of XML nodes. The DeleteRange() method of an XPathNavigator object deletes a range of sibling nodes from the current node to the node specified. But before you can delete the range of nodes, you must find the last node to be deleted.

The code in the solution described above uses the **following-sibling** XPath axis to find the one and only XML node that does not have any sibling XML nodes following it by using an XPath expression filter as follows:

```
XPathNavigator lastChildNode = group1.SelectSingleNode(
  "*[count(following-sibling::my:field1) = 0]", NamespaceManager);
```

Another option would have been to use the position() and last() XPath functions in an XPath expression filter as follows:

```
XPathNavigator lastChildNode = group1.SelectSingleNode(
  "my:field1[position() = last()]", NamespaceManager);
```

Once you have found the last node to be deleted, you must reposition the XPathNavigator object on the first node to be deleted and then call the DeleteRange() method. In the solution described above, you used the MoveToFirstChild() method to move the XPathNavigator object to point to the first child node of the current node (**group 1**) and then delete all of the child nodes as follows:

```
group1.MoveToFirstChild();
group1.DeleteRange(lastChildNode);
```

Once all of the child nodes have been deleted, the XPathNavigator object goes back to pointing to the **group 1** group node. Instead of using the MoveToFirstChild() method, you could have also performed a lookup for the first child node and then deleted all of the child nodes as follows:

```
XPathNavigator firstChildNode = group1.SelectSingleNode(
  "my:field1[1]", NamespaceManager);

firstChildNode.DeleteRange(lastChildNode);
```

The final step in the code is to use the AppendChildElement() method to add the first empty node back to the **group1** group node bound to the multiple-selection list box to restore the control to its original state.

```
group1.AppendChildElement("my", "field1", group1.NamespaceURI, "");
```

44 Validate that at least 3 items have been selected in a multi-select list box

Problem

You have a multiple-selection list box on a form and want to force users to select at least 3 items from the list.

Solution

You can use data validation to force users to select a minimum amount of items from a multiple-selection list box.

To validate that at least 3 items have been selected in a multiple-selection list box:

1. In InfoPath, create a new form template or use an existing one.

2. Add a **Multiple-Selection List Box** to the view of the form template and name it **field1**.

3. Open the **Multiple-Selection List Box Properties** dialog box, leave the **Enter choices manually** option selected, and add the following 5 static value/name pairs as choices to the control: 1 = Item 1, 2 = Item 2, 3 = Item 3, 4 = Item 4, 5 = Item 5. Also select the **At least one selection required** check box on the **Data** tab. Click **OK** when you are done.

4. Click **Data ➤ Form Data ➤ Default Values**.

5. On the **Edit Default Values** dialog box, expand the **group1** node for the multiple-selection list box, deselect the **field1** node under the **group1** node, and click **OK**. With this you have configured the multiple-selection list box not to have one empty item by default.

6. Add an **Optional Section** control to the view of the form template and rename it to **errorMessage**.

7. Open the **Section Properties** dialog box, select the **Do not include the section in the form by default** option on the **Data** tab, deselect the **Allow users to insert the section** check box, and click **OK**.

8. Add a **Text Box** control to the optional section control, name the text box control **value**, and change the text box control into a **Calculated Value** control.

9. Add an event handler for the **Changed** event of the multiple-selection list box control as described in recipe *7 Add an event handler for a control event*.

10. In VSTA, add the following code to the `Changed()` event handler for the multiple-selection list box (*code #: E94351BA-8A6A-4D30-979F-F8CA9109AC67*):

```
XPathNavigator mainDS = MainDataSource.CreateNavigator();
XPathNavigator group1 = mainDS.SelectSingleNode(
```

```
        "/my:myFields/my:group1", NamespaceManager);

    XPathNodeIterator iter = mainDS.Select(
        "/my:myFields/my:group1/my:field1", NamespaceManager);

    if (iter.Count < 3)
    {
      bool exists = false;
      foreach (FormError err in Errors)
      {
        if (err.Name == "MultiSelectErr")
          exists = true;
      }
      if (!exists)
      {
        group1.InsertElementAfter(
          "my", "errorMessage", NamespaceManager.LookupNamespace("my"), "");

        string message = "You must select at least 3 items.";
        XPathNavigator errorMessage = mainDS.SelectSingleNode(
          "/my:myFields/my:errorMessage", NamespaceManager);
        errorMessage.AppendChildElement(
          "my", "value", NamespaceManager.LookupNamespace("my"), message);
        XPathNavigator errorMessageValue = mainDS.SelectSingleNode(
          "/my:myFields/my:errorMessage/my:value", NamespaceManager);

        Errors.Add(errorMessageValue, "MultiSelectErr", message);
      }
    }
    else
    {
      foreach (FormError err in Errors)
      {
        if (err.Name == "MultiSelectErr")
          Errors.Delete(err);
      }

      XPathNavigator errorMessage = mainDS.SelectSingleNode(
        "/my:myFields/my:errorMessage", NamespaceManager);
      errorMessage.DeleteSelf();
    }
```

11. Save and build the project.

12. Preview the form.

When the form opens, select one item in the multiple-selection list box. The optional section with validation error should appear. Select two more items in the multiple-selection list box. The optional section with validation error should disappear.

Discussion

Because the ReportError() method of the XmlValidatingEventArgs object does not have an effect on a multiple-selection list box, the solution described above shows you an alternative for adding data validation to a multiple-selection list box by making use of its **Changed** event, the FormErrorCollection object of a form, and an extra optional section to display an error message for the multiple-selection list box. The benefit of using an optional section to display an error message is that you can delete this section through code to remove the error message and prevent the section from being stored in the Main data source of the form when the form is saved or submitted.

The code in the solution above first retrieves an XPathNavigator object pointing to the **group1** group node of the multiple-selection list box and an XPathNodeIterator object to be able to count how many items have been selected in the multiple-selection list box.

```
XPathNavigator mainDS = MainDataSource.CreateNavigator();
XPathNavigator group1 = mainDS.SelectSingleNode(
  "/my:myFields/my:group1", NamespaceManager);

XPathNodeIterator iter = mainDS.Select(
  "/my:myFields/my:group1/my:field1", NamespaceManager);
```

The code then checks whether less than 3 items have been selected in the multiple-selection list box

```
if (iter.Count < 3)
{
  ...
}
```

and if this is the case, checks whether an error named **MultiSelectErr** has already been added to the FormErrorCollection object of the form.

```
bool exists = false;
foreach (FormError err in Errors)
{
  if (err.Name == "MultiSelectErr")
    exists = true;
}
```

If the error does not exist in the FormErrorCollection object of the form

```
if (!exists)
{
  ...
}
```

the optional section is added to the Main data source of the form using the InsertElementAfter() method of the XPathNavigator object pointing to the multiple-selection list box, since the group node for the optional section should be placed directly after the group node for the multiple-selection list box in the Main data source.

```
group1.InsertElementAfter(
  "my", "errorMessage", NamespaceManager.LookupNamespace("my"), "");
```

Then the **value** field is added to the group node of the optional section and its value is set to be equal to the error message that should be displayed to the user.

```
string message = "You must select at least 3 items.";
XPathNavigator errorMessage = mainDS.SelectSingleNode(
  "/my:myFields/my:errorMessage", NamespaceManager);
errorMessage.AppendChildElement(
  "my", "value", NamespaceManager.LookupNamespace("my"), message);
XPathNavigator errorMessageValue = mainDS.SelectSingleNode(
  "/my:myFields/my:errorMessage/my:value", NamespaceManager)
```

And finally, the error is added to the `FormErrorCollection` object of the form using the `Add()` method of the `Errors` collection.

```
Errors.Add(errorMessageValue, "MultiSelectErr", message);
```

If three or more items have been selected in the multiple-selection list box, so the control contains valid data, the code in the `else` block of the `if`-statement is executed. This code checks whether the **MultiSelectErr** error is present in the `FormErrorCollection` object of the form, and if it is, calls the `Delete()` method of the `Errors` collection to delete the error.

```
foreach (FormError err in Errors)
{
  if (err.Name == "MultiSelectErr")
    Errors.Delete(err);
}
```

In addition, the group node bound to the optional section is also retrieved and deleted using the `DeleteSelf()` method of the `XPathNavigator` object pointing to that group node.

```
XPathNavigator errorMessage = mainDS.SelectSingleNode(
  "/my:myFields/my:errorMessage", NamespaceManager);
errorMessage.DeleteSelf();
```

Bulleted List, Numbered List, and Plain List

45   Add an item to a bulleted list

Problem

You have a bulleted list on an InfoPath form and you want users to be able to enter text in a text box, click a button, and have the text the user entered appear as an item in the bulleted list.

Solution

You can use the `AppendChildElement()` method of the `XPathNavigator` object pointing to the group node bound to the bulleted list to add an item to the list.

To add an item to a bulleted list:

1. In InfoPath, create a new form template or use an existing one.

2. Add a **Text Box** control to the view of the form template and name it **itemToAdd**.

3. Add a **Button** control to the view of the form template and label it **Add Item**.

4. Add a **Bulleted List** control to the view of the form template. Name the group node of the bulleted list **group1** and the repeating field under the group node **field2**.

5. Click **Data** ➤ **Form Data** ➤ **Default Values**.

6. On the **Edit Default Values** dialog box, expand the **group1** node, deselect the check box for the **field2** node, and click **OK**. This should hide the first empty item in the list when the form opens.

7. Add an event handler for the **Clicked** event of the button as described in recipe 7 *Add an event handler for a control event*.

8. In VSTA, add the following code to the `Clicked()` event handler for the button (*code #: AC00C96A-7FD4-4459-AE04-EA37460EBC03*):

```
XPathNavigator mainDS = MainDataSource.CreateNavigator();

string itemToAdd = mainDS.SelectSingleNode(
  "/my:myFields/my:itemToAdd", NamespaceManager).Value;

XPathNavigator group1 = mainDS.SelectSingleNode(
  "/my:myFields/my:group1", NamespaceManager);

if (!String.IsNullOrEmpty(itemToAdd))
  group1.AppendChildElement("my", "field2",
    NamespaceManager.LookupNamespace("my"), itemToAdd);

mainDS.SelectSingleNode(
  "/my:myFields/my:itemToAdd", NamespaceManager).SetValue("");
```

9. Save and build the project.

10. Preview the form.

When the form opens, enter a piece of text in the text box, and then click the button. A new item should appear in the bulleted list.

Discussion

A bulleted list in InfoPath consists of a group node and a repeating field under that group node. So to add an item to a bulleted list, you must add a field that repeats to the group node bound to the bulleted list.

The solution described above uses the `AppendChildElement()` method of the `XPathNavigator` object pointing to the group node bound to the bulleted list to add an item to the list. The code first retrieves the value of the text box control using the following code:

```
XPathNavigator mainDS = MainDataSource.CreateNavigator();

string itemToAdd = mainDS.SelectSingleNode(
  "/my:myFields/my:itemToAdd", NamespaceManager).Value;
```

Then the code retrieves an `XPathNavigator` object pointing to the group node bound to the bulleted list.

```
XPathNavigator group1 = mainDS.SelectSingleNode(
  "/my:myFields/my:group1", NamespaceManager);
```

The `AppendChildElement()` method of the `XPathNavigator` object is then called to create a new node that has the name of the repeating field under the group node bound to the bulleted list and then set the value of the node to be equal to the text that was entered into the text box.

```
if (!String.IsNullOrEmpty(itemToAdd))
  group1.AppendChildElement("my", "field2",
    NamespaceManager.LookupNamespace("my"), itemToAdd);
```

And finally, the text box is cleared in preparation for a new entry.

```
mainDS.SelectSingleNode(
  "/my:myFields/my:itemToAdd", NamespaceManager).SetValue("");
```

46 Remove all items from a bulleted list

Problem

You have a bulleted list on an InfoPath form and you want users to be able to click a button to remove all of the items from the list.

Solution

You can use an `XPathNodeIterator` object and the `DeleteRange()` method of an `XPathNavigator` object pointing to the first item in the list to delete all of the items from a bulleted list.

To remove all items from a bulleted list:

1. In InfoPath, create a new form template or use an existing one.

2. Add a **Bulleted List** control to the view of the form template. Name the group node of the bulleted list **group1** and the repeating field under the group node **field1**.

Figure 23. Nodes of the bulleted list control on the Fields task pane.

3. Add a **Button** control to the view of the form template and label it **Remove All**.

4. Add an event handler for the **Clicked** event of the button as described in recipe 7 *Add an event handler for a control event*.

5. In VSTA, add the following code to the `Clicked()` event handler for the button (*code #: 520DA5EE-CE40-487B-BC20-40597740E70D*):

```
XPathNavigator mainDS = MainDataSource.CreateNavigator();

XPathNodeIterator items = mainDS.Select(
  "/my:myFields/my:group1/my:field1", NamespaceManager);

if (items.Count > 0)
{
  XPathNavigator lastItem = mainDS.SelectSingleNode(
    "/my:myFields/my:group1/my:field1[" + items.Count.ToString() + "]",
    NamespaceManager);

  if (items.MoveNext())
    items.Current.DeleteRange(lastItem);

  mainDS.SelectSingleNode(
    "/my:myFields/my:group1", NamespaceManager).AppendChildElement(
    "my", "field1", NamespaceManager.LookupNamespace("my"), "");
}
```

6. Save and build the project.

7. Preview the form.

When the form opens, add a few items to the list, and then click the button. All of the items should have been deleted from the list.

Discussion

A bulleted list in InfoPath consists of a group node and a repeating field under that group node. So to remove all items from a bulleted list, you must delete all of the fields that are located under the group node bound to the bulleted list.

The solution described above uses the `DeleteRange()` method of the `XPathNavigator` object pointing to the first item in the bulleted list and a reference to the last item in the list to delete all of the items from the list. The code first uses the `Select()` method to retrieve an `XPathNodeIterator` object containing a reference to the node-set for the list items.

```
XPathNavigator mainDS = MainDataSource.CreateNavigator();

XPathNodeIterator items = mainDS.Select(
  "/my:myFields/my:group1/my:field1", NamespaceManager);
```

The code then retrieves the `XPathNavigator` object pointing to the last item in the list

```
XPathNavigator lastItem = mainDS.SelectSingleNode(
  "/my:myFields/my:group1/my:field1[" + items.Count.ToString() + "]",
  NamespaceManager);
```

and then uses the `MoveNext()` method of the `XPathNodeIterator` object to move the `XPathNavigator` object returned by the `XPathNodeIterator` object to point to the first item in the list. The `Current` property of the `XPathNodeIterator` object is then used to retrieve the `XPathNavigator` object pointing to the first item and the `XPathNavigator` object pointing to the last item is then passed to the `DeleteRange()` method of the `XPathNavigator` object pointing to the first item to delete all of the items from the list.

```
if (items.MoveNext())
  items.Current.DeleteRange(lastItem);
```

And because users should still be able to add items to the list after it has been cleared, you must restore the default empty item for the list.

```
mainDS.SelectSingleNode(
  "/my:myFields/my:group1", NamespaceManager).AppendChildElement(
  "my", "field1", NamespaceManager.LookupNamespace("my"), "");
```

Person/Group Picker

47 Set the (default) value of a person/group picker control

Problem

You have a person/group picker control on an InfoPath form and want it to be populated with the names of two users and one group as soon as the form opens.

Solution

You can add items that contain account information for the users and groups you want to display by default to the repeating group node of a person/group picker control in the `FormEvents_Loading()` event handler for a form.

To set the default value of a person/group picker control on an InfoPath form:

1. In InfoPath, create a new form template or use an existing one.

2. Add a **Person/Group Picker** control to the view of the form template.

3. Open the **Person/Group Picker Properties** dialog box and configure the control to get its users and groups from a specific SharePoint site. In addition, select the **Allow multiple selections** check box and the **People and Groups** option, so that the control can store multiple users and groups. Click **OK** when you are done.

4. Add an event handler for the **Loading** event of the form as described in recipe *6 Add an event handler for a form event*.

5. In VSTA, add the following private method to the `FormCode` class (*code #: 28CAEE89-EEA4-41C1-9088-1E5420D8A41B*):

```
private void AddPersonOrGroup(
  string displayName, string accountId,
  string accountType, ref XPathNavigator peoplePickerGroup)
{
  if (peoplePickerGroup != null)
  {
    XmlDocument doc = new XmlDocument();
    XmlElement person = doc.CreateElement(
      "pc", "Person", NamespaceManager.LookupNamespace("pc"));

    XmlElement displayNameElm = doc.CreateElement(
      "pc", "DisplayName", NamespaceManager.LookupNamespace("pc"));
    displayNameElm.InnerText = displayName;
    person.AppendChild(displayNameElm);

    XmlElement accountIdElm = doc.CreateElement(
      "pc", "AccountId", NamespaceManager.LookupNamespace("pc"));
    accountIdElm.InnerText = accountId;
```

```
person.AppendChild(accountIdElm);

XmlElement accountTypeElm = doc.CreateElement(
    "pc", "AccountType", NamespaceManager.LookupNamespace("pc"));
accountTypeElm.InnerText = accountType;
person.AppendChild(accountTypeElm);

doc.AppendChild(person);

peoplePickerGroup.AppendChild(doc.DocumentElement.CreateNavigator());
    }
}
```

6. Add the following code to the `FormEvents_Loading()` event handler (*code #: 28CAEE89-EEA4-41C1-9088-1E5420D8A41B*):

```
XPathNavigator mainDS = MainDataSource.CreateNavigator();
XPathNavigator peoplePickerGroup = mainDS.SelectSingleNode(
    "/my:myFields/my:group", NamespaceManager);

AddPersonOrGroup(
    "Jane Doe", @"DOMAIN\jane.doe", "User", ref peoplePickerGroup);

AddPersonOrGroup(
    "John Doe", @"DOMAIN\john.doe", "User", ref peoplePickerGroup);

AddPersonOrGroup(
    "BizSupportOnline Members", "BizSupportOnline Members",
    "SharePointGroup", ref peoplePickerGroup);
```

where you should replace **DOMAIN** with the correct domain name for your own scenario. In addition, you must use user and group names that exist in your domain.

7. Save and build the project.

8. Preview the form.

When the form opens, two users and one group should appear in the person/group picker control.

Figure 24. Default users and a group in a person/group picker control.

Discussion

In the solution described above, you used code to set the default value of a person/group picker control that allows multiple users or groups to be selected. Note that you are not required to write code to set the default value of a person/group picker control, since you can also use the **Edit Default Values** dialog box (**Data ➤ Form Data ➤ Default Values**) to add default items to the group node that represents the person/group picker control on the InfoPath form.

The code in the solution described above first retrieves the group node that represents the person/group picker control on the form

```
XPathNavigator mainDS = MainDataSource.CreateNavigator();
XPathNavigator peoplePickerGroup = mainDS.SelectSingleNode(
    "/my:myFields/my:group", NamespaceManager);
```

and then it calls a private method named `AddPersonOrGroup()` to add either a person or a group to the group node that represents the person/group picker control on the form

```
AddPersonOrGroup(
  "Jane Doe", @"DOMAIN\jane.doe", "User", ref peoplePickerGroup);

AddPersonOrGroup(
  "John Doe", @"DOMAIN\john.doe", "User", ref peoplePickerGroup);

AddPersonOrGroup(
  "BizSupportOnline Members", "BizSupportOnline Members",
  "SharePointGroup", ref peoplePickerGroup);
```

The `AddPersonOrGroup()` method constructs a **Person** repeating group node

```
XmlDocument doc = new XmlDocument();
XmlElement person = doc.CreateElement(
  "pc", "Person", NamespaceManager.LookupNamespace("pc"));
```

with its three corresponding child elements (**DisplayName, AccountId,** and **AccountType**)

```
XmlElement displayNameElm = doc.CreateElement(
  "pc", "DisplayName", NamespaceManager.LookupNamespace("pc"));
displayNameElm.InnerText = displayName;
person.AppendChild(displayNameElm);

XmlElement accountIdElm = doc.CreateElement(
  "pc", "AccountId", NamespaceManager.LookupNamespace("pc"));
accountIdElm.InnerText = accountId;
person.AppendChild(accountIdElm);

XmlElement accountTypeElm = doc.CreateElement(
  "pc", "AccountType", NamespaceManager.LookupNamespace("pc"));
accountTypeElm.InnerText = accountType;
person.AppendChild(accountTypeElm);

doc.AppendChild(person);
```

and then adds the constructed repeating group node to the group node that represents the person/group picker control on the form.

```
peoplePickerGroup.AppendChild(doc.DocumentElement.CreateNavigator());
```

Note that just like you wrote code in the `FormEvents_Loading()` event handler in the solution above, you can write code in any other event handler to set the value of a person/group picker control on a form.

48 Get the selected user(s) from a person/group picker

Problem

You have a person/group picker control on an InfoPath form that allows multiple users or groups to be selected. You want to display all of the users or groups that have been selected in the person/group picker control in a separate text box on the form.

Solution

You can loop through the repeating group nodes that contain the users or groups to retrieve the selected users or groups from the person/group picker control.

To get the selected user(s) from a person/group picker control on an InfoPath form:

1.   In InfoPath, create a new form template or use an existing one.

2.   Add a **Person/Group Picker** control to the view of the form template.

3.   Open the **Person/Group Picker Properties** dialog box and configure the control to get its users and groups from a specific SharePoint site. In addition, select the **Allow multiple selections** check box and the **People and Groups** option, so that the control can store multiple users and groups. Click **OK** when you are done.

4.   Add a **Text Box** control to the view of the form template and name it **field1**.

5.   Add an event handler for the **Changed** event of the person/group picker control as described in recipe *7 Add an event handler for a control event*.

6.   In VSTA, add the following code to the `group_Changed()` event handler (*code #: 8B075261-6420-4ADC-A9A2-2F35893DF962*):

```
if (e.Operation == XmlOperation.Insert)
{
  XPathNodeIterator accounts = e.Site.Select(
    "pc:Person/pc:AccountId", NamespaceManager);

  System.Text.StringBuilder sb = new System.Text.StringBuilder();

  if (accounts != null)
  {
    while (accounts.MoveNext())
    {
      sb.Append(accounts.Current.Value);
      sb.Append("; ");
    }
  }

  e.Site.SelectSingleNode("/my:myFields/my:field1",
    NamespaceManager).SetValue(sb.ToString());
}
```

7.   Save and build the project.

8.   Preview the form.

When the form opens, select one or more users or groups from the person/group picker control and then click the **Check names** button (the first button behind the text box of the control). The account names should get updated in the text box.

Jane Doe; John Doe; Clovis Carvalho

SYMWONGATON\jane.doe; SYMWONGATON\john.doe; SYMWONGATON\clovis.carvalho;

Figure 25. Selected users from a person/group picker control displayed in a text box.

Discussion

The information for users or groups that are selected from a person/group picker control is stored in repeating group nodes under the main group node that is bound to the person/group picker control. So if you want to retrieve all of the users or groups that have been selected in a person/group picker control, you must loop through the repeating group nodes and retrieve the account information for each group node.

The solution described above uses an XPathNodeIterator object for account ID fields of a person/group picker control

```
XPathNodeIterator accounts = e.Site.Select(
  "pc:Person/pc:AccountId", NamespaceManager);
```

and the MoveNext() method of the XPathNodeIterator object to loop through all of the account ID fields of the person/group picker control

```
if (accounts != null)
{
  while (accounts.MoveNext())
  {
    sb.Append(accounts.Current.Value);
    sb.Append("; ");
  }
}
```

before the results that were stored in a StringBuilder object are written to a text box control.

```
e.Site.SelectSingleNode("/my:myFields/my:field1",
  NamespaceManager).SetValue(sb.ToString());
```

49 Retrieve profile information for a user selected from a person/group picker

Problem

You have a person/group picker control on an InfoPath form and want to use it to select a user and then have profile information for that user (first name, last name, department, and email) appear in other fields on the form.

Solution

You can use the **User Profile Service** web service of SharePoint to retrieve profile information for a user that has been selected from a person/group picker control.

Important:

> Before you call the **User Profile Service** web service, you must ensure that user profiles have been populated with data in SharePoint. An administrator must configure the population of user profiles in SharePoint through SharePoint Central Administration.

To retrieve profile information for a user selected from a person/group picker control:

1. In InfoPath, create a new form template or use an existing one.

2. Add a **Person/Group Picker** control to the view of the form template.

3. Open the **Person/Group Picker Properties** dialog box, configure the control to get its users and groups from a specific SharePoint site, and then click **OK**.

4. Add four **Text Box** controls to the view of the form template and name them **firstName**, **lastName**, **department**, and **email**, respectively.

5. Add a **Button** control to the view of the form template and label it **Retrieve Data**.

6. Select **Data ➤ Get External Data ➤ From Web Service ➤ From SOAP Web Service**.

7. On the **Data Connection Wizard**, enter the URL of the **User Profile Service** web service, for example

   ```
   http://servername/sitename/_vti_bin/UserProfileService.asmx
   ```

   and click **Next**. Here **servername** is the name of the SharePoint server where a site named **sitename** on which the **User Profile Service** web service is located.

8. On the **Data Connection Wizard**, select the **GetUserProfileByName** operation from the list of operations, and click **Next**.

9. On the **Data Connection Wizard**, leave the **AccountName** parameter as is and click **Next**.

10. On the **Data Connection Wizard**, leave the **Store a copy of the data in the form template** check box deselected, and click **Next**.

11. On the **Data Connection Wizard**, leave the data connection name as **GetUserProfileByName**, deselect the **Automatically retrieve data when form is opened** check box, and click **Finish**.

12. Add an event handler for the **Clicked** event of the **Retrieve Data** button as described in recipe *7 Add an event handler for a control event*.

13. In VSTA, add the following code to the `Clicked()` event handler for the button (*code #: 16E28BE9-75CA-49B8-A2FE-030B516FBE28*):

```
XPathNavigator mainDS = MainDataSource.CreateNavigator();

XPathNavigator accountId = mainDS.SelectSingleNode(
  "/my:myFields/my:group/pc:Person/pc:AccountId", NamespaceManager);

DataSource wsDS = DataSources["GetUserProfileByName"];
XPathNavigator wsRoot = wsDS.CreateNavigator();
wsRoot.SelectSingleNode(
  "/dfs:myFields/dfs:queryFields/tns:GetUserProfileByName/tns:AccountName",
    NamespaceManager).SetValue(accountId.Value);
wsDS.QueryConnection.Execute();

XPathNavigator firstName = wsRoot.SelectSingleNode(
"/dfs:myFields/dfs:dataFields/tns:GetUserProfileByNameResponse/tns:GetUserP
rofileByNameResult/tns:PropertyData[tns:Name =
'FirstName']/tns:Values/tns:ValueData/tns:Value",
  NamespaceManager);

XPathNavigator lastName = wsRoot.SelectSingleNode(
"/dfs:myFields/dfs:dataFields/tns:GetUserProfileByNameResponse/tns:GetUserP
rofileByNameResult/tns:PropertyData[tns:Name =
'LastName']/tns:Values/tns:ValueData/tns:Value",
  NamespaceManager);

XPathNavigator department = wsRoot.SelectSingleNode(
"/dfs:myFields/dfs:dataFields/tns:GetUserProfileByNameResponse/tns:GetUserP
rofileByNameResult/tns:PropertyData[tns:Name =
'Department']/tns:Values/tns:ValueData/tns:Value",
  NamespaceManager);

XPathNavigator email = wsRoot.SelectSingleNode(
"/dfs:myFields/dfs:dataFields/tns:GetUserProfileByNameResponse/tns:GetUserP
rofileByNameResult/tns:PropertyData[tns:Name =
'WorkEmail']/tns:Values/tns:ValueData/tns:Value",
  NamespaceManager);


if (firstName != null)
  mainDS.SelectSingleNode("/my:myFields/my:firstName",
    NamespaceManager).SetValue(firstName.Value);

if (lastName != null)
  mainDS.SelectSingleNode("/my:myFields/my:lastName",
```

```
                  NamespaceManager).SetValue(lastName.Value);

      if (department != null)
        mainDS.SelectSingleNode("/my:myFields/my:department",
          NamespaceManager).SetValue(department.Value);

      if (email != null)
        mainDS.SelectSingleNode("/my:myFields/my:email",
          NamespaceManager).SetValue(email.Value);
```

14. Save and build the project.

15. Preview the form.

When the form opens, select a user from the person/group picker control, and then click the **Check names** button (the first button behind the text box of the control). Click the **Retrieve Data** button. The other text boxes on the form should have been populated with the information from the user's profile if this information is available.

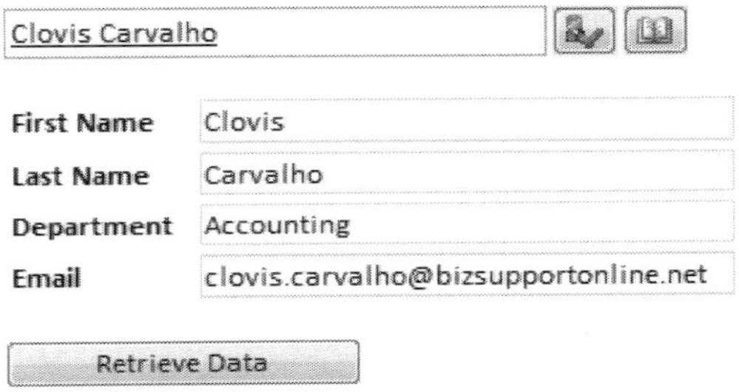

Figure 26. Profile information that was retrieved for a user selected from a person/group picker.

Discussion

In the solution described above, the person/group picker control allows single user selection. This also means that the control returns only one **AccountId** field that contains a value you can pass to the **GetUserProfileByName** method of the **User Profile Service** web service to retrieve user profile information. If you want to configure the person/group picker control to allow multiple selections, you must write code that loops through all of the **pc:Person** group nodes of the control to retrieve the **AccountId** for each user similar to recipe *70 Loop through rows of a repeating table*, before passing this on to the web service to retrieve user profile information.

In the solution described above, the value of the **AccountId** field is first retrieved

```
XPathNavigator mainDS = MainDataSource.CreateNavigator();

XPathNavigator accountId = mainDS.SelectSingleNode(
  "/my:myFields/my:group/pc:Person/pc:AccountId", NamespaceManager);
```

and then this value is used to set the value of the **AccountName** field under the **queryFields** group node in the secondary data source for the web service.

```
DataSource wsDS = DataSources["GetUserProfileByName"];
XPathNavigator wsRoot = wsDS.CreateNavigator();
wsRoot.SelectSingleNode(
  "/dfs:myFields/dfs:queryFields/tns:GetUserProfileByName/tns:AccountName",
    NamespaceManager).SetValue(accountId.Value);
```

Once the value of the query field has been set, you can call the `Execute()` method of the query connection of the secondary data source to retrieve the data for the user's profile (also see recipe *9 Access a secondary data source of a form* for more information about the `Execute()` method and secondary data sources).

```
wsDS.QueryConnection.Execute();
```

After the data has been retrieved, you can get user profile information from fields that are located under the **dataFields** group node of the secondary data source for the web service. The following code retrieves an `XPathNavigator` object pointing to the **Value** field of the **FirstName** property of the user's profile.

```
XPathNavigator firstName = wsRoot.SelectSingleNode(
"/dfs:myFields/dfs:dataFields/tns:GetUserProfileByNameResponse/tns:GetUserProfil
eByNameResult/tns:PropertyData[tns:Name =
'FirstName']/tns:Values/tns:ValueData/tns:Value",
  NamespaceManager);
```

Finally, you can set the values of fields on the form to be equal to the values of properties of the user's profile. The following code sets the value of the **firstName** field to be equal to the value of the **FirstName** property of the user's profile.

```
if (firstName != null)
  mainDS.SelectSingleNode("/my:myFields/my:firstName",
    NamespaceManager).SetValue(firstName.Value);
```

50 Clear a person/group picker control

Problem

You have a person/group picker control on an InfoPath form and you want to allow users to click a button and then have any users or groups that have been selected with the person/group picker control deleted from the control.

Solution

You can use the `DeleteRange()` method of the `XPathNavigator` object pointing to the first repeating group node under the group node of a person/group picker control and pass the last repeating group node to it to clear the control.

To clear a person/group picker control:

1. In InfoPath, create a new form template or use an existing one.

2. Add a **Person/Group Picker** control to the view of the form template.

3. Open the **Person/Group Picker Properties** dialog box, configure the control to get its users and groups from a specific SharePoint site, and then click **OK**.

4. Add a **Button** control to the view of the form template and label it **Clear**.

5. Add an event handler for the **Clicked** event of the button as described in recipe 7 *Add an event handler for a control event*.

6. In VSTA, add the following code to the `Clicked()` event handler for the button (*code #: 409E7BAA-96B8-4BD7-9361-5582C99D134A*).

```
XPathNavigator mainDS = MainDataSource.CreateNavigator();
XPathNodeIterator iter = mainDS.Select(
  "/my:myFields/my:group/pc:Person", NamespaceManager);
int count = iter.Count;

if (count >= 1)
{
  XPathNavigator firstChild = mainDS.SelectSingleNode(
    "/my:myFields/my:group/pc:Person[1]", NamespaceManager);
  XPathNavigator lastChild = mainDS.SelectSingleNode(
    "/my:myFields/my:group/pc:Person[" + count + "]", NamespaceManager);
  firstChild.DeleteRange(lastChild);
}
```

7. Save and build the project.

8. Preview the form.

When the form opens, select one or more users from the person/group picker control and then click the **Check names** button (the first button behind the text box of the control). Click the **Clear** button. The user(s) you selected should disappear from the control.

Discussion

A person/group picker control can be configured to allow single or multiple selections by deselecting or selecting the **Allow multiple selections** check box on the **General** tab of the **Person/Group Picker Properties** dialog box.

If you configure a person/group picker to allow a single person or group to be selected, the main group node that is bound to the control will have only one repeating group node under it, so you can clear the control by either clearing the fields (**DisplayName**, **AccountId**, and **AccountType**) that are located under the repeating group node of the control or by deleting the entire repeating group node.

If you configure a person/group picker to allow multiple persons or groups to be selected, the main group node that is bound to the control may have one or more repeating group nodes under it. So to clear the control, you must first determine how many repeating group nodes are present and then delete them.

The code in the solution above uses the `Count` property of an `XPathNodeIterator` object to find the amount of **pc:Person** repeating group nodes under the main group node bound to the control.

```
XPathNavigator mainDS = MainDataSource.CreateNavigator();
XPathNodeIterator iter = mainDS.Select(
  "/my:myFields/my:group/pc:Person", NamespaceManager);
int count = iter.Count;
```

Once you have determined the amount of repeating group nodes, you can use the `DeleteRange()` method of the `XPathNavigator` object pointing to the first repeating group node to delete all of the repeating group nodes by passing the last repeating group node to it.

```
if (count >= 1)
{
  XPathNavigator firstChild = mainDS.SelectSingleNode(
    "/my:myFields/my:group/pc:Person[1]", NamespaceManager);
  XPathNavigator lastChild = mainDS.SelectSingleNode(
    "/my:myFields/my:group/pc:Person[" + count + "]", NamespaceManager);
  firstChild.DeleteRange(lastChild);
}
```

Note:

When you add a person/group picker control to an InfoPath form, it will have one empty item by default. The code in this recipe does not restore this empty item. You can remove the first empty item from a person/group picker control by deselecting the check box for the **pc:Person** node under the **group** node on the **Edit Default Values** dialog box, which you can access through **Data ➤ Form Data ➤ Default Values**.

File Attachment

The recipes in this section make use of encoding and decoding classes that have been defined in *InfoPathAttachmentEncoder.cs* and *InfoPathAttachmentDecoder.cs* listed in the Appendix to convert the base64-encoded string stored in a file attachment control to and from a `byte` array. Decoding converts a base64-encoded string into a `byte` array, while encoding converts a `byte` array into a base64-encoded string.

51 Load a file from disk into an attachment control

Problem

You have an empty file attachment control on an InfoPath form, and you want to load a specific file that is located on disk into the file attachment control when the form opens.

Solution

You can use the `ReadAllBytes()` method of the `System.IO.File` class to read a file from disk, convert the binary data of the file into a base64-encoded string, and then use the `SetValue()` method of the `XPathNavigator` object of the field bound to the attachment control to load the file into the attachment control.

To load a file from disk and place it in a file attachment control:

1. In InfoPath, create a new form template or use an existing one.

2. Add a **File Attachment** control to the view of the form template and name it **field1**.

3. Add an event handler for the **Loading** event of the form as described in recipe *6 Add an event handler for a form event*.

4. In VSTA, add a new class with the name **InfoPathAttachmentEncoder** to the project and add the code from *InfoPathAttachmentEncoder.cs* listed in the Appendix to the new class file. You can also download the **InfoPathAttachmentEncoder.cs** file from www.bizsupportonline.com and then add it to your VSTA project.

5. Add the following code to the `FormEvents_Loading()` event handler (*code #: 7C977202-AD91-4374-8EB2-352B6230D662*):

```
byte[] bytes = System.IO.File.ReadAllBytes(@"C:\Image.jpg");

if (bytes != null && bytes.Length > 0)
{
  BizSupportOnline.InfoPathAttachmentEncoder encoder =
    new BizSupportOnline.InfoPathAttachmentEncoder("Image.jpg", bytes);

  XPathNavigator mainDS = MainDataSource.CreateNavigator();
  XPathNavigator field1 = mainDS.SelectSingleNode(
    "/my:myFields/my:field1", NamespaceManager);

  if (field1.MoveToAttribute("nil", field1.LookupNamespace("xsi")))
  {
    field1.DeleteSelf();
  }

  field1.SetValue(encoder.ToBase64String());
}
```

where `C:\Image.jpg` is the path to an image stored on disk.

6. Save and build the project.

7.   Preview the form.

When the form opens, the file should appear in the file attachment control.

Image.jpg
JPEG image
39.1 KB

Figure 27. InfoPath form with a file loaded in the file attachment control.

Discussion

The `System.IO.File` class provides static methods for creating, copying, deleting, moving, and opening files, and helps you create `FileStream` objects. You used the `ReadAllBytes()` method of this class in the solution described above to load a file from disk into a `byte` array.

```
byte[] bytes = System.IO.File.ReadAllBytes(@"C:\Image.jpg");
```

You can then take the `byte` array and pass it to initialize an object using a class named `InfoPathAttachmentEncoder`. This class can be used to encode the `byte` array into a base64-encoded string.

```
BizSupportOnline.InfoPathAttachmentEncoder encoder =
  new BizSupportOnline.InfoPathAttachmentEncoder("Image.jpg", bytes);
```

Then you can retrieve an `XPathNavigator` object pointing to the field bound to the file attachment control on the form

```
XPathNavigator mainDS = MainDataSource.CreateNavigator();
XPathNavigator field1 = mainDS.SelectSingleNode(
  "/my:myFields/my:field1", NamespaceManager);
```

and remove the **nil** attribute from the field if it is present

```
if (field1.MoveToAttribute("nil", field1.LookupNamespace("xsi")))
{
  field1.DeleteSelf();
}
```

so that you can set the value of the field bound to the file attachment control to be equal to the base64-encoded string representation of the `byte` array.

```
field1.SetValue(encoder.ToBase64String());
```

52 Load a resource file into an attachment control

Problem

You have 3 documents stored as resource files in an InfoPath form template and you want to be able to retrieve any one of those documents and load it into a file attachment control on a form after a user selects the name of one of those documents and then clicks a button.

Solution

You can use the `OpenFileFromPackage()` method of the `FormTemplate` object to retrieve a document that is stored as a resource file, encode the document, and then load it into a file attachment control.

To load a file that is stored as a resource file in a form template into a file attachment control:

1. In Word, create 3 different documents or use existing ones.

2. In InfoPath, create a new form template or use an existing one.

3. Click **Data ➤ Form Data ➤ Resource Files**.

4. On the **Resource Files** dialog box, click **Add**.

5. On the **Add File** dialog box, browse to and select one of the 3 documents from step 1, and click **OK**.

6. Repeat steps 4 and 5 to add the other 2 documents as resource files to the form template.

7. On the **Resource Files** dialog box, select the first document, and click **Rename**.

8. On the **Rename File** dialog box, enter **Document1.docx** in the **File name** text box, and click **OK**. Repeat this step for the other 2 documents, but rename them to **Document2.docx** and **Document3.docx**, respectively.

9. On the **Resource Files** dialog box, click **OK**. With this you have added the 3 documents as resource files to the form template.

10. Add an **Option Button** control with 3 options to the view of the form template and name it **selectedDocument**.

11. Set the **Value when selected** property of each one of the option buttons to the name you gave each document. The first option button should have its **Value when selected** property set to **Document1.docx**, the second option button should have its **Value when selected** property set to **Document2.docx**, and the third option button should have its **Value when selected** property set to **Document3.docx**. Add these same values as labels to the option buttons.

12. Add a **File Attachment** control to the view of the form template and name it **field2**.

13. Add a **Button** control to the view of the form template and label it **Load Document**.

14. Add an event handler for the **Clicked** event of the button as described in recipe *7 Add an event handler for a control event*.

15. In VSTA, add a new class with the name **InfoPathAttachmentEncoder** to the project and add the code from *InfoPathAttachmentEncoder.cs* listed in the Appendix to the new class file. You can also download the **InfoPathAttachmentEncoder.cs** file from www.bizsupportonline.com and then add it to your VSTA project.

16. Add the following code to the `Clicked()` event handler for the button (*code #: 57A86694-3978-412A-B7C1-1987D5DEAFCB*):

```
XPathNavigator mainDS = MainDataSource.CreateNavigator();
string selectedDocument = mainDS.SelectSingleNode(
  "/my:myFields/my:selectedDocument", NamespaceManager).Value;

if (String.IsNullOrEmpty(selectedDocument))
  return;

using (System.IO.Stream stream =
  (System.IO.Stream)Template.OpenFileFromPackage(selectedDocument))
{
  if (stream == null || stream.Length == 0)
    return;

  byte[] bytes = new byte[stream.Length];
  int numBytesToRead = (int)stream.Length;
  int numBytesRead = 0;
  while (numBytesToRead > 0)
  {
    int n = stream.Read(bytes, numBytesRead, numBytesToRead);

    if (n == 0)
      break;

    numBytesRead += n;
    numBytesToRead -= n;
  }

  BizSupportOnline.InfoPathAttachmentEncoder encoder =
    new BizSupportOnline.InfoPathAttachmentEncoder(
    selectedDocument, bytes);

  XPathNavigator field2 = mainDS.SelectSingleNode(
    "/my:myFields/my:field2", NamespaceManager);

  if (field2.MoveToAttribute("nil", field2.LookupNamespace("xsi")))
  {
    field2.DeleteSelf();
  }

  field2.SetValue(encoder.ToBase64String());
  stream.Close();
}
```

17. Save and build the project.

18. Preview the form.

When the form opens, select the option for one of the documents, and then click the **Load Document** button. The document you selected should appear in the file attachment control.

○ Document1.docx
○ Document2.docx
◉ Document3.docx

Document3.docx
Microsoft Word Document
16.6 KB

Load Document

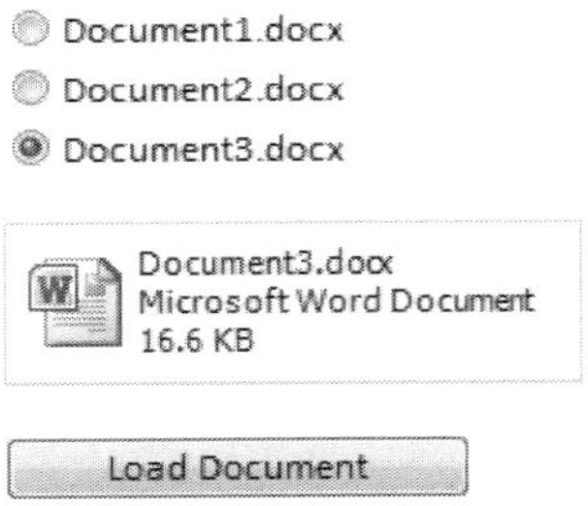

Figure 28. The InfoPath form with Document3.docx loaded in the file attachment control.

Discussion

The `OpenFileFromPackage()` method of the `FormTemplate` object of a form allows you to open files that are stored in the form template (.xsn), including resource files. You can see which files are stored in the form template by extracting its source files via **File ➤ Publish ➤ Export Source Files** or by changing the file extension of the form template from XSN to CAB and viewing the contents of the cabinet file.

In the solution described above, you first added three documents as resource files to the form template. The code retrieves the value of the selected document from the option buttons

```
XPathNavigator mainDS = MainDataSource.CreateNavigator();
string selectedDocument = mainDS.SelectSingleNode(
  "/my:myFields/my:selectedDocument", NamespaceManager).Value;
```

and passes the name of the selected document to the `OpenFileFromPackage()` method to load the document into a `Stream` object.

```
using (System.IO.Stream stream =
  (System.IO.Stream)Template.OpenFileFromPackage(selectedDocument))
{
  ...
}
```

The `Stream` object is then converted into a `byte` array

```
if (stream == null || stream.Length == 0)
  return;
```

```
byte[] bytes = new byte[stream.Length];
int numBytesToRead = (int)stream.Length;
int numBytesRead = 0;
while (numBytesToRead > 0)
{
  int n = stream.Read(bytes, numBytesRead, numBytesToRead);

  if (n == 0)
    break;

  numBytesRead += n;
  numBytesToRead -= n;
}
```

so that it can be passed to an `InfoPathAttachmentEncoder` object to create a base64-encoded string.

```
BizSupportOnline.InfoPathAttachmentEncoder encoder =
  new BizSupportOnline.InfoPathAttachmentEncoder(selectedDocument, bytes);
```

The **nil** attribute (if it is present) is removed from the field bound to the file attachment control.

```
XPathNavigator field2 = mainDS.SelectSingleNode(
  "/my:myFields/my:field2", NamespaceManager);

if (field2.MoveToAttribute("nil", field2.LookupNamespace("xsi")))
{
    field2.DeleteSelf();
}
```

And finally, the base64-encoded string is set as the value of the file attachment control.

```
field2.SetValue(encoder.ToBase64String());
```

Because the solution described above does not prevent users from manually attaching files to the file attachment control, you could extend the solution by clearing the option buttons when a user manually attaches a file to the form. To achieve such functionality through code, you would have to (*code #: AD0BB1A3-1734-47CE-B222-09DCE40358E1*):

1. In InfoPath, add an event handler for the **Changed** event of the attachment control as described in recipe *7 Add an event handler for a control event*.

2. In VSTA, add a new class with the name **InfoPathAttachmentDecoder** to the project and add the code from *InfoPathAttachmentDecoder.cs* listed in the Appendix to the new class file. You can also download the **InfoPathAttachmentDecoder.cs** file from www.bizsupportonline.com and then add it to your VSTA project.

3. Add the following private member variable to the `FormCode` class:

   ```
   private byte[] _previouslySelectedDocument;
   ```

Note that if you created a browser-compatible form template for which its forms should be filled out through a browser, you would have to use the `FormState` dictionary instead of a private member variable. Also see recipe *13 Clear all fields on a form* for an example of using the `FormState` dictionary.

4. At the end of the `Clicked()` event handler for the button, set the value of the private member variable to be equal to the last selected document using the following code:

```
_previouslySelectedDocument = bytes;
```

5. Add the following code to the `field2_Changed()` event handler:

```
if (e.Operation == XmlOperation.ValueChange)
{
  string selectedDocument = e.Site.SelectSingleNode(
    "/my:myFields/my:selectedDocument", NamespaceManager).Value;

  if (!String.IsNullOrEmpty(selectedDocument))
  {
    string fileName = String.Empty;
    byte[] bytesNewFile = null;

    if (!String.IsNullOrEmpty(e.NewValue))
    {
      BizSupportOnline.InfoPathAttachmentDecoder decoder =
        new BizSupportOnline.InfoPathAttachmentDecoder(e.NewValue);

      fileName = decoder.Filename;
      bytesNewFile = decoder.DecodedAttachment;
    }

    if ((fileName.CompareTo(selectedDocument) != 0
      && _previouslySelectedDocument != null
      && bytesNewFile != null
      && _previouslySelectedDocument.Length != bytesNewFile.Length)
      || bytesNewFile == null)
      e.Site.SelectSingleNode("/my:myFields/my:selectedDocument",
        NamespaceManager).SetValue("");
  }
}
```

6. Save and build the project.

7. Preview the form.

When the form opens, select a document from the option buttons, and then click the **Load Document** button. The document should appear in the file attachment control. Hover over the file attachment control, click the paperclip icon when it appears, and select **Attach** from the context menu that appears. Browse to a file and add it to the file attachment control. The option button you last selected should have been cleared and the file you manually attached should have replaced the previously selected document.

53 Save a file from an attachment control to disk

Problem

You have a file attachment control on an InfoPath form and want users to be able to click on a button to save the file that has been attached to the file attachment control to disk.

Solution

You can decode the base64-encoded string of the file that has been attached to the file attachment control and then use the `WriteAllBytes()` method of the `System.IO.File` class to save the attachment to disk.

To save a file from a file attachment control to disk:

1. Follow the instructions from recipe *52 Load a resource file into an attachment control* to create an InfoPath form template with which you can load a file into a file attachment control.

2. Add a **Button** control to the view of the form template and label it **Save Attachment**.

3. Add an event handler for the **Clicked** event of the button as described in recipe *7 Add an event handler for a control event*.

4. In VSTA, add a new class with the name **InfoPathAttachmentDecoder** to the project and add the code from *InfoPathAttachmentDecoder.cs* listed in the Appendix to the new class file. You can also download the **InfoPathAttachmentDecoder.cs** file from www.bizsupportonline.com and then add it to your VSTA project.

5. Add the following code to the `Clicked()` event handler for the button (*code #: 5BCDB255-0569-4A16-87E7-2F0FC1191B23*):

```
XPathNavigator mainDS = MainDataSource.CreateNavigator();

string base64EncodedString = mainDS.SelectSingleNode(
  "/my:myFields/my:field2", NamespaceManager).Value;

if (!String.IsNullOrEmpty(base64EncodedString))
{
  BizSupportOnline.InfoPathAttachmentDecoder decoder =
    new BizSupportOnline.InfoPathAttachmentDecoder(base64EncodedString);

  System.IO.File.WriteAllBytes(
    @"C:\" + decoder.Filename, decoder.DecodedAttachment);
}
```

6. Save and build the project.

7. Preview the form.

When the form opens, select one of the documents from the list of option buttons and click **Load Document** to load the document into the file attachment control. Click **Save**

Attachment. Navigate to the C-drive and verify that the document you selected was saved to disk.

Discussion

The `System.IO.File` class provides static methods for creating, copying, deleting, moving, and opening files, and helps you create `FileStream` objects. You used the `WriteAllBytes()` method of this class in the solution described above to save a `byte` array to disk as a file. But before you can do this, you must first retrieve the base64-encoded string representation of the file from the file attachment control on the form.

```
XPathNavigator mainDS = MainDataSource.CreateNavigator();

string base64EncodedString = mainDS.SelectSingleNode(
  "/my:myFields/my:field2", NamespaceManager).Value;
```

You can then take the base64-encoded string and use it to create an `InfoPathAttachmentDecoder` object.

```
BizSupportOnline.InfoPathAttachmentDecoder decoder =
  new BizSupportOnline.InfoPathAttachmentDecoder(base64EncodedString);
```

This object can be used to decode the base64-encoded string and convert it into a `byte` array. And finally, you can save the file to disk by calling the `WriteAllBytes()` method of the `File` class and making use of the `Filename` and `DecodedAttachment` properties of the `InfoPathAttachmentDecoder` object.

```
System.IO.File.WriteAllBytes(
  @"C:\" + decoder.Filename, decoder.DecodedAttachment);
```

54 Rename a file in an attachment control

Problem

You have a file attachment control on an InfoPath form, which users can use to attach a file to an InfoPath form. You want to enable users to enter a new file name for the file stored in the attachment control and click a button to rename the file.

Solution

You can decode the file that has been added to a file attachment control, extract its data, encode the data for the file using a new file name, and then store the encoded data back into the file attachment control.

To rename a file stored in a file attachment control:

1. In InfoPath, create a new form template or use an existing one.

2. Add a **File Attachment** control to the view of the form template and name it **field1**.

3. Add a **Text Box** control to the view of the form template and name it **newFileName**.

4. Add a **Button** control to the view of the form template and label it **Rename Attachment**.

5. Add an event handler for the **Clicked** event of the button control as described in recipe *7 Add an event handler for a control event*.

6. In VSTA, add a new class with the name **InfoPathAttachmentDecoder** to the project and add the code from *InfoPathAttachmentDecoder.cs* listed in the Appendix to the new class file. You can also download the **InfoPathAttachmentDecoder.cs** file from www.bizsupportonline.com and then add it to your VSTA project.

7. Add a new class with the name **InfoPathAttachmentEncoder** to the project and add the code from *InfoPathAttachmentEncoder.cs* listed in the Appendix to the new class file. You can also download the **InfoPathAttachmentEncoder.cs** file from www.bizsupportonline.com and then add it to your VSTA project.

8. Add the following code to the `Clicked()` event handler for the button (*code #: 9C303486-C22A-4E02-A049-FADC0177A163*):

```
XPathNavigator mainDS = MainDataSource.CreateNavigator();
string newFileName = mainDS.SelectSingleNode(
  "//my:newFileName", NamespaceManager).Value;

XPathNavigator field1 = mainDS.SelectSingleNode(
  "//my:field1", NamespaceManager);
string base64Attachment = field1.Value;

BizSupportOnline.InfoPathAttachmentDecoder decoder =
  new BizSupportOnline.InfoPathAttachmentDecoder(base64Attachment);
byte[] fileData = decoder.DecodedAttachment;

BizSupportOnline.InfoPathAttachmentEncoder encoder =
  new BizSupportOnline.InfoPathAttachmentEncoder(newFileName, fileData);

field1.SetValue(encoder.ToBase64String());
```

9. Save and build the project.

10. Preview the form.

When the form opens, add a file to the file attachment control, enter a new file name (with file extension) in the text box, and then click the **Rename Attachment** button. The name of the file stored in the file attachment control should change to reflect the new file name you entered.

Discussion

To be able to rename a file that is stored in a file attachment control, you must first retrieve the file stored in the file attachment control, decode the file, change the file name, encode the file, and then replace the file stored in the file attachment control with the file that has the new file name.

The code in the solution above first retrieves the value of the new file name

```
XPathNavigator mainDS = MainDataSource.CreateNavigator();
string newFileName = mainDS.SelectSingleNode(
  "//my:newFileName", NamespaceManager).Value;
```

and an `XPathNavigator` object pointing to the field bound to the file attachment control including its value.

```
XPathNavigator field1 = mainDS.SelectSingleNode(
  "//my:field1", NamespaceManager);
string base64Attachment = field1.Value;
```

Then an `InfoPathAttachmentDecoder` object is created and used to decode the base64-encoded string into a `byte` array.

```
BizSupportOnline.InfoPathAttachmentDecoder decoder =
  new BizSupportOnline.InfoPathAttachmentDecoder(base64Attachment);
byte[] fileData = decoder.DecodedAttachment;
```

An `InfoPathAttachmentEncoder` object is then created and used to encode the `byte` array and convert it back into a base64-encoded string, but then with the new file name.

```
BizSupportOnline.InfoPathAttachmentEncoder encoder =
  new BizSupportOnline.InfoPathAttachmentEncoder(newFileName, fileData);
```

And finally, the value of the field bound to the file attachment control is overwritten with the base64-encoded string representation of the file that has the new file name.

```
field1.SetValue(encoder.ToBase64String());
```

55 Restrict the size of a file in an attachment control

Problem

You have an InfoPath form with a file attachment control. You want to allow users to only add files that have a size of less than 2KB to the attachment control.

Solution

You can decode the file that has been added to a file attachment control, extract its data to determine its file size, and then use data validation to determine whether the file that was added to the attachment control is of an acceptable file size.

To restrict a file attachment control to only allow files of a particular file size:

1. In InfoPath, create a new form template or use an existing one.

2. Add a **File Attachment** control to the view of the form template.

3. Add an event handler for the **Validating** event of the attachment control as described in recipe *7 Add an event handler for a control event*.

4. In VSTA, add a new class with the name **InfoPathAttachmentDecoder** to the project and add the code from *InfoPathAttachmentDecoder.cs* listed in the Appendix to the new class file. You can also download the **InfoPathAttachmentDecoder.cs** file from www.bizsupportonline.com and then add it to your VSTA project.

5. Add the following code to the Validating() event handler for the field bound to the file attachment control (*code #: DBF3D876-CC8D-42C9-98D8-7D69F7F1B1D9*):

```
if (!e.UndoRedo && e.Operation == XmlOperation.ValueChange)
{
  string base64String = e.Site.Value;

  if (!String.IsNullOrEmpty(base64String))
  {
    BizSupportOnline.InfoPathAttachmentDecoder decoder =
      new BizSupportOnline.InfoPathAttachmentDecoder(base64String);
    string fileName = decoder.Filename;
    byte[] data = decoder.DecodedAttachment;

    decimal fileSize = Math.Round((decimal)(data.Length / 1024F), 2);
    if (fileSize > 2)
      e.ReportError(e.Site, false, String.Format(
        "The size of '{0}' is {1} KB. It must be less than 2 KB.",
        fileName, fileSize.ToString()));
  }
}
```

6. Save and build the project.

7. Preview the form.

When the form opens, add a file that is larger than 2 KB to the file attachment control. A red dashed border should appear around the file attachment control, and when you hover with the mouse pointer over the file attachment control, you should see a description of the error appear as a tooltip.

Discussion

In the solution described above, you used data validation to prevent users from adding files that are larger than 2 KB to a file attachment control. This involves first detecting whether a change operation and not an undo/redo operation is taking place by checking the UndoRedo and Operation properties of the XmlValidatingEventArgs object. The UndoRedo property returns a value that indicates whether the node being changed is part of an undo or a redo operation, while the Operation property returns an XmlOperation enumeration value that indicates the type of operation (**Delete**, **Insert**, **None**, **ValueChange**) that occurred when the node was changed.

```
if (!e.UndoRedo && e.Operation == XmlOperation.ValueChange)
{
  ...
}
```

You must then retrieve the base64-encoded string representation of the file stored in the file attachment control

```
string base64String = e.Site.Value;
```

and convert it into a `byte` array using an `InfoPathAttachmentDecoder` object.

```
BizSupportOnline.InfoPathAttachmentDecoder decoder =
  new BizSupportOnline.InfoPathAttachmentDecoder(base64String);
```

You can then use the `Filename` and `DecodedAttachment` properties of the `InfoPathAttachmentDecoder` object to extract the name and bytes of the file.

```
string fileName = decoder.Filename;
byte[] data = decoder.DecodedAttachment;
```

And finally, you can determine and check the size of the file.

```
decimal fileSize = Math.Round((decimal)(data.Length / 1024F), 2);
```

If the file turns out to be larger than 2 KB, you can use the `ReportError()` method of the `XmlValidatingEventArgs` object to indicate that a validation error has taken place and to display an error message to the user as a tooltip on the control.

```
if (fileSize > 2)
  e.ReportError(e.Site, false, String.Format(
    "The size of '{0}' is {1} KB. It must be less than 2 KB.",
    fileName, fileSize.ToString()));
```

56 Restrict file types for a file in an attachment control

Problem

You have an InfoPath form with a file attachment control. You want to allow users to only add files that have the JPG file extension to the attachment control.

Solution

You can decode the file that has been added to a file attachment control, extract its file extension, and then use data validation to determine whether the file that was added to the attachment control is of an allowable file type.

To restrict a file attachment control to allow only files of a particular type:

1. In InfoPath, create a new form template or use an existing one.

2. Add a **File Attachment** control to the view of the form template.

3. Add an event handler for the **Validating** event of the attachment control as described in recipe *7 Add an event handler for a control event*.

4. In VSTA, add a new class with the name **InfoPathAttachmentDecoder** to the project and add the code from *InfoPathAttachmentDecoder.cs* listed in the Appendix to the new class file. You can also download the **InfoPathAttachmentDecoder.cs** file from www.bizsupportonline.com and then add it to your VSTA project.

5. Add the following code to the `Validating()` event handler for the field bound to the file attachment control (*code #: 01B070BE-8431-4206-97D5-7756706CF931*):

```
if (!e.UndoRedo && e.Operation == XmlOperation.ValueChange)
{
  string base64String = e.Site.Value;

  if (!String.IsNullOrEmpty(base64String))
  {
    BizSupportOnline.InfoPathAttachmentDecoder decoder =
      new BizSupportOnline.InfoPathAttachmentDecoder(base64String);
    string fileName = decoder.Filename;

    string fileExtension = fileName.Substring(fileName.IndexOf(".") + 1);

    if (fileExtension.ToUpper() != "JPG")
      e.ReportError(e.Site, false, "Only JPG allowed.");
  }
}
```

6. Save and build the project.

7. Preview the form.

When the form opens, add a file that is not a JPG file to the file attachment control. A red dashed border should appear around the file attachment control, and when you hover with the mouse pointer over the file attachment control, you should see a description of the error appear as a tooltip. Attach a file that is a JPG file. The red dashed border should disappear.

Discussion

In the solution described above, you used data validation to prevent users from adding files that do not have a JPG file extension to a file attachment control. This involves first detecting whether a change operation and not an undo/redo operation is taking place by checking the UndoRedo and Operation properties of the XmlValidatingEventArgs object. The UndoRedo property returns a value that indicates whether the node being changed is part of an undo or a redo operation, while the Operation property returns an XmlOperation enumeration value that indicates the type of operation (**Delete, Insert, None, ValueChange**) that occurred when the node was changed.

```
if (!e.UndoRedo && e.Operation == XmlOperation.ValueChange)
{
  . . .
}
```

You must then retrieve the base64-encoded string representation of the file stored within the file attachment control

```
string base64String = e.Site.Value;
```

and load it into an InfoPathAttachmentDecoder object.

```
BizSupportOnline.InfoPathAttachmentDecoder decoder =
  new BizSupportOnline.InfoPathAttachmentDecoder(base64String);
```

You can then use the Filename property of the InfoPathAttachmentDecoder object to extract the name of the file including its extension.

```
string fileName = decoder.Filename;
```

And finally, you can extract the extension of the file from the file name and check it.

```
string fileExtension = fileName.Substring(fileName.IndexOf(".") + 1);
```

If the file does not turn out to have a JPG file extension, you can use the ReportError() method of the XmlValidatingEventArgs object to indicate that a validation error has taken place and to display an error message to the user as a tooltip on the control.

```
if (fileExtension.ToUpper() != "JPG")
  e.ReportError(e.Site, false, "Only JPG allowed.");
```

57 Delete a file from an attachment control

Problem

You have a file attachment control on an InfoPath form, which users can use to attach a file to the form. When users click a button, the file that is present in the file attachment control should be deleted.

Solution

You can use an XPathNavigator object to set the value of the field that is bound to the file attachment control to an empty string and add a **nil** attribute to the field.

To delete a file from a file attachment control:

1. In InfoPath, create a new form template or use an existing one.

2. Add a **File Attachment** control to the view of the form template and name it **field1**.

3. Add a **Button** control to the view of the form template and label it **Clear Attachment**.

4. Add an event handler for the **Clicked** event of the button control as described in recipe *7 Add an event handler for a control event*.

5. In VSTA, add the following code to the Clicked() event handler for the button (*code #: C09B4BF0-2BE1-4EE6-AF8D-AA9C8E609659*):

```
XPathNavigator mainDS = MainDataSource.CreateNavigator();
XPathNavigator field1 = mainDS.SelectSingleNode(
  "//my:field1", NamespaceManager);

field1.SetValue("");

if (!field1.MoveToAttribute("nil",
  NamespaceManager.LookupNamespace("xsi")))
{
  field1.CreateAttribute("xsi", "nil",
    NamespaceManager.LookupNamespace("xsi"), "true");
}
```

6. Save and build the project.

7. Preview the form.

When the form opens, add a file to the file attachment control, and then click the **Clear Attachment** button. The file should disappear from the file attachment control. Save the InfoPath form locally on disk, and then open it in Notepad. In Notepad, check whether the field bound to the file attachment control has the following attribute set on it:

```
xsi:nil="true"
```

Discussion

To be able to properly delete a file from a file attachment control, you must clear the value of the field that is bound to the file attachment control as well as set the value of the **nil** attribute on that field to true.

The code in the solution described above first retrieves an XPathNavigator object pointing to the field bound to the file attachment control

```
XPathNavigator mainDS = MainDataSource.CreateNavigator();
XPathNavigator field1 = mainDS.SelectSingleNode(
  "//my:field1", NamespaceManager);
```

and then sets the value of the field to an empty string and restores its **nil** attribute to have a value equal to `true`.

```
field1.SetValue("");

if (!field1.MoveToAttribute("nil", NamespaceManager.LookupNamespace("xsi")))
{
  field1.CreateAttribute("xsi", "nil",
    NamespaceManager.LookupNamespace("xsi"), "true");
}
```

Picture

58 Load an image from disk into a picture control

Problem

You have an empty picture control that allows an image to be embedded in a form and you want to load an image into that picture control.

Solution

You can use the `Convert.ToBase64String()` method to convert an image to a base64-encoded string, and then use the `SetValue()` method of the `XPathNavigator` object pointing to the field bound to the picture control to set the value of the field equal to the base64-encoded string.

To load an image from disk and place it in a picture control:

1. In InfoPath, create a new form template or use an existing one.

2. Add a **Picture** control to the view of the form template. Select the **Included in the form** option when you add the picture control. Name the picture control **field1**.

3. Add an event handler for the **Loading** event of the form as described in recipe *6 Add an event handler for a form event*.

4. In VSTA, add the following code to the `FormEvents_Loading()` event handler (*code #: 4A32B0A7-AB93-4CC2-8436-2608103BECE6*):

    ```
    byte[] bytes = System.IO.File.ReadAllBytes(@"C:\myImage.jpg");

    string base64 = String.Empty;
    if (bytes != null && bytes.Length > 0)
    {
      base64 = System.Convert.ToBase64String(bytes);
    ```

```
  }

  XPathNavigator mainDS = MainDataSource.CreateNavigator();

  XPathNavigator field1 = mainDS.SelectSingleNode(
    "/my:myFields/my:field1", NamespaceManager);

  if (field1.MoveToAttribute("nil", field1.LookupNamespace("xsi")))
  {
    field1.DeleteSelf();
  }

  field1.SetValue(base64);
```

where `C:\myImage.jpg` is the path to an image on disk.

5. Save and build the project.

6. Preview the form.

When the form opens, the image should appear in the picture control.

Discussion

The method you use to load an image into a picture control depends on the type of picture control you select. There are two ways you can store an image in a picture control in InfoPath 2010:

1. As a link

2. Included in the form

The solution described above uses the second method of saving images in a form.

In the first method the image would not be embedded in the form, while in the second method it would be. A field bound to a picture control in the first method would have the data type **Hyperlink (anyURI)**, and a field bound to a picture control in the second method would have the data type **Picture or File Attachment (base64)**.

The code in the solution described above uses the `ReadAllBytes()` method of the `File` class to retrieve a JPG image named **myImage.jpg** from the local C-drive.

```
byte[] bytes = System.IO.File.ReadAllBytes(@"C:\myImage.jpg");
```

Then the `ToBase64String()` method of the `Convert` class is used to convert the `byte` array of the image into a base64-encoded string.

```
string base64 = String.Empty;
if (bytes != null && bytes.Length > 0)
{
  base64 = System.Convert.ToBase64String(bytes);
}
```

The code then retrieves an `XPathNavigator` object pointing to the field bound to the picture control.

```
XPathNavigator mainDS = MainDataSource.CreateNavigator();

XPathNavigator field1 = mainDS.SelectSingleNode(
  "/my:myFields/my:field1", NamespaceManager);
```

When the picture control does not contain an image, the field it is bound to, has a **nil** attribute set on it, which you must remove before you set the value of the field. You can remove the **nil** attribute using the following code:

```
if (field1.MoveToAttribute("nil", field1.LookupNamespace("xsi")))
{
  field1.DeleteSelf();
}
```

And finally, the code sets the value of the field bound to the picture control equal to the base64-encoded string:

```
field1.SetValue(base64);
```

Tip:

> When you embed an image in an InfoPath form, the image is stored as a string, a base64-encoded string to be more precise. Base64-encoded strings tend to be very long and bulky, so naturally they will also increase the file size of an InfoPath form, and perhaps also cause it to load slower. To prevent images from having a negative impact on form load times and performance, you may want to consider including images as links in forms rather than embedding them in forms.

59 Load an image resource file into a picture control

Problem

You have an image stored as a resource file in an InfoPath form template and you want to be able to retrieve this image and display it in a picture control on the InfoPath form when the form opens.

Solution

You can use the `OpenFileFromPackage()` method of the `FormTemplate` object to retrieve an image from a form template (.xsn), and then convert it to a base64-encoded string using the `System.Convert` class.

To load an image that is stored as a resource file into a picture control:

1. In InfoPath, create a new form template or use an existing one.

2. Click **Data ➤ Form Data ➤ Resource Files**.

3. On the **Resource Files** dialog box, click **Add**.

4. On the **Add File** dialog box, browse to the image you want to include in the form template as a resource file (here you will use an image called **myImage.jpg**), and click **OK**.

5. On the **Resource Files** dialog box, click **OK**. With this you have added an image as a resource file to the form template.

6. Add a **Picture** control to the view of the form template, select the **Included in the form** option on the **Insert Picture Control** dialog box when you add the picture control, and name the picture control **field1**.

7. Add an event handler for the **Loading** event of the form as described in recipe *6 Add an event handler for a form event*.

8. In VSTA, add the following code to the `FormEvents_Loading()` event handler (*code #: 39C70DE8-FACE-43B4-B4AD-85508C759874*):

```
using (System.IO.Stream stream =
   (System.IO.Stream)Template.OpenFileFromPackage("myImage.jpg"))
{
  if (stream == null || stream.Length == 0)
    return;

  byte[] bytes = new byte[stream.Length];
  int numBytesToRead = (int) stream.Length;
  int numBytesRead = 0;
  while (numBytesToRead > 0)
  {
    int n = stream.Read(bytes, numBytesRead, numBytesToRead);

    if (n == 0)
      break;

    numBytesRead += n;
    numBytesToRead -= n;
  }
  numBytesToRead = bytes.Length;

  string base64 = Convert.ToBase64String(bytes);

  XPathNavigator mainDS = MainDataSource.CreateNavigator();
  XPathNavigator field1 = mainDS.SelectSingleNode(
    "/my:myFields/my:field1", NamespaceManager);

  if (field1.MoveToAttribute("nil", field1.LookupNamespace("xsi")))
  {
    field1.DeleteSelf();
  }

  field1.SetValue(base64);

  stream.Close();
}
```

9. Save and build the project.

10. Preview the form.

When the form opens, the image from the resource file should appear in the picture control.

Discussion

The `OpenFileFromPackage()` method of the `FormTemplate` object opens a file contained within the form template (.xsn) file and returns a `Stream` object. You can use it to retrieve a file that has been added as a resource file to the form template as follows:

```
System.IO.Stream stream =
   (System.IO.Stream)Template.OpenFileFromPackage("myImage.jpg")
```

Once you have retrieved the file, you must convert it into a `byte` array

```
byte[] bytes = new byte[stream.Length];
int numBytesToRead = (int) stream.Length;
int numBytesRead = 0;
while (numBytesToRead > 0)
{
   int n = stream.Read(bytes, numBytesRead, numBytesToRead);

   if (n == 0)
     break;

   numBytesRead += n;
   numBytesToRead -= n;
}
numBytesToRead = bytes.Length;
```

so that you can convert that `byte` array to a base64-encoded string using the `Convert.ToBase64String()` method.

```
string base64 = Convert.ToBase64String(bytes);
```

And once converted, you can then retrieve a reference to the field bound to the picture control

```
XPathNavigator mainDS = MainDataSource.CreateNavigator();
XPathNavigator field1 = mainDS.SelectSingleNode(
   "/my:myFields/my:field1", NamespaceManager);
```

and remove the **nil** attribute set on the field bound to the picture control (also see the discussion section of recipe *11 Set the value of a field*)

```
if (field1.MoveToAttribute("nil", field1.LookupNamespace("xsi")))
{
```

```
    field1.DeleteSelf();
}
```

before you set its value to be equal to the base64-encoded string.

```
field1.SetValue(base64);
```

60 Load an image from the web into a picture control

Problem

You have a picture control on a form in which you want to place an image that you retrieve from the Internet when the form opens.

Solution

You can use the `System.Net.WebClient` class to retrieve an image from the Internet as a `byte` array, use the `Convert.ToBase64String()` method to convert the `byte` array into a base64-encoded string, and then use this base64-encoded string to set the value of the picture control.

To load an image from the Internet into a picture control when a form opens:

1. In InfoPath, create a new InfoPath Filler form template or use an existing one.

2. Add a **Picture** control to the view of the form template. Select the **Included in the form** option when you add the picture control, and name the picture control **field1**.

3. Add an event handler for the **Loading** event of the form as described in recipe *6 Add an event handler for a form event*.

4. In VSTA, add the following code to the `FormEvents_Loading()` event handler for the form (*code #: B2C62097-425B-4191-9879-26A390E87442*):

```
XPathNavigator mainDS = MainDataSource.CreateNavigator();
XPathNavigator field1 = mainDS.SelectSingleNode(
   "/my:myFields/my:field1", NamespaceManager);

byte[] bytes = null;
if (Application.MachineOnlineState == MachineState.Online)
{
   System.Net.WebClient wc = new System.Net.WebClient();
   bytes = wc.DownloadData(
      "http://www.bizsupportonline.net/images/beginners-infopath-2010-
book.jpg");
}

if (bytes == null || bytes.Length == 0)
   return;

string base64 = Convert.ToBase64String(bytes);
```

```
if (field1.MoveToAttribute("nil", NamespaceManager.LookupNamespace("xsi")))
{
  field1.DeleteSelf();
}

field1.SetValue(base64);
```

5. Save and build the project.

6. Preview the form.

When the form opens, if Internet connectivity is available, the image should appear in the picture control on the form.

Discussion

In the solution described above, you used the `System.Net.WebClient` class to retrieve an image from the Internet and then added it to a picture control. However, you could retrieve an image from virtually anywhere such as from disk, from SharePoint, or from the form template itself (see recipe *59 Load an image resource file into a picture control*) and add it to a picture control.

The code in the solution above first retrieves an `XPathNavigator` object pointing to the picture control.

```
XPathNavigator mainDS = MainDataSource.CreateNavigator();
XPathNavigator field1 = mainDS.SelectSingleNode(
  "/my:myFields/my:field1", NamespaceManager);
```

Then the code uses the `MachineOnlineState` property of the `Application` object to check the connection state of the client computer before trying to retrieve the image from the Internet.

```
byte[] bytes = null;
if (Application.MachineOnlineState == MachineState.Online)
{
  System.Net.WebClient wc = new System.Net.WebClient();
  bytes = wc.DownloadData(
    "http://www.bizsupportonline.net/images/beginners-infopath-2010-book.jpg");
}
```

Note: Because exceptions can still take place even though the computer is connected to the Internet, you should write code to catch exceptions that may occur. The downloaded `byte` array of the image retrieved from the Internet is then converted into a base64-encoded string.

```
string base64 = Convert.ToBase64String(bytes);
```

The **nil** attribute (if it is present) is removed from the field bound to the picture control.

```
if (field1.MoveToAttribute("nil", NamespaceManager.LookupNamespace("xsi")))
{
  field1.DeleteSelf();
}
```

And finally, the base64-encoded string is used to set the value of the field bound to the picture control.

```
field1.SetValue(base64);
```

The trick for making this solution work is converting an image to a `byte` array or retrieving it as a `byte` array, and then using the `Convert.ToBase64String()` method to convert the `byte` array to a base64-encoded string so that you can use that string to set the value of the field bound to the picture control.

In the solution described above you used the `MachineOnlineState` property of the `Application` object to check whether the client computer had access to the Internet. The `Application` object has a few properties and methods you can use to get information pertaining to the InfoPath application, such as for example:

- `Environment` - Gets a reference to an object that can be used to determine which runtime environment (InfoPath, Web browser, or mobile browser) the form is running in. The `Environment` object provides two properties you can use to check the environment the form is running in: `IsBrowser` gets whether the form template was opened from InfoPath Forms Services in a browser, and `IsMobile` gets whether the form template was opened from InfoPath Forms Services in a browser on a mobile device.

- `MachineOnlineState` - Gets the current connection state of the client computer. It returns one of the following `MachineState` enumeration values:

  - `IEInOfflineState` - Microsoft Internet Explorer is in offline mode.

  - `Offline` - The client computer is not connected to the network.

  - `Online` - The client computer is connected to the network.

  This property is only available for InfoPath Filler Forms and not browser forms.

- `User` - Gets a reference to an object that represents the current user.

- `Quit()` - Quits the InfoPath application without prompting users to save open forms. There is an overload of this method available that accepts a Boolean parameter that indicates whether users should be prompted to save forms before closing the InfoPath application. This method is only available for InfoPath Filler Forms and not browser forms.

Note that only the `Environment` and `User` properties of the `Application` object are available in browser forms. Refer to the MSDN web site or the **Object Browser** in VSTA for the complete documentation and list of all of the properties and methods of the `Application` class.

61 Load an image as a link into a picture control

Problem

You have a picture control on a form and you want to be able to store an image as a link in that picture control.

Solution

You can add a picture control that accepts an URL of an image, and then write code to set the value of the field bound to that picture control to be equal to a valid URL.

To load an image as a link into a picture control:

1. In InfoPath, create a new form template or use an existing one.

2. Add a **Picture** control to the view of the form template, select the **As a link** option on the **Insert Picture Control** dialog box when you add the picture control, and name the picture control **field1**.

3. Add a **Button** control to the view of the form template and label it **Link Image**.

4. Add an event handler for the **Clicked** event of the button control as described in recipe *7 Add an event handler for a control event*.

5. In VSTA, add the following code to the `Clicked()` event handler for the button (*code #: 2A9D4B4D-B8BB-4553-9539-AB94F4C3071E*):

```
XPathNavigator mainDS = MainDataSource.CreateNavigator();
mainDS.SelectSingleNode("/my:myFields/my:field1",
  NamespaceManager).SetValue(
    "http://www.bizsupportonline.net/images/beginners-infopath-2010-
book.jpg ");
```

6. Save and build the project.

7. Preview the form.

When the form opens, click the **Link Image** button. The image should appear in the picture control.

Discussion

The method for loading an image into a picture control depends on the type of picture control you have chosen to use. There are two ways you can store an image in a picture control in InfoPath 2010:

1. As a link
2. Included in the form

The solution described above uses the first method of saving images in a form. See the discussion section of recipe *58 Load an image from disk into a picture control* for the difference between the two methods of saving an image in a picture control.

Because an empty picture control that allows an image to be linked to it does not have a **nil** attribute set on it, you can link an image normally as you would do with any other field in InfoPath by setting the value of the field that is bound to the picture control to be equal to an URL that points to the image.

```
XPathNavigator mainDS = MainDataSource.CreateNavigator();
mainDS.SelectSingleNode("/my:myFields/my:field1",
  NamespaceManager).SetValue(
    "http://www.bizsupportonline.net/images/beginners-infopath-2010-book.jpg ");
```

62   Extract an image from a picture control

Problem

You have a picture control which can be used to embed an image in a form. You want to be able to click a button and save the embedded image to a location on disk.

Solution

You can use the `Convert.FromBase64String()` method to convert the base64-encoded string of an image stored in a picture control into a `byte` array and then use the `System.IO.File.WriteAllBytes()` method to write the `byte` array to a location on disk.

To extract an image from a picture control and save the image to a location on disk:

1.   In InfoPath, create a new form template or use an existing one.

2.   Add a **Picture** control to the view of the form template, select the **Included in the form** option on the **Insert Picture Control** dialog box when you add the picture control, and name the picture control **field1**.

3.   Add a **Button** control to the view of the form template and label it **Save To Disk**.

4.   Add an event handler for the **Clicked** event of the button as described in recipe *7 Add an event handler for a control event*.

5.   In VSTA, add the following code to the `Clicked()` event handler for the button (*code #: 47EB7EC0-4993-4F50-8A3B-D1224AB51D74*):

```
XPathNavigator mainDS = MainDataSource.CreateNavigator();
string base64EncodedString = mainDS.SelectSingleNode(
  "/my:myFields/my:field1", NamespaceManager).Value;

if (!String.IsNullOrEmpty(base64EncodedString))
{
  byte[] bytes = System.Convert.FromBase64String(base64EncodedString);
```

```
        System.IO.File.WriteAllBytes(@"C:\myImage.jpg", bytes);
    }
```

where `C:\myImage.jpg` is the path to a location on disk where the image is saved as **myImage.jpg**.

6. Save and build the project.

7. Preview the form.

When the form opens, add an image to the picture control, and then click the **Save To Disk** button. Open Windows Explorer, navigate to the location where the image should have been saved and verify that it has indeed been saved as **myImage.jpg**.

Discussion

You can store an image in a picture control in InfoPath 2010 either as a link or embedded in the form as a base64-encoded string. A picture control that stores an image as **Included in the form** is stored as a base64-encoded string in the field bound to the picture control.

To extract an image that is stored as an embedded file in a form, you must first get the value of the field that is bound to the picture control

```
XPathNavigator mainDS = MainDataSource.CreateNavigator();
string base64EncodedString = mainDS.SelectSingleNode(
  "/my:myFields/my:field1", NamespaceManager).Value;
```

convert the base64-encoded string that represents the image into a `byte` array

```
byte[] bytes = System.Convert.FromBase64String(base64EncodedString);
```

and then save the `byte` array as a file to disk.

```
System.IO.File.WriteAllBytes(@"C:\myImage.jpg", bytes);
```

Of course you could have also loaded the `byte` array into a `MemoryStream` object for further use in code

```
using (System.IO.MemoryStream ms = new System.IO.MemoryStream(bytes))
{
  // Write your code here
}
```

or load it into an `Image` object to extract information from the image as described in the next recipe.

63 Extract the file extension from a picture control

Problem

You have a picture control on a form. When an image is loaded into the picture control, you want to know what its file extension is, so what type of image (JPG, GIF, etc.) it is.

Solution

You can convert the base64-encoded string of an image that has been loaded in a picture control into a `byte` array, and then use this `byte` array to create an `Image` object that allows you to extract all kinds of information from the image, including its file extension.

To extract the file extension from a picture control:

1. In InfoPath, create a new form template or use an existing one.

2. Add a **Picture** control to the view of the form template, and select the **Included in the form** option on the **Insert Picture Control** dialog box when you add the picture control.

3. Add an event handler for the **Changed** event of the picture control as described in recipe *7 Add an event handler for a control event*.

4. In VSTA, add a reference to the **System.Drawing** assembly.

5. Add the following code to the `Changed()` event handler for the field bound to the picture control (*code #: CFF3AC2F-9050-4D9B-8C17-7B110EC8CD8F*):

```
if (!String.IsNullOrEmpty(e.Site.Value))
{
  string base64 = e.Site.Value;
  byte[] bytes = Convert.FromBase64String(base64);

  if (bytes == null || bytes.Length == 0)
    return;

  string fileExtension = String.Empty;
  using (System.IO.MemoryStream ms = new System.IO.MemoryStream(bytes))
  {
    try
    {
      using (System.Drawing.Image img =
        System.Drawing.Image.FromStream(ms))
      {
        if (img.RawFormat.Equals(System.Drawing.Imaging.ImageFormat.Jpeg))
        {
          fileExtension = "JPG";
        }
        if (img.RawFormat.Equals(System.Drawing.Imaging.ImageFormat.Gif))
        {
          fileExtension = "GIF";
        }
        if (img.RawFormat.Equals(System.Drawing.Imaging.ImageFormat.Emf))
        {
          fileExtension = "EMF";
```

```
      }
      if (img.RawFormat.Equals(System.Drawing.Imaging.ImageFormat.Bmp))
      {
        fileExtension = "BMP";
      }
      if (img.RawFormat.Equals(System.Drawing.Imaging.ImageFormat.Icon))
      {
        fileExtension = "ICO";
      }
      if (img.RawFormat.Equals(System.Drawing.Imaging.ImageFormat.Png))
      {
        fileExtension = "PNG";
      }
      if (img.RawFormat.Equals(System.Drawing.Imaging.ImageFormat.Tiff))
      {
        fileExtension = "TIFF";
      }
      if (img.RawFormat.Equals(System.Drawing.Imaging.ImageFormat.Wmf))
      {
        fileExtension = "WMF";
      }
    }
    ms.Close();
  }
  catch (System.OutOfMemoryException)
  {
    // File does not have valid image format or is not supported by GDI+
    return;
  }
  }
}
```

6. Save and build the project.

7. Preview the form.

Once you have extracted the file extension for the image, you can do other things with it such as add validation to the picture control to force users to select images that have a particular image format.

Discussion

In the solution described above, you used the System.Drawing.Image class to extract an image format through the RawFormat property. The RawFormat property returns a System.Drawing.Imaging.ImageFormat object which has the following image format properties you can check for:

- Bmp - Gets the bitmap (BMP) image format.

- Emf - Gets the enhanced metafile (EMF) image format.

- Exif - Gets the Exchangeable Image File (Exif) format.

- Gif - Gets the Graphics Interchange Format (GIF) image format.

- Icon - Gets the Windows icon image format.

- Jpeg - Gets the Joint Photographic Experts Group (JPEG) image format.

- Png - Gets the W3C Portable Network Graphics (PNG) image format.

- Tiff - Gets the Tagged Image File Format (TIFF) image format.

- Wmf - Gets the Windows metafile (WMF) image format.

Once you have converted an image from a picture control into an `Image` object, you can check other properties of the image such as its width, height, palette, and resolution. Therefore, you can also add validation to a picture control to check these properties.

The code in the solution described above first retrieves the value stored in the picture control.

```
string base64 = e.Site.Value;
```

It then uses the `FromBase64String()` method of the `Convert` class to convert the base64-encoded string of the image stored in the picture control into a `byte` array. The `FromBase64String()` method converts the specified string, which encodes binary data as base64 digits, to an equivalent 8-bit unsigned integer array.

```
byte[] bytes = Convert.FromBase64String(base64);
```

After checking whether the `byte` array is not empty, you can load the `byte` array into a `MemoryStream` object

```
using (System.IO.MemoryStream ms = new System.IO.MemoryStream(bytes))
{
  ...
}
```

which you can then use to create an `Image` object by calling the `FromStream()` method of the `Image` class.

```
using (System.Drawing.Image img = System.Drawing.Image.FromStream(ms))
{
  ...
}
```

You can then use the `Image` object to extract the file extension of the image through the `RawFormat` property.

```
if (img.RawFormat.Equals(System.Drawing.Imaging.ImageFormat.Jpeg))
{
  fileExtension = "JPG";
}
...
```

If you want to add data validation to a picture control, you must first add an event handler for the **Validating** event of the picture control as described in recipe *7 Add an event handler for a control event*, and then use the `ReportError()` method of the

`XmlValidatingEventArgs` object to display a validation error on the picture control. For example, to ensure that the image is a JPEG image, you could add the following code in the `Validating()` event handler for the field bound to the picture control:

```
if (fileExtension != "JPG")
  e.ReportError(e.Site, false, "You must select a JPEG image.");
```

64 Validate the size of an image in a picture control

Problem

You have a picture control on a form and want to prevent users from selecting and using images that are larger than 50 KB.

Solution

You can convert the base64-encoded string of an image that has been loaded in a picture control into a `byte` array, and then use data validation to check and prevent users from selecting images larger than 50 KB.

To validate the size of an image in a picture control and prevent users from selecting images larger than 50 KB:

1. In InfoPath, create a new form template or use an existing one.

2. Add a **Picture** control to the view of the form template, and select the **Included in the form** option on the **Insert Picture Control** dialog box when you add the picture control.

3. Add an event handler for the **Validating** event of the picture control as described in recipe *7 Add an event handler for a control event*.

4. In VSTA, add the following code to the `Validating()` event handler for the picture control (*code #: EDACCEEF-4FB1-4914-A8F9-3E16BA846AE2*):

```
if (!String.IsNullOrEmpty(e.Site.Value))
{
  string base64 = e.Site.Value;
  byte[] bytes = Convert.FromBase64String(base64);

  if (bytes == null || bytes.Length == 0)
    return;

  if (bytes.Length > (50 * 1024))
    e.ReportError(e.Site, false,
      "Image is too large; image must be less than 50 KB.");
}
```

5. Save and build the project.

6. Preview the form.

When the form opens, add an image that is larger than 50 KB to the picture control. A red dashed border should appear around the picture control, and when you hover with the mouse pointer above the image, you should see the error message appear as a tooltip.

Discussion

The `Site` property of the `XmlValidatingEventArgs` object gets the `XPathNavigator` object that is pointing to the node that is being validated. The code in the solution described above first retrieves the value stored in the picture control.

```
string base64 = e.Site.Value;
```

It then uses the `FromBase64String()` method of the `Convert` class to convert the base64-encoded string of the image stored in the picture control into a `byte` array. The `FromBase64String()` method converts the specified string, which encodes binary data as base64 digits, to an equivalent 8-bit unsigned integer array.

```
byte[] bytes = Convert.FromBase64String(base64);
```

And finally, you can use the `Length` property of the `byte` array to check whether the image is larger than 50 KB, which is equivalent to 50 * 1024 bytes, and return an error message if required by using the `ReportError()` method of the `XmlValidatingEventArgs` object (also see chapter 4 for more information on how to validate fields in InfoPath).

```
if (bytes.Length > (50 * 1024))
  e.ReportError(e.Site, false,
    "Image is too large; image must be less than 50 KB.");
```

65 Clear a picture control

Problem

You have a picture control on a form and you want to delete the image that is stored in that picture control when you click a button.

Solution

You can set the field that is bound to the picture control to an empty string and if the picture control allows an image to be embedded, you must also add a **nil** attribute and set its value to `true`.

To clear a picture control:

1.   In InfoPath, create a new form template or use an existing one.

2. Add a **Picture** control to the view of the form template and name it **field1**. If you want to store an image as an URL, select the **As a link** option on the **Insert Picture Control** dialog box when you add the picture control. If you want to store an image as an embedded image, select the **Included in the form** option on the **Insert Picture Control** dialog box when you add the picture control.

3. Add a **Button** control to the view of the form template and label it **Clear Image**.

4. Add an event handler for the **Clicked** event of the **Clear Image** button control as described in recipe *7 Add an event handler for a control event*.

5. In VSTA, add the following code to the `Clicked()` event handler for the button (*code #: 639C7613-C689-4828-9374-11B170C97488*):

    a. If the picture control contains an URL of an image:

    ```
    XPathNavigator mainDS = MainDataSource.CreateNavigator();
    mainDS.SelectSingleNode("/my:myFields/my:field1",
      NamespaceManager).SetValue(String.Empty);
    ```

    b. If the picture control contains an embedded image:

    ```
    XPathNavigator mainDS = MainDataSource.CreateNavigator();
    XPathNavigator field1 = mainDS.SelectSingleNode(
      "/my:myFields/my:field1", NamespaceManager);

    field1.SetValue(String.Empty);
    if (!field1.MoveToAttribute("nil", field1.LookupNamespace("xsi")))
    {
      field1.CreateAttribute("xsi", "nil",
        field1.LookupNamespace("xsi"), "true");
    }
    ```

6. Save and build the project.

7. Preview the form.

When the form opens, add an image to the picture control, and then click the **Clear Image** button. The image should disappear from the picture control. If the picture control allows an embedded image, save the form locally on disk, and then open it in Notepad to check whether the field bound to the picture control has the following attribute set on it:

```
xsi:nil="true"
```

Discussion

You can store an image in a picture control in InfoPath 2010 either as a link or embedded in the form as a base64-encoded string. A picture control that stores an image as **Included in the form** stores it as a base64-encoded string in the field bound to the picture control.

If you store an image as a link in a picture control, so you specify the URL of an image as the value of the field bound to the picture control, you must get a reference to the field that is bound to the picture and set its value to an empty string to be able to clear the picture control.

```
XPathNavigator mainDS = MainDataSource.CreateNavigator();
mainDS.SelectSingleNode("/my:myFields/my:field1",
  NamespaceManager).SetValue(String.Empty);
```

If you store an image as an embedded image in a picture control, you must get a reference to the field that is bound to the picture control

```
XPathNavigator mainDS = MainDataSource.CreateNavigator();
XPathNavigator field1 = mainDS.SelectSingleNode(
  "/my:myFields/my:field1", NamespaceManager);
```

and set the value of the field equal to an empty string.

```
field1.SetValue(String.Empty);
```

You should also add a **nil** attribute to the field and set the value of the **nil** attribute equal to `true` if the picture control is not a required field on the form.

```
if (!field1.MoveToAttribute("nil", field1.LookupNamespace("xsi")))
{
  field1.CreateAttribute("xsi", "nil", field1.LookupNamespace("xsi"), "true");
}
```

Optional Section, Choice Group, and Choice Section

66 Add or remove an optional section when a check box is selected or deselected

Problem

You have a check box and optional section on an InfoPath form. When a user selects the check box, the optional section should appear, and when a user clears the check box, the optional section should disappear.

Solution

You must retrieve the value of the field bound to the check box, and then depending on whether the value indicates that the check box has been selected or deselected, use one of the methods of the XPathNavigator object such as InsertElementAfter() or

`AppendChildElement()` to add the group node bound to the optional section, or use the `DeleteSelf()` method of the `XPathNavigator` object pointing to the group node bound to the optional section to delete the optional section.

To add or remove an optional section when a check box is selected or deselected:

1. In InfoPath, create a new form template or use an existing one.

2. Add a **Check Box** control to the view of the form template and name it **field1**.

3. Add an **Optional Section** control to the view of the form template and name it **group1**. Add some text in the section so that you can see when it is added or removed.

4. Open the **Section Properties** dialog box and then on the **Data** tab, deselect the **Allow users to insert the section** check box, since code should add or remove the optional section and not the user. Click **OK** when you are done.

5. Add an event handler for the **Changed** event of the check box as described in recipe *7 Add an event handler for a control event*.

6. In VSTA, add the following code to the `Changed()` event handler for the field bound to the check box (*code #: 11163FE6-5A93-448A-B914-9557324192B5*):

```
XPathNavigator group1 = e.Site.SelectSingleNode(
  "/my:myFields/my:group1", NamespaceManager);

if (e.Site.Value == "true")
{
  if (group1 == null)
    e.Site.InsertElementAfter(
      "my", "group1",
      NamespaceManager.LookupNamespace("my"), "");
}
else
{
  if (group1 != null)
    group1.DeleteSelf();
}
```

7. Save and build the project.

8. Preview the form.

When the form opens, select the check box. The section should appear. Deselect the check box. The section should disappear.

Discussion

Sections in InfoPath are bound to group nodes. So to add or remove a section, you must add or delete the group node that is bound to the section control. The solution described above uses the `InsertElementAfter()` method of the `XPathNavigator` object pointing to the sibling node preceding the group node bound to the section control to add an optional section control. The preceding sibling node in this case is the field bound to the check box control.

The code first retrieves an XPathNavigator object pointing to the group node bound to the optional section control. Note that the Site property of the XmlEventArgs object returns an XPathNavigator object pointing to the field bound to the check box.

```
XPathNavigator group1 = e.Site.SelectSingleNode(
  "/my:myFields/my:group1", NamespaceManager);
```

When the check box is selected, the optional section should be shown, and when the check box is deselected, the optional section should be removed. So the next step is to check the value of the check box. Check boxes have a value of true or false by default when you add them to an InfoPath form.

So the code goes on to check whether the value of the field bound to the check box is equal to true, and if it is, calls the InsertElementAfter() method of the XPathNavigator object pointing to the field bound to the check box (the field that precedes the group node bound to the optional section in the data source) to add the group node for the optional section control.

```
if (e.Site.Value == "true")
{
  if (group1 == null)
    e.Site.InsertElementAfter(
      "my", "group1", NamespaceManager.LookupNamespace("my"), "");
}
else
{
  ...
}
```

The else block of the if-statement assumes that the value of the field bound to the check box is equal to false, so it calls the DeleteSelf() method of the XPathNavigator object pointing to the group node bound to the optional section to delete the optional section.

```
if (e.Site.Value == "true")
{
  ...
}
else
{
  if (group1 != null)
    group1.DeleteSelf();
}
```

It is very important to remember that the location where you add the group node for the optional section in the data source depends on what has been defined in the XML schema of the form. You cannot add the group node just anywhere in the data source, since this would result in the following error:

Schema validation found non-data type errors.

For example, if you used the `AppendChildElement()` method of an `XPathNavigator` object pointing to the **myFields** group node to add the group node for the optional section, the error above would take place if the group node for the optional section is not defined as the last element in the data source, since the `AppendChildElement()` method always adds an element as the last child element of a node.

In the solution described above, the **field1** node bound to the check box control was the node preceding the **group1** group node (bound to the optional section control) in the Main data source, but if the **group1** group node is located elsewhere in the Main data source in your scenario, you must retrieve the sibling node preceding the **group1** group node and then call the `InsertElementAfter()` method of the `XPathNavigator` object pointing to that sibling node to maintain the correct position of the **group1** group node in the data source. Note that you could also make use of the `InsertElementBefore()` method of the `XPathNavigator` object pointing to the sibling node that immediately follows the group node bound to the optional section control to add the group node if there is such a sibling node in your scenario.

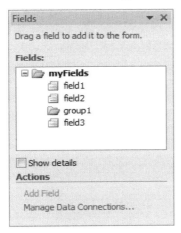

Figure 29. Main data source of an InfoPath form displaying the location of the group1 group node.

For example, if the data source of your form is made up of four nodes: **field1**, **field2**, **group1**, and **field3**, and all nodes are directly located under the **myFields** group node as shown in the figure above, you would have to change the code that adds/removes the **group1** group node to be the following:

```
XPathNavigator field2 = e.Site.SelectSingleNode(
  "/my:myFields/my:field2", NamespaceManager);
XPathNavigator group1 = e.Site.SelectSingleNode(
  "/my:myFields/my:group1", NamespaceManager);

if (e.Site.Value == "true")
{
  if (group1 == null)
    field2.InsertElementAfter(
      "my", "group1", NamespaceManager.LookupNamespace("my"), "");
}
```

173

```
else
{
  if (group1 != null)
    group1.DeleteSelf();
}
```

where **field2** is the sibling node preceding the **group1** group node. Or if you want to use the `InsertElementBefore()` method of the `XPathNavigator` object pointing to the **field3** node, which is the node that is located after the **group1** group node, you could use the following code:

```
XPathNavigator field3 = e.Site.SelectSingleNode(
  "/my:myFields/my:field3", NamespaceManager);
XPathNavigator group1 = e.Site.SelectSingleNode(
  "/my:myFields/my:group1", NamespaceManager);

if (e.Site.Value == "true")
{
  if (group1 == null)
    field3.InsertElementBefore(
      "my", "group1", NamespaceManager.LookupNamespace("my"), "");
}
else
{
  if (group1 != null)
    group1.DeleteSelf();
}
```

67   Add a choice section when a form opens

Problem

You have an InfoPath form with which you want to offer users the ability to submit a travel request or a travel expense, but not both. You want to show the section to enter travel request details by default through code when the form opens.

Solution

You can use a choice group control with two choice section controls, configure the choice group not to display any sections by default, and then write code in the `Loading()` event handler of the form to show the travel request section.

To add a choice section to a choice group when a form opens:

1. In InfoPath, create a new form template or use an existing one.

2. Add a **Choice Group** control to the view of the form template and name the main group node **group1**. Two choice section controls should have automatically been added to the choice group control. Name the group node for the first choice section **travelExpense** and name the group node for the second choice section **travelRequest**. Type the text **Travel Expense** in the **travelExpense** choice section

and the text **Travel Request** in the **travelRequest** choice section.

Figure 30. Choice group with two choice sections on the Fields task pane.

3. Click **Data ➤ Form Data ➤ Default Values**.

4. On the **Edit Default Values** dialog box, expand the **group1** node, deselect the check box for **(Choice)**, and click **OK**. This should prevent any of the two choice sections from appearing when the form opens, so that you can decide which choice section to show through code.

Figure 31. The default choice section removed from the choice group.

5. Add an event handler for the **Loading** event of the form as described in recipe *6 Add an event handler for a form event*.

6. In VSTA, add the following code to the `FormEvents_Loading()` event handler (*code #: 99CC4BB6-595E-4D55-A19C-10DDF8F10B88*):

```
XPathNavigator mainDS = MainDataSource.CreateNavigator();
XPathNavigator group1 = mainDS.SelectSingleNode(
    "/my:myFields/my:group1", NamespaceManager);
```

```
if (group1.HasChildren)
{
  if (group1.MoveToChild(XPathNodeType.Element))
  {
    group1.DeleteSelf();
  }
}

group1.AppendChildElement("my", "travelRequest",
  NamespaceManager.LookupNamespace("my"), "");
```

This code deletes the choice section that is located under the **group1** group node before adding a **travelRequest** choice section to the **group1** group node.

7. Save and build the project.

8. Preview the form.

When the form opens, the travel request choice section should appear.

Discussion

While choice groups display an extra group node named **(Choice)** on the **Fields** task pane in InfoPath Designer 2010, this group node is only a visual indication that the sections below it are mutually exclusive, that is, you can only select one. You do not generally use this group node in code as you saw in the solution described above. For example, the full XPath expression to access the **travelRequest** choice section is

```
/my:myFields/my:group1/my:travelRequest
```

and not

```
/my:myFields/my:group1/my:(Choice)/my:travelRequest
```

Before adding a choice section to a choice group using the `AppendChildElement()` method of the `XPathNavigator` object pointing to the group node bound to the choice group control

```
group1.AppendChildElement("my", "travelRequest",
  NamespaceManager.LookupNamespace("my"), "");
```

you must remove the choice section that is located under the choice group, because a choice group can only have one choice section at a time. You can use the following code to remove the choice section:

```
if (group1.HasChildren)
{
  if (group1.MoveToChild(XPathNodeType.Element))
  {
    group1.DeleteSelf();
```

```
    }
}
```

where **group1** is the XPathNavigator object pointing to the choice group node. Here, the MoveToChild() method is used to move the XPathNavigator object to point to the child element under the group node by using the XPathNodeType.Element enumeration value, and then the DeleteSelf() method is called to delete that child element (the choice section).

68   Add a choice section based on a selected option

Problem

You have an InfoPath form with which you want to offer users the ability to submit a travel request or a travel expense, but not both. You want to allow users to select an option and then have its corresponding section automatically appear on the form.

Solution

You can use a choice group control with two choice section controls, disable all of the choice section commands so that they can only be added to the form through the selection of option buttons, and then write code in the Changed() event handler for the option button control to add either a travel request or a travel expense section to the form, depending on which option the user selected.

To add a choice section based on a selected option:

1.   In InfoPath, create a new form template or use an existing one.

2.   Add an **Option Button** control with 2 option buttons to the view of the form template.

3.   Give the first option button the label **Travel Expense** and change its **Value when selected** property to be equal to **travelExpense** instead of **1**. Also select its **This button is selected by default** property to make it the default selection.

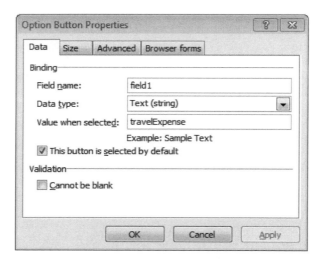

Figure 32. Setting the properties for the first option button.

4. Give the second option button the label **Travel Request** and change its **Value when selected** property to be equal to **travelRequest** instead of **2**.

5. Add a **Choice Group** control to the view of the form template and name it **group1**. Two choice section controls should have automatically been added to the choice group control. Name the group node for the first choice section **travelExpense** and name the group node for the second choice section **travelRequest**. Type the text **Travel Expense** in the **travelExpense** choice section and the text **Travel Request** in the **travelRequest** choice section. Disable all of the section commands (**Insert**, **Remove**, and **Replace With**) for both choice sections (through the **Customize Commands** button on the **Data** tab of the **Choice Section Properties** dialog box for each choice section).

Figure 33. Disabling all of the commands for a choice section.

Note that users would still be able to remove a choice section through the **Cut** command on the choice section menu.

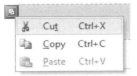

Figure 34. Cut command available on a choice section menu.

6. Add an event handler for the **Changed** event of the option button control as described in recipe *7 Add an event handler for a control event*.

7. In VSTA, add a private member variable named _isOptionDeleteOperation to the FormCode class (*code #: FD26CC9C-132C-4BC3-A58F-583B09746167*):

```
private bool _isOptionDeleteOperation = false;
```

This private member variable will be used to keep track of whether a choice section was manually deleted by a user or by selecting one of the options. Note that if you created a browser-compatible form template for which its forms should be filled out through a browser, you would have to use the FormState dictionary instead of a private member variable. Also see recipe *13 Clear all fields on a form* for an example of using the FormState dictionary.

8. Add the following code to the Changed() event handler for the field bound to the option button control (*code #: FD26CC9C-132C-4BC3-A58F-583B09746167*):

```
string selectedOption = e.NewValue;

XPathNavigator group1 = e.Site.SelectSingleNode(
  "/my:myFields/my:group1", NamespaceManager);

if (group1.HasChildren)
{
  if (group1.MoveToChild(XPathNodeType.Element))
  {
    _isOptionDeleteOperation = true;
    group1.DeleteSelf();
    _isOptionDeleteOperation = false;
  }
}

switch (selectedOption)
{
  case "travelExpense":
    group1.AppendChildElement("my", "travelExpense",
      NamespaceManager.LookupNamespace("my"), "");
    break;
  case"travelRequest":
    group1.AppendChildElement("my", "travelRequest",
      NamespaceManager.LookupNamespace("my"), "");
    break;
  default:
```

```
    // do nothing
    break;
}
```

This code retrieves the value of the newly selected option, deletes the choice section that is present under the **group1** group node, and then adds either a **travelExpense** or a **travelRequest** choice section based on the option that was selected.

9. In InfoPath, on the **Fields** task pane, right-click the **group1** group node, and then select **Programming ➤ Changed Event** to add an event handler for the **Changed** event of the **group1** group node.

10. In VSTA, add the following code to the `group1_Changed()` event handler (*code #: FD26CC9C-132C-4BC3-A58F-583B09746167*):

```
if (e.Operation == XmlOperation.Delete && e.Site.HasChildren)
{
  if (!_isOptionDeleteOperation)
  {
    e.Site.SelectSingleNode("/my:myFields/my:field1",
      NamespaceManager).SetValue("");
  }
}
```

This code ensures that whenever a user removes a choice section by cutting it, the option buttons are updated to show no selected value. The `_isOptionDeleteOperation` variable ensures that when a delete operation is called on the **group1** group node from the `Changed()` event handler for the field bound to the option button control, the option buttons are not reset to show no selected value, since this would result in the `Changed()` event handler for the field bound to the option button control being called again from the `Changed()` event handler for the **group1** group node.

11. Save and build the project.

12. Preview the form.

When the form opens, the travel expense section should appear. Select the **Travel Request** option. The travel request section should appear. Use the **Cut** command on the choice section menu to remove the section from the form. Both option buttons should have been cleared. Select the **Travel Expense** option. The travel expense section should appear.

Discussion

A choice group control allows a user to choose between one of two or more choice sections on an InfoPath form. In the solution described above, you used the `AppendChildElement()` method of the `XPathNavigator` object pointing to the group node bound to the choice group control to add a choice section, and you used the `DeleteSelf()` method of the `XPathNavigator` object pointing to one of the choice sections to remove a selected choice section.

The code uses the `NewValue` property of the `XmlEventArgs` object to retrieve the value of the option that was selected.

```
string selectedOption = e.NewValue;
```

The code then retrieves an `XPathNavigator` object pointing to the group node bound choice group control

```
XPathNavigator group1 = e.Site.SelectSingleNode(
  "/my:myFields/my:group1", NamespaceManager);
```

to be able to remove the choice section that is present under the choice group (see the discussion section of recipe *67 Add a choice section when a form opens* for more information about using the `MoveToChild()` method of the `XPathNavigator` object)

```
if (group1.HasChildren)
{
  if (group1.MoveToChild(XPathNodeType.Element))
  {
    _isOptionDeleteOperation = true;
    group1.DeleteSelf();
    _isOptionDeleteOperation = false;
  }
}
```

before adding the choice section that the user selected.

```
switch (selectedOption)
{
  case "travelExpense":
    group1.AppendChildElement("my", "travelExpense",
      NamespaceManager.LookupNamespace("my"), "");
    break;
  case"travelRequest":
    group1.AppendChildElement("my", "travelRequest",
      NamespaceManager.LookupNamespace("my"), "");
    break;
  default:
    // do nothing
    break;
}
```

While choice sections are being added and removed, the value of a member variable named `_isOptionDeleteOperation` keeps track of whether a choice section is programmatically being removed using the `DeleteSelf()` method in the `Changed()` event handler for the option button. This is necessary to be able to distinguish between a delete operation performed through code and a manual delete operation performed by a user using the **Cut** menu item on the choice section control, because whenever a user manually deletes a choice section, the option buttons should be cleared.

```
if (e.Operation == XmlOperation.Delete && e.Site.HasChildren)
{
  if (!_isOptionDeleteOperation)
  {
    e.Site.SelectSingleNode("/my:myFields/my:field1",
      NamespaceManager).SetValue("");
  }
}
```

When a choice section is deleted from within the Changed() event handler for the option button, the code triggers the Changed() event handler for the group node bound to choice group control. In such a case, you do not want the code in the Changed() event handler for the group node bound to the choice group control to change the value of the option button, since the code in the Changed() event handler for the group node bound to the choice group control should only be triggered by a manual delete operation of a choice section performed by a user. So before calling the delete operation in the Changed() event handler for the option button, a flag (the member variable) is set to indicate that the delete operation was initiated through code. And then when the value of the flag is checked in the Changed() event handler for the group node bound to the choice group control, the option button is not cleared, which would have otherwise caused the Changed() event handler for the option button to be called again and the code to wind up in an endless loop.

Repeating Table and Repeating Section

69   Retrieve a row of a repeating table

Problem

You have a repeating table on an InfoPath form and want to be able to retrieve the values of fields that are located in one specific row of the repeating table.

Solution

You can retrieve rows of a repeating table either by their position within the repeating table, for example the first row or the fourth row, or by the value of a specific field within the repeating table.

To retrieve a row of a repeating table:

1.   In InfoPath, create a new form template or use an existing one.

2.   Add a **Repeating Table** control with 2 columns to the view of the form template.

3.   Add a **Text Box** control to the view of the form template and name it **contents**.

4.   Add a second **Text Box** control to the view of the form template and name it **toSelect**.

5. Add a **Button** control to the view of the form template and place it anywhere outside of the repeating table.

6. Add an event handler for the **Clicked** event of the button control as described in recipe *7 Add an event handler for a control event*.

7. In VSTA, add the following code to the `Clicked()` event handler for the button to retrieve a row of the repeating table (*code #: 3C144335-0D54-4F82-96CB-EFC6E0D03072*):

   a. By position:

```
XPathNavigator mainDS = MainDataSource.CreateNavigator();

string toSelect = mainDS.SelectSingleNode(
  "/my:myFields/my:toSelect", NamespaceManager).Value;

if (String.IsNullOrEmpty(toSelect))
  toSelect = "1";

XPathNavigator row = mainDS.SelectSingleNode(
  "/my:myFields/my:group1/my:group2[" + toSelect + "]",
  NamespaceManager);

System.Text.StringBuilder sb = new System.Text.StringBuilder();
if (row != null)
{
  sb.Append(row.SelectSingleNode("my:field1", NamespaceManager).Value);
  sb.Append("; ");
  sb.Append(row.SelectSingleNode("my:field2", NamespaceManager).Value);
  sb.AppendLine();
}

mainDS.SelectSingleNode("/my:myFields/my:contents", NamespaceManager)
  .SetValue(sb.ToString());
```

   b. By field value:

```
XPathNavigator mainDS = MainDataSource.CreateNavigator();

string toSelect = mainDS.SelectSingleNode(
  "/my:myFields/my:toSelect", NamespaceManager).Value;

XPathNavigator row = mainDS.SelectSingleNode(
  "/my:myFields/my:group1/my:group2[my:field1 = '"
  + toSelect + "']", NamespaceManager);

System.Text.StringBuilder sb = new System.Text.StringBuilder();
if (row != null)
{
  sb.Append(row.SelectSingleNode("my:field1", NamespaceManager).Value);
  sb.Append("; ");
  sb.Append(row.SelectSingleNode("my:field2", NamespaceManager).Value);
  sb.AppendLine();
}

mainDS.SelectSingleNode("/my:myFields/my:contents", NamespaceManager)
  .SetValue(sb.ToString());
```

8. Save and build the project.

9. Preview the form.

When the form opens, add a couple of rows to the repeating table. If the form retrieves rows by position, enter a number in the **toSelect** text box, and click the button. The contents of the row that is located at the position you specified in the **toSelect** text box should be displayed in the text box with the values of the fields separated by semi-colons. If the form retrieves rows by field value, enter a piece of text that is the same as the value of one of the **field1** fields in any row of the repeating table into the **toSelect** text box, and click the button. The contents of the row that has a **field1** field with a value equal to the piece of text you entered into the **toSelect** text box should be displayed in the text box with the values of the fields separated by semi-colons.

Discussion

A row of a repeating table can be retrieved by finding it through its position in the list of rows of the repeating table or through a specific value in one of its fields. In the solution described above, you learned two ways to retrieve a row of a repeating table.

The code first retrieves the value of the **toSelect** text box in which a user can enter either a number (if rows are retrieved by position) or a piece of text that is the same as the value of one of the **field1** fields in the repeating table (if rows are retrieved by field value).

```
XPathNavigator mainDS = MainDataSource.CreateNavigator();

string toSelect = mainDS.SelectSingleNode(
  "/my:myFields/my:toSelect", NamespaceManager).Value;
```

The first method that retrieves a row of the repeating table uses the index number of the row to find the row with row indexes starting at 1 for the first row of the repeating table

```
XPathNavigator row = mainDS.SelectSingleNode(
  "/my:myFields/my:group1/my:group2[" + toSelect + "]", NamespaceManager);
```

and the second method uses a specific value of **field1** in the repeating table to find the row.

```
XPathNavigator row = mainDS.SelectSingleNode(
  "/my:myFields/my:group1/my:group2[my:field1 = '" + toSelect + "']",
  NamespaceManager);
```

Both methods use XPath filter expressions to find the row. Once the row has been found, the contents of the fields in the repeating table row are then retrieved

```
System.Text.StringBuilder sb = new System.Text.StringBuilder();
if (row != null)
{
  sb.Append(row.SelectSingleNode("my:field1", NamespaceManager).Value);
  sb.Append("; ");
  sb.Append(row.SelectSingleNode("my:field2", NamespaceManager).Value);
```

```
    sb.AppendLine();
}
```

and written to the **contents** field on the form.

```
mainDS.SelectSingleNode("/my:myFields/my:contents", NamespaceManager)
  .SetValue(sb.ToString());
```

70   Loop through rows of a repeating table

Problem

You have a repeating table on an InfoPath form and want to sequentially retrieve each row of the repeating table.

Solution

You can use an `XPathNodeIterator` object to loop through rows of a repeating table.

To loop through rows of a repeating table:

1.   In InfoPath, create a new form template or use an existing one.

2.   Add a **Repeating Table** control with 2 columns to the view of the form template.

3.   Add a **Text Box** control to the view of the form template, name it **contents**, and select its **Multi-line** property.

4.   Add a **Button** control to the view of the form template and place it anywhere outside of the repeating table.

5.   Add an event handler for the **Clicked** event of the button control as described in recipe *7 Add an event handler for a control event*.

6.   In VSTA, add the following code to the `Clicked()` event handler for the button (*code #: FD894A64-6E4B-422A-8622-FDAE1C2187B6*):

```
XPathNavigator mainDS = MainDataSource.CreateNavigator();
XPathNodeIterator rows = mainDS.Select(
  "/my:myFields/my:group1/my:group2", NamespaceManager);

System.Text.StringBuilder sb = new System.Text.StringBuilder();
while (rows.MoveNext())
{
  sb.Append(rows.Current.SelectSingleNode(
    "my:field1", NamespaceManager).Value);
  sb.Append("; ");
  sb.Append(rows.Current.SelectSingleNode(
    "my:field2", NamespaceManager).Value);
  sb.AppendLine();
}

mainDS.SelectSingleNode(
```

```
"/my:myFields/my:contents",
NamespaceManager).SetValue(sb.ToString());
```

7. Save and build the project.

8. Preview the form.

When the form opens, add a couple of rows of data to the repeating table, and then click the button. The text box should display all of the data you entered into the fields in the repeating table separated by semi-colons.

Discussion

A repeating table in InfoPath consists of a group node (**group1**), a repeating group node (**group2**), and fields (**field1** and **field2**) under the repeating group node (**group2**).

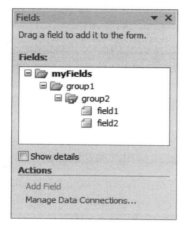

Figure 35. Groups and fields bound to a repeating table control or a repeating section control.

To be able to loop through rows of a repeating table (or sections of a repeating section control), you must retrieve and loop through all of the repeating group nodes (**group2** group nodes).

The XPathNodeIterator class provides an iterator over a selected set of nodes. You can use the Select() method of an XPathNavigator object to return an XPathNodeIterator object for a repeating table, so that you can use it to loop through the rows of the repeating table.

The code in the solution described above first retrieves an XPathNodeIterator object that allows you to loop through all of the **group2** group nodes of the repeating table.

```
XPathNavigator mainDS = MainDataSource.CreateNavigator();
XPathNodeIterator rows = mainDS.Select(
  "/my:myFields/my:group1/my:group2", NamespaceManager);
```

You can then use the MoveNext() method of the XPathNodeIterator object to retrieve each **group2** group node in a while-loop.

```
while (rows.MoveNext())
{
  ...
}
```

The MoveNext() method moves the XPathNavigator object returned by the Current property of the XPathNodeIterator object to the next node in the selected node-set. The value of each field in each row of the repeating table is then retrieved using the Current property and the SelectSingleNode() method, before they are appended to a StringBuilder object.

```
sb.Append(rows.Current.SelectSingleNode("my:field1", NamespaceManager).Value);
sb.Append("; ");
sb.Append(rows.Current.SelectSingleNode("my:field2", NamespaceManager).Value);
sb.AppendLine();
```

Note that because the Current property contains an XPathNavigator object pointing to a **group2** group node, you must use relative XPath expressions that start at **group2** to retrieve **field1** and **field2** located under **group2**.

And finally, the result of the string concatenation is written to the **contents** field on the form.

```
mainDS.SelectSingleNode("/my:myFields/my:contents", NamespaceManager)
  .SetValue(sb.ToString());
```

71 Add a row to a repeating table

The XPathNavigator class has two methods with which you can add a node at the end of a list of nodes of the current node: AppendChild() and AppendChildElement(). You can use either one of these two methods to add a row to a repeating table or a section to a repeating section as the five solutions in this recipe demonstrate.

Use the AppendChildElement() method

Problem

You have a repeating table on an InfoPath form. You want users to be able to click a button to add a new row to the repeating table.

Solution

You can use the AppendChildElement() method of an XPathNavigator object to add a row to a repeating table.

To add a row to a repeating table using the AppendChildElement() method:

1. In InfoPath, create a new form template or use an existing one.

2. Add a **Repeating Table** control with 3 columns to the view of the form template.

3. Click **Data ➤ Form Data ➤ Default Values**.

4. On the **Default Values** dialog box, expand the **group1** node, deselect the check box in front of the **group2** node, and click **OK**. This should remove the first row from the repeating table when the form opens.

5. Add a **Button** control to the view of the form template and label it **Add Row**.

6. Add an event handler for the **Clicked** event of the **Add Row** button control as described in recipe *7 Add an event handler for a control event*.

7. In VSTA, add the following code to the `Clicked()` event handler for the button (*code #: 322E9A28-0655-49E4-9657-DA9BF8CD94A3*):

```
XPathNavigator mainDS = MainDataSource.CreateNavigator();
XPathNavigator group1 = mainDS.SelectSingleNode(
  "/my:myFields/my:group1", NamespaceManager);

group1.AppendChildElement("my", "group2",
  NamespaceManager.LookupNamespace("my"), "");

XPathNodeIterator iter = mainDS.Select(
  "/my:myFields/my:group1/my:group2", NamespaceManager);

int rowCount = 0;
if (iter != null)
  rowCount = iter.Count;

XPathNavigator lastGroup2 = mainDS.SelectSingleNode(
  "/my:myFields/my:group1/my:group2[" + rowCount + "]", NamespaceManager);

if (lastGroup2 != null)
{
  lastGroup2.AppendChildElement("my", "field1",
    NamespaceManager.LookupNamespace("my"), "cell 1");
  lastGroup2.AppendChildElement("my", "field2",
    NamespaceManager.LookupNamespace("my"), "cell 2");
  lastGroup2.AppendChildElement("my", "field3",
    NamespaceManager.LookupNamespace("my"), "cell 3");
}
```

8. Save and build the project.

9. Preview the form.

When the form opens, click **Add Row**. A new row should appear in the repeating table.

Discussion

The `AppendChildElement()` method of an `XPathNavigator` object creates a new child element node at the end of the list of child nodes of the current node using the namespace prefix, local name, and namespace URI specified with the value specified.

The code in the solution described above first retrieves an XPathNavigator object pointing to the **group1** group node, which functions as the container group node for the rows of the repeating table (the **group2** group nodes).

```
XPathNavigator mainDS = MainDataSource.CreateNavigator();
XPathNavigator group1 = mainDS.SelectSingleNode(
  "/my:myFields/my:group1", NamespaceManager);
```

Then the AppendChildElement() method of the XPathNavigator object is used to create a **group2** group node as a child node of the **group1** group node.

```
group1.AppendChildElement("my", "group2",
  NamespaceManager.LookupNamespace("my"), "");
```

Because the AppendChildElement() method does not return a reference to the newly added **group2** group node, you must retrieve the newly added node by retrieving the last child node of the **group1** group node. This can be done using the Select() method of the XPathNavigator object pointing to the **group1** group node and the Count property of the XPathNodeIterator object returned by the Select() method.

```
XPathNodeIterator iter = mainDS.Select(
  "/my:myFields/my:group1/my:group2", NamespaceManager);

int rowCount = 0;
if (iter != null)
  rowCount = iter.Count;

XPathNavigator lastGroup2 = mainDS.SelectSingleNode(
  "/my:myFields/my:group1/my:group2[" + rowCount + "]", NamespaceManager);
```

Note that you could have also used the last() XPath function in the XPath filter expression in the SelectSingleNode() method to get a reference to the last **group2** group node under **group1** as follows:

```
XPathNavigator lastGroup2 = mainDS.SelectSingleNode(
  "/my:myFields/my:group1/my:group2[last()]", NamespaceManager);
```

Once you have a reference to the last **group2** child node of **group1**, you can then add the fields that should be contained within **group2** by using the AppendChildElement() method on **group2**.

```
if (lastGroup2 != null)
{
  lastGroup2.AppendChildElement("my", "field1",
    NamespaceManager.LookupNamespace("my"), "cell 1");
  lastGroup2.AppendChildElement("my", "field2",
    NamespaceManager.LookupNamespace("my"), "cell 2");
  lastGroup2.AppendChildElement("my", "field3",
    NamespaceManager.LookupNamespace("my"), "cell 3");
}
```

Use the AppendChild() method with an XmlDocument object

Problem

You have a repeating table on an InfoPath form. You want users to be able to click a button to add a new row to the repeating table.

Solution

You can pass an XPathNavigator object that is created from an XmlDocument object to the AppendChild() method of the XPathNavigator object pointing to the group node bound to a repeating table to add a row to the repeating table.

To add a row to a repeating table using the AppendChild() method with an XmlDocument object:

1. Follow steps 1 through 6 of *Use the AppendChildElement() method* in this recipe.

2. In VSTA, add the following code to the Clicked() event handler for the button (*code #: 99AEF17E-662D-4B33-859E-F42D4D5187FE*):

```
XmlDocument doc = new XmlDocument();
XmlNode group2 =
   doc.CreateElement("group2",NamespaceManager.LookupNamespace("my"));

XmlNode field =
   doc.CreateElement("field1", NamespaceManager.LookupNamespace("my"));
XmlNode node = group2.AppendChild(field);
node.InnerText = "Cell 1";

field =
   doc.CreateElement("field2", NamespaceManager.LookupNamespace("my"));
node = group2.AppendChild(field);
node.InnerText = "Cell 2";

field =
   doc.CreateElement("field3", NamespaceManager.LookupNamespace("my"));
node = group2.AppendChild(field);
node.InnerText = "Cell 3";

doc.AppendChild(group2);

MainDataSource.CreateNavigator().SelectSingleNode("/my:myFields/my:group1",
   NamespaceManager).AppendChild(doc.DocumentElement.CreateNavigator());
```

3. Save and build the project.

4. Preview the form.

When the form opens, click **Add Row**. A new row should appear in the repeating table.

Discussion

There are four different overloads for the AppendChild() method of the XPathNavigator class. The AppendChild() method in this solution creates a new child element node at the end of the list of child nodes of the current node using the nodes in the XPathNavigator object specified.

The code in the solution described above first creates an XmlDocument object

```
XmlDocument doc = new XmlDocument();
```

that has the structure of a row of the repeating table consisting of a **group2** element

```
XmlNode group2 =
    doc.CreateElement("group2",NamespaceManager.LookupNamespace("my"));
```

that contains 3 elements that represent its fields.

```
XmlNode field =
    doc.CreateElement("field1", NamespaceManager.LookupNamespace("my"));
XmlNode node = group2.AppendChild(field);
node.InnerText = "Cell 1";

field =
    doc.CreateElement("field2", NamespaceManager.LookupNamespace("my"));
node = group2.AppendChild(field);
node.InnerText = "Cell 2";

field =
    doc.CreateElement("field3", NamespaceManager.LookupNamespace("my"));
node = group2.AppendChild(field);
node.InnerText = "Cell 3";

doc.AppendChild(group2);
```

Once the XmlDocument object has been created, its DocumentElement property and the CreateNavigator() method of that document element are used along with the AppendChild() method that accepts an XPathNavigator object to add the **group2** group node with its child fields to the **group1** group node.

```
MainDataSource.CreateNavigator().SelectSingleNode("/my:myFields/my:group1",
    NamespaceManager).AppendChild(doc.DocumentElement.CreateNavigator());
```

Use the AppendChild() method with a string

Problem

You have a repeating table on an InfoPath form. You want users to be able to click a button to add a new row to the repeating table.

Solution

You can pass a string to the `AppendChild()` method of the `XPathNavigator` object pointing to the group node bound to a repeating table to add a row to the repeating table.

To add a row to a repeating table using the `AppendChild()` method with a string:

1. Follow steps 1 through 6 of *Use the AppendChildElement() method* in this recipe.

2. In VSTA, add the following code to the `Clicked()` event handler for the button (*code #: 23852CFD-8CE4-43C7-96B5-6F0BE0387818*):

```
string my = NamespaceManager.LookupNamespace("my");

System.Text.StringBuilder sb = new System.Text.StringBuilder();
sb.AppendFormat("<my:group2 xmlns:my=\"{0}\">", my);
sb.AppendFormat("<my:field1 xmlns:my=\"{0}\">", my);
sb.AppendFormat("{0}</my:field1>", "cell 1");
sb.AppendFormat("<my:field2 xmlns:my=\"{0}\">", my);
sb.AppendFormat("{0}</my:field2>", "cell 2");
sb.AppendFormat("<my:field3 xmlns:my=\"{0}\">", my);
sb.AppendFormat("{0}</my:field3>", "cell3");
sb.Append("</my:group2>");
MainDataSource.CreateNavigator().SelectSingleNode(
    "/my:myFields/my:group1", NamespaceManager).AppendChild(sb.ToString());
```

3. Save and build the project.

4. Preview the form.

When the form opens, click **Add Row**. A new row should appear in the repeating table.

Discussion

There are four different overloads for the `AppendChild()` method of the `XPathNavigator` class. The `AppendChild()` method in this solution creates a new child element node at the end of the list of child nodes of the current node using an XML data string for the child node.

The code in the solution described above first constructs the entire XML for the **group2** group node and the fields it contains using a `StringBuilder` object.

```
string my = NamespaceManager.LookupNamespace("my");

System.Text.StringBuilder sb = new System.Text.StringBuilder();
sb.AppendFormat("<my:group2 xmlns:my=\"{0}\">", my);
sb.AppendFormat("<my:field1 xmlns:my=\"{0}\">", my);
sb.AppendFormat("{0}</my:field1>", "cell 1");
sb.AppendFormat("<my:field2 xmlns:my=\"{0}\">", my);
sb.AppendFormat("{0}</my:field2>", "cell 2");
sb.AppendFormat("<my:field3 xmlns:my=\"{0}\">", my);
sb.AppendFormat("{0}</my:field3>", "cell3");
sb.Append("</my:group2>");
```

Then the `AppendChild()` method that accepts a string is used to add the **group2** group node with its child fields to the **group1** group node.

```
MainDataSource.CreateNavigator().SelectSingleNode(
  "/my:myFields/my:group1", NamespaceManager).AppendChild(sb.ToString());
```

Use the AppendChild() method with an XmlReader object

Problem

You have a repeating table on an InfoPath form. You want users to be able to click a button to add a new row to the repeating table.

Solution

You can pass an `XmlReader` object to the `AppendChild()` method of the `XPathNavigator` object pointing to the group node bound to a repeating table to add a row to the repeating table.

To add a row to a repeating table using the `AppendChild()` method with an `XmlReader` object:

1. Follow steps 1 through 6 of *Use the AppendChildElement() method* in this recipe.

2. In VSTA, add the following code to the `Clicked()` event handler for the button (*code #: 0DA634AA-B09B-4C67-984E-4B2ED241E41F*):

```
string my = NamespaceManager.LookupNamespace("my");

System.Text.StringBuilder sb = new System.Text.StringBuilder();
sb.AppendFormat("<my:group2 xmlns:my=\"{0}\">", my);
sb.AppendFormat("<my:field1 xmlns:my=\"{0}\">", my);
sb.AppendFormat("{0}</my:field1>", "cell 1");
sb.AppendFormat("<my:field2 xmlns:my=\"{0}\">", my);
sb.AppendFormat("{0}</my:field2>", "cell 2");
sb.AppendFormat("<my:field3 xmlns:my=\"{0}\">", my);
sb.AppendFormat("{0}</my:field3>", "cell3");
sb.Append("</my:group2>");

byte[] buffer = System.Text.Encoding.UTF8.GetBytes(sb.ToString());

using (System.IO.MemoryStream ms = new System.IO.MemoryStream(buffer))
{
  using (XmlReader reader = XmlReader.Create(ms))
  {
    MainDataSource.CreateNavigator().SelectSingleNode(
      "/my:myFields/my:group1", NamespaceManager).AppendChild(reader);
    reader.Close();
  }
  ms.Close();
}
```

3. Save and build the project.

4. Preview the form.

When the form opens, click **Add Row**. A new row should appear in the repeating table.

Discussion

There are four different overloads for the `AppendChild()` method of the `XPathNavigator` class. The `AppendChild()` method in this solution creates a new child element node at the end of the list of child nodes of the current node using an `XmlReader` object for the child node.

The code in the solution described above first constructs the entire XML for the **group2** group node and the fields it contains using a `StringBuilder` object.

```
string my = NamespaceManager.LookupNamespace("my");

System.Text.StringBuilder sb = new System.Text.StringBuilder();
sb.AppendFormat("<my:group2 xmlns:my=\"{0}\">", my);
sb.AppendFormat("<my:field1 xmlns:my=\"{0}\">", my);
sb.AppendFormat("{0}</my:field1>", "cell 1");
sb.AppendFormat("<my:field2 xmlns:my=\"{0}\">", my);
sb.AppendFormat("{0}</my:field2>", "cell 2");
sb.AppendFormat("<my:field3 xmlns:my=\"{0}\">", my);
sb.AppendFormat("{0}</my:field3>", "cell3");
sb.Append("</my:group2>");
```

Note that this XML could have been retrieved from anywhere. It is explicitly constructed here for demonstration purposes only. Then the string is converted into a `byte` array using the `GetBytes()` method of the `Encoding` class.

```
byte[] buffer = System.Text.Encoding.UTF8.GetBytes(sb.ToString());
```

And finally, the `byte` array is used to create a `MemoryStream` object from which an `XmlReader` object can be created, which is then subsequently used with the `AppendChild()` method to add a row to the repeating table.

```
using (System.IO.MemoryStream ms = new System.IO.MemoryStream(buffer))
{
  using (XmlReader reader = XmlReader.Create(ms))
  {
    MainDataSource.CreateNavigator().SelectSingleNode(
      "/my:myFields/my:group1", NamespaceManager).AppendChild(reader);
    reader.Close();
  }
  ms.Close();
}
```

Use the AppendChild() method with an XmlWriter object

Problem

You have a repeating table on an InfoPath form. You want users to be able to click a button to add a new row to the repeating table.

Solution

You can pass an XmlWriter object to the AppendChild() method of the XPathNavigator object pointing to the group node bound to a repeating table to add a row to the repeating table.

To add a row to a repeating table using the AppendChild() method with an XmlWriter object:

1. Follow steps 1 through 6 of *Use the AppendChildElement() method* in this recipe.

2. In VSTA, add the following code to the Clicked() event handler for the button (*code #: 93E7E165-B6AC-4562-A72A-CB28D993F4BE*):

```
string my = NamespaceManager.LookupNamespace("my");
using (XmlWriter writer =
  MainDataSource.CreateNavigator().SelectSingleNode(
    "/my:myFields/my:group1", NamespaceManager).AppendChild())
{
  writer.WriteStartElement("group2", my);
  writer.WriteElementString("field1", my, "Cell 1");
  writer.WriteElementString("field2", my, "Cell 2");
  writer.WriteElementString("field3", my, "Cell 3");
  writer.WriteEndElement();
  writer.Close();
}
```

3. Save and build the project.

4. Preview the form.

When the form opens, click **Add Row**. A new row should appear in the repeating table.

Discussion

There are four different overloads for the AppendChild() method of the XPathNavigator class. The AppendChild() method in this solution creates a new child element node at the end of the list of child nodes of the current node using an XmlWriter object that can be used to write the XML for the child node.

The code in the solution described above first creates an XmlWriter object for the **group1** group node by calling the AppendChild() method of the XPathNavigator object pointing to the **group1** group node.

```
string my = NamespaceManager.LookupNamespace("my");
using (XmlWriter writer = MainDataSource.CreateNavigator().SelectSingleNode(
  "/my:myFields/my:group1", NamespaceManager).AppendChild())
{
  ...
}
```

Then the WriteStartElement(), WriteElementString(), and WriteEndElement() methods are used to write the XML for the **group2** group node and its fields.

```
writer.WriteStartElement("group2", my);
writer.WriteElementString("field1", my, "Cell 1");
writer.WriteElementString("field2", my, "Cell 2");
writer.WriteElementString("field3", my, "Cell 3");
writer.WriteEndElement();
```

And finally, the `Close()` method of the `XmlWriter` object is called to close the writer.

```
writer.Close();
```

The `XmlWriter` class has several other methods you can use to create elements and attributes. You are encouraged to go through the list of methods and use the methods that are most suitable for your scenario.

72 Delete rows of a repeating table

Delete a row from a button inside of a repeating table

Problem

You have a repeating table on an InfoPath form and want to be able to delete a row from it.

Solution

You can use the `Source` property of the `ClickedEventArgs` object of the event handler for a button control to get a reference to the row the button is located in and then use this reference to delete the row of the repeating table.

To delete a repeating table row from a button that is located inside of the repeating table:

1. In InfoPath, create a new form template or use an existing one.

2. Add a **Repeating Table** control with 3 columns to the view of the form template.

3. Delete the text box control from the third column and add a **Button** control in its place.

4. Add an event handler for the **Clicked** event of the button as described in recipe *7 Add an event handler for a control event*.

5. In VSTA, add the following code to the `Clicked()` event handler for the button (*code #: 705E3077-4BF8-40B0-B1BF-2F8843271F88*):

```
e.Source.DeleteSelf();
```

where `e.Source` represents an `XPathNavigator` object positioned at the repeating table row that contains the button control that was clicked.

6. Save and build the project.

7. Preview the form.

When the form opens, add a total of 3 rows to the repeating table and number them by entering sequential numbers in the text box in the first column. Click the button that is located in the second row of the repeating table. The second row should now be gone.

Discussion

In the solution described above, e.Source returns the XPathNavigator object positioned at the innermost XML node that contains the button control. So you can use it to retrieve the row of the repeating table that contains the button that was clicked. Once you have done this, it is just a matter of calling the DeleteSelf() method of the XPathNavigator object to delete the repeating table row that contains the button that was clicked.

Delete a row from a button outside of a repeating table

Problem

You have a repeating table on an InfoPath form and want to be able to delete a row from it.

Solution

After identifying which row of a repeating table should be deleted, you can retrieve a reference to that row, and then use the DeleteSelf() method of the XPathNavigator object to delete the row.

To delete a repeating table row from a button that is located outside of the repeating table:

1. In InfoPath, create a new form template or use an existing one.

2. Add a **Repeating Table** control with 3 columns to the view of the form template.

3. Change the text box that is located in the third column of the repeating table into a **Check Box** control and change the data type of the control to **True/False (boolean)** with its **Value when cleared** property set to **FALSE** and its **Value when checked** property set to **TRUE**.

4. Add a **Button** control to the view of the form template and place it anywhere outside of the repeating table.

5. Add an event handler for the **Clicked** event of the button as described in recipe 7 *Add an event handler for a control event*.

6. In VSTA, add the following code to the Clicked() event handler for the button (*code #: 639A6276-F868-4876-BFD4-32ABEF04F4DF*):

```
XPathNavigator mainDS = MainDataSource.CreateNavigator();

XPathNavigator row = mainDS.SelectSingleNode(
  "/my:myFields/my:group1/my:group2[my:field3 = 'true']",
  NamespaceManager);

while (row != null)
{
  row.DeleteSelf();
  row = mainDS.SelectSingleNode(
    "/my:myFields/my:group1/my:group2[my:field3 = 'true']",
    NamespaceManager);
}
```

where **field3** is the field that is bound to the check box control within the repeating table.

7. Save and build the project.

8. Preview the form.

When the form opens, add a total of 3 rows to the repeating table and number them by entering sequential numbers in the text box in the first column. Select the check box that is located in the third cell of the second and third rows. Click the button that is located outside of the repeating table. The second and third rows should now be gone.

Discussion

Before you can delete a specific row or rows of a repeating table by clicking on a button control that is located outside of the repeating table, you must have a way to identify the rows that should be deleted. In the solution described above, a check box was used to identify such rows.

```
XPathNavigator mainDS = MainDataSource.CreateNavigator();

XPathNavigator row = mainDS.SelectSingleNode(
  "/my:myFields/my:group1/my:group2[my:field3 = 'true']", NamespaceManager);
```

The code above only retrieves the first **group2** group node where the **field3** node under it has a value equal to true. And because only one row is retrieved at a time, the code uses a while-loop to continue looking for and deleting all of the **group2** group nodes that satisfy the XPath filter expression until no more **group2** group nodes are found.

```
while (row != null)
{
  row.DeleteSelf();
  row = mainDS.SelectSingleNode(
    "/my:myFields/my:group1/my:group2[my:field3 = 'true']", NamespaceManager);
}
```

The `DeleteSelf()` method of the `XPathNavigator` object pointing to each row found is used to delete the row. If you want to delete a specific row such as for example the first row or the third row of the repeating table, you could use code such as

```
XPathNavigator row = MainDataSource.CreateNavigator().SelectSingleNode(
  "/my:myFields/my:group1/my:group2[1]", NamespaceManager);

if (row != null)
  row.DeleteSelf();
```

to delete the first row of the repeating table, and code such as

```
XPathNavigator row = MainDataSource.CreateNavigator().SelectSingleNode(
  "/my:myFields/my:group1/my:group2[3]", NamespaceManager);

if (row != null)
  row.DeleteSelf();
```

to delete the third row of the repeating table, where **[1]** retrieves the first row of the repeating table and **[3]** retrieves the third row.

Delete all of the rows of a repeating table

Problem

You have a repeating table on an InfoPath form and want to be able to delete all of its rows.

Solution

You can use the `DeleteRange()` method of an `XPathNavigator` object to delete all of the rows of a repeating table by specifying the first and last nodes to delete.

To delete all of the rows of a repeating table:

1. In InfoPath, create a new form template or use an existing one.

2. Add a **Repeating Table** control with 3 columns to the view of the form template.

3. Add a **Button** control to the view of the form template and place it anywhere outside of the repeating table.

4. Add an event handler for the **Clicked** event of the button as described in recipe 7 *Add an event handler for a control event*.

5. In VSTA, add the following code to the `Clicked()` event handler for the button (*code #: 9344D522-B2AD-49C3-9D90-6AE2382C7A6B*):

    ```
    XPathNavigator mainDS = MainDataSource.CreateNavigator();
    XPathNavigator firstRow = mainDS.SelectSingleNode(
      "/my:myFields/my:group1/my:group2", NamespaceManager);
    ```

```
XPathNavigator lastRow = mainDS.SelectSingleNode(
  "//my:myFields/my:group1/my:group2[position() = last()]",
  NamespaceManager);

if (firstRow != null && lastRow != null)
  firstRow.DeleteRange(lastRow);
```

6. Save and build the project.

7. Preview the form.

When the form opens, add a total of 3 rows to the repeating table and number them by entering sequential numbers in the text box in the first column. Click the button that is located outside of the repeating table. All of the rows should now be gone.

Discussion

The solution described above uses the `DeleteRange()` method of an `XPathNavigator` object pointing to the first row of the repeating table to delete all of the rows of the repeating table. Before you can use the `DeleteRange()` method, you must retrieve a reference to the first and last rows that should be deleted. The code in the solution uses

```
XPathNavigator firstRow = mainDS.SelectSingleNode(
  "/my:myFields/my:group1/my:group2", NamespaceManager);
```

to find the first row of the repeating table, and

```
XPathNavigator lastRow = mainDS.SelectSingleNode(
  "//my:myFields/my:group1/my:group2[position() = last()]",
  NamespaceManager);
```

to find the last row that should be deleted, and then uses

```
if (firstRow != null && lastRow != null)
  firstRow.DeleteRange(lastRow);
```

to delete the rows starting from the first row and ending on the last row. Note that the `position()` and `last()` XPath functions are used to find the last row, but you could have also used an `XPathNodeIterator` object to achieve the same results as follows:

```
XPathNodeIterator iter = mainDS.Select(
  "/my:myFields/my:group1/my:group2", NamespaceManager);
XPathNavigator lastRow = mainDS.SelectSingleNode(
  "/my:myFields/my:group1/my:group2[" + iter.Count + "]", NamespaceManager);
```

73 Retrieve the value of a field in the same row of a repeating table

Problem

You have a repeating table on an InfoPath form and want to be able to retrieve the value of a field that is located in the same row as the field that is currently being changed, and copy its value to a text box that is located elsewhere on the form.

Solution

You can use the `Site` property of an `XmlEventArgs` object to retrieve an `XPathNavigator` object for the node being changed, and then use XPath expressions to retrieve sibling nodes.

To retrieve the value of a field that is located in the same row of a repeating table:

1. In InfoPath, create a new form template or use an existing one.

2. Add a **Repeating Table** control with 2 columns to the view of the form template.

3. Add a **Text Box** control to the view of the form template and name it **copiedValue**.

4. Add an event handler for the **Changed** event of **field2**, which is located in the second column of the repeating table, as described in recipe *7 Add an event handler for a control event*.

5. In VSTA, add the following code to the `Changed()` event handler for **field2** (*code #: 61145E6D-7560-4687-A740-E1D6D3E5E3C4*):

```
XPathNavigator field2 = e.Site;
XPathNavigator field1 = field2.SelectSingleNode(
  "../my:field1", NamespaceManager);
XPathNavigator copiedValue = field2.SelectSingleNode(
  "../../../my:copiedValue", NamespaceManager);

if (field1 != null && copiedValue != null)
  copiedValue.SetValue(field1.Value);
```

In this scenario you are copying the value of **field1** over to the **copiedValue** text box when a user changes the value of **field2**.

6. Save and build the project.

7. Preview the form.

When the form opens, enter a piece of text in **field1** in the repeating table, enter a piece of text in **field2** in the repeating table, and then click or tab away from **field2**. The value of **field1** should appear in the **copiedValue** text box on the form.

Discussion

The `Site` property of an `XmlEventArgs` object gets the `XPathNavigator` object that is pointing to the node that is being changed. In the solution described above, you used the `Site` property to retrieve an `XPathNavigator` object pointing to **field2**, which is located in the second column of a repeating table.

```
XPathNavigator field2 = e.Site;
```

You then used **field2** as the context node to find **field1** and **copiedValue** through relative XPath expressions.

```
XPathNavigator field1 = field2.SelectSingleNode(
  "../my:field1", NamespaceManager);
XPathNavigator copiedValue = field2.SelectSingleNode(
  "../../../my:copiedValue", NamespaceManager);
```

And finally, you set the value of **copiedValue** to be equal to the value of **field1** by using the `SetValue()` method and `Value` property of the respective `XPathNavigator` objects pointing to those two fields.

```
if (field1 != null && copiedValue != null)
  copiedValue.SetValue(field1.Value);
```

74 Copy data from a data source to a repeating table

Problem

You have an XML file containing data that you would like to load into a repeating table when a form opens.

Solution

You can use an XSL transformation to convert the data from the XML file into an XML structure that is suitable to replace the XML structure of a repeating table on the form.

To copy data from a data source to a repeating table:

1. In InfoPath, create a new form template or use an existing one.

2. Add a **Repeating Table** control with 2 columns to the view of the form template.

3. Preview the form.

4. Save the form to a location on disk, and then close the form.

5. Navigate to the location on disk where you saved the form and open it in Notepad.

6. Copy the declaration of the **my** namespace.

   ```
   xmlns:my="http://schemas.microsoft.com/office/infopath/2003/myXSD/2011-10-
   03T01:19:26"
   ```

   You will be using it later in the XSL file that performs the transformation. Note: If you want to programmatically set the namespace in the XSL file through code instead of manually as described in the next step, you can use the technique described in recipe *95 Submit repeating table data to a SharePoint list to create new list items*.

7. Open Notepad and add the following contents to it:

   ```
   <?xml version="1.0" encoding="UTF-8" standalone="yes"?>
   <xsl:stylesheet xmlns:xsl="http://www.w3.org/1999/XSL/Transform"
   version="1.0"
   xmlns:my="http://schemas.microsoft.com/office/infopath/2003/myXSD/2011-10-
   03T01:19:26">
     <xsl:output method="xml" />
     <xsl:template match="/">
       <my:group1>
         <xsl:for-each select="/fruits/fruit">
         <my:group2>
           <my:field1><xsl:value-of select="name" /></my:field1>
           <my:field2><xsl:value-of select="color" /></my:field2>
         </my:group2>
         </xsl:for-each>
       </my:group1>
     </xsl:template>
   </xsl:stylesheet>
   ```

   where you should replace the declaration of the **my** namespace with the one you copied earlier. Save the file as **transform.xsl**. You can also download this file from www.bizsupportonline.com.

8. In InfoPath, click **Data ➤ Form Data ➤ Resource Files**.

9. On the **Resource Files** dialog box, click **Add**.

10. On the **Add File** dialog box, browse to and select the **transform.xsl** file, and then click **OK**.

11. On the **Resource Files** dialog box, click **OK**. With this you have added the XSL file as a resource file to the form template.

12. Open Notepad and add the following contents to it:

    ```
    <?xml version="1.0" encoding="UTF-8"?>
    <fruits>
      <fruit><name>Apple</name><color>Red</color></fruit>
      <fruit><name>Banana</name><color>Yellow</color></fruit>
      <fruit><name>Grapes</name><color>Purple</color></fruit>
      <fruit><name>Kiwi</name><color>Brown</color></fruit>
      <fruit><name>Orange</name><color>Orange</color></fruit>
    </fruits>
    ```

Save the file as **Fruits.xml**. You can also download this file from www.bizsupportonline.com.

13. In InfoPath, select **Data ➤ Get External Data ➤ From Other Sources ➤ From XML File** and follow the instructions to add the **Fruits.xml** file as a secondary data source to the form template. Leave the **Automatically retrieve data when form is opened** check box selected and name the data source **Fruits**.

14. Add an event handler for the **Loading** event of the form as described in recipe *6 Add an event handler for a form event*.

15. In VSTA, add the following **using** statements to the **FormCode.cs** file:

```
using System.Xml.Xsl;
using System.IO;
```

16. Add the following code to the `FormEvents_Loading()` event handler (*code #: ABB845A8-6667-4DB2-B349-3445B196DB9A*):

```
using (Stream stream = Template.OpenFileFromPackage("transform.xsl"))
{
  if (stream == null || stream.Length == 0)
    return;

  XPathDocument xslFile = new XPathDocument(stream);
  XslCompiledTransform trans = new XslCompiledTransform();
  trans.Load(xslFile);

  using (MemoryStream ms = new MemoryStream())
  {
    trans.Transform(DataSources["Fruits"].CreateNavigator(), null, ms);

    ms.Position = 0;

    XPathDocument doc = new XPathDocument(ms);

    XPathNavigator group1 =
    MainDataSource.CreateNavigator().SelectSingleNode(
      "/my:myFields/my:group1", NamespaceManager);

    if (group1 != null)
      group1.ReplaceSelf(doc.CreateNavigator());
  }
  stream.Close();
}
```

17. Save and build the project.

18. Preview the form.

When the form opens, all of the fruits from the XML file should appear in the repeating table.

Discussion

In the solution described above, you used an XSL file to transform data from an XML file into a format that was suitable to replace the XML for a repeating table on an InfoPath form. You also used the `OpenFileFromPackage()` method of the `FormTemplate` object to retrieve the XSL file that was stored as a resource file in the form template as a `Stream` object.

```
using (Stream stream = Template.OpenFileFromPackage("transform.xsl"))
{
  ...
}
```

The code uses the `Stream` object returned by the `OpenFileFromPackage()` method to create an `XPathDocument` object that is then used to create an `XslCompiledTransform` object.

```
XPathDocument xslFile = new XPathDocument(stream);
XslCompiledTransform trans = new XslCompiledTransform();
trans.Load(xslFile);
```

And finally, the `Transform()` method of the `XslCompiledTransform` object is called to convert the **Fruits** secondary data source (`DataSources["Fruits"]`) into an XML structure that is suitable to replace the **group1** group node in the form.

```
using (MemoryStream ms = new MemoryStream())
{
  trans.Transform(DataSources["Fruits"].CreateNavigator(), null, ms);

  ms.Position = 0;

  XPathDocument doc = new XPathDocument(ms);

  XPathNavigator group1 =
  MainDataSource.CreateNavigator().SelectSingleNode(
    "/my:myFields/my:group1", NamespaceManager);

  if (group1 != null)
    group1.ReplaceSelf(doc.CreateNavigator());
}
```

Note that an `XPathDocument` object is used for a second time to be able to take the `MemoryStream` object populated by the `Transform()` method of the `XslCompiledTransform` object and create an `XPathNavigator` object, which can then be used in the `ReplaceSelf()` method of the `XPathNavigator` object pointing to the **group1** group node to replace the **group1** group node in the form.

In the solution described above, the XML file contained elements instead of attributes. If you have a data source that contains attributes instead of elements, for example:

```
<?xml version="1.0" encoding="UTF-8"?>
<fruits>
  <fruit name='Apple' color='Red' />
  <fruit name='Banana' color='Yellow' />
  <fruit name='Grapes' color='Purple' />
  <fruit name='Kiwi' color='Brown' />
```

```
  <fruit name='Orange' color='Orange' />
</fruits>
```

you should change the XSL file to have the following contents:

```
<?xml version="1.0" encoding="UTF-8" standalone="yes"?>
<xsl:stylesheet xmlns:xsl="http://www.w3.org/1999/XSL/Transform" version="1.0"
xmlns:my="http://schemas.microsoft.com/office/infopath/2003/myXSD/2011-10-
03T01:19:26">
  <xsl:output method="xml" />
  <xsl:template match="/">
    <my:group1>
      <xsl:for-each select="/fruits/fruit">
      <my:group2>
        <my:field1><xsl:value-of select="@name" /></my:field1>
        <my:field2><xsl:value-of select="@color" /></my:field2>
      </my:group2>
      </xsl:for-each>
    </my:group1>
  </xsl:template>
</xsl:stylesheet>
```

but the code used to perform the transformation should remain the same.

The solution described in this recipe is not restricted to XML files, but can be used with any other type of secondary data source in InfoPath, including secondary data sources for SharePoint lists and web services.

Note that instead of using an XSL transformation, you could have also used a combination of looping through all of the elements in the secondary data source (similar to the technique described in recipe *70 Loop through rows of a repeating table*), copying their values, and adding rows to the repeating table by using one of the methods described in recipe *71 Add a row to a repeating table*.

75 Sort rows of a repeating table

Problem

You have data in a repeating table and you want users to be able to sort this data.

Solution

There are several ways to sort rows of a repeating table, all of which involve first retrieving the data from the repeating table, using a method to sort the data, and then repopulating the repeating table with the sorted data. The following solution significantly reduces the amount of code you would have to write to sort rows of a repeating table by making use of `DataSet` and `DataTable` objects.

To sort rows of a repeating table:

1. In InfoPath, create a new form template or use an existing one.

2. Add a **Repeating Table** control with 2 columns to the view of the form template.

3. Add a few rows with data to the repeating table so that you can test whether the sort functionality is working properly. For example, you could populate the repeating table with titles and colors of Office applications as shown in the table in recipe *81 Create a web service that retrieves data for InfoPath*.

4. Add a **Button** or **Picture Button** control to each one of the two column headers of the repeating table.

5. Add an event handler for the **Clicked** event of the first button as described in recipe *7 Add an event handler for a control event*.

6. In VSTA, add a reference to the **System.Data** assembly.

7. Add the following **using** statements to the **FormCode.cs** file:

```
using System.Data;
using System.IO;
```

8. Add the following private method to the FormCode class (*code #: 5C00C077-A10E-4F56-AA22-D4123BBC5F92*):

```
private void SortRepeatingTable(string fieldName)
{
  XPathNavigator mainDS = MainDataSource.CreateNavigator();
  XPathNavigator group1 = mainDS.SelectSingleNode(
    "/my:myFields/my:group1", NamespaceManager);
  XmlReader reader = group1.ReadSubtree();

  DataSet ds = new DataSet();
  ds.ReadXml(reader);

  DataTable sortedTable = new DataTable();

  if (ds.Tables != null && ds.Tables.Count > 0)
  {
    DataTable dt = ds.Tables[0];
    sortedTable = dt.Copy();
    sortedTable.Clear();

    DataRow[] rows = dt.Select("", fieldName + " ASC");

    foreach (DataRow row in rows)
    {
      sortedTable.Rows.Add(row.ItemArray);
    }
  }

  ds.Tables.Clear();
  ds.Tables.Add(sortedTable);

  using (MemoryStream ms = new MemoryStream())
  {
    ds.WriteXml(ms);

    ms.Position = 0;
    XPathDocument doc = new XPathDocument(ms);
```

```
        group1.ReplaceSelf(doc.CreateNavigator());

        ms.Close();
    }
}
```

What this method does is take the name of the field on which the repeating table should be sorted, and then uses `DataSet` and `DataTable` objects to extract the data from the repeating table and sort it in an ascending order before writing it to a `MemoryStream` object that can be loaded into an `XPathDocument` object that can be used to replace the XML of the repeating table.

9. Add the following code to the event handler for the first button (*code #: 5C00C077-A10E-4F56-AA22-D4123BBC5F92*):

```
SortRepeatingTable("field1");
```

10. In InfoPath, add an event handler for the **Clicked** event of the second button as described in recipe *7 Add an event handler for a control event*.

11. In VSTA, add the following code to the event handler for the second button (*code #: 5C00C077-A10E-4F56-AA22-D4123BBC5F92*):

```
SortRepeatingTable("field2");
```

12. Save and build the project.

13. Preview the form.

When the form opens, click on the button that is located in the header of the first column of the repeating table and verify that the data has been correctly sorted. Do the same for the button that is located in the header of the second column.

Name	Color
Word	Blue
Excel	Green
Access	Red
InfoPath	Purple
PowerPoint	Dark Orange

Insert item

Figure 36. Repeating table before sorting.

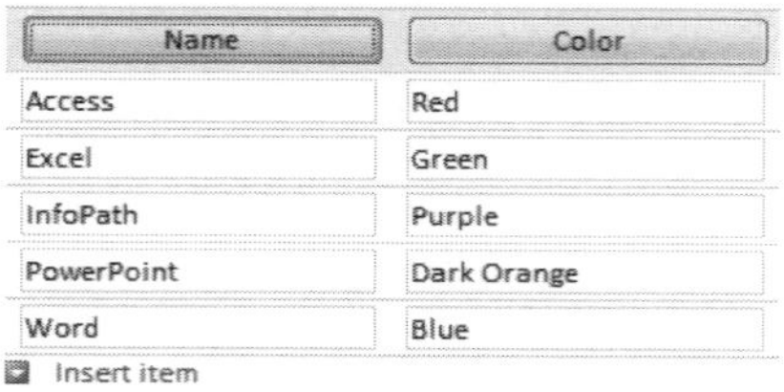

Name	Color
Access	Red
Excel	Green
InfoPath	Purple
PowerPoint	Dark Orange
Word	Blue

Insert item

Figure 37. Repeating table after sorting by the values in the first column.

Figure 38. Repeating table after sorting by the values in the second column.

Discussion

Because the solution described above uses quite a few techniques to manipulate XML from an InfoPath form, let us break down the code in the SortRepeatingTable() method and see what it does. First, the ReadSubtree() method of an XPathNavigator object that points to the **group1** group node of the repeating table is used to return an XmlReader object. The ReadSubtree() method returns an XmlReader object that contains the current node and its child nodes.

```
XPathNavigator mainDS = MainDataSource.CreateNavigator();
XPathNavigator group1 = mainDS.SelectSingleNode(
  "/my:myFields/my:group1", NamespaceManager);
XmlReader reader = group1.ReadSubtree();
```

Next, a DataSet object is created from the XmlReader object that contains the **group1** group node and its child nodes by using the ReadXml() method of a new DataSet object. The ReadXml() method reads the XML schema and data into the DataSet using the specified XmlReader object.

```
DataSet ds = new DataSet();
ds.ReadXml(reader);
```

Next, two DataTable objects are used to sort the data.

```
DataTable sortedTable = new DataTable();

if (ds.Tables != null && ds.Tables.Count > 0)
{
  DataTable dt = ds.Tables[0];
  sortedTable = dt.Copy();
  sortedTable.Clear();

  DataRow[] rows = dt.Select("", fieldName + " ASC");

  foreach (DataRow row in rows)
  {
    sortedTable.Rows.Add(row.ItemArray);
  }
}
```

The first `DataTable` object is retrieved from the `DataSet` object that was created earlier from the repeating table

```
DataTable dt = ds.Tables[0];
```

while the second `DataTable` object named **sortedTable** is created using the `Copy()` method of the first `DataTable` object.

```
sortedTable = dt.Copy();
```

Because the **sortedTable** data table is copied from the original data table that was in the data set, it not only has the same structure, but also contains the same data as the first data table. Therefore, before you populate the **sortedTable** data table you must delete all of the old rows using the `Clear()` method of the data table.

```
sortedTable.Clear();
```

The data is then sorted using the `Select()` method of the first `DataTable` object. While you can also pass a filter to the `Select()` method, the solution described above only makes use of its sort functionality.

```
DataRow[] rows = dt.Select("", fieldName + " ASC");
```

The **sortedTable** data table is then populated by looping through the array of `DataRow` objects returned by the `Select()` method. The `Add()` method of the `DataRowCollection` object of the **sortedTable** data table adds a new row to the end of the collection.

```
foreach (DataRow row in rows)
{
   sortedTable.Rows.Add(row.ItemArray);
}
```

After populating the **sortedTable** data table with the sorted data, the original data table in the data set is replaced with the **sortedTable** data table by first deleting the original data table from the data set using the `Clear()` method of the `DataTableCollection` object, and then adding the sorted data table to the data set using the `Add()` method of the `DataTableCollection` object.

```
ds.Tables.Clear();
ds.Tables.Add(sortedTable);
```

The final step is to write the sorted XML data contained in the data set back to the **group1** group node. To do this, the code first uses the `WriteXml()` method of the data set to store the XML data in a `MemoryStream` object.

```
using (MemoryStream ms = new MemoryStream())
{
  ds.WriteXml(ms);
  ...
}
```

And then the `MemoryStream` object is loaded into an `XPathDocument` object.

```
ms.Position = 0;
XPathDocument doc = new XPathDocument(ms);
```

The `CreateNavigator()` method of the `XPathDocument` object is then used to create an `XPathNavigator` object that is used with the `ReplaceSelf()` method of the `XPathNavigator` object pointing to the **group1** group node to replace its contents with the sorted XML data.

```
group1.ReplaceSelf(doc.CreateNavigator());
```

And finally, the `SortRepeatingTable()` method is called in the event handlers for the buttons used to sort the repeating table by a specific field name.

If you are creating an InfoPath Filler form you could make use of the `DisableAutoUpdate()` and `EnableAutoUpdate()` methods of the `View` object (`CurrentView` property of the `XmlForm` object) at the beginning and end of the `SortRepeatingTable()` method to prevent the view from being updated while the rows in the repeating table are being reordered.

```
private void SortRepeatingTable(string fieldName)
{
  CurrentView.DisableAutoUpdate();

  // Code to perform the sorting goes here

  CurrentView.EnableAutoUpdate();
}
```

This should enhance the user's experience by preventing any flickering of the screen while the repeating table is being repopulated and especially if the repeating table contains a large amount of rows. The `DisableAutoUpdate()` and `EnableAutoUpdate()` methods of the `View` object are not available when you create a browser-compatible form template.

76 Filter rows of a repeating table

Problem

You have data in a repeating table and you want users to be able to perform a wildcard search on the textual data stored in a particular field in the repeating table.

Solution

There are several ways to filter rows of a repeating table, all of which involve first retrieving the data from the repeating table, using a method to filter the data, and then repopulating the repeating table with the filtered data. The following solution significantly reduces the amount of code you would have to write to filter rows of a repeating table by making use of `DataSet` and `DataTable` objects.

To filter rows of a repeating table:

1. In InfoPath, create a new form template or use an existing one.

2. Add a **Text Box** control to the view of the form template and name it **textToSearchFor**.

3. Add a **Button** control to the view of the form template and label it **Filter Data**.

4. Add a **Repeating Table** control with 2 columns to the view of the form template. Name the field in the first column **field1** and the field in the second column **field2**.

5. Add a few rows with data to the repeating table so that you can test whether the filter functionality is working properly. For example, you could populate the repeating table with titles and colors of Office applications as shown in the table in recipe *81 Create a web service that retrieves data for InfoPath*.

6. Add an event handler for the **Loading** event of the form as described in recipe *6 Add an event handler for a form event*.

7. In VSTA, add a reference to the **System.Data** assembly.

8. Add the following **using** statements to the **FormCode.cs** file:

```
using System.Data;
using System.IO;
using System.Text;
```

9. Add the following private member variable to the `FormCode` class (*code #: 45AA7692-D17F-4110-8BEB-FD30B866D684*):

```
private string _group1 = string.Empty;
```

If you are designing a browser-compatible form template that will be published to SharePoint, add the following private property to the `FormCode` class instead of the private member variable (*code #: 45AA7692-D17F-4110-8BEB-FD30B866D684*):

```
private string _group1
{
  get
  {
    return FormState["_group1"].ToString();
  }
  set
  {
    FormState["_group1"] = value;
  }
```

```
}
```

Because you will be modifying the structure of the **group1** group node in the Main data source of the form when you filter, you must store the original structure of the node either in a private member variable or in the FormState dictionary as shown above, so that you can restore the repeating table to its original state when filtering is removed.

10. Add the following code to the FormEvents_Loading() event handler (*code #: 45AA7692-D17F-4110-8BEB-FD30B866D684*):

```
_group1 = MainDataSource.CreateNavigator().SelectSingleNode(
  "/my:myFields/my:group1", NamespaceManager).OuterXml;
```

11. In InfoPath, add an event handler for the **Clicked** event of the **Filter Data** button as described in recipe *7 Add an event handler for a control event*.

12. In VSTA, add the following code to the Clicked() event handler for the **Filter Data** button (*code #: 45AA7692-D17F-4110-8BEB-FD30B866D684*):

```
string group1 = _group1.ToString();
byte[] buffer = Encoding.UTF8.GetBytes(_group1);

XmlReader reader = null;
DataSet ds = new DataSet();
using (MemoryStream ms = new MemoryStream(buffer))
{
  reader = XmlReader.Create(ms);
  ds.ReadXml(reader);
  reader.Close();
  ms.Close();
}

XPathNavigator mainDS = MainDataSource.CreateNavigator();
string textToSearchFor = mainDS.SelectSingleNode(
  "/my:myFields/my:textToSearchFor", NamespaceManager).Value;

DataTable filteredTable = new DataTable();

if (ds.Tables != null && ds.Tables.Count > 0)
{
  DataTable dt = ds.Tables[0];
  filteredTable = dt.Copy();
  filteredTable.Clear();

  DataView dv = new DataView(dt);
  dv.RowFilter = "field1 LIKE '*" + textToSearchFor + "*'";

  foreach (DataRowView drv in dv)
  {
    filteredTable.Rows.Add(drv.Row.ItemArray);
  }
}

ds.Tables.Clear();
ds.Tables.Add(filteredTable);

using (MemoryStream ms = new MemoryStream())
{
```

```
    ds.WriteXml(ms);

    ms.Position = 0;
    XPathDocument doc = new XPathDocument(ms);
    mainDS.SelectSingleNode(
      "/my:myFields/my:group1",
      NamespaceManager).ReplaceSelf(doc.CreateNavigator());

    ms.Close();
  }
```

where **textToSearchFor** is the field used for searching and filtering the repeating table on the value of the **textToSearchFor** field matching the value of any **field1** field in the repeating table.

13. Save and build the project.

14. Publish the form template to a SharePoint form library or preview the form.

When the form opens, enter a piece of text that is contained in one of the **field1** fields in the repeating table and then click the **Filter Data** button. All of the rows that contain the piece of text you entered should be displayed in the repeating table. Clear the text box and click the button again. The repeating table should now be in its original state displaying all of its rows.

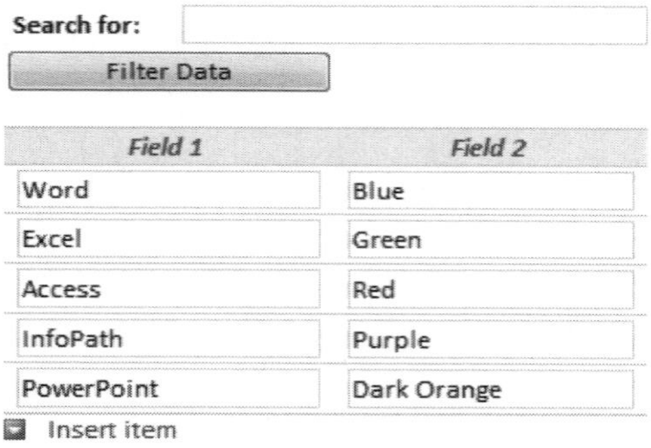

Search for: [   ]

[**Filter Data**]

Field 1	Field 2
Word	Blue
Excel	Green
Access	Red
InfoPath	Purple
PowerPoint	Dark Orange

☑ Insert item

Figure 39. Repeating table before filtering.

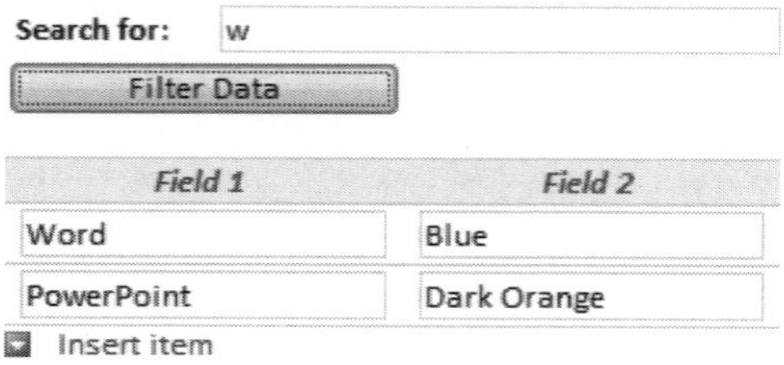

Search for: [w   ]

[**Filter Data**]

Field 1	Field 2
Word	Blue
PowerPoint	Dark Orange

☑ Insert item

Figure 40. Repeating table after filtering on 'w'.

Discussion

The solution described above made use of a DataView object to filter data contained in a repeating table. The RowFilter property of the DataView object was used to set the expression used to filter the rows. Note that the DataView object also has a Sort property, which you could use to sort rows of the repeating table instead of the method described in recipe *75 Sort rows of a repeating table*.

The code in the solution described above first retrieves the XML structure of the **group1** group node of the repeating table and stores it in a _group1 property or member variable when the form opens.

```
_group1 = MainDataSource.CreateNavigator().SelectSingleNode(
  "/my:myFields/my:group1", NamespaceManager).OuterXml;
```

This is done to be able to restore the data in the repeating table to its original state when filtering is removed. Next, in the event handler for the button, the original XML for the **group1** group node is loaded into a DataSet object using a MemoryStream object and an XmlReader object.

```
string group1 = _group1.ToString();
byte[] buffer = Encoding.UTF8.GetBytes(_group1);

XmlReader reader = null;
DataSet ds = new DataSet();
using (MemoryStream ms = new MemoryStream(buffer))
{
  reader = XmlReader.Create(ms);
  ds.ReadXml(reader);
  reader.Close();
  ms.Close();
}
```

Next, the value of the **textToSearchFor** field is retrieved.

```
XPathNavigator mainDS = MainDataSource.CreateNavigator();
string textToSearchFor = mainDS.SelectSingleNode(
  "/my:myFields/my:textToSearchFor", NamespaceManager).Value;
```

Then the repeating table data is filtered using the RowFilter property of a DataView object, and a new DataTable object named **filteredTable** is populated with the filtered rows of data by looping through the DataRowView objects contained in the filtered DataView object.

```
DataTable filteredTable = new DataTable();

if (ds.Tables != null && ds.Tables.Count > 0)
{
  DataTable dt = ds.Tables[0];
  filteredTable = dt.Copy();
  filteredTable.Clear();
```

```
DataView dv = new DataView(dt);
dv.RowFilter = "field1 LIKE '*" + textToSearchFor + "*'";

foreach (DataRowView drv in dv)
{
  filteredTable.Rows.Add(drv.Row.ItemArray);
}
}
```

Note that the **filteredTable** data table is created from the original data table in the data set using the `Copy()` method of the data table in the data set, and then all of the rows of the **filteredTable** data table are deleted using the `Clear()` method of the data table. The filter expression for the `RowFilter` property of the `DataView` object follows the same rules as those for the `Expression` property of a `DataColumn` object, for which you can find documentation on the MSDN web site.

```
dv.RowFilter = "field1 LIKE '*" + textToSearchFor + "*'";
```

And finally, the **group1** group node is replaced and the repeating table populated with the filtered rows by using `MemoryStream` and `XPathDocument` objects combined with the `ReplaceSelf()` method of the `XPathNavigator` object pointing to the **group1** group node as was also done in recipe *75 Sort rows of a repeating table*.

```
ds.Tables.Clear();
ds.Tables.Add(filteredTable);

using (MemoryStream ms = new MemoryStream())
{
  ds.WriteXml(ms);

  ms.Position = 0;
  XPathDocument doc = new XPathDocument(ms);
  mainDS.SelectSingleNode(
    "/my:myFields/my:group1",
    NamespaceManager).ReplaceSelf(doc.CreateNavigator());

  ms.Close();
}
```

Chapter 6: Working with InfoPath Form Data

InfoPath forms contain XML data that can be accessed either internally or externally. This chapter introduces you to a few techniques you can use to access data stored in an InfoPath form either from inside or outside of InfoPath, so that you can for example convert this data into another format or create new InfoPath forms based on an existing form.

77 Sequentially traverse all fields of a form

Use LINQ to XML

Problem

You want to sequentially traverse all of the elements in an InfoPath form.

Solution

You can use LINQ to XML to traverse the XML elements of an InfoPath form.

To sequentially traverse all of the fields of an InfoPath form using LINQ to XML:

1. In InfoPath, create a new form template or use an existing one.

2. Add a couple of controls to the view of the form template.

3. Add an event to the form or a control on the form as described in recipe *6 Add an event handler for a form event* or recipe *7 Add an event handler for a control event*. You will use the event handler for this event to write the code that sequentially traverses the elements in the form.

4. In VSTA, add a reference to the **System.Xml.Linq** assembly.

5. Add the following **using** statements to the **FormCode.cs** file:

```
using System.Xml.Linq;
using System.Collections.Generic;
```

6. Add the following code to the control or form event handler you added earlier (*code #: 9077C8F5-542B-4BE1-804B-461C1331EBF4*):

```
XDocument root =
  XDocument.Parse(MainDataSource.CreateNavigator().OuterXml);
IEnumerable<XElement> elements = root.Descendants();

foreach (XElement element in elements)
{
  string localName = element.Name.LocalName;
  string elementValue = element.Value;
  string ns = element.Name.NamespaceName;
```

```
        string nsprefix = element.GetPrefixOfNamespace(ns);
        bool isGroup = element.HasElements;
        if (element.Parent != null)
        {
          string parent = element.Parent.Name.LocalName;
        }
      }
    }
```

7. Save and build the project.

8. Set a breakpoint and then press **F5** to debug the code.

When the code breaks in VSTA, step through the code and verify that the code is sequentially going through all of the fields and groups of the form.

Discussion

The first step to use LINQ to traverse all elements in an InfoPath form is to use the `Parse` method of the `XDocument` class to create an `XDocument` object from the XML stored in the Main data source of the form.

```
XDocument root = XDocument.Parse(MainDataSource.CreateNavigator().OuterXml);
```

Once you have an `XDocument` object, you can get all of the child elements of the document by using the `Descendants()` method. This method returns a filtered collection of `XElement` objects.

```
IEnumerable<XElement> elements = root.Descendants();
```

Then you can loop through all of the elements in a `foreach`-loop and retrieve the local name, namespace, namespace prefix, value, parent, etc. of each element in the collection.

```
foreach (XElement element in elements)
{
  string localName = element.Name.LocalName;
  string elementValue = element.Value;
  ...
}
```

Note that for repeating structures such as repeating tables and sections, the elements of each row are traversed sequentially and that you can use the `HasElements` property of an element to check whether a node is a group node.

Use a DataSet to convert an InfoPath form to plain text

Problem

You have various fields on an InfoPath form and would like to loop through and display all of these fields and their values in a text box on the form itself.

Solution

You can use a `DataSet` object to extract the data from the Main data source of a form as tables, and then write a recursive function to extract the structure and field values from the tables.

To sequentially traverse all of the fields of an InfoPath form and display the structure of the InfoPath form and its field values as text:

1. In InfoPath, create a new form template or use an existing one.

2. Add a **Text Box** control to the view of the form template, name it **formAsText**, and select its **Multi-line** property.

3. Add any other controls to the view of the form template and populate the fields with default values.

4. Add an event handler for the **Loading** event of the form as described in recipe *6 Add an event handler for a form event*.

5. In VSTA, add a reference to the **System.Data** assembly.

6. Add the following **using** statements to the **FormCode.cs** file:

```
using System.Data;
using System.IO;
using System.Text;
using System.Collections.Generic;
```

7. Add the following private method to the `FormCode` class (*code #: B0CBBD91-E1BF-4286-9F2B-95759D24353A*):

```
private void AddTableData(
  DataSet ds, DataTable dt, int recurLevel, ref StringBuilder sb)
{
  recurLevel++;

  string tableName = dt.TableName;
  for (int i = 1; i < recurLevel; i++)
  {
    sb.Append("\t");
  }
  sb.AppendLine("* " + tableName);

  foreach (DataColumn dc in dt.Columns)
  {
    string columnName = dc.ColumnName;

    if (dc.ColumnMapping == MappingType.Hidden)
      continue;

    for (int i = 0; i < recurLevel; i++)
    {
      sb.Append("\t");
    }
    sb.Append("- " + columnName);

    int j = 0;
```

```
      sb.Append(" [");
      foreach (DataRow row in dt.Rows)
      {
        if (j > 0)
          sb.Append(", ");

        sb.Append(row[columnName].ToString());

        j++;
      }
      sb.Append("]");
      sb.AppendLine();
  }

  List<DataTable> childTables = new List<DataTable>();
  foreach (DataRelation dr in ds.Relations)
  {
    if (dr.ParentTable.TableName == tableName)
    {
      childTables.Add(dr.ChildTable);
    }
  }

  foreach (DataTable childTable in childTables)
  {
    AddTableData(ds, childTable, recurLevel, ref sb);
  }
}
```

8. Add the following code to the `FormEvents_Loading()` event handler (*code #: B0CBBD91-E1BF-4286-9F2B-95759D24353A*):

```
XPathNavigator mainDS = MainDataSource.CreateNavigator();
XmlReader reader = mainDS.ReadSubtree();

DataSet ds = new DataSet();
ds.ReadXml(reader);

StringBuilder sb = new StringBuilder();

if (ds != null && ds.Tables != null && ds.Tables.Count > 0)
  AddTableData(ds, ds.Tables[0], 0, ref sb);

mainDS.SelectSingleNode("/my:myFields/my:formAsText",
  NamespaceManager).SetValue(sb.ToString());
```

9. Save and build the project.

10. Preview the form.

When the form opens, the structure of the form along with its values (displayed between square brackets behind the field names) should be displayed in the **formAsText** text box as shown in the figure below.

```
* myFields
    - textField [This is a sentence]
    - formAsText []
    - dateAndTimeField [2011-10-10T16:44:18]
    - lang [en-us]
    * group1
        * repeatingTable
            - field2 [1, 2, 3]
            - field3 [Apple, Pear, Kiwi]
            - field4 [Red, Green, Brown]
    * group3
        * repeatingSection
            * group5
                * repeatingTableInRepeatingSection
                    - field9 [Section 1 Row 1, Section 1 Row 2, Section 2 Row 1, Section 2 Row 2]
```

Figure 41. InfoPath form data and structure displayed as plain text.

Discussion

When you store the XML of an InfoPath form in a `DataSet` object, each group node becomes a table in the data set, and fields (elements as well as attributes) become table columns.

The solution described above uses the `ReadXml()` method of a `DataSet` object and an `XmlReader` object for the Main data source of the form to convert the form into a `DataSet` object.

```
XPathNavigator mainDS = MainDataSource.CreateNavigator();
XmlReader reader = mainDS.ReadSubtree();

DataSet ds = new DataSet();
ds.ReadXml(reader);
```

Because a group node may contain one or more group nodes, which may in turn also contain one or more group nodes, and so forth, you must use a recursive function to find all group nodes and their respective child group nodes. So a recursive function named `AddTableData()` is called to recursively retrieve all of the tables in the data set and build a `StringBuilder` object.

```
StringBuilder sb = new StringBuilder();

if (ds != null && ds.Tables != null && ds.Tables.Count > 0)
    AddTableData(ds, ds.Tables[0], 0, ref sb);
```

The recursion starts with the table that represents the root node of the InfoPath form (the **myFields** group node). The relationships between the group nodes (tables) are defined and stored in a `DataRelationCollection` object of the data set. You can use this collection to retrieve the child group nodes (tables) of a particular group node (table).

```
List<DataTable> childTables = new List<DataTable>();
foreach (DataRelation dr in ds.Relations)
```

```
{
  if (dr.ParentTable.TableName == tableName)
  {
    childTables.Add(dr.ChildTable);
  }
}
```

Once you have retrieved the child group nodes of a particular group node, you must loop through all of the child group nodes and call the `AddTableData()` recursive function within itself to continue finding and listing the child group nodes of the child group nodes.

```
foreach (DataTable childTable in childTables)
{
  AddTableData(ds, childTable, recurLevel, ref sb);
}
```

And finally, once the code has traversed all of the tables in the data set, the result is written to the **formAsText** field.

```
mainDS.SelectSingleNode("/my:myFields/my:formAsText",
  NamespaceManager).SetValue(sb.ToString());
```

Note that when a table is created in the data set, it is automatically assigned a primary key, which is a hidden column (the `ColumnMapping` property of the `DataColumn` object has a value equal to `MappingType.Hidden`). These columns are excluded from the conversion performed in the solution described above by skipping them when looping through the columns of a table in the `AddTableData()` recursive function.

```
if (dc.ColumnMapping == MappingType.Hidden)
  continue;
```

78 3 Ways to open and read an InfoPath form in memory

Use an XPathDocument object

Problem

You have the `byte` array for an InfoPath form and would like to open this `byte` array in memory and read its contents.

Solution

You can use a `MemoryStream` object and an `XPathDocument` object to open and read an InfoPath form in memory.

To open and read an InfoPath form in memory using an `XPathDocument` object:

1. In InfoPath, create a new form template or use an existing one, and then fill out a form that is based on this form template (if you want to use a sample InfoPath form, you can download and use a file named **LoadMeInMemory.xml** from www.bizsupportonline.com.). This solution makes use of a console application that loads an InfoPath form from disk and stores it in a `MemoryStream` object. However, this solution is not limited to loading a form through code in a console application; you can retrieve a form from anywhere, including a SharePoint document library (see for example recipe *94 Select and add files from a document library as attachments to a form* for how to retrieve files from SharePoint), a SharePoint event receiver (see for example recipe *99 Auto-number InfoPath forms in a form library*), or a SharePoint workflow or workflow activity (see for example recipe *100 Use an InfoPath form to send an email with attachments*). The basic idea is that you should be getting the `byte` array for the form from somewhere and using it to create a `MemoryStream` object.

2. In Visual Studio 2010, select **File ➤ New ➤ Project**.

3. On the **New Project** dialog box, select **Windows** under **Visual C#** from the list of **Installed Templates**, select **.NET Framework 3.5** from the drop-down list box, select **Console Application**, enter a name for the project (for example **GetInfoPathFormConsoleApp**), select a location where to save the solution, enter a name for the solution, and click **OK**.

4. Add the following **using** statements to the **Program.cs** file:

```
using System.IO;
using System.Xml;
using System.Xml.XPath;
```

5. Add the following code to the `Main()` method of the `Program` class (*code #: B092FDB5-BDEF-467D-8CD5-A847D0E17165*):

```
byte[] bytes = File.ReadAllBytes(@"C:\Projects\InfoPath\form.xml");

XPathDocument doc = null;

using (MemoryStream ms = new MemoryStream(bytes))
{
  doc = new XPathDocument(ms);
  ms.Close();
}

if (doc != null)
{
  XPathNavigator root = doc.CreateNavigator();
  root.MoveToFollowing(XPathNodeType.Element);

  string ns = root.GetNamespace("tc");
  XmlNamespaceManager nsMgr = new XmlNamespaceManager(new NameTable());
  nsMgr.AddNamespace("tc", ns);

  string weekOf = root.SelectSingleNode(
    "/tc:timeCard/tc:week/tc:weekOf", nsMgr).Value;
}
```

Note that you should change the path to the InfoPath form
(`C:\Projects\InfoPath\form.xml`), namespace prefix (**tc**), and XPath expression
to suit your own scenario and the form you are using.

6. Save and build the solution.

7. Place breakpoints throughout the code, and then press **F5** to run and debug the
application.

When the code breaks in Visual Studio 2010, step through the code and verify that the
values of the form fields are being retrieved correctly.

Discussion

An `XPathDocument` object provides a fast, read-only, in-memory representation of an
XML document by using the XPath data model.

The code in the solution above first loads an InfoPath form from disk into a `byte` array
by using the `ReadAllBytes()` method of the `File` class.

```
byte[] bytes = File.ReadAllBytes(@"C:\Projects\InfoPath\form.xml");
```

The `byte` array is then used to create a `MemoryStream` object, which is then subsequently
used to instantiate an `XPathDocument` object.

```
XPathDocument doc = null;

using (MemoryStream ms = new MemoryStream(bytes))
{
  doc = new XPathDocument(ms);
  ms.Close();
}
```

Note that because an `XPathDocument` object is read-only, you can only use it to retrieve
data from an InfoPath form. If you wanted to change data in the InfoPath form and then
save those changes, you would have to make use of an `XmlDocument` object instead. The
code for loading an InfoPath form into an `XmlDocument` object is very similar to that for
an `XPathDocument` object.

```
XmlDocument doc = null;

using (MemoryStream ms = new MemoryStream(bytes))
{
  doc = new XmlDocument();
  doc.Load(ms);
  ms.Close();
}
```

After changing data in the `XmlDocument` object, you can use its `Save()` method to save
the changes to a stream, a file, a `TextWriter` object, or an `XmlWriter` object.

The code in the solution above goes on to create an XPathNavigator object pointing to the root node of the InfoPath form.

```
XPathNavigator root = doc.CreateNavigator();
root.MoveToFollowing(XPathNodeType.Element);
```

It then retrieves one of the namespaces used in the InfoPath form and adds it to an XmlNamespaceManager object

```
string ns = root.GetNamespace("tc");
XmlNamespaceManager nsMgr = new XmlNamespaceManager(new NameTable());
nsMgr.AddNamespace("tc", ns);
```

to be able to retrieve the value of a particular field in the form.

```
string weekOf = root.SelectSingleNode(
  "/tc:timeCard/tc:week/tc:weekOf", nsMgr).Value;
```

Note that the way the MemoryStream object is initialized

```
using (MemoryStream ms = new MemoryStream(bytes))
{
  ...
}
```

makes the memory stream non-expandable, which means that if you create an XmlDocument object instead of an XPathDocument object, write to the XmlDocument object, and then try to save it to the same MemoryStream object, you will get the following error:

Memory stream is not expandable.

To be able to save the changes back to the same memory stream, you would have to initialize the MemoryStream object as follows:

```
using (MemoryStream ms = new MemoryStream())
{
  ms.Write(bytes, 0, (int)bytes.Length);
  ms.Position = 0;

  ...
}
```

or save the changes back to a new MemoryStream object (also see *Copy an existing blank InfoPath form and fill it out* in recipe *79 Programmatically create an InfoPath form*).

Use XML deserialization

Problem

You have the `byte` array for an InfoPath form and would like to open this `byte` array in memory and read its contents.

Solution

You can create a class that is based on the XML schema of an InfoPath form and then use XML deserialization to open and read the InfoPath form in memory.

To open and read an InfoPath form in memory using XML deserialization:

1. In InfoPath, create a new form template or use an existing one, and then fill out a form that is based on this form template. If you want to use a sample InfoPath form, you can download and use the files named **LoadMeInMemory.xml** and **LoadMeInMemory.xsd** from www.bizsupportonline.com.

2. Save the form template locally on disk and close InfoPath Designer 2010.

3. Open Windows Explorer and navigate to the location where you saved the form template.

4. Change the file extension of the form template from XSN to CAB.

5. Double-click the cabinet file to open it and view its contents.

6. Right-click the **schema.xsd** file, select **Copy** from the context menu that appears, and paste the file elsewhere locally on disk.

7. Change the file extension of the form template from CAB back to XSN. While you could have used **File ➤ Publish ➤ Export Source Files** from within InfoPath Designer 2010 to extract the form files and then repackage them again as described in recipe *5 Associate a form template with an existing C# project*, the method described in the previous steps is a quick-and-dirty way of getting a file out of the form template.

8. Open the **Visual Studio Command Prompt (2010)**, which is by default located under the **Microsoft Visual Studio 2010 ➤ Visual Studio Tools** program folder.

9. In the **Visual Studio Command Prompt (2010)** window, enter a command to generate a class file from the XSD file, for example:

```
xsd "C:\Projects\InfoPath\schema.xsd" /c /l:cs /o:C:\Temp\
```

This should generate a C# class file named **schema.cs** and place it in the `C:\Temp` folder. This class should allow you to access values of form fields through collections and properties specified on the class. Note: You must change the path to the .xsd file

(C:\Projects\InfoPath\schema.xsd) to the appropriate path for your own scenario.

10. In Visual Studio 2010, select **File ➤ New ➤ Project**.

11. On the **New Project** dialog box, select **Windows** under **Visual C#** from the list of **Installed Templates**, select **.NET Framework 3.5** from the drop-down list box, select **Console Application**, enter a name for the project (for example **GetInfoPathFormConsoleApp**), select a location where to save the solution, enter a name for the solution, and click **OK**.

12. On the **Solution Explorer** pane, add the **schema.cs** file you generated earlier to the project.

13. Add the following **using** statements to the **Program.cs** file:

```
using System.IO;
using System.Xml;
using System.Xml.XPath;
using System.Xml.Serialization;
```

14. Add the following code to the Main() method of the Program class (*code #: 261EB940-EA33-4D09-81E3-C657ED317E25*):

```
byte[] bytes = File.ReadAllBytes(@"C:\Projects\InfoPath\form.xml");

XPathDocument doc = null;

using (MemoryStream ms = new MemoryStream(bytes))
{
  doc = new XPathDocument(ms);
  ms.Close();
}

if (doc != null)
{
  XPathNavigator root = doc.CreateNavigator();

  using (XmlReader reader = root.ReadSubtree())
  {
    reader.MoveToContent();

    XmlSerializer xs = new XmlSerializer(typeof(timeCard));
    timeCard tc = (timeCard)xs.Deserialize(reader);

    DateTime? weekOf = tc.week.weekOf.Value;

    reader.Close();
  }
}
```

timeCard in the code above refers to the name of the class that was generated using the XSD tool. This name will differ in your case and should be the same as the name of the root node in the Main data source of your form (**myFields** by default). Note that you should change the path to the InfoPath form

227

(`C:\Projects\InfoPath\form.xml`) to suit your own scenario and the form you are using.

15. Save and build the solution.

16. Place breakpoints throughout the code, and then press **F5** to run and debug the application.

When the code breaks in Visual Studio 2010, step through the code and verify that the values of the form fields are being retrieved correctly.

Discussion

In the solution described above, you learned how you can generate a class file for an InfoPath form based on its XML schema definition (XSD), and then use this class to deserialize the InfoPath form into an object to be able read data from the form as values of properties of the deserialized object.

The code in the solution above first loads an InfoPath form from disk into a `byte` array by using the `ReadAllBytes()` method of the `File` class.

```
byte[] bytes = File.ReadAllBytes(@"C:\Projects\InfoPath\form.xml");
```

The `byte` array is then used to create a `MemoryStream` object, which is then subsequently used to instantiate an `XPathDocument` object.

```
XPathDocument doc = null;
using (MemoryStream ms = new MemoryStream(bytes))
{
  doc = new XPathDocument(ms);
  ms.Close();
}
```

The code then proceeds to create an `XmlReader` object for the `XPathDocument` object

```
XPathNavigator root = doc.CreateNavigator();
using (XmlReader reader = root.ReadSubtree())
{
  ...
}
```

before using an `XmlSerializer` object and its `Deserialize()` method to deserialize the XML of the InfoPath form into an object.

```
reader.MoveToContent();

XmlSerializer xs = new XmlSerializer(typeof(timeCard));
timeCard tc = (timeCard)xs.Deserialize(reader);
```

And finally, the value of a property of the object (so of a field in the InfoPath form) is retrieved.

```
DateTime? weekOf = tc.week.weekOf.Value;
```

Note that when the XML data of an InfoPath form is deserialized, it loses its XML declaration and XML processing instructions. So if you want to regenerate the InfoPath form later through serialization, you must store the XML processing instructions somewhere, so that they can be retrieved and used at a later stage to reconstruct the InfoPath form (also see *Serialize an object to create an InfoPath form* in recipe *79 Programmatically create an InfoPath form*).

Use LINQ to XML

Problem

You have the `byte` array for an InfoPath form and would like to open this `byte` array in memory and read its contents.

Solution

You can use a `MemoryStream` object with LINQ to XML to open and read an InfoPath form in memory.

To open and read an InfoPath form in memory using LINQ to XML:

1. In InfoPath, create a new form template or use an existing one, and then fill out a form that is based on this form template. If you want to use a sample InfoPath form, you can download and use a file named **LoadMeInMemory.xml** from www.bizsupportonline.com.

2. In Visual Studio 2010, select **File ➤ New ➤ Project**.

3. On the **New Project** dialog box, select **Windows** under **Visual C#** from the list of **Installed Templates**, select **.NET Framework 3.5** from the drop-down list box, select **Console Application**, enter a name for the project (for example **GetInfoPathFormConsoleApp**), select a location where to save the solution, enter a name for the solution, and click **OK**.

4. Add the following **using** statements to the **Program.cs** file:

    ```
    using System.IO;
    using System.Xml;
    using System.Xml.XPath;
    using System.Xml.Linq;
    ```

5. Add the following code to the `Main()` method of the `Program` class (*code #: E2D27E30-3CC2-4862-9284-A79BC08A3B45*):

    ```
    byte[] bytes = File.ReadAllBytes(@"C:\Projects\InfoPath\form.xml");
    ```

```
XPathDocument doc = null;

using (MemoryStream ms = new MemoryStream(bytes))
{
  doc = new XPathDocument(ms);
  ms.Close();
}

if (doc != null)
{
  XPathNavigator root = doc.CreateNavigator();
  root.MoveToFollowing(XPathNodeType.Element);
  string ns = root.GetNamespace("tc");

  XNamespace tc = XNamespace.Get(ns);

  XDocument xdoc =
    XDocument.Load(doc.CreateNavigator().ReadSubtree());

  IEnumerable<string> weeks = from e in xdoc.Descendants(tc + "week")
    where e.Element(tc + "weekOf").Value == "2011-11-11"
    select e.Element(tc + "totalHours").Value;

  foreach (var th in weeks)
  {
    string totalHours = th;
  }
}
```

Note that you should change the path to the InfoPath form
(`C:\Projects\InfoPath\form.xml`), namespace prefix (**tc**), and LINQ expressions
to suit your own scenario and the form you are using.

6. Save and build the solution.

7. Place breakpoints throughout the code, and then press **F5** to run and debug the
application.

When the code breaks in Visual Studio 2010, step through the code and verify that the
values of the form fields are being retrieved correctly.

Discussion

In the solution described above you learned how to load an InfoPath form into a
MemoryStream object and then use classes from the System.Xml, System.Xml.XPath,
and System.Xml.Linq namespaces to access data stored within the form.

The code in the solution above first loads an InfoPath form from disk into a byte array
by using the ReadAllBytes() method of the File class.

```
byte[] bytes = File.ReadAllBytes(@"C:\Projects\InfoPath\form.xml");
```

The byte array is then used to create a MemoryStream object, which is then subsequently
used to instantiate an XPathDocument object.

```
XPathDocument doc = null;

using (MemoryStream ms = new MemoryStream(bytes))
{
  doc = new XPathDocument(ms);
  ms.Close();
}
```

The code then proceeds to retrieve the namespace URI for a specific namespace prefix defined in the form

```
XPathNavigator root = doc.CreateNavigator();
root.MoveToFollowing(XPathNodeType.Element);
string ns = root.GetNamespace("tc");
```

to be able to create an XNamespace object

```
XNamespace tc = XNamespace.Get(ns);
```

that can be used later in the LINQ expression. While there are several ways to instantiate an XDocument object, the code uses the XmlReader object returned by the ReadSubtree() method of the XPathNavigator object for the InfoPath form

```
XDocument xdoc = XDocument.Load(doc.CreateNavigator().ReadSubtree());
```

to create an XDocument object, which can then be used with a LINQ expression to retrieve data from the InfoPath form.

```
IEnumerable<string> weeks = from e in xdoc.Descendants(tc + "week")
  where e.Element(tc + "weekOf").Value == "2011-11-11"
  select e.Element(tc + "totalHours").Value;

foreach (var th in weeks)
{
  string totalHours = th;
}
```

Note that you could have also used lambda expressions in the LINQ to XML code to retrieve data from the InfoPath form.

```
IEnumerable<string> weeks = xdoc.Descendants(tc + "week")
  .Where(e => e.Element(tc + "weekOf").Value == "2011-11-11")
  .Select(e => e.Element(tc + "totalHours").Value);

foreach (var th in weeks)
{
  string totalHours = th;
}
```

79 Programmatically create an InfoPath form

There are several ways to create an InfoPath form from scratch, but in the end, all methods should create an XML file that consists of three main parts:

1. An XML declaration.

2. An mso-infoPathSolution processing instruction and an mso-application processing instruction.

3. An XML fragment representing the contents of the InfoPath form.

While you can use an XmlDocument object to construct an InfoPath form from scratch, you must always first create an InfoPath form template that can be referenced in the mso-infoPathSolution processing instruction of the XML document.

The easiest way to know which values should be assigned to the XML processing instructions is to create a blank InfoPath form that is based on the form template you designed and published, open the blank form in Notepad, and then look at the XML processing instructions at the top of the document.

Once you know these values and have the XML contents of the file, you can instantiate an XmlDocument object and add an XML declaration to it.

```
XmlDocument newDoc = new XmlDocument();
XmlDeclaration dec = newDoc.CreateXmlDeclaration("1.0", "UTF-8", null);
newDoc.AppendChild(dec);
```

Then you must create and add the XML processing instructions using the CreateProcessingInstruction() method of the XmlDocument object.

```
XmlProcessingInstruction pi = newDoc.CreateProcessingInstruction(
  "mso-infoPathSolution", "href=\"C:\\Projects\\InfoPath\\Time Card
2010.xsn\" PIVersion=\"1.0.0.0\" name=\"urn:schemas-microsoft-
com:office:infopath:Time-Card-2010:-sample-TimeCard\"
solutionVersion=\"1.0.0.58\" productVersion=\"14.0.0\"");
newDoc.AppendChild(pi);

pi = newDoc.CreateProcessingInstruction("mso-application",
  "progid=\"InfoPath.Document\" versionProgid=\"InfoPath.Document.3\"");
newDoc.AppendChild(pi);
```

And finally, you can use an XmlDocumentFragment object to load the XML contents of the InfoPath form and add it to the XmlDocument object.

```
XmlDocumentFragment frag = newDoc.CreateDocumentFragment();
frag.InnerXml = timeCardRoot.OuterXml;
newDoc.AppendChild(frag);
```

The last step would be to use the Save() method of the XmlDocument object to save the newly created InfoPath form to a stream, file, TextWriter object, or XmlWriter object.

The following two solutions show two different ways for creating an InfoPath form through code.

Copy an existing blank InfoPath form and fill it out

Problem

You want to create a new InfoPath form through code.

Solution

You can create an InfoPath form template, create a blank form based on this form template, and then use the blank form as the basis to create and fill out a new InfoPath form.

To create an InfoPath form by copying an existing blank form and filling it out:

1. Follow the instructions from step 1 through 4 of *Use an XPathDocument object* in recipe *78 3 Ways to open and read an InfoPath form in memory*. In addition, create a blank InfoPath form that is based on the form template you created; you do not have to prefill it with data if you do not want to.

    The **LoadMeInMemory.xml** file used in recipe *78 3 Ways to open and read an InfoPath form in memory* is linked to a form template named **Time Card 2010.xsn**, which you can also download from www.bizsupportonline.com.

    To use the downloaded form template:

    a. In Windows Explorer, navigate to the location where you saved the form template (.xsn).

    b. Right-click the form template (.xsn), and select **Design** from the context menu that appears. This should open the form template in InfoPath Designer 2010.

    c. In InfoPath, click **Save** and save the form template to a location on disk.

    You should now be able to double-click the form template to open InfoPath Filler 2010 and save an InfoPath form as a blank form.

2. Add the following code to the `Main()` method of the `Program` class (*code #: 50327D80-D162-470B-97CA-0C861FE9CE4B*):

```
byte[] bytes = File.ReadAllBytes(@"C:\Projects\InfoPath\blankForm.xml");

XmlDocument doc = null;

using (MemoryStream ms = new MemoryStream())
{
  ms.Write(bytes, 0, (int)bytes.Length);
  ms.Position = 0;

  doc = new XmlDocument();
```

```
    doc.Load(ms);

    if (doc != null)
    {
      XPathNavigator root = doc.CreateNavigator();
      root.MoveToFollowing(XPathNodeType.Element);

      string ns = root.GetNamespace("tc");
      XmlNamespaceManager nsMgr = new XmlNamespaceManager(new NameTable());
      nsMgr.AddNamespace("tc", ns);

      root.SelectSingleNode(
        "/tc:timeCard/tc:week/tc:weekOf", nsMgr).SetValue("2011-11-11");

      ms.Position = 0;
      doc.Save(ms);

      File.WriteAllBytes(@"C:\Projects\InfoPath\newForm.xml", ms.ToArray());
    }

    ms.Close();
}
```

Note that you should change the path to the blank InfoPath form
(`C:\Projects\InfoPath\blankForm.xml`), the path to the new InfoPath form
(`C:\Projects\InfoPath\newForm.xml`), the namespace prefix (**tc**), and the XPath
expressions to suit your own scenario and the form you are using.

3.   Save and build the solution.

4.   Press **F5** to run the application.

Once the application has run, verify that a new InfoPath form named **newForm.xml** has
been created on disk.

Discussion

The solution described above combines opening an existing blank InfoPath form as
described in recipe *78 3 Ways to open and read an InfoPath form in memory* with creating an
`XmlDocument` object that can be used to change values of fields in the InfoPath form.

The code in the solution above first loads an existing blank InfoPath form from disk into
a `byte` array by using the `ReadAllBytes()` method of the `File` class.

```
byte[] bytes = File.ReadAllBytes(@"C:\Projects\InfoPath\blankForm.xml");
```

The `byte` array is then used to create a `MemoryStream` object, which is then subsequently
used to instantiate an `XmlDocument` object.

```
XmlDocument doc = null;

using (MemoryStream ms = new MemoryStream())
{
  ms.Write(bytes, 0, (int)bytes.Length);
  ms.Position = 0;
```

```
doc = new XmlDocument();
doc.Load(ms);
...
}
```

The code then proceeds to create an `XPathNavigator` object and moves it to point to the root node of the document.

```
XPathNavigator root = doc.CreateNavigator();
root.MoveToFollowing(XPathNodeType.Element);
```

Then it retrieves the namespace URI for a specific namespace prefix defined in the form

```
string ns = root.GetNamespace("tc");
XmlNamespaceManager nsMgr = new XmlNamespaceManager(new NameTable());
nsMgr.AddNamespace("tc", ns);
```

and sets the value of a field.

```
root.SelectSingleNode(
  "/tc:timeCard/tc:week/tc:weekOf", nsMgr).SetValue("2011-11-11");
```

You can use this method to set the value of other fields in the form. Finally, the stream is rewound, so that the changed `XmlDocument` object can be written to the stream using the `Save()` method of the `XmlDocument` object.

```
ms.Position = 0;
doc.Save(ms);
```

The changed InfoPath form in the `MemoryStream` object is then written to disk using the `ToArray()` method of the `MemoryStream` object and the `WriteAllBytes()` method of the `File` class.

```
File.WriteAllBytes(@"C:\Projects\InfoPath\newForm.xml", ms.ToArray());
```

Serialize an object to create an InfoPath form

Problem

You want to create a new InfoPath form through code.

Solution

You can use XML serialization and an `XmlDocument` object to construct a new InfoPath form from an object that was deserialized based on an existing InfoPath form.

InfoPath 2010 Cookbook 3

To create an InfoPath form using XML serialization:

1. Follow the instructions from step 1 through 13 of *Use XML deserialization* in recipe *78 3 Ways to open and read an InfoPath form in memory*.

2. Add the following code to the `Main()` method of the `Program` class (*code #: 7BFAE8FA-A3D2-4D2C-AD8F-88491083231C*):

```
byte[] bytes = File.ReadAllBytes(@"C:\Projects\InfoPath\form.xml");

XPathDocument doc = null;

using (MemoryStream ms = new MemoryStream(bytes))
{
  doc = new XPathDocument(ms);
  ms.Close();
}

if (doc != null)
{
  XPathNavigator root = doc.CreateNavigator();

  Dictionary<string, string> pis = new Dictionary<string, string>();
  while (root.MoveToFollowing(XPathNodeType.ProcessingInstruction))
  {
    pis.Add(root.Name, root.Value);
  }
  root.MoveToRoot();


  using (XmlReader reader = root.ReadSubtree())
  {
    reader.MoveToContent();

    XmlSerializer xs = new XmlSerializer(typeof(timeCard));
    timeCard tc = (timeCard)xs.Deserialize(reader);

    DateTime? weekOf = tc.week.weekOf.Value;
    tc.week.weekOf = DateTime.Now;

    using (MemoryStream oms = new MemoryStream())
    {
      xs.Serialize(oms, tc);
      oms.Position = 0;

      XmlDocument changedDoc = new XmlDocument();
      changedDoc.Load(oms);
      XPathNavigator timeCardRoot =
      changedDoc.CreateNavigator().SelectSingleNode("/");

      XmlDocument newDoc = new XmlDocument();
      XmlDeclaration dec = newDoc.CreateXmlDeclaration(
        "1.0", "UTF-8", null);
      newDoc.AppendChild(dec);

      foreach (string key in pis.Keys)
      {
        XmlProcessingInstruction pi =
          newDoc.CreateProcessingInstruction(key, pis[key]);
        newDoc.AppendChild(pi);
      }
```

```
XmlDocumentFragment frag = newDoc.CreateDocumentFragment();
frag.InnerXml = timeCardRoot.OuterXml;
newDoc.AppendChild(frag);

oms.Position = 0;
newDoc.Save(oms);

File.WriteAllBytes(
    @"C:\Projects\InfoPath\newForm.xml", oms.ToArray());
}

reader.Close();
}
}
```

timeCard in the code above refers to the name of the class that was generated using the XSD tool. This name will differ in your case and should be the same as the name of the root node in the Main data source of your form (**myFields** by default). Note that you should change the path to the existing InfoPath form (`C:\Projects\InfoPath\form.xml`), the path to the new InfoPath form (`C:\Projects\InfoPath\newForm.xml`), the namespace prefix (**tc**), and any other relevant information to suit your own scenario and the form you are using.

3. Save and build the solution.

4. Press **F5** to run the application.

Once the application has run, verify that a new InfoPath form named **newForm.xml** has been created on disk.

Discussion

The deserialization part of the code in the solution above has already been explained in the discussion section of *Use XML deserialization* in recipe *78 3 Ways to open and read an InfoPath form in memory*. The only addition to the deserialization part of the code is using the `MoveToFollowing()` method of an `XPathNavigator` object together with an `XPathNodeType` of `ProcessingInstruction` to save the XML processing instructions in a `Dictionary` object, so that they can be used later to reconstruct a new InfoPath form.

```
Dictionary<string, string> pis = new Dictionary<string, string>();
while (root.MoveToFollowing(XPathNodeType.ProcessingInstruction))
{
  pis.Add(root.Name, root.Value);
}
root.MoveToRoot();
```

The serialization code in the solution above starts by changing a value of a property of the object used to create the InfoPath form.

```
DateTime? weekOf = tc.week.weekOf.Value;
tc.week.weekOf = DateTime.Now;
```

The code then initializes a MemoryStream object

```
using (MemoryStream oms = new MemoryStream())
{
  ...
}
```

that is first used to serialize the object by calling the Serialize() method of an XmlSerialization object.

```
xs.Serialize(oms, tc);
oms.Position = 0;
```

Then an XmlDocument object is initialized to be able to retrieve an XPathNavigator object pointing to the root of the XML data of the object that was serialized.

```
XmlDocument changedDoc = new XmlDocument();
changedDoc.Load(oms);
XPathNavigator timeCardRoot =
  changedDoc.CreateNavigator().SelectSingleNode("/");
```

The code then creates a new XmlDocument object that can be used to construct a new InfoPath form

```
XmlDocument newDoc = new XmlDocument();
```

and proceeds to create and add an XmlDeclaration object to the XmlDocument object.

```
XmlDeclaration dec = newDoc.CreateXmlDeclaration("1.0", "UTF-8", null);
newDoc.AppendChild(dec);
```

The code then loops through the XML processing instructions that were previously stored in a Dictionary object and adds them to the XmlDocument object.

```
foreach (string key in pis.Keys)
{
  XmlProcessingInstruction pi =
    newDoc.CreateProcessingInstruction(key, pis[key]);
  newDoc.AppendChild(pi);
}
```

And finally, the code creates an XmlDocumentFragment object with the value of its InnerXml property set to be equal to the value of the OuterXml property of the XPathNavigator object pointing to the root of the XML data of the object that was serialized.

```
XmlDocumentFragment frag = newDoc.CreateDocumentFragment();
frag.InnerXml = timeCardRoot.OuterXml;
newDoc.AppendChild(frag);
```

The last step is to rewind the `MemoryStream` and then use it to save the contents of the `XmlDocument` object.

```
oms.Position = 0;
newDoc.Save(oms);
```

While you can do anything with the `MemoryStream` object containing the new InfoPath form, the code in the solution described above uses it to create a new InfoPath form on disk by using the `WriteAllBytes()` method of the `File` class.

```
File.WriteAllBytes(@"C:\Projects\InfoPath\newForm.xml", oms.ToArray());
```

80 Convert a form to Word using the Open XML SDK 2.0

Create a Word document that can serve as a template

Problem

You want to use a Word document that can serve as the base template from which to generate Word documents using InfoPath form data.

Solution

You can replace all of the text in a Word document that should be replaced by data entered into an InfoPath form with content controls.

To create a Word document that can serve as a template for generating Word documents from InfoPath forms:

1. In Word 2010, create a new document or use an existing one.

2. If the **Developer** tab is not present on the Ribbon, click **File ➤ Options**. On the **Word Options** dialog box, click **Customize Ribbon**, and then on the right-hand side of the dialog box, select **Main Tabs** from the **Customize the Ribbon** drop-down list box, ensure the **Developer** check box is selected, and then click **OK**.

3. You will use content controls to place data from an InfoPath form throughout the document, so you must replace any text, bulleted lists, images, or tables with content controls that can either be filled or replaced with data from an InfoPath form. Select a piece of text that should be replaced by InfoPath form data, and click **Developer ➤ Controls ➤ Plain Text Content Control**.

Figure 42. The Plain Text Content Control highlighted on the Developer tab in Word 2010.

4. With the content control still selected on the Word document, click **Developer ➤ Controls ➤ Properties**.

5. On the **Content Control Properties** dialog box, enter a unique name in the **Title** field, for example **multilinetext**. This name will be used in code to find the content control. Note that you could also use the XPath expression to the InfoPath form field that should replace the content control as the **Title** for the field.

Figure 43. Setting the properties for a content control in Word 2010.

6. Because the **multilinetext** content control will be getting its data from a multi-line text box control on an InfoPath form, you must select the **Allow carriage returns (multiple paragraphs)** check box on the **Content Control Properties** dialog box.

7. On the **Content Control Properties** dialog box, lock the **multilinetext** content control by selecting the **Content control cannot be deleted** and **Contents cannot be edited** check boxes, and then click **OK**.

8. Add another plain text content control to the Word document, give the content control the title of **singlelineoftext**, and lock the content control. This content control will be populated with data from a normal text box control on an InfoPath form.

9. Add another plain text content control to the Word document, give the content control the title of **richtext**, and lock the content control. This content control will be replaced by data from a rich text box control on an InfoPath form.

10. Add another plain text content control to the Word document, give the content control the title of **picture**, and lock the content control. This content control will be replaced by data from a picture control that contains an embedded image on an InfoPath form.

11. Add another plain text content control to the Word document, give the content control the title of **bulletedlist**, and lock the content control. This content control will be replaced by data from a bulleted list control on an InfoPath form.

12. Add another plain text content control to the Word document, give the content control the title of **repeatingtable**, and lock the content control. This content control will be replaced by data from a repeating table control on an InfoPath form.

13. Because you are going to format the table using a particular style (**Light Shading - Accent 5**), you must add a table to the Word document and apply that style to it. So select **Insert ➤ Tables ➤ Table**, and add a table with 3 rows and 3 columns to the document.

14. Select the table you just added, and then select **Table Tools ➤ Design ➤ Table Styles ➤ Light Shading – Accent 5**.

15. Save the document to a location on disk and name it **template.docx**.

16. Select the table you added in step 13, and press **Backspace** to delete it. Because the table will be constructed through code, you do not need it to be present in the document. The only reason you added it, was to have the style added to the document.

17. Save and close the document.

Discussion

In the solution described above, you saw how you can add content controls to a Word document. You will be using content controls in one of two ways:

1. As containers to which you will write text through code.

2. As markers or placeholders that determine the location of and are replaced by objects such as images, bulleted lists, or tables in the document.

When you add a content control to a document, it does not have style or formatting applied to it. So if you require the text that will be added to a content control through code to have a particular style or formatting, you must apply these to the content control by using one of the following methods:

1. Select the content control and format it as you would normally format text in Word. Note that if you locked the content control, you must first unlock it before trying to apply formatting to it.

2. Select the content control, open its **Properties** dialog box, select the **Use a style to format contents** check box, and then select a style from the **Style** drop-down list box.

3. Use the **Format Painter** command to apply formatting to the content control.

4. Replace existing text that has already been formatted, with a content control. The content control should automatically inherit the formatting from the text it replaced.

DOCX files just like XSN files are packaged files that consist of other files. You can change the file extension of a Word document from DOCX to ZIP, and then open the ZIP file to view its contents. If you do this, you will see that a Word document consists of XML files. These XML files contain settings, definitions, and data used by the Word document. The data entered into a document is stored in a file named **document.xml** that is located in the **Word** folder in the ZIP file.

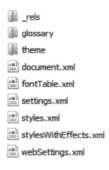

_rels
glossary
theme
document.xml
fontTable.xml
settings.xml
styles.xml
stylesWithEffects.xml
webSettings.xml

Figure 44. Files contained in the Word folder of the ZIP file corresponding to a DOCX file.

When you create a Word document and apply style to it, the styles you use are automatically added to the **styles.xml** file. So if you want to use a particular style in code, for example **LightShading-Accent5** for tables, you must add a table to the Word document that the code will be using as a template to generate documents, apply the style to the table, save the document, delete the table, and save the document again.

Light Shading - Accent 5

Figure 45. Light Shading - Accent 5 table style in Word 2010.

When you delete the table, the style will remain defined in the **styles.xml** file, so that you can apply it to your tables through code (see the next solution for an example of how to generate a table from a repeating table and apply a style to it). You can open the **styles.xml** file and look whether the style you want to use in code is present in the file. For example, for the **LightShading-Accent5**, you would have to look whether the following elements are present in the **styles.xml** file:

```
<w:style w:type="table" w:styleId="LightShading-Accent5">
  <w:name w:val="Light Shading Accent 5" />
  <w:basedOn w:val="TableNormal" />
  ...
</w:style>
```

Once you are done creating a Word document that can serve as a template to generate other documents, added content controls to it, and styled and formatted it as you wish, the next step would be to use the Open XML SDK 2.0 to open the document through code, write to it, and then save it as a new document. You will do this in the next solution.

Important:

> If a particular style you are using in code is not present in the **styles.xml** file, that style will not be applied to the objects in the Word document you generate. In the case of a table, the table would not have any borders, colors, shading, etc. applied to it. So if a table is showing up without style in a document, ensure the style you used in code is present in the **styles.xml** file of the template used to generate the Word document.

Generate a Word document using InfoPath form data

Problem

You want to use data that is stored in an InfoPath form to generate a Word document.

Solution

You can use Open XML to generate a Word document that is based on data from an InfoPath form.

Note:

> This solution requires the Open XML SDK 2.0 to be installed. You can download it from the Microsoft web site.

This solution lists the basic steps for generating a Word document from data stored in an InfoPath Filler form locally on a computer. If you want to generate a Word document from an InfoPath browser form that is submitted to a SharePoint form library and store it in a document library on the SharePoint server, refer to recipe *101 Save a form as a PDF document in a SharePoint document library*, which shows you how to use a SharePoint event receiver to first generate a Word document from an InfoPath form using the same techniques described in this solution, and then schedule a job to have the Word document converted into a PDF file.

To convert an InfoPath form to Word using the Open XML SDK 2.0:

1. In Visual Studio 2010, select **File ➤ New ➤ Project**.

2. On the **New Project** dialog box, select **Windows** under **Visual C#** from the list of **Installed Templates**, select **.NET Framework 3.5** from the drop-down list box, select **Class Library**, enter a name for the project (for example **InfoPathToWordLib**), select a location where to save the solution, enter a name for the solution, and click **OK**.

3. On the **Solution Explorer** pane, rename **Class1.cs** to **InfoPathToWord.cs**.

4. On the **Solution Explorer** pane, right-click the project name, and select **Properties** from the context menu that appears.

5. On the **Properties** window, select the **Signing** tab, select the **Sign the assembly** check box, and then select **<New...>** from the **Choose a strong name key file** drop-down list box.

6. On the **Create Strong Name Key** dialog box, enter a name (for example **InfoPathToWord.snk**), deselect the **Protect my key file with a password** check box, and click **OK**.

7. On the **Solution Explorer** pane, add references to the following assemblies: **DocumentFormat.OpenXml**, **System.Drawing**, and **WindowsBase**.

8. Open the **InfoPathToWord.cs** file and add the following **using** statements to it (*code #: 900125AD-9CB6-4085-B69C-EFDFF3715B8A*):

```
using System.IO;
using DocumentFormat.OpenXml;
using DocumentFormat.OpenXml.Packaging;
using DocumentFormat.OpenXml.Wordprocessing;
using A = DocumentFormat.OpenXml.Drawing;
using DW = DocumentFormat.OpenXml.Drawing.Wordprocessing;
using PIC = DocumentFormat.OpenXml.Drawing.Pictures;
using System.Xml;
using System.Xml.XPath;
```

9. Replace the `InfoPathToWord` class in the **InfoPathToWord.cs** file with the code displayed in *InfoPathToWord.cs* in the Appendix (*code #: C6EE40D6-96BC-485A-A1FD-12511A8E91D2*).

10. Save and build the project.

11. In InfoPath, create a new InfoPath Filler form template or use an existing one.

12. Add a **Text Box** control to the view of the form template and name it **field1**.

13. Add a **Text Box** control to the view of the form template, name it **field2**, and select its **Multi-line** property.

14. Add a **Rich Text Box** control to the view of the form template and name it **field3**.

15. Add a **Picture** control to the view of the form template and name it **field4**. Select the **Included in the form** option when you add the picture control.

16. Add a **Bulleted List** control to the view of the form template and name it **field5**.

17. Add a **Repeating Table** with 4 columns to the view of the form template. Name the repeating group node for the repeating table **group3**.

18. Add a **Button** control to the view of the form template and label it **Print To Word**.

19. Add an event handler for the **Clicked** event of the **Print To Word** button as described in recipe *7 Add an event handler for a control event*.

20. In VSTA, add references to the following assemblies: **DocumentFormat.OpenXml**, **System.Drawing**, **WindowsBase**, and **InfoPathToWordLib**. Note that the **InfoPathToWordLib** assembly refers to the DLL of the class library project you created earlier in Visual Studio 2010.

21. Add the following **using** statements to the **FormCode.cs** file (*code #: B5AD13F8-D982-4DD0-AF9D-219E1C130689*):

```
using System.Collections.Generic;
using System.Text;
using System.IO;
using DocumentFormat.OpenXml;
using DocumentFormat.OpenXml.Packaging;
using DocumentFormat.OpenXml.Wordprocessing;
using InfoPathToWordLib;
```

22. Add the following code to the Clicked() event handler for the **Print To Word** button (*code #: B5AD13F8-D982-4DD0-AF9D-219E1C130689*):

```
XPathNavigator mainDS = MainDataSource.CreateNavigator();

string normalText = mainDS.SelectSingleNode(
  "/my:myFields/my:field1", NamespaceManager).Value;

string multiLineText = mainDS.SelectSingleNode(
  "/my:myFields/my:field2", NamespaceManager).Value;

string rtfValue = String.Empty;
XPathNavigator formNameNode = mainDS.SelectSingleNode(
  "/my:myFields/my:field3", NamespaceManager);
rtfValue = "<html>" + formNameNode.InnerXml + "</html>";

string base64EncodedString = mainDS.SelectSingleNode(
  "/my:myFields/my:field4", NamespaceManager).Value;
byte[] imageBytes = null;
```

```
if (!String.IsNullOrEmpty(base64EncodedString))
{
  imageBytes = System.Convert.FromBase64String(base64EncodedString);
}

XPathNodeIterator iter2 = mainDS.Select(
  "/my:myFields/my:group1/my:field5", NamespaceManager);

XPathNodeIterator iter = mainDS.Select(
  "/my:myFields/my:group2/my:group3", NamespaceManager);

int id = 0;

byte[] copiedBytes =
  File.ReadAllBytes(@"C:\Projects\InfoPath\template.docx");

using (MemoryStream ms = new MemoryStream())
{
  ms.Write(copiedBytes, 0, (int)copiedBytes.Length);

  using (WordprocessingDocument myDoc =
    WordprocessingDocument.Open(ms, true))
  {
    MainDocumentPart mainPart = myDoc.MainDocumentPart;

    List<OpenXmlElement> sdtList = InfoPathToWord.GetContentControl(
      mainPart.Document, "richtext");
    InfoPathToWord.AddRichText(id, rtfValue, ref mainPart, ref sdtList);

    ImagePart imagePart = InfoPathToWord.AddImagePart(
      "rId198", base64EncodedString, ref mainPart);

    long imageWidthEMU = 0;
    long imageHeightEMU = 0;
    Guid imageFormat = Guid.Empty;

    InfoPathToWord.GetImageExtents(base64EncodedString,
      out imageWidthEMU, out imageHeightEMU);

    sdtList = InfoPathToWord.GetContentControl(
      mainPart.Document, "picture");
    string imageType = InfoPathToWord.GetImageType(base64EncodedString);

    OpenXmlElement imageElement = InfoPathToWord.CreateImageElement(
    mainPart.GetIdOfPart(imagePart), "Picture 1", "Pic1." + imageType,
      imageWidthEMU, imageHeightEMU);
    InfoPathToWord.ReplaceContentControl(sdtList, imageElement);

    sdtList = InfoPathToWord.GetContentControl(
      mainPart.Document, "singlelineoftext");
    InfoPathToWord.AddSingleLineText(normalText, ref sdtList);

    sdtList = InfoPathToWord.GetContentControl(
      mainPart.Document, "multilinetext");
    InfoPathToWord.AddMultiLineText(multiLineText, ref sdtList);

    Table table = new Table();

    TableProperties tblProp = new TableProperties();
    TableStyle tblStyle = new TableStyle();
    tblStyle.Val = new StringValue("LightShading-Accent5");
    TableWidth tblWidth = new TableWidth();
```

```
tblWidth.Width = "100%";
tblWidth.Type = TableWidthUnitValues.Pct;
TableLook tblLook = new TableLook();
tblLook.Val = "04A0";
tblLook.FirstRow = true;
tblLook.LastRow = false;
tblLook.FirstColumn = false;
tblLook.LastColumn = false;
tblLook.NoHorizontalBand = false;
tblLook.NoVerticalBand = true;

tblProp.Append(tblStyle);
tblProp.Append(tblWidth);
tblProp.Append(tblLook);

table.AppendChild<TableProperties>(tblProp);

InfoPathToWord.AddTableRow(new string[]
  { "Header 1", "Header 2", "Header 3", "Header 4" }, ref table);
InfoPathToWord.AddRowsToTable(iter, ref table);

sdtList = InfoPathToWord.GetContentControl(
  mainPart.Document, "repeatingtable");
InfoPathToWord.ReplaceContentControl(sdtList, table);

sdtList = InfoPathToWord.GetContentControl(
  mainPart.Document, "bulletedlist");
InfoPathToWord.AddBulletedList("rId200", iter2, ref sdtList,
  ref mainPart);

myDoc.Close();

File.WriteAllBytes(@"C:\Projects\InfoPath\generated.docx",
  ms.ToArray());

ms.Close();

  }
}
```

Note that you should change the path to the Word template (C:\Projects\InfoPath\template.docx) and the path to the newly generated Word document (C:\Projects\InfoPath\generated.docx) to suit your own scenario.

23. Save and build the project.

24. Give the form template Full Trust as described in *Configure an InfoPath form template to have Full Trust* in the Appendix.

25. Preview the form.

When the form opens, fill it out with data, and then click the **Print To Word** button. Navigate to the location on disk where the new document should have been generated, open the Word document, and verify that the data you entered into the form has been written to the Word document.

Discussion

In the solution described above, you learned how to write code that reads data from a text box control, multi-line text box control, rich text box control, picture control, bulleted list, and repeating table control on an InfoPath form to generate a new Word document that is based on a particular base Word document template using the Open XML SDK 2.0. The code can be split into four parts:

1. Retrieve data from the InfoPath form.

2. Retrieve a Word document that can be used as a template to create other documents and open this document so that it can be written to.

3. Write InfoPath form data to the Word document.

4. Close and save the Word document as a new document.

The first part of the code retrieves data from the InfoPath form using classes from the System.Xml and System.Xml.XPath namespaces as you have already seen in almost all of the recipes in this book. For example, the following code retrieves the contents of the rich text box control on the form.

```
string rtfValue = String.Empty;
XPathNavigator formNameNode = mainDS.SelectSingleNode(
  "/my:myFields/my:field3", NamespaceManager);
rtfValue = "<html>" + formNameNode.InnerXml + "</html>";
```

And the following code retrieves the contents of the picture control and converts it into a byte array.

```
string base64EncodedString = mainDS.SelectSingleNode(
  "/my:myFields/my:field4", NamespaceManager).Value;
byte[] imageBytes = null;
if (!String.IsNullOrEmpty(base64EncodedString))
{
  imageBytes = System.Convert.FromBase64String(base64EncodedString);
}
```

After retrieving form field values, the code uses the ReadAllBytes() method of the File class to retrieve the Word document that should serve as a template for creating other documents.

```
byte[] copiedBytes = File.ReadAllBytes(@"C:\Projects\InfoPath\template.docx");
```

And then the byte array for the Word document is used to create a MemoryStream object that is used to instantiate a WordprocessingDocument object, which you can use to write the InfoPath form data to the Word document.

```
using (MemoryStream ms = new MemoryStream())
{
  ms.Write(copiedBytes, 0, (int)copiedBytes.Length);
```

```
using (WordprocessingDocument myDoc = WordprocessingDocument.Open(ms, true))
{
  MainDocumentPart mainPart = myDoc.MainDocumentPart;
  ...
}
}
```

Note that you could have also used a `FileStream` object in this case if you wanted to. A `MemoryStream` object is used here, since it will be required later when you generate Word documents on a SharePoint server (see recipe *101 Save a form as a PDF document in a SharePoint document library*).

The code then uses Open XML SDK 2.0 objects to write InfoPath form data to the Word document and after that it uses the `WriteAllBytes()` method of the `File` class to save the bytes of the Word document to a new file.

```
File.WriteAllBytes(@"C:\Projects\InfoPath\generated.docx", ms.ToArray());
```

The code that writes to the Word document does the following for data from each form field written to the Word document:

1. Gets the data of a form field using `XPathNavigator` or `XPathNodeIterator` objects.

2. Finds the content control that should be written to or replaced by calling the `GetContentControl()` method of the `InfoPathToWord` class. The `InfoPathToWord` class is a static class that was added to a **Class Library** project named **InfoPathToWordLib**, so that its methods could be called from code in an InfoPath Filler form. A **Class Library** project was used in this case, because the code in the `InfoPathToWord` class uses .NET 3.5 features that are not available in VSTA, which is based on .NET 2.0. So by adding the `InfoPathToWord` class to a **Class Library** project, you are able to create a DLL that can be referenced from the code in the InfoPath form template. Note that this DLL automatically becomes part of the form template and is stored in the XSN file as one of the form files when you add it as a reference to the VSTA project.

3. Writes data to the content control or replaces the content control with another object.

Depending on the type of form field, a content control is either written to or replaced. For example, data from InfoPath controls containing a single line of text (such as a text box control) or multiple lines of text (such as a multi-line text box) is written to content controls; while data from InfoPath controls such as a rich text box control, bulleted list, repeating table, or picture control is used to create other Open XML elements to replace specific content controls throughout the Word document.

The code that writes a single line of text from a text box control on the form to a content control in Word resembles the following:

```
sdtList = InfoPathToWord.GetContentControl(
  mainPart.Document, "singlelineoftext");
InfoPathToWord.AddSingleLineText(normalText, ref sdtList);
```

where the `GetContentControl()` method is defined as follows:

```
public static List<OpenXmlElement> GetContentControl(
  Document doc, string name)
{
  List<OpenXmlElement> list = new List<OpenXmlElement>();

  List<SdtBlock> sdtList = doc.Descendants<SdtBlock>()
    .Where(s => name.Contains(s.SdtProperties.GetFirstChild<SdtAlias>()
    .Val.Value)).ToList();

  if (sdtList.Count == 0)
  {
    List<SdtRun> sdtRunList = doc.Descendants<SdtRun>()
      .Where(s => name.Contains(s.SdtProperties.GetFirstChild<SdtAlias>()
      .Val.Value)).ToList();

    foreach (SdtRun sdt in sdtRunList)
    {
      list.Add(sdt);
    }

  }
  else
  {
    foreach (SdtBlock sdt in sdtList)
    {
      list.Add(sdt);
    }
  }

  return list;
}
```

Note that content controls are found by the titles you gave them when you created the Word document (see step 5 in the previous solution). These titles are stored in `SdtAlias` elements. An `SdtAlias` element can be contained in either an `SdtBlock` or an `SdtRun` element. When you place a content control between other text in a paragraph in a document, that content control becomes part of an `SdtRun` element, and when you place a content control on its own (so not within a paragraph of text), that content control becomes part of an `SdtBlock` element. Therefore, the code above first searches for a particular `SdtAlias` element in `SdtBlock` elements, and if it does not find the `SdtAlias` element, it searches for the `SdtAlias` element in `SdtRun` elements, and returns a `List` of `OpenXmlElement` objects, which are generic objects that can be either `SdtBlock` or `SdtRun` objects.

The `AddSingleLineText()` method is defined as follows:

```
public static void AddSingleLineText(
  string singleLineText, ref List<OpenXmlElement> sdtList)
{
```

```
    if (sdtList.Count != 0)
    {
      foreach (OpenXmlElement sdt in sdtList)
      {
        if (sdt.GetType() == typeof(SdtBlock))
        {
          Paragraph p =
            sdt.GetFirstChild<SdtContentBlock>().GetFirstChild<Paragraph>();
          WriteText(singleLineText, ref p);
        }

        if (sdt.GetType() == typeof(SdtRun))
        {
          Run r = sdt.GetFirstChild<SdtContentRun>().GetFirstChild<Run>();
          WriteText(singleLineText, ref r);
        }
      }
    }
}
```

Text coming from a text box control on the InfoPath form is written to a Text element that is contained within a Run element. In the code above, a distinction is made between content controls that stand on their own

```
if (sdt.GetType() == typeof(SdtBlock))
{
  ...
}
```

and content controls that are embedded in other text.

```
if (sdt.GetType() == typeof(SdtRun))
{
  ...
}
```

A content control that stands on its own will contain Paragraph, Run, and Text elements, while a content control that is embedded in other text (so in a Paragraph element) will contain only a Run with a Text element. Therefore, the WriteText() method has two overloads that accept either a Paragraph or a Run element. Refer to *InfoPathToWord.cs* in the Appendix for the code contained in the methods of the InfoPathToWord class.

The code that replaces a content control with data from a repeating table on the form resembles the following:

```
InfoPathToWord.AddTableRow(new string[]
  { "Header 1", "Header 2", "Header 3", "Header 4" }, ref table);
InfoPathToWord.AddRowsToTable(iter, ref table);

sdtList = InfoPathToWord.GetContentControl(mainPart.Document, "repeatingtable");
InfoPathToWord.ReplaceContentControl(sdtList, table);
```

This code adds a header row to a `Table` object by calling the `AddTableRow()` method of the `InfoPathToWord` class, adds the rows from the repeating table to the `Table` object by calling the `AddRowsToTable()` method of the `InfoPathToWord` class, and replaces the content control by calling the `ReplaceContentControl()` method of the `InfoPathToWord` class. Note that the `AddRowsToTable()` method takes an `XPathNodeIterator` object and automatically determines the amount of columns the table contains. The `AddTableRow()` method accepts an array of static strings. It is used here to add a header row to the table.

When the `Table` object is created (before adding rows to it and replacing the content control), it is customized and the **LightShading-Accent5** style is applied to it. Note that this style must be present in the **styles.xml** file mentioned in the previous solution for the document to display the table with a style applied to it.

```
Table table = new Table();

TableProperties tblProp = new TableProperties();
TableStyle tblStyle = new TableStyle();
tblStyle.Val = new StringValue("LightShading-Accent5");
TableWidth tblWidth = new TableWidth();
tblWidth.Width = "100%";
tblWidth.Type = TableWidthUnitValues.Pct;
TableLook tblLook = new TableLook();
tblLook.Val = "04A0";
tblLook.FirstRow = true;
tblLook.LastRow = false;
tblLook.FirstColumn = false;
tblLook.LastColumn = false;
tblLook.NoHorizontalBand = false;
tblLook.NoVerticalBand = true;

tblProp.Append(tblStyle);
tblProp.Append(tblWidth);
tblProp.Append(tblLook);

table.AppendChild<TableProperties>(tblProp);
```

If the table in your generated document does not have a style applied to it, while you have assigned the style through code, open the **styles.xml** file and verify that the style you want to use is present. If it is not present, add a table to the Word document template, apply the style to the table, save the document, delete the table, save the document again, close the document, and verify that the style has been added to the **styles.xml** file. If it has been, try generating the document again using the InfoPath form, and then verify that the style was applied to the table.

The solution described above is not comprehensive in that it does not show you how to add data from each type of control in InfoPath to a Word document. However, the techniques that are applied throughout the code and in the methods of the `InfoPathToWord` class can be used for most of the controls in InfoPath, since they cover basic text controls such as text boxes, drop-down list boxes, date pickers, etc., but also controls that contain repeating fields such as repeating tables, bulleted and numbered lists, and multiple-selection list boxes. In addition, you also saw how to convert an embedded image in an InfoPath form and add it to a Word document.

Because a complete discussion of the Open XML SDK 2.0 is beyond the scope of this book, you are encouraged to consult the Open XML SDK 2.0 documentation to find more solutions if you require adding data from other InfoPath controls that were not covered by this recipe to Word documents.

Chapter 7: Web Service Integration

You can connect an InfoPath form to a web service in one of two ways through code:

1. Add a web service data connection to an InfoPath form and then use the properties and methods of the `WebServiceConnection` class to interact with the web service.

2. Generate a proxy class for the web service by using the **Add Web Reference** command in VSTA or by using the WSDL tool, and then create objects that can be used to interact with the web service.

The first method is the preferred method, since it typically does not require you to give a form template Full Trust as is the case with the second method. In addition, the data connection from the first method can be converted into a data connection file that can be stored in a SharePoint data connection library, whereas the second method does not make use of a data connection added to an InfoPath form; all connection information and credentials are specified through code.

In most cases, you do not have to write code to call web services in InfoPath, but can use rules instead. The only times you may have to write code to call a web service from within an InfoPath form is for example if you are unable to connect to the web service through the user interface of InfoPath Designer 2010 or if you are using a submit data connection for a web service and would like to retrieve results that are sent back by the web service after an operation has completed.

The explanation of working with web services is beyond the scope of this book. Therefore, you must already have a basic understanding of web service programming using Visual Studio 2010 to be able to follow the recipes in this chapter. The recipes in this chapter also require you to have Visual Studio 2010 installed on your computer and to already know how to create and write code for applications using Visual Studio 2010.

InfoPath forms can be connected to SOAP web services, WCF services, and REST web services. The recipes in this chapter cover SOAP web services. Refer to *Create a WCF service that retrieves data for InfoPath* in the Appendix for information about WCF services.

81   Create a web service that retrieves data for InfoPath

Create a web service that returns one value

Problem

You have a SQL Server database table from which you want to retrieve a value from a specific record using a web service.

Solution

You can create a web service that has a web method that accepts a parameter and returns a value from a database record as a specific type.

Suppose you have a SQL Server database table named **OfficeApplications** that contains the following data:

OfficeApplicationId (int)	OfficeApplicationName (nvarchar(50))	OfficeApplicationColor (nvarchar(50))
1	Word	Blue
2	Excel	Green
3	Access	Red
4	InfoPath	Purple
5	OneNote	Purple
6	PowerPoint	Dark Orange

Note:

You can download a file named **OfficeApplications.sql** from www.bizsupportonline.com to create the **OfficeApplications** table for use with this recipe.

To create a web service that returns a value from a database record as a specific type:

1. In Visual Studio 2010, select **File ➤ New ➤ Project**.

2. On the **New Project** dialog box, select **Web** under **Visual C#** from the list of **Installed Templates**, select **.NET Framework 3.5** from the drop-down list box, select **ASP.NET Web Service Application**, enter a name for the project (for example **InfoPathWebService**), select a location where to save the solution, enter a name for the solution, and click **OK**.

3. On the **Solution Explorer** pane, rename **Service1.asmx** to **InfoPathService.asmx**.

4. On the **Solution Explorer** pane, right-click **InfoPathService.asmx**, and select **View Markup** from the context menu that appears.

5. Change the class name in the **InfoPathService.asmx** file from **InfoPathWebService.Service1** to **InfoPathWebService.InfoPathService** as follows (*code #: 21C566C5-08FF-4448-BA7A-35F216553044*):

```
<%@ WebService Language="C#" CodeBehind="InfoPathService.asmx.cs"
Class="InfoPathWebService.InfoPathService" %>
```

6. On the **Solution Explorer** pane, right-click the project name and select **Add ➤ New Item** from the context menu that appears.

7. On the **Add New Item** dialog box, select **Class**, name the file **OfficeApplication.cs**, and click **Add**.

8. Add three public properties named **Id**, **Name**, and **Color** to the `OfficeApplication` class (*code #: 21C566C5-08FF-4448-BA7A-35F216553044*):

```
public class OfficeApplication
{
  public int Id { get; set; }
  public string Name { get; set; }
  public string Color { get; set; }
}
```

9. On the **Solution Explorer** pane, double-click the **Web.config** file to open it.

10. Add the following **connectionStrings** section to the **Web.config** file (*code #: 21C566C5-08FF-4448-BA7A-35F216553044*):

```
<connectionStrings>
  <clear/>
  <add name="InfoPathDB"
    connectionString="Initial Catalog=InfoPathDB;Integrated Security=True;"
    providerName="System.Data.SqlClient" />
</connectionStrings>
```

Remember to replace the value of **Initial Catalog** with the name of your own database in which the **OfficeApplication** table is located.

11. Switch to the **InfoPathService.asmx.cs** file and add the following **using** statements to it:

```
using System.Data.SqlClient;
using System.Configuration;
```

12. Change the namespace for the web service to something suitable, such as for example:

```
[WebService(Namespace =
"http://www.bizsupportonline.net/namespaces/infopathservice/")]
```

13. Rename the class from `Service1` to `InfoPathService`.

```
public class InfoPathService : System.Web.Services.WebService
{
    ...
}
```

14. Replace the `HelloWorld()` web method with the following web method (*code #: 21C566C5-08FF-4448-BA7A-35F216553044*):

```
[WebMethod(Description=
  "Returns the name of an Office application based on its identifier.")]
public string GetOfficeApplicationName(int Id)
{
  OfficeApplication officeApp = new OfficeApplication();
  string connectionString =
    ConfigurationManager.ConnectionStrings["InfoPathDB"].ConnectionString;

  using (SqlConnection conn = new SqlConnection(connectionString))
  {
    SqlCommand cmd = new SqlCommand();
    cmd.CommandType = System.Data.CommandType.Text;
    cmd.CommandText = "SELECT OfficeApplicationName " +
      "FROM OfficeApplications WHERE OfficeApplicationID = @Id";
    cmd.Parameters.Add("Id", System.Data.SqlDbType.Int).Value = Id;
    cmd.Connection = conn;

    try
    {
      conn.Open();

      using (SqlDataReader reader = cmd.ExecuteReader())
      {
        while (reader.Read())
        {
          officeApp.Name = reader.GetString(0);
        }

        reader.Close();
      }
    }
    catch
    {
      // Handle the error using your own preferred error-handling method
    }
    finally
    {
      conn.Close();
    }
  }
  return officeApp.Name;
}
```

15. Click **Build** ➤ **Build Solution** and fix any errors if necessary.

16. Click **Debug ➤ Start Debugging**. This should open a browser window and display the **InfoPathService.asmx** page.

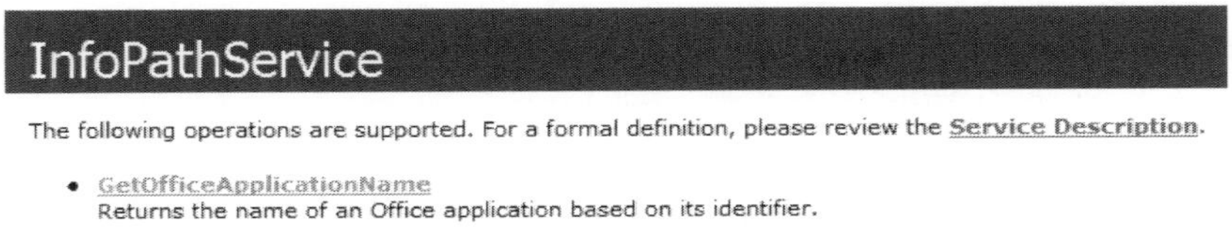

InfoPathService

The following operations are supported. For a formal definition, please review the Service Description.

- GetOfficeApplicationName
  Returns the name of an Office application based on its identifier.

Figure 46. The page for the InfoPathService web service.

17. Click the link for the **GetOfficeApplicationName** web method, enter a valid identifier on the next page, and click **Invoke** to verify that the web method is working properly and returning the correct data.

```
<?xml version="1.0" encoding="utf-8" ?>
<string xmlns="http://www.bizsupportonline.net/namespaces/infopathservice/">Access</string>
```

Figure 47. XML returned by the web method invocation.

18. With the web service still running in debug mode, open InfoPath Designer 2010, and create a new **Blank Form** template.

19. Select **Data ➤ Get External Data ➤ From Web Service ➤ From SOAP Web Service**.

20. On the **Data Connection Wizard**, enter the URL of the web service, for example:

```
http://localhost:24014/InfoPathService.asmx
```

and click **Next**. Note that an URL such as the one specified above should work if you are running the web service and InfoPath on the same computer. Otherwise, you may have to deploy the web service first before you are able to access it in InfoPath.

21. On the **Data Connection Wizard**, select the **GetOfficeApplicationName** operation, and click **Next**. Note that the description you gave the web method should appear in the **Description of operation** box.

22. On the **Data Connection Wizard**, leave the parameter as is, and click **Next**.

23. On the **Data Connection Wizard**, leave the **Store a copy of the data in the form template** check box deselected, and click **Next**.

24. On the **Data Connection Wizard**, leave the data connection name as **GetOfficeApplicationName**, deselect the **Automatically retrieve data when form is opened** check box, and click **Finish**.

25. On the **Fields** task pane, select **GetOfficeApplicationName (Secondary)** from the **Fields** drop-down list box.

26. On the **Fields** task pane, expand the **queryFields** group node, expand the **GetOfficeApplicationName** group node, and then drag-and-drop the **Id** field onto the view of the form template.

27. On the **Fields** task pane, expand the **dataFields** group node, expand the **GetOfficeApplicationNameResponse** group node, and then drag-and-drop the **GetOfficeApplicationNameResult** field onto the view of the form template.

28. Add a **Button** control to the view of the form template and change its **Action** property to **Refresh**.

29. Preview the form.

When the form opens, enter a valid identifier in the **Id** field and then click the **Refresh** button. The name of the Office application that has the identifier you entered should appear in the **GetOfficeApplicationNameResult** text box.

Discussion

When you add a query data connection for a web service in InfoPath, InfoPath creates a secondary data source that has two main group nodes: **queryFields** and **dataFields**. The **queryFields** group node contains fields that correspond to the parameters you can pass to the web service method, while the **dataFields** group node contains fields that correspond to the data returned by the web service method.

Figure 48. The secondary data source for a web service that returns a specific value.

In the solution described above, you created a web service method that takes an integer (**Id** field under the **queryFields** group node) and returns a string (**GetOfficeApplicationNameResult** field under the **dataFields** group node).

```
[WebMethod(Description=
  "Returns the name of an Office application based on its identifier.")]
public string GetOfficeApplicationName(int Id)
{
  ...
}
```

When the InfoPath form calls the web service method and passes an identifier to it, the web service method creates an object of type `OfficeApplication`, retrieves a connection string that is located in the **Web.config** file

```
OfficeApplication officeApp = new OfficeApplication();
string connectionString =
  ConfigurationManager.ConnectionStrings["InfoPathDB"].ConnectionString;
```

and uses it to create a `SqlConnection` object.

```
using (SqlConnection conn = new SqlConnection(connectionString))
{
  ...
}
```

The code then creates a `SqlCommand` object that constructs a SQL SELECT statement that uses the identifier passed to the web service to retrieve the name of an Office application.

```
SqlCommand cmd = new SqlCommand();
cmd.CommandType = System.Data.CommandType.Text;
cmd.CommandText = "SELECT OfficeApplicationName " +
  "FROM OfficeApplications WHERE OfficeApplicationID = @Id";
cmd.Parameters.Add("Id", System.Data.SqlDbType.Int).Value = Id;
cmd.Connection = conn;
```

After a database connection is opened, the query is then executed by calling the `ExecuteReader()` method of the `SqlCommand` object and a `SqlDataReader` object is returned.

```
conn.Open();

using (SqlDataReader reader = cmd.ExecuteReader())
{
  ...
}
```

The `Read()` method of the `SqlDataReader` object allows you to then loop through the records retrieved from the database to retrieve the Office application name.

```
while (reader.Read())
{
  officeApp.Name = reader.GetString(0);
}

reader.Close();
```

And finally, the Office application name is returned to the InfoPath form.

```
return officeApp.Name;
```

Note:

When you are running the web service in debug mode and you create an InfoPath form template as described in the solution above, you can set breakpoints throughout the web service code before performing an action that invokes the web service from within the InfoPath form. This action should hit the breakpoints in Visual Studio so that you can step through the web service code and debug it in Visual Studio.

Create a web service that returns one record

Problem

You have a SQL Server database table from which you want to retrieve a record using a web service.

Solution

You can create a web service that has a web method that accepts a parameter and returns a record from a database table as a group node.

Suppose you have a SQL Server database table named **OfficeApplications** as described in the previous solution.

To create a web service that returns a database record as a group node:

1. Follow steps 1 through 13 of *Create a web service that returns one value* in this recipe.

2. Replace the `HelloWorld()` web method with the following web method or add a new web method if you wish (*code #: F30E0A22-78AF-4AE4-BE31-28725F3EC05F*):

```
[WebMethod(Description=
  "Returns an Office application based on its identifier.")]
public OfficeApplication GetOfficeApplication(int Id)
{
  OfficeApplication officeApp = new OfficeApplication();
  string connectionString =
    ConfigurationManager.ConnectionStrings["InfoPathDB"].ConnectionString;

  using (SqlConnection conn = new SqlConnection(connectionString))
  {
    SqlCommand cmd = new SqlCommand();
    cmd.CommandType = System.Data.CommandType.Text;
    cmd.CommandText = "SELECT OfficeApplicationId, OfficeApplicationName, "
      + "OfficeApplicationColor FROM OfficeApplications "
      + "WHERE OfficeApplicationID = @Id";
    cmd.Parameters.Add("Id", System.Data.SqlDbType.Int).Value = Id;
    cmd.Connection = conn;

    try
    {
```

```
      conn.Open();

      using (SqlDataReader reader = cmd.ExecuteReader())
      {
        while (reader.Read())
        {
          officeApp.Id = reader.GetInt32(0);
          officeApp.Name = reader.GetString(1);
          officeApp.Color = reader.GetString(2);
        }

        reader.Close();
      }
    }
    catch
    {
      // Handle the error using your own preferred error-handling method
    }
    finally
    {
      conn.Close();
    }
  }
  return officeApp;
}
```

3. Click **Build ➤ Build Solution** and fix any errors if necessary.

4. Click **Debug ➤ Start Debugging**. This should open a browser window and display the **InfoPathService.asmx** page.

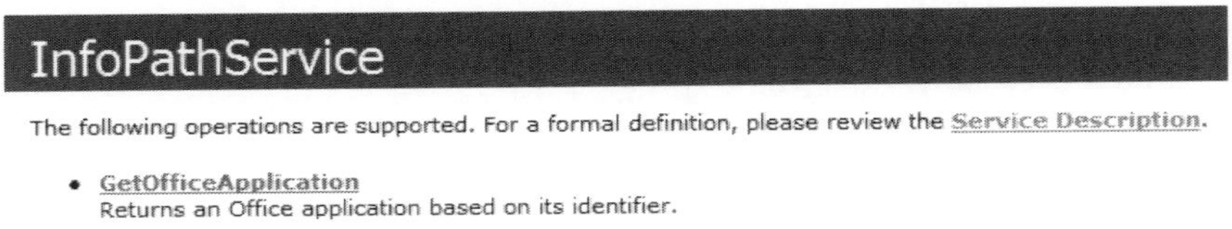

InfoPathService

The following operations are supported. For a formal definition, please review the Service Description.

- **GetOfficeApplication**
  Returns an Office application based on its identifier.

Figure 49. The page for the InfoPathService web service.

5. Click the link for the **GetOfficeApplication** web method, enter a valid identifier on the next page, and click **Invoke** to verify that the web method is working properly and returning the correct data.

```
<?xml version="1.0" encoding="utf-8" ?>
- <OfficeApplication xmlns:xsi="http://www.w3.org/2001/XMLSchema-instance"
    xmlns:xsd="http://www.w3.org/2001/XMLSchema"
    xmlns="http://www.bizsupportonline.net/namespaces/infopathservice/">
    <Id>3</Id>
    <Name>Access</Name>
    <Color>Red</Color>
  </OfficeApplication>
```

Figure 50. XML returned by the web method invocation.

6. With the web service still running in debug mode, open InfoPath Designer 2010, and create a new **Blank Form** template.

7. Select **Data ➤ Get External Data ➤ From Web Service ➤ From SOAP Web Service**.

8. On the **Data Connection Wizard**, enter the URL of the web service, for example:

```
http://localhost:24014/InfoPathService.asmx
```

and click **Next**. Note that an URL such as the one specified above should work if you are running the web service and InfoPath on the same computer. Otherwise, you may have to deploy the web service first before you are able to access it in InfoPath.

9. On the **Data Connection Wizard**, select the **GetOfficeApplication** operation, and click **Next**. Note that the description you gave the web method should appear in the **Description of operation** box.

10. On the **Data Connection Wizard**, leave the parameter as is, and click **Next**.

11. On the **Data Connection Wizard**, leave the **Store a copy of the data in the form template** check box deselected, and click **Next**.

12. On the **Data Connection Wizard**, leave the data connection name as **GetOfficeApplication**, deselect the **Automatically retrieve data when form is opened** check box, and click **Finish**.

13. On the **Fields** task pane, select **GetOfficeApplication (Secondary)** from the **Fields** drop-down list box.

14. On the **Fields** task pane, expand the **queryFields** group node, expand the **GetOfficeApplication** group node, and then drag-and-drop the **Id** field onto the view of the form template.

15. On the **Fields** task pane, expand the **dataFields** group node, expand the **GetOfficeApplicationResponse** group node, and then drag-and-drop the **GetOfficeApplicationResult** group node onto the view of the form template.

16. Add a **Button** control to the view of the form template and change its **Action** property to **Refresh**.

17. Preview the form.

When the form opens, enter a valid identifier in the **Id** field and then click the **Refresh** button. The data for the Office application that has the identifier you entered should appear in the text boxes on the form.

Discussion

When you add a query data connection for a web service in InfoPath, InfoPath creates a secondary data source that has two main group nodes: **queryFields** and **dataFields**. The **queryFields** group node contains fields that correspond to the parameters you can pass to the web service method, while the **dataFields** group node contains fields that correspond to the data returned by the web service method.

Figure 51. The secondary data source for a web service that returns a record.

In the solution described above, you created a web service method that takes an integer (**Id** field under the **queryFields** group node) and returns an `OfficeApplication` object (**GetOfficeApplicationResult** group node under the **dataFields** group node).

```
[WebMethod(Description=
   "Returns an Office application based on its identifier.")]
public OfficeApplication GetOfficeApplication(int Id)
{
   ...
}
```

The code for the web service method in this solution is very similar to the code in the previous solution *Create a web service that returns one value* (refer to the discussion section for a detailed explanation of how the code works). The main difference is what the web service method returns. In *Create a web service that returns one value*, the web service method returned a string value, whereas in this solution the web service method returns an entire object that is serialized into a group node that contains three fields when the result is returned to the InfoPath form.

The query to retrieve data from the database is also slightly different in that it returns all of the information for one particular Office application.

```
SqlCommand cmd = new SqlCommand();
cmd.CommandType = System.Data.CommandType.Text;
cmd.CommandText = "SELECT OfficeApplicationId, OfficeApplicationName, "
   + "OfficeApplicationColor FROM OfficeApplications "
   + "WHERE OfficeApplicationID = @Id";
cmd.Parameters.Add("Id", System.Data.SqlDbType.Int).Value = Id;
cmd.Connection = conn;
```

And because the properties of the `OfficeApplication` object have to be set before it is returned to InfoPath, the code for reading the `SqlDataReader` object is also slightly different.

```
while (reader.Read())
{
  officeApp.Id = reader.GetInt32(0);
  officeApp.Name = reader.GetString(1);
  officeApp.Color = reader.GetString(2);
}
```

And finally, the `OfficeApplication` object is returned to the InfoPath form instead of only a name.

```
return officeApp;
```

The main takeaway of this solution is to know that if you return a serializable object that has properties to an InfoPath form via a call to a web service, that object becomes a group node that contains fields in InfoPath. In the next solution you will see how you can return a repeating group node from a web service to an InfoPath form so that you can bind the data to a repeating table or a repeating section control on the InfoPath form.

Create a web service that returns several records

Problem

You have a SQL Server database table from which you want to retrieve all records using a web service.

Solution

You can create a web service that has a web method that returns all of the records from a database table as a repeating group node.

To create a web service that returns database records in a repeating group node:

1. Follow steps 1 through 13 of *Create a web service that returns one value* in this recipe.

2. Replace the `HelloWorld()` web method with the following web method or add a new web method if you wish (*code #: 69E86FF3-D9DD-44F5-A003-901C101EC4EA*):

```
[WebMethod(Description="Returns all Office applications.")]
public List<OfficeApplication> GetOfficeApplications()
{
  List<OfficeApplication> list = new List<OfficeApplication>();
  string connectionString =
    ConfigurationManager.ConnectionStrings["InfoPathDB"].ConnectionString;

  using (SqlConnection conn = new SqlConnection(connectionString))
  {
    SqlCommand cmd = new SqlCommand();
    cmd.CommandType = System.Data.CommandType.Text;
    cmd.CommandText = "SELECT OfficeApplicationId, OfficeApplicationName, "
      + "OfficeApplicationColor FROM OfficeApplications";
    cmd.Connection = conn;

    try
```

```
{
  conn.Open();

  using (SqlDataReader reader = cmd.ExecuteReader())
  {
    while (reader.Read())
    {
      OfficeApplication offApp = new OfficeApplication();
      offApp.Id = reader.GetInt32(0);
      offApp.Name = reader.GetString(1);
      offApp.Color = reader.GetString(2);
      list.Add(offApp);
    }

    reader.Close();
  }
}
catch
{
  // Handle the error using your own preferred error-handling method
}
finally
{
  conn.Close();
}
}
return list;
}
```

3. Click **Build ➤ Build Solution** and fix any errors if necessary.

4. Click **Debug ➤ Start Debugging**. This should open a browser window and display the **InfoPathService.asmx** page.

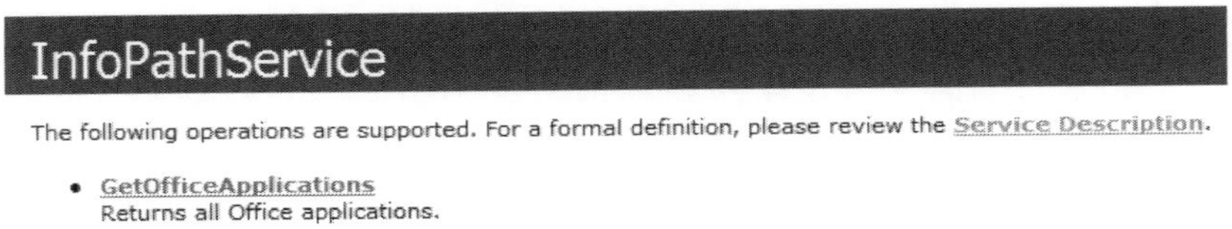

InfoPathService

The following operations are supported. For a formal definition, please review the Service Description.

- GetOfficeApplications
  Returns all Office applications.

Figure 52. The page for the InfoPathService web service.

5. Click the link for the **GetOfficeApplications** web method, and then click **Invoke** to verify that the web method is working properly and returning the correct data.

```
<?xml version="1.0" encoding="utf-8" ?>
- <ArrayOfOfficeApplication xmlns:xsi="http://www.w3.org/2001/XMLSchema-instance"
    xmlns:xsd="http://www.w3.org/2001/XMLSchema"
    xmlns="http://www.bizsupportonline.net/namespaces/infopathservice/">
  - <OfficeApplication>
      <Id>1</Id>
      <Name>Word</Name>
      <Color>Blue</Color>
    </OfficeApplication>
  - <OfficeApplication>
      <Id>2</Id>
      <Name>Excel</Name>
      <Color>Green</Color>
    </OfficeApplication>
  - <OfficeApplication>
      <Id>3</Id>
      <Name>Access</Name>
      <Color>Red</Color>
    </OfficeApplication>
  - <OfficeApplication>
      <Id>4</Id>
      <Name>InfoPath</Name>
      <Color>Purple</Color>
    </OfficeApplication>
  - <OfficeApplication>
      <Id>5</Id>
      <Name>OneNote</Name>
      <Color>Purple</Color>
    </OfficeApplication>
  - <OfficeApplication>
      <Id>6</Id>
      <Name>PowerPoint</Name>
      <Color>Dark Orange</Color>
    </OfficeApplication>
  </ArrayOfOfficeApplication>
```

Figure 53. XML returned by the web method invocation.

6. With the web service still running in debug mode, open InfoPath Designer 2010, and create a new **Blank Form** template.

7. Select **Data ➤ Get External Data ➤ From Web Service ➤ From SOAP Web Service**.

8. On the **Data Connection Wizard**, enter the URL of the web service, for example:

```
http://localhost:24014/InfoPathService.asmx
```

and click **Next**. Note that an URL such as the one specified above should work if you are running the web service and InfoPath on the same computer. Otherwise, you may have to deploy the web service first before you are able to access it in InfoPath.

9. On the **Data Connection Wizard**, select the **GetOfficeApplications** operation, and click **Next**. Note that the description you gave the web method should appear in the **Description of operation** box.

10. On the **Data Connection Wizard**, leave the **Store a copy of the data in the form template** check box deselected, and click **Next**.

11. On the **Data Connection Wizard**, leave the data connection name as **GetOfficeApplications**, deselect the **Automatically retrieve data when form is opened** check box, and click **Finish**.

12. On the **Fields** task pane, select **GetOfficeApplications (Secondary)** from the **Fields** drop-down list box.

13. On the **Fields** task pane, expand the **dataFields** group node, expand the **GetOfficeApplicationsResponse** group node, expand the **GetOfficeApplicationsResult** group node, and then drag-and-drop the **GetOfficeApplication** repeating group node onto the view of the form template. Select **Repeating Table** when you drop the repeating group node.

14. Add a **Button** control to the view of the form template and change its **Action** property to **Refresh**.

15. Preview the form.

When the form opens, click the **Refresh** button. The data for all of the Office applications should appear in the repeating table on the form.

Discussion

When you add a query data connection for a web service in InfoPath, InfoPath creates a secondary data source that has two main group nodes: **queryFields** and **dataFields**. The **queryFields** group node contains fields that correspond to the parameters you can pass to the web service method, while the **dataFields** group node contains fields that correspond to the data returned by the web service method.

Figure 54. The secondary data source for a web service that returns several records.

In the solution described above, you created a web service method that does not take any parameters (there are no fields under the **queryFields** group node) and returns a List of OfficeApplication objects (**GetOfficeApplicationsResult** group node with an **OfficeApplication** repeating group node under the **dataFields** group node).

```
[WebMethod(Description="Returns all Office applications.")]
public List<OfficeApplication> GetOfficeApplications()
{
  List<OfficeApplication> list = new List<OfficeApplication>();
  ...
}
```

The code for the web service method in this solution is very similar to the code in *Create a web service that returns one value* (refer to the discussion section for a detailed explanation of how the code works). The main difference is what the web service method returns. In *Create a web service that returns one value*, the web service method returned a string value, in *Create a web service that returns one record* the web service method returned an OfficeApplication object, and in this solution the web service method returns a List of OfficeApplication objects that is serialized into a repeating group node structure in the InfoPath form.

The query to retrieve data from the database is also slightly different in that it returns all of the Office applications from the database table.

```
SqlCommand cmd = new SqlCommand();
cmd.CommandType = System.Data.CommandType.Text;
cmd.CommandText = "SELECT OfficeApplicationId, OfficeApplicationName, "
  + "OfficeApplicationColor FROM OfficeApplications";
cmd.Connection = conn;
```

And because a List of OfficeApplication objects must be constructed before it is returned to InfoPath, the code for reading the SqlDataReader object is also slightly different.

```
while (reader.Read())
{
  OfficeApplication offApp = new OfficeApplication();
  offApp.Id = reader.GetInt32(0);
  offApp.Name = reader.GetString(1);
  offApp.Color = reader.GetString(2);
  list.Add(offApp);
}
```

And finally, the List of OfficeApplication objects is returned to the InfoPath form instead of only a name.

```
return list;
```

Note that instead of returning a generic List of OfficeApplication objects, you could have also created a separate class named OfficeApplications that inherits from a generic List of OfficeApplication objects.

```
public class OfficeApplications : List<OfficeApplication>
{
}
```

This would have rendered the same results as in the solution described above.

The main takeaway of this solution is to know that if you return a serializable collection of objects to an InfoPath form via a call to a web service, that collection becomes a repeating group node that contains fields in InfoPath.

82   Submit form field values to a web service

Submit form field values as separate parameters

Problem

You have an InfoPath form from which you want to submit values of a few fields to a web service.

Solution

You can add separate parameters for each form field value you want to submit to the web service method used to submit the data.

To submit form field values as separate parameters to a web service:

1. Follow steps 1 through 13 of *Create a web service that returns one value* in recipe *81 Create a web service that retrieves data for InfoPath*.

2. Replace the `HelloWorld()` web method with the following web method or add a new web method if you wish (*code #: AD40689B-83BB-48B9-803D-6D2BD1B28702*):

```
[WebMethod(Description="Adds an Office application to the database.")]
public void AddOfficeApplication(string Name, string Color)
{
  string connectionString =
    ConfigurationManager.ConnectionStrings["InfoPathDB"].ConnectionString;

  using (SqlConnection conn = new SqlConnection(connectionString))
  {
    SqlCommand cmd = new SqlCommand();
    cmd.CommandType = System.Data.CommandType.Text;
    cmd.CommandText = "INSERT INTO OfficeApplications "
      + "(OfficeApplicationName, OfficeApplicationColor) "
      + "VALUES (@Name, @Color)";
    cmd.Parameters.AddWithValue("Name", Name);
    cmd.Parameters.AddWithValue("Color", Color);
    cmd.Connection = conn;

    try
    {
      conn.Open();
      cmd.ExecuteNonQuery();
    }
    catch
    {
      // Handle the error using your own preferred error-handling method
    }
```

```
    finally
    {
      conn.Close();
    }
  }
}
```

3. Click **Build ➤ Build Solution** and fix any errors if necessary.

4. Click **Debug ➤ Start Debugging**. This should open a browser window and display the **InfoPathService.asmx** page.

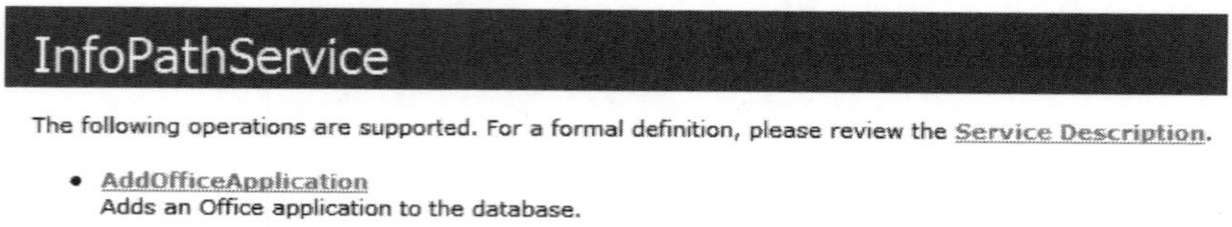

InfoPathService

The following operations are supported. For a formal definition, please review the Service Description.

- **AddOfficeApplication**
  Adds an Office application to the database.

Figure 55. The page for the InfoPathService web service.

5. With the web service still running in debug mode, open InfoPath Designer 2010, and create a new **Blank Form** template.

6. Add two **Text Box** controls to the view of the form template and name them **applicationName** and **applicationColor**, respectively.

7. Select **Data ➤ Submit Form ➤ To Other Locations ➤ To Web Service**.

8. On the **Data Connection Wizard**, enter the URL of the web service, for example:

```
http://localhost:24014/InfoPathService.asmx
```

and click **Next**. Note that an URL such as the one specified above should work if you are running the web service and InfoPath on the same computer. Otherwise, you may have to deploy the web service first before you are able to access it in InfoPath.

9. On the **Data Connection Wizard**, select the **AddOfficeApplication** operation, and click **Next**. Note that the description you gave the web method should appear in the **Description of operation** box.

10. On the **Data Connection Wizard**, ensure the **Name** parameter is selected, and then click the button behind the **Field or group** text box.

11. On the **Select a Field or Group** dialog box, select the **applicationName** field, and click **OK**.

12. On the **Data Connection Wizard**, leave **Text and child elements only** selected in the **Include** drop-down list box, leave the **Submit data as a string** check box deselected, select the **Color** parameter, and then click the button behind the **Field or group** text box.

13. On the **Select a Field or Group** dialog box, select the **applicationColor** field, and click **OK**.

14. On the **Data Connection Wizard**, leave **Text and child elements only** selected in the **Include** drop-down list box, leave the **Submit data as a string** check box deselected, and click **Next**.

15. On the **Data Connection Wizard**, leave the data connection name as **Web Service Submit**, leave the **Set as the default submit connection** check box selected, and then click **Finish**.

16. Preview the form.

When the form opens, enter values into the **Name** and **Color** text boxes, and then click the **Submit** button on the toolbar. Open SQL Server Management Studio and verify that the data was submitted to the database table.

Discussion

Creating a web service to submit data from an InfoPath form is very similar to creating a web service to retrieve data for an InfoPath form. You start by creating a web service method that accepts parameters and returns nothing.

```
[WebMethod(Description="Adds an Office application to the database.")]
public void AddOfficeApplication(string Name, string Color)
{
   ...
}
```

Where parameters are concerned, you can choose to submit separate parameters as shown in the solution above, or you can choose to submit an entire object, whether it is one object (as shown in the next solution), a repeating table (as shown in recipe *83 Submit repeating table data to a web service*), or an entire form (as shown in recipe *84 Submit an entire form to a web service*) to the web service. The code in the solution described above passes separate field values as parameters to the web service method.

The functionality of the web service method that submits data is similar to that of the web service method that retrieves data. The difference in this case lies in using a SQL INSERT statement to submit the data to the database, instead of a SQL SELECT statement to retrieve data from the database.

```
SqlCommand cmd = new SqlCommand();
cmd.CommandType = System.Data.CommandType.Text;
cmd.CommandText = "INSERT INTO OfficeApplications "
  + "(OfficeApplicationName, OfficeApplicationColor) "
  + "VALUES (@Name, @Color)";
cmd.Parameters.AddWithValue("Name", Name);
cmd.Parameters.AddWithValue("Color", Color);
cmd.Connection = conn;
```

In addition, the `ExecuteNonQuery()` method of the `SqlCommand` object is used to execute the query and insert the data into the database table.

```
conn.Open();
cmd.ExecuteNonQuery();
```

Note:

> InfoPath does not create secondary data sources for submit data connections, so even if a web service method returns a value, you would not be able to retrieve this value unless you called the web service through code as demonstrated in recipe *85 Retrieve return values after data has been submitted to a web service.*

Submit form field values as one object

Problem

You have an InfoPath form from which you want to submit values of a few fields as a group to a web service.

Solution

You can create a class that encapsulates the data you want to submit as a group and then use this class as a parameter of the web service method used to submit the data.

To submit form field values as one object to a web service:

1. Follow steps 1 through 13 of *Create a web service that returns one value* in recipe *81 Create a web service that retrieves data for InfoPath*.

2. Replace the `HelloWorld()` web method with the following web method or add a new web method if you wish (*code #: F28A3CC4-F6ED-475F-9EE7-2692768D92B2*):

```
[WebMethod(Description="Adds an Office application to the database.")]
public void AddOfficeApplication(OfficeApplication officeApplication)
{
  string connectionString =
    ConfigurationManager.ConnectionStrings["InfoPathDB"].ConnectionString;

  using (SqlConnection conn = new SqlConnection(connectionString))
  {
    SqlCommand cmd = new SqlCommand();
    cmd.CommandType = System.Data.CommandType.Text;
    cmd.CommandText = "INSERT INTO OfficeApplications "
      + "(OfficeApplicationName, OfficeApplicationColor) "
      + "VALUES (@Name, @Color)";
    cmd.Parameters.AddWithValue("Name", officeApplication.Name);
    cmd.Parameters.AddWithValue("Color", officeApplication.Color);
    cmd.Connection = conn;
```

```
try
{
  conn.Open();
  cmd.ExecuteNonQuery();
}
catch
{
  // Handle the error using your own preferred error-handling method
}
finally
{
  conn.Close();
}
  }
}
```

3. Click **Build ➤ Build Solution** and fix any errors if necessary.

4. Click **Debug ➤ Start Debugging**. This should open a browser window and display the **InfoPathService.asmx** page.

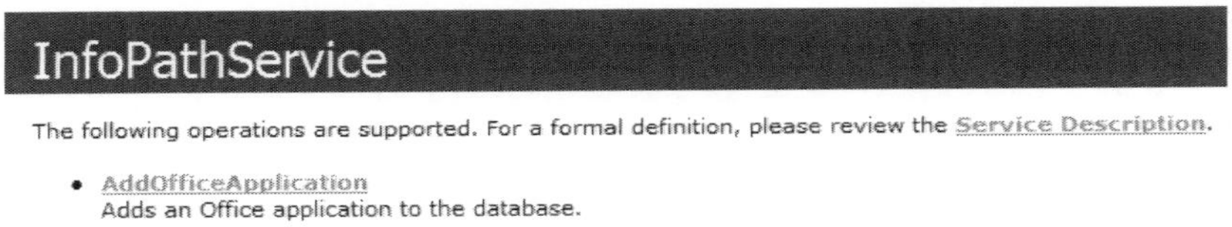

InfoPathService

The following operations are supported. For a formal definition, please review the Service Description.

- AddOfficeApplication
  Adds an Office application to the database.

Figure 56. The page for the InfoPathService web service.

5. Click the link for the **AddOfficeApplication** web method, and then copy the XML from the **soap:Body** element:

```
<AddOfficeApplication
  xmlns="http://www.bizsupportonline.net/namespaces/infopathservice/">
  <officeApplication>
    <Id>int</Id>
    <Name>string</Name>
    <Color>string</Color>
  </officeApplication>
</AddOfficeApplication>
```

Open Notepad, paste the XML you just copied, and save the file as an XML file named **AddOfficeApplication.xml**. Important: Ensure that there are no line-breaks, tabs, or spaces between the elements in the XML file. You can also download the **AddOfficeApplication.xml** file from www.bizsupportonline.com.

6. With the web service still running in debug mode, open InfoPath Designer 2010, and create a new **Blank Form** template.

7. This solution submits an XML fragment containing the data for an Office application to the web service method. You can add the XML fragment either as a secondary data source to the form template or make it part of the Main data source, depending on whether you want to store the data submitted to the web service in the form itself.

If you do not want to store the data as part of the form, create a secondary data source as follows:

a. Select **Data ➤ Get External Data ➤ From Other Sources ➤ From XML File**.

b. On the **Data Connection Wizard**, click **Browse**.

c. On the **Open** dialog box, browse to and select the **AddOfficeApplication.xml** file, and click **Open**.

d. On the **Data Connection Wizard**, click **Next**.

e. On the **Data Connection Wizard**, click **Next**.

f. On the **Data Connection Wizard**, leave the **Automatically retrieve data when form is opened** check box selected, and click **Finish**.

If you want to store the data as part of the form, add the XML fragment to the Main data source as follows:

a. On the **Fields** task pane, right-click the **myFields** group node, and select **Add** from the drop-down menu that appears.

b. On the **Add Field or Group** dialog box, select **Complete XML Schema or XML document** from the **Type** drop-down list box.

c. On the **Data Source Wizard**, click **Browse**.

d. On the **Open** dialog box, browse to and select the **AddOfficeApplication.xml** file, and click **Open**.

e. On the **Data Source Wizard**, click **Next**.

f. On the **Data Source Wizard**, leave the **No** option selected, and click **Finish**.

g. On the **Add Field or Group** dialog box, click **OK**.

8. Select **Data ➤ Submit Form ➤ To Other Locations ➤ To Web Service**.

9. On the **Data Connection Wizard**, enter the URL of the web service, for example:

```
http://localhost:24014/InfoPathService.asmx
```

and click **Next**. Note that an URL such as the one specified above should work if you are running the web service and InfoPath on the same computer. Otherwise, you may have to deploy the web service first before you are able to access it in InfoPath.

10. On the **Data Connection Wizard**, select the **AddOfficeApplication** operation, and click **Next**. Note that the description you gave the web method should appear in the **Description of operation** box.

11. On the **Data Connection Wizard**, ensure the **officeApplication** parameter is selected, and then click the button behind the **Field or group** text box.

12. On the **Select a Field or Group** dialog box, expand all of the group nodes, select the **officeApplication** group node, and click **OK**. Note that if you added the **AddOfficeApplication.xml** file as a secondary data source to the form template in step 7, you would first have to select **AddOfficeApplication (Secondary)** from the **Fields** drop-down list box before you expand all of the group nodes and then select the **officeApplication** group node.

13. On the **Data Connection Wizard**, leave **Text and child elements only** selected in the **Include** drop-down list box, leave the **Submit data as a string** check box deselected, and click **Next**.

14. On the **Data Connection Wizard**, leave the data connection name as **Web Service Submit**, leave the **Set as the default submit connection** check box selected, and then click **Finish**.

15. On the **Fields** task pane, drag-and-drop the **officeApplication** group node (either from the Main or a secondary data source depending on the selection you made in step 7) onto the view of the form template.

16. Preview the form.

When the form opens, enter a **0** in the **Id** text box, enter values into the **Name** and **Color** text boxes, and then click the **Submit** button on the toolbar. Open SQL Server Management Studio and verify that the data was submitted to the database table.

Discussion

The solution described above is similar to the previous solution. The only difference is that in this case the web service method accepts an object instead of two separate parameters.

```
[WebMethod(Description="Adds an Office application to the database.")]
public void AddOfficeApplication(OfficeApplication officeApplication)
{
  ...
}
```

And when constructing the SQL statement for the `SqlCommand` object, the information is extracted from the object instead of from separate parameters.

```
SqlCommand cmd = new SqlCommand();
cmd.CommandType = System.Data.CommandType.Text;
cmd.CommandText = "INSERT INTO OfficeApplications "
  + "(OfficeApplicationName, OfficeApplicationColor) "
  + "VALUES (@Name, @Color)";
cmd.Parameters.AddWithValue("Name", officeApplication.Name);
cmd.Parameters.AddWithValue("Color", officeApplication.Color);
cmd.Connection = conn;
```

Key to making this solution work is using an XML structure in InfoPath that can be deserialized into the object expected by the web service method. In the solution above, the XML structure was copied from the web service page. This XML was then included in the form as either part of the Main data source (using the **Complete XML Schema or XML document** type) or as a secondary data source, and was then used to set the value of the web service operation parameter.

83   Submit repeating table data to a web service

Problem

You have a repeating table on an InfoPath form from which you want to submit its rows to a web service.

Solution

You can use XML serialization attributes on classes the web service uses, so that the XML the web service method expects to receive has the exact same structure as the XML produced by the repeating table on the InfoPath form.

To submit data from a repeating table to a web service:

1. In InfoPath, create a new form template or use an existing one.

2. Add a **Repeating Table** control with 2 columns to the view of the form template, rename the **group1** group node of the repeating table to **Applications**, rename the **group2** repeating group node to **OfficeApplication**, and rename the text boxes within the repeating table to **Name** and **Color**, respectively. Note that these names have not been chosen randomly, but must be the same as the name of the web method parameter (**Applications**) and the class used by the web service to create an `OfficeApplication` object.

Figure 57. Main data source with the nodes for the repeating table.

3. Preview the form and save it locally on disk. Then open the form you saved in Notepad, search for the declaration of the **my** namespace, and copy the namespace URI, for example:

`http://schemas.microsoft.com/office/infopath/2003/myXSD/2011-10-18T22:39:22`

You will be using this namespace URI in the web service, so that the web service is able to recognize the XML sent to it.

4. Follow steps 1 through 13 of *Create a web service that returns one value* in recipe *81 Create a web service that retrieves data for InfoPath*, but at step 8, delete the **Id**

property from the `OfficeApplication` class. The code for the class should now resemble the following:

```
public class OfficeApplication
{
  public string Name { get; set; }
  public string Color { get; set; }
}
```

5. Add the following **using** statement to the **InfoPathService.asmx.cs** file:

```
using System.Xml.Serialization;
```

6. Replace the `HelloWorld()` web method with the following web method or add a new web method if you wish (*code #: AF6DEA96-722D-437C-B545-BC9EC4590475*):

```
[WebMethod(
  Description="Adds one or more Office applications to the database.")]
public void AddOfficeApplications (
  [XmlArray(Namespace =
    "http://schemas.microsoft.com/office/infopath/2003/myXSD/2011-10-
18T22:39:22")]
  List<OfficeApplication> Applications)
{
  string connectionString =
    ConfigurationManager.ConnectionStrings["InfoPathDB"].ConnectionString;

  using (SqlConnection conn = new SqlConnection(connectionString))
  {
    try
    {
      conn.Open();

      foreach (OfficeApplication app in Applications)
      {
        SqlCommand cmd = new SqlCommand();
        cmd.CommandType = System.Data.CommandType.Text;
        cmd.Connection = conn;

        cmd.CommandText = "INSERT INTO OfficeApplications "
          + "(OfficeApplicationName, OfficeApplicationColor) "
          + "VALUES (@Name, @Color)";
        cmd.Parameters.AddWithValue("Name", app.Name);
        cmd.Parameters.AddWithValue("Color", app.Color);
        cmd.ExecuteNonQuery();
      }
    }
    catch
    {
      // Handle the error using your own preferred error-handling method
    }
    finally
    {
      conn.Close();
    }
  }
}
```

where you should replace the namespace URI with the one you copied earlier.

7. Click **Build ➤ Build Solution** and fix any errors if necessary.

8. Click **Debug ➤ Start Debugging**. This should open a browser window and display the **InfoPathService.asmx** page.

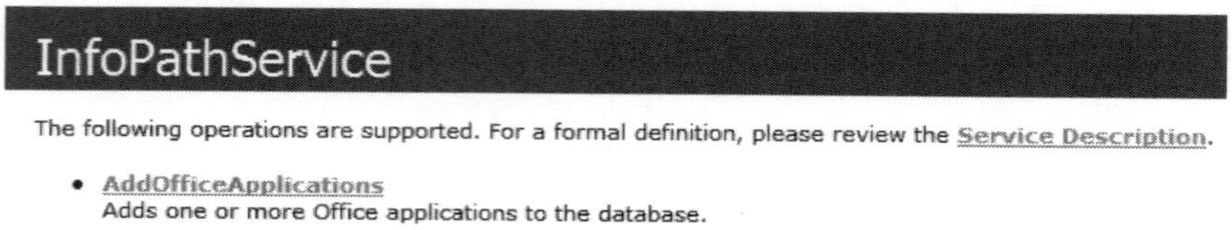

InfoPathService

The following operations are supported. For a formal definition, please review the Service Description.

- **AddOfficeApplications**
  Adds one or more Office applications to the database.

Figure 58. The page for the InfoPathService web service.

9. Click the link for the **AddOfficeApplications** web method. Verify that the XML of the **soap:Body** element contains the namespace URI of the InfoPath form as follows:

```
<AddOfficeApplications
  xmlns="http://www.bizsupportonline.net/namespaces/infopathservice/">
  <Applications
    xmlns="http://schemas.microsoft.com/office/infopath/2003/myXSD/2011-10-
18T22:39:22">
    <OfficeApplication>
      <Name>string</Name>
      <Color>string</Color>
    </OfficeApplication>
    <OfficeApplication>
      <Name>string</Name>
      <Color>string</Color>
    </OfficeApplication>
  </Applications>
</AddOfficeApplications>
```

The namespace of the InfoPath form is defined as the default namespace on the **Applications** element, which is equivalent to the **Applications** group node of the repeating table. All of the child elements of the **Applications** element inherit this default namespace, which results in the same XML structure produced by the repeating table in InfoPath. This should allow the web service to deserialize the XML from the repeating table into an array of `OfficeApplication` objects.

10. With the web service still running in debug mode, in InfoPath, select **Data ➤ Submit Form ➤ To Other Locations ➤ To Web Service**.

11. On the **Data Connection Wizard**, enter the URL of the web service, for example:

```
http://localhost:24014/InfoPathService.asmx
```

and click **Next**. Note that an URL such as the one specified above should work if you are running the web service and InfoPath on the same computer. Otherwise, you may have to deploy the web service first before you are able to access it in InfoPath.

12. On the **Data Connection Wizard**, select the **AddOfficeApplications** operation, and click **Next**. Note that the description you gave the web method should appear in the **Description of operation** box.

13. On the **Data Connection Wizard**, ensure the **Applications** parameter is selected, and then click the button behind the **Field or group** text box.

14. On the **Select a Field or Group** dialog box, select the **Applications** group node of the repeating table, and click **OK**.

15. On the **Data Connection Wizard**, leave **Text and child elements only** selected in the **Include** drop-down list box, leave the **Submit data as a string** check box deselected, and click **Next**.

16. On the **Data Connection Wizard**, leave the data connection name as **Web Service Submit**, leave the **Set as the default submit connection** check box selected, and then click **Finish**.

17. Preview the form.

When the form opens, add rows to the repeating table, enter values into the **Name** and **Color** text boxes, and then click the **Submit** button on the toolbar. Open SQL Server Management Studio and verify that the data was submitted to the database table.

Discussion

The solution described above is similar to the solutions described in recipe *82 Submit form field values to a web service* in that the web service method uses similar code to submit data to the database. The main difference lies in using a generic List object to pass items from a repeating table to the web service. But just like in *Submit form field values as one object* in recipe *82 Submit form field values to a web service*, you must ensure that the piece of XML that comes from the repeating table in InfoPath is accepted by the web service method. Therefore, you must make use of an XmlArray attribute and set its Namespace property to be equal to the namespace URI used by the XML for the repeating table.

The XmlArrayAttribute class specifies that the XmlSerializer must serialize a particular class member as an array of XML elements. You can apply it to a public field or read/write property that returns an array of objects, a collection, or any class that implements the IEnumerable interface. In the solution described above, it was applied to a generic List of OfficeApplication objects.

```
public void AddOfficeApplications(
  [XmlArray] List<OfficeApplication> Applications)
{ ... }
```

In addition, the code used the namespace URI of the InfoPath form to set the Namespace property of the XmlArray attribute.

```
XmlArray(Namespace =
  "http://schemas.microsoft.com/office/infopath/2003/myXSD/2011-10-18T22:39:22")
```

By setting the namespace for the XmlArray attribute to be the same as that of the InfoPath form, the generic List object will have the same namespace as the InfoPath form when it is serialized to XML. And because no explicit namespaces have been defined on the OfficeApplication objects, those objects will inherit the same namespace from their parent List object. This allows you to submit the XML of the repeating table on the InfoPath form to the web service method and have the web service seamlessly deserialize that XML into a generic List object that contains OfficeApplication objects.

84 Submit an entire form to a web service

Use a class for the InfoPath form that has to be submitted

Problem

You have an InfoPath form which you want users to be able to submit in its entirety to a web service.

Solution

You can submit the InfoPath form as an object that is based on the XML schema definition of the InfoPath form and then in the web service method use properties to extract the information you require from the InfoPath form.

To submit an entire form to a web service using a class:

1. Follow steps 1 and 2 of recipe *83 Submit repeating table data to a web service* to create a form template. In addition, rename the **myFields** group node to **InfoPathFormToSubmit**.

Figure 59. The Main data source of the InfoPath form.

2. In InfoPath, click **File ➤ Publish ➤ Export Source Files**.

3. On the **Browse For Folder** dialog box, create a new folder or select an existing folder for saving the source files, and click **OK**.

4. Close InfoPath Designer 2010.

5. Open the **Visual Studio Command Prompt (2010)**, which is by default located under the **Microsoft Visual Studio 2010 ➤ Visual Studio Tools** program folder.

6. In the **Visual Studio Command Prompt (2010)** window, enter a command to generate a class file from the XSD file, for example:

```
xsd "C:\InfoPath\ExportedSourceFiles\myschema.xsd" /c /l:cs /o:C:\Temp\
```

You should change the path to the **myschema.xsd** file (`C:\InfoPath\ExportedSourceFiles\myschema.xsd`) to be the same as the path to the folder where you extracted the form files. This should generate a C# class file named **myschema.cs** and place it in the `C:\Temp` folder. The class should allow you to access values of form fields through collections and properties specified on the class. You can download the **myschema.cs** file from www.bizsupportonline.com to verify its contents against the class file you generated.

7. In Windows Explorer, navigate to the directory that contains the exported source files, right-click the **manifest.xsf** file and select **Design** from the context menu that appears.

8. In InfoPath, click **File ➤ Save As**, and save the form template to a location on disk. This should bundle the exported source files back into an XSN file.

9. Follow steps 1 through 13 of *Create a web service that returns one value* in recipe *81 Create a web service that retrieves data for InfoPath*, but instead of steps 6 through 8, do the following:

   a. On the **Solution Explorer** pane, right-click the project name and select **Add ➤ Existing Item** from the context menu that appears.

   b. On the **Add Existing Item** dialog box, browse to and select the **myschema.cs** file you generated earlier, and then click **Add**.

10. Replace the `HelloWorld()` web method with the following web method or add a new web method if you wish (*code #: 49438B3F-49EB-4CB7-A1AE-9E12B064AA72*):

```
[WebMethod(
  Description = "Submits an InfoPath form of type InfoPathFormToSubmit.")]
public void SubmitForm(InfoPathFormToSubmit InfoPathForm)
{
  string connectionString =
    ConfigurationManager.ConnectionStrings["InfoPathDB"].ConnectionString;

  using (SqlConnection conn = new SqlConnection(connectionString))
  {
    try
    {
      conn.Open();

      foreach (OfficeApplication app in InfoPathForm.Applications)
      {
        SqlCommand cmd = new SqlCommand();
        cmd.CommandType = System.Data.CommandType.Text;
        cmd.Connection = conn;
```

```
        cmd.CommandText = "INSERT INTO OfficeApplications "
          + "(OfficeApplicationName, OfficeApplicationColor) "
          + "VALUES (@Name, @Color)";
        cmd.Parameters.AddWithValue("Name", app.Name);
        cmd.Parameters.AddWithValue("Color", app.Color);

        cmd.ExecuteNonQuery();
      }
    }
    catch
    {
      // Handle the error using your own preferred error-handling method
    }
    finally
    {
      conn.Close();
    }
  }
}
```

11. Click **Build** ➤ **Build Solution** and fix any errors if necessary.

12. Click **Debug** ➤ **Start Debugging**. This should open a browser window and display the **InfoPathService.asmx** page.

13. With the web service still running in debug mode, in InfoPath, select **Data** ➤ **Submit Form** ➤ **To Other Locations** ➤ **To Web Service**.

14. On the **Data Connection Wizard**, enter the URL of the web service, for example:

```
http://localhost:24014/InfoPathService.asmx
```

and click **Next**. Note that an URL such as the one specified above should work if you are running the web service and InfoPath on the same computer. Otherwise, you may have to deploy the web service first before you are able to access it in InfoPath.

15. On the **Data Connection Wizard**, select the **SubmitForm** operation, and click **Next**. Note that the description you gave the web method should appear in the **Description of operation** box.

16. On the **Data Connection Wizard**, ensure the **InfoPathForm** parameter is selected, and then click the button behind the **Field or group** text box.

17. On the **Select a Field or Group** dialog box, select the **InfoPathFormToSubmit** group node, and click **OK**.

18. On the **Data Connection Wizard**, leave **Text and child elements only** selected in the **Include** drop-down list box, leave the **Submit data as a string** check box deselected, and click **Next**.

19. On the **Data Connection Wizard**, leave the data connection name as **Web Service Submit**, leave the **Set as the default submit connection** check box selected, and then click **Finish**.

20. Preview the form.

When the form opens, add rows to the repeating table, enter values into the **Name** and **Color** text boxes, and then click the **Submit** button on the toolbar. Open SQL Server Management Studio and verify that the data was submitted to the database table.

Discussion

If your scenario requires you to submit InfoPath forms that are based on a specific XML schema to a web service, you can use the technique described in the solution above to generate a class that is based on the XML schema of the InfoPath form to be able to submit the entire form to a web service.

The solution described above makes use of the XSD tool of Visual Studio 2010 to generate a class that is based on the XML schema of an InfoPath form. Before you can generate a class file using the XSD tool, you must extract the **myschema.xsd** file from the form template using the **Export Source Files** command in InfoPath or by changing the file extension of the form template from XSN to CAB, and then copying the **myschema.xsd** file from the cabinet file.

After adding the generated C# class file to the web service project, it is then just a matter of using the class as a type for the parameter passed to the web service

```
[WebMethod(
  Description = "Submit an InfoPath form of type InfoPathFormToSubmit.")]
public void SubmitForm(InfoPathFormToSubmit InfoPathForm)
{
  ...
}
```

and then using properties of the C# class within the web method to be able to extract information from the InfoPath form that was submitted to the web service.

```
foreach (OfficeApplication app in InfoPathForm.Applications)
{
  ...
}
```

And finally, you can make use of ADO.NET classes to submit the extracted information to the database as has already been described in previous recipes in this chapter.

Use an XmlDocument object and LINQ to XML

Problem

You have an InfoPath form which you want users to be able to submit in its entirety to a web service.

Solution

You can submit the InfoPath form as a generic `XmlDocument` object to a web service and then use LINQ to XML in the web service method to extract the information you require from the InfoPath form.

To submit an entire form to a web service using an `XmlDocument` object:

1. Follow steps 1 and 2 of recipe *83 Submit repeating table data to a web service* to create a form template.

2. Follow steps 1 through 13 of *Create a web service that returns one value* in recipe *81 Create a web service that retrieves data for InfoPath*, but at step 8, delete the **Id** property from the `OfficeApplication` class. The code for the class should now resemble the following (*code #: 7934A02B-C700-4C0A-A788-642C59B3C121*):

    ```
    public class OfficeApplication
    {
      public string Name { get; set; }
      public string Color { get; set; }
    }
    ```

3. Add the following **using** statements to the **InfoPathService.asmx.cs** file:

    ```
    using System.Xml;
    using System.Xml.XPath;
    using System.Xml.Linq;
    ```

4. Replace the `HelloWorld()` web method with the following web method or add a new web method if you wish (*code #: 7934A02B-C700-4C0A-A788-642C59B3C121*):

    ```
    [WebMethod(Description="Submits an entire InfoPath form.")]
    public void SubmitForm(XmlDocument InfoPathForm)
    {
      XPathNavigator root = InfoPathForm.CreateNavigator();
      root.MoveToFollowing(XPathNodeType.Element);
      string ns = root.GetNamespace("my");

      XDocument xdoc =
        XDocument.Load(InfoPathForm.CreateNavigator().ReadSubtree());

      var my = XNamespace.Get(ns);

      var officeApplications =
        from e in xdoc.Descendants(my + "OfficeApplication")
        select new OfficeApplication
        {
          Name = e.Element(my + "Name").Value,
          Color = e.Element(my + "Color").Value
        };

      string connectionString =
        ConfigurationManager.ConnectionStrings["InfoPathDB"].ConnectionString;

      using (SqlConnection conn = new SqlConnection(connectionString))
      {
        try
        {
    ```

```
        conn.Open();

        foreach (var app in officeApplications)
        {
          SqlCommand cmd = new SqlCommand();
          cmd.CommandType = System.Data.CommandType.Text;
          cmd.Connection = conn;

          cmd.CommandText = "INSERT INTO OfficeApplications "
            + "(OfficeApplicationName, OfficeApplicationColor) "
            + "VALUES (@Name, @Color)";
          cmd.Parameters.AddWithValue("Name", app.Name);
          cmd.Parameters.AddWithValue("Color", app.Color);

          cmd.ExecuteNonQuery();
        }
      }
      catch
      {
        // Handle the error using your own preferred error-handling method
      }
      finally
      {
        conn.Close();
      }
    }
  }
```

5. Click **Build** ➤ **Build Solution** and fix any errors if necessary.

6. Click **Debug** ➤ **Start Debugging**. This should open a browser window and display the **InfoPathService.asmx** page.

7. With the web service still running in debug mode, in InfoPath, select **Data** ➤ **Submit Form** ➤ **To Other Locations** ➤ **To Web Service**.

8. On the **Data Connection Wizard**, enter the URL of the web service, for example:

   ```
   http://localhost:24014/InfoPathService.asmx
   ```

   and click **Next**. Note that an URL such as the one specified above should work if you are running the web service and InfoPath on the same computer. Otherwise, you may have to deploy the web service first before you are able to access it in InfoPath.

9. On the **Data Connection Wizard**, select the **SubmitForm** operation, and click **Next**. Note that the description you gave the web method should appear in the **Description of operation** box.

10. On the **Data Connection Wizard**, ensure the **InfoPathForm** parameter is selected, and then click the button behind the **Field or group** text box.

11. On the **Select a Field or Group** dialog box, select the **myFields** group node, and click **OK**.

12. On the **Data Connection Wizard**, select **XML subtree, including selected element** from the **Include** drop-down list box, leave the **Submit data as a string** check box deselected, and click **Next**.

13. On the **Data Connection Wizard**, leave the data connection name as **Web Service Submit**, leave the **Set as the default submit connection** check box selected, and then click **Finish**.

14. Preview the form.

When the form opens, add rows to the repeating table, enter values into the **Name** and **Color** text boxes, and then click the **Submit** button on the toolbar. Open SQL Server Management Studio and verify that the data was submitted to the database table.

Discussion

If your scenario requires you to submit InfoPath forms that are based on different XML schemas to the same web service (for example if you are storing entire InfoPath forms in the same SQL Server database table as described in recipe *90 Submit an entire InfoPath form to SQL Server*), you can use the technique described in the solution above to make use of a generic XmlDocument object to submit an entire form to a web service.

```
[WebMethod(Description="Submits an entire InfoPath form.")]
public void SubmitForm(XmlDocument InfoPathForm)
{
  ...
}
```

The solution described above makes use of LINQ to XML to read the XML data of the InfoPath form that was submitted by first retrieving the **my** namespace used in the InfoPath form

```
XPathNavigator root = InfoPathForm.CreateNavigator();
root.MoveToFollowing(XPathNodeType.Element);
string ns = root.GetNamespace("my");
```

and then creating an XDocument object

```
XDocument xdoc =
  XDocument.Load(InfoPathForm.CreateNavigator().ReadSubtree());
```

that can be used to extract information (in this case Office applications) from the InfoPath form.

```
var my = XNamespace.Get(ns);

var officeApplications =
  from e in xdoc.Descendants(my + "OfficeApplication")
  select new OfficeApplication
  {
```

```
  Name = e.Element(my + "Name").Value,
  Color = e.Element(my + "Color").Value
};
```

You can then make use of ADO.NET classes to submit the extracted information to the database as has already been described in previous recipes in this chapter.

85 Retrieve return values after data has been submitted to a web service

Use a web service proxy class

Problem

You want to use an InfoPath form to submit data to a web service. The web service returns a value, which you also want to display on the form after the data submission has taken place.

Solution

You must call the web service through code instead of using a data connection to be able to retrieve the value returned by the web service. You can use a web service proxy class to programmatically call a web service.

To programmatically submit data to a web service and get the value returned by the web service:

1. Follow steps 1 through 13 of *Create a web service that returns one value* in recipe *81 Create a web service that retrieves data for InfoPath*.

2. Replace the `HelloWorld()` web method with the following web method or add a new web method if you wish (*code #: F3B2FED7-7E04-4A86-97B1-8A8A8BD282D5*):

```
[WebMethod(Description="Adds an Office application to the database.")]
public int AddOfficeApplication(string Name, string Color)
{
  int Id = -1;

  string connectionString =
    ConfigurationManager.ConnectionStrings["InfoPathDB"].ConnectionString;

  using (SqlConnection conn = new SqlConnection(connectionString))
  {
    SqlCommand cmd = new SqlCommand();
    cmd.CommandType = System.Data.CommandType.Text;
    cmd.CommandText = "INSERT INTO OfficeApplications "
      + "(OfficeApplicationName, OfficeApplicationColor) "
      + "VALUES (@Name, @Color); SELECT @@IDENTITY;";
    cmd.Parameters.AddWithValue("Name", Name);
    cmd.Parameters.AddWithValue("Color", Color);
    cmd.Connection = conn;
```

```
    try
    {
      conn.Open();
      object retVal = cmd.ExecuteScalar();
      if (retVal != null)
        Id = Int32.Parse(retVal.ToString());
    }
    catch
    {
      // Handle the error using your own preferred error-handling method
    }
    finally
    {
      conn.Close();
    }
  }
  return Id;
}
```

This web service method returns the identifier of the record that was inserted into the database.

3. Click **Build ➤ Build Solution** and fix any errors if necessary.

4. Click **Debug ➤ Start Debugging**. This should open a browser window and display the **InfoPathService.asmx** page.

5. Open the **Visual Studio Command Prompt (2010)**, which is by default located under the **Microsoft Visual Studio 2010 ➤ Visual Studio Tools** program folder.

6. In the **Visual Studio Command Prompt (2010)** window, enter a command to generate a class file from the WSDL. For example:

```
wsdl http://localhost:24014/InfoPathService.asmx /l:cs /out:C:\ipWS.cs
```

You should replace the URL of the web service (`http://localhost:24014/InfoPathService.asmx`) with the correct URL for your own scenario. This should generate a C# class file named **ipWS.cs**, which you can use to programmatically call the web service methods from a client application such as InfoPath. You can download the **ipWS.cs** file from www.bizsupportonline.com to verify its contents against the class file you generated.

7. With the web service still running in debug mode, open InfoPath Designer 2010 and create a new form template or use an existing one.

8. Add three **Text Box** controls to the view of the form template and name them **officeApplicationName**, **officeApplicationColor**, and **officeApplicationId**, respectively.

9. Click **Data ➤ Submit Form ➤ Submit Options**.

10. On the **Submit Options** dialog box, select the **Allow users to submit this form** check box, select the **Perform custom action using Code** option, click **Advanced**, select **Leave the form open** in the **After submit** drop-down list box, and then click

Edit Code. This should create a **Submit** event handler for the form. Click **OK** to close the dialog box.

11. In VSTA, on the **Project Explorer** pane, right-click the **References** node and add a reference to the **System.Web.Services** assembly.

12. On the **Project Explorer** pane, right-click the project name, and select **Add ➤ Existing Item** from the context menu that appears.

13. On the **Add Existing Item** dialog box, browse to the **ipWS.cs** file you generated earlier, select it, and then click **Add**.

14. Add the following code to the `FormEvents_Submit()` event handler (*code #: F3B2FED7-7E04-4A86-97B1-8A8A8BD282D5*):

```
XPathNavigator mainDS = MainDataSource.CreateNavigator();

string appName = mainDS.SelectSingleNode(
  "/my:myFields/my:officeApplicationName", NamespaceManager).Value;
string appColor = mainDS.SelectSingleNode(
  "/my:myFields/my:officeApplicationColor", NamespaceManager).Value;

InfoPathService service = new InfoPathService();
int id = service.AddOfficeApplication(appName, appColor);

mainDS.SelectSingleNode("/my:myFields/my:officeApplicationId",
  NamespaceManager).SetValue(id.ToString());

e.CancelableArgs.Cancel = false;
```

15. Save and build the project.

16. Because the code needs the permission of type `System.Net.WebPermission` to call the web service, you must give the form template Full Trust via the **Form Options** dialog box (also see *Configure an InfoPath form template to have Full Trust* in the Appendix.).

17. Preview the form.

When the form opens, enter values in the name and color text boxes, and then click the **Submit** button on the toolbar. The identifier of the newly added record should appear in the **officeApplicationId** text box. Open SQL Server Management Studio and verify that the data was submitted to the database table.

Discussion

In the solution described above, you submitted form data to a SQL Server database via a web service and got the identifier of the newly created record back from the web service. The code in the web service method behaves very much like the code for web services in other recipes in this chapter by using ADO.NET classes to submit and retrieve data from a SQL Server database. The main difference in the solution described above lies in using a `SqlCommand` object with a SQL statement that first inserts a record and then selects the identifier of the newly inserted record.

```
SqlCommand cmd = new SqlCommand();
cmd.CommandType = System.Data.CommandType.Text;
cmd.CommandText = "INSERT INTO OfficeApplications "
    + "(OfficeApplicationName, OfficeApplicationColor) "
    + "VALUES (@Name, @Color); SELECT @@IDENTITY;";
cmd.Parameters.AddWithValue("Name", Name);
cmd.Parameters.AddWithValue("Color", Color);
cmd.Connection = conn;
```

Another crucial difference is using the `ExecuteScalar()` method of the `SqlCommand` object instead of the `ExecuteQuery()` method, since the code must retrieve the value of the identifier returned, so that the web service can return this value to the InfoPath form.

```
object retVal = cmd.ExecuteScalar();
if (retVal != null)
  Id = Int32.Parse(retVal.ToString());
```

On the InfoPath side of this solution, the values of form fields that should be submitted to the database are first retrieved.

```
XPathNavigator mainDS = MainDataSource.CreateNavigator();

string appName = mainDS.SelectSingleNode(
  "/my:myFields/my:officeApplicationName", NamespaceManager).Value;
string appColor = mainDS.SelectSingleNode(
  "/my:myFields/my:officeApplicationColor", NamespaceManager).Value;
```

Then an instance of the web service is created and the web service method is invoked.

```
InfoPathService service = new InfoPathService();
int id = service.AddOfficeApplication(appName, appColor);
```

And finally, the identifier returned by the web service method is written to the **officeApplicationId** field.

```
mainDS.SelectSingleNode("/my:myFields/my:officeApplicationId",
  NamespaceManager).SetValue(id.ToString());
```

Note that the class that was generated by the WSDL tool in step 6 contains a property named **Url**, which you can use to dynamically change the URL of the web service before you make the web service method call.

```
service.Url = "http://servername/InfoPathService.asmx";
```

In the solution described above, the code for submitting form data to the web service was placed in the event handler for the **Submit** event of the form. However, this is not a requirement; you could have also placed this code in a button event handler or the event handler for a field.

A disadvantage of this solution is that you must give the form template Full Trust to be able to call the web service. In the next solution, you will learn how you can programmatically call a web service and get the value returned by the web service without having to give the form template Full Trust.

Use the Execute() method of the WebServiceConnection class

Problem

You want to use an InfoPath form to submit data to a web service. The web service returns a value, which you also want to display on the form after the data submission has taken place.

Solution

You must call the web service through code instead of using rules to be able to retrieve the value returned by the web service. You can use the second overload of the Execute() method of the WebServiceConnection class to pass XPathNavigator objects that can be used as pointers to request and response XML node structures.

To programmatically submit data to a web service and get the value returned by the web service:

1. Use the same web service from the previous solution in this recipe, but change the web service method to be the following (*code #: BBC47E54-E9EB-447E-9144-B19AA03DFBB1*):

```
[WebMethod(Description="Adds an Office application to the database.")]
public AddOfficeApplicationResp AddOfficeApplication(string Name, string
Color)
{
  AddOfficeApplicationResp response = new AddOfficeApplicationResp();
  response.Identifier = -1;

  string connectionString =
    ConfigurationManager.ConnectionStrings["InfoPathDB"].ConnectionString;

  using (SqlConnection conn = new SqlConnection(connectionString))
  {
    SqlCommand cmd = new SqlCommand();
    cmd.CommandType = System.Data.CommandType.Text;
    cmd.CommandText = "INSERT INTO OfficeApplications "
      + "(OfficeApplicationName, OfficeApplicationColor) "
      + "VALUES (@Name, @Color); SELECT @@IDENTITY;";
    cmd.Parameters.AddWithValue("Name", Name);
    cmd.Parameters.AddWithValue("Color", Color);
    cmd.Connection = conn;

    try
    {
      conn.Open();
      object retVal = cmd.ExecuteScalar();
      if (retVal != null)
      {
```

```
            response.Identifier = Int32.Parse(retVal.ToString());
            response.ErrorMessage = "Success";
          }
        }
        catch (Exception ex)
        {
          response.ErrorMessage = ex.Message;
        }
        finally
        {
          conn.Close();
        }
      }
      return response;
    }
```

where you must add a class file named **AddOfficeApplicationResp.cs** that has the following definition to the project:

```
public class AddOfficeApplicationResp
{
  public int Identifier { get; set; }
  public string ErrorMessage { get; set; }
}
```

2. Click **Build ➤ Build Solution** and fix any errors if necessary.

3. Click **Debug ➤ Start Debugging**. This should open a browser window and display the **InfoPathService.asmx** page.

4. With the web service running in debug mode, go to the web service page and click the **AddOfficeApplication** link.

5. Copy the XML fragment from the **soap:Body** element of the web service request, open Notepad, paste the XML, remove all line-breaks, tabs, and spaces between the XML elements in the file, and then save the file as **Request.xml**. A sample XML file would resemble the following:

```
<AddOfficeApplication
xmlns="http://www.bizsupportonline.net/namespaces/infopathservice/"><Name>s
tring</Name><Color>string</Color></AddOfficeApplication>
```

You can also download the **Request.xml** file from www.bizsupportonline.com to compare it against your own file.

6. Copy the XML fragment from the **soap:Body** element of the web service response, open Notepad, paste the XML, remove all line-breaks, tabs, and spaces between the XML elements in the file, and then save the file as **Response.xml**. A sample XML file would resemble the following:

```
<AddOfficeApplicationResponse
xmlns="http://www.bizsupportonline.net/namespaces/infopathservice/"><AddOff
iceApplicationResult><ErrorMessage>string</ErrorMessage><Identifier>int</Id
entifier></AddOfficeApplicationResult></AddOfficeApplicationResponse>
```

You can also download the **Response.xml** file from www.bizsupportonline.com to compare it against your own file.

7.   Open Notepad and create a file named **Fault.xml** that has the following contents:

```
<Fault
xmlns="http://schemas.xmlsoap.org/soap/envelope/"><faultcode/><faultstring/
><detail/></Fault>
```

You can also download the **Fault.xml** file from www.bizsupportonline.com.

8.   With the web service still running in debug mode, open InfoPath Designer 2010 and create a new **Blank Form** template.

9.   Select **Data ➤ Get External Data ➤ From Other Sources ➤ From XML File** and follow the instructions to add a data connection for the **Request.xml** file you created earlier. Leave the **Automatically retrieve data when form is opened** check box selected and name the data connection **Request**.

10.   Select **Data ➤ Get External Data ➤ From Other Sources ➤ From XML File** and follow the instructions to add a data connection for the **Response.xml** file you created earlier. Leave the **Automatically retrieve data when form is opened** check box selected and name the data connection **Response**.

11.   Select **Data ➤ Get External Data ➤ From Other Sources ➤ From XML File** and follow the instructions to add a data connection for the **Fault.xml** file you created earlier. Leave the **Automatically retrieve data when form is opened** check box selected and name the data connection **Fault**.

12.   On the **Fields** task pane, select **Request (Secondary)** from the **Fields** drop-down list box, and then drag-and-drop the **AddOfficeApplication** group node onto the view of the form template.

13.   Add two **Text Box** controls to the view of the form template and name them **identifier** and **errorMessage**, respectively.

14.   Select **Data ➤ Submit Form ➤ To Other Locations ➤ To Web Service**.

15.   On the **Data Connection Wizard**, enter the URL of the web service, for example:

```
http://localhost:24014/InfoPathService.asmx
```

and click **Next**. Note that an URL such as the one specified above should work if you are running the web service and InfoPath on the same computer. Otherwise, you may have to deploy the web service first before you are able to access it in InfoPath.

16.   On the **Data Connection Wizard**, select the **AddOfficeApplication** operation, and click **Next**. Note that the description you gave the web method should appear in the **Description of operation** box.

17. On the **Data Connection Wizard**, ensure the **Name** parameter is selected, and then click the button behind the **Field or group** text box.

18. On the **Select a Field or Group** dialog box, select **Request (Secondary)** from the **Fields** drop-down list box, select the **Name** field under the **AddOfficeApplication** group node, and click **OK**.

19. On the **Data Connection Wizard**, leave **Text and child elements only** selected in the **Include** drop-down list box, leave the **Submit data as a string** check box deselected, select the **Color** parameter, and then click the button behind the **Field or group** text box.

20. On the **Select a Field or Group** dialog box, select **Request (Secondary)** from the **Fields** drop-down list box, select the **Color** field under the **AddOfficeApplication** group node, and click **OK**.

21. On the **Data Connection Wizard**, leave **Text and child elements only** selected in the **Include** drop-down list box, leave the **Submit data as a string** check box deselected, and click **Next**.

22. On the **Data Connection Wizard**, name the data connection **AddOfficeApplication**, deselect the **Set as the default submit connection** check box, and click **Finish**.

23. Add a **Button** control to the view of the form template and label it **Submit Record**.

24. Add an event handler for the **Clicked** event of the **Submit Record** button as described in recipe *7 Add an event handler for a control event*.

25. In VSTA, add the following code to the `Clicked()` event handler for the **Submit Record** button (*code #: BBC47E54-E9EB-447E-9144-B19AA03DFBB1*):

```
XPathNavigator request = DataSources["Request"].CreateNavigator();

XPathNavigator response = DataSources["Response"].CreateNavigator()
  .SelectSingleNode("/ns1:AddOfficeApplicationResponse", NamespaceManager);

XPathNavigator fault = DataSources["Fault"].CreateNavigator()
  .SelectSingleNode("/ns2:Fault/ns2:faultstring", NamespaceManager);

WebServiceConnection ws =
  (WebServiceConnection)DataConnections["AddOfficeApplication"];

ws.Execute(request, response, fault);

string errorMessage = response.SelectSingleNode(
  "//ns1:ErrorMessage", NamespaceManager).Value;
string identifier = response.SelectSingleNode(
  "//ns1:Identifier", NamespaceManager).Value;

XPathNavigator mainDS = MainDataSource.CreateNavigator();
mainDS.SelectSingleNode("/my:myFields/my:identifier",
  NamespaceManager).SetValue(identifier);
mainDS.SelectSingleNode("/my:myFields/my:errorMessage",
  NamespaceManager).SetValue(errorMessage);
```

26. Save and build the project.

27. Preview the form.

When the form opens, enter values in the name and color text boxes, and then click the **Submit Record** button. The identifier of the newly added record should appear in the **identifier** text box and an error message or the text "Success" should appear in the **errorMessage** text box. Open SQL Server Management Studio and verify that the data was submitted to the database table.

Discussion

In the solution described above, you submitted form data to a SQL Server database via a web service and got the identifier of the newly created record back from the web service. You also saw that you can return an object to an InfoPath form after data has been submitted to a web service, and that such an object would allow you to return additional information such as for example an error message to the InfoPath form.

The code in the web service method differs slightly from that in the previous solution in that it returns an `AddOfficeApplicationResp` object instead of an integer.

```
[WebMethod(Description="Adds an Office application to the database.")]
public AddOfficeApplicationResp AddOfficeApplication(string Name, string Color)
{
  ...
}
```

This `AddOfficeApplicationResp` object has two properties: The first property can be used by the web service to return the result of the database record insertion, and the second property can be used to pass an error message back to the client without raising an error.

```
public class AddOfficeApplicationResp
{
  public int Identifier { get; set; }
  public string ErrorMessage { get; set; }
}
```

You may be wondering why you should pass an object that contains error information back to the InfoPath form instead of letting the web service method throw an exception? The reason for this is that whenever you submit data to a web service and the web service throws an exception, a generic COM exception is raised in InfoPath. You could use `try-catch` blocks in InfoPath to catch exceptions raised by web service methods. However, if you use a `try-catch` block in the `FormEvents_Submit()` event handler, InfoPath will still show its own generic error message saying that

The form cannot be submitted because of an error.

The error-handling technique described in the solution above allows you to silently return error messages with proper error descriptions to InfoPath and handle these errors in a way that suits your scenario including in the `FormEvents_Submit()` event handler and prevent InfoPath from displaying its own generic error messages.

The main difference between this and the previous solution lies in how the web service is called and in the fact that you do not have to give the form template Full Trust to run. On the InfoPath side of this solution, the code first retrieves references to the XML node structures that are suitable to be used as the request and response XML fragments for the web service.

```
XPathNavigator request = DataSources["Request"].CreateNavigator();

XPathNavigator response = DataSources["Response"].CreateNavigator()
  .SelectSingleNode("/ns1:AddOfficeApplicationResponse", NamespaceManager);
```

While these XML fragments were added as secondary data sources to the form, you could have also added them to the Main data source of the form using the **Complete XML Schema or XML document** field type as was demonstrated in *Submit form field values as one object* of recipe *82 Submit form field values to a web service*.

The code also retrieves a reference to the **faultstring** field, so that this can be used later in the `Execute()` method of the `WebServiceConnection` object.

```
XPathNavigator fault = DataSources["Fault"].CreateNavigator()
  .SelectSingleNode("/ns2:Fault/ns2:faultstring", NamespaceManager);
```

Finally, the code gets a reference to the **AddOfficeApplication** data connection, casts it to the `WebServiceConnection` type

```
WebServiceConnection ws =
  (WebServiceConnection)DataConnections["AddOfficeApplication"];
```

and then calls its `Execute()` method thereby passing the `XPathNavigator` objects pointing to the request, response, and fault XML fragments to it.

```
ws.Execute(request, response, fault);
```

The first argument of the `Execute()` method is an `XPathNavigator` object that points to the node that should be inserted into the **soap:Body** element of the web service request, which in this case is the **AddOfficeApplication** group node in the **Request** secondary data source. The second argument of the `Execute()` method is an `XPathNavigator` object that points to the node under which the contents of the **soap:Body** returned by the web service should be inserted, which in this case is the **AddOfficeApplicationResponse** node in the **Response** secondary data source. The third argument of the `Execute()` method is an `XPathNavigator` object that points to the node under which to insert the contents of the error text returned in the **Fault** element by the web service, if the operation fails. You can also specify `null` for this argument, so that the error data is not written at all.

Finally, the code retrieves the values that are returned by the web service in the `AddOfficeApplicationResp` object and displays them on the form.

```
string errorMessage = response.SelectSingleNode(
  "//ns1:ErrorMessage", NamespaceManager).Value;
string identifier = response.SelectSingleNode(
  "//ns1:Identifier", NamespaceManager).Value;

XPathNavigator mainDS = MainDataSource.CreateNavigator();
mainDS.SelectSingleNode("/my:myFields/my:identifier",
  NamespaceManager).SetValue(identifier);
mainDS.SelectSingleNode("/my:myFields/my:errorMessage",
  NamespaceManager).SetValue(errorMessage);
```

While the code that calls the web service was placed in the `Clicked()` event handler for a button control, you could have also added it to any other event handler, including the `FormEvents_Submit()` event handler of the form as shown in the previous solution.

Chapter 8: Database Integration

Writing code to connect an InfoPath form to a database can be done either inside or outside of an InfoPath. When you write code inside of InfoPath to connect to a database, you typically write code in the **FormCode.cs** file that uses:

1. `AdoQueryConnection` and `AdoSubmitConnection` classes provided by the InfoPath object model. Because you can only create data connections to either Access or SQL Server from within InfoPath Designer 2010, this option is limited to the two aforementioned database engines.

2. ADO.NET classes. This option can be used with any type of database for which ADO.NET provides types and members.

When you write code outside of InfoPath to connect to a database, you typically write code in a web service that accesses the database and which an InfoPath form can call (see chapter 7). This method involves passing InfoPath form data from fields or from the entire form to a web service, and then writing ADO.NET code in the web service to store data in the database; or writing ADO.NET code in the web service to read data from the database and then calling the web service from within InfoPath to display data on a form. This method can be used with any type of database for which ADO.NET provides types and members, so is not limited to only Access or SQL Server databases. For example, you can use this technique to connect an InfoPath form to an Oracle database through a web service.

The explanation of working with Access or SQL Server is beyond the scope of this book. Therefore, you must already have a basic understanding of database programming for Access or SQL Server using ADO.NET to be able to follow the recipes in this chapter. A few of the recipes in this chapter also require you to have Visual Studio 2010 installed on your computer and to already know how to write code using Visual Studio 2010.

86   Perform a wildcard search on an Access table

Problem

You have an InfoPath form that gets read-only data from an Access database table. You want users to be able to type a piece of text in a text box, click a search button, and then retrieve the records that contain the piece of text you entered.

Solution

Suppose you have an Access database table named **OfficeApplications** that contains the following data:

ID (AutoNumber)	App Name (Text)	App Color (Text)	App Icon (Memo)
1	Access	Red	
2	Excel	Green	
3	InfoPath	Purple	
4	Outlook	Orange	
5	PowerPoint	Dark Orange	
	Word	Blue	

Note:

> You can download a file named **OfficeApplications.accdb** from www.bizsupportonline.com for use with this recipe.

To perform a wildcard search on an Access database table:

1. In InfoPath, click **File ➤ New ➤ Database ➤ Design Form** to create a new **Database** form template.

2. On the **Data Connection Wizard**, click **Select Database**.

3. On the **Select Data Source** dialog box, browse to and select the **OfficeApplications** Access database, and then click **Open**.

4. On the **Data Connection Wizard**, click **Next**.

5. On the **Data Connection Wizard**, leave the name of the data connection as **Main connection**, and then click **Finish**. This connection serves as both a receive and a submit data connection for the database.

6. On the **Fields** task pane, expand the **queryFields** and **q:OfficeApplications** group nodes, drag the **:App_Name** field to the view of the form template, and drop it on the text that says "Drag query fields here". The field should automatically get bound to a text box control.

7. On the **Fields** task pane, expand the **dataFields** group node, drag the **d:OfficeApplications** repeating group node to the view of the form template, and drop it on the text that says "Drag data fields here". Select **Repeating Table** from the context menu that appears when you drop the repeating group node.

8. If you preview the form now, enter part of the name of an Office application in the text box, and click **Run Query**, you should get a message saying:

The specified query did not return any data. You can revise the query, or you can click New Record to enter a new record.

This is because you are only allowed to perform exact match searches when you use the standard query functionality provided by a **Database** form template. So in this solution you are going to write code so that users can perform wildcard searches. Open the **Button Properties** dialog box for the **Run Query** button.

9. On the **Button Properties** dialog box, select **Rules and Custom Code** from the **Action** drop-down list box, change the **Label** of the button to **Run Query**, change the **ID** of the button to **btnRunQuery**, and then click **Edit Form Code**.

10. In VSTA, add the following code to the btnRunQuery_Clicked() event handler (*code #: C77B3EF5-F4CD-4EF1-8972-A7B6B2A14A5D*):

```
CurrentView.DisableAutoUpdate();

XPathNavigator mainDS = MainDataSource.CreateNavigator();
XPathNavigator appNameQueryField = mainDS.SelectSingleNode(
  "/dfs:myFields/dfs:queryFields/q:OfficeApplications/@App_Name",
  NamespaceManager);

AdoQueryConnection conn =
  (AdoQueryConnection)DataSources[""].QueryConnection;

string searchValue = appNameQueryField.Value;
string originalCommand = conn.Command;
string newCommand =
  originalCommand + " WHERE [App Name] LIKE '%" + searchValue + "%'";

conn.Command = newCommand;
appNameQueryField.SetValue("");
conn.Execute();

conn.Command = originalCommand;
appNameQueryField.SetValue(searchValue);

CurrentView.EnableAutoUpdate();
```

11. Save and build the project.

12. Preview the form.

When the form opens, enter part of the name of an Office application to search for in the text box, and then click the **Run Query** button. Only those records that have the text you entered as part of their name should appear in the repeating table.

Discussion

Query and submit connections were first introduced in recipe *9 Access a secondary data source of a form*. If you skipped that recipe, you may want to go back and review it so that you know how to work with the `DataSources` and `DataConnections` properties of a form.

The `Command` property of the `AdoQueryConnection` object gets or sets the SQL command text for the `AdoQueryConnection` object. You can use it in code to dynamically change the SQL statement used to retrieve data from a database.

In the solution described above, you created a **Database** form template, which can be used to retrieve data from or submit data to a database. The Main data source of such a form consists of query fields and data fields. You can use the query fields to query or search for data, while you can use the data fields to display data or enter data for a new record. Because you cannot use the query fields to search for wildcard matches of data in records (only exact matches), you must write code to do so.

The code in the solution above first disables updating of the view to prevent any flickering from occurring while data on the view is being updated.

```
CurrentView.DisableAutoUpdate();
```

Then it retrieves a reference to the Main data source as well as the query field with which you can specify the name of the Office application to search for and return.

```
XPathNavigator mainDS = MainDataSource.CreateNavigator();
XPathNavigator appNameQueryField = mainDS.SelectSingleNode(
  "/dfs:myFields/dfs:queryFields/q:OfficeApplications/@App_Name",
  NamespaceManager);
```

Then the query connection for the Main data source is retrieved and cast to an `AdoQueryConnection` object.

```
AdoQueryConnection conn = (AdoQueryConnection)DataSources[""].QueryConnection;
```

A new command text is then built from the existing command text and a WHERE-clause is appended to the string.

```
string searchValue = appNameQueryField.Value;
string originalCommand = conn.Command;
string newCommand =
  originalCommand + " WHERE [App Name] LIKE '%" + searchValue + "%'";
```

In addition, the original command text is stored in a variable named `originalCommand` so that it can be restored after the query is executed.

Then the value of the `Command` property of the query connection is set to be equal to the new command text

```
conn.Command = newCommand;
```

and the query is executed after clearing the query field.

```
appNameQueryField.SetValue("");
conn.Execute();
```

When you specify values for the query fields in a form that is connected to a database, InfoPath automatically builds the SQL statement with a WHERE-clause to retrieve exact match data. This SQL statement takes precedence over any SQL statement you specify through the `Command` property of the query connection for the Main data source, so you must clear the values of all of the query fields if you want InfoPath to use the SQL statement you specify through the `Command` property of the query connection. Note that this step is not required if you are setting the `Command` property for a query connection that belongs to a secondary data source for a database, since there are no query fields present in such a secondary data source.

Finally, both the query the user specified as well as the original command text are restored

```
conn.Command = originalCommand;
appNameQueryField.SetValue(searchValue);
```

and updates on the view are enabled again.

```
CurrentView.EnableAutoUpdate();
```

Note that you can always statically change the initial SQL statement that is used by InfoPath through the **Data Connection Wizard** as follows:

1. In InfoPath, click **Data ➤ Data Connections**.
2. On the **Data Connections** dialog box, select **Main connection**, and click **Modify**.
3. On the **Data Connection Wizard**, click **Edit SQL**.
4. On the **Edit SQL** dialog box, you should see the following SQL statement listed:

   ```
   select [ID],[App Name] as [App_Name],[App Color] as [App_Color],[App
   Icon] as [App_Icon] from [OfficeApplications] as [OfficeApplications]
   ```

   Change this SQL statement into any valid SQL statement, click **Test SQL Statement**, and then click **OK** on the message box that appears. If there are any errors, fix them. Note that if you change the initial SQL statement, you must alter the code that constructs the new command text in the solution described above to be a valid SQL statement.
5. On the **Edit SQL** dialog box, click **OK**.
6. On the **Data Connection Wizard**, click **Next**.
7. On the **Data Connection Wizard**, click **Finish**.
8. On the **Data Connections** dialog box, click **Close**.

87 Retrieve data from an Access table with Memo field

Problem

You have an Access database table that has a Memo field in which images of Office applications are stored. You want to use an InfoPath form to maintain data in this Access database table, which includes retrieving data from the table.

Solution

You can use classes from the System.Data.OleDb namespace to retrieve data from an Access database table.

Suppose you have an Access database table named **OfficeApplications** as described in recipe *86 Perform a wildcard search on an Access table*.

To retrieve data from an Access database table that contains a Memo field:

1. In InfoPath, create a new InfoPath Filler Form template or use an existing one.

2. Add a **Repeating Section** control to the view of the form template.

3. Open the **Repeating Section Properties** dialog box, deselect the **Show insert button and hint text** check box on the **Data** tab, and then click **Modify**.

4. On the **Section Properties** dialog box, click **Customize Commands**.

5. On the **Section Commands** dialog box, deselect the check boxes for **Insert**, **Insert Above**, **Insert Below**, and **Remove All**, and then click **OK**.

6. On the **Section Properties** dialog box, click **OK**.

7. On the **Repeating Section Properties** dialog box, click **OK**. With this you have set the repeating section to only allow sections to be deleted.

8. Click **Data ➤ Form Data ➤ Default Values**, expand the **group1** node, deselect the check box in front of the **group2** node, and click **OK**. This should prevent the repeating section from having a first empty section.

9. Add two **Text Box** controls within the repeating section and name them **appName** and **appColor**, respectively.

10. Add a **Picture** control within the repeating section. Select the **Included in the form** option when you add the picture control to the repeating section. By selecting this option, you will be storing the image as a base64-encoded string in the form. Name the picture control **appIcon**.

11. On the **Fields** task pane, add a hidden **Field (element)** with the name **ID** and the data type **Text (string)** under the **group2** repeating group node in the Main data source.

Figure 60. Main data source of the form.

12. Add an event handler for the **Loading** event of the form as described in recipe *6 Add an event handler for a form event*.

13. In VSTA, add a reference to the **System.Data** assembly.

14. Add the following **using** statements to the **FormCode.cs** file:

```
using System.Data.OleDb;
using System.Text;
```

15. Add the following private method to the FormCode class (*code #: A86B0D39-888F-4F20-980F-504B130A4CC0*):

```
private void AddSection(
  string id, string appName, string appColor, string appIcon)
{
  XPathNavigator mainDS = MainDataSource.CreateNavigator();

  XPathNavigator group1 = mainDS.SelectSingleNode(
    "/my:myFields/my:group1", NamespaceManager);

  StringBuilder sb = new StringBuilder();
  sb.Append("<my:group2>");
  sb.Append("<my:appName>");
  sb.Append(appName);
  sb.Append("</my:appName>");
  sb.Append("<my:appColor>");
  sb.Append(appColor);
  sb.Append("</my:appColor>");
  if (!String.IsNullOrEmpty(appIcon))
  {
    sb.Append("<my:appIcon>");
    sb.Append(appIcon);
  }
  else
```

```
  {
    sb.Append("<my:appIcon ");
    sb.Append("xsi:nil=\"true\" ");
    sb.Append("xmlns:xsi=\"http://www.w3.org/2001/XMLSchema-instance\">");
  }
  sb.Append("</my:appIcon>");
  sb.Append("<my:ID>");
  sb.Append(id);
  sb.Append("</my:ID>");
  sb.Append("</my:group2>");

  group1.AppendChild(sb.ToString());
}
```

This method is used to repeatedly add a section to the **group1** group node when the code is looping through all of the records from the database table. Note that you can use any one of the methods discussed in recipe *71 Add a row to a repeating table* to add a section to a repeating section in the same way you can add a row to a repeating table.

16. Add the following code to the `FormEvents_Loading()` event handler (*code #: A86B0D39-888F-4F20-980F-504B130A4CC0*):

```
OleDbConnection conn = new OleDbConnection(
  @"Provider=Microsoft.ACE.OLEDB.12.0;" +
  @"Data Source=C:\OfficeApplications.accdb;");

System.Text.StringBuilder sb = new System.Text.StringBuilder();
sb.Append("SELECT OfficeApplications.ID, ");
sb.Append("OfficeApplications.[App Name], ");
sb.Append("OfficeApplications.[App Color], ");
sb.Append("OfficeApplications.[App Icon] ");
sb.Append("FROM OfficeApplications ");

string query = sb.ToString();
OleDbCommand cmd = new OleDbCommand(query, conn);

try
{
  conn.Open();
  OleDbDataReader reader = cmd.ExecuteReader();

  int row = 0;
  while (reader.Read())
  {
    string appID = string.Empty;
    string appName = string.Empty;
    string appColor = string.Empty;
    string appIcon = string.Empty;

    if (!reader.IsDBNull(0))
      appID = reader.GetInt32(0).ToString();

    if (!reader.IsDBNull(1))
      appName = reader.GetString(1);

    if (!reader.IsDBNull(2))
      appColor = reader.GetString(2);

    if (!reader.IsDBNull(3))
```

```
    {
      char[] buffer = null;
      long chars = reader.GetChars(3, 0, buffer, 0, 0);
      if (chars > 0)
      {
        char[] charArray = new char[chars];
        reader.GetChars(3, 0, charArray, 0, (int)chars);
        string pic = new string(charArray);
        appIcon = pic;
      }
    }

    AddSection(appID, appName, appColor, appIcon);

    row++;
  }
  reader.Close();
}
catch (Exception ex)
{
  MessageBox.Show(ex.Message, "An error occurred",
    MessageBoxButtons.OK, MessageBoxIcon.Error);
}
finally
{
  conn.Close();
}
```

Note that you must change the path to the Access database
(C:\OfficeApplications.accdb) to suit your own scenario.

17. Save and build the project.

18. Preview the form.

When the form opens, all of the records from the database table should appear as sections of the repeating section control.

Name	Word
Color	Blue
Icon	

Name	Access
Color	Red
Icon	

Name	Excel
Color	Green
Icon	

Figure 61. InfoPath form displaying the sections for Word, Access, and Excel.

Discussion

Memo fields in Access have the **Memo** data type. You can store very long text in such fields, so they are suitable to store the base64-encoded strings of picture and file attachment controls as well as the contents of for example a rich text box in InfoPath.

In the solution described above, a Memo field was used to store the base64-encoded string of an image, and this image was then retrieved in the Loading() event handler of the form when the database table records were retrieved. The trick for retrieving data from a Memo field is to use the GetChars() method of an OleDbDataReader object as shown in the code below.

```
char[] buffer = null;
long chars = reader.GetChars(3, 0, buffer, 0, 0);
if (chars > 0)
{
  char[] charArray = new char[chars];
  reader.GetChars(3, 0, charArray, 0, (int)chars);
  string pic = new string(charArray);
  appIcon = pic;
}
```

In the code above, the Memo field is the fourth field specified in the SELECT statement, so it can be retrieved using an index number equal to 3. The GetChars() method is called twice: The first time to retrieve the amount of characters that the Memo field contains

```
char[] buffer = null;
long chars = reader.GetChars(3, 0, buffer, 0, 0);
```

and the second time to retrieve the actual contents of the Memo field.

```
if (chars > 0)
{
  char[] charArray = new char[chars];
  reader.GetChars(3, 0, charArray, 0, (int)chars);
  string pic = new string(charArray);
  appIcon = pic;
}
```

The rest of the code to retrieve the data from the database is pretty straightforward. First the code creates an OleDbConnection object.

```
OleDbConnection conn = new OleDbConnection(
  @"Provider=Microsoft.ACE.OLEDB.12.0;" +
  @"Data Source=C:\OfficeApplications.accdb;");
```

Then a SQL SELECT statement is constructed and an OleDbCommand object is created.

```
System.Text.StringBuilder sb = new System.Text.StringBuilder();
sb.Append("SELECT OfficeApplications.ID, ");
sb.Append("OfficeApplications.[App Name], ");
```

```
sb.Append("OfficeApplications.[App Color], ");
sb.Append("OfficeApplications.[App Icon] ");
sb.Append("FROM OfficeApplications ");

string query = sb.ToString();
OleDbCommand cmd = new OleDbCommand(query, conn);
```

The code uses the `Open()` method of the `OleDbConnection` object to open the connection to the database, and then calls the `ExecuteReader()` method of the `OleDbCommand` object to create an `OleDbDataReader` object, with which the data that is returned can be read.

```
conn.Open();
OleDbDataReader reader = cmd.ExecuteReader();
```

And finally, the `Read()` method of the `OleDbDataReader` object is called to loop through and read the data, while a private method named `AddSection()` is used to add a section to the repeating section control for each record that is read.

```
while (reader.Read())
{
  ...
  AddSection(appID, appName, appColor, appIcon);
  ...
}
```

88 Perform create, update, and delete actions on an Access table with Memo field

Add a record to an Access table with a Memo field

Problem

You have an Access database table that has a Memo field in which images of Office applications are stored. You want to use an InfoPath form to maintain data in this Access database table, which includes inserting a record into the table.

Solution

You can use classes from the `System.Data.OleDb` namespace to perform create, update, and delete (CRUD) operations on an Access database table.

Suppose you have an Access database table named **OfficeApplications** as described in recipe *86 Perform a wildcard search on an Access table*.

To add a record to an Access database table that contains a Memo field:

1. In Notepad, create an XML file named **CRUDOperations.xml** that has the following contents:

```
<?xml version="1.0" encoding="UTF-8" ?>
<operations>
  <Coperation></Coperation>
  <Uoperation></Uoperation>
</operations>
```

You can also download the file named **CRUDOperations.xml** from www.bizsupportonline.com. You will use this XML file to keep track of inserts and updates made to the database.

2. In InfoPath, create a new InfoPath Filler Form template or use an existing one.

3. Select **Data ➤ Get External Data ➤ From Other Sources ➤ From XML File** and follow the instructions to create a data connection for the **CRUDOperations.xml** XML file. Name the data connection **CRUDOperations** and leave the **Automatically retrieve data when form is opened** check box selected.

4. Select **Data ➤ Get External Data ➤ From Other Sources ➤ From Database**.

5. On the **Data Connection Wizard**, click **Select Database**.

6. On the **Select Data Source** dialog box, browse to and select the **OfficeApplications.accdb** file, and click **Open**.

7. If the **Select Table** dialog box pops up, select the **OfficeApplications** table, and then click **OK**.

8. On the **Data Connection Wizard**, deselect the **App_Icon (App Icon)** check box, and click **Next**.

9. On the **Data Connection Wizard**, leave the **Store a copy of the data in the form template** check box deselected, and click **Next**.

10. On the **Data Connection Wizard**, name the data connection **OfficeApplications**, leave the **Automatically retrieve data when form is opened** check box selected, and click **Finish**. With this you have added a secondary data source for the **OfficeApplications** Access database table to the form.

11. On the **Fields** task pane, select **OfficeApplications (Secondary)** from the **Fields** drop-down list box, expand the **dataFields** group node, and then drag-and-drop the **d:OfficeApplications** repeating group node onto the view of the form template. Select **Repeating Table** from the context menu that appears when you drop the repeating group node onto the view.

12. Add two **Text Box** controls to the view of the form template and name them **appName** and **appColor**, respectively.

13. Add a **Picture** control to the view of the form template. Select the **Included in the form** option when you add the picture control to the view. By selecting this option, you will be storing the image as a base64-encoded string in the form as well as in the Memo field in the database table. Name the picture control **appIcon**.

14. Add a **Formatting** rule to the **appName** text box with a condition that says:

```
Coperation is blank
and
Uoperation is blank
```

and with a formatting of **Disable this control**. Here, **Coperation** and **Uoperation** are fields located in the **CRUDOperations** secondary data source. What this formatting rule does is disable the **appName** text box if no insert or update operation is taking place.

15. Copy the rule you added to the **appName** text box and paste it on the **appColor** text box and **appIcon** picture control.

16. Add three **Button** controls to the view of the form template and label them **New Record**, **Save Record**, and **Cancel**, respectively.

17. Add a **Formatting** rule to the **New Record** button with a condition that says:

```
Coperation is not blank
```

and with a formatting of **Disable this control**. Here, **Coperation** is a field located in the **CRUDOperations** secondary data source. What this formatting rule does is disable the **New Record** button if an insert operation is taking place.

18. Add a **Formatting** rule to the **Save Record** button with a condition that says:

```
Coperation is blank
```

and with a formatting of **Disable this control**. Here, **Coperation** is a field located in the **CRUDOperations** secondary data source. What this formatting rule does is disable the **Save Record** button if an insert operation is currently not taking place.

19. Add a **Formatting** rule to the **Cancel** button with a condition that says:

```
Coperation is blank
and
Uoperation is blank
```

and with a formatting of **Disable this control**. Here, **Coperation** and **Uoperation** are fields located in the **CRUDOperations** secondary data source. What this formatting rule does is disable the **Cancel** button if neither an insert or update operation is taking place.

20. Add an event handler for the **Clicked** event of the **New Record** button as described in recipe *7 Add an event handler for a control event*.

21. In VSTA, add a reference to the **System.Data** assembly.

313

22. Add the following **using** statement to the **FormCode.cs** file:

```
using System.Data.OleDb;
```

23. Add the following code to the `Clicked()` event handler for the **New Record** button (*code #: A43D534F-25E2-401C-8E12-A71A90E0EEBC*):

```
XPathNavigator mainDS = MainDataSource.CreateNavigator();

mainDS.SelectSingleNode("/my:myFields/my:appName",
  NamespaceManager).SetValue(string.Empty);
mainDS.SelectSingleNode("/my:myFields/my:appColor",
  NamespaceManager).SetValue(string.Empty);

XPathNavigator icon = mainDS.SelectSingleNode(
  "/my:myFields/my:appIcon", NamespaceManager);

if (!icon.MoveToAttribute("nil", icon.LookupNamespace("xsi")))
{
  icon.SetValue(String.Empty);
  icon.CreateAttribute("xsi", "nil", icon.LookupNamespace("xsi"), "true");
}

XPathNavigator crudDS = DataSources["CRUDOperations"].CreateNavigator();
crudDS.SelectSingleNode("/operations/Coperation",
  NamespaceManager).SetValue("1");
crudDS.SelectSingleNode("/operations/Uoperation",
  NamespaceManager).SetValue(string.Empty);
```

The code behind the **New Record** button clears all fields in preparation for entering new data, sets the value of the flag (the **Coperation** field in the **CRUDOperations** secondary data source) that indicates whether an insert operation is taking place to be equal to **1**, and clears the value of the flag (the **Uoperation** field in the **CRUDOperations** secondary data source) that indicates whether an update operation is taking place.

24. In InfoPath, add an event handler for the **Clicked** event of the **Save Record** button as described in recipe *7 Add an event handler for a control event*.

25. In VSTA, add the following code to the `Clicked()` event handler for the **Save Record** button (*code #: A43D534F-25E2-401C-8E12-A71A90E0EEBC*):

```
XPathNavigator mainDS = MainDataSource.CreateNavigator();
string appName = mainDS.SelectSingleNode(
  "/my:myFields/my:appName", NamespaceManager).Value;
string appColor = mainDS.SelectSingleNode(
  "/my:myFields/my:appColor", NamespaceManager).Value;
string appIcon = mainDS.SelectSingleNode(
  "/my:myFields/my:appIcon", NamespaceManager).Value;

OleDbConnection conn = new OleDbConnection(
  @"Provider=Microsoft.ACE.OLEDB.12.0;" +
  @"Data Source=C:\OfficeApplications.accdb;");

OleDbCommand cmd = conn.CreateCommand();
cmd.CommandType = System.Data.CommandType.Text;
System.Text.StringBuilder sb = new System.Text.StringBuilder();
```

```
sb.Append("INSERT INTO OfficeApplications ");
sb.Append("([App Name], [App Color], [App Icon]) ");
sb.Append("VALUES ");
sb.Append("(@AppName, @AppColor, @AppIcon)");
cmd.CommandText = sb.ToString();
cmd.Parameters.AddWithValue("AppName", appName);
cmd.Parameters.AddWithValue("AppColor", appColor);
cmd.Parameters.Add("AppIcon",
    OleDbType.LongVarChar).Value = appIcon;

try
{
  conn.Open();
  cmd.ExecuteNonQuery();
}
catch (Exception ex)
{
  MessageBox.Show(ex.Message, "An error occurred",
    MessageBoxButtons.OK, MessageBoxIcon.Error);
}
finally
{
  conn.Close();
  XPathNavigator crudDS = DataSources["CRUDOperations"].CreateNavigator();
  crudDS.SelectSingleNode("/operations/Coperation",
    NamespaceManager).SetValue(string.Empty);

  DataConnections["OfficeApplications"].Execute();
}
```

The code behind the **Save Record** button inserts a record into the database table, clears the value of the flag (the **Coperation** field in the **CRUDOperations** secondary data source) that indicates whether an insert operation is taking place, and refreshes the **OfficeApplications** secondary data source to display the newly added database record in the repeating table. Note that you must change the path to the Access database (C:\OfficeApplications.accdb) to suit your own scenario.

26. In InfoPath, add an event handler for the **Clicked** event of the **Cancel** button as described in recipe *7 Add an event handler for a control event*.

27. In VSTA, add the following code to the Clicked() event handler for the **Cancel** button (*code #: A43D534F-25E2-401C-8E12-A71A90E0EEBC*):

```
XPathNavigator crudDS = DataSources["CRUDOperations"].CreateNavigator();
crudDS.SelectSingleNode("/operations/Coperation",
  NamespaceManager).SetValue(string.Empty);
crudDS.SelectSingleNode("/operations/Uoperation",
  NamespaceManager).SetValue(string.Empty);
```

The code behind the **Cancel** button clears the value of the flag (the **Coperation** field in the **CRUDOperations** secondary data source) that indicates whether an insert operation is taking place as well as the value of the flag (the **Uoperation** field in the **CRUDOperations** secondary data source) that indicates whether an update operation is taking place.

28. Save and build the project.

29. Preview the form.

When the form opens, all of the records from the Access database table should appear in the repeating table. Click the **New Record** button to enable the fields for entering data for a new record. The **New Record** button should be disabled and the **Save Record** and **Cancel** buttons should be enabled. Enter data for a new Office application in the name and color fields, add an image to the picture control, and then click the **Save Record** button. The newly added record should appear in the repeating table, and after you save the record, the **New Record** button should be enabled and the **Save Record** and **Cancel** buttons should be disabled.

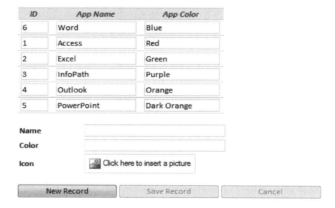

Figure 62. The InfoPath form displaying database records when the form opens.

Figure 63. Entering data for a new record.

ID	App Name	App Color
6	Word	Blue
7	OneNote	Purple
1	Access	Red
2	Excel	Green
3	InfoPath	Purple
4	Outlook	Orange
5	PowerPoint	Dark Orange

Name	OneNote
Color	Purple
Icon	

New Record	Save Record	Cancel

Figure 64. The InfoPath form after the new record has been inserted into the database.

Discussion

There is a lot happening in the solution described above, but most of the code is self-explanatory. The bulk of the functionality and code for adding a record to the database takes place in the Clicked() event handler for the **Save Record** button. This code first retrieves the values that were entered by a user on the form

```
XPathNavigator mainDS = MainDataSource.CreateNavigator();
string appName = mainDS.SelectSingleNode(
  "/my:myFields/my:appName", NamespaceManager).Value;
string appColor = mainDS.SelectSingleNode(
  "/my:myFields/my:appColor", NamespaceManager).Value;
string appIcon = mainDS.SelectSingleNode(
  "/my:myFields/my:appIcon", NamespaceManager).Value;
```

before creating a database connection using an OleDbConnection object.

```
OleDbConnection conn = new OleDbConnection(
  @"Provider=Microsoft.ACE.OLEDB.12.0;" +
  @"Data Source=C:\OfficeApplications.accdb;");
```

An OleDbCommand object is then constructed and its CommandText property is set to be equal to a SQL statement to insert data into the database.

```
OleDbCommand cmd = conn.CreateCommand();
cmd.CommandType = System.Data.CommandType.Text;
System.Text.StringBuilder sb = new System.Text.StringBuilder();
sb.Append("INSERT INTO OfficeApplications ");
sb.Append("([App Name], [App Color], [App Icon]) ");
sb.Append("VALUES ");
sb.Append("(@AppName, @AppColor, @AppIcon)");
cmd.CommandText = sb.ToString();
cmd.Parameters.AddWithValue("AppName", appName);
```

```
cmd.Parameters.AddWithValue("AppColor", appColor);
cmd.Parameters.Add("AppIcon", OleDbType.LongVarChar).Value = appIcon;
```

And finally, the `Open()` method of the `OleDbConnection` object is called to open the database connection, and the `ExecuteQuery()` method of the `OleDbCommand` object is called to add a record to the database.

```
conn.Open();
cmd.ExecuteNonQuery();
```

As shown in the code that sets the values of `OleDbParameter` objects, you can use the `LongVarChar` data type to store the base64-encoded string that represents an image in InfoPath in a Memo field in an Access database.

```
cmd.Parameters.Add("AppIcon", OleDbType.LongVarChar).Value = appIcon;
```

Note that the `finally` block of the `try-catch` block contains code to close the database connection.

```
conn.Close();
```

The code also clears the flag to indicate that the insert operation is not taking place anymore

```
XPathNavigator crudDS = DataSources["CRUDOperations"].CreateNavigator();
crudDS.SelectSingleNode("/operations/Coperation",
  NamespaceManager).SetValue(string.Empty);
```

and refreshes the **OfficeApplications** secondary data source to display the newly added record in the repeating table on the form.

```
DataConnections["OfficeApplications"].Execute();
```

Update a record in an Access table with a Memo field

Problem

You have an Access database table that has a Memo field in which images of Office applications are stored. You want to use an InfoPath form to maintain data in this Access database table, which includes updating a record in the table.

Solution

You can use classes from the `System.Data.OleDb` namespace to perform create, update, and delete (CRUD) operations on an Access database table.

Suppose you have an Access database table named **OfficeApplications** as described in recipe *86 Perform a wildcard search on an Access table*.

To update a record in an Access database table that contains a Memo field:

1. Follow the instructions in the steps of *Add a record to an Access table with a Memo field* in this recipe to create a form template.

2. In InfoPath, add an extra column with a **Button** control to the repeating table and label the button **Select**.

3. Add a **Formatting** rule to the **Select** button with a condition that says:

    ```
    Coperation is not blank
    ```

    and with a formatting of **Disable this control**. Here, **Coperation** is a field located in the **CRUDOperations** secondary data source. What this formatting rule does is disable the **Select** button if an insert operation is taking place.

4. Add an event handler for the **Clicked** event of the **Select** button as described in recipe *7 Add an event handler for a control event*.

5. In VSTA, add the following member variable to the `FormCode` class:

    ```
    string _id = "-1";
    ```

6. Add the following code to the `Clicked()` event handler for the **Select** button (*code #: 1FB607C3-08C4-4D0D-8DE0-3BF61AB156D9*):

    ```
    XPathNavigator mainDS = MainDataSource.CreateNavigator();

    OleDbConnection conn = new OleDbConnection(
        @"Provider=Microsoft.ACE.OLEDB.12.0;" +
        @"Data Source=C:\OfficeApplications.accdb;");

    _id = e.Source.SelectSingleNode("@ID").Value;

    System.Text.StringBuilder sb = new System.Text.StringBuilder();
    sb.Append("SELECT OfficeApplications.[App Name], ");
    sb.Append("OfficeApplications.[App Color], ");
    sb.Append("OfficeApplications.[App Icon] ");
    sb.Append("FROM OfficeApplications ");
    sb.Append("WHERE OfficeApplications.ID = ");
    sb.Append(_id);
    string query = sb.ToString();
    OleDbCommand cmd = new OleDbCommand(query, conn);

    try
    {
      conn.Open();
      OleDbDataReader reader = cmd.ExecuteReader();

      int row = 0;
      while (reader.Read())
      {
        if (!reader.IsDBNull(0))
          mainDS.SelectSingleNode("/my:myFields/my:appName",
            NamespaceManager).SetValue(reader.GetString(0));
    ```

```
    if (!reader.IsDBNull(1))
      mainDS.SelectSingleNode("/my:myFields/my:appColor",
        NamespaceManager).SetValue(reader.GetString(1));

    XPathNavigator icon = mainDS.SelectSingleNode(
      "/my:myFields/my:appIcon", NamespaceManager);

    string pic = string.Empty;
    if (!reader.IsDBNull(2))
    {
      char[] buffer = null;
      long chars = reader.GetChars(2, 0, buffer, 0, 0);
      char[] byteArray = new char[chars];
      if (chars > 0)
      {
        reader.GetChars(2, 0, byteArray, 0, (int)chars);
        pic = new string(byteArray);
      }
    }

    if (!String.IsNullOrEmpty(pic))
    {
      if (icon.MoveToAttribute("nil",
        NamespaceManager.LookupNamespace("xsi")))
        icon.DeleteSelf();

      icon.SetValue(pic);
    }
    else
    {
      icon.SetValue(String.Empty);
      if (!icon.MoveToAttribute("nil",
        NamespaceManager.LookupNamespace("xsi")))
      {
        icon.CreateAttribute("xsi", "nil",
          NamespaceManager.LookupNamespace("xsi"), "true");
      }
    }
    row++;
  }
  reader.Close();
}
catch (Exception ex)
{
  MessageBox.Show(ex.Message, "An error occurred",
    MessageBoxButtons.OK, MessageBoxIcon.Error);
}
finally
{
  conn.Close();
  XPathNavigator crudDS = DataSources["CRUDOperations"].CreateNavigator();
  crudDS.SelectSingleNode("/operations/Uoperation",
    NamespaceManager).SetValue("1");
}
```

The code behind the **Select** button populates the fields on the form with the data from the selected record and then sets the value of the flag (the **Uoperation** field in the **CRUDOperations** secondary data source) that indicates whether an update operation is taking place to be equal to **1**. Note that you must change the path to the Access database (`C:\OfficeApplications.accdb`) to suit your own scenario.

7. In InfoPath, add a **Button** control to the view of the form template and label it **Update**.

8. Add a **Formatting** rule to the **Update** button with a condition that says:

```
Uoperation is blank
```

and with a formatting of **Disable this control**. Here, **Uoperation** is a field located in the **CRUDOperations** secondary data source. What this formatting rule does is disable the **Update** button if no record has been selected to be updated, so if an update operation is not taking place. Note that the **Select** button enables update operations to take place.

9. Add an event handler for the **Clicked** event of the **Update** button as described in recipe *7 Add an event handler for a control event*.

10. In VSTA, add the following code to the `Clicked()` event handler for the **Update** button (*code #: 1FB607C3-08C4-4D0D-8DE0-3BF61AB156D9*):

```
XPathNavigator mainDS = MainDataSource.CreateNavigator();
string appName = mainDS.SelectSingleNode(
  "/my:myFields/my:appName", NamespaceManager).Value;
string appColor = mainDS.SelectSingleNode(
  "/my:myFields/my:appColor", NamespaceManager).Value;
string appIcon = mainDS.SelectSingleNode(
  "/my:myFields/my:appIcon", NamespaceManager).Value;

OleDbConnection conn = new OleDbConnection(
  @"Provider=Microsoft.ACE.OLEDB.12.0;" +
  @"Data Source=C:\OfficeApplications.accdb;");

OleDbCommand cmd = conn.CreateCommand();
cmd.CommandType = System.Data.CommandType.Text;

System.Text.StringBuilder sb = new System.Text.StringBuilder();
sb.Append("UPDATE OfficeApplications ");
sb.Append("SET [App Name] = @AppName, ");
sb.Append("[App Color] = @AppColor, ");
sb.Append("[App Icon] = @AppIcon ");
sb.Append("WHERE ID = ");
sb.Append(_id);

cmd.CommandText = sb.ToString();
cmd.Parameters.AddWithValue("AppName", appName);
cmd.Parameters.AddWithValue("AppColor", appColor);
cmd.Parameters.Add("AppIcon", OleDbType.LongVarChar).Value = appIcon;

try
{
  conn.Open();
  cmd.ExecuteNonQuery();
}
catch (Exception ex)
{
  MessageBox.Show(ex.Message, "An error occurred",
```

```
        MessageBoxButtons.OK, MessageBoxIcon.Error);
    }
    finally
    {
        conn.Close();
        XPathNavigator crudDS = DataSources["CRUDOperations"].CreateNavigator();
        crudDS.SelectSingleNode("/operations/Uoperation",
        NamespaceManager).SetValue(string.Empty);

        DataConnections["OfficeApplications"].Execute();
    }
```

The code behind the **Update** button updates the selected record by writing the values to the database table, clears the value of the flag (the **Uoperation** field in the **CRUDOperations** secondary data source) that indicates whether an update operation is taking place, and refreshes the **OfficeApplications** secondary data source to display the updated data in the repeating table. Note that you must change the path to the Access database (C:\OfficeApplications.accdb) to suit your own scenario.

11. Save and build the project.

12. Preview the form.

When the form opens, all of the records from the Access database table should appear in the repeating table. Click the **Select** button behind one of the records you would like to modify. The data for the record you selected should appear in the fields on the form, the **Save Record** button should be disabled, and both the **Cancel** and **Update** buttons should be enabled. Modify the data for the record, and then click **Update**. The updated record should appear in the repeating table and the **Cancel** and **Update** buttons should be disabled.

ID	App Name	App Color	
6	Word	Blue	Select
1	Access	Red	Select
2	Excel	Green	Select
3	InfoPath	Purple	Select
4	Outlook	Orange	Select
5	PowerPoint	Dark Orange	Select

Name

Color

Icon   Click here to insert a picture

New Record	Save Record	Update	Cancel

Figure 65. The InfoPath form when it first opens.

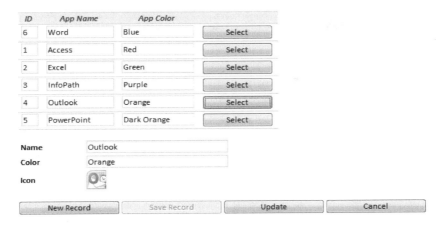

Figure 66. The InfoPath form displaying the selected record.

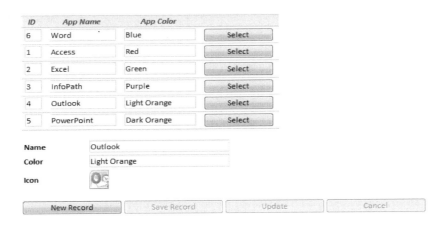

Figure 67. The InfoPath form after the record has been updated.

Discussion

The bulk of the functionality in the solution described above lies in selecting a record from the database, keeping track of the ID of the selected record in a private member variable named _id, and then using the ID to update the record in the database.

The code for selecting a record from the database is pretty straightforward. When the **Select** button is clicked, the ID of the record that is located in the same row of the repeating table in which the button that was clicked is located, is retrieved using the e.Source object.

```
_id = e.Source.SelectSingleNode("@ID").Value;
```

The Source property of the ClickedEventArgs object returns an XPathNavigator object that is positioned at the innermost XML node of the form's underlying XML document that contains the button control. In plain English this means that because the **OfficeApplications** secondary data source contains the button, the Source property returns an XPathNavigator object pointing to the **OfficeApplications** repeating group node (equivalent to a row in the repeating table) in the **OfficeApplications** secondary data source. You can then retrieve the value of the ID in the same row as the button by retrieving the value of the **ID** attribute of the **OfficeApplications** repeating group node.

The code uses the ID to construct a SQL SELECT statement

```
System.Text.StringBuilder sb = new System.Text.StringBuilder();
sb.Append("SELECT OfficeApplications.[App Name], ");
sb.Append("OfficeApplications.[App Color], ");
sb.Append("OfficeApplications.[App Icon] ");
sb.Append("FROM OfficeApplications ");
sb.Append("WHERE OfficeApplications.ID = ");
sb.Append(_id);
string query = sb.ToString();
```

that can then be used with an OleDbCommand object.

```
OleDbCommand cmd = new OleDbCommand(query, conn);
```

A database connection is then opened using the Open() method of the OleDbConnection object, and the ExecuteReader() method of the OleDbCommand object is used to return an OleDbDataReader object, which can then be used to read the data returned from the database.

```
conn.Open();
OleDbDataReader reader = cmd.ExecuteReader();
```

The image that is stored in the Memo field is retrieved by using the GetChars() method of the OleDbDataReader object.

```
string pic = string.Empty;
if (!reader.IsDBNull(2))
{
  char[] buffer = null;
  long chars = reader.GetChars(2, 0, buffer, 0, 0);
  char[] byteArray = new char[chars];
  if (chars > 0)
  {
    reader.GetChars(2, 0, byteArray, 0, (int)chars);
    pic = new string(byteArray);
  }
}
```

And once retrieved, the value is used to set the value of the picture control on the form thereby first removing the **nil** attribute if it is present or adding it if the picture control should be cleared.

```
if (!String.IsNullOrEmpty(pic))
{
  if (icon.MoveToAttribute("nil",
    NamespaceManager.LookupNamespace("xsi")))
    icon.DeleteSelf();

  icon.SetValue(pic);
}
else
{
  icon.SetValue(String.Empty);
  if (!icon.MoveToAttribute("nil",
    NamespaceManager.LookupNamespace("xsi")))
  {
    icon.CreateAttribute("xsi", "nil",
      NamespaceManager.LookupNamespace("xsi"), "true");
  }
}
```

The second part of the solution updates the selected record in the database. This code first retrieves the values of the fields that need to be stored in the database.

```
XPathNavigator mainDS = MainDataSource.CreateNavigator();
string appName = mainDS.SelectSingleNode(
  "/my:myFields/my:appName", NamespaceManager).Value;
string appColor = mainDS.SelectSingleNode(
  "/my:myFields/my:appColor", NamespaceManager).Value;
string appIcon = mainDS.SelectSingleNode(
  "/my:myFields/my:appIcon", NamespaceManager).Value;
```

Then a SQL UPDATE statement is constructed for an `OleDbCommand` object.

```
OleDbCommand cmd = conn.CreateCommand();
cmd.CommandType = System.Data.CommandType.Text;

System.Text.StringBuilder sb = new System.Text.StringBuilder();
sb.Append("UPDATE OfficeApplications ");
sb.Append("SET [App Name] = @AppName, ");
sb.Append("[App Color] = @AppColor, ");
sb.Append("[App Icon] = @AppIcon ");
sb.Append("WHERE ID = ");
sb.Append(_id);

cmd.CommandText = sb.ToString();
cmd.Parameters.AddWithValue("AppName", appName);
cmd.Parameters.AddWithValue("AppColor", appColor);
cmd.Parameters.Add("AppIcon", OleDbType.LongVarChar).Value = appIcon;
```

Note that the value of the Memo field is set through an `OleDbParameter` object using the `LongVarChar` OLE DB data type.

The database connection is then opened using the `Open()` method of the `OleDbConnection` object and the `ExecuteNonQuery()` method of the `OleDbCommand` object is called to update the record in the database.

```
conn.Open();
cmd.ExecuteNonQuery();
```

While the solution described above does not contain functionality to delete a record, you could expand it by adding an extra button control to the repeating table and then writing code similar to the code described in the next solution.

Delete a record from an Access table

Problem

You have an Access database table that has a Memo field in which images of Office applications are stored. You want to use an InfoPath form to maintain data in this Access database table, which includes deleting a record from the table.

Solution

You can use classes from the `System.Data.OleDb` namespace to perform create, update, and delete (CRUD) operations on an Access database table.

Suppose you have an Access database table named **OfficeApplications** as described in recipe *86 Perform a wildcard search on an Access table*.

To delete a record from the Access database table that contains a Memo field:

1. Follow the instructions in recipe *87 Retrieve data from an Access table with Memo field* to create an InfoPath Filler form template that loads data from the **OfficeApplications** database table into a repeating section control.

2. On the **Fields** task pane, click the **group2** group node, and then click on the drop-down arrow that appears on the right-hand side of the name of the group node and select **Programming ➤ Changed Event** from the drop-down menu that appears. This should add an event handler for the **Changed** event of the **group2** group node (which represents a section) to the `FormCode` class.

3. In VSTA, add the following code to the `group2_Changed()` event handler (*code #: CD5DBAAD-1CBE-4554-A8A6-06148289D412*):

```
if (e.Operation == XmlOperation.Delete)
{
  OleDbConnection conn = new OleDbConnection(
    @"Provider=Microsoft.ACE.OLEDB.12.0; " +
    @"Data Source=C:\OfficeApplications.accdb;");

  string id = e.Site.SelectSingleNode("my:ID", NamespaceManager).Value;

  OleDbCommand cmd = conn.CreateCommand();
  cmd.CommandType = System.Data.CommandType.Text;
  cmd.CommandText = "DELETE FROM OfficeApplications WHERE ID = " + id;

  try
  {
```

```
      conn.Open();
      cmd.ExecuteNonQuery();
   }
   catch (Exception ex)
   {
      MessageBox.Show(ex.Message, "An error occurred",
        MessageBoxButtons.OK, MessageBoxIcon.Error);
   }
   finally
   {
      conn.Close();
   }
}
```

Note that you must change the path to the Access database
(C:\OfficeApplications.accdb) to suit your own scenario.

4. Save and build the project.

5. Preview the form.

When the form opens, hover over one of the sections, and then click the down arrow that
appears on the left-hand side of the section and select **Remove group2** from the drop-
down menu that appears. The section should disappear. Open the Access database table
and verify that the record has been deleted from the table.

Discussion

In the solution described above, you used the Changed() event handler of a repeating
section control to first detect a delete operation

```
if (e.Operation == XmlOperation.Delete)
{
  ...
}
```

and then create an OleDbConnection object

```
OleDbConnection conn = new OleDbConnection(
  @"Provider=Microsoft.ACE.OLEDB.12.0; " +
  @"Data Source=C:\OfficeApplications.accdb;");
```

and an OleDbCommand object that uses the **ID** for the section being deleted

```
string id = e.Site.SelectSingleNode("my:ID", NamespaceManager).Value;

OleDbCommand cmd = conn.CreateCommand();
cmd.CommandType = System.Data.CommandType.Text;
cmd.CommandText = "DELETE FROM OfficeApplications WHERE ID = " + id;
```

before using the Open() method of the OleDbConnection object to open the database
connection

```
conn.Open();
```

and execute the query to delete the record by calling the `ExecuteNonQuery()` method of the `OleDbCommand` object.

```
cmd.ExecuteNonQuery();
```

Note that the technique used in the solution above is only one of several ways you can enable a user to delete a record. For example, you could also add a button control to the repeating section and add code to it to delete the section in which the button is located. But whichever method you choose to implement, the code used to delete the record from the database should be pretty similar to the code in the solution above.

89 Retrieve data from SQL Server using a stored procedure

Problem

You want to use a stored procedure to query a SQL Server database table with wildcard queries and have an InfoPath form return only those records that satisfy the search criteria.

Solution

You can change the value of the `Command` property of an `AdoQueryConnection` object for a SQL Server database connection to be equal to a SQL statement for executing a stored procedure, to be able to retrieve data from SQL Server using a stored procedure.

To retrieve data from SQL Server using a stored procedure:

1. In SQL Server, create a new database table named **OfficeApplications** that has three columns of which the first column is an identity column named **OfficeApplicationId**, the second column is a column named **OfficeApplicationName**, and the third column is a column named **OfficeApplicationColor**. You can use the following CREATE script to create the table (*code #: B0CA02A9-C0F4-4A9E-A548-020EFDFCFE54*):

```
CREATE TABLE [dbo].[OfficeApplications](
  [OfficeApplicationId] [int] IDENTITY(1,1) PRIMARY KEY NOT NULL,
  [OfficeApplicationName] [nvarchar](50) NOT NULL,
  [OfficeApplicationColor] [nvarchar(50)] NOT NULL
)
```

Note: You can also download a database script named **OfficeApplications.sql** from www.bizsupportonline.com to create and fill the table with data.

2. Create a new stored procedure named **GetOfficeApplications** that accepts a parameter named **@AppName**. You can use the following CREATE script to

create the stored procedure (*code #: B0CA02A9-C0F4-4A9E-A548-020EFDFCFE54*):

```
CREATE PROCEDURE [dbo].[GetOfficeApplications](@AppName nvarchar(50))
AS
BEGIN
  SELECT * FROM OfficeApplications
  WHERE OfficeApplicationName LIKE '%' + @AppName + '%'
END
```

3. In InfoPath, create a new form template or use an existing one.

4. Select **Data ➤ Get External Data ➤ From Other Sources ➤ From Database**.

5. On the **Data Connection Wizard**, click **Select Database**.

6. On the **Select Data Source** dialog box, click **New Source**.

7. On the **Data Connection Wizard**, select **Microsoft SQL Server**, and click **Next**.

8. On the **Data Connection Wizard**, enter the **Server name** (for example, **(local)**), select the authentication type (for example, **Use Windows Authentication**), and click **Next**.

9. On the **Data Connection Wizard**, select the database from the drop-down list box (for example, **InfoPathDB**), select the table from the list of tables (for example, **OfficeApplications**), and click **Finish**.

10. On the **Data Connection Wizard**, click **Next**.

11. On the **Data Connection Wizard**, leave the **Store a copy of the data in the form template** check box deselected, and click **Next**.

12. On the **Data Connection Wizard**, name the data connection **OfficeApplications**, deselect the **Automatically retrieve data when form is opened** check box, and click **Finish**.

13. Add a **Text Box** control to the view of the form template and name it **field1**.

14. On the **Fields** task pane, select **OfficeApplication (Secondary)** from the **Fields** drop-down list box, expand the **dataFields** group node, and then drag-and-drop the **d:OfficeApplications** repeating group node onto the view of the form template. Bind it to a **Repeating Table** when you drop it.

15. Add a **Button** control to the view of the form template and label it **Get Data**.

16. Add an event handler for the **Clicked** event of the button as described in recipe *7 Add an event handler for a control event*.

17. In VSTA, add the following code to the `Clicked()` event handler for the **Get Data** button (*code #: B0CA02A9-C0F4-4A9E-A548-020EFDFCFE54*):

```
XPathNavigator mainDS = MainDataSource.CreateNavigator();
string field1 = mainDS.SelectSingleNode(
  "/my:myFields/my:field1", NamespaceManager).Value;
```

```
AdoQueryConnection conn =
   (AdoQueryConnection)DataSources["OfficeApplications"].QueryConnection;

string originalCommand = conn.Command;
string newCommand = originalCommand;

if (!String.IsNullOrEmpty(field1))
{
   field1 = field1.Replace("'", "''");
   newCommand = "EXEC GetOfficeApplications '" + field1 + "'";
}

conn.Command = newCommand;
conn.Execute();

conn.Command = originalCommand;
```

18. Save and build the project.

19. Preview the form.

When the form opens, click the **Get Data** button. All of the data from the table should appear in the repeating table. Enter part of the name of an Office application in the text box, and click the button again. The Office applications that contain the text you entered in their names should appear in the repeating table.

Discussion

In the solution described above you learned how to change the Command property of an AdoQueryConnection object to execute a SQL Server stored procedure to return (filtered) data.

The code first retrieves the value of the field that should be used as a parameter for the stored procedure for filtering data on a wildcard match.

```
XPathNavigator mainDS = MainDataSource.CreateNavigator();
string field1 = mainDS.SelectSingleNode(
   "/my:myFields/my:field1", NamespaceManager).Value;
```

It then proceeds to use the DataSources property of the form to retrieve a previously added query connection for a database table. This query connection is then cast to an AdoQueryConnection object, so that the Command property can be exposed.

```
AdoQueryConnection conn =
   (AdoQueryConnection)DataSources["OfficeApplications"].QueryConnection;
```

The code then stores the original command in a variable, so that it can be restored after the query is executed.

```
string originalCommand = conn.Command;
```

The value of the `Command` property of the `AdoQueryConnection` object is then set to be equal to a new command that contains a SQL statement to execute a stored procedure.

```
string newCommand = originalCommand;

if (!String.IsNullOrEmpty(field1))
{
  field1 = field1.Replace("'", "''");
  newCommand = "EXEC GetOfficeApplications '" + field1 + "'";
}

conn.Command = newCommand;
conn.Execute();
```

After the query is executed, the command is then restored to its original value.

```
conn.Command = originalCommand;
```

You could have also used a user-defined function instead of a stored procedure to retrieve data from SQL Server. For example, you could have used the following CREATE script to create a table-valued function

```
CREATE FUNCTION [dbo].[GetOfficeApplicationsFunct] (@AppName nvarchar(50))
RETURNS TABLE
AS
RETURN
(
  SELECT * FROM OfficeApplications
  WHERE OfficeApplicationName LIKE '%' + @AppName + '%'
)
```

and then used the following code to call the table-valued function

```
if (!String.IsNullOrEmpty(field1))
{
  field1 = field1.Replace("'", "''");
  newCommand = "SELECT * FROM GetOfficeApplicationsFunct('" + field1 + "')";
}
```

to return the result as a table with a structure that fits the secondary data source.

While you can use a query data connection for a database to execute a stored procedure to retrieve data from SQL Server, you cannot use it to perform create, update, or delete operations. For the latter, you would either have to write ADO.NET code within an InfoPath form template similar to the technique used to update an Access database in recipe *88 Perform create, update, and delete actions on an Access table with Memo field* or create a web service that can be called to submit data to SQL Server as discussed in recipe *82 Submit form field values to a web service*.

90 Submit an entire InfoPath form to SQL Server

Problem

You want to submit all of the data from an InfoPath form to SQL Server and store it in a table so that the data for the form can be reloaded afterwards in InfoPath.

Solution

You can submit the InfoPath form as a generic XmlDocument object to a web service and then have the web service store the contents of the root node of the InfoPath form in a SQL Server database table column that has the XML data type assigned to it.

To submit an entire InfoPath form to SQL Server:

1. In SQL Server, create a new database table named **InfoPathForm** that has three columns of which the first column is an identity column named **id**, the second column is a **varchar(50)** column named **name**, and the third column is an **xml** column named **form**, as shown in the following script:

    ```
    CREATE TABLE [dbo].[InfoPathForm](
      [id] [int] IDENTITY(1,1) PRIMARY KEY NOT NULL,
      [name] [varchar](50) NOT NULL,
      [form] [xml] NOT NULL
    )
    ```

    You can also download a file named **InfoPathForm.sql** from www.bizsupportonline.com and use it to create the table.

2. In Visual Studio, follow steps 1 through 13 of *Create a web service that returns one value* in recipe *81 Create a web service that retrieves data for InfoPath* to create a web service, but skip steps 6 through 8.

3. Switch to the **InfoPathService.asmx.cs** file and add the following **using** statement to it:

    ```
    using System.Xml;
    ```

4. Replace the HelloWorld() web method with the following web method or add a new web method if you wish (*code #: 8196547D-5ACD-45C7-937B-921B6DEF1E66*):

    ```
    [WebMethod(Description = "Submits an entire InfoPath form to SQL Server.")]
    public void SubmitFormToSQL(string FormName, XmlDocument InfoPathForm)
    {
      string connectionString =
        ConfigurationManager.ConnectionStrings["InfoPathDB"].ConnectionString;

      using (SqlConnection conn = new SqlConnection(connectionString))
      {
        try
        {
          conn.Open();

          SqlCommand cmd = new SqlCommand();
    ```

```
    cmd.CommandType = System.Data.CommandType.Text;
    cmd.Connection = conn;

    cmd.CommandText = "INSERT INTO InfoPathForm (name, form) " +
      "VALUES (@FormName, @Form)";
    cmd.Parameters.AddWithValue("FormName", FormName);
    cmd.Parameters.Add("Form", System.Data.SqlDbType.Xml).Value =
      InfoPathForm.FirstChild.InnerXml;

    cmd.ExecuteNonQuery();
  }
  catch
  {
    // Handle the error using your own preferred error-handling method
  }
  finally
  {
    conn.Close();
  }
  }
}
```

5. Click **Build ➤ Build Solution** and fix any errors if necessary.

6. Click **Debug ➤ Start Debugging**. This should open a browser window and display the **InfoPathService.asmx** page.

7. In InfoPath, create a new form template or use an existing one.

8. Add a **Text Box** control to the view of the form template and name it **formName**. This field will be used to identify a form by name, so that afterwards a user can select and load an InfoPath form from the SQL Server database table (see recipe *91 Retrieve an entire InfoPath form from SQL Server*).

9. Design the form template further as you wish by adding controls or anything else that your scenario requires to it.

10. Select **Data ➤ Submit Form ➤ To Other Locations ➤ To Web Service**.

11. On the **Data Connection Wizard**, enter the URL of the web service, for example:

    ```
    http://localhost:24014/InfoPathService.asmx
    ```

    and click **Next**. Note that an URL such as the one specified above should work if you are running the web service and InfoPath on the same computer. Otherwise, you may have to deploy the web service first before you are able to access it in InfoPath.

12. On the **Data Connection Wizard**, select the **SubmitFormToSQL** operation, and click **Next**. Note that the description you gave the web method should appear in the **Description of operation** box.

13. On the **Data Connection Wizard**, ensure the **FormName** parameter is selected, and then click the button behind the **Field or group** text box.

14. On the **Select a Field or Group** dialog box, select **formName**, and click **OK**.

15. On the **Data Connection Wizard**, leave **Text and child elements only** selected in the **Include** drop-down list box, leave the **Submit data as a string** check box deselected, select the **InfoPathForm** parameter, and then click the button behind the **Field or group** text box.

16. On the **Select a Field or Group** dialog box, select the **myFields** group node, and click **OK**.

17. On the **Data Connection Wizard**, select the **Entire form (XML document, including processing instructions)** option, leave the **Submit data as a string** check box deselected, and click **Next**.

18. On the **Data Connection Wizard**, leave the data connection name as **Web Service Submit**, leave the **Set as the default submit connection** check box selected, and then click **Finish**.

19. Preview the form.

When the form opens, enter a name in the **formName** text box, fill out the form further as you see fit, and then click the **Submit** button on the toolbar. Once the form has been submitted, open SQL Server Management Studio and verify that the data was submitted to the database table.

	id	name	form
▶	1	form01.xml	<?mso-infoPathSolution solutionVersion="1.0....
*	NULL	NULL	NULL

Figure 68. The XML of an InfoPath form stored in a SQL Server database table.

Discussion

When you store XML data in SQL Server, you can store it as either untyped or typed XML. Typed XML data adheres to an XML schema, while untyped XML does not. An XML schema allows you to define validation constraints and data type information for the XML that is to be stored. If you do not want SQL Server to validate the XML data of the entire InfoPath form when it is submitted, use an untyped XML column to store the data as described in the solution above.

```
CREATE TABLE [dbo].[InfoPathForm](
  [id] [int] IDENTITY(1,1) PRIMARY KEY NOT NULL,
  [name] [varchar](50) NOT NULL,
  [form] [xml] NOT NULL
)
```

To create a typed XML column in SQL Server, you must first register an XML schema collection, and then associate that XML schema collection with the table column that has the XML data type assigned to it. When creating the XML schema collection, you must use the XSD file from the InfoPath form template, which you can extract through **File ➤ Publish ➤ Export Source Files** in InfoPath Designer 2010 (also see *Create a typed XML* *column for an InfoPath form* in the Appendix). To learn more about typed vs. untyped XML data in SQL Server, refer to the article entitled *Typed XML Compared to Untyped XML* on the MSDN web site.

The web method in the web service used to submit the entire InfoPath form to SQL Server if pretty straightforward. It has the name of the form and an XML document as its parameters.

```
public void SubmitFormToSQL(string FormName, XmlDocument InfoPathForm)
{
  ...
}
```

The form name is used later to be able to identify a form that a user wants to load by name, and the XML document parameter is used to be able to submit the entire InfoPath form as an XML document to the web service.

A `SqlConnection` object is then used to open a connection to the database (where the connection string information is retrieved from the **Web.config** file).

```
string connectionString =
  ConfigurationManager.ConnectionStrings["InfoPathDB"].ConnectionString;

using (SqlConnection conn = new SqlConnection(connectionString))
{
  conn.Open();
  ...
}
```

A `SqlCommand` object is constructed and `SqlParameter` objects are added to its `Parameters` collection.

```
SqlCommand cmd = new SqlCommand();
cmd.CommandType = System.Data.CommandType.Text;
cmd.Connection = conn;

cmd.CommandText = "INSERT INTO InfoPathForm (name, form) " +
  "VALUES (@FormName, @Form)";
cmd.Parameters.AddWithValue("FormName", FormName);
cmd.Parameters.Add("Form", System.Data.SqlDbType.Xml).Value =
  InfoPathForm.FirstChild.InnerXml;
```

And finally, the code calls the `ExecuteNonQuery()` method of the `SqlCommand` object to insert a record into the SQL Server database.

```
cmd.ExecuteNonQuery();
```

Note that because the XML of an InfoPath form gets encapsulated by a node called **dfs:IPDocument** when you submit it as an **Entire form (XML document, including processing instructions)**, the code in the web method uses the `InnerXml` property of the `FirstChild` property of the `XmlDocument` object to save the InfoPath form to the database, which will exclude the **dfs:IPDocument** node.

```
cmd.Parameters.Add("Form", System.Data.SqlDbType.Xml).Value =
  InfoPathForm.FirstChild.InnerXml;
```

Because the XML schema of an InfoPath form does not contain a definition for the **dfs:IPDocument** node, SQL Server would not be able to validate this node if you used a typed XML column to store the InfoPath forms (see *Create a typed XML column for an InfoPath form* in the Appendix). Therefore, you should exclude the **dfs:IPDocument** node from the XML stored in SQL Server, and the XML that is stored in the XML column in the SQL Server database column should wind up having a format such as the following:

```
<?mso-infoPathSolution name="urn:schemas-microsoft-com:office:infopath:Lib1:-
myXSD-2011-10-26T22-09-21" solutionVersion="1.0.0.202" productVersion="14.0.0.0"
PIVersion="1.0.0.0"
href="http://servername/sitename/Lib1/Forms/template.xsn"?><?mso-application
progid="InfoPath.Document" versionProgid="InfoPath.Document.3"?>
<my:myFields>
  <my:field1>Contents of field 1</my:field1>
  ...
</my:myFields>
```

which is basically the entire InfoPath form including all of its processing instructions, but excluding the **dfs:IPDocument** node. Note that the namespaces have been removed from the XML listed above for clarity reasons.

You could have also chosen to submit the InfoPath form as an **XML subtree, including selected element**, which would have then excluded the processing instructions from the XML stored in SQL Server. The submit method you choose depends on how you want to store the XML data in SQL Server. In addition, you will have to change the code that loads XML data into a form (see recipe *91 Retrieve an entire InfoPath form from SQL Server*) to match the submit method you have chosen to use.

Important:

> Any users who must fill out or open InfoPath forms stored in the database table must have the proper rights in SQL Server to read and write data from/to the database. Consult the SQL Server documentation for instructions on how to give users database permissions.

91 Retrieve an entire InfoPath form from SQL Server

Problem

You have previously stored the XML for InfoPath forms in a SQL Server database table and now you want to retrieve the XML for one of those forms and load it into an InfoPath form.

Solution

You can pass the identifier of a form that should be loaded to a web service, have the web service retrieve the XML data from SQL Server, and then load the data into an InfoPath form by replacing the contents of the root node of the form.

To retrieve an entire form from SQL Server:

1. In Visual Studio, use the web service from recipe *90 Submit an entire InfoPath form to SQL Server*.

2. On the **Solution Explorer** pane, right-click the project name and select **Add ➤ New Item** from the context menu that appears.

3. On the **Add New Item** dialog box, select **Class**, name the file **Item.cs**, and click **Add**.

4. Add the following two classes to the **Item.cs** file (*code #: 031EB338-4B67-4DE4-B2C8-81E0D50EC830*):

```
public class Item
{
  public int Value { get; set; }
  public string DisplayName { get; set; }
}

public class Items : List<Item>
{
}
```

The `Item` class defines an item that can be added to a drop-down list box, combo box, or list box in InfoPath, while the `Items` class defines a `List` of `Item` objects, so makes items "repeating".

5. Add a new web method named **GetFormsList** to the web service using the following code (*code #: 031EB338-4B67-4DE4-B2C8-81E0D50EC830*):

```
[WebMethod(Description = "Retrieves a list of forms as name/value pairs
from SQL Server.")]
public Items GetFormsList()
{
  string connectionString =
    ConfigurationManager.ConnectionStrings["InfoPathDB"].ConnectionString;

  Items items = new Items();
```

337

```
using (SqlConnection conn = new SqlConnection(connectionString))
{
  try
  {
    conn.Open();

    SqlCommand cmd = new SqlCommand();
    cmd.CommandType = System.Data.CommandType.Text;
    cmd.Connection = conn;
    cmd.CommandText = "SELECT id, name FROM InfoPathForm";

    using (SqlDataReader reader = cmd.ExecuteReader())
    {
      while (reader.Read())
      {
        items.Add(
          new Item
          {
            Value = reader.GetInt32(0),
            DisplayName = reader.GetString(1)
          });
      }
      reader.Close();
    }
  }
  catch
  {
    // Handle the error using your own preferred error-handling method
  }
  finally
  {
    conn.Close();
  }
  return items;
}
}
```

This web method is used to retrieve a list of IDs and names of forms that have been stored in the database table, and returns an XML structure that can be used for populating a drop-down list box, combo box, or list box.

6. Add a new web method named **GetFormFromSQL** to the web service using the following code (*code #: 031EB338-4B67-4DE4-B2C8-81E0D50EC830*):

```
[WebMethod(
  Description = "Retrieves an entire InfoPath form from SQL Server.")]
public string GetFormFromSQL(int FormId)
{
  string connectionString =
    ConfigurationManager.ConnectionStrings["InfoPathDB"].ConnectionString;
  string xml = string.Empty;

  using (SqlConnection conn = new SqlConnection(connectionString))
  {
    try
    {
      conn.Open();

      SqlCommand cmd = new SqlCommand();
      cmd.CommandType = System.Data.CommandType.Text;
```

```
cmd.Connection = conn;
cmd.CommandText = "SELECT form FROM InfoPathForm WHERE id = @Id";
cmd.Parameters.Add("Id", System.Data.SqlDbType.Int).Value = FormId;

using (SqlDataReader reader = cmd.ExecuteReader())
{
  while (reader.Read())
  {
    System.Data.SqlTypes.SqlXml formXml = reader.GetSqlXml(0);
    xml = formXml.Value;
  }
  reader.Close();
}
}
catch
{
  // Handle the error using your own preferred error-handling method
}
finally
{
  conn.Close();
}
return xml;
}
}
```

This web method retrieves the XML of an entire form from a SQL Server database table based on an ID.

7. Click **Build ➤ Build Solution** and fix any errors if necessary.

8. Click **Debug ➤ Start Debugging**. This should open a browser window and display the **InfoPathService.asmx** page.

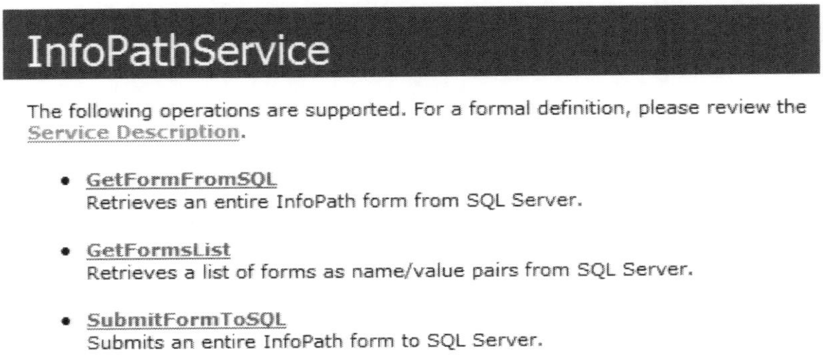

InfoPathService

The following operations are supported. For a formal definition, please review the
Service Description.

- **GetFormFromSQL**
  Retrieves an entire InfoPath form from SQL Server.

- **GetFormsList**
  Retrieves a list of forms as name/value pairs from SQL Server.

- **SubmitFormToSQL**
  Submits an entire InfoPath form to SQL Server.

Figure 69. The page for the InfoPathService web service.

9. In Notepad, create a new file that has the following contents:

```
<SelectedId><Id/></SelectedId>
```

and save the file locally on disk as **SelectedId.xml**. You can also download the **SelectedId.xml** file from www.bizsupportonline.com.

10. In InfoPath, open the form template you created in recipe *90 Submit an entire InfoPath form to SQL Server*.

11. Select **Data ➤ Get External Data ➤ From Other Sources ➤ From XML File** and follow the instructions to add a data connection for the **SelectedId.xml** file. Name the data connection **SelectedId** and leave the **Automatically retrieve data when form is opened** check box selected.

12. Select **Data ➤ Get External Data ➤ From Web Service ➤ From SOAP Web Service**.

13. On the **Data Connection Wizard**, enter the URL of the web service, for example:

```
http://localhost:24014/InfoPathService.asmx
```

and click **Next**. Note that an URL such as the one specified above should work if you are running the web service and InfoPath on the same computer. Otherwise, you may have to deploy the web service first before you are able to access it in InfoPath.

14. On the **Data Connection Wizard**, select the **GetFormFromSQL** operation, and click **Next**. Note that the description you gave the web method should appear in the **Description of operation** box.

15. On the **Data Connection Wizard**, leave the **FormId** parameter as is, and click **Next**.

16. On the **Data Connection Wizard**, leave the **Store a copy of the data in the form template** check box deselected, and click **Next**.

17. On the **Data Connection Wizard**, name the data connection **GetFormFromSQL**, deselect the **Automatically retrieve data when form is opened** check box, and click **Finish**.

18. Select **Data ➤ Get External Data ➤ From Web Service ➤ From SOAP Web Service**.

19. On the **Data Connection Wizard**, enter the URL of the web service, for example:

```
http://localhost:24014/InfoPathService.asmx
```

and click **Next**.

20. On the **Data Connection Wizard**, select the **GetFormsList** operation, and click **Next**.

21. On the **Data Connection Wizard**, leave the **Store a copy of the data in the form template** check box deselected, and click **Next**.

22. On the **Data Connection Wizard**, name the data connection **GetFormsList**, leave the **Automatically retrieve data when form is opened** check box selected, and click **Finish**.

23. On the **Fields** task pane, select **SelectedId (Secondary)** from the **Fields** drop-down list box, right-click the **Id** field under the **SelectedId** group node, drag it to the view, drop it, and select **Drop-Down List Box** from the context menu that appears.

24. Open the **Drop-Down List Box Properties** dialog box, and then on the **Data** tab, select the **Get choices from an external data source** option, select **GetFormsList** from the **Data Source** drop-down list box, and click the button behind the **Entries** text box.

25. On the **Select a Field or Group** dialog box, expand all of the nodes, select the **Item** repeating group node, and click **OK**.

26. On the **Drop-Down List Box Properties** dialog box, ensure **tns:Value** is selected for the **Value** property and **tns:DisplayName** is selected for the **Display name** property, and then click **OK**.

27. Add a **Button** control to the view of the form template and label it **Load Form**.

28. Add an event handler for the **Clicked** event of the button as described in recipe 7 *Add an event handler for a control event*.

29. In VSTA, add the following code to the `Clicked()` event handler for the **Load Form** button (*code #: 031EB338-4B67-4DE4-B2C8-81E0D50EC830*):

```
XPathNavigator mainDS = MainDataSource.CreateNavigator();
string formId = DataSources["SelectedId"].CreateNavigator()
  .SelectSingleNode("/SelectedId/Id", NamespaceManager).Value;

DataSource getFormDS = DataSources["GetFormFromSQL"];
XPathNavigator getFormDSRoot = getFormDS.CreateNavigator();
getFormDSRoot.SelectSingleNode(
  "/dfs:myFields/dfs:queryFields/tns:GetFormFromSQL/tns:FormId",
  NamespaceManager).SetValue(formId);
getFormDS.QueryConnection.Execute();

string xml = getFormDSRoot.SelectSingleNode(
"/dfs:myFields/dfs:dataFields/tns:GetFormFromSQLResponse/tns:GetFormFromSQL
Result", NamespaceManager).Value;

XmlDocument doc = new XmlDocument();
doc.LoadXml(xml);
XPathNavigator docRoot = doc.CreateNavigator().SelectSingleNode(
  "/my:myFields", NamespaceManager);

XPathNavigator root = mainDS.SelectSingleNode(
  "/my:myFields", NamespaceManager);
root.InnerXml = docRoot.InnerXml;
```

30. Save and build the project.

31. Preview the form.

When the form opens, select a form from the drop-down list box, and then click the button. The fields on the InfoPath form should get populated with the data that was retrieved from the database.

Discussion

Before you can retrieve the XML for an entire InfoPath form from SQL Server and load the data to populate an InfoPath form either in InfoPath Filler 2010 or a browser via SharePoint, you must choose a method for identifying the InfoPath form that should be loaded. In the solution above, an extra web method named **GetFormsList** was used to retrieve a list of the forms that are stored in the database, and display these forms in a drop-down list box. The drop-down list box was bound to the field in a secondary data source for an XML file

```
<SelectedId><Id/></SelectedId>
```

so that this field would not become part of the Main data source, since it does not describe actual data within the form itself, but is rather used as a helper field to find the identifier of the InfoPath form that should be loaded.

A user can then select a form from the drop-down list box, and click a button to retrieve the identifier of the form that was selected in the drop-down list box.

```
XPathNavigator mainDS = MainDataSource.CreateNavigator();
string formId = DataSources["SelectedId"].CreateNavigator()
  .SelectSingleNode("/SelectedId/Id", NamespaceManager).Value;
```

The identifier is then used when calling the **GetFormFromSQL** web service method

```
DataSource getFormDS = DataSources["GetFormFromSQL"];
XPathNavigator getFormDSRoot = getFormDS.CreateNavigator();
getFormDSRoot.SelectSingleNode(
  "/dfs:myFields/dfs:queryFields/tns:GetFormFromSQL/tns:FormId",
  NamespaceManager).SetValue(formId);
getFormDS.QueryConnection.Execute();
```

to retrieve the XML of the InfoPath form

```
string xml = getFormDSRoot.SelectSingleNode(
"/dfs:myFields/dfs:dataFields/tns:GetFormFromSQLResponse/tns:GetFormFromSQLResul
t", NamespaceManager).Value;
```

and then extract the XML contents of the **myFields** group node in the InfoPath form.

```
XmlDocument doc = new XmlDocument();
doc.LoadXml(xml);
XPathNavigator docRoot = doc.CreateNavigator().SelectSingleNode(
  "/my:myFields", NamespaceManager);
```

The value of the InnerXml property of the **myFields** group node is then used to populate and display the InfoPath form.

```
XPathNavigator root = mainDS.SelectSingleNode(
  "/my:myFields", NamespaceManager);
root.InnerXml = docRoot.InnerXml;
```

Instead of using a drop-down list box and a button to load a form, you could have also used a query string parameter to pass an ID to an InfoPath form (see recipe *93 Populate form fields from query string parameters*), retrieve the data from SQL Server, and then populate the form with this data.

The **GetFormsList** web method makes use of an `Item` class and an `Items` class with which a repeating XML structure can be constructed that is suitable for use in a drop-down list box, combo box, or normal list box in InfoPath.

```
public class Item
{
  public int Value { get; set; }
  public string DisplayName { get; set; }
}

public class Items : List<Item>
{
}
```

The code for retrieving the XML data and constructing the `Items` collection is pretty straightforward in that it makes use of ADO.NET classes to open a database connection, construct a `SqlCommand` object

```
conn.Open();

SqlCommand cmd = new SqlCommand();
cmd.CommandType = System.Data.CommandType.Text;
cmd.Connection = conn;
cmd.CommandText = "SELECT id, name FROM InfoPathForm";
```

and then use the `ExecuteReader()` method of the `SqlCommand` object to return a `SqlDataReader` object that can be read and used to add `Item` objects to the `Items` collection.

```
Items items = new Items();

using (SqlDataReader reader = cmd.ExecuteReader())
{
  while (reader.Read())
  {
    items.Add(
      new Item
      {
        Value = reader.GetInt32(0),
        DisplayName = reader.GetString(1)
      });
  }
  reader.Close();
}
```

The second web method named **GetFormFromSQL** used in the solution described above, retrieves the actual XML for a specific InfoPath form from the SQL Server database table based on an identifier. The method takes the identifier of the form it should retrieve and returns the XML for that form.

```
public string GetFormFromSQL(int FormId)
{
  string connectionString =
    ConfigurationManager.ConnectionStrings["InfoPathDB"].ConnectionString;
  string xml = string.Empty;

  using (SqlConnection conn = new SqlConnection(connectionString))
  {
    ...
    return xml;
  }
}
```

And then again ADO.NET classes are used to create `SqlConnection`, `SqlCommand`, and `SqlParameter` objects to retrieve the data.

```
SqlCommand cmd = new SqlCommand();
cmd.CommandType = System.Data.CommandType.Text;
cmd.Connection = conn;
cmd.CommandText = "SELECT form FROM InfoPathForm WHERE id = @Id";
cmd.Parameters.Add("Id", System.Data.SqlDbType.Int).Value = FormId;
```

The `ExecuteReader()` method of the `SqlCommand` object returns a `SqlDataReader` object, and then the `GetSqlXml()` method of that `SqlDataReader` object is used to get the XML from the XML table column as a `SqlXml` data type.

```
using (SqlDataReader reader = cmd.ExecuteReader())
{
  while (reader.Read())
  {
    System.Data.SqlTypes.SqlXml formXml = reader.GetSqlXml(0);
    xml = formXml.Value;
  }
  reader.Close();
}
```

If you are calling the web service from a browser form in SharePoint instead of from InfoPath Filler 2010, you may get an error saying that cross-domain access is not allowed. This is likely to occur if the domain name used in the web service URL and the domain name used in the SharePoint server URL differ. If you get this error, you must convert the data connections for the web service methods into data connection files, so that the web service methods can be called from a browser form in SharePoint, and also ensure that cross-domain access has been granted to user forms in SharePoint Central Administration (see *Configure cross-domain access for a web service* in the Appendix).

Note:

The web service, SQL Server, and SharePoint were all located on the same server in the solution described above and Windows Integrated security was used, so "double-hop" security issues should not take place. In a real-world deployment however, you may have to deal with security issues and the forwarding of credentials between services if they are located on different servers. Consult the MSDN documentation to solve such security issues.

Chapter 9: SharePoint Integration

There are several ways you can integrate InfoPath with SharePoint where writing code is concerned:

1. Use the SharePoint client or server object models in code from within InfoPath.

2. Create a SharePoint event handler that runs on a SharePoint form library whenever an InfoPath form is added, edited, or deleted.

3. Create a SharePoint workflow that runs on a SharePoint form library or a content type for an InfoPath form.

4. Use SharePoint web services to retrieve or submit data from within InfoPath.

None of the code you would write for the methods mentioned above, except for the last method, is unique to InfoPath. In fact, the first three methods are all related to SharePoint programming, which is not unique or specific to InfoPath. The only InfoPath-specific functionality when using the first method is that you must give form templates Full Trust when calling into the SharePoint object models. And for the second and third methods, you must know how to retrieve the XML for an InfoPath form from within an event handler or a SharePoint workflow or workflow activity, so that you can read or modify it. Therefore, if you are familiar with writing code for SharePoint, you are already familiar with writing code for the first three methods mentioned above.

The explanation of SharePoint programming and working with SharePoint are beyond the scope of this book. Therefore, you must already have a basic understanding of SharePoint and programming for SharePoint to be able to follow the recipes in this chapter. And because you cannot write code for SharePoint list forms this chapter focuses on writing code for SharePoint form library forms.

92 Add an item to a list using the SharePoint client object model

Problem

You want to use an InfoPath form and the SharePoint client object model to add an item to a SharePoint list.

Solution

You can use the AddItem() method of the List class of the SharePoint client object model to add a new item to a SharePoint list.

Suppose you have a SharePoint list named **OfficeApplications** that has two columns: **Title** and **Color**.

347

InfoPath 2010 Cookbook 3

To add an item to a SharePoint list using the SharePoint client object model:

1. In InfoPath, create a new form template or use an existing one.

2. Add two **Text Box** controls to the view of the form template and name them **title** and **color**, respectively.

3. Add a **Button** control to the view of the form template and label it **Add Item**.

4. Add an event handler for the **Clicked** event of the button as described in recipe *7 Add an event handler for a control event*.

5. In VSTA, add a reference to the **System.Core**, **Microsoft.SharePoint.Client**, and **Microsoft.SharePoint.Client.Runtime** assemblies.

6. Add a **using** statement for the **Microsoft.SharePoint.Client** namespace to the **FormCode.cs** file.

7. Add the following code to the `Clicked()` event handler for the **Add Item** button (*code #: 80CEA868-A1DA-444F-9BFE-545030772F5B*):

```
XPathNavigator root = MainDataSource.CreateNavigator();
string title = root.SelectSingleNode("//my:title", NamespaceManager).Value;
string color = root.SelectSingleNode("//my:color", NamespaceManager).Value;

using (ClientContext clientContext =
  new ClientContext("http://servername/sitename/"))
{
  List officeApplications =
    clientContext.Web.Lists.GetByTitle("OfficeApplications");

  ListItemCreationInformation itemCreateInfo =
    new ListItemCreationInformation();

  ListItem listItem = officeApplications.AddItem(itemCreateInfo);
  listItem["Title"] = title;
  listItem["Color"] = color;
  listItem.Update();

  clientContext.ExecuteQuery();
}
```

Note that you must change the URL of the site where the SharePoint list is located (`http://servername/sitename/`) to suit your own scenario.

8. Save and build the project.

9. Give the form template Full Trust as described in *Configure an InfoPath form template to have Full Trust* in the Appendix.

10. Preview the form.

When the form opens, enter text in the two text boxes and then click the **Add Item** button. In SharePoint, navigate to the SharePoint list to which the item should have been added and verify that this is indeed the case.

Discussion

In the solution described above, you learned how to use classes from the SharePoint client object model to write code that adds an item to a SharePoint list.

The code first retrieves the values of form fields that should be used to create the SharePoint list item.

```
XPathNavigator root = MainDataSource.CreateNavigator();
string title = root.SelectSingleNode("//my:title", NamespaceManager).Value;
string color = root.SelectSingleNode("//my:color", NamespaceManager).Value;
```

It then proceeds to initialize a `ClientContext` object using the SharePoint site URL where the SharePoint list is located.

```
using (ClientContext clientContext =
  new ClientContext("http://servername/sitename/"))
{
  ...
}
```

The code then retrieves a reference to the list by using the `GetByTitle()` method of the `ListCollection` object (`Lists` property) and instantiates a `ListItemCreationInformation` object.

```
List officeApplications =
  clientContext.Web.Lists.GetByTitle("OfficeApplications");

ListItemCreationInformation itemCreateInfo = new ListItemCreationInformation();
```

It then creates a `ListItem` object, populates it with the data from the InfoPath form, and calls the `Update()` method of the `ListItem` object

```
ListItem listItem = officeApplications.AddItem(itemCreateInfo);
listItem["Title"] = title;
listItem["Color"] = color;
listItem.Update();
```

before the entire batch of commands is executed by calling the `ExecuteQuery()` method of the `ClientContext` object.

```
clientContext.ExecuteQuery();
```

Because the code calls into one of the SharePoint assemblies, you must give the InfoPath form template Full Trust to run, otherwise you will see the following error displayed:

The assembly does not allow partially trusted callers.

Giving the form template Full Trust will also force you to publish the form template as an administrator-approved form template if you publish it to SharePoint. If you want to avoid having to do this, you can use for example the **Lists** web service instead of the SharePoint client object model to add list items to a SharePoint list (see recipe *95 Submit repeating table data to a SharePoint list to create new list items*).

The SharePoint client object model also allows you to update and delete list items, as well as upload files to SharePoint. For more information about the SharePoint client object model, consult the SharePoint documentation on the MSDN web site.

93 Populate form fields from query string parameters

Problem

You have a hyperlink to an InfoPath form on a SharePoint page. You want to be able to add query string parameters to the URL of the form, so that when the form opens, the values that were specified through the query string parameters are recognized by the form and used to populate fields on the form.

Solution

You can use the `InputParameters` property of the `LoadingEventArgs` object of the `Loading()` event handler of a browser form to retrieve any query string parameters that were included in the URL of the browser form.

To populate form fields from data passed through query string parameters in an URL:

1. In InfoPath, create a new browser-compatible form template or use an existing one.

2. Add two **Text Box** controls to the view of the form template, and name them **fruitName** and **fruitColor**, respectively.

3. Add an event handler for the **Loading** event of the form as described in recipe *6 Add an event handler for a form event*.

4. Add the following code to the `FormEvents_Loading()` event handler (*code #: 1FFE8DB1-368E-4C04-A33C-71E47BD6CE93*):

```
XPathNavigator mainDS = MainDataSource.CreateNavigator();

if (e.InputParameters != null)
{
  string fruitName = string.Empty;

  if (e.InputParameters.TryGetValue("FruitName", out fruitName))
    mainDS.SelectSingleNode("/my:myFields/my:fruitName",
      NamespaceManager).SetValue(fruitName);

  string fruitColor = string.Empty;
  if (e.InputParameters.TryGetValue("FruitColor", out fruitColor))
    mainDS.SelectSingleNode("/my:myFields/my:fruitColor",
      NamespaceManager).SetValue(fruitColor);
}
```

5. Save and build the project.

6. Publish the form template to a SharePoint form library.

7. In SharePoint, navigate to the form library where you published the form template and add a new form. When the form opens, copy the URL from the browser's address bar, and then close the form.

8. Create a new SharePoint wiki page or use an existing one.

9. Add a hyperlink to the SharePoint wiki page using the URL you copied earlier and add the following two additional query string parameters to the URL (*code #: 1FFE8DB1-368E-4C04-A33C-71E47BD6CE93*):

```
&FruitName=Kiwi&FruitColor=Green%20and%20brown
```

The final URL should look something like the following:

```
http://servername/sitename/_layouts/FormServer.aspx?XsnLocation=http://serv
ername/sitename/libraryname/Forms/template.xsn&SaveLocation=http://serverna
me/sitename/libraryname&Source=http://servername/sitename/libraryname/Forms
/AllItems.aspx&DefaultItemOpen=1&FruitName=Kiwi&FruitColor=Green%20and%20br
own
```

10. Save and close the SharePoint wiki page.

Click on the hyperlink you just added to the SharePoint wiki page. When the form opens, the values for the **FruitName** and **FruitColor** query string parameters should appear in the text boxes on the form.

Discussion

The InputParameters property of the LoadingEventArgs object returns a collection that contains any input parameters specified by using the /InputParameters command-line option, query string parameters in an URL, or one of the NewFromFormTemplateWithInputParameters methods. In the solution described above, the InputParameters property of the LoadingEventArgs object was used to retrieve query string parameters specified in the URL of a new form and then set the values of form fields.

```
string fruitName = string.Empty;

if (e.InputParameters.TryGetValue("FruitName", out fruitName))
  mainDS.SelectSingleNode("/my:myFields/my:fruitName",
  NamespaceManager).SetValue(fruitName);
```

In the code above, the TryGetValue() method of the InputParameters collection returns true if **FruitName** exists in the collection and then writes the value of the **FruitName** item in the collection to a variable named fruitName. The fruitName variable is then used to set the value of the **fruitName** field on the form.

Note that while the solution described above opened a new form, you can use the same technique to pass the values of query string parameters to an existing form.

You could extend the solution described above by creating a second form that has two text box controls (**fruitName** and **fruitColor**) and one hyperlink control on it, and set the default value of the hyperlink control to be equal to a formula that concatenates the URL of another form with the values entered in the text boxes. For example:

```
concat("http://servername/sitename/_layouts/FormServer.aspx?XmlLocation=/sitenam
e/libraryname/form01.xml&Source=http%3A%2F%2Fservername%2Fsitename%2Flibraryname
%2FForms%2FAllItems%2Easpx&DefaultItemOpen=1&FruitName=", fruitName,
"&FruitColor=", fruitColor)
```

This way a user can enter values in fields in one form and then click the hyperlink to open and fill out another form that contains the values of the fields entered in the first form.

While the InputParameters property of the LoadingEventArgs object can also be used with InfoPath Filler forms, the solution above applies to forms that are published to SharePoint and are opened and filled out using a browser.

94 Select and add files from a document library as attachments to a form

Problem

You want users to be able to select a file from a list of files stored in a SharePoint document library and then click a button to download and add the selected file as an attachment to a repeating table on a form.

Solution

You can use the **Copy** web service to download files from a SharePoint document library.

To allow users to select and add files from a SharePoint document library as attachments to a repeating table on a form:

1. In SharePoint, create a new document library or use an existing one. Add a few files to the document library and ensure that the **Title** field of each document contains the file name (plus extension) of the document.

2. In Notepad, create a new file with the following contents:

```
<selectedfile>
  <file/>
</selectedfile>
```

and save it as **SelectedFile.xml**. You can also download this file from www.bizsupportonline.com.

3. In InfoPath, create a new form template or use an existing one.

4. Select **Data ➤ Get External Data ➤ From Other Sources ➤ From XML File** and follow the instructions to add an XML data connection for the **SelectedFile.xml** file. Name the data connection **SelectedFile** and leave the **Automatically retrieve data when form is opened** check box selected.

5. Select **Data ➤ Get External Data ➤ From SharePoint List** and follow the instructions to add a SharePoint list data connection for the document library from step 1. Ensure you select the **Title** and **ID** fields to be included in the data source, name the data connection **Documents**, and leave the **Automatically retrieve data when form is opened** check box selected.

6. On the **Fields** task pane, select **SelectedFile (Secondary)** from the **Fields** drop-down list box, right-click the **file** field, and then drag-and-drop it onto the view of the form template. Select **Drop-Down List Box** from the context menu when you drop the field.

7. Open the **Drop-Down List Box Properties** dialog box, and configure the choices to come from the **Documents** secondary data source. Ensure that **ID** is selected for the **Value** property and **Title** for the **Display name** property. Click **OK** when you are done.

8. Add a **Button** control to the view of the form template and label it **Add File**.

9. Add a **Repeating Table** control with 2 columns to the view of the form template. Rename the text box in the first column to **filename** and change it into a **Calculated Value** control. Delete the text box in the second column (ensure you also delete the field it was bound to from the Main data source), add a **File Attachment** control in its place, and name the file attachment control **file**.

10. Open the **Repeating Table Properties** dialog box, deselect the **Show insert button and hint text** check box on the **Data** tab, and then click **Customize Commands**.

11. On the **Table Commands** dialog box, deselect all of the check boxes except for the **Remove** check box, and then click **OK**.

12. On the **Repeating Table Properties** dialog box, click **OK**.

13. Click **Data ➤ Form Data ➤ Default Values**.

14. On the **Edit Default Values** dialog box, expand the **group1** node for the repeating table, deselect the check box in front of the **group2** node, and click **OK**. With this you have set the repeating table not to start up with a first empty row.

15. Select **Data ➤ Get External Data ➤ From Web Service ➤ From SOAP Web Service**.

16. On the **Data Connection Wizard**, enter the URL of the **Copy** web service, for example:

```
http://servername/sitename/_vti_bin/Copy.asmx
```

and click **Next**. Here **servername** is the name of the SharePoint server where a site named **sitename** on which the **Copy** web service is located.

17. On the **Data Connection Wizard**, select the **GetItem** operation, and click **Next**.

18. On the **Data Connection Wizard**, leave the parameter as is, and click **Next**.

19. On the **Data Connection Wizard**, leave the **Store a copy of the data in the form template** check box deselected, and click **Next**.

20. On the **Data Connection Wizard**, name the data connection **GetItem**, deselect the **Automatically retrieve data when form is opened** check box, and click **Finish**.

21. Add an event handler for the **Clicked** event of the **Add File** button as described in recipe *7 Add an event handler for a control event*.

22. In VSTA, add the following private method to the FormCode class (*code #: 0F0984A7-717D-43AD-BFD7-1137E86AD52D*):

```
private void AddRow(string fileName, string file)
{
  XPathNavigator mainDS = MainDataSource.CreateNavigator();
  XPathNavigator group1 = mainDS.SelectSingleNode(
    "/my:myFields/my:group1", NamespaceManager);

  group1.AppendChildElement("my", "group2",
    NamespaceManager.LookupNamespace("my"), "");

  XPathNodeIterator iter = mainDS.Select(
    "/my:myFields/my:group1/my:group2", NamespaceManager);

  int rowCount = 0;
  if (iter != null)
    rowCount = iter.Count;

  XPathNavigator lastGroup2 = mainDS.SelectSingleNode(
    "/my:myFields/my:group1/my:group2[" + rowCount + "]",
    NamespaceManager);

  if (lastGroup2 != null)
  {
    lastGroup2.AppendChildElement("my", "filename",
      NamespaceManager.LookupNamespace("my"), fileName);
    lastGroup2.AppendChildElement("my", "file",
      NamespaceManager.LookupNamespace("my"), file);
  }
}
```

Also see recipe *71 Add a row to a repeating table* for an explanation of what this code does.

23. Add a new class with the name **InfoPathAttachmentEncoder** to the project and add the code from *InfoPathAttachmentEncoder.cs* listed in the Appendix to the new class file. You can also download the **InfoPathAttachmentEncoder.cs** file from www.bizsupportonline.com and then add it to your VSTA project.

24. Add the following code to the `Clicked()` event handler for the **Add File** button (*code #: 0F0984A7-717D-43AD-BFD7-1137E86AD52D*):

```
string selectedDocID = DataSources["SelectedFile"].CreateNavigator()
  .SelectSingleNode("/selectedfile/file", NamespaceManager).Value;

if (String.IsNullOrEmpty(selectedDocID))
  return;

string fileName =
  DataSources["Documents"].CreateNavigator().SelectSingleNode(
    "/dfs:myFields/dfs:dataFields/d:SharePointListItem_RW[d:ID = "
    + selectedDocID + "]/d:Title", NamespaceManager).Value;

SharePointListRWQueryConnection listConn =
(SharePointListRWQueryConnection)DataSources["Documents"].QueryConnection;
string siteUrl = listConn.SiteUrl.AbsoluteUri;

XPathNavigator getItemDS = DataSources["GetItem"].CreateNavigator();
getItemDS.SelectSingleNode(
  "/dfs:myFields/dfs:queryFields/tns:GetItem/tns:Url",
  NamespaceManager).SetValue(siteUrl + "/DocLib/" + fileName);

DataSources["GetItem"].QueryConnection.Execute();

XPathNavigator stream = getItemDS.SelectSingleNode(
  "/dfs:myFields/dfs:dataFields/tns:GetItemResponse/tns:Stream",
  NamespaceManager);

if (stream != null)
{
  string base64 = stream.Value;

  BizSupportOnline.InfoPathAttachmentEncoder enc =
    new BizSupportOnline.InfoPathAttachmentEncoder(
      fileName, Convert.FromBase64String(base64));

  AddRow(fileName, enc.ToBase64String());
}
```

Note that you should replace **DocLib** with the name of the document library you used in step 1.

25. Save and build the project.

26. Preview the form.

When the form opens, select a file from the drop-down list box, and then click the **Add File** button. The file should be downloaded from the SharePoint document library and added as a file attachment to the repeating table.

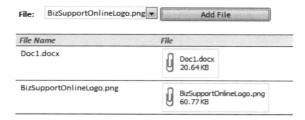

Figure 70. The InfoPath form with the downloaded files embedded in the form.

Discussion

In the solution described above you learned how to use the **GetItem** operation of the **Copy** web service to download a file from a SharePoint document library and store it as an attachment in a form.

The solution makes use of a secondary data source for an XML file named **SelectedFile.xml**, so that the form contains a field that is not part of the Main data source, but that can still be bound to a drop-down list box control to be able to display a list of the documents stored in a SharePoint document library. Since the drop-down list box is only used to select a file and not actually store a selected file in the form, it was bound to a field in a secondary data source instead of a field in the Main data source.

The code in the **Add File** button first retrieves the **ID** of the file that was selected in the drop-down list box.

```
string selectedDocID = DataSources["SelectedFile"].CreateNavigator()
  .SelectSingleNode("/selectedfile/file", NamespaceManager).Value;
```

If no file was selected, the code exits the event handler.

```
if (String.IsNullOrEmpty(selectedDocID))
  return;
```

Because the **GetItem** web service operation expects to receive the full URL of the file it should retrieve, you must first perform a lookup in the **Documents** secondary data source to find the **Title** that corresponds to the **ID** of the file that was selected in the drop-down list box.

```
string fileName =
  DataSources["Documents"].CreateNavigator().SelectSingleNode(
    "/dfs:myFields/dfs:dataFields/d:SharePointListItem_RW[d:ID = "
    + selectedDocID + "]/d:Title", NamespaceManager).Value;
```

The code then retrieves the URL of the SharePoint site where the document library is located by casting the `QueryConnection` property of the `DataSource` object for the SharePoint document library to a `SharePointListRWQueryConnection` object and then retrieving the URL through the `SiteUrl` property of the object.

```
SharePointListRWQueryConnection listConn =
(SharePointListRWQueryConnection)DataSources["Documents"].QueryConnection;
string siteUrl = listConn.SiteUrl.AbsoluteUri;
```

Note that you could have also used either the `ServerInfo` property of the form if the form is opened in the browser (`Environment.IsBrowser`) or a static URL that is based on the SharePoint server and a site name.

```
string siteUrl = String.Empty;
if (Environment.IsBrowser)
  siteUrl = ServerInfo.SharePointSiteUrl.ToString();
else
  siteUrl = "http://servername/sitename/";
```

The `ServerInfo` object provides information about the SharePoint server where the form template of the form is located. `ServerInfo` is defined as a property of the `XmlForm` object, which represents the underlying XML document of a form.

`ServerInfo` has four properties you can use to retrieve SharePoint server information:

1. `SharePointListUrl` – returns a `System.Uri` object that provides the URL of the document library where the form is located.

2. `SharePointServerRootUrl` – returns a `System.Uri` object that provides the root URL of the SharePoint server where the form is located.

3. `SharePointSiteCollectionUrl` – returns a `System.Uri` object that provides the URL of the SharePoint site collection where the form is located.

4. `SharePointSiteUrl` – returns a `System.Uri` object that provides the URL of the SharePoint site where the form is located.

Note that these properties have corresponding InfoPath functions with the same names and which you can use in formulas on an InfoPath form.

Once the site URL has been retrieved, the full URL of the selected document is then used to set the value of the **Url** field that is located under the **queryFields** group node in the **GetItem** secondary data source.

```
XPathNavigator getItemDS = DataSources["GetItem"].CreateNavigator();
getItemDS.SelectSingleNode(
  "/dfs:myFields/dfs:queryFields/tns:GetItem/tns:Url",
  NamespaceManager).SetValue(siteUrl + "/DocLib/" + fileName);
```

The selected document is then retrieved from the document library by calling the `Execute()` method of the **GetItem** query data connection.

```
DataSources["GetItem"].QueryConnection.Execute();
```

Once the web service operation has executed, the **Stream** field that is located under the **dataFields** group node in the **GetItem** secondary data source should contain the base64-encoded string that represents the file that was downloaded.

```
XPathNavigator stream = getItemDS.SelectSingleNode(
  "/dfs:myFields/dfs:dataFields/tns:GetItemResponse/tns:Stream",
  NamespaceManager);
```

The value of this field is then retrieved and encoded to create a base64-encoded string that is suitable for storage in a file attachment control.

```
string base64 = stream.Value;

BizSupportOnline.InfoPathAttachmentEncoder enc =
  new BizSupportOnline.InfoPathAttachmentEncoder(
    fileName, Convert.FromBase64String(base64));
```

And finally, the `AddRow()` method is called to add the file to the repeating table.

```
AddRow(fileName, enc.ToBase64String());
```

Tip:

> The same way you can use the **Copy** web service to download files and store them in a form, you can also download an existing InfoPath form stored in a form library and load its data into another InfoPath form. If you are replacing the data of an entire form (you can use the `InnerXml` property for this), you must ensure that the schemas of the form you are loading and the form that is being populated with data are one and the same.

95 Submit repeating table data to a SharePoint list to create new list items

Problem

You have data in a repeating table which you would like to submit to a SharePoint list as items.

Solution

You can use an XSL transformation to convert the repeating table data into a format that is suitable to be submitted to a SharePoint list through the **Lists** web service.

To submit repeating table data to a SharePoint list:

1. In InfoPath, create a new form template or use an existing one.

2. Add a **Repeating Table** control with 2 columns to the view of the form template. Name the text box in the first column **fruitName** and the text box in the second column **fruitColor**.

3. Open Notepad and add the following contents to it:

```
<?xml version="1.0" encoding="UTF-8" standalone="yes"?>
<xsl:stylesheet xmlns:xsl="http://www.w3.org/1999/XSL/Transform"
version="1.0"
xmlns:my="http://schemas.microsoft.com/office/infopath/2003/myXSD/2011-10-
03T20:49:40">
  <xsl:output method="xml" />
  <xsl:template match="/">
    <xsl:element name="Batch" namespace="">
      <xsl:for-each select="/my:myFields/my:group1/my:group2">
      <xsl:element name="Method" namespace="">
        <xsl:attribute name="Cmd">New</xsl:attribute>
        <xsl:attribute name="ID">
          <xsl:value-of select="count(preceding-sibling::my:group2) + 1" />
        </xsl:attribute>
        <xsl:element name="Field" namespace="">
          <xsl:attribute name="Name">Title</xsl:attribute>
          <xsl:value-of select="my:fruitName" />
        </xsl:element>
        <xsl:element name="Field" namespace="">
          <xsl:attribute name="Name">Color</xsl:attribute>
          <xsl:value-of select="my:fruitColor" />
        </xsl:element>
      </xsl:element>
      </xsl:for-each>
    </xsl:element>
  </xsl:template>
</xsl:stylesheet>
```

Save the file as **TransformRepeatingTable.xsl**. You can also download this file from www.bizsupportonline.com. Note: The namespace URI for the **my** namespace prefix will be corrected later through code.

4. In InfoPath, click **Data ➤ Form Data ➤ Resource Files**.

5. On the **Resource Files** dialog box, click **Add**.

6. On the **Add File** dialog box, browse to and select the **TransformRepeatingTable.xsl** file, and then click **OK**.

7. On the **Resource Files** dialog box, click **OK**. With this you have added the XSL file as a resource file to the form template.

8. In SharePoint, create a new custom SharePoint list named **Fruits** that has a column named **Title** and an extra single line of text column named **Color**.

9. Navigate to the **List Settings** page of the SharePoint list and copy the value of the GUID that is listed after the **List** query string parameter in the URL in the browser's address bar. It should look something like the following:

```
%7B381871EA%2D0275%2D4291%2DA4FE%2D12430EED7B63%7D
```

Replace **%7B** by **{**, **%2D** by **-**, and **%7D** by **}**. The converted GUID should then resemble the following:

```
{381871EA-0275-4291-A4FE-12430EED7B63}
```

Copy the GUID to Notepad, since you will need to use it later in the code.

10. In Notepad, create a new file that has the following contents

```
<SubmitToList>
  <listGuid></listGuid>
  <Batch>
    <Method ID="1" Cmd="New">
      <Field Name="Title"></Field>
      <Field Name="Color"></Field>
    </Method>
  </Batch>
</SubmitToList>
```

and save the file as **SubmitToListBatch.xml**. You can also download this file from www.bizsupportonline.com.

11. In InfoPath, select **Data ➤ Get External Data ➤ From Other Sources ➤ From XML File** and follow the instructions to add an XML data connection for the **SubmitToListBatch.xml** file. Name the data connection **SubmitToListBatch**, and leave the **Automatically retrieve data when form is opened** check box selected.

12. Select **Data ➤ Submit Form ➤ To Other Locations ➤ To Web Service**.

13. On the **Data Connection Wizard**, enter the URL of the **Lists** web service, for example

```
http://servername/sitename/_vti_bin/Lists.asmx
```

and click **Next**. Here **servername** is the name of the SharePoint server where a site named **sitename** on which the **Lists** web service is located.

14. On the **Data Connection Wizard**, select the **UpdateListItems** operation from the list of operations, and click **Next**.

15. On the **Data Connection Wizard**, select the **listName** parameter in the **Parameters** list, and then click the button behind the **Field or group** text box.

16. On the **Select a Field or Group** dialog box, select **SubmitToListBatch (Secondary)** from the **Fields** drop-down list box, select **listGuid**, and click **OK**. With this you have set the **listName** parameter of the web service operation to be equal to the value of the **listGuid** field in the **SubmitToListBatch** secondary data source.

17. On the **Data Connection Wizard**, leave **Text and child elements only** selected in the **Include** drop-down list box, leave the **Submit data as a string** check box deselected, select the **updates** parameter in the **Parameters** list, and then click the button behind the **Field or group** text box.

18. On the **Select a Field or Group** dialog box, select **SubmitToListBatch (Secondary)** from the **Fields** drop-down list box, select the **Batch** group node, and click **OK**. With this you have set the **updates** parameter of the web service operation to be equal to the contents of the entire **Batch** group node in the **SubmitToListBatch** secondary data source.

19. On the **Data Connection Wizard**, select **XML subtree, including selected element** from the **Include** drop-down list box, and click **Next**. This setting will submit the entire XML contents of the **Batch** node including its child nodes and values to the web service.

20. On the **Data Connection Wizard**, name the data connection **SubmitToList**, deselect the **Set as the default submit connection** check box, and click **Finish**.

21. Add a **Button** control to the view of the form template and label it **Submit**.

22. Add an event handler for the **Clicked** event of the button as described in recipe *7 Add an event handler for a control event*.

23. In VSTA, add the following **using** statements to the **FormCode.cs** file:

```
using System.Xml.Xsl;
using System.IO;
```

24. Add the following code to the `Clicked()` event handler for the **Submit** button (*code #: 4B34FE5E-BD8C-4382-9CB4-1C6F6FACA14E*):

```
using (Stream stream = Template.OpenFileFromPackage(
  "TransformRepeatingTable.xsl"))
{
  if (stream == null || stream.Length == 0)
    return;

  XmlDocument xslDoc = new XmlDocument();
  xslDoc.Load(stream);
  xslDoc.DocumentElement.Attributes["xmlns:my"].Value =
    NamespaceManager.LookupNamespace("my");

  using (MemoryStream xslms = new MemoryStream())
  {
    xslDoc.Save(xslms);
    xslms.Position = 0;

    XPathDocument xslFile = new XPathDocument(xslms);
    XslCompiledTransform trans = new XslCompiledTransform();
    trans.Load(xslFile);

    using (MemoryStream ms = new MemoryStream())
    {
      trans.Transform(MainDataSource.CreateNavigator(), null, ms);
      ms.Position = 0;

      XPathDocument doc = new XPathDocument(ms);

      XPathNavigator submitToListDS =
        DataSources["SubmitToListBatch"].CreateNavigator();

      submitToListDS.SelectSingleNode(
        "/SubmitToList/listGuid", NamespaceManager).SetValue(
        "{BE8AAC29-F713-43F3-911F-965D614F0AD6}");
```

```
        submitToListDS.SelectSingleNode(
          "/SubmitToList/Batch", NamespaceManager).ReplaceSelf(
          doc.CreateNavigator());

        DataConnections["SubmitToList"].Execute();

        ms.Close();
      }
    xslms.Close();
    }
}
```

where you must replace the GUID for setting the value of the **listGuid** field with the GUID from step 9.

25. Save and build the project.

26. Preview the form.

When the form opens, add a couple of rows to the repeating table, and then click the **Submit** button. Navigate to the SharePoint list and verify that list items were created using the data you entered into the repeating table.

Discussion

In the solution described above you learned how to transform the XML representation of a repeating table into an XML structure that can be used to pass data to the SharePoint **Lists** web service to be able to add data from rows of a repeating table as new items to a SharePoint list. You thereby made use of XSL to perform the transformation of data.

The XSL file that performs the transformation was added as a resource file to the form template, so the code uses the OpenFileFromPackage() method of the FormTemplate object of the form to retrieve the XSL file as a Stream object.

```
using (Stream stream = Template.OpenFileFromPackage(
  "TransformRepeatingTable.xsl"))
{
  ...
}
```

Once read, the Stream object for the XSL file is then used to create an XmlDocument object.

```
XmlDocument xslDoc = new XmlDocument();
xslDoc.Load(stream);
```

The value of the **my** namespace prefix in the XmlDocument object is then set to be equal to the namespace URI of the form.

```
xslDoc.DocumentElement.Attributes["xmlns:my"].Value =
  NamespaceManager.LookupNamespace("my");
```

If you do not want to programmatically set the namespace in the XSL file, you can also retrieve it and set it manually as described in recipe *74 Copy data from a data source to a repeating table*.

And then the XmlDocument object is saved to a new MemoryStream object

```
using (MemoryStream xslms = new MemoryStream())
{
  xslDoc.Save(xslms);
  xslms.Position = 0;
  ...
}
```

that is subsequently used to create an XPathDocument object that is loaded into an XslCompiledTranform object with which you can transform XML data using the XSL style sheet.

```
XPathDocument xslFile = new XPathDocument(xslms);
XslCompiledTransform trans = new XslCompiledTransform();
trans.Load(xslFile);
```

Because the XSL transformation starts at the root node of the InfoPath form, an XPathNavigator object pointing to the Main data source of the form is passed to the Transform() method of the XslCompiledTranform object.

```
trans.Transform(MainDataSource.CreateNavigator(), null, ms);
ms.Position = 0;
```

The output of the transformation is then stored in a MemoryStream object, which is subsequently loaded into an XPathDocument object.

```
XPathDocument doc = new XPathDocument(ms);
```

This XPathDocument object is used to replace the **Batch** element in the **SubmitToListBatch** secondary data source.

```
XPathNavigator submitToListDS =
DataSources["SubmitToListBatch"].CreateNavigator();

submitToListDS.SelectSingleNode(
  "/SubmitToList/listGuid", NamespaceManager).SetValue(
  "{BE8AAC29-F713-43F3-911F-965D614F0AD6}");

submitToListDS.SelectSingleNode(
  "/SubmitToList/Batch", NamespaceManager).ReplaceSelf(
  doc.CreateNavigator());
```

Note that the code shown above also sets the **listGuid** field in the **SubmitToListBatch** secondary data source to be equal to the value of the GUID of the SharePoint list in which the list items should be created.

And finally, the `Execute()` method of the **SubmitToList** web service data connection is called to submit the data to SharePoint to be able to create the SharePoint list items.

```
DataConnections["SubmitToList"].Execute();
```

While the solution described above makes use of an XSL transformation to construct the XML for the **Batch** element that should be passed to the web service operation, you could also programmatically loop through the repeating table (also see recipe *70 Loop through rows of a repeating table*) and construct the XML for the **Batch** element. You should then add code similar to the following code to the `Clicked()` event handler for the **Submit** button (*code # 11102DDE-F8B1-4783-8921-F231B33FE8F7*):

```
XPathNavigator submitToListDS =
  DataSources["SubmitToListBatch"].CreateNavigator();

submitToListDS.SelectSingleNode(
  "/SubmitToList/listGuid", NamespaceManager).SetValue(
  "{BE8AAC29-F713-43F3-911F-965D614F0AD6}");

XPathNavigator batch = submitToListDS.SelectSingleNode(
  "/SubmitToList/Batch", NamespaceManager);

XPathNodeIterator iter = batch.Select("//Method", NamespaceManager);
XPathNavigator firstChild = batch.SelectSingleNode(
  "//Method[1]", NamespaceManager);
XPathNavigator lastChild = batch.SelectSingleNode(
  "//Method[" + iter.Count + "]", NamespaceManager);
firstChild.DeleteRange(lastChild);

XPathNodeIterator rows = MainDataSource.CreateNavigator()
  .Select("/my:myFields/my:group1/my:group2", NamespaceManager);

int count = 1;
while (rows.MoveNext())
{
  System.Text.StringBuilder sb = new System.Text.StringBuilder();
  sb.AppendFormat("<Method ID=\"{0}\" Cmd=\"New\">", count.ToString());
  sb.AppendFormat("<Field Name=\"Title\">{0}</Field>",
    rows.Current.SelectSingleNode("my:fruitName", NamespaceManager).Value);
  sb.AppendFormat("<Field Name=\"Color\">{0}</Field>",
    rows.Current.SelectSingleNode("my:fruitColor", NamespaceManager).Value);
  sb.Append("</Method>");

  batch.AppendChild(sb.ToString());

  count++;
}

DataConnections["SubmitToList"].Execute();
```

Note that the code above first deletes all of the child elements of the **Batch** element before adding a **Method** element for each row of the repeating table to the **Batch** element.

The **Field** names in the **SubmitToListBatch.xml** file must be the exact internal names (used by SharePoint) for the columns of the SharePoint list you want to submit the data to, otherwise the submission will fail. You can easily find out what the exact name of a column is by going to the edit page of that column in SharePoint and then checking the value that is listed after the **Field** query string parameter in the URL in the browser's address bar. For example, the following URL is for the **Change Column** page of the **Color** column of a SharePoint list:

```
http://servername/sitename/_layouts/FldEdit.aspx?List=%7B381871EA%2D0275%2D4291%
2DA4FE%2D12430EED7B63%7D&Field=Color
```

You must use the same name that is listed after the **Field** query string parameter in the URL for the **Name** attribute of the **Field** element under the **Method** element of the **Batch** element in the XML file.

Tip:

> If you have two lists with the same column names you can switch between submitting to those two lists by switching between the GUIDs of those lists in code. For example, populate a drop-down list box from which the user can select a list to submit data from the repeating table to and use the GUIDs of the lists as the value property of the drop-down list box. Then in code, retrieve the value of the field bound to the drop-down list box and use it to set the **listGuid** field in the secondary data source before submitting the data from the repeating table to SharePoint.

Note that you can also use the **Lists** web service to update or delete items from a SharePoint list. For example, you could add a receive data connection to a SharePoint list and then bind the repeating group node under the **dataFields** group node in the secondary data source for this SharePoint list to a repeating table control on the view of the form template. Once bound, you can add an extra column that contains a button to the repeating table, and then add the following code to the `Clicked()` event handler for that button to update an item from the SharePoint list (*code #: CE3EF56F-83B2-4761-9389-CF9370CB5952*):

```
string id = e.Source.SelectSingleNode("d:ID", NamespaceManager).Value;
string title = e.Source.SelectSingleNode("d:Title", NamespaceManager).Value;
string color = e.Source.SelectSingleNode("d:Color", NamespaceManager).Value;

XPathNavigator submitToListDS =
  DataSources["SubmitToListBatch"].CreateNavigator();

string listGuid = "{BE8AAC29-F713-43F3-911F-965D614F0AD6}";

submitToListDS.SelectSingleNode(
  "/SubmitToList/listGuid", NamespaceManager).SetValue(listGuid);
```

```
XPathNavigator batch = submitToListDS.SelectSingleNode(
  "/SubmitToList/Batch", NamespaceManager);
XPathNodeIterator iter = batch.Select("//Method", NamespaceManager);
XPathNavigator firstChild = batch.SelectSingleNode(
  "//Method[1]", NamespaceManager);
XPathNavigator lastChild = batch.SelectSingleNode(
  "//Method[" + iter.Count + "]", NamespaceManager);
firstChild.DeleteRange(lastChild);

System.Text.StringBuilder sb = new System.Text.StringBuilder();
sb.Append("<Method ID=\"1\" Cmd=\"Update\">");
sb.AppendFormat("<Field Name=\"ID\">{0}</Field>", id);
sb.AppendFormat("<Field Name=\"Title\">{0}</Field>", title);
sb.AppendFormat("<Field Name=\"Color\">{0}</Field>", color);
sb.Append("</Method>");

batch.AppendChild(sb.ToString());

DataConnections["SubmitToList"].Execute();
DataSources["MyList"].QueryConnection.Execute();
```

where **MyList** is the SharePoint list in which you want to update an item and {BE8AAC29-F713-43F3-911F-965D614F0AD6} is its GUID.

Or add the following code to the Clicked() event handler for the button to delete an item from the SharePoint list (*code #: 8CF7B6A6-5964-421C-A695-95ED88F9DF2E*):

```
string id = e.Source.SelectSingleNode("d:ID", NamespaceManager).Value;

XPathNavigator submitToListDS =
  DataSources["SubmitToListBatch"].CreateNavigator();

string listGuid = "{BE8AAC29-F713-43F3-911F-965D614F0AD6}";

submitToListDS.SelectSingleNode(
  "/SubmitToList/listGuid", NamespaceManager).SetValue(listGuid);

XPathNavigator batch = submitToListDS.SelectSingleNode(
  "/SubmitToList/Batch", NamespaceManager);
XPathNodeIterator iter = batch.Select("//Method", NamespaceManager);
XPathNavigator firstChild = batch.SelectSingleNode(
  "//Method[1]", NamespaceManager);
XPathNavigator lastChild = batch.SelectSingleNode(
  "//Method[" + iter.Count + "]", NamespaceManager);
firstChild.DeleteRange(lastChild);

System.Text.StringBuilder sb = new System.Text.StringBuilder();
sb.Append("<Method ID=\"1\" Cmd=\"Delete\">");
sb.AppendFormat("<Field Name=\"ID\">{0}</Field>", id);
sb.Append("</Method>");

batch.AppendChild(sb.ToString());

DataConnections["SubmitToList"].Execute();
DataSources["MyList"].QueryConnection.Execute();
```

where **MyList** is the SharePoint list from which you want to delete an item and {BE8AAC29-F713-43F3-911F-965D614F0AD6} is its GUID. The main changes in the code compared to the solution described in this recipe is that you must use **Update** or **Delete** as the value of the **Cmd** attribute and that you must specify the **ID** of the SharePoint list item to update or delete as a **Field**.

Title	Color		
Apple	Red	Update	Delete
Kiwi	Brown	Update	Delete
Banana	Yellow	Update	Delete
Orange	Orange	Update	Delete
Guava	Green	Update	Delete
Passion Fruit	Red	Update	Delete

Figure 71. Repeating table with Update and Delete buttons.

If you want to perform bulk update and delete operations instead of a single operation, you would have to copy the rows from the secondary data source for the SharePoint list to a repeating structure either in the Main data source or another secondary data source that contains an extra field in which you can specify the operation to perform (**Update** or **Delete**) for each list item, and then construct the XML for the **Batch** node in the **SubmitToListBatch** secondary data source to contain multiple **Method** elements with each performing either an update or a delete operation for a particular item in the list. You can copy rows by either performing an XSL transformation as described in recipe *74 Copy data from a data source to a repeating table* or by looping through rows of the secondary data source and creating new rows in the other repeating structure (see recipe *70 Loop through rows of a repeating table* and recipe *71 Add a row to a repeating table*).

96 Submit a form to libraries on two different sites in the same site collection

Problem

You have an InfoPath form, which you want to submit to a form library on Site A1, Site A2, or both. Users should be able to create a form in the form library on Site A1 and submit the form to form libraries on both Site A1 and Site A2. Likewise, users should also be able to create a form in the form library on Site A2 and submit the form to form libraries on both Site A1 and Site A2. Both Site A1 and Site A2 are subsites of Site A.

Solution

You can use a `FileSubmitConnection` object to submit an InfoPath form to a form library on a chosen SharePoint site. In this scenario, there is a form library named **FormsLib** on both Site A1 and Site A2, and users can submit an InfoPath form to either form library by clicking on buttons. Note: If users are submitting a form to a form library on a different site that is located in the same site collection, they must have the required permissions for submitting forms to the form library on that site.

To submit a form to form libraries on two different SharePoint sites in the same site collection:

1. In InfoPath, create a new SharePoint form library form template or use an existing one.

2. Add a **Text Box** control to the view of the form template and name it **fileName**. Users can use this text box to enter a file name for the form.

3. Select **Data ➤ Submit Form ➤ To SharePoint Library** and add a SharePoint library submit data connection that has the following value for the **Document Library** field:

    ```
    http://servername/siteA1
    ```

    This is the URL of **Site A1** in the SharePoint site collection. Set the **File name** field to the following formula:

    ```
    fileName
    ```

    where **fileName** is the field that is bound to the text box control. Select the **Allow** . **overwrite if file exists** check box, deselect the **Set as the default submit connection** check box, and name the data connection **SharePoint Library Submit**.

4. Add a **Button** control to the view of the form template and label it **Submit to Site A1**.

5. Add an event handler for the **Clicked** event of the **Submit to Site A1** button as described in recipe *7 Add an event handler for a control event*.

6. In VSTA, add the following code to the `Clicked()` event handler for the button (*code #: 6C98E962-C362-488C-A643-B3447EA95CDA*):

    ```
    string fileName = MainDataSource.CreateNavigator()
      .SelectSingleNode("/my:myFields/my:fileName", NamespaceManager).Value;

    FileSubmitConnection submitConn =
      (FileSubmitConnection)(DataConnections["SharePoint Library Submit"]);

    if (String.IsNullOrEmpty(fileName))
      submitConn.Filename.SetStringValue("Form.xml");

    submitConn.FolderUrl = ServerInfo.SharePointSiteCollectionUrl.AbsoluteUri
      + @"siteA1/FormsLib";

    submitConn.Execute();
    ```

7. In InfoPath, add a second **Button** control to the view of the form template and label it **Submit to Site A2**.

8. Add an event handler for the **Clicked** event of the **Submit to Site A2** button as described in recipe *7 Add an event handler for a control event*.

9. In VSTA, add the following code to the `Clicked()` event handler for the button (*code #: 6C98E962-C362-488C-A643-B3447EA95CDA*):

```
string fileName = MainDataSource.CreateNavigator()
  .SelectSingleNode("/my:myFields/my:fileName", NamespaceManager).Value;

FileSubmitConnection submitConn =
  (FileSubmitConnection)(DataConnections["SharePoint Library Submit"]);

if (String.IsNullOrEmpty(fileName))
  submitConn.Filename.SetStringValue("Form.xml");

submitConn.FolderUrl = ServerInfo.SharePointSiteCollectionUrl.AbsoluteUri
  + @"siteA2/FormsLib";

submitConn.Execute();
```

10. Save and build the project.

11. In InfoPath, publish the form template as a site content type to **Site A**, which is the parent site of both **Site A1** and **Site A2**.

12. In SharePoint, create a form library named **FormsLib** on both **Site A1** and **Site A2**, and then associate the content type you created on **Site A** with both form libraries.

In SharePoint, navigate to the **FormsLib** form library on **Site A1** and add a new form. When the form opens, enter a name in the **fileName** text box, and then click the **Submit to Site A2** button. Navigate to the **FormsLib** form library on **Site A2** and verify that the form was saved in the form library. Add a new form to the **FormsLib** form library on **Site A2**. When the form opens, enter a name in the **fileName** text box, and then click the **Submit to Site A1** button. Navigate to the **FormsLib** form library on **Site A1** and verify that the form was saved in the form library.

Discussion

The `FileSubmitConnection` class represents a data connection you create in InfoPath Designer 2010 using the **Data Connection Wizard** to specify information for submitting an InfoPath form to a form library on a SharePoint server. The `FileSubmitConnection` class is available for and works in both InfoPath Filler forms and browser forms. You can access the `FileSubmitConnection` object through the `DataConnections` property of the `XmlForm` object as follows:

```
FileSubmitConnection submitConn =
  (FileSubmitConnection)(DataConnections["SharePoint Library Submit"]);
```

where **SharePoint Library Submit** is the name of the data connection you created through the **Data Connection Wizard**.

The `FileSubmitConnection` object has a property named `Filename`, which returns an `XPathTypedValue` object you can use to either get or set the name that should be used to save the form to the form library. Ordinarily, the information contained in the `Filename` property comes from the information you enter in the **File name** field on the **Data Connection Wizard**, which may be a formula that generates a file name for the form or which references a field on the form as shown in the solution above.

You can use the following code to retrieve the file name that is stored in the `Filename` property:

```
submitConn.Filename.ToString();
```

Note that the `Filename` property automatically appends the **.xml** file extension to a string if it is not already present. And you can use the following code to set the file name to be equal to a specific piece of text:

```
submitConn.Filename.SetStringValue("Form.xml");
```

The latter is used in the solution above to set the value of the `Filename` property if the user did not enter a value in the **fileName** text box. If you wanted to use a formula to generate the file name for the form instead of specifying a static piece of text, you could use the following code to specify the formula using an XPath expression:

```
submitConn.Filename.XPath = "concat('Form_', xdDate:Now())";
```

where the generated file name would consist of the text **Form_** plus the current date and time.

The `FileSubmitConnection` object also has a property named `FolderUrl`, which gets or sets the URL of the folder to which the form should be submitted. The value of the `FolderUrl` property can be either an URL for a root or a sub folder of a form library. In the solution above, the form was submitted to the root folder of the form libraries, but if you wanted to submit the form to a sub folder named **data** in the **FormsLib** form library on **Site A1**, you would have to change the code to be the following:

```
submitConn.FolderUrl = ServerInfo.SharePointSiteCollectionUrl.AbsoluteUri
  + @"siteA1/FormsLib/data";
```

instead of

```
submitConn.FolderUrl = ServerInfo.SharePointSiteCollectionUrl.AbsoluteUri
  + @"siteA1/FormsLib";
```

which submits the form to the root folder of the **FormsLib** form library.

Note that the code above uses the `SharePointSiteCollectionUrl` property of the `ServerInfo` object to return a `System.Uri` object that provides the URL of the

SharePoint site collection where the form is located (also see the discussion section of recipe *94 Select and add files from a document library as attachments to a form*).

And finally, the code calls the `Execute()` method of the `FileSubmitConnection` object to submit the InfoPath form to the form library.

```
submitConn.Execute();
```

97 Use an InfoPath form to add a recurring all day event to a SharePoint calendar

Problem

You want to create an InfoPath form with which you can submit a recurring event to a SharePoint calendar.

Solution

You can use the **Lists** web service to submit a recurring event to a SharePoint calendar.

To add a recurring all day event to a SharePoint calendar using an InfoPath form:

1. In SharePoint, lookup the GUID of the SharePoint calendar you want to submit a recurring event to by going to the **List Settings** page of the calendar and copying the value that is listed after the **List** query string parameter in the URL in the browser's address bar. It should look something like the following:

    ```
    %7B98B1C7C0%2D903E%2D4066%2DA114%2D7D9F3B6923E3%7D
    ```

    Replace **%7B** by **{**, **%2D** by **-**, and **%7D** by **}**. The converted GUID should then resemble the following:

    ```
    {98B1C7C0-903E-4066-A114-7D9F3B6923E3}
    ```

    Copy the GUID to Notepad, since you will be using it later in the code.

2. In InfoPath, create a new form template or use an existing one.

3. Add a **Text Box** control to the view of the form template, name it **title**, and select its **Cannot Be Blank** property to make it a required field.

4. Add two **Date and Time Picker** controls to the view of the form template and name them **startDateTime** and **endDateTime**, respectively. Select the **Cannot Be Blank** property for both date and time picker controls to make them mandatory.

5. Add two **Text Box** controls with the data type **Whole Number (integer)** and the names **timesToRepeat** and **frequencyAmount** to the view of the form template. These text boxes are going to be used to determine whether the event is recurring. In

371

this scenario, the user is going to be able to enter a daily recurrence. The value entered in the **timesToRepeat** field indicates how many times the event should occur within the time period specified, and the value entered in the **frequencyAmount** field indicates the frequency. For example, a **frequencyAmount** of **2** and a **timesToRepeat** of **5** would mean that the event should take place every other day for a total of 5 sessions, and fall within the period specified by **startDateTime** and **endDateTime**.

6. Add a **Check Box** control to the view of the form template and name it **isAllDayEvent**.

7. In Notepad, create a new file that has the following contents

```
<SubmitToCalendar>
  <listGuid></listGuid>
  <Batch>
    <Method ID="1" Cmd="New">
      <Field Name="Title"></Field>
      <Field Name="EventDate"></Field>
      <Field Name="EndDate"></Field>
      <Field Name="fAllDayEvent">0</Field>
    </Method>
  </Batch>
</SubmitToCalendar>
```

and save the file as **Batch.xml**. You can also download this file from www.bizsupportonline.com.

8. Select **Data ➤ Get External Data ➤ From Other Sources ➤ From XML File** and follow the instructions to add an XML data connection for the **Batch.xml** file. Name the data connection **Batch** and leave the **Automatically retrieve data when form is opened** check box selected when you create the data connection.

9. Select **Data ➤ Submit Form ➤ To Other Locations ➤ To Web Service**.

10. On the **Data Connection Wizard**, enter the URL of the **Lists** web service, for example

```
http://servername/sitename/_vti_bin/Lists.asmx
```

and click **Next**. Here **servername** is the name of the SharePoint server where a site named **sitename** on which the **Lists** web service is located.

11. Select the **UpdateListItems** operation from the list of operations, and click **Next**.

12. Select the **listName** parameter in the **Parameters** list and click the button behind the **Field or group** text box.

13. On the **Select a Field or Group** dialog box, select **Batch (Secondary)** from the **Fields** drop-down list box, select **listGuid**, and click **OK**. With this you have set the **listName** parameter of the web service to be equal to the value of the **listGuid** field in the **Batch** secondary data source.

14. On the **Data Connection Wizard**, leave **Text and child elements only** selected in the **Include** drop-down list box, leave the **Submit data as a string** check box deselected, select **updates** in the **Parameters** list, and click the button behind the **Field or group** text box.

15. On the **Select a Field or Group** dialog box, select **Batch (Secondary)** from the **Fields** drop-down list box, select the **Batch** group node, and click **OK**. With this you have set the **updates** parameter of the web service to be equal to the contents of the entire **Batch** group node in the **Batch** secondary data source.

16. On the **Data Connection Wizard**, select **XML subtree, including selected element** from the **Include** drop-down list box, and click **Next**. This setting will submit the entire XML contents of the **Batch** node including its child nodes and values to the web service.

17. On the **Data Connection Wizard**, name the data connection **SubmitEventToCalendar**, ensure the **Set as the default submit connection** check box is selected, and click **Finish**.

18. Click **Data ➤ Submit Form ➤ Submit Options**.

19. On the **Submit Options** dialog box, the **Allow users to submit this form** check box should already be selected, select the **Perform custom action using Code** option, click **Edit Code**, and then click **OK**.

20. In VSTA, add the following code to the `FormEvents_Submit()` event handler (*code #: 16784B00-51BD-4F70-B4E2-FE31992569B0*):

```
XPathNavigator mainDS = MainDataSource.CreateNavigator();

string title = mainDS.SelectSingleNode(
  "/my:myFields/my:title", NamespaceManager).Value;

string startDate = mainDS.SelectSingleNode(
  "/my:myFields/my:startDateTime", NamespaceManager).Value;

string endDate = mainDS.SelectSingleNode(
  "/my:myFields/my:endDateTime", NamespaceManager).Value;

string isAllDayEvent = mainDS.SelectSingleNode(
  "/my:myFields/my:isAllDayEvent", NamespaceManager).Value;

string timesToRepeat = mainDS.SelectSingleNode(
  "/my:myFields/my:timesToRepeat", NamespaceManager).Value;

string frequencyAmount = mainDS.SelectSingleNode(
  "/my:myFields/my:frequencyAmount", NamespaceManager).Value;

string recurrence =
  String.Format(
  @"<recurrence><rule><firstDayOfWeek>su</firstDayOfWeek><repeat><daily
dayFrequency='{0}'/></repeat><repeatInstances>{1}</repeatInstances></rule><
/recurrence>", frequencyAmount, timesToRepeat);

XPathNavigator xmlDS = DataSources["Batch"].CreateNavigator();
```

```
xmlDS.SelectSingleNode(
  "/SubmitToCalendar/listGuid", NamespaceManager).SetValue(
    "{98B1C7C0-903E-4066-A114-7D9F3B6923E3}");

xmlDS.SelectSingleNode(
  "//Field[@Name = 'Title']", NamespaceManager).SetValue(title);

xmlDS.SelectSingleNode(
  "//Field[@Name = 'EventDate']", NamespaceManager).SetValue(startDate +
"Z");

xmlDS.SelectSingleNode(
  "//Field[@Name = 'EndDate']", NamespaceManager).SetValue(endDate + "Z");

if (isAllDayEvent.Equals("true"))
  xmlDS.SelectSingleNode(
    "//Field[@Name = 'fAllDayEvent']", NamespaceManager).SetValue("-1");

if (!(String.IsNullOrEmpty(timesToRepeat) &&
  String.IsNullOrEmpty(frequencyAmount)))
{
  XPathNavigator method = xmlDS.SelectSingleNode(
    "/SubmitToCalendar/Batch/Method", NamespaceManager);

  method.AppendChild(@"<Field Name='EventType'>1</Field>");

  method.AppendChild(@"<Field Name='RecurrenceData'></Field>");

  method.AppendChild(@"<Field Name='UID'>" +
    System.Guid.NewGuid().ToString() + "</Field>");

  method.AppendChild(@"<Field Name='fRecurrence'>-1</Field>");

  xmlDS.SelectSingleNode(
    "//Field[@Name = 'RecurrenceData']",
    NamespaceManager).SetValue(recurrence);
}

DataConnections["SubmitEventToCalendar"].Execute();

e.CancelableArgs.Cancel = false;
```

where you should replace the GUID for the list with the GUID you copied earlier from SharePoint.

21. Save and build the project.

22. Preview the form.

When the form opens, enter information for a new event and click the **Submit** button on the toolbar. In SharePoint, navigate to the SharePoint calendar and verify that the event has been added to the calendar.

Discussion

In the solution described above, you added a daily recurring event to a SharePoint calendar. The recurrence is defined by the following piece of code:

```
string recurrence =
  String.Format(
  @"<recurrence><rule><firstDayOfWeek>su</firstDayOfWeek><repeat><daily
dayFrequency='{0}'/></repeat><repeatInstances>{1}</repeatInstances></rule></recu
rrence>", frequencyAmount, timesToRepeat);
```

You could also change the code to support weekly, monthly, or yearly recurrences. Refer to the article entitled *How to: Add a Recurring Event to Lists on Multiple Sites* on the MSDN web site to get more information about recurring events and the kinds of recurrences you can define.

To be able to actually add a recurring event to the SharePoint calendar, the code in the solution above changes the XML of the **Batch** secondary data source to include four extra **Field** elements with the following **Name** attributes:

1. EventType

2. RecurrenceData

3. UID

4. fRecurrence

These four **Field** elements are added to the XML of the **Batch** secondary data source using the following code:

```
XPathNavigator method = xmlDS.SelectSingleNode(
  "/SubmitToCalendar/Batch/Method", NamespaceManager);

method.AppendChild(@"<Field Name='EventType'>1</Field>");

method.AppendChild(@"<Field Name='RecurrenceData'></Field>");

method.AppendChild(@"<Field Name='UID'>" +
  System.Guid.NewGuid().ToString() + "</Field>");

method.AppendChild(@"<Field Name='fRecurrence'>-1</Field>");

xmlDS.SelectSingleNode(
  "//Field[@Name = 'RecurrenceData']", NamespaceManager).SetValue(recurrence);
```

EventType and **fRecurrence** have static values of **1** and **-1**, respectively, while the value of **UID** is set to be equal to the value of a newly generated GUID using the following code:

```
System.Guid.NewGuid().ToString()
```

The value of **RecurrenceData** is set to be equal to the XML fragment that was previously constructed from the data entered by the user in the **timesToRepeat** and **frequencyAmount** fields on the InfoPath form. The values of the **timesToRepeat** and **frequencyAmount** fields also determine whether a recurring or a normal event should be added to the SharePoint calendar. If both fields are empty, the code assumes that a normal event should be added, so the **Field** elements to make the event recurring should then also be absent from the XML of the **Batch** secondary data source.

```
if (!(String.IsNullOrEmpty(timesToRepeat) &&
  String.IsNullOrEmpty(frequencyAmount)))
{
  ...
}
```

You could change this logic if you wanted to and add for example a check box to the view of the form template to determine whether a recurring event should be added to the SharePoint calendar or not.

The "all day event" part of the solution is implemented through a **Field** element that has a **Name** attribute of **fAllDayEvent** in the **Batch** secondary data source. First the value of the check box on the form is retrieved

```
string isAllDayEvent = mainDS.SelectSingleNode(
  "/my:myFields/my:isAllDayEvent", NamespaceManager).Value;
```

and then it is used later in the code to determine whether to set the value of the **fAllDayEvent** field equal to **-1**, as an indication that the event takes place the entire day and that any times entered should be ignored.

```
if (isAllDayEvent.Equals("true"))
  xmlDS.SelectSingleNode(
    "//Field[@Name = 'fAllDayEvent']", NamespaceManager).SetValue("-1");
```

And just like all other data connections, the `Execute()` method of the `DataConnection` object for the web service is called to perform the actual submit to the SharePoint calendar and create the event.

```
DataConnections["SubmitEventToCalendar"].Execute();
```

After submitting the data, the `Cancel` property of the `CancelableArgs` property of the `SubmitEventArgs` object is set to `false` to indicate that the submit action was successful.

```
e.CancelableArgs.Cancel = false;
```

98   Use an InfoPath form to upload a file to a SharePoint document library

Upload a document stored in a file attachment to SharePoint

Problem

You have a file attachment control on an InfoPath form and want users to be able to upload the file that is stored in the file attachment control to a SharePoint document library.

Solution

You can use the **Copy** web service to upload a file stored in a file attachment control to a SharePoint document library.

To upload a document stored in a file attachment control to a SharePoint document library:

1.   In SharePoint, enter the URL of the **CopyIntoItems** operation of the **Copy** web service in the browser's address bar, for example:

    ```
    http://servername/sitename/_vti_bin/Copy.asmx?op=CopyIntoItems
    ```

2.   Copy the XML fragment that is located in the **soap:Body** element of the SOAP request. For example:

    ```
    <CopyIntoItems xmlns="http://schemas.microsoft.com/sharepoint/soap/">
      <SourceUrl>string</SourceUrl>
      <DestinationUrls>
        <string>string</string>
        <string>string</string>
      </DestinationUrls>
      <Fields>
        <FieldInformation Type="Invalid or Integer or Text or Note or DateTime
    or Counter or Choice or Lookup or Boolean or Number or Currency or URL or
    Computed or Threading or Guid or MultiChoice or GridChoice or Calculated or
    File or Attachments or User or Recurrence or CrossProjectLink or ModStat or
    AllDayEvent or Error" DisplayName="string" InternalName="string" Id="guid"
    Value="string" />
        <FieldInformation Type="Invalid or Integer or Text or Note or DateTime
    or Counter or Choice or Lookup or Boolean or Number or Currency or URL or
    Computed or Threading or Guid or MultiChoice or GridChoice or Calculated or
    File or Attachments or User or Recurrence or CrossProjectLink or ModStat or
    AllDayEvent or Error" DisplayName="string" InternalName="string" Id="guid"
    Value="string" />
      </Fields>
      <Stream>base64Binary</Stream>
    </CopyIntoItems>
    ```

    Open Notepad and paste the XML fragment you just copied, remove all line-breaks and whitespaces between the elements, and then save the file as

CopyIntoItemsRequest.xml. You can also download this file from www.bizsupportonline.com.

3. Copy the XML fragment that is located in the **soap:Body** element of the SOAP response. For example:

```
<CopyIntoItemsResponse
xmlns="http://schemas.microsoft.com/sharepoint/soap/">
  <CopyIntoItemsResult>unsignedInt</CopyIntoItemsResult>
  <Results>
    <CopyResult ErrorCode="Success or DestinationInvalid or DestinationMWS
or SourceInvalid or DestinationCheckedOut or InvalidUrl or Unknown"
ErrorMessage="string" DestinationUrl="string" />
    <CopyResult ErrorCode="Success or DestinationInvalid or DestinationMWS
or SourceInvalid or DestinationCheckedOut or InvalidUrl or Unknown"
ErrorMessage="string" DestinationUrl="string" />
  </Results>
</CopyIntoItemsResponse>
```

Open Notepad and paste the XML fragment you just copied, remove all line-breaks and whitespaces between the elements, and then save the file as **CopyIntoItemsResponse.xml**. You can also download this file from www.bizsupportonline.com.

4. In InfoPath, create a new form template or use an existing one.

5. Select **Data ➤ Get External Data ➤ From Other Sources ➤ From XML File** and follow the instructions to add an XML data connection for the **CopyIntoItemsRequest.xml** file. Leave the **Automatically retrieve data when form is opened** check box selected and name the data connection **CopyIntoItemsRequest**.

6. Select **Data ➤ Get External Data ➤ From Other Sources ➤ From XML File** and follow the instructions to add an XML data connection for the **CopyIntoItemsResponse.xml** file. Leave the **Automatically retrieve data when form is opened** check box selected and name the data connection **CopyIntoItemsResponse**.

7. Add a **Drop-Down List Box** control to the view of the form template, name it **library**, and select its **Cannot be blank** property.

8. Open the **Drop-Down List Box Properties** dialog box, leave the **Enter choices manually** option selected, and then click **Add** to manually enter the names of one or more document libraries which are located on the same SharePoint site to which you will be publishing the form template and to which users are allowed to upload files. Click **OK** when you are done.

9. Add a **File Attachment** control to the view of the form template and name it **document**.

10. Select **Data ➤ Submit Form ➤ To Other Locations ➤ To Web Service**.

11. On the **Data Connection Wizard**, enter the URL of the **Copy** web service, for example

    ```
    http://servername/sitename/_vti_bin/Copy.asmx
    ```

    and click **Next**. Here **servername** is the name of the SharePoint server where a site named **sitename** on which the **Copy** web service is located.

12. On the **Data Connection Wizard**, select the **CopyIntoItems** operation from the list of operations, and click **Next**.

13. On the **Data Connection Wizard**, select **SourceUrl** in the **Parameters** list and click the button behind the **Field or group** text box.

14. On the **Select a Field or Group** dialog box, select **CopyIntoItemsRequest (Secondary)** from the **Fields** drop-down list box, select the **SourceUrl** field, and click **OK**. With this you have set the **SourceUrl** parameter of the web service to be equal to the value of the **SourceUrl** field in the **CopyIntoItemsRequest** secondary data source.

15. On the **Data Connection Wizard**, leave **Text and child elements only** selected in the **Include** drop-down list box, leave the **Submit data as a string** check box deselected, select **DestinationUrls** in the **Parameters** list, and click the button behind the **Field or group** text box.

16. On the **Select a Field or Group** dialog box, select **CopyIntoItemsRequest (Secondary)** from the **Fields** drop-down list box, select the **DestinationUrls** group node, and click **OK**. With this you have set the **DestinationUrls** parameter of the web service to be equal to the value of the **DestinationUrls** group node in the **CopyIntoItemsRequest** secondary data source.

17. On the **Data Connection Wizard**, leave **Text and child elements only** selected in the **Include** drop-down list box, leave the **Submit data as a string** check box deselected, select **Fields** in the **Parameters** list, and click the button behind the **Field or group** text box.

18. On the **Select a Field or Group** dialog box, select **CopyIntoItemsRequest (Secondary)** from the **Fields** drop-down list box, select the **Fields** group node, and click **OK**. With this you have set the **Fields** parameter of the web service to be equal to the value of the **Fields** group node in the **CopyIntoItemsRequest** secondary data source.

19. On the **Data Connection Wizard**, leave **Text and child elements only** selected in the **Include** drop-down list box, leave the **Submit data as a string** check box deselected, select **Stream** in the **Parameters** list, and click the button behind the **Field or group** text box.

20. On the **Select a Field or Group** dialog box, select **CopyIntoItemsRequest (Secondary)** from the **Fields** drop-down list box, select the **Stream** field, and click

OK. With this you have set the **Stream** parameter of the web service to be equal to the value of the **Stream** field in the **CopyIntoItemsRequest** secondary data source.

21. On the **Data Connection Wizard**, leave **Text and child elements only** selected in the **Include** drop-down list box, leave the **Submit data as a string** check box deselected, and click **Next**.

22. On the **Data Connection Wizard**, name the data connection **UploadFile**, deselect the **Set as the default submit connection** check box, and click **Finish**.

23. Add a **Button** control to the view of the form template and label it **Add File**.

24. Add a **Text Box** control to the view of the form template and name it **result**.

25. Add an event handler for the **Clicked** event of the **Add File** button as described in recipe *7 Add an event handler for a control event*.

26. In VSTA, add a new class with the name **InfoPathAttachmentDecoder** to the project and add the code from *InfoPathAttachmentDecoder.cs* listed in the Appendix to the new class file. You can also download the **InfoPathAttachmentDecoder.cs** file from www.bizsupportonline.com and then add it to your VSTA project.

27. Add the following code to the `Clicked()` event handler for the **Add File** button (*code #: 8BFFF78A-ACDA-4B58-B89C-E4D6F93802D2*):

```
string siteUrl = "http://servername/sitename/";

XPathNavigator mainDS = MainDataSource.CreateNavigator();
XPathNavigator secDS =
  DataSources["CopyIntoItemsRequest"].CreateNavigator();

XPathNavigator file = mainDS.SelectSingleNode(
  "/my:myFields/my:document", NamespaceManager);

if (file == null || String.IsNullOrEmpty(file.Value))
  return;

XPathNavigator sourceUrl = secDS.SelectSingleNode(
  "/ns1:CopyIntoItems/ns1:SourceUrl", NamespaceManager);
XPathNavigator destUrl = secDS.SelectSingleNode(
  "/ns1:CopyIntoItems/ns1:DestinationUrls/ns1:string[1]",
NamespaceManager);

XPathNavigator secondDestUrl = secDS.SelectSingleNode(
  "/ns1:CopyIntoItems/ns1:DestinationUrls/ns1:string[2]",
  NamespaceManager);
if (secondDestUrl != null)
  secondDestUrl.DeleteSelf();

XPathNodeIterator fields = secDS.Select(
  "/ns1:CopyIntoItems/ns1:Fields/ns1:FieldInformation", NamespaceManager);
if (fields != null && fields.Count > 0)
{
  int count = fields.Count;
  XPathNavigator firstChild = secDS.SelectSingleNode(
    "/ns1:CopyIntoItems/ns1:Fields/ns1:FieldInformation[1]",
    NamespaceManager);
```

```
   XPathNavigator lastChild = secDS.SelectSingleNode(
     "/ns1:CopyIntoItems/ns1:Fields/ns1:FieldInformation[" + count + "]",
     NamespaceManager);
   firstChild.DeleteRange(lastChild);
}

XPathNavigator stream = secDS.SelectSingleNode(
  "/ns1:CopyIntoItems/ns1:Stream", NamespaceManager);

string libName = mainDS.SelectSingleNode(
  "/my:myFields/my:library", NamespaceManager).Value;

if (!String.IsNullOrEmpty(libName))
{
  BizSupportOnline.InfoPathAttachmentDecoder dec =
    new BizSupportOnline.InfoPathAttachmentDecoder(file.Value);
  string filename = dec.Filename;
  byte[] bytes = dec.DecodedAttachment;

  destUrl.SetValue(siteUrl + libName + "/" + filename);
  sourceUrl.SetValue(destUrl.Value);
  stream.SetValue(Convert.ToBase64String(bytes));

  XPathNavigator response =
    DataSources["CopyIntoItemsResponse"].CreateNavigator()
    .SelectSingleNode("/ns1:CopyIntoItemsResponse", NamespaceManager);

  ((WebServiceConnection)DataConnections["UploadFile"])
    .Execute(secDS, response, null);

  string result = response.SelectSingleNode(
    "//ns1:CopyResult[1]/@ErrorCode", NamespaceManager).Value;

  mainDS.SelectSingleNode(
    "/my:myFields/my:result", NamespaceManager).SetValue(result);
}
```

where you must change the site URL (`http://servername/sitename/`) to point to a valid URL where the document libraries you specified in the drop-down list box are located.

28. Save and build the project.

29. Preview the form.

When the form opens, select a document library from the drop-down list box, add a file to the file attachment control, and click the **Add File** button. The text "Success" should appear in the **result** text box if the file was successfully uploaded. In SharePoint, navigate to the document library to which you uploaded the document and verify that the file is present in the document library.

Discussion

In the solution described above you learned how to use the **Copy** web service and a `WebServiceConnection` object to call the **CopyIntoItems** operation and return its results to an InfoPath form.

The code first specifies a static URL for the site where the document libraries that are listed in the drop-down list box are located.

```
string siteUrl = "http://servername/sitename/";
```

Note that if you will be publishing the form template to SharePoint, you could use the `AbsoluteUri` property of the `SharePointSiteUrl` property of the `ServerInfo` object to set the site URL.

```
string siteUrl = ServerInfo.SharePointSiteUrl.AbsoluteUri;
```

The code then retrieves `XPathNavigator` objects pointing to the Main data source and to the **CopyIntoItemsRequest** secondary data source.

```
XPathNavigator mainDS = MainDataSource.CreateNavigator();
XPathNavigator secDS =
  DataSources["CopyIntoItemsRequest"].CreateNavigator();
```

The code also retrieves an `XPathNavigator` object pointing to the file attachment control.

```
XPathNavigator file = mainDS.SelectSingleNode(
  "/my:myFields/my:document", NamespaceManager);
```

If no document was attached to the file attachment control, the code exits the event handler.

```
if (file == null || String.IsNullOrEmpty(file.Value))
  return;
```

The contents of the secondary data source that is used as the input (request) for the web service operation, is then cleared before it is repopulated with the appropriate data to submit the document to the document library.

```
XPathNavigator sourceUrl = secDS.SelectSingleNode(
  "/ns1:CopyIntoItems/ns1:SourceUrl", NamespaceManager);
XPathNavigator destUrl = secDS.SelectSingleNode(
  "/ns1:CopyIntoItems/ns1:DestinationUrls/ns1:string[1]", NamespaceManager);

XPathNavigator secondDestUrl = secDS.SelectSingleNode(
  "/ns1:CopyIntoItems/ns1:DestinationUrls/ns1:string[2]",
  NamespaceManager);
if (secondDestUrl != null)
  secondDestUrl.DeleteSelf();

XPathNodeIterator fields = secDS.Select(
  "/ns1:CopyIntoItems/ns1:Fields/ns1:FieldInformation", NamespaceManager);
if (fields != null && fields.Count > 0)
{
  int count = fields.Count;
```

```
XPathNavigator firstChild = secDS.SelectSingleNode(
  "/ns1:CopyIntoItems/ns1:Fields/ns1:FieldInformation[1]",
  NamespaceManager);
XPathNavigator lastChild = secDS.SelectSingleNode(
  "/ns1:CopyIntoItems/ns1:Fields/ns1:FieldInformation[" + count + "]",
  NamespaceManager);
firstChild.DeleteRange(lastChild);
}
```

Before repopulating the data source, the code constructs the full URL that the uploaded document should have in SharePoint by using the name of the document library that was selected in the drop-down list box.

```
XPathNavigator stream = secDS.SelectSingleNode(
  "/ns1:CopyIntoItems/ns1:Stream", NamespaceManager);

string libName = mainDS.SelectSingleNode(
  "/my:myFields/my:library", NamespaceManager).Value;

if (!String.IsNullOrEmpty(libName))
{
  BizSupportOnline.InfoPathAttachmentDecoder dec =
    new BizSupportOnline.InfoPathAttachmentDecoder(file.Value);
  string filename = dec.Filename;
  byte[] bytes = dec.DecodedAttachment;

  destUrl.SetValue(siteUrl + libName + "/" + filename);

  ...
}
```

The rest of the values of the fields in the secondary data source that should be submitted to the web service are then set.

```
sourceUrl.SetValue(destUrl.Value);
stream.SetValue(Convert.ToBase64String(bytes));
```

An `XPathNavigator` object pointing to the XML fragment in which the response from the web service can be stored is then retrieved

```
XPathNavigator response =
  DataSources["CopyIntoItemsResponse"].CreateNavigator()
  .SelectSingleNode("/ns1:CopyIntoItemsResponse", NamespaceManager);
```

before the `Execute()` method of the `WebServiceConnection` object is called.

```
((WebServiceConnection)DataConnections["UploadFile"])
  .Execute(secDS, response, null);
```

The `Execute()` method takes `XPathNavigator` objects pointing to the request and response XML fragments that should be used by the web service. The last argument of the `Execute()` method is set to be equal to `null` as an indication that SOAP fault data should not be returned.

And finally, the error code in the response from the web service is retrieved and written to the **result** field on the form.

```
string result = response.SelectSingleNode(
  "//ns1:CopyResult[1]/@ErrorCode", NamespaceManager).Value;

mainDS.SelectSingleNode(
  "/my:myFields/my:result", NamespaceManager).SetValue(result);
```

Note that the base64-encoded string of a file stored in a file attachment control not only contains the actual data that makes up the file, but also header information such as the name of the file. Because the **Stream** parameter of the **CopyIntoItems** operation of the **Copy** web service expects to receive only the actual data of the file encoded as a base64-encoded string, you must first decode the file stored in the file attachment control to extract its file name and the `byte` array for its actual data

```
BizSupportOnline.InfoPathAttachmentDecoder dec =
  new BizSupportOnline.InfoPathAttachmentDecoder(file.Value);
string filename = dec.Filename;
byte[] bytes = dec.DecodedAttachment;
```

and then use the `ToBase64String()` method of the `Convert` class to convert the `byte` array for the actual data into a base64-encoded string, so that you can set the value of the **Stream** parameter of the web service.

```
stream.SetValue(Convert.ToBase64String(bytes));
```

However, had you used a picture control containing an embedded image instead of a file attachment control, you could have passed the value of the field as is to the web service operation, since the base64-encoded string representation of an image does not contain header information. Therefore, you can also use the **Copy** web service to upload images to document or picture libraries without having to convert them before you submit them. For example, if you have a picture control named **image** on a form, you could use the following code:

```
XPathNavigator image = mainDS.SelectSingleNode(
  "/my:myFields/my:image", NamespaceManager);

...

stream.SetValue(image.Value);
```

to set the **Stream** field in the XML for the request sent to the web service. And because the value of a picture control does not have to be changed before it is passed to the **Copy** web service, you could also use rules instead of code to upload an image to SharePoint. The latter cannot be done for a file stored in a file attachment control.

Upload an image from a picture control to SharePoint

Problem

You have a picture control on an InfoPath form and want users to be able to upload the image from the picture control to a SharePoint picture library.

Solution

You can use the **Imaging** web service to upload an image from a picture control to a SharePoint picture library.

To upload an image from a picture control to a SharePoint picture library:

1. In SharePoint, enter the URL of the **Upload** operation of the **Imaging** web service in the browser's address bar, for example:

    ```
    http://servername/sitename/_vti_bin/Imaging.asmx?op=Upload
    ```

2. Copy the XML fragment that is located in the **soap:Body** element of the SOAP request. For example:

    ```
    <Upload xmlns="http://schemas.microsoft.com/sharepoint/soap/ois/">
      <strListName>string</strListName>
      <strFolder>string</strFolder>
      <bytes>base64Binary</bytes>
      <fileName>string</fileName>
      <fOverWriteIfExist>boolean</fOverWriteIfExist>
    </Upload>
    ```

    Open Notepad and paste the XML fragment you just copied, remove all line-breaks and whitespaces between the elements, and then save the file as **ImagingUploadRequest.xml**. You can also download this file from www.bizsupportonline.com.

3. Copy the XML fragment that is located in the **soap:Body** element of the SOAP response. For example:

    ```
    <UploadResponse xmlns="http://schemas.microsoft.com/sharepoint/soap/ois/">
      <UploadResult>string</UploadResult>
    </UploadResponse>
    ```

    Open Notepad and paste the XML fragment you just copied, remove all line-breaks and whitespaces between the elements, and then save the file as **ImagingUploadResponse.xml**. You can also download this file from www.bizsupportonline.com.

4. In InfoPath, create a new form template or use an existing one.

5. Select **Data ➤ Get External Data ➤ From Other Sources ➤ From XML File** and follow the instructions to add an XML data connection for the **ImagingUploadRequest.xml** file. Leave the **Automatically retrieve data when**

form is opened check box selected and name the data connection **ImagingUploadRequest**.

6. Select **Data ➤ Get External Data ➤ From Other Sources ➤ From XML File** and follow the instructions to add an XML data connection for the **ImagingUploadResponse.xml** file. Leave the **Automatically retrieve data when form is opened** check box selected and name the data connection **ImagingUploadResponse**.

7. Add a **Drop-Down List Box** control to the view of the form template, name it **library**, and select its **Cannot be blank** property.

8. Open the **Drop-Down List Box Properties** dialog box, leave the **Enter choices manually** option selected, and then click **Add** to manually enter the names of one or more picture libraries which are located on the same SharePoint site to which you will be publishing the form template and to which users are allowed to upload images. Click **OK** when you are done.

9. Add a **Text Box** control to the view of the form template, name it **filename**, and select its **Cannot be blank** property.

10. Add a **Picture** control to the view of the form template (select the **Included in the form** option when you add the picture control to the view), name it **image**, and select its **Cannot be blank** property.

11. Select **Data ➤ Submit Form ➤ To Other Locations ➤ To Web Service**.

12. On the **Data Connection Wizard**, enter the URL of the **Imaging** web service, for example

```
http://servername/sitename/_vti_bin/Imaging.asmx
```

and click **Next**. Here **servername** is the name of the SharePoint server where a site named **sitename** on which the **Imaging** web service is located.

13. On the **Data Connection Wizard**, select the **Upload** operation from the list of operations, and click **Next**.

14. On the **Data Connection Wizard**, select **strlistName** in the **Parameters** list and click the button behind the **Field or group** text box.

15. On the **Select a Field or Group** dialog box, select **ImagingUploadRequest (Secondary)** from the **Fields** drop-down list box, select **strListName**, and click **OK**. With this you have set the **strListName** parameter of the web service to be equal to the value of the **strListName** field in the **ImagingUploadRequest** secondary data source.

16. On the **Data Connection Wizard**, leave **Text and child elements only** selected in the **Include** drop-down list box, leave the **Submit data as a string** check box deselected, select **strFolder** in the **Parameters** list, and click the button behind the **Field or group** text box.

17. On the **Select a Field or Group** dialog box, select **ImagingUploadRequest (Secondary)** from the **Fields** drop-down list box, select **strFolder**, and click **OK**. With this you have set the **strFolder** parameter of the web service to be equal to the value of the **strFolder** field in the **ImagingUploadRequest** secondary data source.

18. On the **Data Connection Wizard**, leave **Text and child elements only** selected in the **Include** drop-down list box, leave the **Submit data as a string** check box deselected, select **bytes** in the **Parameters** list, and click the button behind the **Field or group** text box.

19. On the **Select a Field or Group** dialog box, select **ImagingUploadRequest (Secondary)** from the **Fields** drop-down list box, select **bytes**, and click **OK**. With this you have set the **bytes** parameter of the web service to be equal to the value of the **bytes** field in the **ImagingUploadRequest** secondary data source.

20. On the **Data Connection Wizard**, leave **Text and child elements only** selected in the **Include** drop-down list box, leave the **Submit data as a string** check box deselected, select **fileName** in the **Parameters** list, and click the button behind the **Field or group** text box.

21. On the **Select a Field or Group** dialog box, select **ImagingUploadRequest (Secondary)** from the **Fields** drop-down list box, select **fileName**, and click **OK**. With this you have set the **fileName** parameter of the web service to be equal to the value of the **fileName** field in the **ImagingUploadRequest** secondary data source.

22. On the **Data Connection Wizard**, leave **Text and child elements only** selected in the **Include** drop-down list box, leave the **Submit data as a string** check box deselected, select **fOverwriteIfExist** in the **Parameters** list, and click the button behind the **Field or group** text box.

23. On the **Select a Field or Group** dialog box, select **ImagingUploadRequest (Secondary)** from the **Fields** drop-down list box, select **fOverwriteIfExist**, and click **OK**. With this you have set the **fOverwriteIfExist** parameter of the web service to be equal to the value of the **fOverwriteIfExist** field in the **ImagingUploadRequest** secondary data source.

24. On the **Data Connection Wizard**, leave **Text and child elements only** selected in the **Include** drop-down list box, leave the **Submit data as a string** check box deselected, and click **Next**.

25. On the **Data Connection Wizard**, name the data connection **UploadImage**, deselect the **Set as the default submit connection** check box, and click **Finish**.

26. Add a **Button** control to the view of the form template and label it **Upload Image**.

27. Add a **Text Box** control to the view of the form template and name it **result**.

28. Add an event handler for the **Clicked** event of the **Upload Image** button as described in recipe *7 Add an event handler for a control event*.

29. In VSTA, add the following code to the `Clicked()` event handler for the **Upload Image** button (*code #: B2CBC07D-D24A-414E-A9AF-D587104C0708*):

```
XPathNavigator mainDS = MainDataSource.CreateNavigator();
XPathNavigator requestDS =
  DataSources["ImagingUploadRequest"].CreateNavigator();
XPathNavigator responseDS =
  DataSources["ImagingUploadResponse"].CreateNavigator();

string picLib = mainDS.SelectSingleNode(
  "/my:myFields/my:library", NamespaceManager).Value;
string filename = mainDS.SelectSingleNode(
  "/my:myFields/my:filename", NamespaceManager).Value;
string image = mainDS.SelectSingleNode(
  "/my:myFields/my:image", NamespaceManager).Value;

requestDS.SelectSingleNode("/ns1:Upload/ns1:strListName",
  NamespaceManager).SetValue(picLib);
requestDS.SelectSingleNode("/ns1:Upload/ns1:strFolder",
  NamespaceManager).SetValue("");
requestDS.SelectSingleNode("/ns1:Upload/ns1:bytes",
  NamespaceManager).SetValue(image);
requestDS.SelectSingleNode("/ns1:Upload/ns1:fileName",
  NamespaceManager).SetValue(filename);
requestDS.SelectSingleNode("/ns1:Upload/ns1:fOverWriteIfExist",
  NamespaceManager).SetValue("true");

XPathNavigator response = responseDS.SelectSingleNode(
  "/ns1:UploadResponse", NamespaceManager);

((WebServiceConnection)DataConnections["UploadImage"])
  .Execute(requestDS, response, null);

XPathNavigator result = response.SelectSingleNode(
  "//ns1:UploadResult/ns1:Upload/@lastmodified", NamespaceManager);

if (result != null)
  mainDS.SelectSingleNode(
    "/my:myFields/my:result", NamespaceManager).SetValue(result.Value);
```

30. Save and build the project.

31. Preview the form.

When the form opens, select a picture library from the drop-down list box, enter a file name with file extension, add an image to the picture control, and click the **Upload Image** button. In SharePoint, navigate to the picture library to which you uploaded the image and verify that the image is present in the picture library.

Discussion

At the end of the discussion section of the previous solution you learned that you can use the **Copy** web service to upload an image to a document library. In the solution described above you learned that you can also use the **Imaging** web service to upload an image to SharePoint. The difference between using either web service for uploading images is that the **Copy** web service allows you to upload images to document and picture libraries, while the **Imaging** web service allows you to upload images to picture libraries.

Note that if you want to use either web service for uploading images, you are not required to write code, since you can also use rules to set the values in the secondary data sources for the XML files that are used as input for the web services, and then submit the data. The only time you may require writing code to upload images is for example if you want to loop through and upload images that have been placed in a repeating table, or if you want to retrieve the information returned by the web service in its response.

In the solution above, you did not have to explicitly set the URL of the SharePoint server or site where the picture library is located, since you specified this information when you created the data connection for the **Imaging** web service.

The technique for calling the **Imaging** web service is similar to the one used in the previous solution in that the code first retrieves references to the Main data source and the data sources that should serve as request and response objects for calling the web service operation.

```
XPathNavigator mainDS = MainDataSource.CreateNavigator();
XPathNavigator requestDS =
  DataSources["ImagingUploadRequest"].CreateNavigator();
XPathNavigator responseDS =
  DataSources["ImagingUploadResponse"].CreateNavigator();
```

The request object is then filled with values.

```
string picLib = mainDS.SelectSingleNode(
  "/my:myFields/my:library", NamespaceManager).Value;
string filename = mainDS.SelectSingleNode(
  "/my:myFields/my:filename", NamespaceManager).Value;
string image = mainDS.SelectSingleNode(
  "/my:myFields/my:image", NamespaceManager).Value;

requestDS.SelectSingleNode("/ns1:Upload/ns1:strListName",
  NamespaceManager).SetValue(picLib);
requestDS.SelectSingleNode("/ns1:Upload/ns1:strFolder",
  NamespaceManager).SetValue("");
requestDS.SelectSingleNode("/ns1:Upload/ns1:bytes",
  NamespaceManager).SetValue(image);
requestDS.SelectSingleNode("/ns1:Upload/ns1:fileName",
  NamespaceManager).SetValue(filename);
requestDS.SelectSingleNode("/ns1:Upload/ns1:fOverWriteIfExist",
  NamespaceManager).SetValue("true");
```

And finally, the `Execute()` method of the `WebServiceConnection` object is called

```
XPathNavigator response = responseDS.SelectSingleNode(
  "/ns1:UploadResponse", NamespaceManager);

((WebServiceConnection)DataConnections["UploadImage"])
  .Execute(requestDS, response, null);
```

and the result of the call written to the **result** field on the form.

```
XPathNavigator result = response.SelectSingleNode(
  "//ns1:UploadResult/ns1:Upload/@lastmodified", NamespaceManager);

if (result != null)
  mainDS.SelectSingleNode(
    "/my:myFields/my:result", NamespaceManager).SetValue(result.Value);
```

99 Auto-number InfoPath forms in a form library

Problem

You want users to be able to submit InfoPath forms to a SharePoint form library and then have the forms automatically get incremental numbers assigned to them in their file names.

Solution

You can use an event receiver on a SharePoint form library to rename and sequentially number InfoPath forms as they are submitted to the form library.

To auto-number InfoPath forms in a SharePoint form library:

1. In InfoPath, create a new browser-compatible form template or use an existing one.

2. On the **Fields** task pane, add a hidden **Field (element)** with the data type **Text (string)**, and the name **formName** to the Main data source of the form.

3. Click **Data ➤ Submit Form ➤ To SharePoint Library**.

4. On the **Data Connection Wizard**, enter the URL of the form library to which forms will be submitted, and then click the formula button behind the **File name** text box.

5. On the **Insert Formula** dialog box, click **Insert Field or Group**.

6. On the **Select a Field or Group** dialog box, select **formName**, and click **OK**.

7. On the **Insert Formula** dialog box, click **OK**.

8. On the **Data Connection Wizard**, select the **Allow overwrite if file exists** check box, and click **Next**.

9. On the **Data Connection Wizard**, leave the data connection name as **SharePoint Library Submit**, leave the **Set as the default submit connection** check box selected, and click **Finish**.

10. Click **Data ➤ Submit Form ➤ Submit Options**.

11. On the **Submit Options** dialog box, select the **Perform custom action using Code** option, click **Edit Code**, and then click **OK**.

12. In VSTA, add the following code to the `FormEvents_Submit()` event handler (*code #: 20695A4E-271E-43B1-B786-5A9A095A84C8*):

```
XPathNavigator mainDS = MainDataSource.CreateNavigator();
XPathNavigator formName = mainDS.SelectSingleNode(
  "/my:myFields/my:formName", NamespaceManager);

if (String.IsNullOrEmpty(formName.Value))
{
  formName.SetValue(System.Guid.NewGuid().ToString());
}

DataConnections["SharePoint Library Submit"].Execute();

e.CancelableArgs.Cancel = false;
```

This code checks whether the **formName** field is empty (as is the case for new forms) and if it is, generates a GUID to be used as the form name.

13. Save and build the project.

14. In InfoPath, click **File ➤ Info ➤ Form Options**.

15. On the **Form Options** dialog box, ensure **Web Browser** is selected in the **Category** list, deselect the check boxes for **Save** and **Save As**, and then click **OK**.

16. Publish the form template to the SharePoint form library you chose in step 4.

17. In Visual Studio 2010, select **File ➤ New ➤ Project**.

18. On the **New Project** dialog box, select **SharePoint ➤ 2010** under **Visual C#** from the list of **Installed Templates**, select **.NET Framework 3.5** from the drop-down list box, select **Event Receiver**, enter a name for the project (for example **AutoNumberEventReceiver**), select a location where to save the solution, enter a name for the solution, and click **OK**.

19. On the **SharePoint Customization Wizard**, enter the URL of the site where the form library is located, select **Deploy as a sandboxed solution**, and click **Next**.

20. On the **SharePoint Customization Wizard**, select **List Item Events** in the first drop-down list box, select **Form Library** in the second drop-down list box, select the check box in front of **An item was added**, and click **Finish**.

21. Add the following **using** statements to the **EventReceiver1.cs** file:

```
using System.IO;
using System.Data;
using System.Xml;
using System.Xml.XPath;
using System.Text;
```

22. Replace the code in the `ItemAdded()` method with the following code (*code #: 20695A4E-271E-43B1-B786-5A9A095A84C8*):

```
try
{
  this.EventFiringEnabled = false;

  if (properties.List.Title != "LibrayWithAutoNumberedForms")
  {
    properties.Cancel = true;
    return;
  }

  int lastNumber = 0;
  int count = properties.List.ItemCount;
  if (count > 1)
  {
    DataTable table = properties.List.Items.GetDataTable();
    DataRow[] rows = table.Select("LinkFilename LIKE 'Form_*'", "ID ASC");
    DataRow lastRow = null;

    if (rows != null && rows.Length > 0)
      lastRow = rows[rows.Length - 1];

    string lastItem = String.Empty;
    if (lastRow != null)
      lastItem = lastRow["LinkFilename"].ToString();

    lastItem = lastItem.Replace(".xml", "");

    Int32.TryParse(lastItem.Substring(
      lastItem.IndexOf("_") + 1), out lastNumber);
  }

  string newName = String.Format("Form_{0}.xml", lastNumber + 1);

  SPListItem item = properties.ListItem;

  if (item != null && item.File != null)
  {
    byte[] bytes = item.File.OpenBinary();
    using (MemoryStream ms = new MemoryStream(bytes))
    {
      XmlDocument doc = new XmlDocument();
      doc.Load(ms);

      XPathNavigator root = doc.CreateNavigator();
      root.MoveToFollowing(XPathNodeType.Element);
      string ns = root.GetNamespace("my");

      XmlNamespaceManager nsMgr = new XmlNamespaceManager(new NameTable());
      nsMgr.AddNamespace("my", ns);
      XPathNavigator formNameNode = root.SelectSingleNode(
        "my:formName", nsMgr);

      if (formNameNode != null)
      {
        formNameNode.SetValue(newName);
      }

      item.File.SaveBinary(
```

```
            Encoding.UTF8.GetBytes(doc.CreateNavigator().OuterXml));
          item.File.MoveTo(item.ParentList.RootFolder.Url
            + "/" + newName, true);
          item.File.Item["Name"] = newName;
          item.File.Update();

          ms.Close();
        }
      }
    }
  }
  catch (Exception ex)
  {
    properties.Status = SPEventReceiverStatus.CancelWithError;
    properties.ErrorMessage = ex.Message;
    properties.Cancel = true;
  }
  finally
  {
    this.EventFiringEnabled = true;
  }
```

where you should change the **LibrayWithAutoNumberedForms** to be the name of the form library where you published the form template.

23. Click **Build ➤ Build Solution** and solve any errors if necessary.

24. Click **Build ➤ Deploy Solution** to deploy the solution to SharePoint.

In SharePoint, navigate to the form library where you published the form template and add a new form. Submit the form and after a couple of seconds, refresh the view and verify that the name of the form has been automatically changed and auto-numbered. Add a second form, submit it, and verify that the auto-numbering process works correctly.

Discussion

In the solution described above, you learned how to use a SharePoint event receiver to automatically sequentially number forms that are submitted to a form library using a base name of **Form_** with a number.

You first created an InfoPath form and configured it to be submitted to a form library using a file name that is stored in a hidden field named **formName** in the form itself. When the form is submitted, an XPathNavigator object pointing to the **formName** field is created in the FormEvents_Submit() event handler

```
XPathNavigator mainDS = MainDataSource.CreateNavigator();
XPathNavigator formName = mainDS.SelectSingleNode(
  "/my:myFields/my:formName", NamespaceManager);
```

and then the value of the field is checked. If the field is empty, it means that the form being submitted is a newly created form, so a GUID should be generated and used as a temporary name for the form. If the field is not empty, the name should not be overwritten.

```
if (String.IsNullOrEmpty(formName.Value))
{
  formName.SetValue(System.Guid.NewGuid().ToString());
}
```

And finally, the form is submitted to the form library by calling the Execute() method of the submit data connection for the SharePoint form library.

```
DataConnections["SharePoint Library Submit"].Execute();

e.CancelableArgs.Cancel = false;
```

Once the form has been submitted, a SharePoint event receiver runs and renames the form that was submitted to have a name such as for example **Form_12.xml**, with **12** being the highest number of all the forms that start with **Form_** in the form library.

The code for the event receiver is pretty straightforward. When the ItemAdded() method runs, the code first checks whether the correct form library triggered the call, and if it was a different form library, the event is canceled.

```
if (properties.List.Title != "LibrayWithAutoNumberedForms")
{
  properties.Cancel = true;
  return;
}
```

After counting the amount of list items in the list and ensuring that the list is not empty

```
int lastNumber = 0;
int count = properties.List.ItemCount;
if (count > 1)
{
  ...
}
```

the code goes on to retrieve a DataTable object by calling the GetDataTable() method of the SPListItemCollection object

```
DataTable table = properties.List.Items.GetDataTable();
```

to filter and sort the items in the list.

```
DataRow[] rows = table.Select("LinkFilename LIKE 'Form_*'", "ID ASC");
```

The filter in the Select() method of the DataTable object filters the items on the LinkFilename (which is equivalent to the name of the form) starting with **Form_** and then sorts the results in an ascending order by the ID of the list item, which may differ from the actual number in the name of the form, but which nonetheless should allow all forms to be sorted in an ascending numerical order.

Once the filtered `DataRow` objects have been retrieved, the file name of the last item is determined and its number extracted and stored in a variable named `lastNumber`.

```
DataRow lastRow = null;

if (rows != null && rows.Length > 0)
  lastRow = rows[rows.Length - 1];

string lastItem = String.Empty;
if (lastRow != null)
  lastItem = lastRow["LinkFilename"].ToString();

lastItem = lastItem.Replace(".xml", "");

Int32.TryParse(lastItem.Substring(lastItem.IndexOf("_") + 1), out lastNumber);
```

The `lastNumber` variable is then used to construct a new file name.

```
string newName = String.Format("Form_{0}.xml", lastNumber + 1);
```

Once a new file name has been generated, the code then retrieves the list item the event receiver is running on through the `SPItemEventProperties` object.

```
SPListItem item = properties.ListItem;
```

InfoPath forms that are submitted to a form library are stored as attachments of list items. So if you want to retrieve the actual contents of an InfoPath form, you must use the `File` property of the `SPListItem` class.

```
if (item != null && item.File != null)
{
  ...
}
```

And then you can use the `OpenBinary()` method of the `SPFile` object together with `MemoryStream` and `XmlDocument` objects to retrieve the actual values of fields in the form.

```
byte[] bytes = item.File.OpenBinary();
using (MemoryStream ms = new MemoryStream(bytes))
{
  XmlDocument doc = new XmlDocument();
  doc.Load(ms);
  ...
}
```

The code reads the contents of the `XmlDocument` object and retrieves an `XPathNavigator` object pointing to the **formName** field so that it can set its value to be equal to the new file name that was previously generated.

```
XPathNavigator root = doc.CreateNavigator();
root.MoveToFollowing(XPathNodeType.Element);
string ns = root.GetNamespace("my");

XmlNamespaceManager nsMgr = new XmlNamespaceManager(new NameTable());
nsMgr.AddNamespace("my", ns);
XPathNavigator formNameNode = root.SelectSingleNode("my:formName", nsMgr);

if (formNameNode != null)
{
  formNameNode.SetValue(newName);
}
```

And finally, the `SaveBinary()` method of the `SPFile` object is used together with the `GetBytes()` method of the `Encoding` class to write the modified contents of the InfoPath form back to the list item.

```
item.File.SaveBinary(Encoding.UTF8.GetBytes(doc.CreateNavigator().OuterXml));
```

This effectively has the SharePoint event receiver saving the generated file name in the InfoPath form itself. You could have also created a solution, where as soon as a user opens the form, the file name is retrieved in the `Loading()` event handler of the form, and when the form is resubmitted this value is permanently stored in the form. The code in the `Loading()` event handler would look something like the following:

```
if (Environment.IsBrowser)
{
  string loc = string.Empty;

  e.InputParameters.TryGetValue("XmlLocation", out loc);

  if (!String.IsNullOrEmpty(loc))
  {
    string[] locParts = loc.Split('/');
    int count = locParts.Length;
    if (count > 0)
    {
      MainDataSource.CreateNavigator()
        .SelectSingleNode("/my:myFields/my:formName", NamespaceManager)
        .SetValue(locParts[count - 1]);
    }
  }
}
```

The code above uses the `InputParameters` property of the `LoadingEventArgs` object to search for the value of the `XmlLocation` parameter. If this parameter is present, the filename is then extracted from its value and then used to set the value of the **formName** field. When the form is resubmitted, the code that generates a GUID will be skipped, since the **formName** field is not blank anymore, and the file name that was generated by the SharePoint event receiver will be used to submit the form.

But by having the SharePoint event receiver update the InfoPath form field, you remove the dependency from any user having to reopen and resubmit the form for the

formName field to have a value that is the same as the actual file name of the InfoPath form in the form library.

The last step is to use the MoveTo() method of the SPFile object, the **Name** field of the SPListItem object, and the Update() method of the SPFile object to rename the file in the form library.

```
item.File.MoveTo(item.ParentList.RootFolder.Url + "/" + newName, true);
item.File.Item["Name"] = newName;
item.File.Update();
```

The SharePoint event receiver in the solution described above was deployed as a sandboxed solution. To debug a sandboxed solution:

1. In Visual Studio 2010, click **Debug ➤ Attach to Process**.

2. On the **Attach to Process** dialog box in the **Available Processes** list, locate the **SPUCWorkerProcess.exe** process, and then click **Attach**.

3. Add one or more breakpoints anywhere in the code in the ItemAdded() method.

4. In SharePoint, navigate to the form library where you published the form template, add a new form, and then submit it. The debugger should break in Visual Studio 2010.

Note that the **Microsoft SharePoint Foundation Sandboxed Code Service** must be running for sandboxed solutions to work. You can start this service via **System Settings ➤ Manage services on server** in SharePoint Central Administration. For more information about working with sandboxed solutions, consult the SharePoint documentation on the MSDN web site.

Tip:

> If you made changes to and redeployed an event receiver, but the changes do not seem to have taken effect, increase the version of the assembly in the **AssemblyInfo.cs** file or set it to be equal to **1.0.***, redeploy the event receiver, and try again.

100 Use an InfoPath form to send an email with attachments

Problem

You want to allow users to submit an InfoPath form to a SharePoint form library and then have a workflow run to send an email to one or more users using the data that was entered into the InfoPath form including any attachments.

Solution

You can create a custom workflow activity that makes use of the `MailMessage` class to send an email with attachments when a form is submitted to a form library.

This solution consists of the following three parts:

1. Create an InfoPath form that can serve as a form to enter information contained in an email.

2. Create a custom workflow activity that makes use of the `MailMessage` class to send an email with attachments.

3. Create a SharePoint Designer workflow that makes use of the custom workflow activity.

To create an InfoPath form that can serve as an email form:

1. In InfoPath, create a new form template or use an existing one.

2. Add a **Text Box** control to the view of the form template and name it **subject**.

3. Add a **Rich Text Box** control to the view of the form template and name it **body**.

4. On the **Fields** task pane, right-click the **body** field, and select **Add** from the drop-down menu that appears.

5. On the **Add Field or Group** dialog box, enter **isHtml** in the **Name** text box, select **True/False (boolean)** from the **Data type** drop-down list box, leave **FALSE** selected in the **Default value** drop-down list box, and click **OK**.

6. Drag-and-drop the **isHtml** field from the **Fields** task pane onto the view of the form template and bind it to a **Check Box** control.

7. Add a **Repeating Table** control with one column to the view of the form template.

8. On the **Fields** task pane, delete the field that is located under the repeating group node of the repeating table. Delete the corresponding text box control from the repeating table on the view, and then add a **File Attachment** control in its place. Name the file attachment control **file**.

9. Click **Data ➤ Form Data ➤ Default Values**.

10. On the **Edit Default Values** dialog box, expand the group node (**group1**) for the repeating table, deselect the check box in front of the repeating group (**group2**) node for the repeating table, and click **OK**. This should prevent the repeating table from having a first empty row.

11. Publish the form template to a SharePoint form library named **SendEmailOnSubmitLib**.

To create a custom workflow activity that can send an email with attachments:

1. In Visual Studio 2010, select **File ➤ New ➤ Project**.

2. On the **New Project** dialog box, select **Workflow** under **Visual C#** from the list of **Installed Templates**, select **.NET Framework 3.5** from the drop-down list box, select **Workflow Activity Library**, enter a name for the project (for example **BizSupportOnlineWFActionsLib**), select a location where to save the solution, enter a name for the solution, and click **OK**.

3. On the **Solution Explorer** pane, right-click the project name, and select **Properties** from the drop-down menu that appears.

4. On the **Properties** window, select the **Signing** tab, select the **Sign the assembly** check box, and then select **<New...>** from the **Choose a strong name key file** drop-down list box.

5. On the **Create Strong Name Key** dialog box, enter a name (for example **BizSupportOnlineWFActionsLib.snk**), deselect the **Protect my key file with a password** check box, and click **OK**.

6. On the **Properties** window, select the **Application** tab, change the **Assembly name** to **BizSupportOnlineWFActionsLib**, and the **Default namespace** to **BizSupportOnlineWFActionsLib**.

7. On the **Solution Explorer** pane, add references to the **Microsoft.SharePoint** and **Microsoft.SharePoint.WorkflowActions** assemblies.

8. On the **Solution Explorer** pane, add a new class with the name **InfoPathAttachmentDecoder** to the project and add the code from *InfoPathAttachmentDecoder.cs* listed in the Appendix to the new class file. You can also download the **InfoPathAttachmentDecoder.cs** file from www.bizsupportonline.com and then add it to your project.

9. On the **Solution Explorer** pane, rename **Activity1.cs** to **SendEmailActivity.cs**, and then right-click it and select **View Code** from the context menu that appears.

10. Add the following **using** statements to the **SendEmailActivity.cs** file (*code #: 5D7A725A-E9BD-41D4-8BBB-E51C07A74F61*):

```
using Microsoft.SharePoint;
using Microsoft.SharePoint.WorkflowActions;
using System.Collections.Generic;
using System.Xml;
using System.Xml.XPath;
using System.IO;
using System.Diagnostics;
using System.Net.Mail;
```

11. The class should have a namespace of `BizSupportOnlineWFActionsLib` and a name of `SendEmailActivity`.

```
namespace BizSupportOnlineWFActionsLib
{
  public partial class SendEmailActivity : SequenceActivity
  {
    public SendEmailActivity()
    {
      InitializeComponent();
    }
  }
}
```

Register the following dependency properties in the `SendEmailActivity` class (*code #: 5D7A725A-E9BD-41D4-8BBB-E51C07A74F61*):

```
public static DependencyProperty __ContextProperty =
  DependencyProperty.Register(
  "__Context", typeof(WorkflowContext), typeof(SendEmailActivity));

public static DependencyProperty ListIdProperty =
  DependencyProperty.Register(
  "ListId", typeof(string), typeof(SendEmailActivity));

public static DependencyProperty ListItemProperty =
  DependencyProperty.Register(
  "ListItem", typeof(int), typeof(SendEmailActivity));

public static DependencyProperty SubjectFieldXPathProperty =
  DependencyProperty.Register(
  "SubjectFieldXPath", typeof(string), typeof(SendEmailActivity));

public static DependencyProperty BodyFieldXPathProperty =
  DependencyProperty.Register(
  "BodyFieldXPath", typeof(string), typeof(SendEmailActivity));

public static DependencyProperty AttachmentFieldXPathProperty =
  DependencyProperty.Register(
  "AttachmentFieldXPath", typeof(string), typeof(SendEmailActivity));

public static DependencyProperty ToUsersProperty =
  DependencyProperty.Register(
  "ToUsers", typeof(System.Collections.ArrayList),
  typeof(SendEmailActivity));

public static DependencyProperty SmtpServerProperty =
  DependencyProperty.Register(
```

```
    "SmtpServer", typeof(string), typeof(SendEmailActivity));

public static DependencyProperty ToListIdProperty =
    DependencyProperty.Register(
    "ToListId", typeof(string), typeof(SendEmailActivity));

public static DependencyProperty IncludeFormLinkProperty =
    DependencyProperty.Register(
    "IncludeFormLink", typeof(string), typeof(SendEmailActivity));
```

12. Add a get/set property for each dependency property you registered (*code #: 5D7A725A-E9BD-41D4-8BBB-E51C07A74F61*):

```
[Description("Context")]
[ValidationOption(ValidationOption.Required)]

[Browsable(true)]
[DesignerSerializationVisibility(DesignerSerializationVisibility.Visible)]
public WorkflowContext __Context
{
  get
  {
    return ((WorkflowContext)base.GetValue(
      SendEmailActivity.__ContextProperty));
  }
  set
  {
    base.SetValue(SendEmailActivity.__ContextProperty, value);
  }
}

[Description("ListId")]
[ValidationOption(ValidationOption.Required)]
[Browsable(true)]
[DesignerSerializationVisibility(DesignerSerializationVisibility.Visible)]
public string ListId
{
  get
  {
    return ((string)base.GetValue(SendEmailActivity.ListIdProperty));
  }
  set
  {
    base.SetValue(SendEmailActivity.ListIdProperty, value);
  }
}

[Description("ListItem")]
[ValidationOption(ValidationOption.Required)]
[Browsable(true)]
[DesignerSerializationVisibility(DesignerSerializationVisibility.Visible)]
public int ListItem
{
  get
  {
    return ((int)base.GetValue(SendEmailActivity.ListItemProperty));
  }
  set
  {
    base.SetValue(SendEmailActivity.ListItemProperty, value);
  }
}
```

```
[Description("SubjectFieldXPath")]
[ValidationOption(ValidationOption.Required)]
[DesignerSerializationVisibility(DesignerSerializationVisibility.Visible)]
public string SubjectFieldXPath
{
  get
  {
    return ((string)(base.GetValue(
      SendEmailActivity.SubjectFieldXPathProperty)));
  }
  set
  {
    base.SetValue(SendEmailActivity.SubjectFieldXPathProperty, value);
  }
}

[Description("BodyFieldXPath")]
[ValidationOption(ValidationOption.Required)]
[DesignerSerializationVisibility(DesignerSerializationVisibility.Visible)]
public string BodyFieldXPath
{
  get
  {
    return ((string)(base.GetValue(
      SendEmailActivity.BodyFieldXPathProperty)));
  }
  set
  {
    base.SetValue(SendEmailActivity.BodyFieldXPathProperty, value);
  }
}

[Description("AttachmentFieldXPath")]
[ValidationOption(ValidationOption.Required)]
[DesignerSerializationVisibility(DesignerSerializationVisibility.Visible)]
public string AttachmentFieldXPath
{
  get
  {
    return ((string)(base.GetValue(
      SendEmailActivity.AttachmentFieldXPathProperty)));
  }
  set
  {
    base.SetValue(SendEmailActivity.AttachmentFieldXPathProperty, value);
  }
}

[Description("ToUsers")]
[ValidationOption(ValidationOption.Required)]
[Browsable(true)]
[DesignerSerializationVisibility(DesignerSerializationVisibility.Visible)]
public ArrayList ToUsers
{
  get
  {
    return ((ArrayList)base.GetValue(SendEmailActivity.ToUsersProperty));
  }
  set
  {
    base.SetValue(SendEmailActivity.ToUsersProperty, value);
```

```
    }
  }

  [Description("SmtpServer")]
  [ValidationOption(ValidationOption.Required)]
  [DesignerSerializationVisibility(DesignerSerializationVisibility.Visible)]
  public string SmtpServer
  {
    get
    {
      return ((string)(base.GetValue(SendEmailActivity.SmtpServerProperty)));
    }
    set
    {
      base.SetValue(SendEmailActivity.SmtpServerProperty, value);
    }
  }

  [Description("ToListId")]
  [ValidationOption(ValidationOption.Required)]
  [Browsable(true)]
  [DesignerSerializationVisibility(DesignerSerializationVisibility.Visible)]
  public string ToListId
  {
    get
    {
      return ((string)base.GetValue(SendEmailActivity.ToListIdProperty));
    }
    set
    {
      base.SetValue(SendEmailActivity.ToListIdProperty, value);
      }
  }

  [Description("IncludeFormLink")]
  [ValidationOption(ValidationOption.Required)]
  [DesignerSerializationVisibility(DesignerSerializationVisibility.Visible)]
  public string IncludeFormLink
  {
    get
    {
      return ((string)(base.GetValue(
        SendEmailActivity.IncludeFormLinkProperty)));
    }
    set
    {
      base.SetValue(SendEmailActivity.IncludeFormLinkProperty, value);
    }
  }
```

13. Override the `Execute()` method:

```
protected override ActivityExecutionStatus Execute(
  ActivityExecutionContext executionContext)
{
  return base.Execute(executionContext);
}
```

14. Replace the code in the `Execute()` method of the `SendEmailActivity` class with the following code (*code #: 5D7A725A-E9BD-41D4-8BBB-E51C07A74F61*):

```
List<MemoryStream> msList = new List<MemoryStream>();

try
{
  SPSite site = (SPSite)__Context.Site;
  SPWeb web = (SPWeb)__Context.Web;
  SPList list = web.Lists[new Guid(this.ListId)];
  SPListItem item = list.GetItemById(this.ListItem);
  ArrayList users = this.ToUsers;

  SPFile file = item.File;

  if (file == null)
    throw new System.ArgumentNullException("file");

  byte[] xmlFormData = null;
  xmlFormData = file.OpenBinary();

  XPathDocument ipForm = null;

  if (xmlFormData != null)
  {
    using (MemoryStream ms = new MemoryStream(xmlFormData))
    {
      ipForm = new XPathDocument(ms);
      ms.Close();
    }
  }

  if (ipForm == null)
    throw new System.ArgumentNullException("ipForm");

  XPathNavigator ipFormNav = ipForm.CreateNavigator();

  ipFormNav.MoveToFollowing(XPathNodeType.Element);
  XmlNamespaceManager nsManager =
    new XmlNamespaceManager(new NameTable());

  foreach (KeyValuePair<string, string> ns
    in ipFormNav.GetNamespacesInScope(XmlNamespaceScope.All))
  {
    if (ns.Key == String.Empty)
    {
      nsManager.AddNamespace("def", ns.Value);
    }
    else
    {
      nsManager.AddNamespace(ns.Key, ns.Value);
    }
  }

  string from = __Context.InitiatorUser.Email;
  string subject = String.Empty;
  string body = String.Empty;
  bool isHtml = false;

  XPathNavigator nodeNav = ipFormNav.SelectSingleNode(
    this.SubjectFieldXPath, nsManager);
```

```
if (nodeNav != null)
{
  subject = nodeNav.Value;
}

string currentItemUrl = __Context.CurrentItemUrl;

nodeNav = ipFormNav.SelectSingleNode(
this.BodyFieldXPath, nsManager);
if (nodeNav != null)
{
  string isHtmlVal = nodeNav.GetAttribute(
    "isHtml", nodeNav.NamespaceURI);
  if (isHtmlVal == "true")
    isHtml = true;

  if (isHtml)
  {
    body = nodeNav.InnerXml;

    if (this.IncludeFormLink == "1")
      body = body + "<br/></br>Form Location: " + currentItemUrl;
  }
  else
  {
    body = nodeNav.Value;

    if (this.IncludeFormLink == "1")
      body = body + "\n\nForm Location: " + currentItemUrl;
  }

  XPathNodeIterator iter = ipFormNav.Select(
    this.AttachmentFieldXPath, nsManager);

  using (MailMessage msg = new MailMessage())
  {
    msg.From = new MailAddress(from);
    msg.Subject = subject;
    msg.Body = body;
    msg.IsBodyHtml = isHtml;

    for (int i = 0; i < users.Count; i++)
    {
      SPUser user = web.SiteUsers[users[i].ToString()];
      if (user != null && !String.IsNullOrEmpty(user.Email))
      {
        msg.To.Add(new MailAddress(user.Email));
      }
    }

    if (iter != null && iter.Count > 0)
    {
      while (iter.MoveNext())
      {
        if (String.IsNullOrEmpty(iter.Current.Value))
          continue;

        BizSupportOnline.InfoPathAttachmentDecoder dec =
          new BizSupportOnline.InfoPathAttachmentDecoder(
          iter.Current.Value);
        string fileName = dec.Filename;
        byte[] data = dec.DecodedAttachment;
```

```
            MemoryStream ms = new MemoryStream(data);
            msList.Add(ms);
            Attachment attachment = new Attachment(ms, fileName, null);
            msg.Attachments.Add(attachment);

            SPDocumentLibrary docLib =
               (SPDocumentLibrary)web.Lists[new Guid(this.ToListId)];
            docLib.RootFolder.Files.Add(fileName, data, true);
         }
      }

      SmtpClient smtp = new SmtpClient(this.SmtpServer);
      smtp.Send(msg);
   }
  }
}
catch (Exception ex)
{
  string source = "BizSupportOnline Custom SPD Action";

  if (!EventLog.SourceExists(source))
  {
    EventLog.CreateEventSource(source, "Application");
  }

  EventLog log = new EventLog("Application");
  log.Source = source;
  log.WriteEntry(ex.Message, EventLogEntryType.Error);
}
finally
{
  foreach (MemoryStream m in msList)
  {
    m.Close();
    m.Dispose();
  }
}

return ActivityExecutionStatus.Closed;
```

15. Change the compilation mode to **Release**, and build the solution.

16. Open the **Visual Studio Command Prompt (2010)**, which is by default located under the **Microsoft Visual Studio 2010 ➤ Visual Studio Tools** program folder.

17. In the **Visual Studio Command Prompt (2010)** window, type **cd**, enter the path to the **Release** folder under the **bin** folder of the project, and press **Enter**. For example:

```
cd C:\Projects\SharePoint
2010\SendEmailWithAttachmentActivity\SendEmailWithAttachmentActivity\bin\Re
lease
```

18. Retrieve the public key token of the DLL by entering the following into the command-prompt window and pressing **Enter**:

```
sn -T BizSupportOnlineWFActionsLib.dll > key.txt
```

This should write the public key token to a text file named **key.txt**.

19. Open the **key.txt** file and copy the public key token.

20. Add the DLL to the Global Assembly Cache (GAC) by entering the following into the command-prompt window and pressing **Enter**:

```
gacutil -i BizSupportOnlineWFActionsLib.dll
```

21. Open Windows Explorer, and navigate to the **Workflow** folder under the SharePoint root:

```
C:\Program Files\Common Files\Microsoft Shared\Web Server
Extensions\14\TEMPLATE\1033\Workflow
```

22. Add a new text file named **BizSupportOnline.ACTIONS** to the **Workflow** folder, open the file in Notepad, and then add the following XML to it (replace the public key token with the public key token you copied earlier) (*code #: 5D7A725A-E9BD-41D4-8BBB-E51C07A74F61*):

```xml
<?xml version="1.0" encoding="utf-8"?>
<WorkflowInfo Language="en-us">
<Actions Sequential="then" Parallel="and">
  <Action Name="Send an Email with Attachments from InfoPath"
          ClassName="BizSupportOnlineWFActionsLib.SendEmailActivity"
          Assembly="BizSupportOnlineWFActionsLib, Version=1.0.0.0,
Culture=neutral, PublicKeyToken=cf7727cfa09f8cfe"
          AppliesTo="all" Category="BizSupportOnline Actions">
    <RuleDesigner
    Sentence="Send an email with %1 and %2 and %3 from %4 to %5 using %6
and upload the attachments to %7 and %8 a link to the form">
        <FieldBind Field="SubjectFieldXPath" DesignerType="TextArea"
                Text="this subject" Id="1" />
        <FieldBind Field="BodyFieldXPath" DesignerType="TextArea"
                Text="this body" Id="2"/>
        <FieldBind Field="AttachmentFieldXPath" DesignerType="TextArea"
                Text="this attachment" Id="3" />
        <FieldBind Field="ListId,ListItem" Text="this form"
                DesignerType="ChooseListItem" Id="4" />
        <FieldBind Field="ToUsers" Text="these users" DesignerType="Person"
                Id="5"/>
        <FieldBind Field="SmtpServer" DesignerType="TextArea"
                Text="this SMTP server" Id="6"/>
        <FieldBind Field="ToListId" DesignerType="ListNames"
                Text="this library" Id="7" />
        <FieldBind Field="IncludeFormLink" DesignerType="Dropdown"
                Text="(do not) include" Id="8">
          <Option Name="include" Value="1"/>
          <Option Name="do not include" Value="0"/>
        </FieldBind>
    </RuleDesigner>
    <Parameters>
      <Parameter Name="SubjectFieldXPath" Type="System.String, mscorlib"
                Direction="In" />
      <Parameter Name="BodyFieldXPath" Type="System.String, mscorlib"
                Direction="In" />
      <Parameter Name="AttachmentFieldXPath" Type="System.String, mscorlib"
                Direction="In" />
```

```
            <Parameter Name="__Context"
                     Type="Microsoft.SharePoint.WorkflowActions.WorkflowContext"
                     Direction="In" />
            <Parameter Name="ListId" Type="System.String, mscorlib"
                     Direction="In" />
            <Parameter Name="ListItem" Type="System.Int32, mscorlib"
                     Direction="In"  />
            <Parameter Name="ToUsers"
                     Type="System.Collections.ArrayList, mscorlib"
                     Direction="In" />
            <Parameter Name="SmtpServer" Type="System.String, mscorlib"
                     Direction="In" />
            <Parameter Name="ToListId" Type="System.String, mscorlib"
                     Direction="In"  />
            <Parameter Name="IncludeFormLink"  Type="System.String, mscorlib"
                     Direction="In" />
        </Parameters>
      </Action>
    </Actions>
  </WorkflowInfo>
```

Save and close the file.

23. In Windows Explorer, and navigate to the **80** folder for SharePoint:

```
C:\inetpub\wwwroot\wss\VirtualDirectories\80
```

24. Create a backup of the **web.config** file and then open it in Notepad.

25. Locate the **authorizedTypes** section and add the following XML fragment to it (*code #: 5D7A725A-E9BD-41D4-8BBB-E51C07A74F61*):

```
<authorizedType Assembly="BizSupportOnlineWFActionsLib, Version=1.0.0.0,
Culture=neutral, PublicKeyToken=cf7727cfa09f8cfe"
Namespace="BizSupportOnlineWFActionsLib" TypeName="*" Authorized="True" />
```

Ensure you change the values for the `Assembly`, `PublicKeyToken`, and `Namespace` attributes to the correct values for your own assembly. Save and close the **web.config** file.

26. Reset Internet Information Services (IIS) by entering the following into the command-prompt window:

```
iisreset
```

To create a SharePoint Designer workflow that uses the custom workflow activity:

1. In SharePoint Designer 2010, click **File ➤ Sites ➤ Open Site**.

2. On the **Open Site** dialog box, browse to and select the site on which the **SendEmailOnSubmitLib** form library is located or enter the URL of the site in the **Site name** text box, and click **Open**.

3. Once the site has been opened in SharePoint Designer 2010, click **Site ➤ New ➤ List Workflow** or select **Workflows** in the left **Navigation** pane and then click

Workflows ➤ New ➤ List Workflow on the Ribbon, and select **SendEmailOnSubmitLib** from the drop-down menu that appears.

4. On the **Create List Workflow** dialog box, type **SendEmailWF** in the **Name** text box, and click **OK**. This should open the workflow editor with one step (**Step 1**) already added.

5. Click on the text in **Step 1** to place the cursor inside of **Step 1**, click **Workflow ➤ Insert ➤ Action**, and select **Send an Email with Attachments from InfoPath** under the **BizSupportOnline Actions** category.

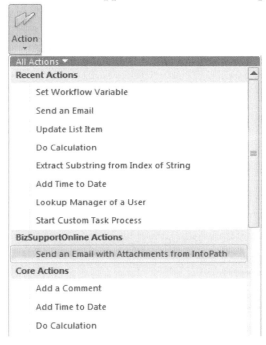

Figure 72. The custom activity listed in the list of actions in SharePoint Designer 2010.

6. Click **this subject** in the sentence for the workflow action, and then enter the following XPath expression in the text box:

    ```
    //my:subject
    ```

7. Click **this body** in the sentence for the workflow action, and then enter the following XPath expression in the text box:

    ```
    //my:body
    ```

8. Click **this attachment** in the sentence for the workflow action, and then enter the following XPath expression in the text box:

    ```
    //my:file
    ```

9. Click **this form** in the sentence for the workflow action.

10. On the **Choose List Item** dialog box, leave **Current Item** selected in the **List** drop-down list box, and click **OK**.

11. Click **these users** in the sentence for the workflow action.

12. On the **Select Users** dialog box, select the users who should receive an email from the list of existing users and groups, and click **Add**. Click **OK** when you are done.

13. Click **this SMTP server** in the sentence for the workflow action, and then enter the name of the SMTP server you want to use in the text box. For example:

```
win-ji2o5062vat
```

14. Click **this library** in the sentence for the workflow action, and then select a document library from the drop-down list box to which the attachments that are extracted from the InfoPath form should be uploaded.

15. Click **(do not) include** in the sentence for the workflow action, and then select **include** from the drop-down list box that appears if you want to include a link to the InfoPath form in the body of the email or select **do not include** from the drop-down list box if you do not want to include a link.

The final sentence for the workflow action should say something like:

```
Send an email with //my:subject and //my:body and //my:file from Current
Item to Jane Doe using win-ji2o5062vat and upload the attachments to DocLib
and include a link to the form
```

16. Click **Workflow ➤ Manage ➤ Workflow Settings**.

17. On the workflow settings page under **Start Options**, select the **Start workflow automatically when an item is created** check box. This will allow the workflow to run whenever a new form is added to the form library. Leave the **Allow this workflow to be manually started** check box selected so that the workflow can also be manually started in case you want to run it again on a form or in case it failed to run.

18. Click **Workflow Settings ➤ Save ➤ Publish** to publish the workflow.

In SharePoint, navigate to the form library where you published the form template and add a new form. Fill out the form with relevant data and add one or more file attachments to it. Save or submit the form to the form library. Once the workflow has completed, verify that the email was sent and that the documents were uploaded to the document library specified in the workflow.

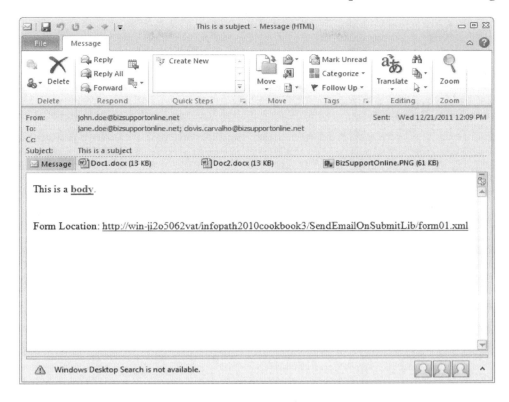

Figure 73. The email that was sent by the workflow as it appears in Outlook 2010.

Discussion

In the solution described above, you learned how you can use classes from the `System.Net.Mail` namespace in a custom workflow activity to send an email with attachments that are extracted from an InfoPath form when the InfoPath form is submitted to a form library. In addition, it also showed you how you can use the SharePoint server object model to upload the extracted attachments to a document library.

The basic steps for creating a workflow activity that can be used in a SharePoint Designer workflow are:

1. Create a workflow activity library project in Visual Studio 2010.

2. Register dependency properties that should be used to communicate with the workflow activity.

3. Create a get/set property for each dependency property you register.

4. Override the `Execute()` method of the workflow activity and add code to it.

5. Sign the assembly with a strong name.

6. Deploy the assembly to the Global Assembly Cache (GAC).

411

7. Add an **AuthorizedType** element for the assembly to the **web.config** file of SharePoint.

8. Create an .ACTIONS file that can be used to hook up the workflow activity to the SharePoint Designer interface.

9. Reset IIS.

The workflow activity in the solution described above implements a couple of techniques that have already been explained throughout this book. In particular, it shows you how to retrieve an InfoPath form (also see recipe *78 3 Ways to open and read an InfoPath form in memory*) from within a workflow activity using `SPFile`, `XPathDocument`, and `MemoryStream` objects.

```
SPFile file = item.File;

if (file == null)
  throw new System.ArgumentNullException("file");

byte[] xmlFormData = null;
xmlFormData = file.OpenBinary();

XPathDocument ipForm = null;

if (xmlFormData != null)
{
  using (MemoryStream ms = new MemoryStream(xmlFormData))
  {
    ipForm = new XPathDocument(ms);
    ms.Close();
  }
}
```

It also shows you a different way for retrieving the namespaces used in an InfoPath form by using the `GetNamespacesInScope()` method of an `XPathNavigator` object.

```
XPathNavigator ipFormNav = ipForm.CreateNavigator();

ipFormNav.MoveToFollowing(XPathNodeType.Element);
XmlNamespaceManager nsManager =
  new XmlNamespaceManager(new NameTable());

foreach (KeyValuePair<string, string> ns
  in ipFormNav.GetNamespacesInScope(XmlNamespaceScope.All))
{
  if (ns.Key == String.Empty)
  {
    nsManager.AddNamespace("def", ns.Value);
  }
  else
  {
    nsManager.AddNamespace(ns.Key, ns.Value);
  }
}
```

And finally, it shows you how you can loop through the attachments stored in a repeating table (also see recipe *70 Loop through rows of a repeating table*), decode them, and upload them to a document library using the SharePoint server object model instead of a web service (see recipe *98 Use an InfoPath form to upload a file to a SharePoint document library*).

```
if (iter != null && iter.Count > 0)
{
  while (iter.MoveNext())
  {
    if (String.IsNullOrEmpty(iter.Current.Value))
      continue;

    BizSupportOnline.InfoPathAttachmentDecoder dec =
      new BizSupportOnline.InfoPathAttachmentDecoder(iter.Current.Value);
    string fileName = dec.Filename;
    byte[] data = dec.DecodedAttachment;

    MemoryStream ms = new MemoryStream(data);
    msList.Add(ms);
    Attachment attachment = new Attachment(ms, fileName, null);
    msg.Attachments.Add(attachment);

    SPDocumentLibrary docLib =
      (SPDocumentLibrary)web.Lists[new Guid(this.ToListId)];
    docLib.RootFolder.Files.Add(fileName, data, true);
  }
}
```

Because the `Attachment` class does not have a constructor that has a `byte` array parameter (only a stream or a file path), the file attachments that are extracted from the InfoPath form are placed in a generic `List` of `MemoryStream` objects

```
List<MemoryStream> msList = new List<MemoryStream>();
```

so that `Attachment` objects can be created and added to the `Attachments` collection of the `MailMessage` object.

```
MemoryStream ms = new MemoryStream(data);
msList.Add(ms);
Attachment attachment = new Attachment(ms, fileName, null);
msg.Attachments.Add(attachment);
```

The `MemoryStream` objects that were stored in the generic `List`, are then closed and disposed of in the `finally` block of the `try-catch` block.

```
finally
{
  foreach (MemoryStream m in msList)
  {
    m.Close();
    m.Dispose();
  }
}
```

413

The solution described above enables sending emails that contain HTML by using a rich text box with an attribute named **isHtml**. The value of this attribute is retrieved in code using the `GetAttribute()` method of the `XPathNavigator` object pointing to the field bound to the rich text box

```
nodeNav = ipFormNav.SelectSingleNode(this.BodyFieldXPath, nsManager);
if (nodeNav != null)
{
  string isHtmlVal = nodeNav.GetAttribute("isHtml", nodeNav.NamespaceURI);
  ...
}
```

and then the value of the `IsBodyHtml` property of the `MailMessage` object is set to be equal to the value of the **isHtml** attribute.

```
msg.IsBodyHtml = isHtml;
```

The value of the `From` property of the `MailMessage` object is populated based on the email address of the person who initiates the workflow.

```
string from = __Context.InitiatorUser.Email;
...
msg.From = new MailAddress(from);
```

The workflow initiator can be retrieved from the workflow context (**__Context** dependency property) through the `InitiatorUser` property. What is also retrieved from the workflow context is the URL of the InfoPath form the workflow is running on through the `CurrentItemUrl` property.

```
string currentItemUrl = __Context.CurrentItemUrl;
```

And depending on the value that is set through SharePoint Designer for the **IncludeFormLink** dependency property, the URL of the InfoPath form is or is not included in the body of the email.

```
if (isHtml)
{
  body = nodeNav.InnerXml;

  if (this.IncludeFormLink == "1")
    body = body + "<br/></br>Form Location: " + currentItemUrl;
}
else
{
  body = nodeNav.Value;

  if (this.IncludeFormLink == "1")
    body = body + "\n\nForm Location: " + currentItemUrl;
}
```

The .ACTIONS file serves as the glue for connecting the workflow activity to SharePoint Designer. This file consists of XML elements that define information for the connection. The general structure looks as follows:

```
<WorkflowInfo>
  <Actions>
    <Action>
      <RuleDesigner>
        <FieldBind />
        <FieldBind />
        ...
      </RuleDesigner>
      <Parameters>
        <Parameter />
        <Parameter />
        ...
      </Parameters>
    </Action>
  </Actions>
</WorkflowInfo>
```

The **RuleDesigner** element contains one or more **FieldBind** elements with each having an **Id** attribute that is referenced in the workflow sentence. A **FieldBind** element also defines the type of control shown in the SharePoint Designer interface and the **Text** that should appear in the workflow sentence for the dependency property the field is bound to. For example:

```
<FieldBind Field="SubjectFieldXPath" DesignerType="TextArea" Text="this subject"
Id="1" />
```

is bound to a dependency property named **SubjectFieldXPath**, it appears as a **TextArea** in SharePoint Designer with the text **this subject** underlined in the workflow sentence. Because its **Id** is equal to **1,** the value of its **Text** attribute will appear where **%1** appears in the workflow sentence, which is defined as an attribute named **Sentence** on the **RuleDesigner** element.

```
Sentence="Send an email with %1 and %2 and %3 from %4 to %5 using %6 and upload
the attachments to %7 and %8 a link to the form"
```

Each **FieldBind** element is also linked to a **Parameter** element under a **Parameters** element. The **Parameter** element defines the type of data that is passed to the workflow activity or that is received from the workflow activity. For example:

```
<Parameter Name="SubjectFieldXPath" Type="System.String, mscorlib"
Direction="In" />
```

defines the **SubjectFieldXPath** dependency property to be a System.String object and it is passed into (Direction="In") the workflow activity. Several types of fields were used in the .ACTIONS file to show you how you can define fields which users can use to select users, select a value from a drop-down list box, or enter normal text when creating a SharePoint Designer workflow.

Tip:

> The **Workflow** folder under the SharePoint root (`C:\Program Files\Common Files\Microsoft Shared\Web Server Extensions\14\TEMPLATE\1033\Workflow`) contains a file named **WSS.ACTIONS**, which you can open in Notepad and search for clues on how to define fields so that they appear as a particular control in a workflow sentence in SharePoint Designer. Do not modify this file, but only use it as a "cheat sheet".

Debugging a workflow activity is similar to debugging a SharePoint event receiver (see recipe *99 Auto-number InfoPath forms in a form library*) in that you must attach the debugger to the worker process as follows:

1. In Visual Studio 2010, set the compilation mode to **Debug** instead of **Release**.

2. Deploy the assembly to the GAC as described in the solution above. Ensure you deploy the DLL that is located in the **Debug** folder under the **bin** folder.

3. In Visual Studio 2010, set breakpoints throughout the code in the `Execute()` method of the workflow activity.

4. Select **Debug ➤ Attach to Process** and attach the debugger to the **w3wp.exe** process for SharePoint.

5. In SharePoint, start the workflow that makes use of the workflow activity by either adding a new form to the form library or manually starting the workflow on an existing form.

Once the workflow is started, the debugger should break in Visual Studio 2010 for you to debug the code.

101 Save a form as a PDF document in a SharePoint document library

Problem

You want users to be able to submit InfoPath forms to a SharePoint form library and then have PDF documents corresponding to those InfoPath forms automatically created in a SharePoint document library.

Solution

You can use the Open XML SDK to convert an InfoPath form into a Word document (see recipe *80 Convert a form to Word using the Open XML SDK 2.0*) and then use Word Automation Services to convert the Word document into a PDF document and store that PDF document in a document library.

Note:

> Word Automation Services must be running on your SharePoint server for this solution to work.

While you could use a web service or a workflow to schedule a Word Automation Services job to convert InfoPath forms that have been converted into Word documents to PDF, in this solution you will use a SharePoint event receiver to schedule jobs.

To save a form as a PDF document in a document library when the form is submitted:

1. In Word 2010, create a new document or modify an existing one as described in *Create a Word document that can serve as a template* of recipe *80 Convert a form to Word using the Open XML SDK 2.0*. Name the document **template.docx**.

2. In SharePoint, create a new SharePoint document library named **DocLib**, and upload the **template.docx** Word document to the document library.

3. In InfoPath, create a new browser-compatible form template as described in *Generate a Word document using InfoPath form data* of recipe *80 Convert a form to Word using the Open XML SDK 2.0*, but do not add the **Print To Word** button or code to the form template, and publish the form template to a SharePoint form library.

4. In Visual Studio 2010, select **File ➤ New ➤ Project**.

5. On the **New Project** dialog box, select **SharePoint ➤ 2010** under **Visual C#** from the list of **Installed Templates**, select **.NET Framework 3.5** from the drop-down list box, select **Event Receiver**, enter a name for the project (for example **ConvertToPDFEventReceiver**), select a location where to save the solution, enter a name for the solution, and click **OK**.

6. On the **SharePoint Customization Wizard**, enter the URL of the site where the form library is located, select **Deploy as a farm solution**, and click **Next**.

7. On the **SharePoint Customization Wizard**, select **List Item Events** in the first drop-down list box, select **Form Library** in the second drop-down list box, select the check box in front of **An item was added**, and click **Finish**.

8. On the **Solution Explorer** pane, add references to the **Microsoft Office 2010 component (Microsoft.Office.Word.Server)**, **DocumentFormat.OpenXml**, **WindowsBase**, and **System.Drawing** assemblies.

9. Add a class named **InfoPathToWord** to the project as described in steps 8 and 9 of *Generate a Word document using InfoPath form data* of recipe *80 Convert a form to Word using the Open XML SDK 2.0*.

10. Add the following **using** statements to the **EventReceiver1.cs** file (*code #: 8F24FD3E-F07D-49D4-A737-7D97B9743684*):

```
using Microsoft.Office.Word.Server.Conversions;
using System.IO;
using System.Xml;
using System.Xml.XPath;
using DocumentFormat.OpenXml;
using DocumentFormat.OpenXml.Packaging;
using DocumentFormat.OpenXml.Wordprocessing;
using System.Collections.Generic;
```

11. Add a private method named `ConvertInfoPathToWord()` that is defined by the following code to the `EventReceiver1` class (*code #: 8F24FD3E-F07D-49D4-A737-7D97B9743684*):

```
private byte[] ConvertInfoPathToWord(MemoryStream ms, SPFile file)
{
  byte[] bytes = file.OpenBinary();

  using (MemoryStream msInternal = new MemoryStream(bytes))
  {
    XmlDocument doc = new XmlDocument();

    doc.Load(msInternal);

    XPathNavigator root = doc.CreateNavigator();
    root.MoveToFollowing(XPathNodeType.Element);
    string ns = root.GetNamespace("my");

    XmlNamespaceManager nsMgr = new XmlNamespaceManager(new NameTable());
    nsMgr.AddNamespace("my", ns);

    string normalText = root.SelectSingleNode(
      "/my:myFields/my:field1", nsMgr).Value;

    string multiLineText = root.SelectSingleNode(
      "/my:myFields/my:field2", nsMgr).Value;

    string rtfValue = String.Empty;
    XPathNavigator formNameNode = root.SelectSingleNode(
      "/my:myFields/my:field3", nsMgr);
    rtfValue = "<html>" + formNameNode.InnerXml + "</html>";

    string base64EncodedString = root.SelectSingleNode(
      "/my:myFields/my:field4", nsMgr).Value;
    byte[] imageBytes = null;
    if (!String.IsNullOrEmpty(base64EncodedString))
    {
      imageBytes = System.Convert.FromBase64String(base64EncodedString);
    }

    XPathNodeIterator iter2 = root.Select(
      "/my:myFields/my:group1/my:field5", nsMgr);
```

```
XPathNodeIterator iter = root.Select(
  "/my:myFields/my:group2/my:group3", nsMgr);

int id = 0;

using (WordprocessingDocument myDoc =
  WordprocessingDocument.Open(ms, true))
{
  MainDocumentPart mainPart = myDoc.MainDocumentPart;

  List<OpenXmlElement> sdtList = InfoPathToWord.GetContentControl(
    mainPart.Document, "richtext");
  InfoPathToWord.AddRichText(id, rtfValue, ref mainPart, ref sdtList);

  ImagePart imagePart = InfoPathToWord.AddImagePart(
    "rId198", base64EncodedString, ref mainPart);

  long imageWidthEMU = 0;
  long imageHeightEMU = 0;
  Guid imageFormat = Guid.Empty;

  InfoPathToWord.GetImageExtents(base64EncodedString,
    out imageWidthEMU, out imageHeightEMU);

  sdtList = InfoPathToWord.GetContentControl(
    mainPart.Document, "picture");
  string imageType = InfoPathToWord.GetImageType(base64EncodedString);

  OpenXmlElement imageElement = InfoPathToWord.CreateImageElement(
  mainPart.GetIdOfPart(imagePart), "Picture 1", "Pic1." + imageType,
    imageWidthEMU, imageHeightEMU);
  InfoPathToWord.ReplaceContentControl(sdtList, imageElement);

  sdtList = InfoPathToWord.GetContentControl(
    mainPart.Document, "singlelineoftext");
  InfoPathToWord.AddSingleLineText(normalText, ref sdtList);

  sdtList = InfoPathToWord.GetContentControl(
    mainPart.Document, "multilinetext");
  InfoPathToWord.AddMultiLineText(multiLineText, ref sdtList);

  Table table = new Table();

  TableProperties tblProp = new TableProperties(
    new TableStyle() { Val = "LightShading-Accent5" },
    new TableWidth() { Width = "100%",
                       Type = TableWidthUnitValues.Pct },
    new TableLook() { Val = "04A0", FirstRow = true,
                      LastRow = false, FirstColumn = false,
                      LastColumn = false, NoHorizontalBand = false,
                      NoVerticalBand = true }
  );

        table.AppendChild<TableProperties>(tblProp);

  InfoPathToWord.AddTableRow(new string[]
    { "Header 1", "Header 2", "Header 3", "Header 4" }, ref table);
  InfoPathToWord.AddRowsToTable(iter, ref table);

  sdtList = InfoPathToWord.GetContentControl(
    mainPart.Document, "repeatingtable");
  InfoPathToWord.ReplaceContentControl(sdtList, table);
```

```
            sdtList = InfoPathToWord.GetContentControl(
              mainPart.Document, "bulletedlist");
            InfoPathToWord.AddBulletedList("rId200", iter2, ref sdtList,
              ref mainPart);

          myDoc.Close();
        }
        msInternal.Close();
    }
    return ms.ToArray();
}
```

12. Replace the code in the `ItemAdded()` method with the following code (*code #: 8F24FD3E-F07D-49D4-A737-7D97B9743684*):

```
try
{
  this.EventFiringEnabled = false;

  string siteUrl = properties.WebUrl;
  SPListItem item = properties.ListItem;

  SPWeb web = properties.Web;
  SPList lib = web.Lists["DocLib"];
  SPFile file = lib.RootFolder.Files["template.docx"];
  string generatedDoc = "";

  if (file != null)
  {
    byte[] templateBytes = file.OpenBinary();

    using (MemoryStream ms = new MemoryStream())
    {
      ms.Write(templateBytes, 0, (int)templateBytes.Length);

      byte[] convertedDocBytes = ConvertInfoPathToWord(ms, item.File);

      generatedDoc = item["LinkFilename"].ToString().Replace(
        "xml", "docx");
      SPFile newFile =
        lib.RootFolder.Files.Add(generatedDoc, convertedDocBytes, true);

      ms.Close();
    }
  }

  string fileName = generatedDoc;
  string pdfFileName = fileName.Replace("docx", "pdf");

  string sourceUrl = siteUrl + "/DocLib/" + fileName;
  string destUrl = siteUrl + "/DocLib/" + pdfFileName;

  string wordAutomationServiceName = "Word Automation Services";

  using (SPSite spSite = new SPSite(properties.SiteId))
  {
    ConversionJob job = new ConversionJob(wordAutomationServiceName);
    job.UserToken = spSite.UserToken;
    job.Settings.UpdateFields = true;
    job.Settings.OutputFormat = SaveFormat.PDF;
    job.AddFile(sourceUrl, destUrl);
```

```
        job.Start();
      }
    }
    catch (Exception ex)
    {
      properties.Status = SPEventReceiverStatus.CancelWithError;
      properties.ErrorMessage = ex.Message;
      properties.Cancel = true;
    }
    finally
    {
      this.EventFiringEnabled = true;
    }
```

13. Click **Build ➤ Build Solution** and solve any errors if necessary.

14. Click **Build ➤ Deploy Solution** to deploy the solution to SharePoint.

In SharePoint, navigate to the form library where you published the form template, add a new form, and then save or submit the form. Depending on how you have configured Word Automation Services, you must wait a certain amount of time (15 minutes if you are using the default settings) until the **Word Automation Services Timer Job** has run, and after it has run, navigate to the **DocLib** document library and verify that a Word document and a PDF document were created for the InfoPath form you submitted.

Discussion

In the solution described above you learned how you can create a SharePoint event receiver that runs during the **ItemAdded** event to retrieve an InfoPath form that is submitted to a form library, extract data stored within that form and generate a Word document, save the Word document to a document library, and then have a timer job convert the Word document into a PDF document.

The code uses a base Word document named **template.docx**, which was uploaded to a document library named **DocLib**, to generate a new Word document based on data from the InfoPath form that was saved or submitted to a form library.

```
SPWeb web = properties.Web;
SPList lib = web.Lists["DocLib"];
SPFile file = lib.RootFolder.Files["template.docx"];
string generatedDoc = "";
```

After retrieving the Word document template using the `SPFileCollection` object of the `SPFolder` object for the root folder of the document library, the code goes on to use the `OpenBinary()` method of the `SPFile` object to create a `byte` array from the Word document that was retrieved

```
byte[] templateBytes = file.OpenBinary();
```

and then writes this `byte` array to a `MemoryStream` object that can be used to write the InfoPath form data to a Word document.

```
using (MemoryStream ms = new MemoryStream())
{
  ms.Write(templateBytes, 0, (int)templateBytes.Length);
  ...
}
```

The code then calls a method named `ConvertInfoPathToWord()`, which opens the InfoPath form that was submitted, loads it into an `XmlDocument` object

```
byte[] bytes = file.OpenBinary();

using (MemoryStream msInternal = new MemoryStream(bytes))
{
  XmlDocument doc = new XmlDocument();

  doc.Load(msInternal);
  ...
}
```

extracts the namespace and creates an `XmlNamespaceManager` object

```
XPathNavigator root = doc.CreateNavigator();
root.MoveToFollowing(XPathNodeType.Element);
string ns = root.GetNamespace("my");

XmlNamespaceManager nsMgr = new XmlNamespaceManager(new NameTable());
nsMgr.AddNamespace("my", ns);
```

so that data can be read from the InfoPath form and then written to the Word document using the Open XML SDK 2.0, and returned to the calling method as a `byte` array.

```
byte[] convertedDocBytes = ConvertInfoPathToWord(ms, item.File);
```

The code in the `ConvertInfoPathToWord()` method is similar to the code used and discussed in recipe *80 Convert a form to Word using the Open XML SDK 2.0*. It makes use of the same `InfoPathToWord` class described in the Appendix, so if you require background information on what it does, refer to the aforementioned recipe.

Once the `byte` array for the converted document has been created, it is used to create a new `SPFile` object that has the same name as the InfoPath form, but with a file extension of DOCX instead of XML. This file is then written back to the same document library where the original Word document template is located by using the `Add()` method of the `SPFileCollection` object.

```
generatedDoc = item["LinkFilename"].ToString().Replace("xml", "docx");
SPFile newFile =
  lib.RootFolder.Files.Add(generatedDoc, convertedDocBytes, true);
```

Once the new Word document has been generated, the code goes on to generate a new file name for the PDF document that should be created from the Word document.

```
string fileName = generatedDoc;
string pdfFileName = fileName.Replace("docx", "pdf");
```

Since the PDF document is to be stored in the same document library (**DocLib**) as the original Word document, two full paths for both documents are generated, where the Word document URL is the source URL and the PDF document URL is the destination URL.

```
string sourceUrl = siteUrl + "/DocLib/" + fileName;
string destUrl = siteUrl + "/DocLib/" + pdfFileName;
```

And finally, a Word `ConversionJob` object is created to schedule a timer job for converting the Word document into a PDF document.

```
string wordAutomationServiceName = "Word Automation Services";

using (SPSite spSite = new SPSite(properties.SiteId))
{
  ConversionJob job = new ConversionJob(wordAutomationServiceName);
  job.UserToken = spSite.UserToken;
  job.Settings.UpdateFields = true;
  job.Settings.OutputFormat = SaveFormat.PDF;
  job.AddFile(sourceUrl, destUrl);
  job.Start();
}
```

For more information about using Word Automation Services to convert documents, refer to the article entitled *Developing with SharePoint 2010 Word Automation Services* on the MSDN web site.

Appendix

Create a WCF service that retrieves data for InfoPath

Problem

You have a SQL Server database table from which you want to retrieve a value of a specific record using a web service.

Solution

You can create a WCF service that has a web method that accepts a parameter and returns a value of a database record as a specific type.

Suppose you have a SQL Server database table named **OfficeApplications** as described in recipe *81 Create a web service that retrieves data for InfoPath*.

To create a WCF service that retrieves data for InfoPath:

1. In Visual Studio 2010, select **File ➤ New ➤ Project**.

2. On the **New Project** dialog box, select **WCF** under **Visual C#** from the list of **Installed Templates**, select **.NET Framework 3.5** from the drop-down list box, select **WCF Service Application**, enter a name for the project (for example **InfoPathWCFService**), select a location where to save the solution, enter a name for the solution, and click **OK**.

3. On the **Solution Explorer** pane, rename **Service1.svc** to **InfoPathService.svc**.

4. On the **Solution Explorer** pane, right-click **InfoPathService.svc**, and select **View Markup** from the context menu that appears.

5. Change the class name in the **InfoPathService.svc** file from **InfoPathWCFService.Service1** to **InfoPathWCFService.InfoPathService** as follows:

    ```
    <%@ ServiceHost Language="C#" Debug="true"
    Service="InfoPathWCFService.InfoPathService"
    CodeBehind="InfoPathService.svc.cs" %>
    ```

6. On the **Solution Explorer** pane, rename **IService1.cs** to **IInfoPathService.cs**, and then double-click the file to open it.

7. Replace the code enclosed within the curly brackets for the namespace with the following code (*code #: C32D7D9B-982B-410E-AF0A-FF3960DEBC55*):

    ```
    [ServiceContract]
    public interface IInfoPathService
    {
      [WebGet(UriTemplate = "officeapplications")]
      [OperationContract]
    ```

```
  List<OfficeApplication> GetOfficeApplications(string appName);
}

[DataContract]
public class OfficeApplication
{
  [DataMember]
  public int ID { get; set; }

  [DataMember]
  public string Name { get; set; }

  [DataMember]
  public string Color { get; set; }
}

[CollectionDataContract]
public class OfficeApplications : List<OfficeApplication>
{
  public OfficeApplications() { }
  public OfficeApplications(
    List<OfficeApplication> officeApplications) : base(officeApplications)
  { }
}
```

8. Switch to the **InfoPathService.svc.cs** file and add the following **using** statements to it:

```
using System.Data.SqlClient;
using System.Configuration;
```

9. Rename the class from `Service1` to `InfoPathService`.

10. Replace the code within the `InfoPathService` class with the following code (*code #: C32D7D9B-982B-410E-AF0A-FF3960DEBC55*):

```
public List<OfficeApplication> GetOfficeApplications(string appName)
{
  List<OfficeApplication> list = new List<OfficeApplication>();
  string connectionString =
    ConfigurationManager.ConnectionStrings["InfoPathDB"].ConnectionString;

  using (SqlConnection conn = new SqlConnection(connectionString))
  {
    SqlCommand cmd = new SqlCommand();
    cmd.CommandType = System.Data.CommandType.Text;
    cmd.CommandText = "SELECT * FROM OfficeApplications "
      + "WHERE OfficeApplicationName LIKE @AppName";
    cmd.Parameters.AddWithValue("AppName", appName.Replace("*", "%"));
    cmd.Connection = conn;

    try
    {
      conn.Open();

      using (SqlDataReader reader = cmd.ExecuteReader())
      {
        while (reader.Read())
        {
          OfficeApplication offApp = new OfficeApplication();
          offApp.ID = reader.GetInt32(0);
```

```
        offApp.Name = reader.GetString(1);
        offApp.Color = reader.GetString(2);
        list.Add(offApp);
      }
      reader.Close();
    }
  }
  catch
  {
    // Handle the error using your own preferred error-handling method
  }
  finally
  {
    conn.Close();
  }
}
return list;
}
```

11. On the **Solution Explorer** pane, double-click the **Web.config** file to open it.

12. Add the following **connectionStrings** section to the **Web.config** file (*code #: C32D7D9B-982B-410E-AF0A-FF3960DEBC55*):

```
<connectionStrings>
  <clear/>
  <add name="InfoPathDB"
    connectionString="Initial Catalog=InfoPathDB;Integrated Security=True;"
    providerName="System.Data.SqlClient" />
</connectionStrings>
```

Remember to replace the value for **Initial Catalog** with the name of your own database in which the **OfficeApplication** table is located.

13. Add the following **service** element to the **services** section in the **Web.config** file (*code #: C32D7D9B-982B-410E-AF0A-FF3960DEBC55*):

```
<service name="InfoPathWCFService.InfoPathService"
    behaviorConfiguration="InfoPathWCFService.InfoPathServiceBehavior">
  <endpoint address="" binding="basicHttpBinding"
    contract="InfoPathWCFService.IInfoPathService"  />
</service>
```

14. Add the following **behavior** element to the **serviceBehaviors** section in the **Web.config** file (*code #: C32D7D9B-982B-410E-AF0A-FF3960DEBC55*):

```
<behavior name="InfoPathWCFService.InfoPathServiceBehavior">
  <serviceMetadata httpGetEnabled="true"/>
  <serviceDebug includeExceptionDetailInFaults="false"/>
</behavior>
```

15. Click **Build ➤ Build Solution** and fix any errors if necessary.

16. With the **Web.config** file window still in focus, click **Debug ➤ Start Debugging**. This should open a browser window displaying a list of files. Click **InfoPathService.svc** to display the WCF service page.

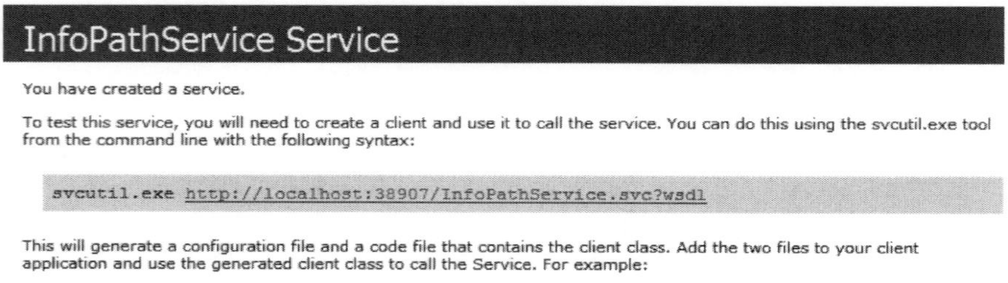

InfoPathService Service

You have created a service.

To test this service, you will need to create a client and use it to call the service. You can do this using the svcutil.exe tool from the command line with the following syntax:

```
svcutil.exe http://localhost:38907/InfoPathService.svc?wsdl
```

This will generate a configuration file and a code file that contains the client class. Add the two files to your client application and use the generated client class to call the Service. For example:

Figure 74. The page for the InfoPathService WCF service.

17. With the WCF service still running in debug mode, open InfoPath Designer 2010, and create a new **Blank Form** template.

18. Select **Data ➤ Get External Data ➤ From Web Service ➤ From SOAP Web Service**.

19. On the **Data Connection Wizard**, enter the URL of the web service, for example:

```
http://localhost:38907/InfoPathService.svc
```

and click **Next**. Note that an URL such as the one specified above should work if you are running the web service and InfoPath on the same computer. Otherwise, you may have to deploy the web service first before you are able to access it in InfoPath.

20. On the **Data Connection Wizard**, select the **GetOfficeApplications** operation, and click **Next**.

21. On the **Data Connection Wizard**, leave the parameter as is, and click **Next**.

22. On the **Data Connection Wizard**, leave the **Store a copy of the data in the form template** check box deselected, and click **Next**.

23. On the **Data Connection Wizard**, name the data connection **GetOfficeApplications**, deselect the **Automatically retrieve data when form is opened** check box, and click **Finish**.

24. On the **Fields** task pane, select **GetOfficeApplications (Secondary)** from the **Fields** drop-down list box.

25. On the **Fields** task pane, expand the **queryFields** group node, expand the **GetOfficeApplications** group node, and then drag-and-drop the **appName** field onto the view of the form template.

26. On the **Fields** task pane, expand the **dataFields** group node, expand the **GetOfficeApplicationsResponse** group node, expand the **GetOfficeApplicationsResult** group node, and then drag-and-drop the **OfficeApplication** repeating group node onto the view of the form template. Select **Repeating Table** from the context menu when you drop it.

27. Add a **Button** control to the view of the form template and change its **Action** property to **Refresh**.

28. Preview the form.

When the form opens, enter the full or partial name (plus asterisks) of an Office application in the **appName** field and then click the **Refresh** button. All of the Office applications that contain the piece of text you entered in their name should appear in the repeating table. To return all of the Office applications, enter an asterisk (*) and then click the **Refresh** button.

Discussion

Creating a WCF service that can be called from an InfoPath form is similar to creating an ASP.NET web service that can be called from an InfoPath form (see chapter 7). The main difference lies in the configuration of the WCF service in the **Web.config** file.

To be able to connect InfoPath to a WCF service, the WCF service must have an endpoint configured with a **basicHttpBinding** binding.

```
<system.serviceModel>
  <services>
    <service name="InfoPathWCFService.InfoPathService"
        behaviorConfiguration="InfoPathWCFService.InfoPathServiceBehavior">
      <endpoint address=""
        binding="basicHttpBinding"
        contract="InfoPathWCFService.IInfoPathService" />
    </service>
  </services>
  <behaviors>
    <serviceBehaviors>
      <behavior name="InfoPathWCFService.InfoPathServiceBehavior">
        <serviceMetadata httpGetEnabled="true"/>
        <serviceDebug includeExceptionDetailInFaults="false"/>
      </behavior>
    </serviceBehaviors>
  </behaviors>
</system.serviceModel>
```

Note:

When you are running the WCF service in debug mode and you create an InfoPath form template as described in the solution above, you can set breakpoints in the WCF service code before performing an action that invokes the WCF service from within the InfoPath form. This action should hit the breakpoints in Visual Studio so that you can step through the WCF service code and debug it in Visual Studio.

Create a digital certificate to sign an InfoPath form template

Problem

You have an InfoPath form template, which you want to configure to have Full Trust.

Solution

You can use Active Directory Certificate Services to create a digital certificate that can be used to digitally sign an InfoPath form template when you assign Full Trust to it. Before you can create a digital certificate that can be used to sign an InfoPath form template, you must:

1. Have a root Certification Authority (CA) set up on a Windows Server.
2. Enable a certificate template that can be used to issue digital certificates that are suitable to sign InfoPath form templates.

Important:

> An administrator must set up the Active Directory Certificate Services role on a Windows Server before you can create digital certificates for InfoPath. Refer to the article entitled *Active Directory Certificate Services Step-by-Step Guide* on the MSDN web site for more information about how to set up Active Directory Certificate Services.

To enable a certificate template that can be used to issue digital certificates that are suitable to sign InfoPath form templates:

1. In Windows Server 2008, open **Server Manager**.

2. On the **Server Manager** window, expand the **Roles** node, expand the **Active Directory Certificate Services** node, and expand the node for the CA.

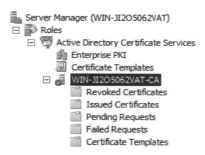

3. Click the **Certificate Templates** folder and check whether a **Code Signing** template is present. If it is not, right-click the **Certificate Templates** folder and then select **New ➤ Certificate Template to Issue** from the context menu that appears.

4. On the **Enable Certificate Templates** dialog box, select **Code Signing**, and click **OK**.

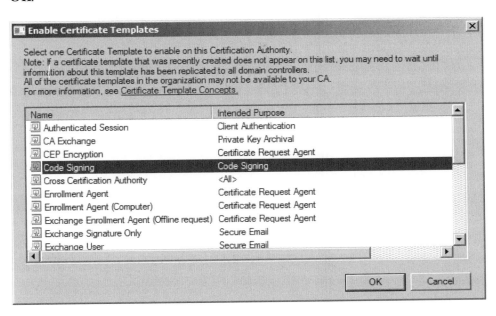

Once you have set up the CA and enabled the **Code Signing** certificate template, users should be able to use the **Certificates** snap-in to be able to request a certificate.

To open the **Certificates** snap-in:

1. In Windows 7 or Windows Server 2008, click the Windows or **Start** button, type **mmc** in the **Search programs and files** text box, and press **Enter**.

2. On the **Console** window, click **File ➤ Add/Remove Snap-in**.

3. On the **Add or Remove Snap-ins** dialog box, select **Certificates** in the list of **Available snap-ins**, and click **Add**.

4. On the **Certificates snap-in** dialog box, leave the **My user account** option selected, and click **Finish**.

5. On the **Add or Remove Snap-ins** dialog box, click **OK**.

To request a digital certificate from the **Certificates** snap-in:

1. Open the **Certificates** snap-in as described in the steps outlined above.

2. On the **Console** window, expand the **Certificates – Current User** node, and then right-click the **Personal** folder and select **All Tasks ➤ Request New Certificate**.

3. On the **Certificate Enrollment** dialog box, on the **Before You Begin** screen, click **Next**.

4. On the **Certificate Enrollment** dialog box, on the **Select Certificate Enrollment Policy** page, select **Active Directory Enrollment Policy**, and click **Next**.

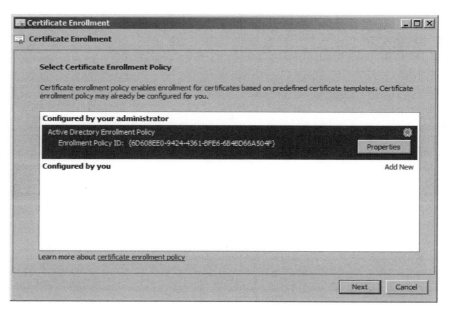

5. On the **Certificate Enrollment** dialog box, on the **Request Certificates** page, select **Code Signing**, and click **Enroll**.

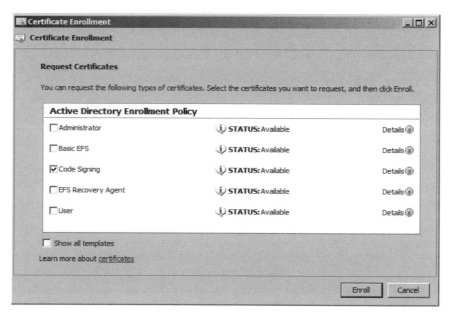

6. On the **Certificate Enrollment** dialog box, on the **Certificate Installation Results** page, click **Finish**.

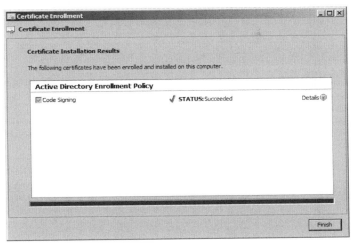

7. On the **Console** window, press F5 to refresh the screen, expand the **Personal** folder, click the **Certificates** folder under the **Personal** folder, and verify that the certificate you requested is present.

8. Double-click the certificate to open it, and then on the **Certificate** dialog box, ensure that the following purposes are listed:

   a. Ensures software came from software publisher

   b. Protects software from alteration after publication

   and that you have a private key that corresponds to the certificate.

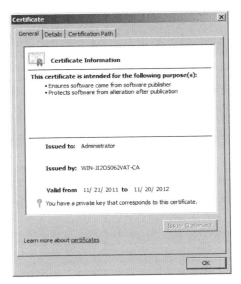

9. On the **Certificate** dialog box, click **OK**.

Note that for you to be able to use a certificate to digitally sign InfoPath form templates, the following conditions must be met:

1. The **Key Usage** attribute value must include **Digital Signature** or **Non-Repudiation**. Note that certificates with the value set to **Exchange** cannot be used to sign data in InfoPath forms.

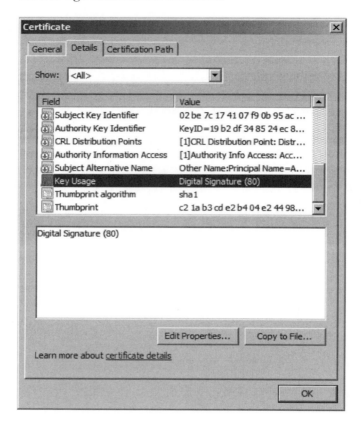

Figure 75. The Key Usage attribute highlighted on the Certificate dialog box.

2. The certificate must not be expired or revoked, and the date of issue must be in the past. Check the **Valid from ... to ...** period on the **General** tab of the **Certificate** dialog box.

3. The certificate must be associated with a private key on the user's computer. Check for the key icon with the text "You have a private key that corresponds to this certificate" at the bottom of the **General** tab of the **Certificate** dialog box.

4. The certificate authority that issued the certificate must be in the **Trusted Root Certification Authorities** store on the user's computer for the certificate to be

trusted. On the **Console** window, expand the **Trusted Root Certification Authorities** folder, click the **Certificates** folder, and then verify that the certificate for the CA that issued the certificate is present.

To find out which CA issued a certificate, click the **Certification Path** tab on the **Certificate** dialog box of the certificate you want to check. The CA that issued the certificate should be listed at the top of the tree. You can also click the **Details** tab on the **Certificate** dialog box and check the value of the **Issuer** attribute.

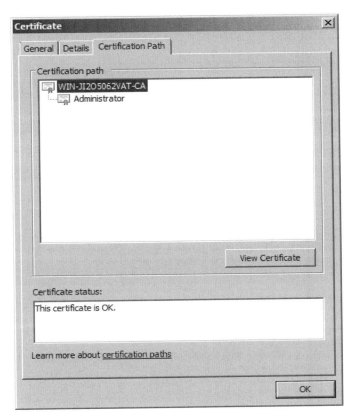

Figure 76. The issuer highlighted at the top of the certification path.

A self-signed certificate (the type of temporary certificate you can create from within InfoPath Designer 2010) is generally not trusted, since a trusted root CA certificate is absent from the **Trusted Root Certification Authorities** store.

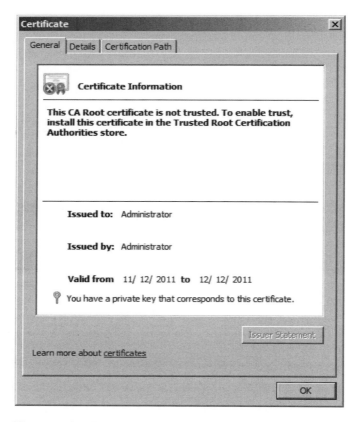

Figure 77. A self-signed certificate without a trusted root certification authority.

Certificates can be issued on several different ways. If you requested a certificate and installed it on your computer, but it is not appearing on the dialog box after you click **Select a Certificate** on the **Form Options** dialog box under **Security and Trust** (see the next recipe), it is highly likely that it does not satisfy one or more of the four conditions listed above.

Configure an InfoPath form template to have Full Trust

Problem

You have written code for an InfoPath form template that requires you to give the form template Full Trust.

Solution

You can select the Full Trust option as the security level and digitally sign the form template with a certificate.

To configure an InfoPath form template to have Full Trust:

1. In InfoPath, open the form template to which you want to give Full Trust.

2. Click **File ➤ Info ➤ Form Options**.

3. On the **Form Options** dialog box, select **Security and Trust** in the **Category** list.

4. On the **Form Options** dialog box, deselect the **Automatically determine security level (recommended)** check box, select the **Full Trust** option, select the **Sign this form template** check box, and click **Select certificate**.

5. On the **Windows Security** dialog box, select the certificate you want to use, and click **OK**. If you see a message saying "No certificate available", refer to the previous recipe.

6. On the **Form Options** dialog box, click **OK**.

Publish an InfoPath form template as administrator-approved

Problem

You gave a form template Full Trust and are now forced to publish it as an administrator-approved form template.

Solution

Publishing an InfoPath form template as an administrator-approved form template involves performing the following four steps:

1. In InfoPath Designer 2010, select the administrator-approved option when publishing the form template.

2. In SharePoint Central Administration, upload the form template.

3. In SharePoint Central Administration, activate the form template to a site collection.

4. In SharePoint, add the form template as a content type to a form library.

To publish an InfoPath form template as an administrator-approved form template:

1. In InfoPath, open the form template you want to publish as an administrator-approved form template.

2. Click **File ➤ Publish ➤ SharePoint Server**.

3. On the **Publishing Wizard**, enter the URL of the SharePoint server, and click **Next**.

4. On the **Publishing Wizard**, select the **Administrator-approved form template (advanced)** option, and click **Next**.

5. On the **Publishing Wizard**, click **Browse**.

6. On the **Browse** dialog box, browse to a network location that can be accessed by the administrator that needs to upload the form template to the SharePoint server, enter a name for the form template in the **File name** text box, and click **Save**.

7. On the **Publishing Wizard**, click **Next**.

8. On the **Publishing Wizard**, promote fields or create web part connection parameters if your form template calls for it, and then click **Next**.

9. On the **Publishing Wizard**, click **Publish**.

10. On the **Publishing Wizard**, click **Close**.

After you have published the form template from within InfoPath Designer 2010, an administrator must upload it to SharePoint via SharePoint Central Administration.

To upload a form template to SharePoint:

1. In SharePoint Central Administration, under **General Application Settings**, click **Manage form templates**.

2. On the **Manage Form Templates** page, click **Upload form template**.

3. On the **Upload Form Template** page, click **Browse**.

4. On the **Choose File to Upload** dialog box, browse to and select the form template that was previously published from within InfoPath, and then click **Open**.

5. On the **Upload Form Template** page, click **Upload**.

6. On the **Upload Form Template** page, click **OK**.

7. On the **Manage Form Templates** page, refresh the page and wait until the **Status** for the form template says **Ready**.

After the form template has been uploaded and has a status of **Ready**, the next step is to activate the form template to a site collection so that it can be associated as a content type to one or more form libraries.

To activate a form template to a site collection:

1. In SharePoint Central Administration, under **General Application Settings**, click **Manage form templates**.

2. On the **Manage Form Templates** page, hover with the mouse pointer over the form template that needs to be activated, click the drop-down arrow on the right-hand side of the name of the form template, and select **Activate to a Site Collection** from the drop-down menu that appears.

3. On the **Activate Form Template** page, under **Activation Location**, select the site collection you want to activate the form template to. If an incorrect site collection is being shown, click the site collection URL, select **Change Site Collection** from the drop-down menu that appears, and follow the instructions to change the site collection.

4. On the **Activate Form Template** page, click **OK**.

After the form template has been activated to a site collection, it should appear in the **FormTemplates** document library of the top-level site in the site collection to which it was activated and a corresponding site content type should be present under the **Microsoft InfoPath** group on the **Site Content Types** page of the top-level site in the site collection. The final step is to associate the content type for the form template to a SharePoint form library.

To associate the content type for the administrator-approved form template to a form library:

1. In SharePoint, create a new form library or navigate to an existing one on a site in the site collection to which the form template was activated.

2. Click **Library Tools ➤ Library ➤ Settings ➤ Library Settings**.

3. On the **Form Library Settings** page under **General Settings**, click **Advanced settings**.

4. On the **Advanced Settings** page, under **Content Types**, select the **Yes** option for **Allow management of content types**, and click **OK**.

5. On the **Form Library Settings** page under **Content Types**, click **Add from existing site content types**.

6. On the **Add Content Types** page, select **Microsoft InfoPath** from the **Select site content types from** drop-down list box, select the content type for the form template from the **Available Site Content Types** list box, click **Add**, and then click **OK**.

You should now be able to use the form template to create InfoPath forms in the form library.

Configure cross-domain access for a web service

Problem

You want to call a web service from a browser form in SharePoint, but are getting an error saying that cross-domain access is required.

Solution

If the web service is located on another server or is accessed through an URL that uses a domain name that is different from the domain name used in the SharePoint server URL, you can allow cross-domain access via SharePoint Central Administration. In addition, you must convert and save the data connection as a data connection (UDCX) file in a SharePoint data connection library.

To enable cross-domain access in SharePoint Central Administration:

1. In SharePoint Central Administration, click **General Application Settings**.

2. On the **General Application Settings** page under **InfoPath Forms Services**, click **Configure InfoPath Forms Services**.

3. On the **Configure InfoPath Forms Services** page, under **Cross-Domain Access for User Form Templates**, select the **Allow cross-domain data access for user form templates that use connection settings in a data connection file** check box, and click **OK**.

Before you convert the data connection for a web service into a data connection file, you must have a SharePoint data connection library in which you can save the file. You can create a SharePoint data connection library as follows:

1. In SharePoint, navigate to the site where you published the form template, and click **Site Actions > More Options**.

2. On the **Create** page, select **Library** under **Filter By**, select **Data Connection Library**, enter a **Name**, and click **Create**.

Once you have a SharePoint data connection library, you can save the (receive or submit) data connection for a web service as a data connection file in the SharePoint data connection library on the site where the form template is published as follows:

1. In InfoPath, click **Data > Data Connections**.

2. On the **Data Connections** dialog box, select the data connection you want to convert into a data connection file, and click **Convert to Connection File**.

3. On the **Convert Data Connection** dialog box, click **Browse**.

4. On the **Browse** dialog box, browse to and select the data connection library you created earlier, enter a name for the data connection file or accept the default name, and click **Save**.

5. On the **Convert Data Connection** dialog box, leave the **Relative to site collection (recommended)** option selected, and click **OK**. Note that unlike the relative to site collection option, if you choose the **Centrally managed connection library (advanced)** option, you will be forced to publish the form template as an administrator-approved form template.

6. Repeat steps 2 through 5 for each data connection that should be converted.

7. On the **Data Connections** dialog box, click **Close**.

8. Publish or republish the form template to a SharePoint form library.

9. In SharePoint, navigate to the data connection library where you stored the data connection file.

10. The data connection file you saved should have an **Approval Status** of **Pending**. This approval status must be changed to **Approved** before you can use the data connection file, so hover over the name of the data connection file, click on the drop-down arrow that appears on the right-hand side of the file, and select **Approve/Reject** from the drop-down menu that appears.

11. On the **Approve/Reject** page, select the **Approved** option, and click **OK**. The data connection file you just saved should have an **Approval Status** of **Approved**.

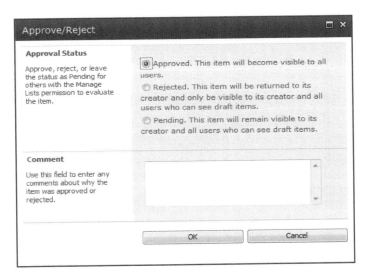

Figure 78. Approving a data connection file in SharePoint 2010.

Test the InfoPath form to see whether the data connection for the web service is working as expected.

Create a typed XML column for an InfoPath form

Problem

You want to store InfoPath forms in their entirety in a SQL Server database column that has the XML data type, but that is also validated by SQL Server using an XML schema.

Solution

Before you can create a typed XML column for an InfoPath form in SQL Server, you must have the XML schema definition (XSD) for the InfoPath form. To get the XSD file that defines the InfoPath form:

1. In InfoPath, open the form template for which you want to create a typed XML column in SQL Server.

2. Click **File ➤ Publish ➤ Export Source Files**.

3. On the **Browse For Folder** dialog box, browse to a location on disk where you can store the form files, and click **OK**.

4. Open Windows Explorer, and navigate to the location where you exported the files. You should see a file named **myschema.xsd**.

5. Open the **myschema.xsd** file in Notepad and copy all of its contents to the Windows clipboard.

Once you have the XML schema definition for the InfoPath form, you must register an XML schema collection in SQL Server as follows:

1. In Microsoft SQL Server Management Studio, click **New Query** to open a new query window.

2. Enter the following script in the query window (*code #: 8D319760-7A35-49A8-8CE7-B0651E9754C2*):

```
CREATE XML SCHEMA COLLECTION InfoPathSchemaCollection AS
'<Your XML schema definition goes here>';
GO
```

For example:

```
CREATE XML SCHEMA COLLECTION InfoPathSchemaCollection AS
'<?xml version="1.0" encoding="UTF-8" standalone="no"?>
<xsd:schema
targetNamespace="http://schemas.microsoft.com/office/infopath/2003/myXSD/20
11-10-26T22:09:21" xmlns:xsi="http://www.w3.org/2001/XMLSchema-instance"
xmlns:xhtml="http://www.w3.org/1999/xhtml"
xmlns:dfs="http://schemas.microsoft.com/office/infopath/2003/dataFormSoluti
on" xmlns:tns="http://www.bizsupportonline.net/namespaces/infopathservice/"
xmlns:d="http://schemas.microsoft.com/office/infopath/2003/ado/dataFields"
xmlns:http="http://schemas.xmlsoap.org/wsdl/http/"
xmlns:soap12="http://schemas.xmlsoap.org/wsdl/soap12/"
xmlns:mime="http://schemas.xmlsoap.org/wsdl/mime/"
xmlns:soapenc="http://schemas.xmlsoap.org/soap/encoding/"
xmlns:tm="http://microsoft.com/wsdl/mime/textMatching/"
xmlns:soap="http://schemas.xmlsoap.org/wsdl/soap/"
xmlns:wsdl="http://schemas.xmlsoap.org/wsdl/"
xmlns:my="http://schemas.microsoft.com/office/infopath/2003/myXSD/2011-10-
26T22:09:21" xmlns:xd="http://schemas.microsoft.com/office/infopath/2003"
xmlns:xsd="http://www.w3.org/2001/XMLSchema">
  <xsd:element name="myFields">
    <xsd:complexType>
      <xsd:sequence>
```

```
          <xsd:element ref="my:field1" minOccurs="0"/>
          <xsd:element ref="my:field2" minOccurs="0"/>
          <xsd:element ref="my:field3" minOccurs="0"/>
          <xsd:element ref="my:group1" minOccurs="0"/>
          <xsd:element ref="my:formName" minOccurs="0"/>
          <xsd:element ref="my:field7" minOccurs="0"/>
        </xsd:sequence>
        <xsd:anyAttribute processContents="lax"
namespace="http://www.w3.org/XML/1998/namespace"/>
      </xsd:complexType>
    </xsd:element>
    <xsd:element name="field1" type="xsd:string"/>
    <xsd:element name="field2">
      <xsd:complexType mixed="true">
        <xsd:sequence>
          <xsd:any minOccurs="0" maxOccurs="unbounded"
namespace="http://www.w3.org/1999/xhtml" processContents="lax"/>
        </xsd:sequence>
      </xsd:complexType>
    </xsd:element>
    <xsd:element name="field3" nillable="true" type="xsd:date"/>
    <xsd:element name="group1">
      <xsd:complexType>
        <xsd:sequence>
          <xsd:element ref="my:group2" minOccurs="0" maxOccurs="unbounded"/>
        </xsd:sequence>
      </xsd:complexType>
    </xsd:element>
    <xsd:element name="group2">
      <xsd:complexType>
        <xsd:sequence>
          <xsd:element ref="my:field4" minOccurs="0"/>
          <xsd:element ref="my:field5" minOccurs="0"/>
          <xsd:element ref="my:field6" minOccurs="0"/>
        </xsd:sequence>
      </xsd:complexType>
    </xsd:element>
    <xsd:element name="field4" type="xsd:string"/>
    <xsd:element name="field5" type="xsd:string"/>
    <xsd:element name="field6" type="xsd:string"/>
    <xsd:element name="formName" type="xsd:string"/>
    <xsd:element name="field7" type="xsd:string"/>
</xsd:schema>';
GO
```

and click **Execute**. Note that you must use the contents of the XSD file you copied earlier in your own script. If you get an error saying "XML parsing: line 1, character 54, unable to switch the encoding", ensure that you did not prepend an **N** to the text for the XML schema. If you did, remove it and try again.

3. Use the following statements to verify that the XML schema collection and XML namespace for the InfoPath form were registered (*code #: 8D319760-7A35-49A8-8CE7-B0651E9754C2*).

```
select * from sys.xml_schema_collections
select name from sys.xml_schema_namespaces
```

Note that the instructions given above are for SQL Server 2008 R2. For more information about XML schema collections, refer to the article entitled *CREATE XML SCHEMA COLLECTION (Transact-SQL)* on the MSDN web site.

Once you have registered the XML schema collection, you can use it to create an XML column as follows:

1. In Microsoft SQL Server Management Studio, click **New Query** to open a new query window.

2. Enter the following script in the query window (*code #: 8D319760-7A35-49A8-8CE7-B0651E9754C2*):

```
CREATE TABLE [dbo].[InfoPathForm](
    [id] [int] IDENTITY(1,1) NOT NULL,
    [name] [varchar](50) NOT NULL,
    [form] [xml] (InfoPathSchemaCollection) NOT NULL
);
GO
```

and click **Execute**.

You should now be able to store entire InfoPath forms in the typed XML column. If you want to store more than one type of InfoPath form in the XML column, you must register an XML schema collection that defines two or more different XML schemas. For more information about XML schema collections, refer to the article entitled *CREATE XML SCHEMA COLLECTION (Transact-SQL)* on the MSDN web site.

InfoPathAttachmentDecoder.cs

```
using System;
using System.IO;
using System.Text;

namespace BizSupportOnline
{
  public class InfoPathAttachmentDecoder
  {
    private const int SP1Header_Size = 20;
    private const int FIXED_HEADER = 16;

    private int fileSize;
    private int attachmentNameLength;
    private string attachmentName;
    private byte[] decodedAttachment;

    public InfoPathAttachmentDecoder(string base64EncodedString)
    {
      byte[] data = Convert.FromBase64String(base64EncodedString);
      using (MemoryStream ms = new MemoryStream(data))
      {
        BinaryReader reader = new BinaryReader(ms);
        DecodeAttachment(reader);
        reader.Close();
        ms.Close();
```

```
    }
  }

  private void DecodeAttachment(BinaryReader reader)
  {
    byte[] headerData = new byte[FIXED_HEADER];
    headerData = reader.ReadBytes(headerData.Length);

    fileSize = (int)reader.ReadUInt32();
    attachmentNameLength = (int)reader.ReadUInt32() * 2;

    byte[] fileNameBytes = reader.ReadBytes(attachmentNameLength);

    Encoding enc = Encoding.Unicode;
    attachmentName =
      enc.GetString(fileNameBytes, 0, attachmentNameLength - 2);
    decodedAttachment = reader.ReadBytes(fileSize);
  }

  public void SaveAttachment(string saveLocation)
  {
    string fullFileName = saveLocation;

    if (!fullFileName.EndsWith(Path.DirectorySeparatorChar.ToString()))
      fullFileName += Path.DirectorySeparatorChar;

    fullFileName += attachmentName;

    if (File.Exists(fullFileName))
      File.Delete(fullFileName);

    using (FileStream fs = new FileStream(fullFileName, FileMode.CreateNew))
    {
      BinaryWriter bw = new BinaryWriter(fs);
      bw.Write(decodedAttachment);
      bw.Close();
      fs.Close();
    }
  }

  public string Filename
  {
    get { return attachmentName; }
  }

  public byte[] DecodedAttachment
  {
    get { return decodedAttachment; }
  }
 }
}
```

InfoPathAttachmentEncoder.cs

```
using System;
using System.Text;
using System.IO;
using System.Security.Cryptography;
```

```
namespace BizSupportOnline
{
  public class InfoPathAttachmentEncoder
  {
    private string base64EncodedFile = string.Empty;
    private string fileName;
    private byte[] fileData;

    public InfoPathAttachmentEncoder(string fileName, byte[] fileData)
    {
      if (fileName == string.Empty)
        throw new ArgumentException("Must specify file name", "fileName");

      if (fileData.Length == 0)
        throw new ArgumentNullException("fileData", "File is empty");

      this.fileName = fileName;
      this.fileData = fileData;
    }

    public string ToBase64String()
    {
      if (base64EncodedFile != string.Empty)
        return base64EncodedFile;

      using (MemoryStream ms = new MemoryStream())
      {
        using (MemoryStream msOld = new MemoryStream(fileData))
        {
          using (BinaryReader br = new BinaryReader(msOld))
          {
            string fileName = this.fileName;

            uint fileNameLength = (uint)fileName.Length + 1;

            byte[] fileNameBytes = Encoding.Unicode.GetBytes(fileName);

            using (BinaryWriter bw = new BinaryWriter(ms))
            {
              bw.Write(new byte[] { 0xC7, 0x49, 0x46, 0x41 });

              bw.Write((uint)0x14);
              bw.Write((uint)0x01);
              bw.Write((uint)0x00);

              bw.Write((uint)br.BaseStream.Length);
              bw.Write((uint)fileNameLength);
              bw.Write(fileNameBytes);
              bw.Write(new byte[] { 0, 0 });

              byte[] data = new byte[64 * 1024];
              int bytesRead = 1;

              while (bytesRead > 0)
              {
                bytesRead = br.Read(data, 0, data.Length);
                bw.Write(data, 0, bytesRead);
              }
            }

            br.Close();
          }
```

```
          using (MemoryStream msOut = new MemoryStream())
        {
          using (BinaryReader br =
            new BinaryReader(new MemoryStream(ms.ToArray())))
          {
            ToBase64Transform tf = new ToBase64Transform();

            byte[] data = new byte[tf.InputBlockSize];
            byte[] outData = new byte[tf.OutputBlockSize];

            int bytesRead = 1;

            while (bytesRead > 0)
            {
              bytesRead = br.Read(data, 0, data.Length);

              if (bytesRead == data.Length)
                tf.TransformBlock(data, 0, bytesRead, outData, 0);
              else
                outData = tf.TransformFinalBlock(data, 0, bytesRead);

              msOut.Write(outData, 0, outData.Length);
            }

            br.Close();
          }

          msOut.Close();

          base64EncodedFile = Encoding.ASCII.GetString(msOut.ToArray());
        }

        msOld.Close();
      }

      ms.Close();
    }

    return base64EncodedFile;
    }
  }
}
```

InfoPathToWord.cs

```
public static class InfoPathToWord
{
  public enum ListStyle
  {
    Bullets = 1,
    Numbers = 2
  }

  public static List<OpenXmlElement> GetContentControl(
    Document doc, string name)
  {
    List<OpenXmlElement> list = new List<OpenXmlElement>();
```

```
  List<SdtBlock> sdtList = doc.Descendants<SdtBlock>()
    .Where(s => name.Contains(s.SdtProperties.GetFirstChild<SdtAlias>()
    .Val.Value)).ToList();

  if (sdtList.Count == 0)
  {
    List<SdtRun> sdtRunList = doc.Descendants<SdtRun>()
      .Where(s => name.Contains(s.SdtProperties.GetFirstChild<SdtAlias>()
      .Val.Value)).ToList();

    foreach (SdtRun sdt in sdtRunList)
    {
      list.Add(sdt);
    }

  }
  else
  {
    foreach (SdtBlock sdt in sdtList)
    {
      list.Add(sdt);
    }
  }

  return list;
}

public static void ReplaceContentControl(
  List<OpenXmlElement> sdtList, OpenXmlElement element)
{
  if (sdtList.Count != 0)
  {
    foreach (OpenXmlElement sdt in sdtList)
    {
      OpenXmlElement parent = sdt.Parent;
      parent.InsertAfter(element, sdt);
      sdt.Remove();
    }
  }
}

public static void WriteText(string textToWrite, ref Paragraph par)
{
  List<Run> runs = par.Elements<Run>().ToList();
  int count = runs.Count;

  foreach (Run run in runs)
  {
    if (count == 1)
    {
      Text t = run.GetFirstChild<Text>();
      t.Text = textToWrite;
    }
    else
    {
      run.Remove();
    }
    count++;
  }
}

public static void WriteText(string textToWrite, ref Run run)
```

```
{
  Text t = run.GetFirstChild<Text>();
  t.Text = textToWrite;
}

public static void AddSingleLineText(
  string singleLineText, ref List<OpenXmlElement> sdtList)
{
  if (sdtList.Count != 0)
  {
    foreach (OpenXmlElement sdt in sdtList)
    {
      if (sdt.GetType() == typeof(SdtBlock))
      {
        Paragraph p =
          sdt.GetFirstChild<SdtContentBlock>().GetFirstChild<Paragraph>();
        WriteText(singleLineText, ref p);
      }

      if (sdt.GetType() == typeof(SdtRun))
      {
        Run r = sdt.GetFirstChild<SdtContentRun>().GetFirstChild<Run>();
        WriteText(singleLineText, ref r);
      }
    }
  }
}

public static void AddMultiLineText(
  string multiLineText, ref List<OpenXmlElement> sdtList)
{
  string[] lines = multiLineText.Split(new char[] { '\n' });
  if (sdtList.Count != 0)
  {
    foreach (OpenXmlElement sdt in sdtList)
    {
      for (int i = 0; i < lines.Length; i++)
      {
        Paragraph p =
          sdt.GetFirstChild<SdtContentBlock>().GetFirstChild<Paragraph>();

        if (i == 0)
        {
          InfoPathToWord.WriteText(lines[i], ref p);
        }
        else
        {
          Paragraph pNext = sdt.AppendChild((Paragraph)p.Clone());
          InfoPathToWord.WriteText(lines[i], ref pNext);
        }
      }
    }
  }
}

public static void AddRichText(int id, string rtfValue,
  ref MainDocumentPart mainPart, ref List<OpenXmlElement> sdtList)
{
  if (sdtList.Count != 0)
  {
    id++;
    string altChunkId = "AltChunkId" + id;
```

```
    AlternativeFormatImportPart chunk =
      mainPart.AddAlternativeFormatImportPart(
      AlternativeFormatImportPartType.Xhtml, altChunkId);

    using (MemoryStream ms =
      new MemoryStream(System.Text.Encoding.UTF8.GetBytes(rtfValue)))
    {
      chunk.FeedData(ms);
      ms.Close();
    }

    AltChunk altChunk = new AltChunk();
    altChunk.Id = altChunkId;

    InfoPathToWord.ReplaceContentControl(sdtList, altChunk);
  }
}

public static ImagePart AddImagePart(string id, string base64EncodedString,
  ref MainDocumentPart mainPart)
{
  string imageType = GetImageType(base64EncodedString);

  ImagePart imagePart = null;

  switch (imageType)
  {
    case "JPG":
      imagePart = mainPart.AddImagePart(ImagePartType.Jpeg, id);
      break;
    case "GIF":
      imagePart = mainPart.AddImagePart(ImagePartType.Gif, id);
      break;
    case "EMF":
      imagePart = mainPart.AddImagePart(ImagePartType.Emf, id);
      break;
    case "BMP":
      imagePart = mainPart.AddImagePart(ImagePartType.Bmp, id);
      break;
    case "ICO":
      imagePart = mainPart.AddImagePart(ImagePartType.Icon, id);
      break;
    case "PNG":
      imagePart = mainPart.AddImagePart(ImagePartType.Png, id);
      break;
    case "TIFF":
      imagePart = mainPart.AddImagePart(ImagePartType.Tiff, id);
      break;
    case "WMF":
      imagePart = mainPart.AddImagePart(ImagePartType.Wmf, id);
      break;
    default:
      imagePart = mainPart.AddImagePart(ImagePartType.Jpeg, id);
      break;
  }

  byte[] imageBytes = System.Convert.FromBase64String(base64EncodedString);
  using (MemoryStream ms = new MemoryStream(imageBytes))
  {
    imagePart.FeedData(ms);
    ms.Close();
  }
```

```csharp
    return imagePart;
}

public static string GetImageType(string base64String)
{
  byte[] bytes = Convert.FromBase64String(base64String);

  if (bytes == null || bytes.Length == 0)
    return null;

  string fileExtension = String.Empty;
  using (System.IO.MemoryStream ms = new System.IO.MemoryStream(bytes))
  {
    try
    {
      using (System.Drawing.Image img = System.Drawing.Image.FromStream(ms))
      {
        if (img.RawFormat.Equals(System.Drawing.Imaging.ImageFormat.Jpeg))
        {
          fileExtension = "JPG";
        }
        if (img.RawFormat.Equals(System.Drawing.Imaging.ImageFormat.Gif))
        {
          fileExtension = "GIF";
        }
        if (img.RawFormat.Equals(System.Drawing.Imaging.ImageFormat.Emf))
        {
          fileExtension = "EMF";
        }
        if (img.RawFormat.Equals(System.Drawing.Imaging.ImageFormat.Bmp))
        {
          fileExtension = "BMP";
        }
        if (img.RawFormat.Equals(System.Drawing.Imaging.ImageFormat.Icon))
        {
          fileExtension = "ICO";
        }
        if (img.RawFormat.Equals(System.Drawing.Imaging.ImageFormat.Png))
        {
          fileExtension = "PNG";
        }
        if (img.RawFormat.Equals(System.Drawing.Imaging.ImageFormat.Tiff))
        {
          fileExtension = "TIFF";
        }
        if (img.RawFormat.Equals(System.Drawing.Imaging.ImageFormat.Wmf))
        {
          fileExtension = "WMF";
        }
      }
      ms.Close();
    }
    catch (System.OutOfMemoryException)
    {
      // File does not have valid image format or is not supported by GDI+
      return null;
    }
  }

  return fileExtension;
}
```

```
public static void GetImageExtents(
  string base64EncodedString, out long imageWidthEMU, out long imageHeightEMU)
{
  imageWidthEMU = 0;
  imageHeightEMU = 0;

  if (String.IsNullOrEmpty(base64EncodedString))
    return;

  byte[] imageBytes = System.Convert.FromBase64String(base64EncodedString);

  using (MemoryStream ms = new MemoryStream(imageBytes))
  {
    System.Drawing.Image imageFile = System.Drawing.Image.FromStream(ms);

    imageWidthEMU =
      (long)((imageFile.Width / imageFile.HorizontalResolution) * 914400L);

    imageHeightEMU =
      (long)((imageFile.Height / imageFile.VerticalResolution) * 914400L);

    ms.Close();
  }
}

public static OpenXmlElement CreateImageElement(
  string relationshipId, string picName, string picFileName, long width,
  long height)
{
  OpenXmlElement element =
    new Drawing(
      new DW.Inline(
        new DW.Extent() { Cx = width, Cy = height },
        new DW.EffectExtent()
        {
          LeftEdge = 0L,
          TopEdge = 0L,
          RightEdge = 0L,
          BottomEdge = 0L
        },
        new DW.DocProperties()
        {
          Id = (UInt32Value)1U,
          Name = picName
        },
        new DW.NonVisualGraphicFrameDrawingProperties(
          new A.GraphicFrameLocks() { NoChangeAspect = true }),
        new A.Graphic(
          new A.GraphicData(
            new PIC.Picture(
              new PIC.NonVisualPictureProperties(
                new PIC.NonVisualDrawingProperties()
                {
                  Id = (UInt32Value)0U,
                  Name = picFileName
                },
                new PIC.NonVisualPictureDrawingProperties()
              ),
            new PIC.BlipFill(
              new A.Blip(
                new A.BlipExtensionList(
```

```
                        new A.BlipExtension()
                        {
                          Uri = "{28A0092B-C50C-407E-A947-70E740481C1C}"
                        })
                    )
                    {
                      Embed = relationshipId,
                      CompressionState = A.BlipCompressionValues.Print
                    },
                    new A.Stretch(
                      new A.FillRectangle())),
                new PIC.ShapeProperties(
                    new A.Transform2D(
                      new A.Offset() { X = 0L, Y = 0L },
                      new A.Extents() { Cx = width, Cy = height }),
                    new A.PresetGeometry(
                      new A.AdjustValueList()
                    ) { Preset = A.ShapeTypeValues.Rectangle }))
              ) { Uri = "http://schemas.openxmlformats.org/drawingml/2006/picture"
                })
        )
        {
          DistanceFromTop = (UInt32Value)0U,
          DistanceFromBottom = (UInt32Value)0U,
          DistanceFromLeft = (UInt32Value)0U,
          DistanceFromRight = (UInt32Value)0U,
          EditId = "50D07946"
        });

  return element;
}

public static void AddRowsToTable(XPathNodeIterator rows, ref Table table)
{
  while (rows.MoveNext())
  {
    TableRow row = new TableRow();

    XPathNodeIterator iter =
      rows.Current.SelectChildren(XPathNodeType.Element);

    while (iter.MoveNext())
    {
      TableCell cell = CreateTableCell(iter.Current.Value, 2400);
      row.AppendChild(cell);
    }

    table.AppendChild(row);
  }
}

public static void AddTableRow(string[] rowValues, ref Table table)
{
  if (rowValues == null)
    return;

  TableRow row = new TableRow();

  for (int i = 0; i < rowValues.Length; i++)
  {
    TableCell cell = CreateTableCell(rowValues[i], 2400);
    row.AppendChild(cell);
```

```
    }

    table.AppendChild(row);
  }

  public static Paragraph CreateListParagraph(
    string listItemText, ListStyle listStyle)
  {
    Paragraph par = new Paragraph() {
      RsidParagraphAddition = "004E66CD", RsidParagraphProperties = "001D690E",
      RsidRunAdditionDefault = "001D690E"
    };

    ParagraphProperties parProps = new ParagraphProperties();
      parProps.SpacingBetweenLines = new SpacingBetweenLines() { After = "0" };
    ParagraphStyleId parStyleId =
      new ParagraphStyleId() { Val = "ListParagraph" };

    NumberingProperties numProps = new NumberingProperties();
    NumberingLevelReference numLevelRef = new NumberingLevelReference() {
      Val = 0
    };
    NumberingId numId = new NumberingId() { Val = (int)listStyle };

    numProps.Append(numLevelRef);
    numProps.Append(numId);

    parProps.Append(parStyleId);
    parProps.Append(numProps);

    Run run = new Run(new Text() { Text = listItemText });

    par.Append(parProps);
    par.Append(run);

    return par;
  }

  public static void AddBulletedList(string id, XPathNodeIterator listItems,
    ref List<OpenXmlElement> sdtList, ref MainDocumentPart mainPart)
  {
    NumberingDefinitionsPart numDefPart =
    InfoPathToWord.AddNumberingDefinitionsPart(id, ref mainPart);

    if (sdtList.Count != 0)
    {
      foreach (OpenXmlElement sdt in sdtList)
      {
        OpenXmlElement parent = sdt.Parent;

        while (listItems.MoveNext())
        {
          Paragraph par = InfoPathToWord.CreateListParagraph(
            listItems.Current.Value, InfoPathToWord.ListStyle.Bullets);
          parent.InsertBefore(par, sdt);
        }

        sdt.Remove();
      }
    }
  }
```

```
private static NumberingDefinitionsPart AddNumberingDefinitionsPart(
  string id, ref MainDocumentPart mainPart)
{
  if (mainPart.NumberingDefinitionsPart == null)
  {
    NumberingDefinitionsPart numPart =
      mainPart.AddNewPart<NumberingDefinitionsPart>(id);
    GenerateNumberingDefinitionsPart1Content(numPart);
    return numPart;
  }
  else
  {
    return mainPart.NumberingDefinitionsPart;
  }
}

private static TableCell CreateTableCell(string contents, int cellWidth)
{
  TableCell cell = new TableCell(new Paragraph(new Run(new Text(contents))));
  cell.AppendChild(new TableCellProperties(
    new TableCellWidth()
      { Type = TableWidthUnitValues.Dxa, Width = cellWidth.ToString() }));

  return cell;
}

private static void GenerateNumberingDefinitionsPart1Content(
  NumberingDefinitionsPart numberingDefinitionsPart1)
{
  // Generate the code for this method using the instructions in the Appendix
  // of InfoPath 2010 Cookbook 3
}
}
```

You must generate the code for the GenerateNumberingDefinitionsPart1Content()
method and add it to the InfoPathToWord class as follows:

1. Create a blank Word document and add a bulleted list that has a few items to the
   document.

2. Save and close the Word document.

3. Open the **Open XML SDK 2.0 Productivity Tool** (which is located under the
   Microsoft Office Open XML SDK 2.0 program folder), and click **Open File**.

4. On the **Open** dialog box, navigate to the Word document you created in step 1,
   select the document, and then click **Open**.

5. Once the document has been loaded in the **Open XML SDK 2.0 Productivity
   Tool**, click **Reflect Code**.

6. Once the code has been generated on the right-hand side of the window, search for a
   GenerateNumberingDefinitionsPart1Content() method, select the code it
   contains, copy the code, and then paste the code in the corresponding method in the
   InfoPathToWord class.

Index

V

W

X

Printed in Great Britain
by Amazon.co.uk, Ltd.,
Marston Gate.